douglas gomery

university of maryland

• •

movie history:
a survey

• •

• wadsworth publishing company • belmont, california •
a division of wadsworth, inc.

Communications Editor: Kristine M. Clerkin
Editorial Assistant: Nancy Spellman
Production Editors: Harold P. Humphrey
  and Karen Garrison
Designer: Andrew H. Ogus
Print Buyer: Karen Hunt
Copy Editor: Stephanie Prescott
Photo Researcher: Sarah Bendersky
Compositor: Jonathan Peck Typographers
Cover Design: Andrew H. Ogus and Anne Kellejian
Cover Photographer: Lara Hartley
Signing Representative: Rochelle Turoff
Cover photograph courtesy of Renaissance Rialto Inc.

Printed in the United States of America   34

  2 3 4 5 6 7 8 9 10—94 93 92 91

Library of Congress Cataloging-in-Publication Data

Gomery, Douglas.
  Movie history: a survey / Douglas Gomery.
    p.   cm.
  Includes bibliographical references.
  Filmography: p.
  IBSN 0-534-12294-9
  1. Motion pictures—History. I. Title.
PN1993.5.A1G636   1991   90-77219
791.43′09—dc20   CIP

table of
contents

• •

preface

• • • • • • • • • • • • • • • • • • •

section i
the silent cinema:
1895–1927

• • • • • • • • • • • • • • • • • • •

• **chapter 1** •
**the invention and innovation
of the movies 3**

• chapter 2 •
the triumph of hollywood 31

• chapter 3 •
hollywood establishes
the classic narrative style 67

• chapter 4 •
influential alternatives to hollywood:
european cinema 103

• • • • • • • • • • • • • • • • • • • •

section iii
the television era:
1951–1975

• • • • • • • • • • • • • • • • • • • •

• **chapter 10** •
television, wide-screen,
and color 279

• chapter 11 •
a transformation
in hollywood moviemaking 311

• chapter 12 •
the art-cinema alternative 347

• chapter 13 •
searching for alternative styles 389

• chapter 14 •
an epilogue:
contemporary film history 423

• appendix 1 •
guide to further reading 442

• appendix 2 •
filmography 469

index 493

preface

• •

• some background •

We have many forms of communication and expression. The motion picture as a technological possibility began during the 1890s and for the first half of the twentieth century represented a dominant form of popular culture throughout the world. Today the cinema still attracts vast millions to theatrical screenings and reaches still more people through television and video presentation. Most people see thousands of films as children and teenagers, and thousands more as adults.

Scholars around the world have in recent years discovered new ways to help us understand how films have shaped our lives and influenced our world. *Historical analysis* is one method. This book is a history of cinema in one volume, aimed for the reader who has never closely examined cinema's past. I cover what I hope will be useful for the uninitiated reader to begin his or her own study.

To select what information to use and what to omit brings us face to face with historiography, the philosophy and method of history. In *Movie History: A Survey* I lay out my historiographic methods and follow them consistently as a model for the reader. Thus, this survey not only examines cinema's past but also serves as an example of appropriate ways to ask and answer questions about film history. This book is not a survey of my favorite films, but an application of what I think are the most useful and powerful methods to study film's past.

My historiographic approach to cinema goes beyond the traditional aesthetic approach. Certainly film has had dozens of artists of first rank who have fashioned many complex, unified, and intense art works that rank with the best of music, painting, theatre, or literature. But film is different from means of expression that preceded it: it is based on highly complicated technologies, expensive to make and present, and shown to large numbers of people. Therefore, this book treats not only the aesthetic aspect of movie history but also its technology, economics, and sociology. Let me touch on these four elements.

Motion pictures are based on a special technology. But that technology, first brought forth in 1895, has not remained static. There have been (1) the coming of sound in the late 1920s; (2) the coming of wide-screen and color images and television in the 1950s; and (3) the development of cable television, satellite transmission, and home video in the 1970s. These three major transformations in the technology of filmmaking and presentation serve to structure the book.

But we need more than a simple list of technological changes. This book assumes that in Hollywood and capitalist film industries around the world, new movie technologies have been adopted to increase profits. To understand the economic history of film requires two models.

First, in the West (in capitalist countries) films are created, distributed, and shown by profit-making companies. The American film industry (Hollywood) has long represented the apotheosis of creating films for profit and has exported its films into Europe, Asia, Africa, and the rest of the Americas. These nations found themselves in a quandary: their citizens loved the films Hollywood provided them, but as long as Hollywood monopolized the market, native-based filmmakers had no chance to ply their craft, to develop an indigenous film industry. Thus, in the end, all nations save the United States fought back with government prohibitions against Hollywood and subsidies to help native filmmakers.

In socialist nations, however, government authorities make the majority of economic decisions; film is utilized as part of a socialist development of the nation, principally as part of an educational and cultural sector. Thus, it is best to examine filmmaking, film distribution, and film exhibition as extensions of government policy. The contradiction is that although Hollywood certainly represents the worst of the capitalist world, its films seem to draw enthusiastic support from the USSR, China, and other socialist nations.

The basic technology and economics of the movies have led to important influences on society. The social history of the movies flows from its economic status. In the United States, this has meant a mass cultural form, defining stereotypes and collective images in the consciousness of adults and children alike. In turn this has led to battles over censorship and the control of images and sounds. Indeed, most countries of the Western world have some system of control either maintained by the film industry itself or by government agencies. In socialist countries the movies have served to promote state propaganda, communicate information, and accentuate specialized artistic movements—all to advance the interests of the state and the worldwide socialist revolution. This has often been done by stressing reality, while in the West the fictional form (what we call theme feature films) has dominated.

Considering conditions of technology, economics, and sociology, we are able to tackle the question of the history of film as an art form. The book does this first by considering how Hollywood established and maintained the dominant form of expression, and then by analyzing how alternative cinematic traditions developed. That is, one aesthetic mode of filmmaking, often labeled the Classic Hollywood Narrative style, has defined accepted moviemaking style and form in the United States since the late 1910s. Filmmakers interested in experimenting with other modes have had to work against audience expectations of the Classic Hollywood Narrative style. This book examines the history of this style and the major alternatives from abroad and within the United States, including contributions in documentary, experimental, and animated film.

Movie History: A Survey thus integrates technological, economic, social, and aesthetic questions to survey all phases of cinema's past. We begin with Hollywood because, simply put, the American cinema has so long dominated world cinema in terms of technological change, economic power, aesthetic standards, and social impact that it provides *the* benchmark by which other means of filmmaking have to be evaluated. That is not to say that Hollywood conquered the world, but rather that Hollywood's success around the world has long defined what is possible.

From this benchmark, I move on to examine particular non-Hollywood filmmaking alternatives, or movements. Films made within a movement share common traits of form and style, common production systems, and common assumptions about what makes an important film. That is not to say that movements exist wholly outside Hollywood. Indeed, they have long influenced the look and style (but not the fundamental principles) of the Classic Hollywood Narrative cinema.

• structure of the book •

To implement this four-part approach to technological, economic, social, and aesthetic history, *Movie History: A Survey* is divided into three major sections:

    I. "The Silent Cinema, 1895–1927"
    II. "The Hollywood Studio Era, 1928–1950"
    III. "The Television Era, 1951–1975"

The initial chapter in each section describes and analyzes technological change in the movies, first in the United States and then in its export to film industries throughout the world.

Once the technology was in place, Hollywood could develop as an industry and social entity. Economic and social history provides the second unit of analysis in each section, whether as an individual chapter (Chapter 2 in Section I) or as the second part of the initial chapter, as in Sections II and III.

But Hollywood has long stood for more than its available technologies, massive corporate entities, and seemingly pervasive social impact. The American film also has long set a dominant aesthetic standard—the Classic Hollywood Narrative style. This form and style of motion picture leads to feature-length films (usually one and a half to two hours) that tell patterned stories (Westerns or musicals, for example) with highly publicized stars photographed from certain acceptable camera angles, and compiled within certain editing schemes. The aesthetic history of Hollywood constitutes the third chapter of Section I and the second chapters in Sections II and III.

With an understanding of the technology, economics, sociology, and style of Hollywood in the silent era, the studio period, and the television age, we can comprehend and appreciate the major alternatives posed by foreign cinema. Once an influential native cinema has been identified, its economic and social conditions are outlined and then its unique aesthetic contributions (of style and form) are analyzed. Chapters on important alternative movements from all parts of the world conclude Sections I, II, and III.

All histories must cut off at some date. This book ends, as a history, in 1975, when Hollywood again began to initiate technological change with the increasing use of cable television and home video to present movies.

In the final segment of the book—"An Epilogue: Contemporary Film History"—I examine what *seem to be* the major technological, economic, social, and aesthetic changes in the past decade. Chapter 14 is not history in the same vein as the rest of the book, because we lack the perspective needed to identify fundamental shifts and patterns.

• in conclusion •

Finally, let me comment on several important practical matters. Around the world, thousands of features are being made and shown in theatres and on television every year. Even more documentaries, animated works, and experimental films are also being turned out. To locate up-to-the-minute reading, look to the journals and periodicals noted in the "Guide to Further Reading" at the end of the book.

The "Guide" also gives the sources that proved useful in writing this book. No historian of the cinema can do all the primary research for a survey history that covers millions of films made and shown in different countries throughout the world. He or she must rely on the fine work of others. In some cases we have wonderful studies, but in some places vast holes exist for further research. Like all writers of survey histories before me, I have integrated my own research and writings with what I consider the best writing in film history today. I profoundly thank all those authors mentioned in the "Guide to Further Reading."

The "Guide" also lists the paper materials that make up primary documentation of film history, where one can find studio records, or the documents of social film history, or technological data for sound, color, and widescreen. As more and more archives open up collections that contain valuable papers and records, and as microfilm records of important papers go into distribution, it becomes easier and easier to borrow (often through interlibrary loan) the written record of film history. The "Guide" offers a beginning for the reader to initiate his or her own research.

No book can deal with all the films ever made. Based on the principles outlined above, I selected those films of greatest importance within this perspective of the historical analysis of film. In the "Filmography" at the end of the book, I list additional credits under the categories established in the text. I also describe the best ways to see films and the pitfalls of film viewing.

Whenever possible, the date for a film is the year of its theatrical release in the country of origin. Film titles are given in English unless the common usage in English-speaking countries retains the original title.

This book contains about twenty stills per chapter as illustrations. In a few cases they are frame enlargements—these are the best "quotations" because they are from the films themselves. In other cases, however, I could only use publicity materials.

Let me emphasize that there is no substitute for examining the films themselves. In the early 1970s, when I entered film studies, owning a film was an expensive and often illegal activity. The only real choice was to buy 16mm copies at hundreds of dollars per film from dealers who often winked at the copyright laws. The coming of home video has made television viewing of films much less expensive. Thousands of classics can be rented from a local video store or through the mail. Names of mail-order renters and sellers of tapes can be found in the "Filmography."

But remember that seeing a film on videotape is not the same thing as the theatrical experience. Often, home videotapes have been edited or censored. They rarely contain the full image, particularly for wide-screen productions. Worst of all, color and sound may have been added to make a more attractive television show.

It is best to see a film shown in the gauge in which it was made, and on the sound system for which it was intended, uncut, uninterrupted.

But often the video is the only inexpensive way to conduct repeated viewings and thus gather the data needed for aesthetic and social history. I strongly recommend that you see the film at least once as it was intended to be seen and heard, and then use alternative sources, such as home video, for re-viewing.

• acknowledgments •

I wish to thank the many people who helped with this book. Let me single out a select few.

The text was immeasurably improved through the readings and criticism of Henry B. Aldridge, Eastern Michigan University; Drew Caspar, University of Southern California; Jeffery Chown, Northern Illinois University; Charles H. Harpole, Ohio State University; Audrey Kupferberg, Yale University; Hugh McCarney, Western Connecticut State University; Suzanne Regan, California State University, Los Angeles; Dave Viera, California State University, Long Beach; and Marion Weiss, American University.

I thank Sarah Bendersky and the following institutions for help with the photographs: the Museum of Modern Art, New York; the Kobal Collection; the Bison Archives; the Wisconsin Center for Film and Theatre Research; and the Motion Picture and Television Photo Archive, Los Angeles. Every effort was made to locate appropriate images, but it was not possible to be completely faithful to the precise filmic image. Reader, please forgive the limitations of the modern publication process.

To the staff at Wadsworth I shall always be grateful: Kristine Clerkin, editor; production editors Hal Humphrey and Karen Garrison; Andrew Ogus, designer; and many others in Belmont. Making a book is a collaborative process.

One person made this book possible: Marilyn Moon. With her wise counsel, I was able to accomplish a great deal. Oh, that the world had a few more with the wisdom, understanding, warmth, and intelligence of Marilyn. Anyone who reads this book and has reached the age of sixty-five ought to whisper a soft "thank you" that Marilyn chose to expend most of her efforts to revamp our nation's health care system.

Douglas Gomery
Chevy Chase, Maryland

••••••••••••••••••••••

movie history

••••••••••••••••••••••

I

• • • • • • • • • • • • • • • • • • • •

the silent cinema
1895 to 1927

• • • • • • • • • • • • • • • • • • • •

1895
1896
1897
1898
1899
1900
1901
1902
1903
1904
1905
1906
1907
1908
1909
1910
1911
1912
1913
1914
1915
1916
1917
1918
1919
1920
1921
1922
1923
1924
1925
1926
1927

. . . .

1

••

the invention
and innovation
of the movies

In the beginning the cinema was simply just another technological marvel. Through the decade of the 1890s into the early days of the twentieth century, inventors worked with the first filmmakers and exhibitors to convince a skeptical public to embrace the movie show. In the process these inventor/entrepreneurs set the stage for a social, economic, and cultural revolution which would fundamentally alter the way we know our world.

To study the introduction of this new technology, we must acknowledge that the movies became a business in which inventors became entrepreneurs to make money with their new inventions within U.S. capitalism. But inventors did not operate in a vacuum during the last decade of the nineteenth century, seeking to create some ideal new enterprise. Rather, at first they sought to sell their discoveries to some existing entertainment industry, be it vaudeville, theatre, or the phonograph model. But first the necessary new apparatus had to be created. For cinema this meant a camera to record images, and a printer to transfer them to the film strip. (Once the vaudeville and theatre proved to be the proper models, then a projector was needed to show movies to large groups of people.)

There is no law which dictates that necessary inventions need be made for any one purpose. Many times people create new knowledge for one goal, and then it becomes used for quite another (for example, the zoom lens was invented to improve the accuracy of bomb dropping during the Second World War). And frequently entrepreneurs do not recognize the purposes even once the new information is available (for example, wide-screen movies were available decades before they became commonplace in the 1950s).

A second step occurs when this apparatus is taken to the marketplace, that is, it is innovated. For the movies this meant a set of marketing strategies by which to convince the public to part with its money. Risk and timing weigh heavily on the prospective innovator. Will waiting help? Should one try to be first or learn from the mistakes of others? What will potential competitors do? The process of innovation is one of juggling new information with projected and real costs, with the demands of the potential audience. It took time to find ways to use the new motion pictures at low enough costs to please audiences of the day.

Finally, once the innovation has been established, it takes time to convince the rest of the world to adopt it. Indeed the very diffusion of the cinema throughout the world took more than ten years to become a mass leisure time activity. Many would try, but not until the 1910s would Hollywood convince the world that cinema could become a mass art form, not simply a passing fad. The diffusion of the technology was accomplished when the movies became an industry of influential, profitable enterprises.

This chapter charts the invention, innovation, and diffusion of the movies in the years before the cinema became a worldwide phenomena. We shall discover how the movies came to be invented, and how inventors turned entrepreneurs brought the new cinematic technology to a mass public audience.

the invention of the movies

During the years at the end of the nineteenth century scientists and inventors around the world were working on aspects of the design for "photographic images with motion." But the history of the invention of the cinema centers in the United States and France, and we focus our survey there.

• early knowledge •

Because moving images depend on individual still photographs appearing in rapid succession, certain technological requirements had first to be met. That is, the development of photography had logically to precede the development

An early experiment in motion photography by Eadweard Muybridge.

of the movies. During the nineteenth century a series of discoveries were gradually perfected, beginning with the recording of images on paper coated with light-sensitive particles. But at first, after being removed from the camera, these recorded images would continue to darken to all black. By the 1830s a method was discovered to chemically "fix" the silver salts so that they would not continue to be affected by light; positives could then be made from these negatives.

Early photographs, such as those taken by Mathew Brady during the Civil War, required lengthy exposures, at first as long as thirty min-

utes. Refinements lowered necessary exposure time to a few minutes, then a few seconds. By the 1870s inventors had begun to utilize exposures as fast as one–twenty-fifth of a second on glass plates. But glass plates were of no help to those who envisioned "moving pictures." A new base was required to enable one to capture movement in time, not simply photographic recordings of single images.

In the late 1870s Eadweard Muybridge, an American photographer, made a pioneering series of photographs on glass plates in order to show precisely how a horse ran. He did this with a battery of cameras activated by threads to trip the shutters stretched across the track, coupled with a neutral white background. We finally could see an animal in motion. Thus, capturing movement was possible, but not on a moving strip. In 1882 Frenchman Etienne-Jules Marey invented a camera that recorded twelve separate images on the edge of a re-volving disc of film. Six years later he built the first camera to use a long strip of flexible film, this time on a paper base. His purpose, like that of Muybridge, was simply to break down and analyze the movements of animals.

The pioneering photography company in the United States, Eastman Kodak of Rochester, New York, in 1889 introduced a flexible film base, celluloid. With such a malleable base the creation of a lengthy continuous set of frames recording motion became possible. This would be the basis for the movie camera. But by then the knowledge for such a camera was available in a number of countries, and any number of scientists began to work to invent the cinema: Thomas Edison and Thomas Armat in the United States; Etienne-Jules Marey, Louis Le Prince, and Louis and Auguste Lumière in France; Ottomar Anschutz, Max Skladanowsky and Oskar Messter in Germany; and William Friese-Greene and Robert Paul in Great Britain. All could legitimately make some claim that they had a part in inventing the movie camera.

But the cinema—to become a mass spec-tator experience—also required a means to present the film—a movie projector. Projectors had existed before 1889, indeed, throughout the nineteenth century, to present photographic slides. These magic lanterns were modified with a series of shutters, cranks, and other mechanisms to project a continuous strip of photos on a screen. To make the images seem to "move," the photos on the strip had to be stopped for a short time and viewed—or pro-jected on a screen. This process needed to be repeated at least twelve times a second to avoid flicker.

After any number of frustrations, inventors working independently in a number of coun-tries around the world perfected a projector with the necessary intermittent motion capa-bility. Films thus could be recorded (the cam-era), and then shown (the projector). Although many claim to have invented the cinema, two important inventors, because of the status of their countries at the time, became the most influential, helping spread their inventions throughout the world: Thomas Alva Edison of the United States, and the brothers August and Louis Lumière of France.

• thomas alva edison •

Through the latter half of the nineteenth cen-tury, the famous American inventor Thomas Alva Edison worked on and off on the movies as he did on any number of inventions. He did not envision creating cinema per se, but wished to invent a visual accompaniment to his vastly successful phonograph. In the 1890s phono-graphs were popular arcade items; patrons dropped in coins to hear the latest of Edison's marvels. It was in this context that he sought to build a moving picture show to go along with his penny arcade money-maker.

During the 1870s Edison acquired a ste-reopticon, a device that projected three-dimen-sional still pictures. He soon thereafter installed a photographic darkroom in both his Menlo Park and West Orange, New Jersey laboratories. In February 1888, Edison met Eadweard Muy-bridge who at the time was working at the Uni-versity of Pennsylvania in nearby Philadelphia.

Adolph Zukor (right) meeting with Thomas Alva Edison.

● ●

Inspired by Muybridge's experiments, Edison sought to combine their study of "movement" (still frame by still frame) with the sounds of his phonograph. Edison bought ninety Muybridge plates picturing horses, deer, and naked humans in motion. The problem was how to run them in continuous motion and then couple that with the phonograph sounds.

But always restless, Edison moved on to other projects, and ordered twenty-eight–year–old William Kennedy Laurie Dickson to find a solution. Dickson, an amateur photographer, was a logical choice to work on the moving pictures project. George Eastman's development of the celluloid-based photographic film provided Dickson with new possibilities. He also learned of Marey's photography of motion on paper strips. Dickson set off to invent the movies in what might best be categorized as a brilliant job of synthesis, rather than a burst of totally original creation. He designed the camera, the Kinetograph, to record the images which would be projected along with the sounds of a phonograph. The result was a popular arcade peep-show attraction using short films.

Always the businessman, Edison strove to exploit his company's new invention by placing it in amusement parlors throughout the United States. From the beginning he envisioned that movies would be linked with sound, and he instructed Dickson to develop what came to be called the Kinetoscope to present short films to individual viewers. At this point Edison felt movies (with or without sound) would be a passing arcade fad; therefore he did not create a system to project films onto a screen.

By 1892 the vertical feed Kinetograph (the viewer) was ready; two years later the first set of machines reached Broadway amusement arcades. The fifty-foot loops of film moved through the machine in less than a half minute. The machine utilized two important ideas: a stop-motion device to insure discontinuous but regular movement of the film, and a perforated celluloid strip. The use of celluloid allowed it all to happen many times per second.

It was only in 1893 that Edison re-assigned Dickson back to the Kinetograph. The size of the original camera was that of an upright piano. So a studio, the Black Maria, was built around it. The roof opened to adjust the light, and the film was exposed at forty frames per second (versus today's twenty-four). Dickson chose as his first film subjects entertainers who could be persuaded to journey across the Hudson River to the New Jersey studio: denizens of Broadway vaudeville theatres, circus performers, trained animal acts, dancers, and comics. Early film titles included *The Gaiety Girls Dancing*, *Trained Bears*, and *Highland Dance*. Numerous vaudeville stars and celebrities of the day (for example, Buffalo Bill Cody and Annie Oakley) appeared before Edison's camera.

An early kinetoscope parlor, approximately 1894–1895.

● ●

In April 1894 Andrew Holland opened the first Kinetoscope parlor in a converted shoe store on Broadway in New York City. He charged twenty-five cents per person (later falling to a nickel) for access to Edison peep-show viewers, each of which contained a single loop. Soon other Kinetoscope parlors were opened across the United States, all showing shorts which lasted just sixteen seconds. The shorts were produced exclusively by the Edison Company and sold for ten to fifteen dollars per print.

At this point Edison ceased to be a cinema inventor per se and became a cinema innovator. That is, he turned from creating the knowledge which gave rise to the cinema camera, developer, and printer and turned to making money

from these new machines. (Indeed, he had no projector at the time.) In a later section we shall look at Edison the innovator, who in 1896 with more assistants (most notably Edwin S. Porter) sought methods to produce and sell and thus make money from the new inventions.

• the brothers lumière •

Edison concentrated on the camera, ignoring the projector. But others envisioned the projector as an important part of the mix. Three fundamental requirements—a lamp for light, a lens to magnify the images, and a mechanism

Louis and Auguste Lumière in their laboratory.

● ●

The original Lumière cinematographe camera.

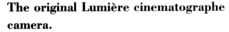

for intermittent motion—were needed. The German Oskar Messter, the Englishman William Friese-Green, and the Frenchman Louis Aime Augustin Le Prince all worked on the projector, often inspired by what they had learned from Edison. But by far the most important of these early inventors were the brothers Lumière of Lyons, France: Louis and Auguste.

They operated a factory which manufactured photographic equipment. After a thorough study of Edison machines, the Lumières constructed their own version of a camera, projector, and printer. In December 1895 the brothers Lumière publicly introduced their Cinematographe by projecting ten short motion pictures on a screen in the basement of the Grand Café in Paris. Although Edison was clearly first, the Lumières developed the system that would endure—projection of film onto a screen. They were so successful that Edison soon abandoned his peep show and like the Lumières made equipment and movies for public presentation.

Much smaller and lighter, the Lumières' sixteen-pound (versus Edison's five-hundred–pound apparatus) hand-cranked Cinematographe permitted ease of camera movement and placement. It could follow events. The Lumières could take their camera to the world. And since their camera was hand-cranked, films could be made and shown at speeds which varied from fourteen to twenty-four frames per second. Only with the coming of sound was film speed standardized at twenty-four frames per second.

As one might expect, the first Lumière films were simple, usually consisting of only a single shot. The Lumières took their lightweight, manually operated cameras to the parks, gardens, and any number of other public places in and around France to record everyday activities and, when possible, important events of the day. (Edison's was motor driven and heavy and required an electrical power supply.) The titles of their most famous early films (*Arrival of a Train at a Station*, *Baby's Lunch*, and *Workers Leaving the Factory*) accurately describe the interest in recording ordinary happenings of life. These two tactics—the Lumières' recording of actual events and Edison's films of entertainment—would define the principal forms of film as a mass medium. The Lumières' Cinemato-graphe screenings and their initial popularity signaled the end of the invention phase of the movies.

But Edison and the Lumières were hardly alone in working on the movies. Almost overnight many others claimed to have invented their own apparatus. In Germany Max and Emile Skladanowsky developed their own projector called the Bioscope and made a public performance in Berlin in November 1895. In 1896 a manufacturer of scientific instruments in Great Britain, Robert W. Paul, patented his own version of the movie projector. The technology for the silent movie show, which would last until the late 1920s, was in place. It was now up to businessmen and women to figure out the best way to use the devices to make money. Filmmaking and viewing might be faddishly popular initially, but what form and shape would they take in the long run?

the strategy of innovations

There were three different strategies by which early movie entrepreneurs tried to bring movie entertainment to the masses. We shall focus our attention on the United States, although cases in others countries provided variations on the same theme.

1. First the inventors of the technology tried to make money with their new gadgets. But they needed somewhere to show the films.

2. This would lead them to vaudeville theatres, which needed attractions to fill their seats; theatre owners were happy to try a new gimmick to draw in patrons. Vaudeville business operators convinced the entertainment world of the drawing power of the movies.

3. So, entertainers from all aspects of show

business began to see filmmaking as a way to find a place in show business, and hundreds entered the new film industry and became the first filmmakers. This would lead to storefront or nickelodeon theatres.

• inventors as entrepreneurs •

Inventors rarely play in their laboratories for the fun of it. They seek fortune and fame. This was certainly the case with the pioneering work in the movies. In particular, Edison and the Lumière brothers offer us clear examples of how successful inventors attempted to bring their inventions to the world of show business. Both tried to capture the market through control of the new movie technology.

Edison began in the movie business as a man interested in repeating his successes with the phonograph. He was a hardware person interested in selling equipment, not entertainment. He argued that if one sold projectors which could be used to show films to hundreds if not thousands, who would buy equipment after the first sales wave? He wanted to make a killing, as fast as possible, on the sale of his invention and then move on. Thus, he refused to pay the necessary $150 to secure international protection for his patents and so made possible the borrowing and adapting of his ideas.

Edison marketed his peep shows through a company established by Norman C. Raff and Frank R. Gammon. But the peep show proved only a novelty and could never make very much money since only one person could use it at a time. Raff & Gammon searched for a projector to integrate into the Edison system so they could display to large crowds. They saw what

Edison did not: more profits from movies as a form of theatre.

Raff & Gammon had learned of the European success of the Lumières' Cinematographe, and so in December of 1895 when they learned of a projector designed by C. Francis Jenkins and Thomas Armat, two Americans, which had been demonstrated at the Cotton States Exposition in Atlanta, they bought the exclusive rights. Edison Manufacturing Works would build it. (Armat had incorporated the Latham loop, which enabled films of great lengths to be shown without risking breakage of the film strip.) The new projector was called the Vitascope.

Raff & Gammon had bought the rights to the Vitascope not to exhibit films themselves, but to peddle the right to do so to others. They sought to franchise the Vitascope state by state. The first screening under this system took place in New York City at Koster and Bial's Music Hall in April 1896 as "Edison's Vitascope," to take advantage of the fame of America's best-known inventor. Indeed, since the Cinematographe had been booked in New York, Raff & Gammon were under considerable pressure to demonstrate their "new technological wonder." The Vitascope became a permanent vaudeville attraction as the nation turned into the twentieth century.

But Raff & Gammon ran into constant problems. For one thing, the machine's motor was incompatible with electric supplies in many cities around the United States. During the fall of 1896 Edison stepped in to develop his own projector and sell it outright, not through Raff & Gammon. In time Edison bought out his cash-poor partners; the Wizard of Menlo Park had entered the entertainment business in a big way.

From 1896 onward, the Edison Company sold films to exhibitors on a first-come, first-

Filming an early Edison short.

• •

served basis. Edison's business strategy envisioned maximizing the number of exhibitors served while producing the films directly or through license agreements. If Edison could have made a large number of small exhibitors dependent on its services and machines, it could have achieved a dominant market share.

But there were competitors. Producers such as Philadelphia's Sigmund Lubin and New York's American Mutoscope and Biograph Company, plus foreign imports (from companies including Lumière of France, among others), flooded the American market. As more and more films became available, having a direct relationship with Edison proved irrelevant, if unnecessary.

In response Edison went to court to try to curtail all production of movies in the United States, since, as his lawyers argued, he controlled the necessary patents. Unfortunately for Edison, exhibitors throughout the country were able to easily acquire films from abroad; all his suit did in the short run was to increase the flood of foreign films into the United States.

In 1900 the Edison Company decided to pay closer attention to the films it distributed. In October of 1900 Edison began building a studio in New York City on East 21st Street. From such a base it had access to the best vaudeville talent. Production at the new studio commenced in February 1901 with Edwin S. Porter as the most important of the early filmmakers.

Near the end of 1901, as the Edison studio was beginning to regularly turn out films, Edison's lawyers won an important victory which upheld the company's patent position. Temporarily, Lubin left for Germany; Vitagraph stopped making films and reverted back to its original exhibition business. Edison seemed in control of American moviemaking. Taking advantage of its position, the Edison Company pursued an extremely conservative policy, concentrating on news films and topical attractions. Thomas Edison was glad his invention was again making money; now he could turn his energies to other projects.

Taking no chances operating as a monopolist, Edison kept the industry in a steady position. But his monopoly was short-lived. In March of 1902, a higher court reversed the favorable 1901 decision, and Edison's heyday was doomed. The company was forced to make longer, more spectacular films to keep up with its competitors. This new direction led to the narrative experiments for which Edison's ace filmmaker, Edwin S. Porter, became famous, including *The Life of an American Fireman* and *The Great Train Robbery*, both made in 1903, the year following the defeat in the courts.

Across the Atlantic, the brothers Lumière were matching Edison's early success as they too attempted to turn their inventions into profits. The Lumières had sufficient capital and managerial skill to market their new apparatus with considerable success, both in France and around the world. Indeed their projector was the first to achieve worldwide success. Others, in particular Edison, had focused all their energies on reproducing vaudeville numbers. The Lumières continued to stress real-life activities. They shot working men and women, actual events around them, indeed their own family.

They concentrated on work related activities (*Tearing Down a Wall*), societal rituals (countless military and governmental ceremonies), and travelogues, especially of interest in the era of the railroad train. The Lumières' father had been a successful portrait photographer and passed on an understanding of what subjects sold best. But for the Lumières the filming of documentary actualities was simply a way to generate publicity to help sell Cinematographe equipment.

After the first public demonstration of the Cinematographe in Paris in 1895, the Lumières worked to create a demand for their cameras and projectors. They traveled to photographic congresses and called on the editors of popular science magazines, all to promote interest in this latest wonder of science. They proclaimed a product superior to simple black and white still photographs. These were industrialists selling the movies as a new, improved industrial product, not as a substitute for mass entertainment as Edison was doing in the United States.

The logical extension of this publicity campaign was to tender the first newsreels. The Lumières would film writers and famous scientists and impress these influential members of the scientific community by projecting their moving images on a screen. In turn the scientists and writers praised the new invention which had made them "stars." So finally, when a big premiere was set for December 1895, curiosity spilled over to the general public. People wanted to see the Cinematographe they had read about in magazines and newspapers in the preceding months, "moving pictures" hailed by scientists as the greatest marvel of the age. Indeed, as early as 1896, the Lumière name signified films of important people and recordings of events from daily life.

The Lumière camera was lightweight and could easily be taken to its subjects. Technological superiority to Edison's immobile camera enabled the French brothers to extract full advantage from their business strategy. (Eventually the camera would be used for fictional filmmaking.) Since they did not have the existing link to financing, they had to effect a low-cost way to innovate the movies. The Lumières financed most of their growth without borrowing from banks. But in the end, because of a lack of permanent support, they were never able to become a power in the very industry they created. They sensed this and from the beginning concentrated on exploiting the market as quickly as they could.

• selling the movies through vaudeville •

In the United States it took vaudeville entrepreneurs to provide a permanent home to the movies. Indeed, when the new movie technology first became available in 1894, vaudeville stood at the apex of commercialized popular entertainment. The first American movie audiences often were found in vaudeville theatres. The Edison/Armat Vitascope, the Lumières' Cinematographe, and the other versions of movies all made their debuts in New York vaudeville theatres in the 1896–1897 season (September to May) as single fifteen-minute acts among eight others on the bill. Until the explosive growth of the nickelodeon in 1906, American vaudeville theatres provided the movie industry regular access to potential patrons.

Vaudeville theatre consisted of eight or more acts aimed at a middle-class audience.

These ten- to twenty-minute bits of entertainment were generally unrelated in form and content. The vaudeville bill aimed to please as many patrons as possible with Irish tenors, trained seals, inspirational poetry readings, troops of acrobats, pairs of comics, professors with magic lantern slides, and "playlets" of condensed versions of popular dramatic hits from Broadway. Managers of vaudeville houses tried to book a little something for everyone.

One reason folks flocked to vaudeville entertainment in the 1890s was that it had moved into theatres whose architecture and interior design nearly matched the best theatres in town. So with the opening of Proctor's Pleasure Palace on Labor Day of 1895 in New York City, patrons were made to feel at home in a large auditorium, a roof garden, a German cafe, and a barber shop, with a Turkish bath and flower and booksellers in the basement. Once they paid their admission, patrons could enjoy a continuous show in the main auditorium (ten in the morning until midnight) or make use of some other part of Proctor's offerings.

The 1890s saw the building of chains of vaudeville theatres: the Keith's in major cities in the eastern part of the United States; the Pantages and Orpheum circuits west of the Mississippi. But competition was most keen in New York City, then the largest American city. To keep their theatres filled, Keith's, Proctor's, Tony Pastor, and Koster and Bials, among others, had to find newer, ever-different acts.

One source they looked to were visual spectacles such as puppetry, shadowgraphy (the making of shadow figures with hands), magic illusions, living pictures (famous scenes recreated by poses of live actors), and magic lantern presentations. During the 1895–1896 vaudeville season, the new movies offered a version of this form of spectacle.

One of America's earliest vaudeville theatres, Providence, Rhode Island, 1888.

● ●

In the movies vaudeville theatre owners found a new attraction. The latest marvel of the Edison factory could be marketed under the name of the greatest inventor in the world. The Lumières' Cinematographe made its American debut in June of 1896, two months after the Edison Vitascope, at Keith's Union Square vaudeville theatre. Keith's, the major vaudeville power in the eastern United States, dropped Vitascope and signed up the Lumières to service its theatres. From a New York office the Lumières supplied theatres with a projector,

a technician, and films—a complete "act" in the vaudeville parlance.

The Lumières' act could ride the circuit just like a juggler or a comic team. And the Cinematographe was hand cranked, not dependent on the multitude of different electrical sources in American cities of the time. Finally, the Lumières cleverly coupled short travelogs of foreign lands (for example, their native France) with local footage filmed by the traveling projectionist/cameraman as he moved from city to city.

By the end of the 1896–1897 season the pattern for commercial exhibition of movies as a vaudeville act had been established which would endure for a decade. Movies were best known to patrons as vaudeville acts until the rise of the nickelodeon in 1906. In vaudeville the movies found a way to reach the middle class. Indeed, vaudeville presented the forum by which Americans were introduced to the movies.

The films of this era served this vaudeville audience. For example, the American Mutoscope and Biograph Company continued the Lumières' practice of filming local activities. Audiences in city after city saw their own home town through films of local sporting teams, new buildings going up, or maneuvers of the fire department. Travel films, in the tradition of the magic lantern show, also presented moving pictures of faraway places. The travelogue was an important form for the movies between 1896 and 1903.

A variant was the news film. The clearest indication of its popularity came during the first war recorded on film—the Spanish-American conflict. During the winter of 1898, Americans were subjected to a constant barrage of public invective, especially from the newspapers of William Randolph Hearst, against the supposed

Spanish repression of Cuba. On 15 February 1898, the United States Navy's battleship *Maine* was sunk while at anchor in Havana's harbor under questionable circumstances; within two months the United States and Spain were at war. The actual incursion lasted only ten weeks, but problems persisted the following year in the Philippines.

Filmmakers recorded images of all number of war-related activities. The movies became so identified with news of the Spanish-American War that Edison renamed his projector the "Wargraph." To keep costs down, filmmakers "re-created" the battle of Manila Bay with cut-out photographs and judiciously placed smoke in makeshift studios. Fully one-third of all the movies made during 1898 and 1899 were news films, principally of the various Spanish-American War activities.

If war films sparked the early interest in seeing movies in vaudeville theatres, their very nature posed an essential problem. No one could count on or predict when war or news of urgent interest would happen. The movies proved highly successful vaudeville acts when a war was on, but otherwise they cost too much relative to their limited popularity. Vaudeville entrepreneurs began to seek new forms of movies to show. Thus, as the movie and vaudeville industries moved into the twentieth century, more and more comic films were made. These comic narratives on film became staples of America's vaudeville theatres by the 1902–1903 season (September through May).

The next season, moviemakers turned to dramatic stories, but the growth of this genre was slower. Some dramatic films, however, proved exceptionally popular. When Edwin S. Porter's *The Life of an American Fireman* was initially presented at Keith's vaudeville theatre in Boston during the summer of 1903, it was a major hit, as was a successor, Porter's *The Great Train Robbery*.

Vaudeville theatre crowds loved the magical trick films of Georges Méliès which began to appear in the United States during the fall of 1902. Méliès films such as *A Trip to the Moon*, *Little Red Riding Hood*, and *Cinderella* were held over, an unprecedented ploy at the time. Magicians had long been a vaudeville staple, and moviemakers integrated spectacular stage effects into familiar narratives. By 1904, there was an equal mix of films of actuality (news and documentary films) with films of comedy, drama, and magic. Such a mix guaranteed a constant stream of attractions. Fictional works could be created in the regular, low-cost, predictable fashion desired by vaudeville theatre owners.

What all this change and increased popularity did was open up the market for movie shows. If movies could be hits in vaudeville theatres, could they stand on their own? In a movie-only theatre? The nickelodeon would answer a resounding "yes" to these questions. By 1910, there would be more than ten thousand movie-only theatres, signaling the success of the innovation of movies. The vaudeville theatres had done their job. Movies had become a permanent part of the mass-entertainment landscape. The nickelodeon would signal the beginning of the diffusion of the movies in the United States.

• filmmakers as innovators •

Once films began to be made and presented in vaudeville houses, the fledgling film industry began to attract men and women to moviemaking. We can see in the careers of Americans

Edwin S. Porter, pioneer filmmaker.

● ●

Edwin S. Porter, J. Stuart Blackton, Albert E. Smith, and Sigmund Lubin, in the actions of the American Mutoscope and Biograph Company, and in the significant innovations of Frenchman Georges Méliès how filmmakers helped innovate the movies. All offer us fascinating examples of how filmmakers struggled to make movies a vital part of American mass entertainment.

Edwin S. Porter stands as one of the most important of early American filmmakers. His *The Life of an American Fireman* (1903) and *The Great Train Robbery* (1903) certainly rank as the most famous of pre-nickelodeon films. Porter began his career as a traveling projectionist, two months after the premiere of Edison's Vitascope at Koster and Bial's Music Hall in April 1896. He worked in California, Indiana, and Ontario, Canada.

Early in 1898 he settled in New York City to work at the Eden Musée, an early center of film exhibition, and was heavily involved in putting together packages of films from the Spanish-American War during the height of popularity of that film genre. In 1900 Porter moved to the Edison studio to become a cameraman as Edison began to experiment with story films. *Terrible Teddy the Grizzly King* (1901) burlesqued vice-president–elect Theodore Roosevelt. *The Finish of Bridget McKeen* (1901) presented a two-shot comedy in which Porter dissolved from one shot to another to provide the necessary continuity for the joke.

These and other early films share a common style. The first shots are self-contained presentations, constructed like single-shot films so common in this period. The significant difference is the addition of the tag, a short fragment which could stand alone but commented on the earlier shot. There is no continuity linkage yet; in some cases a live narrator standing beside the screen helped stitch the story together.

Through 1901 and 1902 Porter continued to experiment with comic, vaudeville-oriented films. In 1902, Porter began several notable experiments: *Appointment by Telephone* (1902), *Jack and the Beanstalk* (1902), *How They Do Things in the Bowery* (1902), and *The Life of an American Fireman* (1903). *Appointment by Telephone* is a three-shot, one-hundred-foot film which tells of a wife confronting her husband who is "stepping out." It makes use of interior and exterior spatial relationships, creating a fictional world. *Jack and the Beanstalk*, inspired by Méliès' success, is a ten-shot narrative which took six weeks to make. *Jack and the Beanstalk* anticipated many of the narrative film devices so celebrated in *The Life of an American Fireman*. This film was certainly not the first to tell a story, but one of the first to make the story so tightly drawn that an exhibitor need not rearrange it as was common in vaudeville theatres. The exhibitor was reduced to a simple programmer.

The Life of an American Fireman represents the consolidation of Porter's development as a filmmaker. As with *Jack and the Beanstalk*, Porter chose a subject with which audiences were quite familiar through lantern slide shows. Indeed, *Bob the Fireman* was a hit as a lantern slide presentation in the 1902–1903 entertainment season, and Porter simply transferred it to the movies. (Edison had made fire rescue films as early as 1896.) The use of the narrative attractiveness of a dramatic rescue, from a well-known story, predated and anticipated *The Great Train Robbery* (1903) and *Rescued from an Eagle's Nest* (1907). Porter showed audiences shots of racing fire engines and burning buildings. This success with the power of telling gripping stories would become the basis of the Classic Hollywood cinema, the foundation of the studio system.

Porter continued to develop his powers of storytelling, through somewhat sophisticated editing techniques, in his best-known film, *The Great Train Robbery*. Intentionally or not he employed cross-cutting to imbibe a greater feeling of dramatic tension into a simple western tale of robbery and rescue. Others would follow Porter's lead. He had made his contribution by suggesting a number of possibilities of how the new medium might be used to tell stories.

But early on Porter ceased making important contributions as a filmmaker. He would remain a mainstream director for another decade, working at the end for Famous Players–Lasky, the company which would do so much to spread the Classic Hollywood narrative film around the world. Porter then turned to designing cameras, including the Simplex, and until his death in 1941 worked on the periphery of the industry he had done so much to help start.

J. Stuart Blackton and **Albert E. Smith** were rivals to Porter. Before their involvement in the cinema, they worked together in mass entertainment, Blackton as a cartoonist and Smith as a magician. The duo traveled the Lyceum circuit of churches and YMCAs putting on an evening's entertainment with ventriloquism, magic, and a magic lantern presentation. Blackton painted the slides and provided the monologue for the magic lantern act. Their entry into the new movie industry came as a straightforward extension of the magic lantern act.

Blackton visited Edison's Black Maria studio in 1896, and one year later he and Smith purchased a projector and incorporated as the Vitagraph Company, to play off the name of the Edison *Vita*scope. Movies became central to their act; Vitagraph began only as an exhibitor of early movies. The spark that made the company grow was the great interest in 1898 in the Spanish-American War. At first, Smith and Blackton took advantage of the best available war footage and integrated it into their vaudeville act. Later, Vitagraph went into production so Blackton and Smith could differentiate their product from what Edison and others were offering. In May 1898, using a modified Edison camera, they filmed *The Battle of Manila Bay* on a table with careful manipulation of photographs of ships and battle scenes amid flashes of gunpowder and fireworks.

Vitagraph not only made Spanish-American War films. It also recorded the New York Naval Parade in August 1898, Albert Smith as a magician in *The Vanishing Lady* (a Méliès-like disappearing act), and *The Burglar on the Roof*, with Blackton as the burglar, an evocation of a

J. Stuart Blackton (left) and Alfred E. Smith working on an early production.

newspaper comicstrip character. These films were shown in various New York City vaudeville theatres. Vitagraph got in trouble duplicating (or duping) Edison films, and rather than fight the charge, it became a licensee of the Edison Company. Edison, however, as the licensor owned Vitagraph's films, and made copies and sold them to any exhibitor who might ante up the money. Vitagraph only had exclusive rights for the first three months. During 1899, this symbiotic relationship thrived, so that by May of 1899, Vitagraph declared itself one of the largest movie concerns in the United States. At this point both Edison and Vitagraph made money, Edison from selling apparatus and films, Vitagraph from exhibition and filmmaking. But the exhibition end proved less lucrative and stable, so Vitagraph concentrated on filmmaking to make consistent profits.

Success did not come easily. Lighting problems frustrated recordings of boxing matches, but such films proved consistent draws and helped Vitagraph obtain a permanent exhibition contract with Tony Pastor's Theatre on Union Square in New York City. Vitagraph recorded Admiral Dewey's successful return from the Philippines. As can be seen from these two examples, Vitagraph specialized in topical films with current news value. News films could be rushed to a theatre and fully exploited before the competition could duplicate them. Otherwise, Vitagraph imitated Méliès' trick and magic films and presented distinctive comedies, in particular a series with "Happy Hooligan" played by Blackton.

But Edison wanted a full and complete monopoly and was not content to depend on Vitagraph or any other "upstart." In 1900, the two broke ranks, and in April of that year Vitagraph came out with its own catalog. As it battled Edison in the courts, Vitagraph survived by importing films from abroad, in particular from France. For a time between January 1901 and March 1902, an unfavorable court ruling even prevented Vitagraph from making films. But Vitagraph remained in the filmmaking business and began to prosper with the commencement of the nickelodeon era. In 1906 Vitagraph built a studio in Brooklyn to make longer works; by 1910, it was releasing some three reels of film per week, thus establishing itself as a major company in the film business. Edison may have tried to monopolize film through control of the technology, but showmen like Blackton and Smith, with experience in providing entertainment to the masses, still succeeded and, indeed, prospered.

The American Mutoscope and Biograph Company (hereafter AMB), based in New York, was able to make a go of it because it had established an ongoing relationship with the Keith's vaudeville chain. In 1895, the Magic Introduction Company, owned by Bernard Koopman, joined with manufacturers Henry Marvin and Herman Casler, from upstate New York, and with W. K. L. Dickson, Edison's assistant, to form the AMB. The goal was to produce the equipment for short subjects to be presented on flip cards for mutoscope machines in amusement parks and dime museums. But quickly the company expanded to produce movies for vaudeville theatres as well. In October 1896, AMB presented movies at Hammerstein's Olympic Music Hall, including short films of William McKinley running for President of the United States.

But like all of these early Edison competitors, AMB had to be aggressive to survive and prosper. Edison threatened lawsuits, while AMB sought to try different types of movies which included comedies, dramas, and films with sensational themes as well as the travelogues, religious films, and films based on classical literature. By 1899 AMB was making dozens of films each year, usually about twenty-five to fifty feet in length, running scarcely more than a minute in time. In 1900 the company made more than 350 titles, of which half were shot on location and dealt with news events or travel. The other half were vaudeville-inspired entertainments. Most of the filming, done outdoors, was completed between May and October.

As with Vitagraph, once freed from Edison's legal threats AMB began to make longer entertainment films. In 1903 came *The American Soldier in Love and War* in three parts, *Kit Carson* in thirteen parts, and *The Pioneers* in six parts. The latter two were made on location in New York state's Adirondack Mountains. These were AMB's entries in the year that Edison's Edwin S. Porter made *The Life of an American Fireman* and *The Great Train Robbery*. In 1904 AMB continued with longer films, up to one reel. Fewer titles were released, but with more time and money allocated to production values. Billy Bitzer, later to become world famous as D. W. Griffith's cameraman, signed up and recorded films about the Westinghouse plant in Pittsburgh, Pennsylvania, and the St. Louis World's Fair.

But the number of news films, tied so closely to actual interesting events, fell after 1904. As with most companies of the time, AMB made longer and longer fictional works to entice the newly forming nickelodeons. Production changed as well. More and more films were shot indoors where lighting and stage conditions could be more easily controlled. AMB moved away from the improvisational style of filmmaking which had worked well with short, one-shot films. Fewer cameramen were involved on fewer set productions. These type of production conditions would set the industry standard in New York City until the move to California at the end of the decade.

Sigmund Lubin was an early moviemaker who did not begin in vaudeville. In 1898, Lubin of Philadelphia was offering Edison a great deal of competition. Lubin had come to the United States from Berlin, Germany, not as an uneducated peasant, but with a university degree in optics. He settled in Philadelphia to set up an optical shop, which led him to an interest in the movies. During his stay as a visiting

professor at the University of Pennsylvania, Eadweard Muybridge exhibited his animal locomotion studies, which attracted a great deal of attention, including that of Lubin. On Christmas Day in 1895 Latham's eidoloscope was shown at Keith's Bijou Theatre, right across the street from Lubin's shop. Six months later, Edison's Vitascope played the same theatre, followed two months later by the Lumières' Cinematographe. Lubin felt he could do better and began to manufacture moving picture equipment and produce films to compete on the vaudeville circuit with these competitors. His projector could present slides and films in a continuous program, which gave him "a leg up" in terms of programming flexibility.

At first Lubin as filmmaker followed the Edison model by recording Philadelphia's vaudeville talent, including *Mlle. Rosina Venus, Queen of the Invisible and Dancing Tightwire,* and *Professor Kriesel's Trained Dogs.* As an avid boxing fan, he re-created with actors many of the great prize fights of the era. Lubin's Cineograph projector weighed less than fifty pounds, small enough to be used easily by traveling exhibitors. It was not dependent, as were Edison's original models, on electricity, but could be run with acetylene gas, calcium, or electricity. Lubin was offering a Cineograph projector, two films, two Monarch records, and a Victor phonograph—all for less than one hundred dollars.

By 1897, Lubin had nearly three hundred films in the can; a year later the total topped one thousand titles. These included the usual news footage, recordings of vaudeville acts, prize fights, and trick films. Lubin built an early theatre in 1899 on the midway of the National Export Exposition in West Philadelphia. By 1908, he had a chain of some one hundred theatres along the East Coast. (These would later be taken over by the Stanley chain and then Warner Bros.) Many of the early Lubin films were simple duplicates of films by Edison, Méliès, and AMB. Indeed, Lubin, operating out of the main New York circle, duped to a greater degree than almost any competitor, angering the Wizard of Menlo Park. Edison thus took direct aim at Lubin, filing suit in 1898. The two battled in court off and on until 1908, when both joined forces to effect their own monopoly with the Motion Picture Patents Company. Lubin, with Edison and other pioneers, suffered through this alliance and, with the rise of Hollywood, Lubin receded to the background.

Georges Méliès offered the greatest challenge to both his fellow countrymen, the brothers Lumière, as well as to filmmakers around the world. Méliès was a professional magician who owned and operated the Theatre Robert-Houdin in Paris. He had been using magic lantern projections in his conjuring acts for years. When he saw a presentation of the Lumières' Cinematographe in 1895, he sought to incorporate their device into his acts. But the Lumières would not sell a machine to a competitor. So Méliès, a mechanic, photographer, and stage designer, purchased a projector from pioneering British inventor Robert William Paul and modified it for use as camera and projector. By April of 1896, his Theatre Robert-Houdin had become the first public movie theatre.

In what may be an apocryphal story, Méliès, one day while filming the Paris Opera House, had his camera jam, and so he recorded one event "on top of" another. When projected, one set of objects seemed to disappear, then another magically appeared. However true, Méliès needed a way to control these accidents. He drew on his background as a magician and

Georges Méliès, magician and filmmaker.

• •

helped pioneer a whole series of special effects. During the spring of 1897 Méliès built his first "glasshouse" studio on the grounds of his home in suburban Paris. The building measured fifty-five by twenty feet and twenty feet high and was glass-enclosed to admit maximum sunlight, then cinema's only effective light source.

In his studio, Méliès began to fashion elaborate settings to create fantasy worlds for use as mise-en-scène in his short films. The studio was a small, crammed building complete with theatrical machinery, balconies, trap doors, and sliding backdrops. There, he could plan and stage action for the camera. Gradually, he moved from simple trick effects (a man disappearing, for example) to story "tableaux," still consisting of only one shot. Whereas the Lumières seemed to run out of material in the late 1890s, Méliès grew more inventive and bold. In 1899, he produced the 13 minute *The Dreyfus Affair*, a major example of the then favored genre of the reconstructed newsreel.

Méliès created a totally imaginary world on film. Only in such a controlled environment could he make *The Mermaid* (1903), in which an undersea world is manufactured from an actress in costume, a fish tank placed in front of the camera, and additional sets and apparatus. Only with careful preparation and design knowledge from his years on the stage, could Méliès have fashioned the illusion of *The Man with the Rubber Head* (1901), in which he "inflated" his own head. (He did it by moving his own image in relationship to the camera, all photographed against a neutral background.) This master of mise-en-scène gave rise to a cinema of imagination which continues to this day with tricks abetted by computers.

Méliès told stories on film based on his knowledge of the theatre. He conceived of his films as dramatic scenes played out in a single shot. Editing occurred between single-shot scenes. The camera remained static to imitate a spectator in the theatre. But within this rigid formula Méliès perfected the fade-out/fade-in and the dissolve to distinguish one scene from another.

Méliès made many films, but certainly his most influential and famous was *A Trip to the Moon* (1902). Inspired by a Jules Verne novel of the same name, this film was a spectacle of fourteen minutes (three times the average Edison or Lumière product). It contains thirty separate scenes, connected by lap dissolves, in which we see "moon people" disappear and a spaceship fly to the moon.

To sell his films, Méliès organized the Star Film Company. Between 1897 and 1913, Méliès produced, directed, photographed, and even acted in some five hundred films, many of which were released hand-colored. By 1902, Méliès stood at the crest of his fame as the most successful early filmmaker. Star Film had become one of the world's largest suppliers of motion pictures. His films became very popular and through free trade in the cinema of the time freely circulated around the world. The New York office of Star Films was headed by his brother, Gaston. Other agencies were opened in London, Berlin, and Barcelona.

Méliès' objective was to create spectacle, bringing to the nascent medium elaborate studio sets, makeup, costumes, and trick effects. He wanted to overwhelm with an appreciation of the special effects. So when the actors in *A Trip to the Moon* bow and recognize the audience, it is not, as has often been suggested, merely a naive misunderstanding of the distinction between stage and screen, but an explicit recognition and respect for an audience accustomed to the conventions of the stage.

Méliès relied on certain forms of editing to help achieve his tricks. Indeed there are instances of rapid editing long before D. W. Griffith would make it famous in *The Birth of a Nation*. In *A Trip to the Moon*, there is a sequence of four shots in less than twenty seconds. The episode deals with the return of the rocket and contains scenes (1) on the moon, (2) in space, (3) above the ocean, and (4) at the bottom of the sea. This technique was not common but showed that Méliès was able to use editing to link together his special effects in ever-different ways to please his audiences.

• • • • • • • • • • • • • • • •

bringing the movies to the masses

• • • • • • • • • • • • • • • •

By the first decade of the twentieth century, the American public had taken to the movies, but not in a significant way. What happened next would make the movies into a major industry, a big business.

Hollywood as a powerful center of filmmaking did not exist. Films freely circulated from country to country. Film pioneers in industrialized countries throughout the world obtained or built cameras and made recordings of life and fantasies for entertainment. The coming of Hollywood would signal the end of such free trade in the cinema. To best understand how the United States fully embraced the movies, we need to closely examine change in the three facets of the film business: film production, film distribution, and film exhibition.

• film production •

Despite the efforts of Thomas Edison, filmmaking during the first decade of the twentieth century was a competitive situation. There were lots of small moviemakers, albeit Edison, AMB, Lubin, and Vitagraph were the most famous. Scores of filmmakers set up shop. In Chicago, for example, there was Essanay, Selig, and a score of smaller companies. Further off the beaten track were the Prudential Film Company

of Worcester, Massachusetts, and the United States Motion Picture Company of Wilkes-Barre, Pennsylvania. Prior to the arrival of Hollywood, motion picture production companies worked all over the United States. We must not make the mistake of only remembering the companies which made "great" films or the "first" of some type.

Films became more complicated. The simplest form, the film of one shot, can be said to have been inaugurated by the earliest films of Edison and Lumière and included those thousands of single take recordings of vaudeville attractions. This was the simplest way to record a vaudeville act. But as soon as the novelty of this simple one-shot form wore off, filmmakers began to make films with two and then more shots. We might have expected these to be the earliest form of Hollywood-like continuity filmmaking, but often filmmakers emphasized the discontinuity or disruption in the story. Films might have one long shot of some action and then a second, shorter shot of someone waking in bed, obviously having had a dream. The humor of discontinuity, so familiar in vaudeville routines, provided cinema with models for more complicated structures.

Narratives of continuity came through early chase films. The end of one shot is signalled by characters leaving the frame, while the next shot is inaugurated by their reappearance. The

Natural light illuminating an early film studio.

● ●

prototypes of this genre seem to stem from the popularity and influence of *A Trip to the Moon*. The journey provided the structure to create a simple continuity. By 1904, comic chase films made the continuity structure a widespread practice, with such titles as AMB's *The Maniac Chase*. Hundreds of imitators followed, instituting any number of situations in which characters could be motivated to run after each other.

In the earliest years New York City, as the mecca for vaudeville entertainment and America's largest city, became the center for film production. Most studios, former warehouses or stores, were located near Union Square on 14th Street in lower Manhattan. But New York City itself offered a multitude of possible locations, from slums to the homes of the upper class, from urban parks to beaches beside the ocean. When it became necessary to go out to the countryside, filmmakers ventured to unsettled New Jersey, scene for any number of early Westerns.

• film distribution •

Early films were traded in an open marketplace. Numerous jobbers sold the early films not as single units touted for their great stars as we might today, but by the foot or meter. It was not until 1904 or so that formal wholesalers, known as film exchanges, appeared. Early major companies (Edison, AMB, and the like) provided vaudeville theatres with a full-service attraction: the film, projectors, and even projectionists. Thus there was no need for a separate distribution mechanism between producer and theatre owner. The institution of film distribution was created with the rise of smaller companies after 1900 who simply made movies, who needed some mechanism to sell their footage to theatres around the United States, and if possible to theatres in other nations around the world.

European film companies provided models for distribution. For example, prior to 1902 Méliès' Star Films used an American company, AMB, to handle its sales in the United States. Since international copyrights were not enforced, filmmakers strove to maximize revenue as quickly as possible. But with so many lost sales due to illegal duplication of *A Trip to the Moon* (1902), Méliès established an American branch of Star Film Company in New York in 1902 under the management of his older brother Gaston. In July 1904 Pathé Frères, another French company, set up an office in the United States. Edison saw this as a threat and

sued both Pathé and Méliès in November 1904. By 1908 Pathé had become the largest single source for U.S. theatres.

Pathé commenced by sending representatives to sell equipment and films where none existed. By encouraging local entrepreneurs to open theatres it created demand for its films. Pathé would then open up an exchange and saturate the area. So throughout the first decade of the twentieth century, reports filtered back from the Middle East and China that Pathé had established the movies where none had existed before. Pathé moved to London, New York, Moscow, Brussels, Berlin, St. Petersburg, Amsterdam, Barcelona, Milan, Budapest, Warsaw, Calcutta, and Singapore.

• film exhibition •

Expanded film production and distribution depended on increased attendance at theatres. For film exhibition in the United States, at first there were only vaudeville houses and, in the summer, amusement parks. What gave impetus to the extraordinary rise in the movie business in the United States was the innovation of a theatre which only presented movies—the nickelodeon. These theatres set off an explosion in the demand for and impact of the movies as mass culture.

There had always been nickelodeons. Indeed, Raff & Gammon, Edison's agents in the 1890s, had franchised to any number of folks who rented storefronts and showed movies there. These small theatres offered brief programs of just film entertainment for a small admission charge—usually a nickel. But the number of nickelodeons never grew very large until vaudeville had first established the popularity of the movies as an entertainment form. Once that was done, an industry was ready to provide the films which could make up a program of entertainment which could stand on its own.

The nickelodeon was a small, uncomfortable, makeshift theatre, usually a converted cigar store, pawnshop, or restaurant made over to look like a vaudeville theatre. Out front were large hand-painted posters announcing the movies for the day; there were no advertisements in newspapers or reviews to guide potential patrons. (Advertisements and reviews would not start on a regular basis until 1912 or so.) Inside, the show of a number of news, documentary, comedy, fantasy, and dramatic shorts lasted about one hour. The show usually began with a sing-along, with words illustrated on hand painted, color magic lantern slides. But the bulk of the program was films.

But once the nickelodeon movement began in earnest, its popularity grew rapidly. In 1904 there were only a handful; the vaudeville remained the mainstay of film exhibition. By October 1906 there were more than one hundred in Chicago alone; a year later the figure in the United States topped two thousand; by 1910 some placed the number over ten thousand. One estimate claimed some twenty-six million attended each week in 1910, fully one-fifth of the adult population. Gross receipts reached into the millions of dollars.

The nickelodeon business was an easy one to enter. The experiences of the brothers Warner, Adolph Zukor (later head of Paramount), and Marcus Loew (creator of MGM) testified over and over again to the free-for-all in the nickelodeon world. Only a few thousand dollars in capital was required, little training, and

no special connections. Laws existed only to prevent highly flammable nitrate film from exploding into fire. There were no unions, rules, or regulations. The early days of the movie business were a golden opportunity for anyone who wanted to take a chance.

The front of the nickelodeon was its most important feature. There was no newspaper advertising and so the theatre's facade had to sell the show to the passing public—a myriad of lights with a prominent ticket booth. The name of the theatre was spelled out prominently surrounded by gaudy, often melodramatic posters. Electric lights played an important role in signs and displays. Often barkers stood outside and hawked the wares of the early theatres.

The inside was more sedate, even simple, for it was little more than a bare screening room, long and narrow and holding between fifty and three hundred folks. There were wooden chairs, with no stages. The screen was simply attached to the back wall. A piano accompanied the silent film, but in the better establishments, there might also be a violinist and players of other instruments (a total of three or four). The screen was typically twelve by nine feet. The projection booth was set off in the rear. With increasing worry about fires, a separate booth was required.

The nickelodeon explosion increased the number of movie outlets from the three hundred vaudeville theatres to thousands of movie-only theatres. By 1908 the nickelodeon had replaced the vaudeville theatre as the primary outlet for movie presentation in the United States, but vaudeville theatres continued to show movies as one of their regular acts. "Nickel madness" rode a wave of economic prosperity, both for the nation as a whole and the entertainment business in particular. With

The O. K. Nickelodeon, approximately 1906. Note the 5-cent admission price.

• •

its price several times less than the typical vaudeville show, it is not surprising to learn that early devotees of the nickelodeon came from the poorer folks in a city. This gave rise to the expression of "democracy's theatre."

Once the movies became so popular, the converted store fronts were abandoned for theatres with separate lobbies, grand architecture, stages, fine seats, and separate projection booths. The model was the legitimate theatre. This transformation coincided with the coming of longer films, while the early nickelodeons were just series of shorts. But there were from the beginning illustrated song slides with frequent changes of programs and lecturers who explained the movies.

As early as 1907 reports indicated that there seemed to be just too many theatres. So nickelodeon owners turned to vaudeville acts to differentiate their shows from the ones down the street. This was the rise of what has been called small-time vaudeville. By moving their nickelodeon operations into their own theatres, movie exhibitors could have a stage and offer live acts as well as movies. But these were movie theatres first, with vaudeville added, not vaudeville with movies which had been the case before 1905. With a thousand-seat theatre the owners increased possible revenues and could demand more at the boxoffice. With this new wave the *nickel*odeon was over, at least in terms of cost to patrons. Small-time vaudeville charged a dime to fifty cents.

This increase in admission fees meant a change in the movie audience. Granted, in the short span of the nickelodeon craze (1906 to 1909) moviegoers were not rich folks. But theatre owners did not want to count on the poor as their basic audience. Middle-class Americans had more time and money and thus could make up a more stable audience. Moreover, poorer audiences often consisted of rowdy youths who disrupted shows and caused others to stay away. Theatre owners moved to cater to the middle class and draw them away from vaudeville entertainment.

To lure the family trade, theatre owners focused on the mother and her children on a shopping break or after school. If a theatre owner could draw this type of audience, he could make more money and gain a favorable image in the community. Thus women and children saw half-price afternoon specials and stories in the movies which catered to them.

Filmmakers began to draw on respected authors such as Emile Zola, Edgar Allan Poe, Victor Hugo, and even William Shakespeare for inspiration. These stories were free of copyright costs and signaled social respectability. There was no longer any fear that the movie show was some sort of fad or passing phenomenon. By 1910 the movie show, in more and more beautiful theatres, now represented an accepted part of the matrix of American show business. The pure nickelodeon disappeared by 1920.

But the nickelodeon had provided the platform which seduced a nation of moviegoers. This initial home for movies was recalled years later with a nostalgic innocence celebrating a populist shrine. The nickelodeon also gave a platform for the beginnings of the careers of many of Hollywood's founders. William Fox, for example, began with a Brooklyn nickelodeon in 1906, but by 1910 he was operating fourteen small-time vaudeville/movie shows in the environs of New York City. Marcus Loew would form MGM in 1924. He had begun twenty years before with penny arcades and then moved to nickelodeons and small-time vaudeville/movie shows. By 1910 he had twelve such operations in New York alone and was beginning to spread to other major American cities.

By 1905 the movies stood at a threshold. In the United States and Western Europe, there were filmmakers, a network of distribution, and theatres to show movies. Less developed countries would take on the cinema, following the dictates of the American and European companies, over the next dozen years. Into this early mix would come Hollywood. The American film industry would come to dominate the world, first through its economic muscle (freed by the chaos of World War I to enter country after country) and simultaneously by setting the standard for proper moviemaking.

2

• •

the triumph of hollywood

Within the decade of the 1910s, Hollywood arose to define the cinema in the United States as well as throughout the world. Stars like Charlie Chaplin and Mary Pickford were among the most famous people of their era. Inexorably the American cinema came to dominate and indeed define the world film as a production center, industrial form, and social force. Hollywood was (and still is) more than a set of moviemaking companies all nestled together in southern California. Hollywood defines its strength by distributing films around the world and controlling theatres in which to present the films to the public.

Any movie-making industry—Hollywood or other—includes the production, distribution, and exhibition of films:

1. *Production:* First, films must be created. Since the early 1910s this has been done in studios in and around Los Angeles—an area generically known as Hollywood although it encompasses more than that city section: Culver City for MGM (today Lorimar), Universal City for Universal Studios, Burbank for Warner Bros., and an actual Hollywood address for Paramount.

2. *Distribution:* Then these companies peddle their films. Indeed, worldwide distribution

has long been the basis of Hollywood's power. No other film industry has been so far-reaching.

3. *Exhibition:* Finally, the theatres. Prior to the television age, films were shown principally in theatres, from nickelodeons to movie palaces.

To analyze Hollywood or any film industry we will proceed in two steps. First, we shall establish who owned the principal companies which controlled production, distribution, and exhibition. Hollywood, from 1920 to 1950, was defined by a small set of companies that dominated all three aspects ("the studios").

Once we understand ownership and control, we seek to learn how these companies operated in this particular historical context. In the United States, Hollywood ruled with an iron hand. Abroad, native industries had to react to Hollywood's invasion and then constant presence. That is not to say that film industries outside the United States did not reflect the imperatives and interests of their cultural heritage. It only states that despite varying cultural contexts, Hollywood came to dominate in markets from England to Ethiopia, from South America to Africa to Asia. That was not necessarily a "good thing," simply a fact of international movie economics even to the present day.

the coming of hollywood

Hollywood commenced with the failure of the Motion Picture Patents Company. That attempt to monopolize the film business began in 1908 when ten leading producers of movies and manufacturers of cameras and projectors combined to form a cartel to set prices of equipment they alone would manufacture. The Trust sought to squeeze out all possible profits from the production, distribution, and exhibition of motion pictures. The Motion Picture Patents Company sought to set artificial restraints of trade, stop the free flow of equipment and films, and then charge artificially high prices and reap the accordant benefits.

Taking their cue from the steel, oil, and legitimate theatre industries of the day, a number of the early owners of basic movie patents put aside their differences to form a cartel by pooling and control of patents. Only cooperating companies licensed by the Patents Trust could manufacture "legal" movies and movie equipment. Eastman Kodak agreed to supply film stock only to Patents Trust members and allies. The Patents Trust extracted profits by charging for use of its patents. So, for example, to be legally able to manufacture projectors one had to pay the Trust five dollars a week. To rightfully use projectors, exhibitors needed to pay two dollars a week. To make movies, producers paid a half cent for approved film stock.

The central problem for the Trust was to find ways to supervise and maintain control. To monitor middlemen the Trust actually went into the business of film distribution with the General Film Company. For a time around 1909 they seemed to be on the verge of succeeding. It looked as if there would be only one film company in the United States, operating along the lines of a public utility. But it failed, in part because members of the Trust, like many a cartel before and after, chafed under the terms of the shotgun marriage of ten companies: some members wanted to go the way of longer, feature-length films, while others seemed content making millions with short subjects.

The actual formation of the Patents Trust in 1908 resulted from a settlement between two hostile factions: allies of the Edison Manufacturing Company on one hand, and those linked with the American Mutoscope and Biograph Company on the other. For more than ten years these two had been fighting to establish hegemony over the basic patents for moviemaking and movie exhibition. The Patents Company pooled patents for cameras, film, and projectors to increase the power of all. Constituent members, the leading companies of the day, realized that it was better to divide up existing profits than lose increasing shares to outsiders.

The Trust never tried to own all moviemaking companies nor all theatres. It simply made life so difficult that it assumed that in time the independents would fall into line rather than fight a losing battle. In classic monopolistic fashion, it tried to limit production, distribution, and exhibition, but it simply proved impossible to keep out independents when the demand was increasing, and there was so much money to be made.

It was the rise of the independent which would create Hollywood as we know it today. Adolph Zukor would put together Paramount; Marcus Loew would create Loew's and MGM; William Fox fashioned his movie empire. The expectations of enormous riches gave these and other self-reliant entrepreneurs an incentive. From the start, license violations were frequent. Theatre owners wanted to book films and not pay the royalties to the Trust. Outlaw producers set up shop to supply these needs.

In 1910, the General Film Company aggressively sought to clog the distribution of films that the independents wanted. Anyone who distributed films outside the General Film Company was in obvious violation. For a time it looked as if this strategy would succeed, for it was difficult and costly to resist. But independent exhibitors and movie makers persisted. They sought to differentiate their products. They raided popular magazines, famous novels, and successful plays for plots. Westerns were among the most popular of these initial genres and helped spark interest in shooting on location "out West." Indeed, the independents found California, with its temperate climate, cheap land, and lack of unions, an ideal place to make low-cost movies.

The independents used other methods to get films for theatres. In Chicago, Carl Laemmle, later head of Universal, began to import films from Europe. He went into production using Lumière film stock. Indeed the Lumière Company and its New York agent succeeded in developing a sizable business selling French film stock to the independents. Although the quality may have been unreliable and the supply un-

Members of the Motion Pictures Patent Company, including Thomas Alva Edison (second left, front row).

• •

dependable, it did offer an alternative to the Kodak monopoly. By early 1911 Lumières' agent was selling more than thirty-five million feet of positive movie film per year, when Kodak was selling more than ninety million. Soon Kodak was losing so much business that it began in 1911 to sell film stock to independents. This was the first break in the monopoly strategy of the Motion Picture Patents Company.

By 1912 the independent movement was in full swing. There was enough production that theatres could rely solely on independent films to fill their bills. Distribution networks outside the General Film Company reached nation-wide size. The Patents Trust had failed for fundamental reasons, ones which would set up the principles underlying the economics of Hollywood.

First, the new Hollywood companies began to differentiate their products. Gone were the days when film was sold by the foot. Each movie became a unique product so that it could be heavily advertised. Differentiation was accom-

plished by emphasizing popular stories and then developing movie stars to act in them.

Second, the movies were marketed in as many places as possible. Remember, this was the era of the silent cinema when it was easy to translate intertitles and produce versions in French, Spanish, German, and other widely spoken tongues.

Third, Hollywood learned to take control of exhibition in the United States without having to buy all the theatres (more than twenty thousand). This was possible because theatres in big cities, showing first-run motion pictures, captured the bulk of the boxoffice take. Own these theatres (about 10 percent) and one could control more than three-quarters of the revenues of any film. The Hollywood studios developed chains of movie palaces which dominated the theatre business in the major urban areas of the United States.

In short, the most successful independents succeeded at what the Patents Trust failed to accomplish—control of production, distribution, and exhibition. In the process they took over the world of cinema and created the hegemony—Hollywood.

Make no mistake about it: the Patents Company introduced changes in the movie business which would be adopted by the independents. The Trust brought an end to litigation over the technological base of the movies; it involved bankers in the fledgling industry; it established a true national market for the movies. It was the Trust which united movie selling, through the General Film Company, into one national market, so thereafter moviegoers throughout the United States would be presented the same movies. By 1920, Hollywood's films would play the entire globe.

This worldwide popularity in turn created a demand which required year-round production. To meet this requirement year-round sunshine was found in southern California. The nearby mountains and flatlands provided varied locations. Thus, a small Los Angeles suburb of some seven hundred folks in 1903 became the movie center of the world. By the late 1910s, Hollywood Boulevard had become the hottest of the hot spots, a symbol of glamour the world over. It drew thousands who sought to move from dreary small towns to the glamour capital of the world.

By 1925, Hollywood had more press representatives than any other place in the United States except New York City, even exceeding the nation's capital. The social impact was staggering. As early as 1920, the Hollywood Chamber of Commerce was running advertisements begging aspiring actors and actresses to stay away: "Don't Try to Break into the Movies." Gone were the days of free and easy access to filmmaking, the uninhibited flow of films, and the ease of entry into the theatre business. Hollywood products, featuring well-known stars, were in demand in cinemas throughout the world.

the hollywood production system

With the demise of the Trust, independents congregating in Hollywood sought ways by which to stabilize, control, and even dominate the business of making movies. During the 1910s, the successful companies, led by Famous Players–Lasky, developed a system by which to manufacture popular, feature-length films. This method came to be known as the Hollywood system of production. Through the principles of the feature film, the star system, and the studio method of filmmaking, Hollywood companies taught the world how to make profitable movies. Many contributed to the development of the Hollywood system of production; only Adolph Zukor fully exploited it.

• the rise of the feature film •

Independents sought to offer their audiences something different. This meant a longer work which could stand on its own and not need be a part of a vaudeville show. Films had at first been fit into vaudeville programs. Nickelodeons had gone one step further by collecting short films, and presenting them in collections lasting an hour or so. The legitimate theatre, in turn, had always presented one play, for a two-hour (or longer) show. The feature film would follow this latter model and center on one, longer film. Short newsreels or animated subjects might provide a compliment, but it would be the two hour movie which would sell the show.

What this meant was that the feature film had to be a story of unusual interest, produced at a cost far in excess of what had been available in the past. Inspiration came from the serial. Indeed, a Motion Picture Patents Company member, Vitagraph, had released a four-part version of Victor Hugo's *Les Miserables* over a span of three months in 1909. Serials provided important ways to test new audiences for longer forms.

Foreign features repeatedly demonstrated that longer films drew sizable audiences. The influx of foreign photoplays began in 1911, as independents imported epics from European filmmakers who did not care about the Patents Trust and were happy to have the extra business. Classic tales from Italy such as *The Fall of Troy*, *Dante's Inferno*, and *Jerusalem Delivered* proved there was a market for longer fare and even met with the approval of doubting reformers and educators.

Dante's Inferno, a Milano Film production imported by P. P. Craft, for example, enjoyed successful extended engagements in New York, Boston, and Washington in 1911. Where the average film may have played two days, *Dante's Inferno* was held over for two weeks. Where the average film was shown in a two-hundred seat nickelodeon, *Dante's Inferno* was presented in thousand-seat (rented) legitimate theatres for a dollar per admission.

Craft followed up with another Milano epic, *Homer's Odyssey*. To publicize the fact that the filmmakers had spent nearly a quarter of a million dollars to reconstruct an entire Greek city, he inaugurated a national advertising campaign, again booked the film only into legitimate theatres, and raised admission prices to an unheard of two dollars. In the lobbies, employees hawked plaster busts of Homer, postcards from Greece, and souvenir programs. Craft mixed the techniques which had worked well in his previous job as publicist for Buffalo Bill's Wild West Show with the practices common in legitimate stage.

A number of Trust members broke ranks to import the longer works. George Kleine was the most successful. In 1913 alone, Kleine had four feature-length hits: *Quo Vadis?*, *The Betrothed*, *The Last Days of Pompeii*, and *Anthony and Cleopatra*. These movies were sold to well-to-do, educated folks. Indeed, with the coming of the feature film, the selling of films moved into an new arena. It was not simply enough to announce the movies as an act in a vaudeville show or to promote a new set of movies each day through posters outside the nickelodeon show. The investment in a feature film required

***Dante's Inferno* (1911).**

• •

a special and individualized promotional effort. The movie industry was moving from selling "the movies" as a novelty to peddling the merits of individual titles.

Distribution changed. Franchising through agents, region by region, gave way to placing films in legitimate theatres. (Picture palaces would be built once this need had been demonstrated.) By 1914 one-fifth of Broadway's theatres were showing feature-length movies. Indeed, the most influential of feature films, *The*

Birth of a Nation, opened the following year at a New York legitimate theatre and ran nearly a year at an admission price of two dollars.

• the star system •

But what was the best way to construct and sell these elaborate, expensive feature films? What was needed was a way to make each new film

Quo Vadis? (1913).

● ●

special, a product which would sell itself. To effect such a strategy, Hollywood simply aped the vaudeville industry and initiated the star system. Everyone recognized that vaudeville (and legitimate theatre before that) had long used headliners to sell the show. As early as 1909, the Edison Company publicized its acquisition of important theatrical talent from Broadway impresarios David Belasco, Charles Frohman, and Otis Skinner. In 1910, Kalem and Vitagraph introduced lobby card displays featuring the headline players. Thus the star system began with the Patents Trust but was fully exploited and developed by independents.

Independents were more aggressive in promoting possible stars. For example, Carl Laemmle hired away Florence Lawrence and renamed the former "Biograph Girl" the "IMP Girl" after his Independent Motion Picture Company. He then sent his "new" star on tour and planted story after story in the newspapers, often blaming the Trust for spreading false in-

● ●

An autographed picture of Mary Pickford at the height of her popularity.

● ●

formation about her. Laemmle announced in every town that would have him and his press agents that "Florence Lawrence was indeed alive and could be seen in the new IMP production of. . . ." Stars provided a means of differentiating films and boosting sales.

Filmmakers also turned to the legitimate theatre for the first famous players. By 1913, a number of companies specialized in filming popular Broadway plays. Adolph Zukor's Famous Players in Famous Plays would be the most noted of these because it alone would survive into the studio era of the 1930s. Zukor and his partners' early successes included *The Count of Monte Cristo* starring James O'Neill, father of the famous playwright, *The Prisoner*

of Zenda starring James Hackett, *Queen Elizabeth* starring Sarah Bernhardt, and *Tess of the d'Urbervilles* starring Minnie Maddern Fiske. There were also David Belasco's Motion Picture Drama Company, Playgoer's Film Company, and Broadway Film Company.

The new, independent movie producers realized they would eventually have to begin to develop their own stars. Consider the career of Mary Pickford. This Canadian-born vaudeville performer saw her salary increase accordingly:

1909: $100 per week
1910: $175 per week
1914: $1000 per week
1915: $2000 per week
1916: $10,000 per week
1917: $15,000 per week

Famous Players was willing to pay Mary more than a million dollars per year in 1917 because her films drew so many folks to the box office. Fans went to her films religiously, lining up as soon as the boxoffice opened.

Mary's success pushed Hollywood companies to develop their own "Little Marys" and then "ink" them to exclusive, long-run contracts so that the player could not seek a higher salary elsewhere. The Hollywood company would advertise the star and milk the profits from the films. Studios regularly issued feature-length attractions with elaborately prepared scenarios widely advertising these releases. Soon the narratives, mise-en-scène, camerawork, and editing were all centered around the star.

The star system established a milestone on 15 January 1919 when three of the biggest stars in the business—Charlie Chaplin, Douglas Fairbanks, and Mary Pickford—joined with director D. W. Griffith to create United Artists. This company of stars issued a declaration of independence from their former employers, announcing the formation of their own distribution company so they could fully extract the riches of their fame and their drawing power at the box office. For the first time ever, motion picture performers acquired complete autonomy over their work, controlling a corporate apparatus which set in motion approved promotion, advertising, and publicity.

The new United Artists did not lack for popular films: *The Mark of Zorro* (1920, Fairbanks), *Robin Hood* (1922, Fairbanks), *Little Lord Fauntleroy* (1921, Pickford), and *The Gold Rush* (1925, Chaplin). Unfortunately UA did not regularly release enough films to fill any theatre for a year. Even though theatre owners wanted Chaplin, Fairbanks, and Pickford films, they could not afford to go dark to wait for them. Thus in the long run United Artists never was able to fully exploit its stars or develop new ones. As the marquee value of Pickford, Fairbanks, and Griffith began to fade, United Artists was forced to become a haven for independent producers (some good, some bad) fleeing from the strict confines of an MGM, Paramount, Fox, or Warner Bros.

• the studios •

Indeed as the Hollywood system of feature films with major stars developed, it necessitated an apparatus to guarantee the shipment of such films to theatres on a weekly basis. Hollywood studios needed to develop efficient and cost-effective production methods. At the same time, to attract customers, the feature film had to meet a certain standard of quality. To do this with one-reel films had been easy. Once the switch was made to features, a new organization for production was needed: the studio system.

In the days before the feature film, there were two standard methods of making one-reel movies. For "reality" subjects, a cameraman (with possibly an assistant or two) would journey to the subject, record the action with appropriate camera angles and then edit it together as quickly as possible. This could be done overnight since little preplanning was required. There were no scripts, just assignments. Go get that story and bring me the finished film, the owner of the company would say.

For films inspired by vaudeville acts or literary sources, movie companies employed a director to stage the scenes and a cameraman and assistants to record them. Gradually, as more and more films were needed, specialists were hired to assist the director make movies faster. These included writers to think up story ideas, scenic artists to paint backgrounds, and designers to create costumes. Workers were added, using as a model a theatre production to be staged for a camera operator.

But as more and more films were needed, the disadvantages of aping the legitimate theatre became evident. Filmmakers realized that if they shot all scenes of one locale at one time, money would be saved. That is, it was less expensive to shoot the story "out of order" rather than record the scenes as they might be staged in a theatre. Once all planned scenes were filmed, in whatever order, an editor could reassemble them, following the dictates of the script. All this required a carefully thought out, prearranged plan to calculate the minimum cost in advance. Such a plan became known as the shooting script.

The shooting script was based on a story which pleased the audience. The filmmaker

Director Harry Beaumont in the old Warner Brothers studio on Sunset, Hollywood, approximately 1923.

thus had to fashion shooting scripts which would turn out to be popular films. Interesting stories fashioned with correct verisimilitude and clarity became the standard for the well-made movie. Gradually, as features became longer, stories became more complicated and appealing, requiring ever more complex shooting scripts. It was impossible to "fit" everything into a short subject; a feature needed more and more time to tender a complete story.

The solution to faster feature filmmaking was to pay careful attention to preparing the shooting script. Through careful planning, the director could make a careful estimate of the necessary footage for each scene and then add them so they fit together in the end. Gradually filmmakers developed tricks so few shots ever had to be redone. Intertitles were often added to eliminate scenes while making the story as tight as possible.

Thus, both efficient filmmaking (always now shot "out of order") and a standard of clearly articulated, exciting, continuously appealing stories with fascinating characters became the norms filmmakers sought. The typical script noted its genre (comedy or drama, for example), cast of characters, and a synopsis of the story, and only then went on to a scene-by-scene scenario including intertitles.

The director could estimate how long shooting would take and what resources would be required. From this proposed plan, the head of the film company could decide if he or she wanted to make this movie. A line producer could, once the project was approved, re-do the shooting script to fashion the actual order of production. From about 1908 to 1917 Hollywood developed this studio method of making movies. No one person sat down and invented the Hollywood system. Earlier means of production methods were not inferior or primitive, just less efficient. The Hollywood method proved the way to minimize the costs of making movies and hence maximize profits.

In particular, screen writers focused on ways to establish major transitions in time and space. Techniques were developed to make films look real in both sets and lighting. But above all, the story had to flow together. For inspiration early filmmakers began to draw on and adapt novels and plays. These subjects (from *The Fall of Troy* to *A Tale of Two Cities* to *Enoch Arden* to *Faust*) could stand on their own as feature attractions. Exhibitors could charge more, and with a hit film, everyone could make more money.

The writing departments of the Hollywood companies prepared the scripts. By 1911 such units were established to adapt material and, ever more frequently, to create original screenplays. Most work was done in-house to regularize the production of scripts and avoid copyright hassles. By 1913 writing departments even had subunits expert in adapting the classics or providing original material. Additional experts then took the screenplays and estimated costs of production and needed sets and

allocated the time of stars, supporting players, and men and women behind the camera, all of whom were under contract. Once the process was complete, a detailed plan existed that was familiar to everyone and best utilized the resources at hand. Under this system, the director lost much of the power he or she had a decade earlier. The director was required to simply make the movie as planned by others.

Thomas Ince set in motion a standard working procedure involving a producer who worked from the continuity script. Script approval set projects in motion utilizing available buildings in the studio and scores of technical workers and specialists organized by department. The studio factory contained buildings housing sets, wardrobes, directors, screenwriters, and management plus stages and a backlot with standing sets and even a water tank. Police, a fire department, plus all sorts of maintenance workers made this a veritable city within a city.

A program of films was planned for a year in advance by the studio boss and his or her assistants. Experts planned the films, supervised creation of the scripts, and worked on the coordination of the myriad of details to make the films. Sets would be used over and over again, adapted for different stories. Art directors handled the building of the sets; costumers planned what stars and extras would wear; casting directors found the talent; makeup artists perfected the best dyes and bases for the proper movie look; and cinematographers were picked who worked fast and efficiently on the type of film being made.

The actual shooting was always done out of order. Time was of the essence. Large complicated sets were used near the end of filming, because they took longer to be completed. Actors were shuttled from film to film to make the best use of their time under contract. Often multiple cameras were used for complicated shots so not to have to stage them twice. This was nearly always the case for battlefield sequences. And always present was the continuity clerk, who checked that when this film being made out of order was reassembled, shots would "match" and the story make sense.

The final print of the film was assembled by a team of editors following guidelines set by the producer. Previews were often held to test if actual audiences liked the work; the film was recut if low-cost improvements could be made. Music was developed to be sent out to silent film orchestras. By 1920 all these functions were standardized. The coming of sound would actually call for few changes, for already in place was an efficient, cost-effective way to make films which appealed to large audiences.

At his peak Ince made stars, for example William S. Hart and Charles Ray. He deserves credit for making Frank Borzage into a director of the first rank and producing a number of films starring Sessue Hayakawa. *Civilization* (1916) would be his last great film, an uneven plea for pacifism, released near the end of the First World War. Ince died in 1924, under strange circumstances, and ought to be best remembered as a pioneer of the studio system of making movies.

• the paramount way •

If Thomas Ince pioneered the Hollywood studio system, it was Adolph Zukor and his Famous Players' Company which taught the world how to fully exploit it. By 1921 Zukor had turned Famous Players into the largest film company in the world. In 1916 Zukor had merged twelve smaller producers and the distributor Paramount to form Famous Players–Lasky Corporation. As the feature length film with a number of headlining stars became more and more the dominant attraction and motivation for the profits, Famous Players became the dominant force in the industry. Zukor had begun in exhibition in New York City and then turned to production with Famous Players in Famous Plays. By 1917 his new company included stars such as Mary Pickford, Douglas Fairbanks, Gloria Swanson, Pauline Frederick, Blanche Sweet, and Norma and Constance Talmadge.

Famous Players then, recognizing that not all theatres were equal, began to charge more for showings at larger, new movie palaces located in big cities and less for rental to small-town movie houses. Large theatres paid five hundred to seven hundred dollars a week for a five-reel feature while small houses might pay less than fifty dollars. Still theatres booked what made money, and so of the estimated twenty thousand theatres in the United States in 1919, a quarter were regularly presenting Famous Players films.

Famous Players took advantage of this popularity and began to block book. That is, if a theatre wanted to show the films of Mary Pickford, it had to take pictures with less well-known stars. In turn, Famous Players used this guaranteed booking as a cushion to test and develop new stars and to try new stories. When major theatre owners began to form alternative booking cooperatives, Zukor reacted in 1919 by entering the theatre business. Such a large venture could not, however, be financed with the cash on hand, however well the company was doing. This was a real estate venture of the largest magnitude, and so Famous Players borrowed ten million dollars with the help of the Wall Street banking house of Kuhn, Loeb and was listed on the New York Stock Exchange.

Zukor and associates had hit the big time.

Zukor moved quickly, and by the mid-point of 1921 Paramount owned three hundred theatres. Four years later it merged with Balaban & Katz, the most important and innovative theatre chain in the United States at the time. In the space of six years Paramount had moved from a minor participant in the world of theatres to the dominant operator. And, by purchasing so many circuits, it doomed its major competitors. By 1931 Paramount's newly named Publix theatre circuit would be the largest in the world, double the size of its nearest competitor.

Paramount was so successful in its thrust toward dominance that the United States Justice Department began to receive hundreds of complaints of suspected anti-trust violation. After six years of investigation it was found that Paramount and its affiliated companies did violate the law. It did this by threatening theatre owners and through ownership, control, and access to first-run theatres. But the Republican administrations of the 1920s did nothing. It would not be until 1938 that the Justice Department of President Franklin D. Roosevelt filed the suit that would force Paramount and the other major Hollywood companies to sell their theatres.

· · · · · · · · · · · · · · · ·

world distribution

· · · · · · · · · · · · · · · ·

It was not enough for the Hollywood companies to simply control all the movie stars and studios. Their long-run economic security depended on the construction and maintenance of networks for national and international distribution. Once a feature film was made, the majority of its cost had been accumulated. It then cost relatively little to market throughout the world. If somehow the producer could expand the territory to include greater and greater portions of the world, the additional revenues overwhelmed any extra costs. This is a simple application of economies of scale.

The rise of Hollywood thus also required the exporting of the American cinema to all parts of the globe. While other national cinemas, as we shall see in later chapters, were restricted to their own countries, Hollywood took on the world as its proper marketplace. But first Hollywood had to conquer the United States. Before 1910, films were sold regionally through what was called "state's rights distribution." The Patents Trust's General Film Company constituted the first national market for the cinema. A member of the Trust could sell the films to all parts of the United States at one time.

The next step was to change the system from sales to rentals. Under the new system a theatre would book the film for a certain number of days and split the proceeds with the distributor, based on some agreed-upon formula. Downtown picture palaces would pay the most for an exclusive first run of a film; a rural theatre with a few hundred seats would pay far less, playing the film months after it had run downtown.

Beginning in 1914 Paramount began to take full advantage of the new national market to rent its feature films. A former General Film salesman, W. W. Hodkinson, had convinced eleven regional state's rights exchanges to join forces to create Paramount. Hodkinson's plan necessitated a steady supply of feature films, and thus he sought out producers such as Adolph Zukor and Jesse Lasky, the duo who would eventually oust Hodkinson and take over the company.

Although the average cost for Paramount's features ranged up to thirty thousand dollars, revenues regularly topped one hundred thousand dollars. Quickly, other national distributors were formed: Lewis Selznick's (David O.'s father) World Film Corporation, Louis B. Mayer's Metro Pictures, the Triangle Corporation (whose producers included D. W. Griffith, Thomas Ince, and Mack Sennett), Universal, and Fox Film Corporation. But Famous Players, ever aggressive, led the way, and was to effect a stranglehold on the marketplace.

In 1917 a group of powerful exhibitors fought back. Led by Thomas Tally of Los Angeles, Jules Mastbaum of Philadelphia, and A. H. Blank of Des Moines, Iowa, twenty-six banded together to finance independent productions and then distribute them nationally. Each powerful theatre owner was granted a monopoly for his region of the country. Under such a plan, it was reasoned, they could beat Zukor at his own game. The new company's name: First National Exhibitor's Circuit. The initial franchise holders represented theatres from Philadelphia to Los Angeles, Chicago to New Orleans. First National went after the biggest stars by bidding Charlie Chaplin away from Mutual and Mary Pickford from Famous Players, each for salaries in excess of one million dollars a year.

By 1920 the Hollywood companies had firmly established their distribution offices throughout the United States, indeed throughout all of North America. The First World War significantly curtailed the production and distribution power of European moviemakers, and into that gap stepped Hollywood.

Prior to 1910, American film companies had sold films abroad through agents. The movie company would find a representative in a foreign country and sell him or her films to market as they might wish. This provided uneven coverage around the world. The first company to open offices abroad was Vitagraph, in Paris and London in 1906. But with the formation of the Motion Picture Patents Company in 1909, American movie companies began a systematic push into foreign markets that accelerated with the opening of the First World War, which spread over Europe in late July 1914.

By September of that year, war had engulfed the continent. The ultimate effect on the world's trade in films was to reduce greatly what was coming out of France and Italy, the leading producers on the continent. This allowed the American exporters to take over markets abandoned by France and Italy. By the latter half of 1915,

A German movie theatre.

● ●

Hollywood was capturing a greater and greater share of film screen time in Latin America, Asia, and Africa.

The French film industry was particularly hard hit. Not only was the economy in shambles, but for a time all theatres were shut down. Germany also was hit. American films immediately flooded in, since at this point America was officially neutral. As the war dragged on, Hollywood prospered and Europe suffered irreversible declines. The war surprisingly did not disrupt the flow of films outside Europe. One change did take place. With Britain at war, the center of trade shifted from London to New York. After the war there was talk of a shift back to London to "business as usual." But the damage had been done. Indeed, as early as 1916 the center of the film export world had moved to New York City.

In 1916 Hollywood began to adopt new strategies, open more subsidiary offices, and

thereby established a dominance which was not easily changed after the war. Hollywood moved to the Far East, South America, indeed all over the world. The key to Hollywood's success during the war was that it avoided relying too much on Europe and turned to other markets. In 1913 Hollywood took nearly all its money from Europe and North America, with the bulk of the remainder coming from Australia and New Zealand. But in 1916 sizable monies were being drawn from other parts of the world. For example, South America's and Asia's purchases increased eightfold.

By the end of hostilities, Hollywood settled down into a comfortable hegemony. Exhibitors around the world seemed eager for Hollywood films, especially in countries with no native film production. During the 1920s, prior to the coming of sound, Hollywood solidified itself firmly in all parts of the world. Only the Soviet Union, with a Marxist government, Germany with the rise of nationalism and then fascism, and Japan, with a strong nationalist economy and film industry of its own, were able to keep the Americans at bay.

Hollywood formed an association, the Motion Picture Producers and Distributors Association of America, and hired former Postmaster General Will H. Hays to facilitate international relations. One of Hays' tasks was to make sure that foreign countries permitted Hollywood to operate with an open hand. He functioned as a foreign ambassador, helped by a cooperative State Department under Presidents Harding, Coolidge, and Hoover.

During the 1920s, no film industry could challenge Hollywood. In Great Britain, Canada, and Australia (with a common language) Hollywood controlled some 85 percent of screen time; in France, Poland, Hungary, Yugoslavia, and Rumania about two-thirds. The case was the same in South America, the Caribbean, and Central America. By 1922 Argentina and Brazil entered Hollywood's top five markets. The film world of the 1920s was an American market almost wherever anyone cared to journey. The world was Hollywood's marketplace.

But this was more than simple success for Hollywood. The international distribution of Hollywood and its unique ability to maintain this international control had a great effect on the history of world cinema. Other countries had to struggle not simply to please their native movie fans, but also to somehow "better" Hollywood, which had become the de facto world standard. From this economic base, Hollywood would define appropriate standards of film style, form, and content. In chapter after chapter of this survey of film history we shall see the effects of the Hollywood international distribution monopoly.

movie palace exhibition

The production and distribution of films were only two of the foundation pegs of the institution Hollywood. Movie moguls knew the money came through the theatrical boxoffice and thus sought some measure of control over that sector of the film business. If Hollywood could be found in its studios and offices for distribution throughout the world, it could also be located in the movie palaces situated on main streets from New York to Los Angeles, Chicago to Dallas.

The modern movie palace began with Roxy's opening of the three-thousand–seat Strand Theatre in 1914 in New York. With opening night, Samuel F. "Roxy" Rothapfel set in place a program adapted and copied by Sid Grauman in Los Angeles and A. J. and Barney Balaban and Sam Katz in Chicago. Roxy went back to the roots of the film industry and tendered a live vaudeville show plus a movie show. But this time the movies were the centerpiece and the vaudeville a "plus" to attract audiences away from other entertainments.

Roxy's shows opened with the house orchestra playing the national anthem followed by some popular classical composition. (No need to have to pay extra fees for musical rights, simply use public domain works.) Then came a newsreel, a travelogue, and a comic short. Finally came the feature film, accompanied by a full orchestra, usually of fifty to one hundred members. For the opening of the Strand, Roxy booked the Selig production of *The Spoilers* starring William Farnum.

But there was more to the idea of the movie palace. Added in was the splendor of the legitimate theatre's architecture and the touch of class of ushers to effect a fantasyland never available before or since in moviegoing. It took Samuel Rothapfel (the p was dropped during World War I, when Germanic names were not fashionable) and Sid Grauman to make picture palace entertainment the industry standard. Then Hollywood swooped in and purchased these theatres to truly control production, distribution, and exhibition.

Samuel Rothapfel (always Roxy to his public) opened his first nickelodeon in Forest City, Pennsylvania on New Year's Day of 1908. His immediate and overwhelming success took him on the road to become a consultant for theatre owners. In city after city he helped make owners more money while he developed his ideas for how to program a movie palace.

Roxy became a true national figure with his success in 1913 with the Regent Theatre in New York. He improved projection, put the musicians on the stage and made them into stars, improved the ventilation, and added vaudeville

acts. He showed only "high-class" films, typically filmed versions of classical plays or novels, such as George Kleine's production of *The Last Days of Pompeii*. Charging only fifteen cents, Roxy had to turn away customers.

By April 1914 Roxy moved his movie-house formula to Broadway's Strand, to offer what some described as an experience like going to a presidential reception or an opening night at the opera. Roxy serviced his guests with an army of ushers whom he had drilled with the rigor and show he learned in the Marines. The seats were upholstered in the coziest Pullman-car fashion.

He had yet another hit. The movies made him the first *movie*-theatrical impresario. Ever restless, Roxy moved to fashion the Rialto in 1916 into a "Temple of the Motion Picture." Thomas Lamb provided a handsome interior modeled after the Adam style from Britain. The ushers wore scarlet tunics piped in gold and tassels. Opening-day advertisements proclaimed "The World's Largest Organ—Most Wonderful System of Electrical Effects Ever Installed in Any Theatre—15 cents—25 cents—50 cents—no higher." One writer stated: "The manager [of the movie palace] is engaged in selling motion picture entertainment only incidentally. He is selling his theatre."

Roxy went on to the Rivoli in 1917, the Capitol in 1920, his own radio show in 1922, and in 1927 his own Roxy theatre. The Regent had an Italian Renaissance loggia and an arcade of store fronts reminiscent of the Palazzo del Consiglio in Verona. Roxy's Rialto was in the English Adam style; his Rivoli had a facade like the Parthenon, with white glazed terra cotta columns and a pediment; the Roxy was a Spanish wonder palace. All had specially constructed domes and recesses, richly colored drapery, plaster detail with gold and silver trim, marble statues and

The rotunda of the Roxy Theatre, New York City, 1927.

● ●

extensive drapes and other wall decorations. A massive crystal chandelier hung from the center of the ceiling and illuminated the entire auditorium. The Roxy, a six-thousand–seat dream palace, would represent the finest in movie theatre entertainment to Americans in the years immediately preceding the Great Depression.

Roxy's final project was the art deco masterwork, Radio City Music Hall, which opened in 1932. But even before this theatre was built, Roxy ran out of money and ideas in the face of the Great Depression. Roxy had great ideas and brought the movie theatre out of the age of the nickelodeon into the age of the movie palace, but he was always making money for others

and never was able to construct a system for maximizing profits from movie exhibition.

A similar scenario was playing out on the West Coast with Sid Grauman, who in 1917 built the first major movie palace in Los Angeles, the Million Dollar Theatre. During the 1920s few theatres in the United States were more famous than his Egyptian and Chinese on Hollywood Boulevard, making Sidney Patrick Grauman the leading movie palace impresario west of Chicago. His special innovation was the prologue, a type of stage show which preceded the first-run film and was linked to it in story and theme so to provide a complete, unified show.

But Grauman, like Roxy three thousand miles to the east, never was able to sustain his economic enterprises. Both Roxy and Grauman were forced to sell out before 1931 and work for others. On the other hand, Balaban & Katz in Chicago developed a system for making millions with the movie palace entertainment. In the period immediately after the end of World War I, pioneering exhibitors took their cues for maximizing profits from the extraordinary success of this Chicago corporation. Indeed, once Balaban & Katz merged into Famous Players in 1925, it became the cornerstone of the most successful and powerful theatre enterprise of its day and set the standard for Hollywood's presence on Main Street.

Balaban & Katz's success commenced when the Central Park Theatre opened in October 1917. This mighty picture palace was an immediate success, and Sam Katz, as corporate planner and president, opened a second picture palace in the fashionable Uptown district of Chicago's far North Side: the Riveria. At this point Katz put together a syndicate of backers who all were doing so well in their own Chicago-based businesses that they had some extra cash to invest: Julius Rosenwald, head of

Sears-Roebuck; William Wrigley, Jr., of chewing gum fame; and John Hertz, Chicago's taxi king.

With this financial support, Balaban & Katz opened the four-thousand–seat Tivoli Theatre in February 1921 and the equally large Chicago Theatre downtown in October 1921. By closely examining how Balaban & Katz was able to expand so rapidly, so successfully, we can understand why the movie exhibition business moved from a marginal leisure-time industry to center stage in the business of entertainment.

Balaban & Katz carefully considered the *location* of its theatres. Before, theatre owners had followed the prevailing tendencies of entertainment districts. Balaban & Katz constructed the locus of its power by going to the new audiences for the movies who lived in what were then the suburbs of America's biggest cities. Balaban & Katz demonstrated that it was not enough to simply seek middle-class audiences by happenstance; one had to take the movie show to their transportation crossroads. What gave Balaban & Katz its opening was the construction of urban mass transit trolley and elevated lines at the turn of the century. Rapid mass transit enabled the middle class and the rich to move to the edge of the city to the first true suburbs (although many were actually within city boundaries).

Balaban & Katz took full advantage of this revolution in mass transit by building its first three movie palaces in the heart of outlying business centers of Chicago, not downtown. The company's first movie palace, the Central Park, illustrates this principle of location. North Lawndale, in what was then the far West Side of Chicago, was the neighborhood to which the middle class aspired to move. The elevated train had reached North Lawndale in 1902 and within two decades this lightly populated outpost had grown into a teeming neighborhood, princi-

pally of Jews who had fled Maxwell Street. Their children had acquired a strong desire for upward mobility from education in public school, from reformers such as Jane Addams, and from newly acquired gentile friends. This new generation ate nonkosher food, attended synagogue less frequently, and spoke Yiddish only at home. And as part of this cultural assimilation, they also fell in love with the movie show.

But it was not enough to select the optimal crossroads to locate one's theatre. A movie company had to offer a good show. And that show began with the *building* which housed the movies—the picture palace. Balaban & Katz sought to make their buildings attraction unto themselves. With the pride associated with the

Left, Sid Grauman, owner and creator of the Chinese Theatre (above) on Hollywood Boulevard.

opening of a world's fair or new skyscraper, Chicagoans of the 1920s proclaimed and heralded their movie palaces as the finest in the world. Balaban & Katz theatres spelled opulence to the average Chicago moviegoer, symbolizing a special treat, more than simply "going-out-to-the-movies."

The Chicago architectural firm headed by the brothers George and C. W. Rapp designed the Central Park Theatre, and from that day forward for nearly two decades their drawing boards were not without at least one major project for Sam Katz. Rapp & Rapp mixed design elements from nearly all eras, including French, Spanish, Italian, Moorish and, later, Art Deco renderings. Among their trademarks were the

main facade's triumphal arch, the monumental staircase (inspired by the Paris Opera House), and the grand, column-lined lobby (inspired by the Hall of Mirrors in Versailles).

The architecture of the movie palace was designed to insulate the public from the outside world and provide a stage for the entertainment. The theatrical aspect of the movie palace entertainment commenced long before one went inside. Indeed, it began on the street as one first gazed upon strong vertical lines accentuated by ascending pilasters, windows, and towers, lifting high above the shop fronts. The building was a rigid, steel shell, with an inner core on which the plaster decoration was hung. Massive steel trusses were used to support the necessary thousands in a balcony that had no obstructions. Here was a structure unlike any one might find elsewhere in the city. The brilliant terra-cotta purples, golds, azures, and crimsons glowed day and night.

Outside, massive electric signs set up "bright light" centers, seen for miles by those on trolleys. The upright signs towered several stories in height and flashed their messages in several colors. Behind the upright signs were stained-glass windows which reflected the lights into the lobby. These exterior lights reminded many of the glories of the Columbian Exposition (a world's fair of 1892 held in Chicago to celebrate the discovery of America), when serious electrical light displays were first introduced into the city. Light displays were still unusual enough to demand public comment to a culture in which electricity had been in cities for only a few decades. The stained-glass windows evoked an era of church architecture, linking with traditional, respected institutional architecture of the past.

Once inside, the patrons weaved through a series of vestibules, foyers, lobbies, lounges, promenades, and waiting rooms designed to impress, even excite. The lobbies and foyers were, if anything, more spectacular than the architectural fantasy outside. Decorations included opulent chandeliers lighting every major room, classical drapery on walls and entrances, luxurious chairs and fountains, and grand spaces for piano and/or organ accompaniment for waiting crowds. And since there always seemed to be a waiting line, keeping newly arriving customers happy was as important as entertaining those already in the auditorium. Inside, everyone had a perfect view of the screen, and careful acoustical planning ensured the orchestral accompaniment to the silent films could be heard even in the farthest reaches of the balcony. This was a dignified

Sam Katz, creator and operator of the greatest chain of movie palaces in motion picture history.

● ●

setting, and patrons responded accordingly.

The publicity for these theatres emphasized the "class" to the average moviegoer. One commentator compared these Balaban & Katz theatres to baronial halls or grand hotels in which one might have tea or attend a ball. They were planned to make Balaban & Katz's upwardly mobile patrons feel as if they were at home with a king or in the haunts of a modern business tycoon.

Balaban & Katz had a policy of treating the movie patron as a king or queen. Its theatres tendered *services* to customers including free child care, smoking rooms, and painting galleries in the foyers and lobbies. In the basement of each movie palace was a complete playground which included slides, sandboxes, and

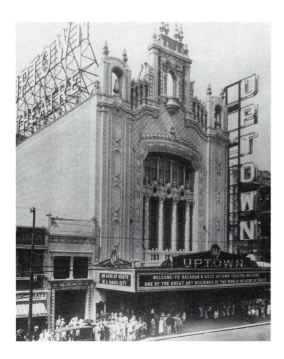

Chicago's 5000 seat Uptown Theatre on opening day. Note the sign on the marquee.

• •

other objects of fun one rarely saw outside a traditional play yard. Children were left in the care of nurses while their families were at the show upstairs. Indeed, there were special afternoon tea shows for women who went shopping with small children and infants.

Ushers maintained a quiet decorum in the theatre. They guided patrons through the maze of halls and foyers, assisted the elderly and small children, and handled any emergencies which might arise. A picture palace had forty ushers and doormen in attendance. Balaban & Katz recruited its corps from male college students, dressed them in red uniforms with white gloves and yellow epaulets, and demanded they be obediently polite even to the rudest of patrons. All requests had to end with a "thank you;" under no circumstances were tips to be accepted. The special service was free, part of the price of admission.

Balaban & Katz emphasized *stage shows*. They became small-time vaudeville entrepreneurs, developing local talent into stars who could then make the circuit in its theatres. If the company could mount popular but tasteful shows, it could attract the middle-class audience who had grown up on vaudeville. The strategy worked. In time, Balaban & Katz became more famous for impressive stage attractions, orchestras, and organists than any movies it presented.

Balaban & Katz stage shows were elaborate mini-musicals with spectacular settings and intricate lighting effects. These stage shows stood as a separate package of entertainment, emphasizing themes rather than individual stars. There were shows to celebrate holidays, fads of the day, heroic adventures, indeed all the highlights of the Roaring Twenties from the Charleston to Lindbergh to the radio. In the trade this strategy was known as the "pure presentation," as opposed to Grauman's prologues that linked dramatically and thematically to the movie which followed, or the Loew's strategy of a typical five-act headliner vaudeville show.

For its orchestras and organists who provided music for the silent films, Balaban & Katz depended on the star system. Jesse Crawford became an organist as well known as any Chicagoan of the 1920s. In 1923 Crawford's wedding to fellow organist Helen Anderson was the talk of Chicago's tabloids. The couple began to perform together and by 1925 had their radio show and recording contract. When Sam Katz took the pair to New York, the newspapers mourned the loss in the same way they would the loss of a sports star from the Bears or Cubs.

Each of the four characteristics noted above could be easily copied by any theatre chain

The Paradise Theatre in Chicago. Its marquee was reputed to be the largest in the world.

willing to make the necessary investment. But through the early 1920s, Balaban & Katz offered the only air-conditioned movie theatres in the world, providing summer time comfort no middle-class American could resist. After 1926 most important movie places either installed air conditioning or built the new theatre around it.

The Central Park Theatre, opened in 1917, was the first mechanically air-cooled theatre in the world. There had been crude experiments with blowing air across blocks of ice, but these never functioned without severe breakdown. Prior to the Central Park, most movie houses in the Midwest, South, and Far West simply closed during the summer or opened to small crowds. Great progress toward safe mechanical cooling was made during the first two decades of the twentieth century, and the changes centered in Chicago because of the importance of cooling in the meat processing industry.

The air-conditioning apparatus took up a room in the basement the size of two restrooms. For the Chicago Theatre the equipment included more than fifteen thousand feet of heavy-duty pipe, giant 240-horsepower electric motors, and two 1000-pound flywheels.

Once in place these air-cooled fantasy worlds became famous as summertime escapes from the brutal Chicago summers. Balaban & Katz's publicity constantly reminded Chicagoans of the rare treat in store inside. Icicles were hung from all newspaper advertisements. The city's public health commissioner proclaimed that Balaban & Katz theatres had purer air than Pike's Peak and that anyone with a lung disease ought to regularly spend time at the movies.

The results were nothing short of phenomenal. Movie trade papers noted the consistently high grosses during the summer months and could find no better explanation that the comfort inside. Indeed, the take at the box office in the summer regularly exceeded the take during the normally peak months during the winter.

Location, architecture, service, stage shows, and air conditioning made the movie palace into an American institution. Sometimes it seemed the movies themselves simply did not matter. With its five-part system of mass entertainment Balaban & Katz made more money than any chain of movie houses in the world. Their theatres were filled from morning to night, nearly every day of the week. Prices had soared past five and ten cents, sometimes reaching a dollar for the best seats on Saturday and Sunday nights. This was no makeshift nickelodeon, but a carefully crafted package of pleasure designed to maximize profits.

With the merger with Famous Players, Sam Katz was able to successfully transfer the Balaban & Katz system to Paramount's national chain of theatres. Soon the newly christened Publix chain was the world's largest, most profitable, and most imitated. It stretched from North Carolina to Texas, from Michigan to Iowa. Through Famous Players Canadian, Publix also dominated movie exhibition north of the United States border. An estimated two million folks attended Publix theatres each day. And at the head of this operation, Sam Katz decided on everything from the patterns of the carpets to appropriate music to film booking. He ranked as the most powerful executive in the movie business, although few movie fans would ever recognize him on the street.

All decisions were made in New York based on information passed up the line. Costs fell, but so did the contact with the public and the feeling of the theatre as a part of the community. Movie shows were now just another chain store, next to a Woolworth's five and dime and the Sears department store. The Publix slogan summed it all up: "You don't need to know what's playing at a Publix House. It's bound to be the best show in town."

● ● ● ● ● ● ● ● ● ● ● ● ● ●
the social reaction to hollywood
● ● ● ● ● ● ● ● ● ● ● ● ● ●

When movies were first introduced in the United States there was little thought of what impact they would have on the society and culture in general. Yet by the 1920s, their influence was seen everywhere, their effects debated in all manner of publication and venue.

Everyone seemed to see movies as the cause for any number of social problems from juvenile delinquency to communicating diseases to tearing the nation's religious and moral base apart. Educators pleaded for the movies to educate; religious leaders wanted movies to foster spiritual values. By the mid-1920s, it seemed everybody had a solution for the proper way to "improve" the movies.

Thus, for almost as long as audiences have been seeing movies, journalists, educators, religious leaders, social scientists, and other well-meaning reformers have wondered what the movies' effects were on all those people spending all those hours in the dark. Historians have sorted these into three types of questions:

1. *Who made movies and why?* Here we examine the filmmaking industry from a sociological point of view. Racists have asserted an evil Jewish influence over Hollywood, others see Hollywood as a collection of condescending shysters once again trying to prove that a sucker is born every minute. More thoughtful analysis has looked at the backgrounds of the filmmakers, the social networks that make up Hollywood, and the motivation of film artists.

2. *Who watched the movies and why?* Since movies have a mass audience, many have long wondered who actually attended. Indeed, early reformers worried that the first audiences were composed only of children who should be in school. They reasoned that movies served as a powerful drug which lured the nation's youth away from true educational activities. More objective studies have revealed that patterns of moviegoing have been constantly changing through the history of film.

3. *What did films tell us about the changing ideas and beliefs of a society?* Historians have focused on how the movies explicitly and implicitly send messages about a society at a particular time. For example, what can the rash of adult Westerns made during the 1950s tell us about the United States in the cold war? On the surface, newsreels and

documentaries seem to show us the world directly, but fictional films tell the historian a great deal about broader ideological constructs, that is, assumptions held dear by a society. This type of study is usually labeled "film as history," treating the movies as a set of cultural documents in the same way we might use novels, plays, or other forms of expression.

This latter form of study has been the dominant form of the analysis of the effects of movies. So, for example, Thomas Cripps' *Slow Fade to Black* examined the external pressures at work behind the representations of blacks in American films made before 1942. He presumed that "popular art is an expression of deep seated values and attitudes," but not in any automatic or direct way. And Cripps went further, to examine how and why Hollywood as a social institution dealt with pressures, attitudes, and beliefs to form its portraits of black America. Civil rights groups, he found, by 1942 had pressured Hollywood to change to more positive images. Cripps could, but did not, look at audiences for films made by and starring blacks for the period he considered.

These three approaches structure the work of the social historian of film. In our survey below, utilizing all the forms of social historical analysis, we shall see how Americans responded to the coming of Hollywood.

• the progressive era •

At the turn into the twentieth century, movies in the U.S. met head-on the myriad of social forces which historians have labeled the Progressive Era. The Progressives were dedicated to the idea that there was progress in this world and that all technical changes ought to be used to improve the human condition. More fundamentally, Progressivism was bound up with urbanization and industrialization (as were the movies), but coupled with the ideals of nineteenth century agrarian idealism. That is, they wanted change which led to a world only available in the past. The crowding of America's cities, the development of governmental bureaucracies, and even the coming of the movies only made life more difficult for the individual seeking a correct path through life.

A new force arose to deal with these problems, a professional middle class dedicated to making the world a better place. They wanted to use scientific methods of psychology, sociology, economics, political science, and education to teach students to adapt to a fast-changing world. The school became a site for social change, the educator a social reformer. And hopefully the marvel of the movies could teach us all to better understand our world, make sense of our role in it, and rise to greater glories as a society.

Social workers, trained in the new social sciences, fanned out to "do good" in America's cities. Using the settlement house as a base of operations, they quickly despaired that the new movie house down the street was out of their control. They could positively affect schools and even religious institutions to some degree, but this new force of the motion pictures was in private hands, and its poorly educated owners did not care to make the movies a force for social good. The struggles between the Progressives and the leaders of the movie industry brought this debate out in the open. Could the movies be controlled? Or would the movies simply stagnate as another social evil?

Almost from the moment of the surge of the nickelodeon in 1905, the motion picture industry found itself under close scrutiny. This was no organized mass movement, but a total response by interested sectors of society to what was evident in a powerful tool of communication and entertainment. The criticisms and reactions seemed to center on four issues: the effects on children, the potential health problems, the negative influences on morals and manners, and the lack of a proper role for educational and religious institutions in the development of the movies.

If Progressivism had a central theme, it was to seek better health, education, and urban conditions for children. The child symbolized all that the Progressives held dear. Only through youngsters, with their innocence and freedom, could scientific, rational concepts mold a better society. Within this context the movies provided their incalculable lure to the young on every street corner. Once this was realized, early on, social workers, educators, and clergymen kept an eye on the conditions of the theatres, the explicit and implicit messages perceived in the photoplays, and the degree of the competition for a child's time, especially as compared to schoolwork.

Consider the experience of probably the most famous Progressive, Jane Addams of Chicago. In her book *The Spirit of Youth and City Streets* (1909) she devoted a chapter to the new "House of Dreams." Although she praised the opportunity for another recreational outlet in crowded Chicago, she voiced considerable skepticism because of possible harmful effects. The movies, she argued, taking a tact which would be repeated countless times, provided an illusionary dream world. The world of the movies simply provided a cruel illusion which warped the moral and social lessons her Hull House staff was trying to teach. There seemed to be a tinge of jealously because the movie house was doing what the settlement house was trying to accomplish: draw children to a center for fun and learning.

Many echoed Addams' fears and sentiments. The movies were compared to a disease which would sap the strength and moral energy of a generation. Others found it to be the new century's most disturbing social problem. Still others argued the movies encouraged criminal behavior and unwanted sexual activity. Think of it: here was a darken room filled with children of all ages and all sexes. Such an image sent fear into the hearts of Progressives, who wanted to remold the world with Victorian standards of decorum and courtship.

The impact of the early movies, Progressives argued, threaded its way through all areas of life, from the development of a "normal" sense of humor to the encouragement of sadistic and violent tendencies. Even when the feature film commenced, with its instant versions of classic literature, the Progressives complained. The new movies were simply too strong a force, growing too fast, to be able to be scientifically molded in any reasonable way.

No matter that these complaints of the nature and influence of the movies upon the children of America were themselves little more than hasty generalizations (not scientific conclusions of any sort). They did indicate that many citizens of the United States, especially leaders in social work, education, and religion, had became greatly concerned about the new movies early on, a concern that continued until television in the 1950s replaced the movies as *the* mass media threat.

One solution seemed to lie in attempting to take over film exhibition. For example, in the 1910s Jane Addams began her own rival nickelodeon, showing educational films. Chicago's nickelodeons suffered no loss in business. Soon Addams switched to other tactics.

Others suggested that the cities of America initiate municipal theatres, under the direction of museum boards and school districts. There educators could program for the benefit of children who could know no better. This too was not widely adopted. Popular Hollywood films easily outdrew any fare offered in the classroom or museum. Such failures only frustrated the Progressives and made them try harder to look for ways to control the movies.

If there was a controversy that symbolized the coming of the age of the movies, the recognition of a power so great the powers-to-be need worry, it became clear with the release of D. W. Griffith's *The Birth of a Nation*. Before that film opened in 1915, the opponents of the movies had to point to scattered evidence of the evils of the new medium. But with the premiere and run of that film throughout 1915, detractors and defenders of the medium acknowledged its power. Within four days of the opening of the film, the National Association for the Advancement of Colored People announced that it intended to wage a fight against what it considered a racist portrait of black men and women. This only drew more people to see the film and inflamed the controversy.

When the film opened in Boston, protestors demanded it be stopped. The president of Harvard denounced it; Griffith felt necessary to publish a booklet, *The Rise and Fall of Free Speech in America*, to defend himself. (He would make *Intolerance* the following year to explore the subject of morals and free speech in four different cultures.) Whatever side one took, the movies had moved from the periphery of American culture to the center of public debate.

But there were other objections to these feature films. One was the unsanitary conditions of the storefront theatres. The Progressives liked outdoor activity, with the clean air and open space usually not found in crowded city slums. While Progressives pleaded for more playgrounds, the youth of America hustled into dark, seemingly unsanitary spaces to feast their eyes on movies, hours on end.

In many instances, the fears of social workers, clergy, and public health workers were well founded. The early nickelodeons were simply reconstructed vacant stores, put together with little regard for ventilation, safety, or sanitary conditions. But this was corrected by 1915, first because of a flood of safety ordinances, then a spate of building theatres especially designed for the movies. There were few real health problems in America's movie houses after 1915. Still, the nation's theatres were closed in 1918 with the national flu epidemic, and if Progressives ever ran out of reasons to attack the movies, a simple charge of "unhealthfulness" would do.

The arena of debate shifted during the 1910s to the effects of American movies on the overall morals and manners of a nation's youth. Hundreds of formal and informal studies were conducted. The issue was debated in nearly every legislative forum, including the United States House of Representatives and United States' Senate. Yet never was any satisfactory conclusion—harmful or good—drawn. All lamented that the potential of the movies was not more fully realized as a force for education. The popular view of the day was that because children spent hour upon hour in the movie house, their values were somehow changed. In the end there was no simple consensus of what was wrong, only that something was amiss. Groups attacked films dealing with crime and delinquency, sexual license, and misinformation. There were others who saw the movies in a more positive light. They stressed that the movies were bringing culture to the masses, an entertainment alternative not available before.

But the opponents of the movies held the day and thus immediately jumped to debate systems for censorship.

• the coming of censorship •

Progressive forces could not stop the movies, so they settled for content control. This struggle for censorship began first on the local level then moved to state legislatures, governor's offices, and finally the halls of the United States Congress, the White House, and the United States Supreme Court.

Progressive reformers were able to defend the censorship of the movies because they declared this medium a business, a pleasure, an exploitation of the masses, not a means of speech or art form. More than ninety cities, from New York to Milwaukee, would eventually embrace this argument and before 1920 establish local controls over the movies. The initial struggle commenced in Chicago. In 1907, the city, second in the United States in population, had more than one hundred nickelodeons. There had been less than a dozen a mere four years earlier. The *Chicago Tribune* attacked the problem; Jane Addams advocated regulation of movie houses. In November 1907 the Chicago City Council passed an ordinance which empowered the superintendent of police to issue permits for the exhibition for movie shows.

New York City struggled through the debate a year later, and after a well-publicized hearing and even the temporary closing of all nickelodeons, the only action taken was to limit by age who could go to the movies. This proved unworkable and the struggle continued. The nation's first comprehensive municipal law was passed in New York in August 1913, covering not only censorship but also ventilation, fire laws, exits, and other aspects of the operation of a movie house.

These and many other laws on the local level proved ineffective at best. The reason was that by the mid-1910s the film industry had informally agreed to cooperate with the Progressives. Still, Pennsylvania created a state board of censors in 1911, followed by Ohio in 1913, Kansas in 1914, Maryland in 1916, Virginia in 1922, and New York state in 1922. Indeed, the United States Supreme Court established the precedent that state and local laws were acceptable in a 1915 case of the Mutual Film Company versus the Ohio censors. The Supreme Court placed movies (until overturned in 1952) in the same category as circuses, "a business pure and simple," not covered by free speech standards.

At the same time, the battle was fought for federal control. As early as 1915 a law was proposed, but not passed. Several more attempts were made, but no sweeping federal censorship was ever passed. (This made the United States the exception around the world.) There were prohibitions against obscene movies and prize fights (until 1940) but nothing as comprehensive as the Progressives' victory with the Volsted Act, which prohibited alcoholic drink.

• the hays office •

Millions of American moviegoers loved Hollywood films, but the moral and religious leaders of the United States criticized the negative, harmful influences of the movies and called for governmental censorship. In response the leaders of the film industry established the Motion Picture Producers and Distributors Association under Will Hays to monitor and police the movies. Hollywood wished to minimize the unfavorable publicity surrounding the lifestyles of the early movie stars, and the scandals of Hollywood.

Hays was one of the most famous public figures of his day. In 1920 he was heralded as a member of the "Ohio Gang," which elected Warren G. Harding president of the United States in the greatest landslide to that point in American political history. As his reward, Hays served for the first year of the hugely popular Harding administration as one of the more visible and respected postmaster generals. Hays also served as an unofficial White House advisor.

In 1921, while Hays was in the process of reforming the Postal Service, the American film industry was entering a crucial phase of its growth. Hollywood had expanded from a limited presence into one of the more visible institutions within the society. Filmmakers were churning out more than five hundred films per year, which appeared on screens throughout the world. But with success had come scandal. Religious and educational leaders began to raise protest against the news they saw coming out of Hollywood.

In 1920 Mary Pickford, America's beloved sweetheart, had secretly divorced her husband, minor star Owen Moore, and wed a star of her own rank—Douglas Fairbanks. Movie magazines and yellow journalists of the day screamed foul. They claimed the Nevada divorce was a fraud. The next year, an unknown movie extra, Virginia Rappe, died during a wild party given over Labor Day weekend in a San Francisco hotel by one of the three highest-paid stars in Hollywood, Roscoe "Fatty" Arbuckle. Arbuckle was tried (but never convicted) in a series of sensational trials. The scandal sheets and gossip

Will Hays, president of the Motion Picture Producers and Distributors Association of America, 1922–1945.

● ●

hounds had a field day: "Arbuckle had raped Rappe during a drunken orgy."

Hollywood was labeled Sin City. This was an era when the Klu Klux Klan was gaining power, fundamentalist preachers such as Billy Sunday were roaming the country preaching fire and brimstone, and the United States Department of Justice in its Palmer Raids was arresting anyone not considered a true-blue American. The scandals reached the highest levels of Hollywood in November, 1924 when Thomas Ince, one of the founders of Hollywood itself, mysteriously died aboard William Randolph Hearst's yacht.

Aroused by these scandals, the forces of morality of the right, fresh from their triumph of adding prohibition against alcohol to the

United States' Constitution, prepared to challenge the film world. Voices began to call for a federal commission to oversee the movies or at least much stricter censorship laws. The movie industry needed some sort of leader to help them put their house in order, much as major league baseball had enlisted Judge Kenesaw Mountain Landis a couple of years earlier to put the Black Sox scandals behind the "national pastime."

Will Hays would be their man. In January 1922 he accepted a salary of more than one hundred thousand dollars per annum (plus an unlimited expense account) to became the first president of the Motion Picture Producers and Distributors Association of America. Hays went immediately to work, using his political clout

Hollywood Boulevard in its heyday.

● ●

to help turn aside an impending crisis facing the movie industry that spring. The Massachusetts legislature was about to pass a strict law censoring the movies. It seemed that if this precedent was established, it would be only a matter of time before the equally morally rigid states in the South and Midwest would follow.

Hays sent an army of political operatives to Massachusetts and was able to force a public referendum on the issue. Through shrewd manipulation of the press and other forces of public opinion, Hays convinced the voters of the Bay State to reject the proposed law by a two-

to-one margin. The tide had turned and Hays was able to use the same arguments and political muscle to turn back censorship bills pending in twenty-two other state legislatures.

Hays then moved to create a formal public relations arm of his Motion Picture Producers and Distributor's Association to deal with the religious groups, educational organizations, and other parties so concerned with the presumed negative influence of the movies. Hays himself became the point man, speaking before countless groups trying to convince them that the movies could be used for positive good. He was a skillful speaker and more than held his own in tangles with reformers and Bible-belt conservatives.

Hays proved as successful in improving relationships within the movie business itself. Following the principles which had worked so well in the Post Office department, he sought to institute more efficiency and uniformity of relations among producers, distributors, and exhibitors. Specifically he pushed for the introduction of standardized exhibition and distribution contracts and for arbitration procedures to settle disputes. In 1927 he established the Copyright Protection Bureau to register the growing number of titles of films.

He also worked hard to improve labor relations, albeit with a favorable tilt toward management. These efforts resulted in a company union—the Academy of Motion Picture Arts and Sciences—in 1927. Today the Academy is world famous as the organization which gives out the Oscars, but it began as a company-sponsored forum for resolving labor disputes, and would service that need through the prosperous 1920s. Once the Great Depression struck, however, serious unions were formed in Hollywood and the Academy reverted to largely ceremonial functions.

• the social institution of hollywood •

By 1925 the American motion picture industry stood as one of the larger cultural industries in the country, with an investment of over one billion dollars, principally in theatre buildings and properties. To make the necessary films, distribute them around the world, and present them in theatres in the United States and Can-

ada, a handful of important companies emerged to dominate. These major corporations, with studios in Hollywood and beyond and offices in New York City, formed the corporate Hollywood, with power that the Motion Picture Patents Company only dreamed of.

On top were the Big Three of Famous Players–Lasky, Loew's (with its more famous production arm, MGM), and First National, in that order of importance. After that came a group of five midsized companies led by Fox and Universal, followed by Producers Distributing Corporation, Warner Bros., and Film Booking Office. In a special category of its own somewhere between the Big Three and Mid-Five was United Artists, a distributor for the films of its stars. But with United Artists' close ties to Loew's (a Schenck brother ran each), UA was a true insider. All nine companies had international distribution. Most owned theatres.

Below the nine came a number of independent producers, all of whom distributed their films regionally through state's rights jobbers. In 1925 the independents made about one-third of Hollywood's films, but only on the low cost end. These were the cheap serials and Westerns turned out for small independent theatres, not tied to the important nine companies. For all intents and purposes the important nine companies represented Hollywood to the world.

Corporate Hollywood, with its immense production, international distribution, and powerful theatre chains, dictated a strict cycle of film release. The exhibition season began in late August and ran until May. Throughout most of the country (Chicago, with Balaban & Katz's air conditioning, the exception) the summer meant scaling back of attendance and even the closing of some theatres. To feed this schedule, the Hollywood companies sold their array of films in a frenzy which lasted from the preceding March to May. The major season for making movies was spring through the fall.

The institutional apparatus began with the widely publicized sales convention, staged to introduce films which were in scenarios but usually not finished. (Hollywood liked to make the sales and then make the films.) The exhibition season commenced with heavy advertising. Hollywood publicized its work, in this pretelevision era, through general interest magazines such as *Saturday Evening Post*, newspapers, and numerous fan publications.

But Hollywood by 1925 relied on more than the twenty thousand theatres in the United States for the bulk of its revenues. The foreign market was estimated at one hundred million dollars per year by the mid-1920s, about a third of the expected take of a major film. At the time, Hollywood represented an important exporter for the United States; indeed, with autos, movies were one of the best and brightest parts of expanding export trade. The new movies even topped such long term export favorites as paper and electrical supplies.

Hollywood represented the film business to most Americans, but the bulk of the industry's investment was actually on Main Street in the form of theatres. The key to understanding the theatres in the United States was that not all were equal. Most of the twenty thousand were located in small towns with five thousand people or less, bringing in precious little in the way of dollars. Hollywood looked to the major cities (one hundred thousand people or more) to garner the bulk of their monies. These big cities had less than a quarter of the theatres, but recorded more than half the patrons and even a greater share of the dollar intake. In 1926, on average, half of the patrons in United States theatres could be found in movie houses in the nation's seventy-nine cities with one hundred

Rudolph Valentino, star of *Four Horsemen of the Apocalypse* (1920).

● ●

thousand people or more. In other words, half the movie patrons attended only a fifth of the theatres.

And by-and-large, these very theatres were owned by Hollywood companies. They saw no need to buy rural theatres because so little could be made per house. In turn, Hollywood favored its theatres with the best films first. Only weeks, often months later, was a small neighborhood house or a theatre in a small town able to book the same film.

Indeed, the mid-1920s saw Hollywood's important companies initiate a buying wave, adding to the theatres they had purchased in the early 1920s. Famous Players, as one might expect, started this wave of expansion in the spring of 1925 with the initiation of construction of some twenty major picture palaces, including the flagship Paramount in Times Square. But it was in the fall of 1925, when Zukor merged Balaban & Katz into Famous Players, that Paramount was created, the greatest movie company in the world. The subsidiary Publix chain had more than five hundred theatres and was now being run by the man most considered the shrewdest operator in the business, Sam Katz of Chicago.

But Famous Players was not alone. Loew's, in 1926, initiated the construction of more than twenty new theatres (principally picture palaces) and Fox, with a small circuit, began to play serious catch-up. It set out on a twenty-million-dollar spree to build more than thirty wonder theatres, including some of the finest movie palaces ever built in the United States: the Foxes in Philadelphia, St. Louis, Detroit, and San Francisco. It even took over the Roxy in New York, then the finest movie theatre in the world.

Once the institution of Hollywood was established, its style of filmmaking became the world's standard. One filmmaker seemed to symbolize Hollywood's success and excess: Cecil B. deMille, who after the First World War led the way to a different type of image of morality on film, openly portraying the material and sensual pleasures which would become known as the "Roaring Twenties."

Now Progressivism as a broad-based social movement began to fade. Former villains became heroes. Consider the case of Rudolph Valentino. Before the war, his dark "foreign" features would have made him an ideal evil man whose eroticism would have threatened a "good" society. Yet a reversal occurred in some of the most popular early films of the 1920s; frank sexuality made stars of such men as Valentino.

The films which launched the career of Valentino demonstrate the source of this new popularity. In *The Four Horsemen of the Apocalypse* (1921), he played the son of an Argentine businessman. In the opening scene we see Valentino, as Julio, dancing the tango in a smoke-filled cabaret, dressed in tight pants and a gaucho hat. Through all his movie adventures Valentino continued to be the dark foreign lover, as in *The Sheik* (1921), in which he plays an Arab who seduces an emancipated English woman. Although the hero might pay for his sins in the end, the fascination of the audience was with his adventures of sin throughout.

Cecil B. deMille took advantage of this trend. His formula was to take the desires projected onto foreign lovers and bring them into American culture. Instead of reforming the external world, he explored the sexuality of marriage in *Old Wives for New* (1918), *Don't Change Your Husband* (1919), *Male and Female* (1919), *Why Change Your Wife?* (1920), *Forbidden Fruit* (1921), and *The Affairs of Anatol* (1921). The stories in these genre-like films begin with a bored husband or wife trapped in a routine job or social position. Seeking excitement outside this confinement, he or she would turn to cabarets, jazz music, and/or a foreign lover. The marriage dissolves and the hero goes out to explore, in the bulk of the film, the excesses of the Roaring Twenties. But in the end, he or she remarries and the family remains intact. Indeed the marriage is presumed happier for the experience.

These important films of deMille all were made within the confines of strict rules, in what has come to be labeled the Classic Hollywood Narrative style, the defining aesthetic standards for cinema around the world.

···

3

· ·

hollywood establishes the classic narrative style

During the 1910s and into the 1920s Hollywood developed a style of filmmaking which would become the accepted form for "correct" moviemaking throughout the world. This Classic Hollywood Narrative style took its origins from a number of sources in popular culture but surpassed all of them in popularity by 1925. Directors such as D. W. Griffith and Cecil B. deMille became household names. Great American filmmakers such as Charlie Chaplin, Buster Keaton, Ernst Lubitsch, and King Vidor worked within this artistic mode to fashion masterpieces. Rejecting this style, isolated colonies of documentary filmmakers outside of Hollywood developed a cinema of reality they declared superior to the artifice produced by Hollywood.

To understand the Classic Hollywood Narrative style, we need some terms of analysis. To many the aesthetic analysis of film history means the identification and evaluation of great cinematic works. Instead, we shall focus on film as art, exploring the changing set of relationships both within individual films and between films and filmmakers. How have the elements of the cinema (editing, camerawork, and mise-en-scène in the silent film days) been used in particular ways at different points? Certain styles such as the Classic Hollywood Narrative model have been used for decades while others (for example, German Expressionism and French Impressionism) lasted less than ten years.

Film style is composed of a pattern of editing (the joining of shots), camerawork, mise-en-scène (lighting, behavior of figures, and manipulation of costume and decor) and, after 1927, sound. Filmmakers have combined these elements of the cinema in a multitude of different ways, stressing certain parameters over others. For example, Hollywood has long stressed continuity editing; the German Expressionists of the 1920s concentrated on the distortion of the mise-en-scène. Film style is the way filmmakers manipulate the available elements of the medium; aesthetic historians examine how film style has changed over time.

On a broader level, style relates to the general organization of the film. This usually means telling a story (narrative construction). Since Hollywood has so long denoted story as the proper structure, we will divide the history of the aesthetics of cinema into narrative and non-narrative components.

Finally there is the level of theme: the general ideas incorporated into a film. For example, Hollywood has long stressed the unity of the family and the happy resolution of familial problems as proper themes. On the other hand, surrealist filmmakers of the 1920s stressed themes of the disorganization and discontinuity of the world. John Ford specialized in Westerns about the clash and confrontation of different cultures (European versus Native American). We shall see how different themes have helped define certain periods of cinematic history.

the nature of the classic hollywood style

Since the end of World War I, Hollywood has produced a consistent style of filmmaking. That is not to say all films have looked the same. Film genres clearly present differences: the Western, the musical, or the science fiction film. But all genre films follow the rules of the Classic Hollywood cinema, specifying a certain set of characters, themes, narratives, and mise-en-scène within the framework of the Hollywood style. Filmmakers have used genre elements to fashion complex films, just as classical poets and composers did centuries ago. Certain filmmakers (those we call *auteurs*) were able to work within the Hollywood studio system to make highly complex, moving films. A John Ford Western, a Vincente Minnelli musical, a Sam Fuller war film are all recognizable because of certain intricate narrative combinations of camerawork, sound, mise-en-scène, and editing. Still, all follow the rules for the proper Hollywood film.

We shall first consider the history and development of the Classic Hollywood Narrative cinema. After that, we can then turn to consider the works of a number of auteurs, not because they were the greatest artists, but because auteurism offers a useful way to make sense of the massive number of Hollywood films of the silent era.

To keep the product flowing and the theatres full, Hollywood needed a regular source and style of films. Each one should be different enough to attract millions of patrons, but still be easily understood and turned out at the lowest possible cost. This regularity of feature-film production and style became the cornerstone of the Hollywood film. Historians call this regular style the Classic Hollywood cinema.

Hollywood represented a certain way to combine the camerawork, editing, and mise-en-scène into stories which audiences were willing to pay for year after year. The Classic Hollywood style offered a unique artistic mode of cinematic practice, one which thrived within the industrial conditions described in the previous chapter.

With Hollywood, beginning in the 1920s, we have a set of norms upon which an industry agreed. These norms were a unified system with bounded alternatives. For example, a filmmaker could light a scene with high or low lighting to underscore the action of the story, but the filmmaker could not light the scene so low the viewer could not see anything. Likewise, the length of a shot ought to be motivated by the story, not be "too short" or "too long." There were hundreds upon hundreds of alternatives within the system, but rigid and definable boundaries. The Hollywood cinema developed a set of cues to tell the viewer to

expect something. Often these cues were intentionally redundant to ensure that the viewer would not miss a moment of the unfolding story. In short, the Classic Hollywood Narrative system was a standardized flexible formula.

Hollywood films have not lacked aesthetic value, and just because the avant-garde breaks with the Hollywood norms does not make great art. Indeed, filmmakers working within the Classic Hollywood style must be judged in terms of skill in using the established norms and, when possible, in terms of the ability of the filmmaker to modify the rules in a complex, intense, and unified way. Always, narrative causality ruled; the cinema had to be manipulated to tell a story.

By 1920 spectators and filmmakers alike came to the Hollywood narrative film with a set of expectations. Characters acted in a certain way; action and problems introduced in the beginning would be fully resolved by the end; the story flowed along in a manner which tried to hold the audience's interest. Hollywood had to convince the public to attend its tales rather than rely on those found in books, newspapers, magazines, or the theatre. The Classic Hollywood system would define the aesthetics of the American cinema and provide the norms by which filmmakers fashioned alternative styles.

To fully understand the Classic Hollywood Narrative, consider some basic terms. The distinction between a *plot* (the series of actions we see on the screen) and the *story* (the chain of events as we reconstruct cause-effect relationships or, to use another term, the narrative) is fundamental. In the plot, action takes place in chronological order; in a narrative, we have linkages, motivations, twists, and turns. So, for example, a murder occurs, a man drives around in a car and visits people, then a suicide occurs; here we have only a series of events. But if we see the murder and murderer, and we learn the driver is a detective who seeks out the criminal who, just before he finds her, commits suicide, then we have a story, a common yarn told over and over again with various heroes, locations, and historical contexts.

Thus, a story is constituted as a cause-effect relationship between the figures as characters, time, and space. Viewers are expected to make sense of the narrative by noting various events and actions and linking them together. Some events may not be in the plot, but viewers are expected to infer them. So, within the two-hour film we need not see every action of our detective, but we infer the (unseen) driving to visit the next possible witness or his actions unrelated to the mystery to be solved. Filmmakers in Hollywood have long struggled to fashion interesting stories. What should be shown, what could be left out? A two-hour feature film could not show and tell everything. Viewers came to appreciate filmmakers who could entertainingly construct stories which told enough to hold interest, but did not reveal too much.

Since the 1920s Hollywood has used the *characters* to hold stories together. These characters need not even be human (for example, Lassie or R2-D2). What makes them characters in Hollywood stories are a set of character traits. A major character is expected to be (according to dominant ideological standards) good-looking, possess wit and keen insight, and go through a series of adventures "larger than life." A minor character need only be identified by body type or a certain costume. Major characters must have enough interesting traits to propel the story along. If the character does something "out-of-character," it is because we are just learning of a new trait. But traits must be consistent with what we have come to expect. For example, detectives must be logical

individuals who can piece together evidence which others fail to understand. They need not look like Sherlock Holmes, but they will not ring true unless they can think and act according to expectations.

The characters in the Classic Hollywood cinema are placed in situations which, after some conflicts, trials, and tribulations, are resolved. The story ought to hold interest until the action is resolved. But there are certain Hollywood forms that work even when we know the end. For example, in a Western, conventionally the hero triumphed over the villain. Yet people flocked to westerns. That was to see *how* the hero would vanquish the villain. In other words, they wanted to know through what actions, in what order, with what twists and turns the filmmaker would resolve the narrative, even though they knew the outcome.

Within this now-familiar use of characters in stories, Hollywood evolved a set of norms for the use of cinematic *time* and *space*. The plot flowed along in real time, lasting about two hours. Some films might run longer, but a feature film is, by definition, not a short. The story, however, could roam across days, months, years, even centuries. For example, the life of Jesus lasted more than thirty years but has been told on screen in slightly over two hours. The plot cannot possibly relate every event in the story, and it is part of the Hollywood filmmaker's art to manipulate "story time" to hold the audience's interest. We might have a flashback, telling us of actions in the past. We might even have a flash-forward, relating action in the future. In whatever combination, the filmmaker needed to provide cues to indicate what had been skipped over.

The filmmaker also can manipulate space. Events in the plot occur in some locale, what we have come to call the setting. We even associate certain characters with certain settings. Sherlock Holmes plied his trade in foggy London, Superman in a New York–like Metropolis, Rhett Butler and Scarlett O'Hara in the South. If editing is associated with the manipulation of time, it is the camerawork and mise-en-scène (figures, costume, decor, and lighting) with which we associate the manipulation of cinematic space. Normally in the Classic Hollywood cinema, the setting is established early on, and then the characters play out their actions within that arena. But that not need always be the case. In *Star Wars*, the characters roam from one galaxy to another, creating new mythical settings which in the 1970s became part of the mythical culture.

Within this scheme of story and plot, time and space, the Hollywood filmmaker had a great range of possibilities. There can be searches, such as that of our detective, who seeks the solutions to specific crimes and finds the answers at the end. But all Hollywood narrative films must end within a prescribed period of time. So at the end of the Hollywood film, the detective will have solved the crime, the Western hero will have brought the community back to normalcy. Hollywood tied up all loose ends in its stories and then asked the viewer to come back again. There had to be complete closure, with no loose ends hanging about; the fate of each major character, the answer to each important question or problem, the outcome of each significant conflict had to be resolved.

The Classic Hollywood cinema assumes that characters serve as the agents of action within the story. Physical changes such as hurricanes or snowstorms may serve as a precondition for action. Likewise, changes in society, wars, or economic transformations can serve as catalysts for action, but the center of the film rests with the decisions and actions of a finite set of characters.

Frequently the film begins with an enigma or problem which affects the life of the major character. He or she then wants to solve the crime, escape, or do something to reach a certain, defined goal. But the goal cannot be reached until the narrative is over. There are forces of opposition to the central character's desire; actions are necessary to reach the desired conclusion. So the criminal must be caught, the enemy defeated, the evil, land-grabbing rancher brought to jail. Order must be restored. The active, goal-oriented protagonist is at the center of the Hollywood version of storytelling, often motivated by certain psychological traits (desire to make the world safe or to complete the journey into the unknown, for example).

In the Classic Hollywood cinema, cinematic elements of story construction are tied together by continuity editing. The physical break between the hundreds of shots which make up a feature film could be disturbing, ever disrupting the flow of the story. In the years before the First World War, filmmakers in Hollywood developed ways to stitch together the story as coherently and clearly as possible. The purpose was (and is) to provide a smooth flow from shot to shot, scene to scene, sequence to sequence. The graphic, rhythmic, spatial, and temporal relations in time were molded into a system which seemed to make each shot flow smoothly into the next.

Thus, graphically the shots had to match. If a space was specified, it could not be "jumbled up" unless there was some motivation in the plot. Indeed, once a locale was established, continuity was maintained until the scene was over. Figures and props were balanced in the frame, and the lighting remained constant, highlighting the central characters. Shots should be held long enough to provide crucial information. If we have a long shot (in distance) to establish the action, the shot must be held on the screen far longer than the shot of a face of a familiar character.

Hollywood developed a series of guidelines to preserve the continuity of space. We are expected to see the action from the same side of a 180-degree line; to cross over that imaginary line would violate continuity of background space within a scene. If this rule was broken, we might see "new backgrounds" behind the characters, and become disoriented as to precisely where they were. By preserving this central axis, the filmmaker was required to be sure that when characters moved, they did so in the same general direction. All rules about the proper use of cinematic space sought to ensure that the story flowed along without disruption, that characters were ever the center of our focus. The viewer should not be distracted by the mechanics of filmmaking, once he or she had learned the Classic Hollywood rules.

To be sure, the Classic Hollywood Narrative film is only one way to organize a film. Films can be orchestrated like music, around a certain set of temporal rhythms, or around visual shapes and designs. Filmmakers can construct arguments to persuade viewers to take certain action. This is not the place to describe all the possibilities, but to note that the Classic Hollywood narrative is simply one way, a choice among many.

But this particular choice has dominated the Hollywood cinema since the 1910s. And with Hollywood's power and popularity around the world, the Classic Hollywood Narrative cinema has come to stand for the "proper" way to make a film. This single possibility, among many, be-

came the dominant mode of moviemaking in the world. Other possibilities can then be seen as distinct alternatives posed in opposition to the Classic Hollywood Narrative system. Thus, it is "classical" because it has dominated world filmmaking for so long. It is "Hollywood" because it was developed by the American film industry and continues to be championed in the United States.

Stylistically, from the late 1910s on, the Classic Hollywood cinema has dominated filmmaking. Some films used the system before 1917, but in that year and after, the Classic Hollywood style became the standard. This coincided with the rise of the the studio system, which organized a set of procedures whereby filmmakers created scripts which laid out the plan for the plot, others shot the film, while others assembled the final copy, all under the supervision of studio managers. The studio system was as much a set of buildings and necessary equipment as it was a particular organization of labor into the specialties of script writers, unit managers, art directors, electricians, cinematographers, and editors, to name but a few of the subspecialties. By the late 1910s Hollywood had a strict division of labor involving hundreds of workers, most of whom were not known to the general public, but who followed orders of the producers who supervised their projects.

The typical silent Classic Hollywood feature film of the 1920s contained between five hundred and one thousand shots, between nine and eighteen sequences, not including the credits. This was less than what would become the norm in the sound era. Remarkably, the differences between studios were minimal. But with directors there were differences. Maurice Tourneur and Buster Keaton, for example, used comparatively long takes throughout, while

D. W. Griffith and Erich von Stroheim employed unusually rapid cutting styles. Yet in the end, all differences had to be formulated within a common style, the Classic Hollywood Narrative style.

the sources of the classic hollywood film

The Classic Hollywood cinema did not just appear magically one day on the doorstep of a studio in Culver City, California. Indeed, in the 1890s through the emergence of the nickelodeon, movies looked very different stylistically from the Classic model—so much so that these films have been labeled by some as "primitive." Clearly there was a profound difference between shorts, meant to fill vaudeville turns, and the longer Classic Hollywood fare released after 1917. It was not the work of a lone genius who perfected the Classic Hollywood style, but rather the labors of any number of filmmakers, ever seeking a system which would efficiently produce films the public would seek out year after year.

The transformation to the Classic style took place during the 1910s. Within the new studio structure, filmmakers exchanged information through articles in trade journals and seminars; concurrently, the distribution and exhibition sectors were offering feedback as to the devices which seemed to do the best job.

The primitive cinema, as we look back, was neither better nor worse than what followed. Primitive (or what we shall call "early") cinema assumed a theatrical model. As part of vaudeville turns the mise-en-scène was set up as in the theatre, and actors and actresses moved as if on stage. The camera was placed to give each spectator "the best seat in the house." The continuity editing system, the basis of the Classic Hollywood model, was unnecessary since one scene followed another as on the stage. Often a complete film was only a single shot.

The first films were modeled on vaudeville acts. There were variety turns, travelogues, views of current events (sometimes recorded on location, often staged later), and films based on magic acts. By 1903, these genres had seemed to run their course, and so thereafter filmmakers began to experiment with simple, causally linked stories. The length grew, the production time increased, the complexity of creation expanded, with interior and exterior shots.

A chase frequently provided the modus operandi for the action and, with it, a simple story structure: provocation, chase, rescue. But there was another form of vaudeville—the playlet, condensed versions of famous stage plays, with stage stars recreating their famous roles. When moviemakers also turned to narratives, it was with the playlet model in mind. It is as if they sought a *Reader's Digest* version of *Uncle Tom's Cabin*, the plays of Shakespeare, or the novels of Charles Dickens.

But with the rise of the nickelodeon theatre and the demand for more movies, a system needed to be developed for regular mass production. The reasons for the choice of the narrative model were many. One involved the film industry's desire to imitate the novel and legitimate theatre, the artistic forms favored by the middle-class patrons the movie theatre owners wanted to attract. With greater length came the possibility for the type of character development popular in novels and plays. In addition, longer films underscored the need to unify films through editing. The process of change was one of experimentation, then adaptation, then normalization. Gradually, from 1905 to 1917, the Classic Hollywood system became the standard.

Films of the 1910s aimed for a middle-class audience with the time and money to attend movies on a regular basis. But these audiences could also digest stories in magazines (the popular *Saturday Evening Post*, for example), dime novels, and the live drama of the legitimate stage. To compete, filmmakers borrowed heavily from existing plays, novels, and short fiction. As the movies grew in popularity, companies began to bid away theatrical stars and hire popular fiction writers, often writers for tabloid newspapers, who could turn any situation into a gripping yarn.

Movies borrowed narrative principles from all media. The short story and the play were meant to be consumed in a single sitting, as was the movie show. This required sustained unity. But the feature film had many more characters and moved about in space and time in the manner of a novel which would often be read over a period of days, even weeks. The novel thus allowed an interweaving of action and more complex character development than could a film. Consequently, the film should be organized around a single theme, a vivid impression to hold the viewer at the edge of his or her chair.

To do all this, the screenwriter was admonished to introduce no unrelated elements and to motivate, clearly, all action and change. Characters ought to be vivid and lasting in impression, developed and true. The character became the wellspring of the action. The feature film did not have the time to develop character as fully as the novel; instead it borrowed from the theatre to present instant, vivid impressions. The models for the Classic Hollywood film came from the popular short story, the dime novel, and popular theatre.

The early pre-Hollywood films consisted of a single incident; longer films developed a pattern: enigma, crisis, climax, and resolution, all tied together with cause-effect linkages. Unity of story required a coherent, gripping pattern of action. Motivation of character and narrative causality became more and more important as films became longer and longer.

Director D. W. Griffith is rightly praised for the short films he made before *The Birth of a Nation* precisely because he integrated multiple lines of action. By 1909 he began (through parallel editing) to blend together seemingly unrelated actions, cutting between two threads of actions (say from rescuers to the potential victims of some imminent disaster). With films like his *The Drive for Life* (1909) Griffith began to cut to interrupt the action at a crucial point, in the middle of a gesture. In *The Drive for Life* a woman has been sent a box of poisoned candy. Her lover discovers the deed and rushes off in an automobile to warn her. Griffith cuts from the speeding car to the innocent girl about to eat the chocolates, back and forth. At the end of each shot of the fiancee, she is caught in the middle of an action, usually holding the piece of candy near her lips, about to eat. Of course, when we cut back to her, she has not actually eaten the poisoned candy. In this way Griffith built suspense by "holding" action and elongating tension. While today we take such conventions for granted, these devices had to be created.

Griffith perfected the art of building non-suspense sequences as well. A famous early example can be found in *A Corner in Wheat* (1909) when he cuts from the capitalists successfully controlling the wheat market for huge financial gain, to suffering farmers. We see the lavish entertainment of the "Wheat King" contrasted to poor folks unable to even buy bread. In this case the primary thrust of the editing underscored a vivid contrast, to make a thematic point. Griffith would make similar points in *The Usurer* (1910), *Gold Is Not All* (1910), and *One Is Business, the Other Crime* (1912). The interweaving of images of wealth and poverty in these films, the exploiter and exploited, is underscored by pairs of shots in sharp contrast.

By the mid-1910s dual sets of plot lines had become common. In *The Cheat* (1915) Cecil B. deMille skillfully interweaves a wife's flirtation with an evil Japanese merchant with her husband's desire for fame and fortune. Indeed, the second line of a dual plot line was often a tale of romance. But Griffith's *Intolerance* (1916)

experimented with four lines of parallel action—a convention that proved too complex for popular use.

Characters motivated the action in the Classic Hollywood cinema. Hollywood filmmakers became adept at establishing as many traits as needed in a short amount of time. Flashbacks, dreams, and visions became common devices to alert viewers. The star system aided in quick character identification. Stars played types, and so as early as 1914 everyone "knew" that Mary Pickford was a pure child figure with golden curls. Stories were crafted with these character traits in mind: no use fashioning a story of "Little Mary" as the evil spinster stepsister. Stars even became associated with standard goals. Mary Pickford always rescued her family; Western hero Harry Carey, Sr., invariably saved the town; Douglas Fairbanks "won the girl." The pleasure of the story became seeing how the filmmaker would have a favorite star overcome the odds and do "the right thing."

This silent Classic Hollywood narrative used intertitles to establish action, relate dialogue, and help characters express themselves. Many early short films had no intertitles because none were necessary to explain a single action. But with the coming of the need to establish complex characters and their interrelations, more and more dialogue titles came into use. Quotation marks and the movement of lips before cutting to the intertitle signaled the audience that important words were about to be spoken and they should pay attention.

By 1917, the goal of the Classic Hollywood cinema became to relate important dialogue in as clever a way as possible. Noted screenwriter Anita Loos popularized the idea that intertitles could contribute to the art of the film, and with her titles for D. W. Griffith's *Intolerance* (1916) she provided jokes, elaborate descriptions,

***Wild and Woolly* (1917), starring Douglas Fairbanks, Sr.**

even asides. Loos continued in this tradition with the popular comedies of Douglas Fairbanks: *Reaching for the Moon* (1917) and *Wild and Woolly* (1917).

Intertitles used painted backgrounds in what came to be referred to as the art title card. The Triangle Film Company innovated this strategy, and by 1920 it had become the standard. A painted backdrop could establish a scene or provide crucial information. In Douglas Fairbanks' *When the Clouds Roll By* (1919), the various parts of New York City are cleverly established, not with establishing shots but with intertitles.

Acting styles were also adapted to the Classic Hollywood model. With cause-effect narration supplying much of the impetus of the story, the sweeping gestures of pantomime of the early cinema gave way to more subtle, restrained gestures and facial movements. The secret was to have enough exaggeration but not so much as

to look unnatural. Better lighting, faster film stocks, and improved filmic makeup made it easier for the viewer to appreciate subtle gestures, even when the camera was in medium or long shot.

It was with this new acting style that D. W. Griffith probably made his greatest contribution to the Classic Hollywood cinema. In particular, he assembled a repertory company including Mary Pickford, Dorothy and Lillian Gish, and Blanche Sweet and with them worked to perfect a sustained performance style centered on subtle facial expressions in close-ups. Griffith, a former stage actor, was particularly interested in the problem of appropriate cinematic acting, replacing the whole figure gesture (common on the stage of the day) with the facial gesture, only possible in the cinema.

Editing rules were needed to make the Classic Hollywood system work efficiently. The long shot established the scene; cutting analyzed its action. Indeed, by 1917, the long shot as establishing shot was so formulaic that it could be played with in comic fashion. In *Wild and Woolly* (1917) one scene begins with a medium shot of the Fairbanks hero dressed in cowboy attire, sitting in an Indian tepee. Later in the scene we learn that he is actually in his bedroom, far from the Old West.

The shift to the Classical Hollywood cinema also changed the way Hollywood used space. While early cinema had been generally flat, the new Hollywood staged scenes in depth. Painted backdrops gave way to authentic-looking props and sets photographed more and more in deep focus, with appropriate lighting and center framing of the important action. The Classic cinema demanded a series of beautifully framed and lit shots, stitched one after another rather than one expensive, elaborate tracking shot. Indeed, during the 1910s establishing and re-establishing shots, cut-ins, consistent screen direction, shot/reverse shot, crosscutting, and matching looks and action were set into play. Such techniques permitted the plot to proceed along in clearly defined sets of space while making the story flow in coherent, lively fashion.

Storytelling, through editing, was honed to a precise, consistent, efficient set of practices.

By 1917 these elements had been codified in the Classic Hollywood model. The industry subdivided the work into subspecialties including the art director, master editor, cinematographer, and assistants. Through the 1920s the Classic model had reached a firm degree of stability, as filmmakers became more skilled at matching on action, lighting for emphasis, motivating character action, and editing for continuity.

By the early 1920s the rules were well-known. Veterans of the studios of the 1910s taught newcomers. The Classic Hollywood system would survive (indeed, prosper) with the introduction of sound. The Classic cinema quietly and completely incorporated other technological transformations as well. Panchromatic film stock captured the yellows and reds that orthochromatic could not. The Moviola replaced simple cutting with scissors and a light box, and thus made editing simpler and more cost-effective in time and labor. It also made it easier to adhere to the rules of matching on action and maintaining story continuity.

• • • • • • • • • • • • • • • • •

the director's stamp

• • • • • • • • • • • • • • • • •

To understand differentiation within the Classic Hollywood system it helps to begin with the role of the director. To locate a specific set of stylistic techniques, manipulations of the story and plot, and considerations of complex themes is to seek to understand the tendencies of the Classic Hollywood Narrative system. Some directors manipulated stylistic elements, others the story elements, some both. Although the Classic Hollywood system had a finite set of rules, it permitted a nearly infinite set of possible strategies within those rules. The standards could even be violated momentarily, but then things quickly had to return to normal.

The directors discussed below have one trait in common. They all learned their craft as the Classic model was being perfected during the 1910s, and in their own individual way proved that the system was subtle enough to accommodate individual looks. They sensed they had to fit their "touches" into the accepted set of norms.

• d. w. griffith •

Griffith is the filmmaker whom most label as the "father of the American cinema." And in his heyday (1914 through 1921) he certainly was important. But his glory proved short-lived and a decade later he was an outcast. Griffith certainly pioneered a new form of more naturalistic acting; he certainly proved film had important social effects; but in the end he failed to adapt to the studio system of the 1920s.

Griffith deserves credit for being the first filmmaker to extensively employ principles of narration in the Hollywood cinema, particularly in his early features. Through the power of historical stories, he voiced his view of the world. Indeed he was one of a number of pioneers who carefully experimented with emerging rules. He and his cameramen Billy Bitzer and Henrik Sartov gave the world soft photography in *Broken Blossoms* (1919). The softening of the images of Lillian Gish and the gauzy shots of the harbor struck many as a great breakthrough in its day. At first this posed a distinct alternative to the classic style of sharp focus, but seemingly overnight soft focus was incorporated into the Classic Hollywood model to make actresses more attractive.

Perhaps no other director has generated a greater reaction than Griffith. His work is usually allocated a full, hallowed chapter in histories of film. But his contributions to the Classic Hollywood cinema were certainly limited. Directors were inspired by him, but few copied a style which was passé by 1925. Indeed, with *Broken Blossoms* in 1919 and *Way Down East* a year later, Griffith directed his last important films. His final films were too often simply routine studio works. That was precisely the problem. Griffith could not, like deMille or other Hollywood professionals, adapt to the Classic Hollywood cinema and make complex, popular works within Hollywood's rules.

It must be noted that Griffith has also been attacked as the supreme Hollywood racist. His *The Birth of a Nation* (1915) has prompted modern critics to label his work vulgar, inane, moralizing, and sexist. In his own day Griffith was attacked by the NAACP and other liberal organizations. But despite his detractors, then and now, D. W. Griffith certainly ranked as the first "name" Hollywood director, the first filmmaker whose name above the title meant something. As such, when three of the biggest stars of the day (Charlie Chaplin, Douglas Fairbanks, and Mary Pickford) joined forces to create United Artists in 1919, few were surprised when Griffith was invited to be a founding partner.

Griffith began his directing career in 1908 and within the following five years made some 485 films, principally one- and two-reelers for the Biograph Company. In these apprentice works he developed a complex use of parallel editing and innovative acting techniques, as discussed above. His last-minute rescues and dramatic cross-cutting climaxed in *Intolerance*, one of the most spectacular films from early

The Babylon set from D. W. Griffith's *Intolerance* (1916).

● ●

Hollywood. Indeed his pioneering shorts displayed a remarkable sophistication, and today many critics find them more complex than his later feature film work. He certainly mined the theme of the solidarity of the family in a confused and disordered world in *The Musketeers of Pig Alley* (1912), *A Corner in Wheat* (1909), *The Girl and Her Trust* (1912), and *The Battle at Elderbush Gulch* (1914).

The peak of his personal popularity came with the features he made between 1915 and 1920: *The Birth of a Nation, Intolerance, Hearts of the World, Broken Blossoms*, and *Way Down East. Hearts of the World* is not often cited in surveys of Griffith's career, but during the First World War it was among the most popular of war films and rivaled *The Birth of a Nation* in

financial success. (*The Birth of a Nation*, based on sketchy data, was considered the all-time box office champion until the coming of the talkies.) *Hearts of the World* skillfully praised America's entry into the First World War.

But Griffith's reputation rests with *The Birth of a Nation* and *Intolerance*. One is a racist defense of a pre-Civil war Southern life-style, the other a plea for universal understanding. Griffith seems to be a tradition-bound bigot in the former, a crusading liberal in the latter. Yet these two epics share some characteristics. They both imply that history serves best as a chaotic background for a fictional drama of separation and unification. Griffith was at his best using cinema to create passion as he moved his narratives to spectacular endings. He continued to rework this same ground in later years, with less and less financial success.

His subsequent works of pastoral romance (*True-Heart Susie* and *The Greatest Question*) lacked the narrative fire of the earlier work. The stories seemed thin on plot as if he was experimenting with the Classic Hollywood system at the very time it was reaching the initial crest of its power. He wanted the mood and atmosphere to dominate story development. The 1920s in Hollywood was not the proper time for such experiments. Critics of the day complained of repetition of shots, thin plots, loose ends, and dangling characters. Today those qualities are recognized as an alternative to the Hollywood cinema; in the 1920s they meant Griffith's career was doomed to failure, ending at an age when many were doing their finest work.

• cecil b. demille •

Within the development of the Classic Hollywood Narrative style, more importance should be attached to someone like Cecil B. deMille, who was then ace director for the top company in Hollywood. DeMille worked within the rules and made world-famous films. To the public deMille represented the archetypical imperious, Germanic director, but he made Famous Players–Lasky millions and millions of dollars turning out films of all sorts. Indeed, working for Famous Players, a company he had a hand in creating, deMille helped fashion the fundamental rules for the Classic Hollywood film. If Griffith finally rejected the Classic rules, deMille embraced them. No individual alone pioneered the Classic Hollywood system, but certainly deMille led the way as much as anyone.

No deMille film of the 1910s can be called typical, but few had as much influence at the time as *The Cheat*. Released the same year as *The Birth of a Nation*, *The Cheat* was far more influential in helping to develop the rules of the Classic Hollywood cinema. *The Cheat* is a melodrama in which a society woman, Mrs. Richard Hardy, attempts to save her husband from financial ruin by borrowing the needed funds from a wealthy Japanese man she knows. But he demands favors in return. Mrs. Hardy returns the money, but this simply enrages him and he brands her on the shoulder with a red-hot iron. Richard Hardy attacks the Japanese man (changed to Burmese in later prints to increase foreign export potential), and in a final courtroom sequence is about to be judged guilty of this crime when his wife reveals the wound on her shoulder.

This is pure Classic Hollywood Narrative tale, highlighted by the subtle acting of stars Fannie Ward and Sessue Hayakawa. Indeed, into what could have been a hackneyed melodrama, deMille added complex lighting, with mottled shadows and patterns of shadow suggestive of jail bars. Characters are surrounded by smoke, silhouetted behind screens, and appear from nowhere amidst pitch black. This is a tour de force of lighting. In deMille's hands *The Cheat* became an intricate study of individual responsibility handled with subtlety and sophistication. Though the plot involved the threat of infidelity, for example, the film seems entirely free of sentimentality. In addition, the acting style is remarkably modern, direct but without sweeping gestures.

With *The Cheat* deMille showed he was a master of the film narrative. During the remainder of the silent era he made comedies and dramas, capturing an American society in transition. His initial works brought well-

A production still from Cecil B. deMille's *The Cheat* (1915), starring Fannie Ward.

known plays to the screen for Famous Players—*Rose of the Rancho*, *The Girl of the Golden West*, *The Squaw Man*, and *The Virginian*. These films starred such proven players as James O'Neil from Broadway and Geraldine Farrar from the operatic stage. At the end of the First World War came a series of comedies, unlike *The Cheat* in story form, but very similar in faithfulness to the newly established Hollywood rules: *Old Wives for New* (1918), *We Can't Have Everything* (1918), *Male and Female* (1919), *Why Change Your Wife?* (1920) and *Saturday Night* (1922). Ernst Lubitsch, much more famous for his comedies of manners, singled out deMille from this era as a major influence. All Hollywood owed deMille a debt for helping

lead the way to an understanding of how to make films which would be popular around the world.

• the hollywood professionals •

But Cecil B. deMille was hardly the lone successful professional working in Hollywood of the silent era. John Ford, James Cruze, King Vidor, William Wellman, Henry King, Raoul Walsh, and Allan Dwan, among others, represent directors who worked skillfully in the Classic Hollywood Narrative style. Such pros served as the backbone of the Hollywood studio system, making great films within specified genres

John Ford's *The Iron Horse* (1924).

and specific Classic rules. Together they over-saw the creation of the most popular films of the silent era.

John Ford grew up with the American cinema. Early on his older brother Francis had moved west to work for Universal, and John joined him in 1914. For the next three years, the very formative period of the Classic Hollywood cinema, John Ford apprenticed as an actor, stuntman, and assistant director. In 1917 he was promoted to contract director to fashion low-budget Westerns for Universal, starring Harry Carey, Sr. *Straight Shooting* (1917), for example, contains any number of compositions which evoke later Ford Westerns such as *Fort Apache* (1948) and *The Searchers* (1956).

In 1921 Ford moved to the Fox Film Company and added to his growing reputation. *The Iron Horse* (1924), a Western spectacular, provided Fox's answer to Famous Players–Lasky's *The Covered Wagon* (1923). More importantly, *The Iron Horse* established the young director's place in Hollywood. In it Ford laid down the blueprints for his fifty-year interest in the Western. Other early work such as *Four Sons* (1928) proved Ford could not only create optimistic visions of the family in America but also craft darker portraits as well. Yet his films of the 1920s were more often positive hymns to America's past.

In his silents, we can see the development of the style of a Hollywood master. Ford composed with a formality, a symmetry that would seem to be expected from a filmmaker who valued order in society. Ford's images seem to be neatly bisected by tent poles, hitching rails,

James Cruze's *The Covered Wagon* (1923).

• •

gateways, and rail lines, all working to engender a set of visual delights within the Classic Hollywood Narrative style. We also see an emerging interest in formal events which link men and women to society. Even nonritualized activities frequently are turned into rituals through careful positioning and framing of characters within complex settings. In *Three Bad Men* (1926) there is a sequence in which one of the central characters carries his dead sister down the stairs of a saloon. This act is turned into a funeral rite through careful framing, composition, and lighting.

James Cruze was another of Hollywood's ace directors during the 1920s. For *The Covered Wagon* (1923), *Ruggles of Red Gap* (1923), *Merton of the Movies* (1924), and *Old Ironsides* (1926), he earned some seven thousand dollars

per week. Like his fellow professionals, Cruze grew up with the cinema, beginning as an actor in the 1910s and then later moving into directing.

No one accuses him of making great films. Some have argued that Cruze was not even a complex employer of the techniques of the Classic Hollywood cinema. But in the pre-sound era, his work was very popular. He made his name with *The Covered Wagon*, a spectacular Western shot on location. This elaborate use of mise-en-scène, filmed almost entirely in Utah and Nevada, offered a striking contrast to the usual studio shooting of the day. The formulaic tale of the Western journey positioned the setting in equal strength to the characters. The story remained clear, but the mise-en-scène provided the possibility of a complexity

King Vidor's *The Big Parade* (1925).

● ●

later enveloped into the Classic Hollywood style.

Cruze helped spark interest in big-budget Westerns. The genre had always been popular in silent serials and low-budget fare. Cruze's *The Covered Wagon* and *The Pony Express* (1925) proved the genre could make money. Although the great migration westward across the United States during the nineteenth century had been the subject of earlier Westerns such as William S. Hart's *Wagon Tracks* (1919), *The Covered Wagon* represented the first time the experience was set to epic scale in a Hollywood film. There were seven hundred Indians, thousands of local extras, and five hundred wagons which were left from the actual crossings, not built for the movie. Jesse Lasky, realizing Famous Players' nearly total domination of the

film industry at the time, poured five times the normal budget into this massive project. The camerawork often simply recorded the elaborate mise-en-scène, stressing an almost newsreel realism. Camera position, from the top of a bluff or straight-on or capturing charging Indians, set up the spectacle of this film.

King Vidor also made his reputation filming the spectacular, but in this case a war film, *The Big Parade* (1925). *The Big Parade* changed Vidor's status from contract director to courted screen talent. Produced by Irving Thalberg, the film was one of the biggest hits of 1925–1926, playing as a special attraction for weeks on end. Although Vidor would make attempts at films which experimented with the basic tenets of the Classic Hollywood system (the reactions of "everyman" to the anonymous city in *The*

William Wellman's *Wings* (1927), starring Richard Barthelmas (center) and Clara Bow.

● ●

Crowd (1928) pleased critics), he kept bread and butter on the table by continuously producing box-office attractions.

The Big Parade is remembered as the first antiwar war film of note following World War I, the first which made enormous amounts of money. It is the story of the single soldier who experiences the horrors of war. This suited Vidor's interest in playing the individual against the crowd, both at the level of the narrative and at the level of style in terms of elaborate use of mise-en-scène. *The Big Parade* took on its authentic look through carefully re-created realism. Still, Vidor was able to make an intimate, moving story on an epic scale.

The Crowd caught this theme of the individual trapped in a world out of control in the simple tale of a man going to the city and trying to make it. This was considered an experiment because there was no glamorous star or gripping tale of suspense. The style, however, remained Classic, stressing an unusual theme. Here was a rare serious effort at capturing the realism of marriage, of a man and woman trying to survive in the modern world. It made little money, and Vidor returned to more mainstream efforts.

William Wellman broke into films through his friendship with Douglas Fairbanks and directed such popular fare as *The Vagabond Trail* (1924), *The Circus Cowboy* (1924), and *The Cat's Pajamas* (1926). The newly christened Paramount (formerly Famous Players–Lasky) hired him to direct *Wings* (1927), surely the most spectacular war film made during the silent era and the winner of the first Academy Award. *Wings* made Paramount millions and placed Wellman near the top of the purveyors of the Classic Hollywood style.

Wings was shot on location in Texas, including its recreated World War I battle scenes on the ground, and spectacular dog fights in the air. It was the placement of the camera in planes (Wellman was a pilot in World War I) and the carefully staged air battles which, in the months before and after Lindbergh's flight across the Atlantic, captured the public's fancy. The story of two boyhood pals who become flyers, experience a war, and love the same woman (Clara Bow) was routine at best. But within the Classic Hollywood cinema, the use of the camera and mise-en-scène was spectacular. In one scene, there were twenty-eight planes flying everywhere. This could all be done with computer coordination today, but it was a massive operation in the 1920s. Moreover, with so much going on in any one shot, it was difficult to keep the action straight.

Raoul Walsh was a pupil of D. W. Griffith, yet by the mid-1920s he had surpassed his teacher to become a studio favorite and would remain on top for nearly forty years. Walsh was the consummate action director. He reached an initial pinnacle in 1924 with *The Thief of Bagdad*, starring Douglas Fairbanks. But it was

Alan Dwan's *Robin Hood* (1922), starring Douglas Fairbanks, Sr. (second from right).

• •

What Price Glory? (1926) which vaulted Walsh to the top of his profession. *What Price Glory?* was among the genre of popular World War I tales of realism which seemed to dominate at the box office during the mid-1920s. It had been a stage success, but no one expected a realistic story of two rugged marines brawling over a French girl to work on film. Walsh continued his success with *Sadie Thompson* (1928) and *The Cock-Eyed World* (1929), a sequel to *What Price Glory?*

Allan Dwan, a trained electrical engineer (Notre Dame, 1907), began with Essanay, writing stories for that Chicago film company in 1909. He worked for one of the first California film companies (Santa Barbara's Flying "A"), and toiled also for Universal and Triangle. For Grif-

fith, he designed a traveling elevator device on tracks used for the famous overhead shots of Babylon in *Intolerance*. He did eleven pictures with Douglas Fairbanks, culminating in *Robin Hood* in 1922. His reputation at Famous Players–Lasky rested with films starring Gloria Swanson, Bebe Daniels, and Rod LaRocque. The eight films with Swanson, in particular *Manhandled* in 1924, were among the most successful box-office attractions of the silent era. Few aside from deMille participated more fully in the development of the Classic Hollywood style than Allan Dwan.

Henry King grew up in the world of the circus, burlesque, and vaudeville. Like many of his fellow professionals, he entered the movie business during the 1910s. By 1915 he was di-

● ●

Janet Gaynor in Frank Borzage's *Seventh Heaven* (1927).

● ●

Tourneur (see below). He apprenticed at Universal in the early 1920s and then made his name directing two big budget features for United Artists: *The Eagle* (1925, with Rudolph Valentino), and *Kiki* (1926, starring Norma Talmadge, then wife to head of United Artists, Joseph M. Schenck). Brown then signed with MGM, lorded over at the time by Joseph Schenck's brother, Nicholas, and directed *Flesh and the Devil* (1927, starring Greta Garbo), and *Anna Christie* (1930, Garbo's first talkie).

Frank Borzage began his career with Thomas Ince, working as an actor in Westerns and comedies. In 1916 he began directing for Universal and later worked at Paramount and First National. His *Seventh Heaven* (1927), starring Charles Farrell and Janet Gaynor, was among the most popular films of the late 1920s. *Seventh Heaven* (1927) won him the award as the best director at the first Academy Awards. Borzage earned his reputation as a director of melodrama. This is a difficult type of story form to work in because it can become so maudlin. Borzage made it big box-office. His melodramas were different from Griffith's because they revolved around spirituality, the salvation of his characters. He presented inner beauty through exterior expression, and thus a certain type of performer was crucial for his films.

Fred Niblo joined Thomas Ince in 1918, after a long career in the theatre. He then directed *The Mark of Zorro* (1920, with Douglas Fairbanks) and *The Three Musketeers* (1921, also with Fairbanks). These two hits put him on the map, and he went on to direct a number of the most popular films of the 1920s: *Blood and Sand* (1922, with Rudolph Valentino), *Ben-Hur* (1926, which earned the new MGM a great deal

● ●

recting for Pathé, Mutual, the American Film Company, Paramount, Goldwyn, and United Artists. During the 1920s he had no major hits such as *The Covered Wagon*, *Wings*, or *The Big Parade*, but he did turn out consistently fine work for United Artists: *The White Sister* (1923, starring Lillian Gish and Ronald Colman), *Stella Dallas* (1925, script by Francis Marion, also starring Ronald Colman), and *The Winning of Barbara Worth* (1926, a Western again written by Marion and again starring Colman). Henry King provides an example of the Hollywood professional who, working closely with one star, one screenwriter and one production company, could regularly turn out popular fare.

Clarence Brown directed his first feature in 1920, after serving as an assistant to Maurice of money), and *The Temptress* (1926, with Greta Garbo). He certainly will be most remembered for *Ben-Hur*, one of the most popular of Hollywood's silent films. The biblical novel, first published in 1880, was an immediate best-seller and successful on the stage. Niblo demonstrated with his *Ben-Hur* that with fast-paced action and elaborate mise-en-scène, Hollywood could craft spectacles which could draw in millions to the boxoffice.

Tod Browning served as an assistant director on D. W. Griffith's *Intolerance* (1916). In 1919 he joined Universal and soon became the resident director for that studio's major star and man of a thousand disguises, Lon Chaney, Sr. Both moved to MGM to film a string of features, from *The Unholy Three* (1925) through *Where East Is East* (1929). Chaney became famous as the master of the disguise: In *The Unholy Three* he played a crook who dressed up as an old woman, in *The Unknown* (1927) he was Alanzo the Armless, and in *London After Midnight* (1927) he played both a policeman and a vampire. Like Henry King, Browning proved it was possible to prosper under the studio system— even when supervised by the iron-fisted Irving Thalberg—with the right combination of story and star.

• the comic stylists •

It was hard to be too inventive within the Classic Hollywood system, but most successful in doing so were the comics. They worked within the system but still were able to consistently "break" the rules as part of their comedy. Charlie Chaplin, Buster Keaton, and their compatriots "got away" with probing and manipulating the Classic Narrative style because the comedy genre permitted a limited amount of carefully

constructed breaking with societal norms. From the beginning, the short comedy sketch, borrowed from vaudeville, was a standard of the movies. It continued in popularity and was absorbed into the Classic Hollywood cinema during the 1910s.

Mack Sennett perfected an action-oriented comedy based on stereotypical characters. His big break came with *The Curtain Pole* (1909), directed by D. W. Griffith. By 1910 Sennett was in charge of his own comedy unit, directing *The Lucky Toothache* that October. He then moved on to his own studio in California. There he established regular production of two-reelers with the Keystone Kops and others, drawing inspiration from comic strips, French slapstick cinema, vaudeville, pantomime, and burlesque. He signed many of the top comics of the era. Fatty Arbuckle became a baby-faced giant, Ben Turpin a cross-eyed "leading man." Also on the lot was the beautiful Mabel Normand, the villainous Ford Sterling, the burly Mack Swain, and the tiny Chester Conklin. He helped initiate the careers of Charlie Chaplin, Harold Lloyd, and Harry Langdon, all discussed below. He was in the end a consummate producer of comedies, one who understood the developing Classic Hollywood Narrative style and how to work madcap traditions of comic farce into it.

Sennett was no sophisticated comic stylist; he emphasized the brash, the vulgar, and burlesque. He parodied hit feature films and stage plays of the day, always turning serious dramas into outrageous nonsense. He made jokes of all ethnic, social, and sexual stereotypes, building series around material which many would find offensive today: the German Heinie, the Jewish Cohen, and the black Rastus. His Keystone Kops were meant as parody of the police as a moral force of order. Sennett sped up the action, manipulating humans in the same way he worked with automobiles, pies, or other

Charlie Chaplin, director and star of
***The Gold Rush* (1925).**

comic props. Later directors sought to develop comic characters; Sennett stuck with comic action. Sennett relied on the broadest-based humor possible. He was not an innovator, but an adaptor, throwing jokes and humorous skits at the audience as fast as possible, hoping something would work.

Charlie Chaplin was undoubtedly Sennett's greatest gift to cinema. Surely one of the most popular figures of his day, Chaplin was that rare star who by the 1920s had total control over his work. This English-born vaudevillian came to the United States in 1913 and apprenticed with Sennett for two years. His first film, *Making a Living* (1914), in which he was dressed as a dubious dandy, was well received, but it was in his second, *Kid Auto Races at Venice* (1914) that he adopted the costume which made him world famous: the baggy pants, cane, derby hat, oversized shoes, the undersized jacket, and mustache.

Charlie Chaplin, director and star of
***The Gold Rush* (1925).**

Once Chaplin struck out on his own, he became a great star and through a series of deals progressed to longer films and more and more control of what he turned out. By 1919 he was a full partner in the new United Artists and would produce, write, and direct all the films he would make during the next forty years. He was the cinema's first true international superstar, a filmmaker who caused millions of waiting fans to flock to theatres, while also drawing praise from such normally movie-hating intellectuals as George Bernard Shaw and H. G. Wells.

Chaplin worked well within the Classic Hollywood narrative framework. His first step was to establish a universally loved character, the Little Tramp. He endowed his beloved tramp with a flexible set of traits he could carefully manipulate through film after film: always the little guy, an easy target for the bullies of the world, but so agile, quick-witted, and ingenious in using found objects. Through struggle after struggle, the Little Tramp was able to survive in a mean, cruel world. The Tramp could be lecherous as he tried to win the girl, but more often than not he ended up alone, drawing the audience's profound empathy.

The complex Chaplin character began to take shape with *A Dog's Life* (1918), in which he developed social satire by drawing contrast between the Little Tramp and his faithful mongrel friend. *Shoulder Arms* (1918) poked fun at the First World War, and *The Kid* (1921) presented a world of poverty in a contrasting funny and tragic way.

But only with the end of his obligations at First National did Chaplin begin to turn out his best work. *The Gold Rush* (1925) was Chaplin's favorite amongst his own films. Inspired by the stories of the Donner Party and the popularity of the documentary *Nanook of the North* (see below), Chaplin took his Tramp to the frozen gold fields where humans endured great hardships in search of even greater wealth. This film contains a string of Chaplin's best comic sequences. In one of his most famous transpositions of objects, the starving Tramp cooks his own shoe. He carefully boils it, constantly testing for tenderness, and then carves it up like a roast, twirling the shoestrings around his fork like spaghetti. The film is filled with pathos. When the Tramp dreams he is entertaining the elusive girl, he dances with forks as his legs and dinner rolls as oversized feet. This "Oceana Roll," with his playful face coyly appearing over the tops of these two dancing legs, remains one of the most memorable images in the entire Chaplin canon.

Within his series of comedies (longer and more elaborate as his fame steadily grew), Chaplin served up some of the greatest social criticism the Hollywood system permitted. But in the end Chaplin ought to be remembered as a filmmaker who created one of the greatest characters—Little Charlie. But even with budgets big enough for three typical films, Chaplin worked within a narrow range of the possibilities of the cinema, even of the Classic style. He had the best-loved character in the cinema and stuck to telling simple stories, in a straightforward style. The Little Tramp remains one of the most famous images in the history of the movies.

Buster Keaton was considered in the 1920s a silent comic of a lower rank than Chaplin. But today Keaton is praised as one of the great stylists of the cinema. His cinema of long takes (in time and space) stretched the Classic Hollywood style to its limits, and at times even looked almost experimental. Protected by his producer, brother-in-law Joseph M. Schenck, from 1922 with *Cops* to 1928 with *The Cameraman*, Buster Keaton directed, wrote, and acted in a series of comic masterworks, often taking only credit as the star.

Keaton was brought into the movies by Fatty Arbuckle, who by 1914 was a featured Sennett player and director. Keaton had spent his whole life in his family's vaudeville act. Through years of practice he developed his incredible athletic ability, and the skill to perform a gag with a "great stone face." As the physical universe seemed to be closing in on him, the Keaton figure, with remarkable physical skill, could always find a way out.

Keaton served his filmmaking apprenticeship during the late-1910s, and by 1920 began to make a series of two-reelers under his own name. He displayed an inventive comic wit from the beginning, and many recognize these early shorts as among the greatest of the era, whether the Keaton figure is spooked by bizarre mechanical gadgets (*The Haunted House*, 1921) or is chased by every sort of character (*Cops*, 1922).

From 1923 to 1928 Keaton created a series of two features per year. This regular schedule (while Chaplin was taking longer and longer between films) was the work of a man who sought to turn out entertainments, not artistic masterworks. He employed familiar stories from the Civil War romance (*The General*, 1927) to feuding mountain families (*Our Hospitality*, 1923) to Westerns (*Go West*, 1925). Keaton could exploit these well-known genres (buttressed with the ever-struggling Keaton character trying to win the love of some helpless heroine) to construct seemingly endless comic sequences.

Using his own extraordinary athletic prowess, oppressive surroundings, and threatening

Our Hospitality (1923), directed by and starring Buster Keaton.

● ●

situations, Keaton expressed a visual style built on the camera as a recording device, not simply a tool to tell stories. In *Seven Chances* (1925) he battles a rock slide; in *The Navigator* (1924) the enemy is a complete (empty) ocean liner; in *Go West*, a herd of cattle. Perhaps the most admired today is his *Sherlock, Jr.* (1924), in which the opponent is cinema itself. Buster plays a projectionist who falls asleep and then becomes a prisoner within the film he is showing, trapped by unknowing shifts in time and space.

But primarily Keaton will be remembered as the master of the mise-en-scène. He used long takes and long shots to take optimal advantage of the great coordination and athletic skill he possessed. In *Our Hospitality* he made complete use of decor, costume, lighting, and figures (especially himself) to fashion a complex comedy, but one that still fit within the established bounds of the Hollywood system. In a takeoff of the Hatfields-McCoys feud, we see that the McKay estate which Keaton's character as a child had envisioned as a mansion is really a tumbledown shack. The Canfield house is a mansion.

When the inevitable chases occur, because he as a McKay loves the Canfield daughter, the contrast becomes part of the comedy of juxtaposition, in costume as well as alternations of light and dark. In one chase, a murder takes place in complete darkness, only punctuated by

The Kid Brother (1927), produced by and starring Harold Lloyd.

• •

the light emitting from the gunshots. But the brilliance of the film, as with all of Keaton's silent feature-length comedies, comes with layered gags performed with various planes of the depth of field. We constantly see Willie in the foreground and his pursuers in the background, all in the same shot yet hidden from each other. In but one example, Willie is sitting on some rocks when a waterfall suddenly washes over and hides him, for just a crucial moment, from his pursuers.

Harold Lloyd was another of the popular silent comics in his day. In 1923 he formed his own company, and though others may have directed, *The Freshman* (1925) and *The Kid Brother* (1927) were certainly his creations. As

producer and star, Lloyd had the final say. He would satirize college life in *The Freshman* (1925) and extend a comedy of thrills, hanging from buildings in *Safety Last* (1923). Many rank *The Kid Brother*, made for Paramount, as his finest work. But in the end he was a conservative traditionalist who sought to fit into the safety of the Classic Hollywood system.

Harry Langdon, under the direction of Frank Capra, made *Tramp, Tramp, Tramp* (1926), *The Strong Man* (1926), and *Long Pants* (1927), all capturing the innocence of a child-like man caught in the modern world. He is passive, dealing without a will. Langdon had worked in vaudeville since 1903, playing his baby-face role for some twenty years. His screen persona was the awestruck innocent, the world's oldest baby, found perplexed in an adult world full of sophisticated women, gangsters, and everyday gadgets which never seemed to work. But he never was able to work this magic once he began to direct himself. (His best work came under the direction of Frank Capra, who would become a major filmmaker of the 1930s.) The Langdon comedies were the work of a team and provided the model for studio comedy of the 1930s. Unlike Lloyd, Chaplin, and Keaton, Harry Langdon's career at the top lasted but three years.

• transplanted europeans •

A number of the most exciting talents of Hollywood's silent cinema were European émigrés. In this category we showcase two Germans (Ernst Lubitsch and F. W. Murnau) and two Swedes (Victor Seastrom and Mauritz Stiller). They brought experience from a foreign film industry to a Hollywood which sought the artistic respectability associated with the European film. But it took a great deal of flexibility for any émigré to survive and prosper.

The Classic Hollywood system of filmmaking permitted only occasional tracking, panning, and reframing shots. They were simply too expensive. It was easier and faster to create one carefully balanced and beautifully lit static composition and with continuity editing link it up with hundreds to follow. Typical was one the most beautiful films of the early 1920s, Rex Ingram's *The Four Horsemen of the Apocalypse* (1921), which contained only a handful of tracking shots during Rudolph Valentino's tango dancing scenes.

The coming of the Germans changed all that; directors began to move their cameras as often and as freely as they could. New elevators, dollies, and cranes were built to provide the camera the flexibility to imitate the effects of German films such as F. W. Murnau's *The Last Laugh* (1924). The Classic Hollywood Narrative system quickly absorbed these possibilities, assigning them as substitutions for editing. Charles Rosher and Karl Struss used camera movements for stunning effect in F. W. Murnau's Hollywood debut, *Sunrise* (1927).

Ernst Lubitsch initiated the German wave into Hollywood. Born in Berlin, Lubitsch was known for his costume epics starring the Polish "bombshell" Pola Negri. One in particular, *Madame Dubarry* (1919), made his international reputation, and he was brought over to make *Rosita*, starring Mary Pickford, a costume drama. But it was another genre which made his name in the United States. Working for Warner Bros., then a small independent operation, he made five films from 1924 to 1927 which dealt with sexual and psychological relationships in and out of marriage while refraining from conventional moral judgments. This European view was permitted so long as things all came out "correctly" in the end with the wicked being punished. They always did. Lubitsch was hailed a genius.

F. W. Murnau failed to adapt. This star director of the German Expressionist cinema (see chapter 4) had become a world-famous figure when in 1926 Fox studios signed him up and brought him to the United States. Murnau was a master of light and shadow, of the moving camera. At Fox he received the red carpet treatment: he was allowed to bring over his own craftspeople from Germany. His team's initial feature, made just before the coming of sound, was the highly regarded *Sunrise* (1927), a touching story of a young farm couple (played by Janet Gaynor and George O'Brien) who make their first trip to the big city. *Sunrise* is a simple, moving tale, complete with some of the most complex camera movements ever recorded in a Hollywood film. With such elaborate camerawork, *Sunrise* is justifiably praised as one of the most beautiful films in Hollywood history.

Sunrise's mise-en-scène was German-inspired. The architecture of the city was distinctly Bauhaus. Murnau also made expressive use of light and dark, distorting the mise-en-scène to express emotion and conflict. Subtle oppositions of light and shadow set up the contrasts of evil and good. Light dramatically breaks through into the church when the husband and wife are reconciled in the wedding scene; the artificial light of the amusement park foreshadows the near tragedy of the boating accident; the horror-film-like darkness of the marsh overlays meetings between the husband and his temptress.

Sunrise represented the quintessential Hollywood art film of the late silent era. It won an Academy Award for Artistic Quality of Production, an award never given out again. But it also made very little money, and thus Fox supervised Murnau closely for *Four Devils* (1928). Murnau then co-directed *Tabu* with Robert Flaherty. Tragically, Murnau died in 1931. The coming of sound required even more rigid adherence to the rules of the Classic Hollywood system, permitting little opportunity to fashion an art film. *Sunrise* could have only been made when Hollywood was riding high and the studio chiefs felt they needed a dose of artistic respectability. If there is a film which symbolized the German invasion of Hollywood, it was F. W. Murnau's *Sunrise*.

Paul Leni was another German who started his career in set design. As the result of di-

George O'Brien and Janet Gaynor starring in F. W. Murnau's *Sunrise* (1927).

• •

recting *Waxworks* (1924), he was hired by Universal and came to Hollywood to make four films: *The Cat and the Canary* (1927), *The Chinese Parrot* (1927), *The Man Who Laughs* (1928), and *The Last Warning* (1929, his only talkie). These thrillers employed elaborate makeup to create grotesque creatures. They also displayed a complex use of set design, a direct incarnation of German Expressionism. *The Man Who Laughs* stands as the most relentlessly Germanic film to come out of Hollywood in its late silent film phase. Leni, like Lubitsch, tried to redefine Expressionism in the Classic Hollywood cinema and do it with the horror film, but he tragically died in 1929.

Victor Seastrom was one of the great Swedish directors (see chapter 4). In 1922 he was contacted by the Goldwyn Company and left a year later for Hollywood as part of the European exodus. Through the remainder of the silent era he directed films for MGM (into which the Goldwyn Company had merged), and at that point his name (Sjöström) was "Americanized" to Seastrom. He achieved a measure of critical success with *The Scarlet Letter* (1927, starring Lillian Gish), and *The Wind* (1928, again starring Gish). But Hollywood was much too rigid for him, and he returned to Sweden in 1930. He ended up becoming one of that nation's most famous actors, best known in the United States for his featured role in Ingmar Bergman's *Wild Strawberries* (1957).

Mauritz Stiller had a career which paralleled Seastrom's, his friend and fellow countryman. In Sweden he discovered Greta Garbo for *The Story of Gösta Berling* (1923). Their success brought them to Hollywood, but after several disputes over Garbo's role in *The Temptress* (finished by Fred Niblo in 1926), and Pola Negri's in *Hotel Imperial* (notable for its spectacular hotel set over which a camera suspended from a rail surveyed the action), Stiller died in 1928. It seems Stiller had been long accustomed to having his own way while working in Sweden, was largely used to filming in an improvised, almost chaotic manner, and so never fit the requirements for preplanning and tight scheduling of the Classic Hollywood cinema.

Benjamin Christensen was a Dane who worked in Hollywood during the late 1920s. Christensen was known for sophisticated lighting, exquisite panning and tracking shots, and an interest in realistic decor. His success with *Witchcraft Through the Ages* (1922) led to such Hollywood assignments as *The Devil's Circus* (1926) and *Seven Footprints to Satan* (1929).

But none of his horror films made enough of a dent in the box office, and Christensen returned to Denmark to resume his career.

Paul Fejos was a Hungarian who made his way to Hollywood. With *The Last Moment* (1928) he caught the interest of Charlie Chaplin and was offered a contract at Universal. In 1930 he made French and German versions of early talkies (for export purposes) for MGM, but then returned to Europe in 1931. He was too interested in experimenting with cranes, elaborate camera movements, and "starless" realism. His *Lonesome* (1928) combined superimpositions with camera movements inspired by Murnau's *The Last Laugh*. But with the coming of the Great Depression, experimentation was out, and like so many others from Europe, Fejos left Hollywood.

• outsiders •

The Classic Hollywood system demanded strict obedience to the rules. It took a strong personality to try to buck the powers-that-be; most who tried, despite turning out fine complex works, were forced to leave the industry, for example Erich von Stroheim, Maurice Tourneur and Rex Ingram. Either you accepted the economics and the stylistics of the system, or you were forced to flee to Europe to try to find a less rigid arena for film production.

Erich von Stroheim took his first bit part in the movies in 1914. That year he began to work for D. W. Griffith as actor and assistant on *The Birth of a Nation*. He would continue to act, off and on, for the rest of his life. In 1918 he directed *Blind Husbands* for Universal, and he worked there until 1922. What von Stroheim is most remembered for is the realism of his films in Hollywood in the mid-1920s. In witty, risqué, European-like love triangles, he seemed obsessed with the details of the boudoirs, banquet halls, and social ceremonies. Von Stroheim wanted to create his own world on film, with details Hollywood considered frivolous for lean, inexpensive story construction.

In *Greed* he went a step further, attempting a Naturalistic twelve-hour tale of lust for riches. Based on Frank Norris' novel *McTeague*, von Stroheim stressed the ugly and bizarre parts of human nature in the study of avarice and degradation in a mismatched couple. The system struck back in the form of producer Irving Thalberg, who re-cut it to fit the Classic Hollywood rules. The version we see contains only hints of von Stroheim's directoral touches. Unlike the Hollywood professionals, von Stroheim's career was doomed to failure. Still, he was able to go on to create *The Merry Widow* (1925), *The Wedding March* (1927), and *Queen Kelly* (1928) before leaving for Europe.

Maurice Tourneur went to work for Jesse Lasky in 1917, but disagreements arose, and he moved on to Universal. Tourneur is considered by his advocates one of the great pictorial stylists, having been influenced by his study with the sculptor Rodin in Paris. But from the beginning, his association with Hollywood was doomed, since he had made a number of public pronouncements against the rigidity of the Classic Hollywood style. He did direct Mary Pickford in *Pride of the Clan* (1917) and *The Poor Little Rich Girl* (1917). For a time he was the director Famous Players relied on to produce great movies for the masses: *A Doll's House* (1918, based on the Ibsen play), *Victory* (1919, based on the Joseph Conrad novel), and *Treasure Island* (1920, with Lon Chaney, Sr.). But the money and fame were not enough; he wished to work in a style that stressed pictorial image, not the story. Typical of this Tourneur was *The Blue Bird* (1918), filled with excesses of pictorialism which were wonderful to look at but clearly outside the Classic Hollywood system. If Hollywood wanted art, it would go to Germany and hire a Murnau.

Rex Ingram has an early career profile not unlike many of the Hollywood professionals discussed above. In 1913 he began with Edison, then wrote several scenarios for pioneer filmmaker J. Stuart Blackton, moved to Vitagraph, then Fox, Universal, and Metro. At this stop he directed *The Four Horsemen of the Apocalypse*, the first smash hit of the new decade of the 1920s. With *The Four Horsemen of the Apocalypse*, Ingram stood at the top of his profession, having provided Rudolph Valentino with the vehicle which made him a star. He then went on—with cameraman John Seitz and editor Grant Whytock—to make a dazzling series of films for Metro: *The Conquering Power* (1921, script by June Mathis, again starring Valentino), *Turn to the Right* (1921, starring Alice Terry), *The Prisoner of Zenda* (1922, starring Terry and Lewis Stone) and *Scaramouche* (1923, starring Ramon Novarro, Terry, and Stone). These films of adventure made enormous amounts of money and were of such quality that critics of the day ranked Ingram with deMille and von Stroheim.

Ingram sacrificed narrative continuity and characterization for pictorial beauty. He used his star Alice Terry's pale Nordic look to visually contrast with the dark foreign features of Rudolph Valentino and Ramon Novarro. Many ranked him with the top creative figures of his day; filmmakers such as Yasujiro Ozu in Japan and David Lean in England have acknowledged debts to Ingram. He went to great lengths to make his costume, decor, and lighting create just the right look. This set him into conflict with the efficiency and cost minimizing of the studio system. He eventually quit and moved to the south of France to make Hollywood-like films there. Such was his standing that for a time MGM permitted such radical behavior. But soon there were enough new talents on the scene in southern California who were willing to bend to the studio wishes. So in 1932 Ingram left filmmaking for good, not yet forty years old.

the documentary movement

Not all American silent films were Hollywood-made features. There was a rudimentary animation industry which would not reach full flower until the coming of sound. More important during the 1920s as shorter works were newsreels. With radio only beginning and newspapers the sole source of news, newsreel scenes from around the world became an important cornerstone of the commercial American film industry. The newsreel was Hollywood's bow to reality cinema. But the newsreel had to entertain as well as inform. The typical newsreel was a ten-minute potpourri of recorded news footage, released twice a week to theatres from 1911 on. It was a photographic news source which inherited the mantle of the actualities which had been so popular with vaudeville audiences in the first decade of the history of cinema.

Indeed the newsreel—a regular compilation of news footage organized as stories as in a magazine—began in France and England. It was the French Pathé company which introduced the idea into the United States as part of the service of the Motion Picture Patents Company. In 1911 came Pathé's Weekly, a reel of international news scenes issued every Tuesday. The model was straightforward enough. Pathé would strive to produce an illustrated magazine on film, regularly bringing the news of the world to moving picture theatres. Promised (and delivered) were shots of Queen Victoria from London, marching troops in France and Germany, Navy battleships, horse shows, sailing regattas, sporting events, funerals of the famous, and the exploits of early aviators. These subjects would become standard items, and proved so popular that Pathé increased issues frequently to twice a week. By 1914 Pathé had thirty-seven full-time cameramen in North America alone. Around the world it maintained sixty offices from which enough footage for two features was sent to its headquarters in Jersey City, New Jersey to be edited into one gripping reel. Demand was so strong that in 1914 Pathé introduced a daily newsreel service.

But Pathé was hardly alone in the newsreel market during the 1910s. Vitagraph had long produced actualities, but not until 1911 did it begin a regular news service. The Vitagraph Monthly of Current Events focused on the sensational, even buying old locomotive engines and staging crashes for the "news" reel cameras. In 1913 the newspaper organization of the wide-flung Hearst newspaper chain began its own newsreel with the inauguration of President Woodrow Wilson. Joining in 1914 with William Selig, the movie producer, the Hearst-Selig News Pictorial became a twice-a-week offering. Hearst provided the reporters to scoop exclusives; Selig provided the experience in the moviemaking field. But in 1918, after several other attempted alliances, Hearst ventured on its own and became the International Newsreel. Hearst released its product first through Universal and then MGM.

Slowly during the 1910s a number of major services appeared to rival Pathé and International. In 1913 Universal introduced The Universal Animated Weekly. During the fall of 1919 came Fox News. To offset the advantages Hearst had, Fox affiliated with the United News Service. Issued on Wednesdays and Saturdays, Fox had more than a thousand cameramen around the world by 1922. Scoops included unique footage of Mexican revolutionary Pancho Villa, exclusives of the Klu Klux Klan, and aerial shots of the Grand Canyon.

Fox would adroitly use the coming of sound to boost its newsreel (retitled Fox Movietone News) into first place among the various competitors. Its success was so great it forced the largest movie company in the world at the time, Paramount, to begin its own news service rather than buy from Fox. With Paramount's introduction (guaranteed a success because of its ownership of so many important movie theatres), in 1930 the lineup of newsreels stood this way: Pathé (distributing through RKO), Hearst (through MGM), Universal, Paramount, and Fox. There were also a number of local services which operated on the fringe of the industry.

A significant boost to interest in newsreels came with America's entry into the First World War. In April 1917 the United States declared war on Germany, and whatever American cameramen were covering the foreign war were replaced by the United States Army Signal Corps. The administration of President Woodrow Wilson wanted to sell the American public on the war, and so it produced all the battle footage for the newsreel companies. It even edited and compiled a final product to be sent out. Unflattering footage was simply shelved, but what film made it through was well received and created more interest in newsreels.

By the mid-1920s, just before the introduction of sound, the newsreel was standard fare in nearly every theatre in the country. Picture palaces, in fact, subscribed to a number of services (including local ones) and compiled their own "topical specials." Theatres paid according to size, with picture palaces getting exclusive first-runs and then passing down the footage to lower-rung competitors. The newsreel followed the tenets of Classic Hollywood continuity storytelling, although its "characters" were selected from public popularity. Best was to get exclusive footage of the important, interesting actions of a major popular figure such as Charles Lindbergh, Babe Ruth, or the King and Queen of England.

But newsreels were not the lone entry in the field of nonfiction moviemaking in the United States. After the First World War, there grew up a small documentary movement. The dominance of the Hollywood cinema and its alliance with the newsreel left precious little space for documentary films. A true documentary should not be staged, a growing body of filmmakers argued; it ought to permit the camera to record the mise-en-scène as is. Then, if one wanted to cut it together in a Classical Hollywood fashion, fine.

One particular documentary genre did achieve a measure of popularity: the travel film. The travelogue had been a mainstay of the early cinema, beginning with the simple adventures of a Hales Tour's car "taking" passengers via news footage from Tacoma to Tokyo, from Vesuvius to Pike's Peak. But the major break came in 1909 when at the end of his presidency Theodore Roosevelt announced he was going on an African safari. The trip was filmed and was a hit. In 1912 Paul Rainey's *African Hunt*, in the same genre, ran for fifteen months in New York and made its distributor, Carl Laemmle, a fortune. *Hunting Big Game in Africa with Gun and Camera* ran for three months at New York's Lyric Theatre. This success set off a wave of interest in bringing back real footage from the primitive world.

For a time in the 1920s Osa and Martin Johnson made a career of films about the wilds of Africa. They would shoot footage and then come back to the United States and do lecture tours, or in some cases they were able to obtain national release. Their 1928 production of *Simba*, made under the auspices of the American Museum of Natural History, recorded their safari to "the Dark Continent," but with a measure of fakery to excite the audience. Their skillful editing put Osa Johnson in many a tight scrape which, in reality, was never the case. Martin Johnson simply roused and goaded animals and then edited in shots of his wife. Japanese director Akira Kurosawa remembered seeing the Johnsons' films in his youth. Indeed, their *Cannibals of the South Seas* was a hit in 1912, paving the way for Flaherty's *Nanook of the North*.

There was the same spirit of adventure in Merian C. Cooper's *Grass* (1925) and *Chang* (1927). Here the goal was to make the far-off land seem friendly, inviting, even familiar. In many theatres during the 1920s travelogues were regularly shown along with comic and animated shorts plus newsreels, all before the feature would start. *Grass* recorded the lives of obscure peoples in what then was called Asia Minor (today Turkey and parts of the USSR). It was a tale of men and women struggling against nature, complete with title cards expressing their reactions ("B-r-r-r"). *Chang* surveyed Siam (today Thailand), presenting an often condescending view of foreign culture.

This interest in the exotic, the foreign was best exploited by Robert Flaherty. Flaherty made the genre a hit with his *Nanook of the North*, and from there he took movie fans to the South Seas, the coast of Ireland, and then the swamps of Louisiana. He worked and reworked the story of man versus nature in a way many found appealing as the United States was becoming the mightiest industrial power in the world. Robert Flaherty is still probably the most famous documentary filmmaker, this despite his making only five major films, two in the silent era: *Nanook of the North* (1922) and *Moana* (1926). He began with the romantic tradition of the travelogue and taught the first generation of American documentary filmmakers how to use motion pictures to make statements and comments about the world. He demonstrated that there was an alternative to the Classic Hollywood feature film.

Flaherty was born in a world without the cinema, in 1884 in Iron Mountain, Michigan, the son of an owner-manager of an iron ore mine. His interest in nature in a world of growing urbanism and industrialism would provide the theme and continuity of idea for his whole

Robert Flaherty's *Nanook of the North* (1922).

life. As America turned into the twentieth century, young Flaherty became an explorer, a maker of maps, and a mining engineer. In 1910 he set out on his first exploration of the Hudson Bay to determine the possibilities of ore deposits. It was on his third trip in 1913 to this uncharted territory that Flaherty took along a new, portable Bell and Howell camera.

After a number of setbacks, in 1920 he began to make a film about the Eskimos he knew so well. He convinced Revillon Frères, the French furriers, to back him in making what the company wanted as a publicity film. He took seventy-five thousand feet of film, two Akeley cameras, a printing machine, a Haulberg electric light plant, and a projector with him on his

expedition in June 1920 to Cape Dufferin on the northeast coast of Hudson Bay, eight hundred miles to the north of the rail frontier in northern Ontario. There he worked for more than a year capturing the lives, times, and suffering of a group of non-industrialized men and women on the North American continent.

He staged some scenes because the conditions of filming did not permit him to capture them "live." In many ways *Nanook of the North* was a costume picture, capturing the past as well as the present. It was like the Wild West shows of Wild Bill Cody. Flaherty took pains to procure genuine Innuit clothes to "correctly dress" his cast. Like a modern art director who seeks to avoid television antennae in a work set in the 1920s, Flaherty sought to paint a portrait of the past. His sequence of the walrus hunt was staged at Nanook's request.

Flaherty tried to convince Paramount and other movie companies to distribute the film, with no success. But the theatre impresario Samuel Rothefel saw it, and backed it. *Nanook of the North* was booked throughout the United States and proved to be the first documentary to so widely play. The film is the tale of a year in the life of one character, Nanook. Much of the film established the exotic scene; the end saw Nanook kill (in a staged fight) a walrus. Flaherty, through Classic Hollywood editing, fashioned a tale of a character who struggled against nature and won.

The success of *Nanook* captured the attention of Jesse Lasky, the head of production at Famous Players–Lasky, then the most powerful movie studio in the United States. He wanted Flaherty to duplicate *Nanook* for the South Seas, certainly a more pleasing exotic locale. Flaherty spent three years making *Moana*, but not as another *Nanook*. Flaherty had no experience in the South Seas and, besides, the tale of struggle for survival seemed implausible on a tropical isle. After shooting some forty thousand feet of orthochromatic footage, he switched to panchromatic and in 1926 completed the film for which John Grierson first coined the term documentary as we use it today.

Moana was a travelogue, complete with episodes of fishing, harvesting coconuts, hunting turtles, and coming of age. Flaherty experimented with lens and camera techniques as well as film stocks, giving the film added camera movement and shots with depth. But in the end the simple style, letting the mise-en-scène "speak for itself," remained. Flaherty tried to convince Paramount to sell *Moana* as an art work to a special audience, but the company chose to release it in general run in the same manner it might promote a thrilling feature film length tale of adventure in the South Pacific.

• • • • •

From the perspective of Hollywood, the art film, during the 1920s, came from Europe, in particular France, Germany, and the USSR. There filmmaking was not as much a business as an extension of the intellectual and cultural world of the fine arts. European filmmakers had to face the economic and technological constraints of film production and exhibition, but chose to fulfill a different social dimension with films which often did not seek to be popular on a mass scale or necessarily make extraordinary profits. The silent cinema of Europe, an alternative to the Classic Hollywood Narrative style, is the subject of the following chapter.

4

● ●

influential alternatives to hollywood: european cinema

After World War I, filmmakers in other countries struggled against the domination of Hollywood. They labored within their own relatively small industries to develop alternative genres and styles to counter the popularity of Hollywood movies within their own nations' theatres. Native cinemas in two European capitals established art cinemas which reached full development in the silent era: German Expressionism in Berlin and French Impressionism in Paris.

Alternatives to Hollywood were required in the 1920s because the American film industry captured the world market. The majority of theatres throughout the world presented Hollywood films, leaving precious little time for the native creations. Some industries tried to imitate Hollywood, others took the position that only a new and different type of cinema could offer any hope. It is the glories of that second tradition which we celebrate in this chapter.

Before we examine the work of the European filmmakers, especially the French and Germans, we ought to clearly formulate the nature of a film movement. A movement consists of a set of films and filmmakers working in a common style and from common ideas. This includes writings and theories as well as films.

A movement invariably begins by positioning its work against the dominant strain, in this case Hollywood. Such a "revolt" requires some sort of institutional support from the film industry, and/or wealthy sponsors, and/or the government to provide the necessary financing. The analysis of any film movement properly begins with historical analysis of the industrial and societal conditions which provided the conditions for its creation.

From this institutional base comes a unified style. Since Hollywood and its Classic Narrative style so defined the cinema world, it is most productive to examine the efforts of the European cineastes in terms of their differences from Hollywood films, including differences in camerawork, editing, mise-en-scène, and their use of narrative to convey their particular thematic concerns. Within each of the movements certain key filmmakers emerged. That is not to say that they were the only ones, but their films defined the movement's core.

All movements come to an end. Economic and social conditions change, or a new technology is introduced. The principal movements considered in this chapter, those in France and Germany, ended because of a combination of economic calamity (the coming of the Great Depression) and the ability of Hollywood to bid away key filmmakers.

No chapter could cover all possible movements, in all possible countries, even for a period as short as the silent film era. A selection must be made, here concentrating on two nations: France and Germany. But there were other movements in Europe, and first we shall examine the traditionalists, the Swedes, who continued in the art of nineteenth-century realism.

• • • • • • • • • • • • • • •

swedish cinema

• • • • • • • • • • • • • • •

At the turn of the century, Sweden began to develop a thriving film industry. By 1910 Charles Magnusson was leading the Swedish film company AB Svenska Biografteatern to international fame. Probably no other nation of such a comparatively small population had a cinema that could match the fame of the Swedish cinema of the 1910s and 1920s.

Since the country was so small, one man could make a major difference, and that was Magnusson. He had entered the industry at nineteen after he had seen the first exhibitions of the Lumière films in Malmo in 1896. By 1905 he was considered a top newsreel cameraman. Five years later he took charge of AB Svenska Biografteatern, a producer of fiction films as well as travel films and newsreels from its studio in Stockholm. In 1912 Magnusson's company was responsible for some twenty-five films, nine of which were directed by Victor Sjöström or Mauritz Stiller. Through the 1910s Magnusson stressed the production of high-quality films because he knew that was the only way to compete with Hollywood on its own terms. Magnusson was anxious to have cinema gain a respectable place in Swedish society, and to provide the films with a distinctive look began to send his directors off to shoot more and more on location.

Sweden's neutrality enabled film production to continue during World War I as the rest of European filmmaking turned to propaganda works. The Roda Kvarn, a luxury cinema built in 1915, denoted that the film industry had taken hold in Sweden and symbolized the seriousness with which the Nordic country treated the new art form. By 1920 Sjöström and Stiller had completed more than fifty films between them, often based on the work of noted Swedish novelist Selma Lagerlof and Norwegian playwright Henrik Ibsen.

During World War I Sweden built up its native production, taking advantage of its neutral position. Through this period of opportunity, a brief flowering of the Swedish cinema took place, which ended when Sjöström and Stiller left for Hollywood. Magnusson would remain the head of production until 1928, but with the coming of sound, the Swedish film industry, like that of nearly all countries in Europe, simply became another colony for Hollywood exhibition.

The films of the Swedish Golden Age of the 1910s typified Swedish Realism, an alternative style to Hollywood based on location shooting, and an interest in outdoor mise-en-scène. As Hollywood gradually moved indoors to control costs and standardize production, the more flexible Swedish industry was going outside to take full advantage of the wonderful landscapes and lighting textures. The Swedish cinema was always small, and although there were more than twenty filmmakers regularly working in the country during the late 1910s and early 1920s, the two principal filmmakers on whose reputation the Swedish cinema rests were Mauritz Stiller and Victor Sjöström.

Mauritz Stiller was born in Helsinki, Finland and in 1904 emigrated to Sweden to escape service in the Russian army. (At the time Finland was under Russian control.) He worked in the theatre and then moved to the cinema in 1912. Victor Sjöström was a native of Sweden, and earned a reputation as a top actor in the theatre. He too moved to the cinema, and during the 1910s he learned his craft in the studio just outside Stockholm. Stiller's output seemed more varied, and in keeping with his dandyish public persona. His early work consisted of thrillers and comedies; in this context, he learned his craft.

Victor Sjöström cut his teeth on literary adaptations. Together, Stiller and Sjöström directed more than fifty films between 1912 and 1916, most of which have been lost. Sjöström's *Give Us This Day* (*Ingeborg Holm*, 1913), however, has survived to attest to this director's early interest in realism and social change. It dealt with poverty and the need for the state to help the poor. *Give Us This Day* is credited with securing aid for lower-income families in Sweden.

By 1917 Stiller and Sjöström were entering their most influential phase. In that year Sjöström took a tiny crew and acting company to the mountains of Lapland to shoot *The Outlaw and His Wife* (*Berg-Ejvind och Hans Hustru*, 1918), a dour story of a man (played by Sjöström himself) who had to steal sheep to feed his starving family. The horrors of nature at least

A studio portrait
of Mauritz Stiller.

Victor Sjöström (right) at work.

• •

granted the outlaw and his wife a brief refuge together, huddled in their mountain hideout as they pondered better days through a series of flashbacks.

The Outlaw and His Wife offered an example of the country's landscape fully integrated within the melodramatic saga, not simply serving as an interesting backdrop as would have been the case with the Classic Hollywood cinema. The impact of the natural environment on humans was intensified by the texture of the cinematography, the use of deep focus lensing, complex lighting, double and triple exposures, and a slow-paced rhythmic editing. Long shots enabled the viewer to absorb the varied mise-en-scène as the characters struggled their way

through life. Louis Delluc, noted French critic and filmmaker of the day, declared *The Outlaw and His Wife* the most beautiful film in the world, praising the way Sjöström was able to stitch the beautiful Swedish landscape into an element of the story the equal of any character.

In *The Phantom Chariot* (*Korkarlen*, 1921) Sjöström again employed flashbacks to examine the drunken past of hero David Holm (played by Sjöström), who awaited (in a churchyard) "death's wagon" to bear him away. Julius Jaenzon's skillful cinematography enabled Sjöström to offer the viewer a ghost-like effect as Holm's soul seems to take leave of his body. But in the very next year Sjöström was to take his leave to Hollywood. Charles Magnusson

Victor Sjöström's *The Outlaw and His Wife* (1918).

supported the idea because he wanted for AB Svenska Biografteatern the sole distribution rights to MGM films in Sweden.

Stiller remained in Sweden through 1924. In *Bonds That Chafe* (*Erotikon*, 1920) Stiller established a pattern of sophisticated upper-class comedy in the manner of a Cecil B. deMille or Ernst Lubitsch. In *Thomas Graal's Best Film* (*Thomas Graal's Basta Barn*, 1917) he created a comedy examining the foibles of mankind as revealed by various comic, but also very realistic, situations. The couple in the film are not married for more than a few minutes (and are just riding away from the wedding) when they begin to argue whether their child will be a boy or girl. They end up spending their honeymoon apart. Later Stiller derived humor from both bedroom doors, separated by a hallway, being opened, then closed, then opened—simultaneously. The Swedes did not simply make the melancholy films which we so often associate with Sjöström and then, later in the 1950s, Ingmar Bergman, but great comedies as well.

But it was *The Saga of Gösta Berling* (1923), based on Swedish author Selma Lagerlof's novel, which would turn out to be Stiller's most successful film. *The Saga of Gösta Berling* in its original form ran nearly four hours, shown in two parts. Its .plot centers on the search for redemption by Gösta Berling, a defrocked priest, and the several women who disastrously fall in love with him. It represents both the peak and the swan song of the Golden Age of the Swedish silent cinema.

With epic sweep and overflowing narrative, *The Saga of Gösta Berling* evokes a nineteenth-century Swedish life in a lyrical, vibrant way. The film seems to sum up the fine use of natural landscape which had been part of the films of Stiller and Sjöström. *The Saga of Gösta Berling* is set in Varmland, on the Norwegian border, an area dominated by lakes. Not only in the famous pursuit by the wolves in the climax, but throughout the film, Stiller used the forests, the ever-present frozen water, and the vast landscapes of his native land to define his complex narrative.

Indeed, Stiller worked on an acting style which fit into, not overwhelmed, the landscape. Upon this vast fresco of life, Greta Garbo played her second movie role. Contrary to popular belief Stiller did not discover Garbo. He simply needed two young actresses and sent to Stockholm's Royal Dramatic Academy Theatre for its two best. Stiller engaged both and shortened the latter's last name from Gustafsson to Garbo. Stiller's Garbo was a fresh young Swedish girl, not the "sleeky dame" (to quote Variety) of later MGM fame.

the experimentalists

The Swedish realists were hardly the only alternative to Hollywood of the silent era. If the Swedes adhered to the past dictates of realism, then the experimentalists, principally in France, sought to completely break with the past and begin anew. The Cubists, Dadaists, and Surrealists each had their own principles, all founded by artists who, after working in painting or theatre, would then venture into filmmaking.

The years prior to the First World War were characterized by intense activity in the modern arts. In Paris and Milan the Italian Futurists issued a record number of manifestos. The poet Apollinaire in Paris defended Cubism. By 1913

several modern artists had begun to consider film seriously for its kinetic dynamism. For example, painter Pablo Picasso, an avid movie-goer, toyed with the idea of using film for the representation of movement. The Surrealists would look to film as fantasy, the ability through juxtaposition to conjure up a completely new world. By the close of the First World War, film was being considered a medium for serious expression.

Cubist, Dadaist, and Surrealist filmmakers broke completely with the commercial system of filmmaking. To survive economically they made very short films (generally five to twenty minutes in length at most), and they rarely used established actors or industry-connected technicians. Instead they relied on friends. Thus they needed little in the way of financing, using their own money or what could be borrowed or scraped together from rich patrons of the arts. They did not distribute to established theatres but staged special avant-garde "events."

The beginning of the **Cubist** movement in modern art is usually tied to the exhibition of Picasso's *Demoiselles d'Avignon* in 1907. The Cubists were concerned with *form*; they questioned the value of traditional pictorial and narrative procedures and values. The 1920s saw the Cubist film movement emerge as artists-turned-filmmakers pushed the concept of pure form toward non-representational mise-en-scène and non-narrative structure.

In 1912 Hans Richter, after finishing at the Weimar Academy of Art, began to write about modernism in art for *Aktion* journal. After serving in the First World War and being wounded, he journeyed to Switzerland to become a painter. Stymied by the limits of canvas and brush, he sought out a three-dimensional forum with a time dimension—motion pictures. He is most famous for his first work *Rhythmus 21* (1921–1924), an animated work exploring fundamental shapes and sizes. Richter sought to bring the cinema to its basics, to remove all considerations save shape and design. Film should be a kinetic composition of rectangular forms of grays, blacks, and whites. The frame was not a window through which to view a story, but rather a canvas on which to adjust the shapes and designs from a Cubist point of view.

Viking Eggeling also began as a painter. During the early 1920s he became interested in line as a formal element and tried to reduce art to its basic components in the way music can be enscribed as notes and tones. Eggeling learned animation so he could literally turn a painting

into a film. In *Diagonal Symphony* (1921–1923), a "moving drawing," one motif follows another with the diagrammatic clarity of a blackboard drawing, all arranged along a diagonal axis. Simple patterns lead to more complex ones and back again.

Walter Ruttman, an architect, was also interested in shape, design, and space, and so turned to cinema because he did not want to be constrained by time. His desire to set a Cubist painting in motion resulted in a series of abstract films he made in Germany in the early 1920s. In his workshop outside Munich (as Richter and Eggeling were working outside Berlin), he made *Opus I* (1921), an animated film filled with triangles, circles, squares, and ellipses; bubbles, globes, and clouds; and rhythmically flickering light and darkness—music made visible. Ruttman also crafted *Opus II*, *Opus III*, and *Opus IV*, all variations on the same theme.

Fernand Léger, the French Cubist painter, also made films. His discovery of the comedies of Chaplin precipitated his interest in the cinema, and, in collaboration with Dudley Murphy, he made *Le Ballet Mécanique* (1924), an abstract film reminiscent of a Cubist painting. He would go on to prepare other films (including an episode in Hans Richter's *Dreams That Money Can Buy*) but *Le Ballet Mécanique* remains one of the most influential, widely seen of the experimental works of the 1920s.

In *Le Ballet Mécanique*, Murphy, a young American journalist, and Léger explored the impact of the age of machines on the world at large. Instead of a human ballet, we see the rhythms and movements of objects made to move mechanically. Indeed, relatively few of the multitude of objects in the film are actual machines, but through careful manipulation, hats, bottles, canes, and faces almost become mechanical objects. The structure of the film is musical: Objects are introduced, manipulated, and juxtaposed in a careful rhythm through time. Through graphic matches and repetitions, we see that the film itself has a mechanical structure, but no story; it is a Cubist alternative to the Classic Hollywood storytelling.

The **Dada** movement was christened in Switzerland but spread quickly after the First World War to Germany, France, and even the United States. It was a reaction to the war, a revolt against agony, death, greed, and materialism. So, for example, a Dada performance artist might fire a pistol into the audience, then deliver a lecture, and finally simply undress. Marcel Duchamps, under the pseudonym R. Mutt, entered a urinal, which he called *Fountain*, in an art exhibition. Dadaists sought to shock, to bewilder, to mock.

Important Dada films included Rene Clair's *Entr'acte* (1924) and Marcel Duchamp's *Anemic Cinema* (1926). These two films carried illogic to an extreme. *Entr'acte*, a comic fantasy, was an integral part of Francis Picabia's ballet *Relâché*, which premiered in December 1924. The film opened the performance as a sort of prologue that featured Picabia and the ballet's composer, Erik Satie, descending from the sky in slow motion to load a cannon aimed at the audience. Most of *Entr'acte* was shown at the ballet's intermission, to a rising chorus of boos and howls of disgust.

Entr'acte is a loose series of shots, defying logical narrative connections, unified only through visual links. For example, a ballerina, photographed in slow motion from below, is transformed into an opening and closing flower, an image which matches the inflation and deflation of balloons with faces drawn on them shown later. This technique exemplifies some of the Dadaist spirit of anarchy and mockery toward any serious interpretaion of the world. The film ends in a chase, seemingly in-

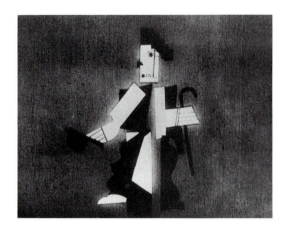

Fernand Léger and Dudley Murphy's *Le Ballet Mécanique* (1924). This is their vision of Charlie Chaplin.

• •

spired by a Mack Sennett Keystone Kops comedy, which includes a camel-drawn hearse. In its day, *Entr'acte* was seen as an assault on the French society; today, the film is considered a film in the Dadaist mode, that is, pure fun.

Surrealism, built on the ruins of Dada, had a goal of positive action. For Dada, in negating everything, ended by negating itself. To the Surrealists the bourgeoisie was the enemy; the Surrealists continued Dada's attack on traditional art but as an organized movement. They sought a "superior" (or sur-) reality. In 1924 Andre Breton's *Surrealist Manifesto* and the first issue of the Surrealist review, *La Révolution Surréaliste*, appeared. The Surrealist filmmakers worked mostly in and around Paris, but outside the regular commercial film industry in France. They received their monies from rich patrons and screened their work to a select few.

Surrealists sought to examine a "super" reality through thoughts hidden in the unconscious. They wanted to go beyond reason, beyond normal conceptions of aesthetics and morality, to a world of the bizarre. As filmmakers, this meant deliberately avoiding the Classic Hollywood style. Yet the Surrealists were greatly inspired by Hollywood. For example, the untamed madness which seemed to be the constant theme of the comedies of Mack Sennett was much admired by the Surrealists Man Ray, Salvador Dali, and Antonin Artaud.

But Surrealist stories were not told according to strict cause-effect rules, which they identified with the rational thought of the normal world. Instead, the Surrealist filmmakers sought to make films with *no* causal connections. This philosophy is best exemplified in the most famous Surrealist film of the 1920s, Salvador Dali and Luis Buñuel's *Un Chien Andalou* (*An Andalusian Dog*, 1928). In this film human figures pull two pianos stuffed with dead donkeys across a room, appear on a beach, then ride down a street, in no logical narrative order.

The Surrealists juxtaposed events to shock normally complacent, relaxed audiences. If Hollywood attempted to be entertaining, then the Surrealists attempted to be disturbing: They actually wished to send their audiences out the door. In the most famous image of all, in *Un Chien Andalou*, Buñuel and Dali make it appear that a human eye has been slit. (It was actually the eye of a dead animal that was cut.)

Un Chien Andalou ran in Paris for nine months through late 1929 into 1930, in part because it was so attacked by the right-wing press of the day. Buñuel sought free associations, playing with narrative style from titles ("Once upon a time," and "Eight years later,"), randomly juxtaposing events. The film has human figures, but no characters with names or motivations. It shocks for no other purpose than to shock. It is a film filled with objects: canes, a severed hand, a striped box. But only the theme of the discontinuity of desire with a middle-class world seems to tie the film together. *Un Chien Andalou* is a film of disunity, of non-expression, of assault on the normal, traditional view of the world.

• • • • • • • • • • • • • • •

an individualist

• • • • • • • • • • • • • • •

But not all filmmakers worked in movements, be they national enterprises as found in Sweden or artistic spinoffs as found in Cubism, Dadaism, and Surrealism. There were individualists who struggled alone, outside of an established movement. Consider the case of the noted Danish director Carl Dreyer.

Dreyer began his career as a screenwriter at Nordisk in his native Denmark and made his directorial debut with *The President* (*Praesidenten*, 1919). He then went out on his own with *The Parson's Widow* (1920) in Sweden and then worked in Germany and France. He truly was a director of international scope. He operated on a film-by-film basis, working on a single project for a single company on whatever terms he could favorably negotiate. Between 1920 and 1926, he made seven films in five countries, no two of them for the same company. His most famous work was *The Passion of Joan of Arc*, a German production made in France. (The same company had backed Abel Gance's *Napoleon* and Jean Epstein's *Finis Terrae*, both discussed below.)

The Passion of Joan of Arc is one of the most famous silent films and one of the biggest failures at the boxoffice. Filming began in 1927 and was completed by the end of the year. The film is a symphony of faces that tell of Joan's trial and burning at the stake as a witch. Dreyer pushed the flatness of the image to an untried limit with straight-on camera angles, contorted framings, and constant graphic matches.

The script was taken from the actual trial, and the sets (frequently unseen) were based on historical designs. But the events, which in fact spread over a year or more, are condensed into a day. Using panchromatic film to heighten the contrasts between the costume and face, Dreyer cruelly exposed emotion through facial expression and looks. He seemed to want the close-up to move into the inner reaches of the soul. He literally tortured his Joan, actress Renée Falconetti. This film of both realism and artifice was the vision of one man and seemed to push the silent film to its limit. Many argue that it signaled the end of the silent era.

french impressionism

Between 1918 and 1928 an influential movement emerged and flourished in France which many have come to call French Impressionism. In Paris there were clubs established to screen these new works and writers who attempted to explain the new cinema and its place in culture. The French Impressionists, through production and exhibition, and through their writings, were able to convince the artists and intellectuals of Paris of the 1920s to take film seriously. They argued that film need not simply be Hollywood stars and stories, but, could be, as Louis Delluc maintained, a unique and vital art form on its own.

The French Impressionists stressed that the filmmakers could transform nature, through careful manipulation of camerawork, to express the mental and emotional states of characters. They did not reject storytelling per se, only the narrow way Hollywood chose to tell its tales. The style of the French Impressionists was characterized by the expanded vision of camera-

Carl Dreyer at work.

• •

work they used to express such mental states. Abel Gance, Louis Delluc, Germaine Dulac, Marcel L'Herbier, and Jean Epstein, among others, emphasized subjective camerawork and optical devices, as well as rhythmic editing, to convey in a new way the emotional development of their characters.

• french film industry and society •

The particular economic and social fabric of France of the 1920s defined the nature of this alternative film tradition. As it did throughout Europe, the coming of the First World War in 1914 meant the French film industry effectively closed down. Workers left to fight; factories turned to war production. Although movie theatres did not close, they turned increasingly to the Hollywood films of Douglas Fairbanks and Cecil B. deMille, serials of Pearl White, Westerns

of William S. Hart, and comedies of Charlie Chaplin. The movies proved as popular in France as they were in the United States at the time. By 1918, when the war ended, Hollywood had taken complete hold of the French market.

Young French talents wanted to try to move beyond Hollywood to transform film into an art form, making movies which would compare to the best in poetry, painting, and music. These filmmakers were young, in their twenties and thirties, just beginning their artistic careers. They sought to craft their own scripts and work as independently as possible. But they distributed their films through the traditional commercial channels to mainstream theatres, in part because they wished to offer mass audiences an alternative to Hollywood. They did not rebel against the cinema as business, but instead wished to create an alternative—an "art cinema" business.

As in the United States, the status of film in France had changed dramatically from the years before the First World War. In 1912 French newspapers did not regularly list film showings. By 1925 not only were films well publicized, there were a half-dozen magazines devoted solely to the cinema. The First World War may have disrupted the production of films, but it only encouraged interest in them as entertainment. Gradually artists began to consider the possibilities for the new medium.

The key year seems to have been 1915, when Hollywood films first flooded French screens. Prior to that the French had done exceedingly well in their own market. During the early 1910s only one American company, Vitagraph, had any success in France, and Vitagraph's John Bunny was one of the few American players known in Paris. By 1920 Hollywood films outnumbered French product by sometimes as much as eight to one. In the 1920s the French would establish quotas to protect native production, but by then Hollywood had too firm a hold.

The intellectuals who became the founders and proponents of the French Impressionist movement built upon this interest in the cinema through the creation of ciné-clubs which could show all sorts of films. They began publishing journals to express their love for the new art and to examine its complexity. The first journal, *Le Film*, had begun in 1914 as a trade paper, but in 1917 Louis Delluc became its editor and began turning out impassioned pleas on behalf of the newest art of the twentieth century. It became the goal of a small group of activists led by Delluc to persuade Parisians that cinema was an art form equal to any other. By the mid-1920s there were a number of journals circulating in Paris with serious work about the cinema, long before any such writing was commonplace in the United States.

With ciné-clubs, students of the cinema could come together to see the films discussed in journals and hear lectures from experts. German and Swedish films, and the best of Hollywood, were exhibited by Louis Delluc and his friends in the first ciné-club created in 1920. Because ciné-clubs were private they could show films banned by authorities, such as Russian Sergei Eisenstein's *Battleship Potemkin*, an avowedly radical work. By the late 1920s there were more than a half-dozen such ciné-clubs in Paris and more in Nice, Marseilles, Lyon, Reims, and other cities and towns around the country.

• impressionist film style •

French Impressionist filmmaking presented an alternative style to Hollywood's. What made it different was its stress on camerawork and editing and its lack of emphasis on story continuity. The new Parisian film enthusiasts stressed film ought to stand on its own as an art of suggestion and feeling. So they placed the character's psychological state at the center of a film. Viewers should focus on the impression of feelings and emotions, not the drama of a story. To depict memories, they used flashbacks. To penetrate consciousness they used dream sequences. Germaine Dulac's *The Smiling Madame Beudet*, for example, is a study of the fantasy life of its female central character, how she escaped from a dull marriage through daydream and memory.

The Impressionists also experimented with cinematography and editing to better convey mental states. In Impressionist films, masking the frame and superimpositions traced and delineated the thoughts and feeling of central characters. In Jean Epstein's *Coeur Fidèle* (1923), the heroine looks out a window, and the superimposition of the foul air from the nearby waterfront harbor conveys her feelings of dejection in being a simple barmaid. In the Impressionist film, objects are seen from the point of view of a specific character; they may even be out of focus if the character is drunk or sick.

French Impressionist filmmakers also made use of rhythmic editing, not (like Hollywood) to tell a story in more exciting fashion, but to capture feeling and emotion. In Abel Gance's *La Roue* (1923), an impending train wreck is presented in an ever-accelerating pace; shot lengths get shorter and shorter to make us "feel" the crash. The Impressionists believed that just as music uses the length and tone of its notes, film should use spatial, graphic, rhythmic, and temporal editing.

The Impressionists developed a specific film aesthetic. They argued that art is the transformation of nature by the imagination, that is, an expression of feelings. To them film seemed to be capable of expressing a new and exciting view of the world, distinct from the view projected by the Classical Hollywood cinema. To express this aesthetic, they coined the term *photogenie*, the ability to transform reality through the cinema. This concept was based on the special power of the camera to blur images, superimpose images, slow down motion, in short to give "reality" a new look. In narrative films they believed the tale ought to be told from the point of view of one character; close-ups and a variety of camera angles should be used to isolate objects and gestures, adding to a new-found sense of subjectivity.

Impressionists also made great use of optical devices, including masks around the frame, dissolves, superimpositions, out-of-focus shots, irises, wipes, and fades—in and out. These devices—coupled with fast and slow motion—heightened the denotation of subjectivity and emphasized dramatic moments. By stylizing images, these cinematic alternatives brought out all the possibilities of the pictorial qualities of the cinema. This style enriched the narrative film form by revealing characters' inner states. Reveries, fantasies, and memories were expressed through such stylistic options as dissolves, superimpositions, fade-ins and fade-outs, selective focus, and slow motion. In an extreme extension of the style, Impressionist filmmakers distorted point of view to denote blindness and stark terror.

Editing was also carefully manipulated to underline a character's point of view. In particular, rhythmic editing structured the pace of an experience as the character underwent it, expressing his or her inner feelings. Editing was simply one more way filmmakers were able to exploit the mechanical means of the cinema to express their view of the nature of feelings, the core of *photogenie*.

These stylistic manipulations first began to appear in films at the end of the First World war. Abel Gance's *J'Accuse* (1919), for example, uses superimposed images to underscore a character's fears and imaginings. Memories and fantasies interrupt his story, and vivid point-of-view shots (for example, down the barrel of a gun) project that character's particular viewpoint. Gance also drew symbolic parallels in *J'Accuse*. He likened a war parade to a dance macabre and an actual battle to a painting. *J'Accuse* announced to the world the new style of filmmaking that was developing in France. Similiar stylistic uses of camerawork and editing can be found in Marcel L'Herbier's *Rose-France* (1918), *Le Carnival des Vérités* (1920), *L'Homme du Large* (1920), *El Dorado* (1921), and *Don Juan and Faust* (1922), as well as in Louis Delluc's *La Fête Espagnole* (1919), *Fièvre* (1921), and *La Femme de Nulle Part* (1922) and in Germaine Dulac's *The Smiling Madame Beudet* (1923).

This impetus to experiment with new uses of camerawork and editing began to undergo significant changes as early as 1923. While continuing the interest in experimenting with camerawork, new works stressed even more rhythmic montage to indicate the flow of a character's experience, frequently by means of accelerated cutting. Jean Epstein's *L'Auberge Rouge* and *Coeur Fidèle* (both 1923), Marcel L'Herbier's *L'Inhumaine* (1924), Germaine Dulac's *Le Diable dans la Ville* (1924), and Abel Gance's *Napoleon* (1927) offer fascinating examples. All were inspired by Gance's *La Roue*, released in February 1923, with its innovative use of rhythmic editing, climaxing with shots only one frame long. After *La Roue* rhythmic editing was considered an important building block of French Impressionist filmmaking.

The peak of the movement seems to have come in the years immediately preceding the coming of sound and the Great Depression. During this period, experiments with camerawork were pushed to the limit. For example, Abel Gance's *Napoleon* (1927) employed any number of hand-held camera shots and structured a climax with the employment of three screens or a triptych. Marcel L'Herbier began to experiment with length tracking and crane shots, culminating in his *L'Argent* (1929), where the camera prowls through corridors and floats along ceilings. Jean Epstein began to try purely visual, titleless sequences. His *Six et Demi-Onze* (1927), for example, had only seven titles in the first half-hour. But all of these experiments remained just that, never capturing the attention of other filmmakers in the way that earlier ruminations of camerawork and rhythmic editing had.

The French Impressionists never were able to survive economically. Eventually, the companies headed by Gance, L'Herbier, and Epstein went out of business. With the coming of sound and a world-wide depression, experiments in the cinema were not financially as possible as before in the French film industry. The French Impressionist filmmakers continued to work, but all believed their best work lay behind them. They had briefly flourished as an alternative to Hollywood. But unlike Hollywood, they were unable even to dominate their own market.

• noted french directors •

Louis Delluc, in the years immediately following the end of the First World War, was one of the more significant figures in the revival of French cinema, making contributions as a writer, a theorist, and a filmmaker. The film which opened his eyes to the possibilities of the cinema was Cecil B. deMille's *The Cheat* (1915). Through this work from Hollywood, Delluc could envision vast potential for the cinema as the twentieth century's art form. As a critic and writer, he tried to make sense of the work of D. W. Griffith, Thomas Ince, Charlie Chaplin, and deMille. He coined new critical vocabulary such as *cinéastes*, and attempted to better understand the nature of the cinema and its proper relationship to the other arts. He championed the French Impressionist filmmakers; he saw the cinema as a popular, not an elite, art form.

Eventually Delluc turned to filmmaking. Between 1919 and his premature death in 1924, he scripted one film, *La Fête Espagnole* (1919, directed by Germaine Dulac), and directed eight others. *Fièvre* (1921) drew heavily on the French theatre and also the films of William S. Hart and D. W. Griffith. It is a drama set in a run-down bistro in Marseilles in which old passions are rekindled, feuds ignited, and men killed. With its realistic mise-en-scène, *Fièvre* impressed the critics of the day with its exploration of the powerful versus the powerless. Predating the dark films of the French cinema made just before World War II, Delluc struck a cord with his portrait of a society gone amok after the "war to end all wars."

L'Inondation (1923), Delluc's final film, was another realist film set in the French provinces. Probably inspired by another of his favorites, Swedish filmmaker Victor Sjöström's *Karin, Daughter of Ingmar* (1920), *L'Inondation* includes murder and an evocative mise-en-scène. Shot on location in the Rhone valley, Delluc wasted (as Hollywood saw it) a portion of his narrative by describing the village of Vaucluse, its festivals and complex culture. Here again was an evocative work, again foreshadowing the lyricism so common to the French cinema of the 1930s.

Abel Gance's *J'Accuse* (1919).

● ●

Abel Gance was another innovator who tried to utilize all combinations of the new film technologies to better convey the world of his characters. In his epic *Napoleon* (1927), Gance alternated long lenses to capture more distance and shorter ones to capture depth. He pioneered early wide screen with three images lined up side by side (Polyvision). He strapped cameras to cars and people to capture their point of view. In *Napoleon* he even placed his camera operator on roller skates to move around among the characters.

Gance came to the cinema as an actor. By 1911 he had organized his own production company, Le Film Français. After the First World War he went on to make several of the most famous films: *J'Accuse* (*I Accuse*, 1919), *La Roue* (*The Train*, 1923), and the magnificent *Napoleon*. The massive financial failure precipitated

by *Napoleon* thrust him to the periphery of the film industry, although he continued to regularly work well into the 1950s.

As early as 1916, with the unreleased *La Folie du Docteur*, Gance had begun to experiment, purposely distorting the use of the lens to reveal the emotional states of his characters. He reached an initial peak with *J'Accuse*, a provocative film about the recent world war and a huge financial success. Released in four parts, *J'Accuse* was inspired by D. W. Griffith's *Intolerance*, which Gance had seen in 1917. *J'Accuse* is a bleak film—two men go off to war, and both are killed by the film's end—but it is a powerful film about the futility of the call to arms.

Gance strove to capture his characters feeling the pain of war. We look down the barrel of a gun and then see the same instrument used

Abel Gance's *La Roue* (1923).

• •

to kill innocent birds. Directly inspired by *Intolerance* Gance sustains an often shocking rhythmic montage in the final battle sequence. As a soldier reads letters he will never send, the fighting progresses with cannon fire, troops massing for attack, and night battles punctuated by blinding flashes of gunfire. This impressive montage, as well as quieter ones such as the festival scene in which we are introduced to the two central characters, prefigure *La Roue*.

Gance certainly established his reputation with *La Roue*. This tale of the railroads and rail workers began as a simple melodrama, but the longer he worked on the project, the more meaning it took on for him. With the death of his wife, Gance interrupted filming and journeyed to the United States to meet his hero

D. W. Griffith. This meeting inspired a work which would run some eight hours, in four parts. It became the most expensive film made to date in France.

The December 1922 premiere of *La Roue* marked a high point of the French Impressionist movement. No film since *The Cheat* had so stunned the French filmmaking and critical community. The tale of a locomotive engineer (Sisif) and an orphaned girl he adopts, Norma, sprawls over tragedy after tragedy, ending with peace found in Sisif's death. *La Roue* is a realistic tale of the rail industry and the lives of its workers, but Gance concentrates on the inner life of its two central characters. When Sisif goes blind, for example, close-ups of his eyes and face are intercut with his blurring vision of

Abel Gance's *Napoleon* (1927). Two examples of the triptych.

● ●

tables, his pipe, a clock, his face in a mirror, and the distant mountain. The scene eventually fades to black.

But the film would be most praised for its powerful use of time achieved through rhythmic editing, rapid montages, and acceleration usually associated only with a musical composition. Gance developed catastrophe after catastrophe in the rail industry as trains constantly accelerated toward danger. Such repetition might border on cliché today, but five years after *Intolerance*, it stunned the world with a powerful and fresh brand of moviemaking.

The success of *La Roue* inspired Gance to plunge into a project of vast proportions: *Napoleon*. This narrative sprawls over the life of

the French military leader, from his career as a young cadet through his triumphal march into Italy. Gance twisted history to present an extremely positive image of his subject. He skillfully employed a vast array of cinematic parameters: rapid cutting, tinting, superimpositions, wide-angle lenses, hand-held cameras, and a new triple-screen, wide-screen image process called Polyvision. This film is a masterwork of visual experimentation. Gance commenced planning in 1924, began shooting in 1925, and wrapped a year and half later. The six-hour film opened on 7 April 1927, marking the end of the French Impressionist movement.

Jean Epstein also was drawn to cinema through the impact of viewing films of Griffith, Ince, and Chaplin. A native of Poland, he settled in France in 1908, studied medicine, and then worked as a translator for Auguste Lumière. He began, like Delluc, as a film critic, celebrating the directorial style of deMille, the slapstick comedies of Mack Sennett, the acting of Lillian Gish and Sessue Hayakawa. Intrigued by the unique properties of film art, he began making films, eager to explore all possible technical variations. He wanted to fashion films in which all the various means at his disposal might be merged into a new aesthetic form.

Epstein's major films are *L'Auberge Rouge* (1923), *Coeur Fidèle* (1923), *Le Lion des Mogols* (1924), and *La Chute de la Maison Usher* (*The Fall of the House of Usher*, 1928). He developed a style which de-emphasized the story by presenting events in a nonchronological sequence and by having actors underplay all scenes. His camerawork and lighting gave a meticulous polish to each shot. To convey characters' points of view, Epstein utilized out-of-focus shots that created dream-like textures. He also experimented with the rhythms of time, space, and graphic qualities. Since Epstein believed that humans perceived reality only through symbols, he saw film as the quintessential representation of reality, a symbol of a symbol. He also claimed that the cinema offered a unique forum to express feelings and emotions.

When Epstein began making films, he had two mentors, Delluc and Gance. His first fiction film, *L'Auberge Rouge*, was inspired by Delluc; his second, *Coeur Fidèle*, by *La Roue*. *Coeur Fidèle*, a story of down-and-out workers in Marseilles, became famous for its intercutting and accelerated montage. (Indeed the film resembles Delluc's *Fièvre*, and helped inspire Julian Duvivier's *Pépé Le-Moko* (1937) and Marcel Carné's *Quai des Brumes* (1938).) But the film offered far more than simply rapid editing. In its famous carnival sequence, Epstein tried to do with the merry-go-round what Gance had

done with the railroad wheel in *La Roue*. Even more accomplished in terms of acting and setting was the evocative dark world of *La Chute de la Maison Usher*. This tale of love and madness is told in a marvelously controlled style which makes extensive use of slow motion and multiple superimposition. Epstein was at his subjective best as his hero refuses to accept the distinction between life and death, and, through an act of will, summons back the woman he has killed.

Marcel L'Herbier is often considered the most representative of the French Impressionist directors. While Louis Delluc focused on the screenplay and Gance on the skillful use of the available technology, L'Herbier, like Epstein, manipulated camerawork to create an alternative style. In *El Dorado*, for example, a story of a young Swedish painter, L'Herbier systematically blurred his images.

L'Herbier decided to become a filmmaker when he saw *The Cheat* by deMille. His first film, *Rose-France* (1918), was no Hollywood melodrama like *The Cheat*, but rather an effort at visual music. It has a drawing-room plot, but because of its maskings, superimpositions, and process shots, it projects the experimental feel of discontinuous narrative. It was as if L'Herbier realized the reigning power of the narrative early on and wanted to depose it.

After *Rose-France*, L'Herbier turned to routine mainstream filmmaking at Gaumont, one of the largest studios in France. It seems *Rose-France* inspired him to learn more of his craft, and Gaumont was willing to teach. *L'Homme du large* (1920) was interesting for its experiments with low-key lighting, foreground and background contrasts, and unusual wipes and masking. One additional remarkable feature was that intertitles were superimposed over images rather than placed on separate cards between shots.

Marcel L'Herbier's *L'Inhumaine* (1924).

• •

El Dorado (1921), a melodramatic tale of a dancer's woes, was L'Herbier's first important work. Through careful placement of the camera, L'Herbier captured the subjective point of view of the dancer to convey her feelings through subjective inserts and flashbacks. Although Gaumont found the film too often out of focus, the critics in the ciné-clubs praised its fascinating use of camera technique. This was an important film because it broke with the Hollywood narrative but was still relatively popular.

By the mid-1920s L'Herbier felt he was ready to venture on his own. He left Gaumont and made his two most famous works: *L'Inhumaine* and *L'Argent* (1929). In *L'Inhumaine*, a serial adventure romance, the story is a pretext for experimental filmmaking. It was produced, in part, to make a dent in the United States' market for art films, which had been opened up earlier in the decade by *The Cabinet of Dr. Caligari*. The tale of a celebrated singer is constantly ruptured, suspended, and "broken" to call attention to the process of filmmaking itself. Not only does the film include all the experiments of camerawork L'Herbier had attempted to that time, but it incorporates an editing style reminiscent of Abel Gance. *L'Argent*, inspired by Emile Zola's novel, was more radical in its theme—it is an attack on capitalism—than in

Germaine Dulac's *La Souriante Madame Beudet* **(1924).**

• •

its style. Along with Gance's *Napoleon* it marked the end of the French Impressionist film movement in France of the 1920s, several months before the economic calamity which is foreseen in the film.

Germaine Dulac began her career as a writer for the feminist French journal *La Française* in 1909, then moved into the early film industry as a camerawoman. By 1918 she formed her own production company. After work in ciné-clubs and a visit to the United States in the early 1920s (including a meeting with D. W. Griffith), she made *La Souriante Madame Beudet* (*The Smiling Madame Beudet*, 1923) which established her reputation. In 1928, in collaboration with noted Surrealist writer Antoin Artaud, she created *La Coquille*

et le Clergyman (*The Seashell and the Clergyman*, 1927).

Dulac directed her first film in 1915, in part because so many men were going to war. Her early films were conventional stories, aimed at the general French audience. Gradually she experimented more and more, and with *La Souriante Madame Beudet* moved into the heart of the French Impressionist movement. This film depicts the life and dreams of a small-town woman who was trapped in a marriage to a coarse, repulsive businessman. In characteristic Impressionist style, Dulac used slow-motion cinematography to get inside the head of the woman and to articulate her condition. For example, in one scene, Beudet's point of view is conveyed through a careful use of dissolves,

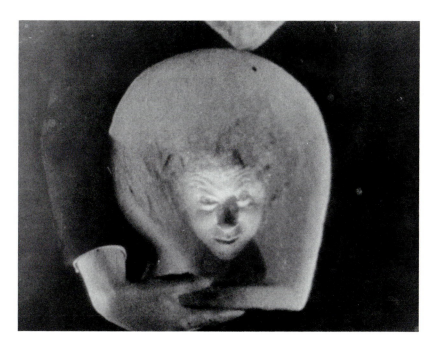

Germaine Dulac's *La Coquille et le Clergyman* (1927).

● ●

and a distorted use of lenses, double exposures, and slow motion. As she is reading a magazine, she comes upon a photo of a champion tennis player. Suddenly, in a slow-motion superimposition, he breaks out of his stance to serve the ball and becomes, through superimposition again, her husband.

In 1927 Dulac switched course and abandoned the French Impressionist style. With Antoin Artaud handling the script, she directed a Surrealist-like film, *La Coquille et le Clergyman*, which, in its dream structure, lacked the typical Impressionist concern with narrative. In this film three characters interact, but with space and time so fractured that any sort of Hollywood-like continuity is negated. There are no intertitles to guide the viewer or fades which punctuate sequences. It seems as if the techniques of subjectivity which Dulac had used so effectively earlier in the decade are being questioned. This seems to be a film *about* the Impressionist style of filmmaking.

During the following two years Dulac's work intersected with that of another avant-garde movement, the Cubist cinema. Her *Disque 927* (1928), *Themes and Variations* (1928), and *Etude Cinégraphique sur une Arabesque* (1929) all bear the influence of Ferdinand Leger. But as was the case with the other French Impressionist filmmakers, her sources of finance dried up with the coming of the world depression, and she was able to make few of her own films during the 1930s. She then turned to directing newsreels for Gaumont.

• • • • • • • • • • • • • • • •

german
expressionism

• • • • • • • • • • • • • • • •

During the 1920s there was one European nation that offered Hollywood a true challenge. Germany was the only country with enough resources, a large enough native market, and the added support of the government which could provide films to woo native audiences away from Hollywood's best. The particular economic and social fabric of Germany defined the nature of its particular alternative tradition, but even with all the German cinema's advantages, Hollywood would still prove too strong. Ernst Lubitsch and F. W. Murnau were lured away even before the Nazis drove most other talents to flee. Nevertheless, through the 1920s German Expressionism provided audiences with films which were a valid alternative to those of Hollywood.

• industry and society •

As with all its European neighbors, the German film industry had to somehow deal with Hollywood. Before the advent of the First World War, the German film industry ranked as one of the most productive in the world. But the war changed all that. The German war government began to subsidize the film industry and required its native theatres to show only German films. With the absence of French, Italian,

American, and other European films, the German film companies thrived. Fully aware of the propaganda value of the cinema, in December 1917 the German government sponsored Universum Film AG (hereafter UFA) by bringing together a set of film companies. The most powerful organization in the German film industry, UFA was instantly a world force in the cinema, certainly the most powerful in all Europe.

At this point the Germans began to think seriously about exporting films. Erich Pommer, of Decla-Bioscop, the second ranking company, was convinced that this additional export could only be done successfully with art films, not clones of Hollywood. Decla's *The Cabinet of Dr. Caligari* (1919) certainly was the film which brought fame to the German cinema. But the German film industry also made spy and detective films, historical epics, and even for a time sex exploitation films. Ernst Lubitsch's *Madame Dubarry*, an epic about the French Revolution (released in the United States as *Passion*), paved the way. It received great reviews and enjoyed widespread popularity. By 1923 UFA had taken over Decla, and Pommer had become one of the most powerful movie producers in the world.

Throughout the 1920s UFA continually absorbed a number of smaller companies and dominated the market for the most expensive, most spectacular films. What gave UFA special force were the same factors which buttressed Hollywood: extraordinary power in distribution and exhibition. Like Hollywood companies, UFA owned a large chain of theatres. With its considerable economic muscle, UFA was the *one* company equal in power in its nation to Hollywood's major studios.

When the war ended, Hollywood moved into Germany. The Germans, who had had their screens to themselves for about a decade, now saw Hollywood films flood the market. By the late 1920s, even UFA was in trouble. In the long run, the Classic Hollywood cinema prevailed and the German Expressionist films, aimed at audiences throughout the world, were phased out. They simply cost too much and took in too little. Fritz Lang's famous science fiction film, *Metropolis* (1927), is a case in point. Lang had employed some eight hundred actors and actresses, thirty thousand extras, and taken nearly a year to film. UFA managers hoped it would be a hit in the United States, but the film ended up losing so much money that UFA was reorganized under new management.

In order to protect themselves, the German companies began to make a series of agreements with Hollywood. In 1927 UFA formed a joint venture with Paramount and MGM. Under this arrangement, UFA's most important theatres would exhibit twenty of Paramount's and twenty of MGM's films in Germany and, in exchange, the American companies would handle ten UFA pictures in the United States. Other German companies made similar agreements with American companies, including Tera (with Universal), and Rex (with United Artists). Most of these agreements did not survive the coming of sound.

The German government tried to help its film industry by passing a law restricting the importing of Hollywood films. The coming of sound seemed to provide just the opportunity for the Germans to take back native screens because the manufacturers of the sound equipment in Germany were as strong as those in the United States. But the German electrical manufacturers were unable to best Western Electric and RCA for world domination of talkies. In 1930 the German and American manufacturers of sound equipment agreed to divide up the world market. Only a dictator like Adolph Hitler could throw Hollywood out of the country, and return German screens to German filmmakers (see chapter 8).

• stylistic traits •

Between 1919 and 1930 a number of films were made in Germany which constituted the movement called German Expressionism. Expressionism (a term borrowed from painting and theatre) refers to an extreme stylization of the mise-en-scène: chiaroscuro lighting, surrealist settings, stylized acting, and frequently a camera moving about this "unreal" world. The gothic appearance of these films is often accompanied by macabre, low-life subject matter. The overall effect is of a world filled with angst, paranoia, and nonrational phenomena; a world of pointed criticisms of the Hollywood bourgeois universe.

After the war a number of small film companies such as Erich Pommer's Decla-Bioscop reappeared to challenge UFA. These companies had to take chances on unconventional material since UFA had the German market essentially locked up. One of Pommer's strategies was to produce an off-beat script by Carl Mayer and

The Cabinet of Dr. Caligari (1919).

● ●

Hans Janowitz. Pommer recruited three set designers—Hermann Warm, Walter Reimann, and Walter Rohrig—to provide a new look. These designers decided to model the film after German Expressionism, an avant-garde movement which had been going strong for more than a decade in German painting, theatre, literature, and architecture.

When *The Cabinet of Dr. Caligari* (1919) appeared, it was considered unlike any film that had been made to that time. But to those familiar with Expressionism in other arts, this film provided no shock. It was a surprise only to the mass audiences generally unfamiliar with the German avant-garde. *The Cabinet of Dr. Caligari* is no tentative essay in the Expressionist style, but rather a full-fledged work. Why? Where did the Expressionism in *The Cabinet of Dr. Caligari* come from?

Only after Expressionism had been established in painting, literature, and drama did the film industry embrace it. This style had its origins in a revolt against the arts of the nineteenth century. Painters such as Vincent Van Gogh and Paul Gauguin rejected the aesthetic of absolute fidelity to the external appearance of the world and began to express their personal, subjective visions. In Germany, painter Edvard Munch began to paint severely distorted figures and completely abandoned nineteenth century realistic detail. Proponents of Expressionism criticized not only nineteenth century art and its obsession with realism, but also the Prussian state. Through a vague idealism, they sought a somehow better world.

Expressionism began to appear in literature and drama during the 1910s. Expressionistic literature, like Expressionist art, was a reaction against the naturalism which had come to dominate German writing of the 1890s. Expressionistic playwrights in particular wanted to create dramas emphasizing the spiritual aspects of humanity. They penned extremely stylized plays of deep subjectivity and self-expression. Actors became symbols who interacted with the decor, costumes, and lighting and used unrestrained gestures, with broad, exaggerated facial expressions. The sets were nonrealistic and often overtly symbolic.

The First World War offered a key turning point. If anything, the horrors of war exacerbated the dissolution and despair that had been the impetus behind the Expressionist movement. At the end of the war, the Expressionistic movement ceased to be simply an avant-garde style of the few; it became an important movement in the arts of a defeated nation. Government museums began to purchase the Expressionistic paintings they had ignored a few years earlier; the most prominent theatrical companies began to stage Expressionist plays. Indeed, in the years immediately after the war, there was a great unity among the artists of Germany. There seemed, even on the political level, hope for a better world through the new democratic Weimar government, created in 1920.

Now that Expressionism had gained popular acceptance and had reached its pinnacle in the traditional arts, the profit-seeking film industry adopted its principles. Since there had been no Expressionistic films before *The Cab-*

inet of Dr. Caligari, the film's creators had to draw on the other arts for inspiration. The three set designers started out as if they were painting sets for the Expressionist theatre and the actors drew from their experience on the Expressionist stage. The result was an important, innovative film, certainly one of the first to attempt to portray a purely subjective world on the screen.

The stars of the German Expressionist style may have been its set designers. Walter Reimann, Walter Rohrig, and Hermann Warm in *The Cabinet of Dr. Caligari* helped perfect a method of predirection which enabled them to visualize a film before shooting. Thus the film's director, Robert Wiene, was swept along by the Expressionism of his designers. Similarly, the work of Paul Leni, first as a designer then as a highly influential film director, dominated the creation of *Carlos and Elizabeth* (1924). Leni's influence is manifest not only in the decor, but in the lighting, in certain bits of stage business, even in the acting. The film's director, Richard Oswald, never did so well again.

The Cabinet of Dr. Caligari initiated a trend in German filmmakers. They looked for new ways to project subjectivity on the screen; instead of simply having actors or actresses show anger, filmmakers attempted to use cinematic means to convey rage. So, for example, *The Cabinet of Dr. Caligari*, by presenting the world seen entirely through the eyes of a medium, could offer a distorted world from the point of view of a madman. In this film all the elements of cinema were made to play an active role in conveying the meaning of emotions or feelings. Following the lead of Expressionism in the other arts, filmmakers in Germany abandoned all attempts at realism or subtlety. Instead they used distortion to bring to life the soul of a defeated nation.

So when we see Francis for the first time in the insane asylum courtyard as he stops to look around, we are given a visual representation of his madness through the set design. The lines radiating out from him indicate that this world is a vision of his own making. We see, as we do throughout the film, vertical lines and horizontal planes disturbing the "normal" sense of space. Actors wear costumes which clash—as do their gestures—with disjointed sets. Makeup also conveys the inner feelings of the characters, even symbolically at times. When the main character is not in the insane asylum, he wears ordinary, Hollywood-approved silent film makeup. In the insane asylum sequences he has heavy makeup around his eyes and mouth to indicate that he is under the spell of the mad doctor. *The Cabinet of Dr. Caligari* seems to be a painting in motion, far from a Classic Hollywood film in which characters operate in a space of visual continuity. Expressionism projected a world of discontinuity.

The success of *The Cabinet of Dr. Caligari* provided a new look for the German cinema, vaulting it to a place unequaled outside Hollywood in the 1920s. The film served as a model for further experiment with camerawork and editing. But *The Cabinet of Dr. Caligari* was not the only Expressionist work. In 1920 *The Golem*, purely through the use of Expressionist sets, created a complex horror film. The transformation of traditional genres, in this case the horror film, by Expressionist filmmakers spread quickly, affecting commercial productions far removed from any intellectual concern. In 1923 Expressionism reached its peak with Fritz Lang's *Die Nibelungen*, Arthur Robison's *Warning Shadows*, Robert Wiene's *Raskolnikow*, and G. W. Pabst's debut with *The Treasure*. In 1924 the world hailed *The Last Laugh* and *Waxworks* as masterworks. But with

Dupont's *Variety* in 1925 the movement began to come apart. The Great Depression and Adolph Hitler assured its conclusion.

• noted german directors •

Ernst Lubitsch is probably best known for his comedies made in Hollywood, but from 1911 to 1922 he was a major force in German filmmaking. In 1911 Lubitsch began his career as an actor in the Max Reinhardt theatre company. A year later he began to make one-reelers, first as a writer, then as a writer-director. His ethnic slapstick comedies inspired Chaplin's "Charlie." In *The Immigrant*, Chaplin comes to New York by boat the same as Lubitsch, as Siegmund Lachmann in *Der Stolz der Firma* (*The Pride of the Firm*, 1914), arrived in Berlin from Ravitsch, a Prussian province. Sigmund, like "Charlie," is hungry, counts his pennies, and flirts with the ladies. The music hall origins of storytelling farce link Lubitsch and Chaplin at this point.

Lubitsch called *The Oyster Princess* (1919) his first comedy with his famous wit. The narrative lampooned the American nouveaux riche who, for all their wealth, were still uncouth and uncultured. This comedy of manners is a farce about Americans trying to become members of European royalty. In this film he depicts a world in which everyone consumes to excess. The famous Lubitsch trademark (action we can't see behind closed doors) occurs in this film as the father tries to observe the wedding night of his daughter through a keyhole. But through all this Lubitsch's characters remain delightfully human.

The Oyster Princess was a big hit, so popular UFA officials complained that they could not make enough prints to keep up with demand.

Lubitsch planned *Madame Dubarry* (*Passion* in the United States, 1919) as the "greatest German film of all time." Although he demanded that certain details be true to the period (star Pola Negri, as Dubarry, and the rest of Louis XV's court were draped in the finest silk and Brussels lace), he played fast and loose with the historical facts. The result was a spectacular drama about the French Revolution that opened to an ecstatic audience at the premiere of the UFA-Palast am Zoo cinema, a grand picture palace, in September 1919. The only criticism was the leftist press's complaint that Lubitsch had drained the film of all political and social content.

Between 1918 and 1923 Lubitsch made eighteen more German films. In the process, he became world famous, along with Pola Negri, who starred in his historical spectacles. Indeed, in December, 1920 *Passion* broke the blockade against German films coming into the United States, and introduced stars Negri and Emil Jannings and director Lubitsch to America. Within a year Lubitsch's *Anna Boleyn* (*Deception*), *Carmen* (*Gypsy Blood*), and *Sumurun* (*One Arabian Night*) had been shown in New York and, along with *Passion*, were deemed by a number of newspaper and magazine critics among the best films of the year.

Fritz Lang in the 1920s certainly was one of the most important Expressionist directors. Born in Vienna and trained as an engineer, Lang did not turn to film until 1918 when he moved to Berlin and joined Decla as a reader and story editor. He scripted and directed his first film, *Halbblut* (*Half Caste*) in 1919. In 1922 *Doktor Mabuse, der Spieler* (*Dr. Mabuse, the Gambler*) effected a total regeneration of the serial (as *The Golem* had done with the horror film). Everything which had been unconscious in the genre became conscious. The film was a sensation in its day, making Lang a famous talent worldwide.

Lang then went on to make any number of classics: *Die Nibelungen* (1924, in two parts), *Metropolis* (1927), *Spies* (1928), and *M* (1931). Indeed when Lang made *Das Testament des Dr. Mabuse* (*The Testament of Dr. Mabuse*, 1933), the Nazis banned the work in one of their first official acts. Afraid the Nazis might discover his Jewish background, Lang fled the country to work in Hollywood.

If *The Cabinet of Dr. Caligari* was built on graphic contrasts, from sets, makeup, acting, and mise-en-scène, Lang's German films reflected a more plastic style. In *Siegfried* (1924) he built settings that gave a sense of realistic three-dimensional space but were not realistic in any other terms and possessed abstract, symmetrical, monumental qualities. Their design was more than simply decorative. The universe in the film is deterministic; the figures go through an inevitable series of consequences.

Lang's *Metropolis* is his epic. It took a year to film at the UFA studios and cost an astronomical two million dollars to make at a time when even the average Hollywood film cost no more than two hundred thousand dollars. In this utopian film, Lang realized a vision of a city of the future with looming skyscrapers, vast suspension bridges, and a society of plenty. However, below ground, masses of nameless workers function as no more than cogs to keep the prosperous world above humming along. Eventually the workers revolt, but in the end there is a reconciliation and the two strata come together.

In *Metropolis* the elements of Expressionism are used to distort the normal ways of using figures, lighting, decor, and costume. Stark lighting, formless costumes, and mechanistic decor underscore the portrayal of the workers

Fritz Lang's *Metropolis* (1927).

• •

as an anonymous mass. Extreme stylization characterizes the scenes in which the workers, like machines, change shifts. The spiritual creator of this divided world, the scientist Rotwang, lives in the shadows of the skyscrapers, almost between the two worlds.

Friedrich Wilhelm (F. W.) Murnau also came to the cinema after the First World War. After making his first film, *The Boy in Blue* in 1919, he went on to direct some twenty films in Germany before, in 1926, he was drawn to Hollywood. Murnau is most famous for his pioneering work, *The Last Laugh* (1924), starring Emil Jannings. His camera moved upstairs and down, indoors and out, overwhelming the story of a proud commissionaire falling into the life of a lavatory attendant. Murnau skillfully dis-

torted the mise-en-scène of a modern city to initially situate the life of a hotel bellman who, although he must serve the rich, is still admired by by his fellow tenement dwellers because of the status implied by his uniform. After he loses this job he sinks lower and lower. He is saved at the end (in the film's lone intertitle) by the wishes of an eccentric American millionaire who, having willed his fortune to the last man who served him, dies in the hotel lavatory where the bellman was working. In the end the hero gets the last laugh.

The Last Laugh was hailed as a masterpiece both in Germany and abroad, and Murnau was lauded for liberating the camera. In a famous drunk scene, for example, the camera records the bellman's distorted, staggering point of

F. W. Murnau's *The Last Laugh* (1924), starring Emil Jannings.

• •

view. In the dream scene which follows, Murnau suggests an even more subjective experience using a host of Expressionist distortions of decor, costume, lighting, and figures. In a studio, Murnau created a city of angled, dark buildings, flashing neon, reflecting car windows, and wet pavements.

Murnau made other German films. In *Nosferatu* (1922), a faithful version of Bram Stoker's novel *Dracula*, he uses Expressionistic lighting, acting, and sets. The monster is tall, cadaverously thin, bald, bat-eared, and rabbit-toothed and moves in short, jerky steps. The effect is at once ludicrous, chilling, and pathetic. Most disturbing is the scene in which Nosferatu approaches Nina's bedroom but is seen only as a huge, tormented, spiderlike shadow.

Tartuffe (1925), the second-to-last film he made in Germany, is a screen adaptation of Molière's black comedy, again starring Jannings. His final German film was *Faust* (1926) with Jannings as Mephistopheles and a distinguished cast from the European stage. Again the camera moved and soared, capturing the world of light and dark. After these triumphs he was drawn to Hollywood where he finished the remainder of his too-short career.

Georg Wilhelm (G. W.) Pabst was educated as an engineer, became an actor, fought in World War I, and afterwords became an Expressionist film director. The highlight of his long career came in the 1920s with *Secrets of a Soul* (1925), *The Love of Jeanne Ney* (1927), *Pandora's Box* (1928), *Westfront 1918* (1930), and *The Threepenny Opera* (1931). He was an exponent of the Expressionist style, not an innovator. Expressionism can be defined as manipulation of mise-en-scène: Pabst's films deal with one aspect of mise-en-scène, the careful use of actors and actresses. He did appropriate all elements of the Expressionist style: to illustrate the workings of the human unconscious in *Secrets of a Soul* (1925), he employed a shapeless, womblike house, and extreme contrasts of light and shadow. But he is best remembered for his ability to find and direct acting talents: Asta Nielsen and Greta Garbo in *The Joyless Street*, Brigitte Helm in *The Love of Jeanne Ney*, and Louise Brooks in *Pandora's Box*.

Ewald Andre (E. A.) Dupont began as a film critic in Berlin in 1911. In 1916 he sold his first scenario and the following year directed his first film, *The Secret of the American Docks* (1917). He would work consistently in the German cinema through 1926, when he moved to Hollywood to work for Universal on the strength of his most important film, *Variety* (1925). He directed in Hollywood until 1928. Then he went to England, Germany, and back to Hollywood, where he would work sporadically in and outside the film industry until his death in 1956.

Some directors can maintain a steady flow of interesting films; others are remembered for a single film. The latter is the case with Dupont. That film was *Variety* (or *Vaudeville*), a tale of death and jealousy among trapeze artists. The film, which features another masterful performance by Emil Jannings, is remembered for its powerful realism and visual fluidity. Cinematographer Karl Freund, set designer Paul Leni, and actor William Dieterle, later a noted Hollywood director for Warner Bros., all contributed to this masterwork. *Variety* seemed to be

E. A. Dupont's *Variety* (1925), starring Emil Jannings (right).

• •

a subtle summation of various devices of Expressionist mise-en-scène manipulation. It raised the status of the German cinema to the highest peg in the world and profoundly increased the international awareness of the Expressionist movement.

German Expressionism began to decline as a movement in the mid-1920s. Yet even though fewer films were being made, many of the tendencies were retained. Even in a comparatively realistic social film such as G. W. Pabst's *Pandora's Box* (1928), the lighting and sets expressionistically are conveyed in several scenes, in particular the final Jack the Ripper section. But in the end the power and influence of Hollywood proved too strong. Hollywood studios began to lure away the best of the German talent. Mary Pickford tempted Ernst Lubitsch in 1923. After supervising Fritz Lang's *Metropolis*, Erich Pommer made his way to California to work for Paramount. F. W. Murnau, after *Faust* (1926), moved to Fox to make *Sunrise*. Actors

Conrad Veidt and Emil Jannings, cinematographers Karl Freund and director Fritz Lang left by the early 1930s. Indeed, if the money of Hollywood was not enough of a draw, then by 1933 the policies of the Nazis were. Lang's *The Testament of Dr. Mabuse* (1933) counted as the final film of the German Expressionist movement.

German Expressionism did have a significant impact on the Classic Hollywood Narrative style, especially through horror films of the 1930s and the *film noir* of the 1940s. Indeed, of all the alternative European cinemas, German Expressionism had the greatest impact on Hollywood. This was the case in part because the Expressionist directors were used to working in a controlled studio environment similar to Hollywood's. In addition certain Expressionist techniques (distorted lighting and camerawork) were easily absorbed into the Classic Hollywood cinema.

But the Hollywood movie moguls were hardly willing to accept all the traits of the distortion of mise-en-scène; they selectively approved the use of German low-key lighting for horror films and in mystery stories, distorted mise-en-scène in science fiction and horror films, and swooping camera movements and angles for shock effects in a selected number of cases. The influence of German Expressionism reached its height in Hollywood in the *film noir* of the 1940s. This category of mystery story is characterized by the internal conflict in characters, unhappy endings, and night locations filled with distorted shadows. Hollywood chose carefully from the traits of German Expression-

ism, combined them with the traditional rules, and then meshed them with the narrative traits of the hard-boiled detective novel. The result was a type of film which proved popular through the 1940s and into the 1950s, often directed by German expatriates.

It should not be assumed that German Expressionism, French Impressionism, or any of the other movements we have just discussed operated in a vacuum, restricted to a single country. Just the opposite was the actual case. The Germans saw and were influenced by the work of the French and vice versa. Thus we see Expressionist mise-en-scène in the work of French filmmaker Marcel L'Herbier in *Don Juan and Faust* (1922). In turn, Germans such as F. W. Murnau used subjective camerawork very effectively in *The Last Laugh* (1924) as the French had been doing for a number of years. An independent, Carl Dreyer, actually borrowed from all these movements. The production designer of his most famous film, *The Passion of Joan of Arc*, was Hermann Warm, one of the trio who had worked on *The Cabinet of Dr. Caligari*, and his swinging camera movements were straight from French Impressionism. All of these contributions made the silent film one of the most international of art forms. But one cinema tradition operated outside these capitalist industries, the radical and influential cinema of the USSR. The silent Soviet cinema of the post revolutionary period is the subject of the next chapter.

....

5

· ·

the soviet experiment in filmmaking

The major European alternatives to Hollywood were all based in the capitalist mode of profit production. The Russian Revolution spawned a cinema based in socialist economics and radical cultural experimentation. The new Soviet society effected a film movement which crested at the end of the silent era. *Battleship Potemkin* and *Ten Days That Shook the World* made any number of artists and intellectuals of the 1920s sit up and take notice of the movies as an art form. Directors Sergei Eisenstein, Dziga Vertov, Esther Shub, Vsevolod Pudovkin, and Alexander Dovzhenko worked within the new Soviet society to create extraordinary films, true alternatives to the Classic Hollywood Narrative style.

the russian revolution: a new society

In 1917 the Russian Revolution established a new government in the USSR, one which faced the difficult task of reshaping and controlling all sectors of life in the new society. Like other industries, filmmaking underwent changes in production, distribution, and exhibition. Although the pre-Revolutionary Russian film industry had not figured prominently in world cinema, there certainly was a film industry, producing principally in Moscow and Petrograd. Before 1907 the French film companies had invaded Russia and supplied early theatres with cinematic fare. In 1907 the first Russian production company, Drankov, was established; a decade later there were some twenty Russian film companies feeding the home market with literary adaptations, costume epics, and other forms of Hollywood-like narrative films.

The October Revolution changed this system radically and fundamentally. Many veteran directors, actors, and technicians fled as the new Bolshevik government declared film a vital tool in its revolutionary struggle, an industry which could educate and help restructure the new society. In November 1917 a centralized subsection of the State Department of Education, Nakompros, was established. In July 1918 the Soviets clamped strict controls on existing supplies of raw film stock. As a result, all remaining Russian film producers took their equipment, and fled west, hoping the Russian Revolution would prove short-lived and in the near future, things would return to normal.

The transition from the capitalist czarist film industry to Soviet state control of film production, distribution, and exhibition proved a difficult and slow process. There were too few supplies and too little equipment and film stock. Nonetheless, by the summer of 1918, trains, specially equipped to show films, left for the eastern front to disseminate political information to Soviet troops still at war. By 1919 the

world war had ended but Soviet film production had dwindled to a trickle. Through his New Economic Policy in 1921, Lenin encouraged a limited return to private filmmaking to at least fill some screens. But this limited capitalism in the cinema proved short-lived, and by 1923 the government had created a formal state monopoly of all film production, distribution, and exhibition.

Vladimir Ilyich Lenin, Russia's inspirational revolutionary leader, held the cinema in high regard. In a statement quoted repeatedly Lenin maintained that: "Of all the arts, for us [the new Soviet government] the cinema is the most important." Lenin felt that cinema should be an integral tool for teaching new Soviet citizens how best to adapt to a communist state. The first films the new government created were documentaries and newsreels; fictional films came later. Production increased from a mere eleven films in 1921 to more than 150 three years following. This increase permitted the government to consider reopening the market for imports and cycling revenues from theatres back into the production of Soviet films. Studios in all regions began to expand; Goskino, the Soviet cinema state authority, was established. In 1923 a special propaganda production unit, Proletkino, was formed specifically to produce political films to support particular arty interests and causes.

Until 1924 the films coming from Soviet studios remained conventional in style, untouched by the avant-garde experiments taking place in other arts in post-Revolutionary Russia. But in 1925 the Soviet government decided to permit increased freedom in the arts, and the Soviet cinema opened up and began to explore new possibilities. Thereafter, through the final years of the silent era the USSR became one of the most important and influential filmmaking nations in the world.

Lenin intended that the cinema first and foremost should provide the new revolutionary regime with its most effective weapon of agitation, propaganda, and education. By the time the Bolshevik revolutionaries had seized power in October 1917, the cinema was the most popular form of entertainment in the urban areas of Russia. No one had to sell the movies to the Russians found in the nation's largest cities. But in the countryside, the movies were still very much a novelty, and the Soviet Union of the early 1920s was still very much a rural country.

Lenin wanted his cinema industry to help reach people in all sectors of his vast country. The silent cinema, with its stress on visual images rather than written language, was a particularly attractive tool for the new Soviet government since the majority of its citizens were illiterate. Furthermore, there was no common language. In the years right after the Revolution, the new Soviet government needed to instruct the populace in fundamental principles of Marxism; the silent film, properly used, would offer access unavailable through traditional means.

To minimize the need for intertitles, a special burden was placed on visual elements. Stories had to be straightforward and easily understood. To help spread the principles of the Revolution, the government established agitation-propaganda trains, which presented speakers, theatrical performances, and film screenings as they toured the country. These "agit-trains" toured constantly during the years after the Revolution as the Soviets consolidated power, featuring films that were short, simple, and direct. As they took the message from the cities to the provinces, workers gathered film material for hundreds of newsreels and longer works which celebrated the October Revolution. Eisenstein and Vertov, to name but two, learned much of their craft on such agit-trains.

By the mid-1920s all studios, including Goskino (renamed Sovkino in 1925), Proletkino, Sevzapkino, and Mezhrabpom-Russ, finally had the resources to begin to assemble staffs of directors, cinematographers, editors, and other needed personnel. Talents began to be identified with particular organizations. Pudovkin worked at Mezhrabpom-Russ, Sergei Eisenstein at Sovkino, and Alexander Dovzhenko at VUFKU, to name but three of the major directors who would emerge in the 1920s.

With the success of Eisenstein's *Battleship Potemkin* and Pudovkin's *Mother* in 1926, the Soviet film industry turned to its most ambitious set of projects, the celebration of the tenth anniversary of the October Revolution. The impulse to produce the best, as well as the first, of the anniversary films resulted in a race involving Esther Shub and Sergei Eisenstein at Sovkino and Vsevolod Pudovkin at Mezhrabpom-Russ. Pudovkin won and launched his *The End of St. Petersburg*. Weeks later, Sovkino completed two films re-creating Russia's pre-Revolutionary history entirely from archive footage—*The Great Road* and *Fall of the Romanov Dynasty*, both directed by Shub.

But the most famous of these so-called Jubilee films was Sergei Eisenstein's *October* (in the west, *Ten Days That Shook the World*). At Sovkino, he and his coworkers were ordered to abandon their current production, *The General Line* (later entitled *The Old and the New*), to create *October* as quickly as possible. Not released until 1928, *October* turned out to be the last of the celebrations of the Revolution. This delay was due in part to the film's revisions to reflect recent Soviet history, which by 1927 was the subject of intense ideological scrutiny and reevaluation in the wake of Lenin's death and Leon Trotsky's expulsion from the Communist party. *October* was extensively edited and re-edited with references to the role of Stalin's opponents in the Revolution eliminated.

Unfortunately for Eisenstein and his fellow filmmakers the politics of the Soviet Union were changing. The Communist party leadership after Lenin had become hostile to experiments taking place in the cinema, labeling the new style too "formalist." The government, then moving toward control by Josef Stalin, seemed to want a conservative, Hollywood-like realist style which treated state-approved, "correct" subjects. This signaled the end of the age of experimentation, a termination of the golden age of the Soviet montage movement. The final years of the 1920s functioned as a transition to the style of socialist realism, a more conservative style which embraced the politically acceptable view of the "reality" of the Communist movement.

Upon completing *October*, Eisenstein returned to the unfinished *The General Line* and decided to simplify his experimentation so his new film could be easily understood by a mass Soviet audience. Eisenstein did not completely abandon his use of montage, but he did not break any new ground with experiments in symbols and the creation of ideas which he had used so effectively in *October*. Indeed the title, *The General Line*, was later changed to *The Old and the New* because some felt the original title implied some sort of high-level official sanction.

Other filmmakers working outside Moscow managed to continue to experiment for a bit longer. Dovzhenko's *Earth* (about the land and reform) was declared "counter-revolutionary," and "defeatist," though it managed to escape

outright prohibition. Vertov completed his highly experimental *Man with a Movie Camera* (1929) at VUFKU in the Ukraine. In 1927 Vertov had been ordered to leave Sovkino in Moscow because, in part, he, like Eisenstein, was considered too formalist. Vertov, his editor wife Elizoveta Svilova, and cameraman brother, Mikhail Kaufman (*Cinema Eye's* Council of Three) were able, for a time, to make films in the Ukraine. VUFKU employed Vertov, his wife, and brother on the condition that they first complete *The Eleventh Year*, the Vertov trio's contribution to the 1927 tenth year anniversary of the Revolution.

Soviet authorities felt they should dictate the appropriate political task of the cinema. When the new regime developed the USSR's first five-year plan (1928–1932) to industrialize the country, as part of that plan, the Communist party defined for the first time the precise responsibilities of film workers. Such direct political control proved difficult to enforce because of the coming of sound. But in the long run, the authorities needed obedient filmmakers, ones who would follow their dictates.

Before this the Bolsheviks had maintained a delicate balance between full direct control and a limited free market policy to keep screens full and to foster native production. During the 1920s the majority of films shown in the USSR were foreign; indeed, most were from Hollywood. If we imagine that Soviet citizens watched only the great Eisenstein and Vertov classics, we are wrong; they also viewed the silent comedies of Charlie Chaplin and Buster Keaton and the adventures of Douglas Fairbanks and Mary Pickford.

The Soviets began importing from the United States, Germany, and France after World War I. During the heaviest period of importation (the mid-1920s), more than three-quarters of the films presented were from non-Soviet filmmakers. For example, of the more than two hundred films presented in Leningrad theatres during 1924, only two were Soviet film products. Anatoli Lunacharsky, the people's commissar for the cinema, preferred that audiences come voluntarily to the theatres and see propaganda newsreels as part of the show. Hollywood, he argued, drew audiences into theatres, and Soviet newsreels educated them. Indeed, when Douglas Fairbanks and Mary Pickford visited the USSR in 1926, they were mobbed by fans just as they were when they toured the heartland of the United States. A Soviet-produced feature film, *The Kiss of Mary Pickford* (1927), was made around the time of their visit from an idea by Commissar Lunacharsky himself. And the praise of Fairbanks and Pickford helped sell *Battleship Potemkin* to moviegoers in the USSR.

The Soviets used monies from paying audiences to help finance the film industry Lenin deemed so important. (Indeed we must re-member Lenin did not think it was as important to finance film production as it was to support the steel industry or farming, for example.) In January 1922 Lenin formally authorized the commissar of foreign trade to import large numbers of feature films and to plow the monies back into the film industry. The Soviet authorities charged their citizens a relatively high price for the privilege of viewing what they deemed "decadent" American products.

Hollywood films had long been popular in Russia. They drew sizable audiences, particularly in the major cities of Moscow and Leningrad. *Intolerance* had a special run in Petrograd in 1919 to raise money for victims of the civil war famine. Since the Soviets did not recognize international copyright, they bought and did not rent films. Thus a typical program would include films from Hollywood mixed with a number of Soviet educational films and newsreels.

the new soviet film style

In spite of the shortages of equipment and difficult economic and social conditions after the war, young men and women moved into the film industry in hopes of creating a new art form. **Dziga Vertov** began his film ca-reer recording documentary footage of the First World War and by age twenty was in charge of compiling newsreels for the new government. **Lev Kuleshov** began teaching in the new state film school on cinema, and performed a series of valuable editing experiments. **Sergei Eisenstein** worked on trains carrying propaganda to troops, and then in workers' theatre before moving into the cinema. **Vsevolod Pudovkin** began as an actor and was inspired by D. W. Griffith's *Intolerance* (1916) to go into filmmaking. These four plus other talented filmmakers, in particular **Esther Shub** and **Alexander Dovzhenko**, took the Soviet film of the 1920s to center stage in the world of cinema. None had worked in the czarist film industry; they had discovered the virtues of the cinema as part of their experience in the Russian Revolution, which changed the lives of all citizens in some way.

To fashion a new cinema, filmmakers emphasized the power of editing in writings, teachings, and discussions. With the proper formulation of montage, they could make powerful statements on behalf of revolutionary change. As was true of many of the transformations taking place in the USSR at the time, there was constant argument about fundamental principles. V. I. Pudovkin, for example, believed shots in a film should be joined together like bricks in a building. Sergei Eisenstein argued that the maximum effect could be gained only if the shots did not fit together smoothly, but instead jolted the spectator. He went so far as to argue that with the proper juxtaposition of shots, the filmmaker could convey abstract ideas in what he called "intellectual montage."

During the mid-1920s this new formulation of the cinema of montage did not develop in isolation but came into productive collusion with the energetic theoretical and artistic activity taking place in the other arts. The work of poet Vladimir Mayakovsky and theatre director Vsevolod Meyerhold, for example, profoundly influenced the early work of Sergei Eisenstein,

in particular his *Battleship Potemkin* (1925). But it was the movement in painting and design known as Constructivism which influenced the Soviet montage school of filmmaking most profoundly.

For some years, even prior to the Russian Revolution, the predominantly representational traditions of Russian painting had been under attack by young artists. Inspired by the abstract forms emerging from European modernist movements such as Cubism and Futurism, the Constructivists sought to effect a unique combination of technology, science, and art in the new Soviet society. Artists, intellectuals, and workers could labor side by side to make a new culture, a new society, a new economy. Art, like any other productive activity, should be geared to the needs of the working people.

Iconoclastic abstraction, the hallmark of the avant-garde in Europe, gave way to the idea of art as production, as work in the service of the masses. According to the Soviet Constructivists, the artist should seek to bridge the gap between the traditional tenets of the creative process and the needs of engineering design and functional design in a new Socialist society. Using art as a tool to build a radical new society had not been tried before, certainly not on such a large scale. Until Constructivism, no movement in modern art had been so thoroughly an expression of Marxist ideology or so closely connected with a true revolution.

Constructivism was meant to be neither an abstract style in art nor even art per se. It was first an expression of a deeply motivated conviction that the artists could contribute to the enhancement of the physical and intellectual needs of the society. The film artist could do this by utilizing the tools of cinema for communication and education in the new Soviet society. Constructivists aimed to radicalize the art of cinema and to educate a revolutionary proletariat.

For Constructivists in the USSR, a new world had been created. They believed artists (or more accurately, creative designers) should take a productive place in society alongside other workers, including scientists and traditional engineers. This was not a novel concept. Architects like Louis Sullivan and Frank Lloyd Wright in the United States had argued that the engineer stood at the frontier of the new twentieth century art. Constructivists believed the artist should locate the fundamental elements of his or her medium and then use it to its best possible advantage for social progress.

The utility of all the people was the main objective. Gone was art for art's sake. The new Soviet social order demanded new means and forms of expression based on science and engineering. The new means of expression in the cinema was particularly attractive, but Constructivists were also fascinated with architecture, poster and furniture design, and magazine illustration.

Film, because of its complex technological base, its industrialized mode of production, and its process of assembly, provided the ideal test case for developing an art for the new Soviet society. The penetrating arguments and analysis of Sergei Eisenstein, Lev Kuleshov, and Vsevolod Pudovkin captured the moment for those who sought new ways to organize film materials through montage, to shock and excite audiences. These filmmakers and film theorists believed that art should serve the interests of the working class and that the artist, as a technician, should seek the most appropriate ways to communicate Socialist ideas. Soviet films made between the release of Sergei Eisenstein's *Strike*

in 1925 and Alexander Dovzhenko's *Earth* in 1930 offered example after example of an alternative to the Hollywood method of constructing a motion picture.

In Soviet Montage, cinema graphic and rhythmic editing provided the key connections between shots. Eisenstein, in particular, wished to use the power of editing to manipulate the emotions of the spectator. All his films tell a story, yet the editing assumes much greater importance than Hollywood would find acceptable. Although the Soviet films did employ a narrative structure, they tended to downplay a character's psychological development. Instead they stressed social forces as the root causes of change in people's lives. Stories were the vehicles to help Soviets better understand the effects of the forces of economic change and social transformation, not to entertain. Often large groups served as a "collective hero," as in Eisenstein's *October* (1928) and *The General Line* (1929).

This theory of film form had many consequences. For instance, because of the deemphasis of individual personalities, the Soviet system developed no stars. Filmmakers cast unknowns, individuals who best reflected the look of the figures in the script. This concept of *typage* focused on stature and gestures rather than fame and reknown. If there is a hero or central character in Soviet film, it is the Soviet people, the proletariat as a group.

In particular, the films of Sergei Eisenstein laid a foundation for a complex system of editing, one in which meaning is expressed through the juxtaposition of shots rather than the manipulation of the mise-en-scène (as in German Expressionism) or the manipulation of camerawork and optical devices (as in French Impressionism). Through editing, the Soviets pushed cinema far beyond the borders of traditional Hollywood ideas. This can be seen again and again: in the slaughter sequence in Eisenstein's *Strike*; in the battlefront–stock exchange sequence in Podovkin's *The End of St. Petersburg* (1927); in the "degradation of the gods" sequence in Eisenstein's *October*.

With the Soviet Montage cinema, filmmaking and exhibition began to take on a greater and greater importance in the new Soviet, post-Revolutionary society. The significant turning point came when Eisenstein was commissioned to produce a film commemorating the aborted revolution in 1905. This film, *Battleship Potemkin*, premiered at the Moscow's Bolshoi Theatre, a testament to its importance to state officials. Yet it took the prodding of influential writers, journalists, and party officials to induce Sovkino to send it abroad. *Battleship Potemkin* proved an international success. Just as *The Cabinet of Dr. Caligari* was to alert audiences around the world to German Expressionism, *Battleship Potemkin* signaled to those interested in film art that they ought to pay attention to the new Soviet Montage movement.

But Eisenstein was not the only filmmaker who thought about the power of editing. Alexander Dovzhenko envisioned a cinema marked by a kind of plasticity of image which stressed both the composition within the frame and the juxtaposition among images. He used a stronger narrative system, but one that was still far from the absolute continuity sought by Hollywood. For example, a distinctive mark of the Dovzhenko version of Soviet Montage is "creative geography," in which a character's action is matched over two shots, while the setting changes. For example, in *Earth* at one point the father of a dead boy is transported from his son's death bed (shot one) to a hilltop (shot two), all while he continues to grieve. Holly-

Lev Kuleshov's *The Extraordinary Adventures of Mr. West in the Land of the Bolsheviks* (1924).

● ●

wood would have required a signal for the new setting. The Soviet Montage style did not.

● lev kuleshov ●

If there was one figure who pioneered the Soviet Montage movement, it was director-theorist-teacher Lev Kuleshov. Trained as a painter, before the Revolution he had chosen a career as a stage-set designer. With the coming of the Russian Revolution, he moved to film, initiating theories which led to a famous series of editing experiments. He made his most significant contribution in helping to form the Soviet's film school. Kuleshov never made the famous films his compatriots did, but his impact as a teacher, certainly in the early days, is seen in the works of such noted pupils as Eisenstein and Pudovkin.

In the heady days of the 1920s, propaganda trains and puppet shows, endless manifestos, debates, and experimental workshops seemed to be everywhere. Filmmakers searched through all forms of popular art, from pantomime to the circus to detective thrillers, for techniques to appropriate for filmmaking. Kuleshov introduced serious discussion of montage as an organizing principle. Influenced by all the sources noted above as well as by Hollywood figures such as D. W. Griffith, he tried to formulate a socialist theory of film. Having been in on the founding of the VGIK, the official film school, Kuleshov was given his own workshop in which to conduct experiments. He manipulated time and space, and tested the effects of various graphic and rhythmic techniques.

Kuleshov wanted to prove cinema was superior to other means of art and communication. Thus he conducted various experiments which suggested to him that each shot acquired meaning from its immediate context, that is, from the shots which preceded and followed it on the screen. The ideas of the cinema were built up from this fundamental principle. By altering the context of the shot, he could experiment with different effects. From valuable experience on the agit-prop trains in the early 1920s, he collected, along with Vertov and Eisenstein, material for films such as *On the Red Front* (1920), a compilation work.

His first fiction film was the remarkable satire, *The Extraordinary Adventures of Mr. West in the Land of the Bolsheviks* (1924), followed by *Death Ray* (1925) and *By the Law* (1926). *The Extraordinary Adventures of Mr. West in the Land of the Bolsheviks* is an eighty-minute comedy for which Pudovkin cowrote the scenario and helped with the production design. It was conceived originally as one of Kuleshov's experimental films and thus provided the first test of Kuleshov's theories. Mr. West (Porfiri Podobed) is the typical American reacting to a socialist culture during a trip to the Soviet Union. The comedy revolves around underplaying, inspired by the Soviets' love for Buster Keaton and Harold Lloyd.

Kuleshov's importance went far beyond his talents as a filmmaker. As the master teacher of the Soviet Montage movement, he influenced almost all other filmmakers, not only with his ideas of montage but also with his insistence on nonstylized acting. In his search for proper film acting, Kuleshov's experiments resembled those of theatre director Vsevolod Meyerhold who used biomechanics to train actors and actresses to use their bodies for the theatre.

sergei eisenstein: theorist and filmmaker

Sergei Eisenstein was the most important figure of the Soviet Montage school. Born in Latvia two years before the end of the nineteenth century, Eisenstein was educated in St. Petersburg in civil engineering and architecture. His career was interrupted by the October

Revolution, and by 1920 he had joined the Pro letkult theatre in Moscow as a scenic artist. A year later he was part of Meyerhold's directors workshop for the theatre. Meyerhold's Constructivist theatre project functioned as a vehicle for political propaganda and a testing ground for avant-garde techniques of artistic expression. In this Constructivist theatre, art was a branch of production in the service of the state, for the advancement of the Revolution.

To better understand and improve theatrical performance, Eisenstein drew from such diverse sources as American slapstick comedy, the circus, classical mime, and the Italian tradition of *commedia dell'arte*, all to make fun of capitalists and capitalism. He called his method: a montage of attractions. He drew attention to the construction of a stage play rather than hiding its means of production and pretending that it was a magical creation. Eisenstein argued that the theatre should express the rage of the oppressed, and he drew on ideas from psychologists Pavlov and Freud to craft an aggressive assault on the audience, to shock them into political awareness. He and his theatrical compatriots took to the street, actively seeking to influence the working-class audiences.

In 1924 Eisenstein turned to the cinema. His first film, *Strike*, brought together violently conflicting ideas in a series of sketches which examined the idea of class so basic to Marxist thought. Eisenstein's purpose was to teach the Soviet working class to unite to protest the inequities of the past. In *Strike* he attempted to merge what he had learned in the theatre with Kuleshov's principles of editing to fashion a new cinematic form. In particular, he rejected orthodox stage acting in favor of typage, the view that characters should represent stock types which are immediately recognizable to the audience. Thus, the film actor and actress

had no independent existence but functioned as part of the mise-en-scène, which when combined with camerawork yielded strips of film that could be edited together to generate important ideas.

Eisenstein theorized that the individual shot was film's basic unit of construction. Meaning came from the juxtaposition of shots. Unlike Pudovkin, whose idea of montage involved the linkage of shots for narrative purposes, Eisenstein favored the collision of contradictory shots, to shock and agitate his audiences. He identified five kinds of montage: metric, rhythmic, tonal, overtonal, and intellectual. These dealt with the length of the shots, the rhythm and tones created as shots clashed, and the creation of ideas which came about as shots were combined in certain formations.

Envisioning a film which would both reflect and embody the essence of the October Revolution, the 26-year-old Eisenstein planned *Strike* as one of eight projects in a state-sponsored series examining the struggles of the working class before the October Revolution. The film's opening shot of factory smokestacks sets the tone. Then Eisenstein cut to shots of written communications urging "workers of the world unite." Factory machinery and workers seem united as one in shots which combine the two, creating a harmony which forces of capitalism crush in scene after scene.

Eisenstein's next film was perhaps the most famous of the Soviet Montage era. *Battleship Potemkin* (1925) was commissioned to commemorate the abortive 1905 revolution which had been crushed by the czar. Eisenstein focused on sailors on one particular battleship who had staged an unsuccessful mutiny, depicting this rebellion as a central metaphor for the October Revolution of 1917. Eisenstein constructed the script, directed it, and edited it.

The fundamental principle behind Eisenstein's editing was to join together disparate elements to produce new ideas. History and events were the motivating forces, not individual characters or stars. Certainly the most memorable and harrowing sequence in *Battleship Potemkin* comes in the Odessa steps massacre, which has become one of the more celebrated sequences in the history of the cinema. Eisenstein and his crew had moved south to Odessa because of problems with filming in Leningrad from poor weather. To make up time, Eisenstein decided to film a single event to symbolize the hopes, triumphs, sufferings, and ultimate failure of the revolution.

The Odessa steps sequence was part of this strategy and illustrates Eisenstein's idea of montage. Long shots convey confusion and alarm as people scramble down the steps when the Cossacks come down to crush them. Confusion and alarm are intercut with eyes of terror, lips in silent scream, feet stumbling, a bouquet crushed, a broken umbrella, and a woman losing her baby carriage. Throughout the scene, the relentless soldiers march down the stairs and kill, their military order in dramatic contrast to the disorder of the fleeing crowd. The tempo quickens in a horrifying crescendo of death and disaster. This scene, like the entire film, is constructed with complex rhythms and dramatic contrasts of image, light, and mood.

All types of montage can be found in *Battleship Potemkin*. In the Odessa steps massacre sequence we see metric montage at work: as the massacre intensifies, the editing tempo increases. Rhythmic montage occurs as Eisenstein cuts between the steady marching of the soldiers and the chaotic scramble of the fleeing crowd. Tonal montage can be seen in the conflicts of planes, masses, and lights as the shadows of the soldiers' rifles and uniforms intersect

the light reflecting off fleeing citizens. Intellectual montage underscores the end of the sequence, when the Battleship Potemkin responds to the massacre by firing three times toward the czarist headquarters. Three images of marble lions—the first sleeping, the second waking, the third rising—appear as a single beast, aroused as the Russian masses will be ten years later against czarist oppression.

When *Battleship Potemkin* was first released early in 1926, it drew mixed reactions in the USSR. Many praised it, but an equal number denounced it as too "formalist," a charge Eisenstein would hear more and more as his career progressed. Audiences in Berlin and in other capitals in Europe, however, embraced the new "experimental" film, and with this foreign acceptance, Soviet officials began to support the film. Soon *Battleship Potemkin* became a cornerstone of the prestige then associated with the Soviet school of montage.

October, Eisenstein's next film, was an anniversary film, commissioned to celebrate the ten-year anniversary of the Russian Revolution. It combined actual newsreel footage with reconstructed scenes to dramatize events which led up to the Bolshevik Revolution in 1917. *October* (or *Ten Days That Shook the World* as it was titled in the West) was released in January 1928. Eisenstein directed his script, and filmed it during the spring of 1927 in Leningrad. *October* was not the anticipated popular successor to *Battleship Potemkin*, but it was one of the boldest experiments in Soviet montage, the peak, some would argue, of Soviet filmmaking of the 1920s.

Preparation for *October* included research into newspaper reports, photographs, newsreels, as well as John Reed's book, *Ten Days That Shook the World*. The initial scenario called for covering all the events leading up to

Sergei Eisenstein's *October* (1928).

the 1917 Revolution. Although this plan was narrowed, an abundance of detail remains, which, according to some detractors, weakens the film. There is too much data for the mass audience, they claim; *October* is an intellectual exercise, with too much to comprehend in one viewing. The film was also caught up in the politics of the day, as the leaders of the two divided Soviet political factions vied to have themselves portrayed positively. Josef Stalin's allies triumphed over Leon Trotsky's followers. As a result of squabbling and re-editing, *October* was finally released in March 1928, four months after the anticipated premiere.

October forced to the surface the complex, mixed reactions to Eisenstein's films. Intellectuals and filmmakers tended to love it. Party officials and the masses were indifferent. There was too much there to comprehend, and it was certainly not in the style of the still-popular Hollywood cinema. The use of typage is abundant in this work, and the representation of Lenin brought much criticism. The worker chosen to represent the nation's great revolutionary leader certainly resembled Lenin physically, but many complained that he lacked the "inner drive and brilliance" of the designer of the Russian Revolution.

October marked Eisenstein's move to an intellectual cinema in which reason and passion are co-equal. He believed that the Marxist dialectical conflict and the resulting synthesis of opposites could be applied to editing to rigorously examine ideas fundamental to the Rev-

Sergei Eisenstein's *The General Line* (1929).

olution. Thus, intellectual montage abounds in *October*. For example, God is compared to a primitive idol, and the moderate leader Kerensky is linked to Napoleon. Eisenstein also juxtaposed czarist soldiers and the common folks and set up rhythms like music and graphic qualities which emphasized the distinction between the powerful and the powerless. He sought to move his audience, first emotionally and then intellectually, to examine the fate of their country under the capitalists, the Czar, and the new Soviet socialist regime.

The General Line (1929) was Eisenstein's next film and the last which was clearly identified as his work in the Soviet Montage school. In this film, he experimented with "sensual montage." *The General Line* was designed to bring out the underlying associations between images, a method which would force emotional reverberations between images more than associations between ideas. The fundamental emotional responses of the audience would be engaged by this process.

In *The General Line*, his last silent film, Eisenstein traced the transformation of a poor Russian farm village into a prosperous collective farm. Under pressure from the state authorities he used an individual hero, a peasant woman who struggles for the establishment of the collective. Eisenstein was willing to construct a hero because the state had begun to denounce this most famous filmmaker as too formalist, accusing him of preferring to promote the aesthetics of montage over the content

Sergei Eisenstein's *Ivan the Terrible* **(1944, 1946).**

of the works. Still *The General Line*, like *October*, had to be cut to fit the dictates of the political moment.

After completing *The General Line*, Eisenstein embarked on a tour of Western Europe and North America to meet with other filmmakers and intellectuals and to learn the technology of talkies. In Hollywood he worked on several projects for Paramount Pictures, but none moved past the script stage. For example, he wanted to make a film from Theodor Dreiser's novel *An American Tragedy*, which, as he saw it, showed how adverse social conditions led to murder. Paramount wanted a melodramatic love story. He then turned to the ill-fated *Que Viva Mexico!*, a joint venture with American socialist Upton Sinclair, and never finished yet another project, *Bezhin Meadow*.

Upon his return to the USSR he was denounced by the Stalinist regime. Only when he began to toe the party line was he accepted back to make *Alexander Nevsky* (1938) and the two parts of *Ivan the Terrible* (1944 and 1946), the final films of his career. *Alexander Nevsky* (1938) is an historical epic about a thirteenth-century Russian hero. Eisenstein used professional actors and a brilliant score by Sergei Prokofiev to counterpoint sound and image and fashioned a popular success. *Alexander Nevsky* represents a fundamental turning point in his career. In the 1920s he had been the radical filmmaker, seeking to explore and develop a new language of the cinema. In the 1930s he attempted to moderate his "radical" film theories to fit then-acceptable standards of socialist realism. With *Alexander Nevsky* Eisenstein entered a new phase in which his films centered on heroes and a new sense of montage accenting, not overwhelming, the storyline.

Ivan the Terrible is a two-part work. Part I was released in 1944, and the second part not until 1958. Eisenstein directed and wrote the script; Tisse did the cinematography; Prokofiev composed the music. *Ivan the Terrible* was conceived as a trilogy: *Part I, Ivan the Terrible*; *Part II, The Boyars*; *Part III, Ivan's Struggles*. Only the first two parts were finished, and only Part I was released before the director's death.

Throughout his career, and particularly during the Soviet Montage era of the 1920s, Eisenstein argued that a revolutionary society needed a revolutionary culture that would instill a new consciousness into the workers, who simply wanted a better life than was available under the czar. To this end he was more than simply a master filmmaker. He was the cinema's first major theoretician. His ideas of montage inspired a generation of Soviet filmmakers and even experimental filmmakers of the day in the West. From ideas drawn from Japanese culture

and language, the psychological theories of Freud and Pavlov, the theatrical precepts of Meyerhold, the social and economic theories of Karl Marx, and the cinema of D. W. Griffith, Eisenstein sought to understand the unique properties of the cinema.

Eisenstein's ideas changed as did his films. Many treat his voluminous writings as if they are one body, but as his silent films were different from his talkies, so was his film theory of the 1920s different from his theory in the 1930s and 1940s. The early Eisenstein was avowedly materialist, and sought a theory of the cinema based on the building block of the individual shot. The new Eisenstein of the 1930s was more interested in psychological states or "inner speech." The desire to build a film shot by shot was replaced by a romantic interest in human nature and emotional associations. Interest in conflict was replaced by fascination with organic unity; Richard Wagner, the noted German composer, became Eisenstein's inspiration, not the Constructivists.

experiments in realism: dziga vertov and esther shub

Dziga Vertov released the first in a series of newsreels called *Kino-Pravda*, less than a year after Lenin's famous decree praising the cinema. For the Soviet Montage era's alter-

native to the newsreel in the west, Vertov compiled footage shot on the streets and mixed in animation, laboring to locate an editing style appropriate to films of persuasion. He went far beyond the typical Hollywood newsreel, employing superimpositions and title cards to considerable symbolic effect. Vertov wanted to catch the attention of his viewers and then convince them of the importance of Revolutionary commitment and zeal.

Dziga Vertov was born Denis Kaufman and educated as a musician. After the Russian Revolution he took the name Dziga Vertov which roughly translates as "spinning top" and turned to cinema, dramatically announcing a "sentence of death" to all existing cinematic forms, in particular Hollywood. Vertov was determined to fight for "cinema truth" to the exclusion of all other modes. He wanted to make a clean sweep of the past and begin again anew.

In 1919 he began his task as chief editor of *Kinonedielia* (*Film Weekly*), a series of newsreel-like programs which he organized, compiled, and edited. This work gave him a chance to experiment with ideas of montage since that was the lone variable with which a film compiler could work. In 1921, he moved to a mobile, agit-prop unit that included a theatrical troop, a cinema, cinematographers, a film laboratory, an editing room, a library, political lecturers, and a printing press, which traveled through the USSR from April 1919 through November 1921. The film, *Agit-Train*, documented this journey by incorporating footage taken by the unit's cinematographers, including Vertov himself. Indeed throughout the early 1920s Vertov spread his message of film reality on agit-steamboats and agit-trains to take newsreels directly to the people.

Vertov's pro-reality stance earned him praise in high places. Early in 1922 Lenin is said to have told his commissar of education, Anatoli Lunacharsky, that all film programs in the USSR ought to include newsreels to reflect the new reality of the changing socialist nation. With Lenin's support, Vertov launched, in May 1922, his famous *Kino-Pravda* (*Film Truth*) newsreel series, a regular monthly release. With this series his wife, Elizoveta Svilova, became his editor and his brother Mikhail Kaufman his chief cinematographer.

Kino-Pravda sent its camera operators to record the rebuilding of railroads and streetcar lines, the creation of airports and hospitals. These "fragments of reality" were juxtaposed through superimpositions, split screens, and slow motion to various bits of the truth about the change in the new society. Often *Kino-Pravda* films were the only items in Soviet cinema programs which dealt directly with the daily reality of the workers in the audience.

The editing in *Kino-Pravda* was dazzling. In one sequence in the eighteenth issue, Vertov skillfully juxtaposed shots of various machines and striking workers singing the "Internationale." Indeed by the thirteenth issue Vertov and his comrades had altogether abandoned the news format for a series of documentary films on current concerns in the quest for the true communist state. To convey a sense of the breadth of the Revolution, he included aerial footage of cities, factories, and villages in his vast nation to capture "life caught unawares." Sometimes he would use a hidden camera; sometimes he stayed so long on site that people forgot he was there.

Before *Kino-Pravda* ended in 1925, Vertov moved to *Kino-Glaz* (*Cinema Eye*, 1924). Again working with his brother and wife, Vertov was able to fuse his interest in the formal aspects of the cinema with his political preoccupations. *Cinema Eye* contains an astonishing play between testimony and evidence: there are process shots, rhythmic montage, frenzied accelerations, repetitions, and ellipses—all the possible tools of the cinema editor playing with

Dziga Vertov's *Kino-Pravda*, launched May 1922.

his art and craft. Vertov wanted to define the nature of the cinema by stripping bare preconceptions of its use.

To make maximum use of all the footage he was accumulating, Vertov began to reassemble it into longer and longer films. Among the most successful of these compilation films was *A Sixth of the World* (1926), in which he used short intermittent intertitles to address the audience: "You in the small villages. . . . You on the oceans. . . . You Uzbeks. . . . You Kalmiks. . . ." Vertov also directly addressed various occupations, age groups, and other classifications of the Soviet society. The film ended by reminding Soviet citizens that "You are owners of one-sixth of the world." The incantation style is reminiscent of Walt Whitman, whom Vertov much admired.

Vertov's *Man with a Movie Camera* (1929) offered the full realization of his decade of experiments, a theory of film on film. This is a film about filmmaking and the illusions it can create. The film's central figure is a cameraman, traveling through Moscow. He involves himself in its daily dawn-to-dusk activities, observing all walks of life. Vertov orchestrated superimpositions, animation, split screens, fast motion, seemingly all possible camera angles, and moving camera shots, all cut together in a rhythm which gives this film a unique vitality.

Consider the opening. We see an empty theatre; the audience arrives; the projectionist readies the film; the orchestra begins to play; the film comes to the screen—indeed the very film we are about to watch. Throughout *Man with a Movie Camera* the viewer is constantly reminded of the camera's presence. In Hollywood, reflections of the camera in a window would be considered "mistakes." In Vertov's film, they are part of the very structure and theme. We see the cameraman, with his bulky apparatus, edging up a smokestack, climbing out of a beer mug, being hoisted by a crane, walking into the sea, running across rooftops, and working down in a mine shaft. Some of these shots (by a second camera operator) were shot live; others done through superimpositions in the post-production process.

The self-reflexive aspect of the film becomes more and more complex as it progresses. For instance, a shot of a motorcyclist is followed by a shot of the cinematographer filming the motorcyclist and then the same sequence being projected in the theatre. Later, in the midst of more activity, the frame freezes and is followed by a series of stills; then these same frames are shown in the hands of an editor. We see the editor hang the strip of film on a drying rack along with other strips, some from sequences we have already seen.

Man with a Movie Camera ends with a return to the theatre. The camera and tripod "assemble" on the screen, "take a bow," and "walk off." The finale includes a jumbling of shots from previous scenes intercut with shots of the audience watching those scenes; finally, the camera lens turns toward the audience. Vertov's theme is clear—he has shown us a part of the world, but only "reality" on film.

Greeted in 1929 as an exciting view of the future of the cinema, *Man with a Movie Camera* still seems experimental because its vision was never realized. It remains a sophisticated, complex alternative to the Hollywood cinema. Unfortunately, after *Man with a Movie Camera*, Vertov fell out of political favor. His disinterest in scenarios was labeled "antiplanning"; his experiments in editing were declared too formalistic. Vertov, his wife, and brother exited to studios in the Ukraine, apparently to set some distance between them and the powers-that-be in Moscow. There they did make a number of innovative early sound films, including *Enthusiasm* (1931) and *Three Songs of Lenin* (1934). But like the other giants of the Soviet Montage school, Vertov and company simply became state workers, grinding out newsreels on predictable schedules, adhering to the dictates of state-approved content and style.

Esther Shub also compiled newsreels to create vivid portraits of Soviet history. Her films depended upon original newsreel material which she re-edited to instruct audiences of the time. Shub is noted for two principal montage works. *Fall of the Romanov Dynasty* (1927) is a pioneering example of the compilation film. Shub spent enormous amounts of time and energy to research and collect film material, a difficult, frustrating process since much of the archival footage was in such bad shape. By editing together the pieces she was able to achieve effects of irony, absurdity, and pathos in a playful, ironic look at the fall of the Czarist regime.

The Great Road (1927), another compilation film, was her anniversary effort. But there was too much missing (or never shot) about the crucial events of the Russian Revolution and so she had to reconstruct certain events. In the official reaction of the day, Shub was praised for her efforts while Eisenstein, for *October*, was condemned. She was seen as faithful to the official history, while Eisenstein was damned for putting too much of his own personality into the work. Fifty years later, it can be argued that Shub was as manipulative as Eisenstein.

Esther Shub was born in the Soviet Ukraine and educated in literary studies in Moscow. During the Revolution she took a position with the theatre department of the People's Branch of Education and worked with Meyerhold. In 1922 she joined Goskino to help re-edit imported films for Soviet distribution. She finished her training by working with Eisenstein on *Strike* and *Battleship Potemkin*. From 1927 to 1928 she created her trilogy about revolutionary transformation: *The Russia of Nicholas II and Leo Tolstoy*, *Fall of the Romanov Dynasty*, and *The Great Road*.

If the Soviet Montage school was based on principles of editing, one of the foremost editors in the USSR during the 1920s was Esther Shub. After gaining considerable reputation and experience re-editing imports, she became the master of the compilation film. She brought to the genre, based solely on editing pre-existing footage, a flare for using all sorts of seemingly odd pieces to create stunning effects. With the coming of sound and the Stalin regime, Shub turned to fiction cinema and created the approved young communist hero for *Komsomol—Leader of Electrification* (1932). She embraced socialist realism, with its stress on a straight-forward, non-experimental, almost Hollywood sense of editing. Only occasionally was she able to reproduce that former flare: self-reflexive moments of characters looking directly into the lens, microphones visible in the scene, to remind viewers that this was a movie, not real life.

the traditionalist: vsevolod pudovkin

Vsevolod I. Pudovkin was the most conventional of the Soviet filmmakers of the 1920s. Since all the major talents of the Soviet silent era, in one way or another, conformed to the montage style, it is easy to see their work and writings as homogeneous. But there were significant differences, both in their theories and in their films. This certainly was the case for Pudovkin, the most traditional of the group, who rejected the radical editing style of Eisenstein while retaining the Marxist themes.

Vsevolod Illarionovitch Pudovkin was educated in physics and chemistry at Moscow University, and after being wounded in World War I, had his comfortable life forever shattered by the Russian Revolution. In 1920 Pudovkin entered film school to learn to become an actor. Lev Kuleshov was his teacher. Once he graduated, Pudovkin settled on directing, although frequently, like Alfred Hitchcock, he did appear in a small part in his own films and later acted in Eisenstein's *Ivan the Terrible*.

Vsevolod Pudovkin's *Mother* (1926).

As Kuleshov's student, Pudovkin's first films were mixtures of the documentary and fiction genres. *Chess Fever* (1925) is a short comedy which incorporates both documentary footage (from an international chess tournament) and acted scenes. *Mechanics of the Brain* (1926) aimed to popularize Pavlov's theories of conditioned reflexes and thus to fit into the scientific-educational film mode of film documentary. But three fictional works—*Mother* (1926), *The End of St. Petersburg* (1927), and *Storm over Asia* (1928)—would make his reputation.

All three of these films were popular in the USSR since they were built on the techniques developed by Hollywood. That is, Pudovkin sought to fashion popular works on revolu-tionary subjects. Here was a director who never ventured too far with his cinematic experiments. As a consequence, although he is associated with Eisenstein and Vertov, Pudovkin's work might very well be closer to such films as *The Living Corpse* (1929), based on a Tolstoy play, directed by Fyodor Otsep and *The Girl with the Hatbox* (1927), a satirical comedy, directed by Boris Barnet, both of which drew audiences almost as large as did imported Hollywood films.

While *Mother*, *The End of St. Petersburg*, and *Storm over Asia* were concerned with various aspects of the Revolution, they focused on the involvements and conflicts of one individual, not the mass hero of Eisenstein. *Mother*, based on a Maxim Gorky novel, was set during the

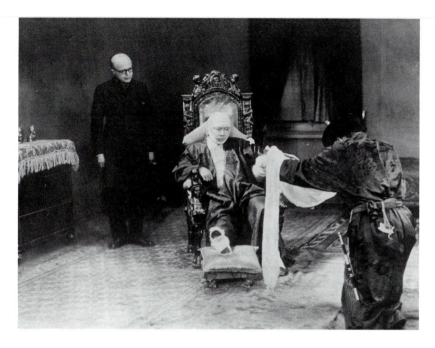

Vsevolod Pudovkin's *Storm over Asia* **(1928).**

• •

aborted 1905 revolution. Rather than concentrate on a shipload of sailors as Eisenstein did in *Battleship Potemkin*, *Mother* chronicles the plight of the title character, who inadvertently causes her politically active son to be sentenced to prison, and eventually shot as he tries to escape. With his death, his mother's consciousness is raised, but in the end she too is killed, trampled to death by a Czarist army which attacks as workers protest.

Although the theme of a mother's love for her son is stretched to fit into a propaganda framework, the film is edited to produce harmony like a musical composition, not to promote conflict. Pudovkin sought to merge together pieces of film to make a synthetic whole. For example, when the son receives

some happy news while in prison, his hands are seen energetically in motion, and a close-up of the bottom part of his face is intercut with shots of a sunlit stream, birds cavorting in a pond, and a happy child.

The End of St. Petersburg was Pudovkin's contribution to the tenth anniversary of the Russian Revolution. Unlike *October*, which celebrated the mass of Russians who rebelled, Pudovkin centered his tale on the political education of an inexperienced young peasant, skillfully blending a realistic setting with a fictional tale. As with *Mother*, Pudovkin charted the emergence of his central figure from political naivety to committed Marxist consciousness. *Storm over Asia* is about the Civil War in Mongolia, detailing the activities of the English army of occupation in Mongolia (called the White Russian army in foreign prints). The film focuses on a young Mongol trapper who is radicalized by unfolding events after he is cheated out of a prized fox fur by a European merchant.

Like Eisenstein, Pudovkin was more than a film actor and director; he was fascinated with this new medium and wrote a great deal about it. Lev Kuleshov introduced him to montage as a force in the cinema, and Pudovkin, in his writings and films, explored the power of intercutting seemingly different images together. His essays on film theory, most notably "The Film Scenario," and "Film Director and Film Material," stress the power of editing.

In Pudovkin, for instance, it was unnecessary for a film actor or actress to overperform or overgesture as a stage actor or actress may have. Figures in films should "underplay," and the editor then can juxtapose their images to create the proper effect. Pudovkin saw montage as an interaction of many and various elements, including the script, acting, and later, color and sound. He contended that montage, as the highest form of editing, was the foundation of film art, that montage revealed the relationship between film and real life.

the outsider: alexander dovzhenko

Alexander Dovzhenko stood outside the mainstream of Soviet experimentation. Through emotional and poetic expression, almost melancholy in simplicity and style, he celebrated the farmers and agriculture of his native Ukraine. Dovzhenko stressed the image more than his famous associates of the 1920s, he did not bombard the viewer with harsh images, but with lyrical ones. His reputation rests on two films: *Arsenal* (1929) and *Earth* (1930). *Arsenal* tells of the tumultuous period of Soviet history after the First World War. In *Earth*, he relates the story of a peasant leader who is

killed by a landowner after the farmers in a small Ukrainian village band together to demand a tractor. But the events of the story simply serve as a backdrop for a tremendously moving panorama of rustic life and the inevitability of death even in the new Soviet society of the 1920s.

As a Ukrainian, Dovzhenko stands apart from the other Soviet directors. Educated in science and economics in the years immediately preceding the Russian Revolution, he worked as a high school teacher (and organized demonstrations), served in the army in the First

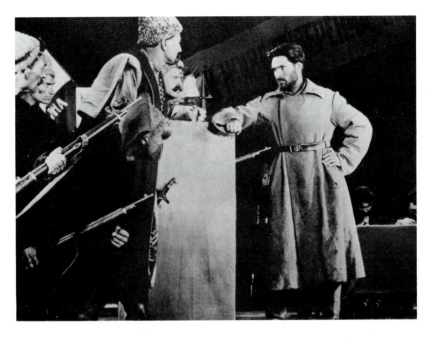

Alexander Dovzhenko's *Arsenal* (1929).

World War, and then became an artist and cartoonist. He came to film late, not making his reputation until 1929 with *Arsenal* and 1930 in *Earth*. He was able to learn from Eisenstein's *Strike* and *Battleship Potemkin*, Pudovkin's *Mother* and *The End of St. Petersburg*, Vertov's *Cinema Eye* and *A Sixth of the World*, as well as many of the most praised works of German Expressionism and French Impressionism. All influenced his complex, unique style.

Arsenal (subtitled: *The January Uprising in Kiev in 1918*) was made for VUFCO and released in Kiev in February 1929. It was filmed in and around Kiev in the latter half of the previous year. Dovzhenko did the editing, scenario, and direction. In many ways *Arsenal* is a more radical text than even *October*. For example, in *October* Eisenstein used montage to

create meaning within the space and time of the accepted events of the Russian Revolution. In *Arsenal*, the symbolism is purposely esoteric, with seemingly deliberate barriers to cloud the viewer's perception, so that it is not clear, even after a number of viewings, precisely what is going on. Dovzhenko's theme of the horror of war, as symbolized by an arsenal of weapons, seems to fly in the face of the necessity of armed struggle that was at the very foundation of the Russian Revolution.

Earth seems to be Dovzhenko's most accessible film, moving between static shots of remarkable beauty and dynamic narrative episodes: the opening sea of grain, the moonlit lovers, a farmer posed between two massive oxen. But the introduction of the tractor prepares the way for an accelerating montage of reaping and processing grain which recalls the cream separator sequence in Eisenstein's *The General Line*.

Indeed, *Earth* ends with one of the longest and most elaborate examples of parallel montage in film history. The sequence begins as Vassily's father, converted from his conservative state of mind by his son's death, rejects the offices of the town's priest. Crowds of people, who were first seen as onlookers at the tractor's arrival, begin to mill together and march at the dead man's funeral. The father joins them as they begin to sing. Their ranks swell until another young man, who will lead them in the social transformation in place of the now-dead Vassily, begins to make a speech.

Throughout the march and speech, Dovzhenko repeatedly cuts away to the murderer fleeing from the village. As the speech begins, the murderer shouts his confession from the graveyard, unheard. Other elements intervene. As the crowd passes Vassily's house, his pregnant mother goes into labor and gives birth. At the end of this striking sequence Dovzhenko cuts rapidly from images of the singing crowds to the labor pains of the mother to the fleeing killer to the open casket, in a breathtaking rhythmic orchestration. The film ends with the ripe fruit, rain, new lovers, and a total reaffirmation of the earth as the source of all power. Individuals may die, but the earth goes on.

Earth, released in April 1930 in Kiev, is a tribute to life in the Ukraine, the birthplace of Dovzhenko. It is a film of the rural life, of the struggles of a single village. There is no formal story, but the structure of the film revolves around the triumph of modern farm equipment over primitive methods of agriculture. Youthful peasants join together to purchase a tractor to more efficiently operate their farms. Men and women fasten together stalks cut from the earth, a threshing machine toils in the fields, and

eventually the peasants produce an abundant harvest. Dovzhenko captures the meaning of the earth to these people, who believe the land must be lovingly nurtured so that all can be fed. The earth as a provider goes on, one generation to another.

But *Earth* is not apolitical. It was meant to herald a new beginning to Soviet farm life. As we might expect from a film of such complexity, it was controversial in its day. Many complained that the style of the film overwhelmed its message of the superiority of the collective mechanized farm. It failed, some noted, to directly deal with the specific concerns of the Revolution; its themes were too universal.

Earth represented an unusual project because it did attempt a broader-than-usual outlook on the transformation of the Soviet society. This is evident in the film's prologue and epilogue. The prologue opens with a series of beautiful shots of fields of ripened fruit, some fallen, some still on the trees. It is a time of harvest, and a family group ranging over four generations is gathered around the eldest, the patriarch. He is about to die, surrounded by the fruits of his labor. It is old making way for the new, the cycle of nature. The epilogue of *Earth* succinctly reiterates the enduring nature of the land. Storms come but the cycle of growth and plenty continue, as the fields in the end of the film give way to the sunshine.

The pace of the film seems to reflect this lack of frenzy. If Vertov was the "spinning top," Dovzhenko was a slow, contemplative director. *Earth* is not paced or structured like a typical Soviet montage, but neither is it paced like a Hollywood film. So, for instance, after the killing of Vassily, there is a fade into a shot of his father sitting before a table with his head resting against one of his hands, seemingly pondering his son's death. The shot has no change for more than a minute. This is not the speed of

Alexander Dovzhenko's *Earth* (1930).

Vertov, the intellectual montage of Eisenstein, or the drama of Hollywood. It is an alternative, a new way to situate the impact of the death.

Dovzhenko's films were not simply projections of personal and private visions; they referred to specific historical settings. He was more than the cinematic equivalent of a romantic poet, dominated by a pastoral vision of life and embodying an ahistorical and timeless set of themes. He borrowed and organized material from the society and culture in which the film was made. His films were marked by a tension between his concern for Soviet modernism and his enduring loyalty to the peasant tradition. He was also a part of the strident, revolutionary cinema of the USSR of the 1920s.

Dovzhenko is a difficult director with whom to deal. Whereas Eisenstein and Pudovkin, for example, studied Western cinema and in Mos-

cow participated in the mainstream Constructivist movement, Dovzhenko operated outside, in Kiev, within the deep roots of his Ukrainian background and culture. Unlike his more cosmopolitan contemporaries, Dovzhenko took material from such esoteric sources as regional folklore, thus making them much more difficult for outsiders to analyze. Yet Dovzhenko constantly produced films which alluded to historical and cultural settings. His films did take up issues of immediate concern to his fellow countrymen and women. Of those made in the 1920s, only *Zvenigora* and *Arsenal* were set outside the time of the film's production, and they were historical dramas dealing with recent Soviet political and social history.

Few filmmakers from the USSR showed such concern for shifts in national policy and fashioned such a referential collection of works.

If Eisenstein had his *The General Line*, about the mechanization of agriculture, it seemed appropriate that a year later Dovzhenko would come out with *Earth*. Indeed, Dovzhenko examined three sectors of Soviet industrial change: *Earth*'s agriculture, *Ivan*'s heavy industry, and *Aerograd*'s land development in the Soviet Far East. Later, as Eisenstein was glorifying past heroes in *Alexander Nevsky* and *Ivan the Terrible*, Dovzhenko followed the same trend with his *Shchors* (1939), about a martyr of the Revolution, and *Michurin* (1948), about a leading Russian horticulturist. In short he followed the broad changes demanded by Stalin.

The Soviet Montage movement drew to a close when a changing Soviet government consolidated under Josef Stalin in the 1930s. The new regime sought a new approach to the cinema. The montage style was criticized as too formalist, too esoteric. The new government wanted simple films that would be readily understandable to all audiences. Stylistic experimentation and nonrealistic subject matter were denounced, censored, or simply not funded.

In 1934, the government, by then directly under Stalin, called for a new style of cinema called Socialist Realism, grounded in a Hollywood-like style but projecting the accepted Soviet world view. As a movement, the Soviet Montage school ceased in the early 1930s with the completion of Vertov's *Enthusiasm*

(1931) and Pudovkin's *Deserter* (1933). In 1930, when Sovkino was dissolved, it was replaced by Soyuzkino, a government agency responsible to the Politburo's Economic (rather than, as previously, its Education) Department. Stalin's appointee, Boris Shumyatsky, formally adopted Socialist Realism as the official policy, stressing traditional, non-experimental, realist films.

The coming of sound, and thus the film industry's need for a financial infusion for new equipment, guaranteed total acceptance. Musicals and literary adaptations would come to dominate the cinematic output as well as any number of biographical films about the successes of Stalin and Lenin. This signaled the end of the experiments which, with the worldwide applause for Eisenstein's *Battleship Potemkin*, had made Soviet film one of the best known alternatives to Hollywood. Indeed the coming of sound drew to a close the first phase of film history. The silent cinema had consisted of three elements: mise-en-scène, camerawork, and editing. (Music, noises, and infrequently spoken lines were added live in the theatrical setting.) Recorded sound, including dialogue, added a fourth major element, and with it a new phase in the history of film would begin.

II

the hollywood studio era
1928 to 1950

· ·

6

··

the coming of sound and the studio system

During the late 1920s the technology of the cinema changed in a fundamental way. During the silent era, mammoth picture palaces used seventy-five–piece orchestras, complete with several members whose sole job was to provide sound effects and noises. Every neighborhood house had a hardworking piano player plunking out a musical accompaniment. But inventors had long sought to develop a mechanical sound system to supply needed music and even dialogue. Indeed, Thomas Edison originally conceived of his version of cinema as image and sound.

During the first two decades of the twentieth century scientists (including Edison) struggled to mechanically link phonograph technology to the silent motion picture. But this marriage never worked because early efforts to maintain synchronization of speaker and speech failed. No one could coordinate sound and image recorded on incompatible equipment. Furthermore, as movie theatres grew into picture palaces, there was no adequate loudspeaker system that could fill all parts of a large auditorium.

Between 1907 and 1913 inventor-entrepreneurs presented film audiences with the Vivaphone, Synchroscope, Chronophone, the

Cameraphone, and the Cinephone. Each tried to mechanically link silent cinema and the phonograph; each failed. In 1913 Thomas Edison, then America's most famous inventor, proclaimed he had the answer. His Kinetophone employed a powerful amplifier and a sophisticated system of pullies and controls to synchronize sound and image. Heralded by notice after notice, the world premiere of this marvel from the workshop of the Wizard of Menlo Park was presented by the Keith-Albee vaudeville organization. Edison's American Talking Picture Company was set up expressly to produce and distribute movies with sound.

Unfortunately audiences found the Kinetophone inferior to even the average movie house orchestra. At Keith's Union Square theatre in New York City, patrons actually booed the latest Edison miracle, with good reason. Its synchronization failed more often than it succeeded; music came out in harsh and tinny tones; spectators at the back of the hall could not hear. It had taken Thomas Edison himself to demonstrate once and for all that a simple marriage of the phonograph to silent film technology would never work. It seemed that if America's greatest inventor could not create talkies, no one could. The *silent* cinema remained the standard, but not for a lack of trying to create movies with sound.

• • • • • • • • • • • • • • • •

the coming
of sound

• • • • • • • • • • • • • • • •

The coming of sound required three phases of change: invention, innovation, and diffusion. As with the very introduction of the movies themselves, first scientists had to develop apparatus that would record and synchronize sound and image with a quality and tone suitable for presentation to large audiences. At the innovation phase, companies had to figure out how to market sound films to the public, knowing of the inherent risk in trying to sell something everybody *knew* would not work. Finally, the major movie companies had to decide to accept the new technology and substitute it for the standardized silent film.

This three-phase transformation took place between 1926 and 1930. Seemingly overnight the silent film era ended; Hollywood switched completely to talkies. In 1925 silent filmmaking was the standard; a mere five years later Hollywood produced *only* films with sound. The speed of the transition surprised almost everyone. Within thirty-six months, formerly perplexing technical problems were resolved, marketing and distribution strategies were reworked, soundproof studios were constructed, and fifteen thousand theatres were wired for sound. Since Hollywood so dominated the film business throughout the world, no foreign film industry dared not adopt sound, and by 1935 sound-on-film had become the world standard.

The transformation to sound films did not begin in Hollywood. It took one of the world's largest corporations, American Telephone & Telegraph, to overcome the frustrating technological problems Edison could not resolve. During the 1910s AT&T's scientists, working in a unit that would later become known as Bell Labs, perfected an electronic sound-on-disc recording and reproducing system to monitor and test its new long distance telephone network. As a spin-off of this research, AT&T scientists invented the first true loudspeaker and sound amplifier. Combining these inventions with movie technology produced a system which could record and project clear, vibrant sounds to audiences even in theatres as large as the newly built Capital in Times Square with its five thousand seats. In 1922 AT&T had begun to try to sell its new sound technology. But despite the technical reputation of AT&T and its financial muscle, the barons of the American film industry, fully cognizant of the multitude of embarrassing failures of talkies a decade earlier as well as the substantial investment required, passed when initially offered the new equipment.

A minor Hollywood company, Warner Bros., took up the challenge. The brothers Warner (led by eldest Harry, assisted by Abe in distribution and Jack and Sam in production) had come a long way from their nickelodeon days in Ohio but still had not grown to one-hun-

dredth of the size of Famous Players–Lasky. Warners sought a means by which to grow to challenge the dominant triumvirate of Famous Players, Loew's/MGM, and First National. In 1924 the brothers Warner expanded into more expensive feature film production, worldwide distribution, and theatre ownership, backed by the Wall Street banking house of Goldman Sachs.

During this phase of corporate growth, Sam Warner learned of AT&T's inventions. He was immediately smitten but somehow had to persuade the head of the family, Harry, to approve. Harry saw a demonstration, and soon the four brothers were working up a strategy to use sound to help them build up their company. Deciding not to rock the feature film boat, the company made recordings of vaudeville acts and offered them as novelties to exhibitors along with their feature length films. Warner's sales pitch stressed that these so-called vaudeville sound shorts could substitute for the then omnipresent stage shows offered by picture palaces around the country. Thus, the very first "talkers" were short recordings of the acts of top musical, comic, and variety talent then touring the United States.

Warner Bros. set in motion its strategy of using these vaudeville shorts to innovate sound films in September, 1925. It took a year to work out the bugs, but at the beginning of the next movie season in August 1926 Warners was ready to premiere the marvel it called *Vitaphone*. The studio's public relations experts launched a media splash. Newspapers around the world hailed the latest technological wonder of the Roaring Twenties. First-nighters anted up ten dollars for a seat (equivalent to fifty dollars sixty years later). The cream of New York society came to witness operatic favorites sung—on film—by such stars as Metropolitan Opera tenor Giovanni Martinelli. The presentation of the silent film *Don Juan* (1926), with music on a sound track replacing the usual live orchestra, followed.

As Warner Bros. developed more packages (silent feature films with orchestral music on disc plus "vaudeville" shorts), it tested audience preferences. The brothers Warner quickly realized the moviegoing public preferred recordings of popular musical acts to those of opera stars. Al Jolson and Elsie Janis, two of the biggest names in the music business during the 1920s, moved to the head of the line to become the first stars of Vitaphone "vaudeville" shorts. Logically and systematically, Warner Bros. inserted vaudeville-style sequences into its feature films.

This set of feature-length films interpolated with Vitaphoned sequences commenced with Al Jolson as *The Jazz Singer*, which premiered in October 1927. Despite this film's fabled reputation, *The Jazz Singer* was not an instant hit. In fact, it was only when the film (plus accompanying Vitaphone shorts) moved outside New York City into the American heartland that the public began to take more than a passing interest. Extended runs in Charlotte, North Carolina; Reading, Pennsylvania; and Baltimore, Maryland—to name but three prominent examples—made film industry leaders sit up and take notice. When in April 1928 the New York Roxy booked *The Jazz Singer* for an unprecedented second run and it grossed one hundred thousand dollars per week, it seemed only a matter of time before other studios would try Vitaphone.

During those first months of 1928, Warner Bros. had only one true competitor—the Fox Film Corporation. Fox had adapted a version of AT&T's pioneering technology to record

sound-*on-film*. (In the 1930s sound-on-film would become the industry standard.) In 1926 William Fox had signed with AT&T to use this technology to improve his company's newsreel business. Like the brothers Warner, William Fox did not believe there was a future for feature-length talkies, but the veteran showman reasoned that the public certainly might prefer newsreels with sound to silent offerings.

William Fox never made a better business decision in his career. Fox Film engineers labored to integrate sound-on-film with accepted silent newsreel techniques. On the final day of April 1927, five months before the opening of *The Jazz Singer*, Fox Film presented its first sound newsreels at the ornate, five-thousand–seat Roxy Theatre located at the crossroads of the entertainment world on Times Square. Less than a month later, Fox stumbled across the publicity coup of the decade when it screened the only footage *with sound* of the takeoff and triumphant return of aviator Charles Lindbergh. The enormous popularity of Lindbergh's hop across the Atlantic undoubtedly contributed handily to Fox's success with sound newsreels. Fox newsreel cameramen soon spread to all parts of the globe in search of stories "with a voice." Theatre owners queued up to have their houses wired simply to be able to show Fox Movietone newsreels. To movie fans of the day, Movietone News offered as big an attraction as any movie star.

The major movie companies, led by Paramount, did not want to be left behind. For more than a year, a committee of experts from Paramount, MGM, First National, and United Artists met secretly to study their options. They examined AT&T's sound-on-film technology, were wooed by rival RCA, and drew up plans to anticipate all the problems they thought they

Al Jolson in *The Singing Fool* (1928).

● ●

might encounter. After nearly six months of haggling over terms, early in May 1928 the four movie companies signed with AT&T. Once this collective decision had been made, the rush to produce and sell talkies began in earnest.

The wide-spread adoption of sound—its diffusion—took place within a remarkably short span. The major Hollywood companies had too much at stake to procrastinate. On the corporate level, the planning committee had done its work so well that industry chieftains were surprised at how few unanticipated difficulties arose. Within the framework of the Acad-

emy of Motion Picture Arts and Sciences, the major studios cooperated to resolve any remaining problems as quickly as possible. The big studios continued to prosper; smaller producers could not afford the new cost, and were either taken over by larger concerns or simply went out of business.

The diffusion of films with sound proceeded logically and systematically. First, at the beginning of the movie season that September of 1928, Paramount, MGM, and the other major studios came out with "scored features." That is, they simply added recorded musical tracks to silent films already in the can. Movie house owners immediately let go resident orchestras, freeing funds to help pay for the necessary wiring. Musicians' unions protested, but by 1930 only a handful of theatres in America's largest cities still maintained a house orchestra and organist.

By January 1929, a little over six months after Paramount, MGM, First National, and United Artists had signed their original contracts with AT&T, the majors began to show 100 percent talkies. In September 1928 Warner Bros. led the way with *The Singing Fool* starring Al Jolson. First-nighters paid a record eleven dollars for tickets to its premiere. *The Singing Fool* proved such a hit that professional Broadway scalpers departed from custom and brokered blocks of tickets to a movie. Two songs from the film, "Sonny Boy" and "There's a Rainbow 'Round My Shoulder," went on to become the first million-selling records of the talkie era. *The Singing Fool* cost only two hundred thousand dollars, but drew an unprecedented five million dollars. *The Singing Fool* proved to all doubters that talkies were here to stay.

Ten days before the majors even signed with AT&T, the Academy of Motion Picture Arts and

Sciences, founded a year earlier and not yet world famous for giving out Oscars, sponsored its first seminar on sound. Less than a month later twenty committees had been established to gather and distribute information, hire experts, and hold seminars. Irving Thalberg, production chief at MGM, supervised these vital coordinating activities. The Hollywood studios went on a building boom, doubling studio space in less than two years. Several companies reopened studios near New York City to accommodate Broadway stage talent unwilling to trek to California. Paramount's complex in Long Island City (now home to the American Museum of the Moving Image), a simple commute from Manhattan across the East river, was the largest. Stars such as the Marx Brothers worked at Paramount-East during the day and on Broadway at night.

Theatres owned by Hollywood companies received their sound installations first; smaller, independently owned houses had to sign up and then wait sometimes more than a year. The major Hollywood companies could hardly keep track of the millions rolling in. Warner Bros. and Fox moved to the top of the industry. A new major company, Radio-Keith-Orpheum (RKO), was formed. In a rush to compete with AT&T, the Radio Corporation of America (RCA) developed its own version of sound-on-film but could not convince the major Hollywood companies to sign up for its Photophone.

To make the best of this situation, RCA founder and president David Sarnoff turned to a friend, financier Joseph P. Kennedy, father of President John F. Kennedy and patriarch of the Kennedy political family. At the time the elder Kennedy owned a small Hollywood studio, the Film Booking Office (FBO). During the last six months of 1928 Sarnoff and Kennedy merged

RCA's sound equipment with the FBO studio and added the theatres from the Keith-Albee-Orpheum vaudeville theatre empire to create Radio-Keith-Orpheum. RKO drew its strength from RCA's financial strength and radio talent, FBO's production experience in Hollywood, and a well-located chain of theatres throughout the United States.

The public's infatuation with talkies set off the greatest rush to the boxoffice in the history of American movies. At its peak, every person over the age of six in the United States went to the movies on average once a week. Profits for the major Hollywood companies soared. In 1929 merger became the order of the day. Warner Bros. took over First National; Fox (temporarily, it turned out) took control of Loew's and MGM. A year later, once the dust had cleared, there were five major players in Hollywood—Paramount, Loew's/MGM, Warner Bros., Fox, and RKO—and three minor studios—Columbia, Universal, and United Artists. The latter group, unlike their larger cousins, owned no theatres. The coming of sound had set in place a corporate structure which would define the studio era of the 1930s and 1940s— the Golden Age of Hollywood.

The coming of sound did not confine itself to the United States. In 1928 Hollywood distributed its films throughout the world, and in many countries Hollywood films filled more than half of the available time on movie screens. Once Hollywood decided to switch to talkies, European theatre owners scrambled to wire their theatres and book the latest attractions from America. Seeking to sell sound movie equipment all over the world, AT&T and RCA accommodated foreign producers and exhibitors as quickly as they could. They soon established a world standard of sound-on-film.

• • • • • • • • • • • • • • •

hollywood's
major studios

• • • • • • • • • • • • • • •

The coming of sound solidified Holly-wood's control over the world market and moved the United States into the Studio Era in which filmmaking, film distribution, and film exhibition were dominated by five corporations: (1) Paramount, (2) Loew's (parent company for the more famous MGM), (3) Fox Film (later Twentieth Century–Fox), (4) Warner Bros., and (5) RKO. They ruled Hollywood during the 1930s and 1940s and operated around the world as fully integrated business enterprises. The Big Five owned the most important movie theatres in the United States. By controlling picture palaces in all of America's downtowns, they took in three-quarters of the average boxoffice take. Only after they granted their own theatres first-run and soaked up as much of the boxoffice grosses as possible did they then permit smaller, independently owned theatres to scramble for the remaining bookings, sometimes months, or even years, after a film's premiere.

• paramount •

Throughout the 1940s Paramount represented the most profitable and powerful Hollywood company. In the 1930s Paramount had to struggle to meet the oppressive mortgage obliga-tions of its huge theatre chain, but thereafter it quickly regained the economic power it had maintained throughout the 1920s. More than any other member of the Big Five, Paramount relied on its chain of more than one thousand theatres to maintain its corporate might. Paramount's movie houses held dominion throughout the heartland of the United States from Chicago to New Orleans.

A Chicago theatre man, Barney Balaban stood at the top of this corporate colossus. Chicago's Balaban & Katz had merged with Paramount in 1926 and still served as the cornerstone of Paramount's theatrical empire. Balaban ruled with an iron hand, requiring his signature for all significant corporate expenditures, whether for a wig for Bing Crosby or a new popcorn machine for a theatre in Omaha. Balaban's conservative corporate strategy made him a darling of Wall Street. Indeed, in 1946 Paramount earned a record forty-million–dollar profit, a figure which would stand unmatched for two decades.

By the mid-1940s Barney Balaban had formulated a corporate strategy for producing the popular fare to fill Paramount's theatres. It had not always been thus. In the early 1930s, unlike MGM (with Louis B. Mayer), Warner Bros. (with brother Jack) or Twentieth Century–Fox (with Darryl F. Zanuck), Paramount did not have a strong executive in charge of production. Jesse

L. Lasky and B. P. Schulberg left in 1932; Emmanuel Cohen, who signed Mae West, left in 1934.

Balaban wanted his own man in California, so he placed Y. Frank Freeman in charge of production from 1937 through the remainder of the studio era. Freeman had been a theatre man, and it was his assistants who actually ran the day-to-day show. One, Henry Ginsberg, from 1944 through 1950, was able to make a significant impact with his sponsorship of the Crosby-Hope films and the work of Cecil B. deMille.

Freeman relied on already proven concepts and stars. For example, Paramount plucked its two biggest stars—Bing Crosby and Bob Hope—from radio. We do not vividly associate this duo with the movies, yet by the measure of box-office receipts they represented the height of 1940s Paramount stardom. Their five *Road* pictures of the 1940s all raked in millions. Individually, Crosby also did *Holiday Inn* (1942), *Going My Way* (1944), *The Emperor Waltz* (1948), and *A Connecticut Yankee in King Arthur's Court* (1949). Hope starred in a series of comedies including *My Favorite Blonde* (1942), *My Favorite Brunette* (1947), *Monsieur Beaucaire* (1946), and *The Paleface* (1948). From 1944 to 1949 either Crosby or Hope (usually the former) ranked as the top male box-office attraction in the United States in an annual poll of exhibitors.

Other filmmakers helped Barney Balaban drive Paramount toward millions in profits. Director Cecil B. deMille, for example, created one hit after another. *Union Pacific* (1939), *North West Mounted Police* (1940), *The Story of Dr. Wassell* (1944), and *Unconquered* (1947) were all among the ten most financially successful films of their respective years and poured millions into Paramount's coffers. A

Barney Balaban (left) meets James Cagney, Nicholas Schenck, and Spyros Skouras.

● ●

deMille protégé, Mitchell Leisen, directed *I Wanted Wings* in 1941, to tie in to the Second World War. That war also boosted the careers of Paramount players William Holden, Ray Milland, and Veronica Lake. But the filmmaker who draws the most praise today is writer-director Preston Sturges with his *The Great McGinty* (1940), *The Lady Eve* (1941), and *The Miracle of Morgan's Creek* (1944). These comedies sparkle with wit and represent the best of 1940s Hollywood.

Like all its fellow members of the Big Five, Paramount offered exhibitors fifty-two features per year starring such favorites as Fredric March, Barbara Stanwyck, Gary Cooper, and Betty Hutton. In addition, Paramount's newsreels were considered the best in the business, and Popeye the Sailor cartoons added a bit of flare. But it was the Hope-Crosby midbrow musical comedies which provided the steady stream of profits, year-in year-out. Critics may never have counseled him thus, but Barney Balaban kept his eye directly on the boxoffice take, not on cinematic complexity.

The Metro-Goldwyn-Mayer studio lot, approximately 1935, Culver City, California.

• •

As a result, Paramount maintained its corporate supremacy with films that were loved by fans of the time but often forgotten today. Indeed, we more recall the studio's fare from its money-losing days of the early 1930s. Although the comedies of Mae West (*I'm No Angel*, 1933 and *Belle of the Nineties*, 1934) and the Marx Brothers (*The Cocoanuts*, 1929 and *Horse Feathers*, 1932) never matched the box-office take of Paramount films of the 1940s, they have left a more lasting aesthetic legacy, as have the films of Marlene Dietrich, the musicals of Maurice Chevalier, and the sparkling comedies of Ernst Lubitsch.

• loew's/mgm •

Metro-Goldwyn-Mayer, with its internationally famous symbol of the roaring Leo the Lion, was surely the most famous of the Hollywood studios of the 1930s. From a purely business perspective, MGM simply functioned as a suc-

cessful unit within the larger enterprise of Loew's, Inc. A fully integrated movie company, Loew's owned a movie studio, a network for international distribution, and a highly profitable theatre chain centered in the five boroughs of New York City. Indeed, Loew's management, led by Nicholas M. Schenck, ran the company as if it were simply a chain of movie houses supplied with MGM's films.

In Culver City, California, a suburb of Los Angeles, MGM had a complete movie factory with twenty-seven sound stages on 168 acres. The epitome of studio facilities, MGM's laboratories could process 150 thousand feet of film each day, and its property rooms contained more than fifteen thousand items to be used in movie after movie. Sound studios in Culver City, Paris, Barcelona, and Rome created tracks for dozens of films (dubbed in more than one dozen languages) that were shipped to all parts of the globe.

Nicholas M. Schenck presided over the Loew's empire from 1927 until 1956. Known as the General, Schenck took over from founder Marcus Loew. A trusted team of assistants, many of whom remained loyal to Schenck for more than thirty years, executed his every order. Louis B. Mayer, head of the Hollywood lot, may have been more famous to the public at large, but ran all but the most trivial decisions past the General in New York. Because of Loew's longtime fiscally conservative business practices, the company was burdened by few costly mortgages during the Great Depression, and thus never experienced any red ink during that economic calamity. During the early 1930s Loew's/MGM stood at the top of the world's movie business.

MGM's method of film production reflected Schenck's conservative business philosophy. Schenck played it close to the vest. During the early 1930s the studio created only top-drawer feature films. Other films that Loew's distributed were pick-ups, principally from the Hal Roach Studio (short subjects) and Hearst Enterprises (newsreels). Only after the Great Depression had run its course did Loew's feel bold enough to permanently ally with these operations.

For its feature film productions, MGM publicly projected an image as the Tiffany of studios: a high-class, elegant operation. Through the 1930s Greta Garbo and Norma Shearer headlined in a series of high-gloss, sophisticated melodramas, guaranteed to improve the studio's image among those who scorned the movies. But Schenck, sitting in his office atop the Loew's State building in the heart of Times Square, covered all bets. He had his studio make a wide variety of feature films, many of which we would hardly classify as high-class.

In fact, in MGM's best years, the early 1930s, the studio's star who most often was ranked highest in popularity polls was none other than sixty-one-year-old, gruff Marie Dressler. Dressler played older women with a heart of gold in *Min and Bill* (1930) and *Tugboat Annie* (1933), two hits of the period. That she reached the peak of her stardom at MGM with inelegant movie roles did not matter to Schenck. He liked the monies which continuously flowed in at the boxoffice.

MGM used a variety of stars to realize its great profits. Indeed, during the 1930s MGM presented jungle adventures (the *Tarzan* series), slapstick comedies (Stan Laurel and Oliver Hardy in *Sons of the Desert*, 1933), and the satire and burlesque of the Marx Brothers (*A Night at the Opera*, 1935, and *A Day at the Races*, 1937). But year-in, year-out, through the two decades of the Golden Age of Hollywood, Clark Gable and Spencer Tracy were the stu-

A studio portrait of Clark Gable.

● ●

dio's most long-lived stars, two rugged actors whose roles came to define the ideal American male.

During the 1940s MGM became closely associated with a certain brand of Technicolor musical. *Meet Me In St. Louis* (1944) with Judy Garland and directed by her husband Vincente Minnelli, *Easter Parade* (1948) with Garland and Fred Astaire, and the innovative *On the Town* (1949) starring Gene Kelly and codirected by Kelly and Stanley Donen are engaging films and attracted large audiences. Perhaps more than any other genre, the Hollywood musical relies upon a collaborative production system: performers, composers, lyricists, set designers, and choreographers are needed as well as a director, screenwriter, cinematographer, editor, and producer.

In MGM's case Arthur Freed, former composer and lyricist, produced a number of the best musicals of the late 1940s and early 1950s. He was able to integrate the talents of directors Vincente Minnelli, Stanley Donen, and Gene Kelly; performers Kelly, Fred Astaire, Judy Garland, and Frank Sinatra; and many others assembled at MGM as the studio era drew to a close.

MGM made millions with the low budget "B" *Dr. Kildare* and *Hardy* family series. *Our Gang* comedy shorts made millions for Loew's in the 1930s. In the 1940s the studio developed the popular *Tom and Jerry* cartoon series. MGM did not create its own newsreels. Rather, it developed a long-term relationship with the newspaper organization of William Randolph Hearst, which had a worldwide network of stringers to scoop the competition.

• twentieth century—fox •

In the hierarchy of studio power in the 1930s and 1940s, Twentieth Century—Fox ranked behind Paramount and MGM. Although the Great Depression did not prove kind to the fortunes of Fox Film, after it merged with Twentieth Century Pictures in 1935 the new amalgamation prospered. Founder William Fox was out, replaced by new managers and part-owners, Darryl F. Zanuck and Joseph M. Schenck (in Los Angeles) and during the 1940s Spyros Skouras (in New York). Zanuck, Schenck, and Skouras resurrected the company.

Studio boss Darryl F. Zanuck surely earned more public notoriety than Schenck or Skouras. At Warners Zanuck had become a top production executive, but he could never hope to move beyond Jack Warner. In 1933 Zanuck left Warner Bros. to form (with Joseph M. Schenck) Twentieth Century Pictures, an independent production company. Zanuck proved an authoritative studio boss, one prone to public excesses. Frequently at premieres and other public gatherings he was heard bellowing to sycophants: "Don't say yes until I finish talking!"

However, Zanuck knew enough to stay in the good graces of his senior partner Joseph M. Schenck. In the film business Schenck possessed far more clout. Joseph M. Schenck's younger brother Nicholas had supplied the needed finances to complete the merger of the tiny Twentieth Century Pictures and the ailing Fox Film. The Schenck brothers worked closely together to make sure Twentieth Century—Fox and Loew's/MGM continually ranked at or near the top of the American movie business.

Analyzing the filmmaking strategy at Fox during the 1930s and 1940s is a straightforward task, since there were only two heads of production: Winfield Sheehan until 1935, and Darryl F. Zanuck thereafter. Sheehan had organized the Fox Film studio in 1914, and his rare successes in the early 1930s came with features starring Shirley Temple and Will Rogers. Indeed by 1935 the adorable child actress and the vaudeville veteran from Oklahoma stood atop the annual polls of star popularity taken by movie exhibitors.

Zanuck took over as production chief during the summer of 1935 and supervised Twentieth Century—Fox's studio production well into the 1950s. He quickly developed new stars. The first seems like an unusual choice, but in her day, skating champion Sonja Henie was a movie

Darryl F. Zanuck (left) argues with Joseph M. Schenck (center), while Sidney Kent (second from left) and two underlings listen.

queen. Her first feature, *One in a Million* (1937), was a smash, and during her salad days of the late 1930s Henie reliably drew in millions at the boxoffice for her employer. Zanuck imported two more stars from the Broadway stage. Alice Faye had been struggling in New York but became a crowd favorite at Fox with her portraits of the girl-next-door in both musicals and dramas. Tyrone Power is the best remembered of Zanuck's early stars. Through films such as *In Old Chicago* (1938) and *Suez* (1938), Power moved to the top rank of studio players and remained there except for a stint in the Marine Corps during World War II.

Zanuck brought Twentieth Century–Fox its greatest prosperity during the 1940s with Technicolor musicals starring Betty Grable. He established a durable formula during the 1940s when Grable ranked as Hollywood's top female star. Moviegoers seemed unable to get enough of this blonde woman who by her own admis-

sion was a marginal singer and dancer. Starring in *Moon Over Miami* (1941), *Song of the Islands* (1942), *Coney Island* (1943), *The Dolly Sisters* (1945), *Mother Wore Tights* (1947), and *When My Baby Smiles at Me* (1948), Betty Grable made her studio more money than any single other performer of the studio era. Critics hailed Zanuck's serious films (such as *Gentlemen's Agreement*, 1947 and *Pinky*, 1949), but studio chieftains Schenck and Skouras much preferred Grable musicals.

Throughout the Studio Era Twentieth Century–Fox did produce low-budget or "B" films. During the 1930s *Charlie Chan* was probably Fox's best-loved series. Exhibitors also clamored for Fox's newsreels. Indeed, Fox's "March of Time" quasi-documentary series became an icon of the era, with its exposés inspired by *Time* magazine and the booming voice of narrator Westbrook Van Voorhis. Traditional Movietone News also stood at the top

Harry Warner (second from right) and brother Abe (left) and two exhibitors waiting for the premiere of *The Lights of New York* (1928).

● ●

of its field. Announcer Lowell Thomas became a household name, and stringers in fifty-one countries (reporting to nine editing centers around the globe) dug up scoop after scoop. Many times Twentieth Century–Fox was able to sell a theatre its features simply on the strength of the drawing power of Movietone newsreels.

● warner bros. ●

Warner Bros. (always abbreviated unless referring to the four men themselves) was the only true family-run operation among the major movie studios. Eldest brother Harry was the president, middle brother Abe supervised distribution, and the "baby," Jack, headed the stu-

dio in California. (Sam died in 1927.) The family struggled to make money and succeeded only as a result of their innovation of sound, and then later sharing in the prosperity of the era of the Second World War.

Historians celebrate Warner Bros. for its social exposé films (*I Am a Fugitive from a Chain Gang*, 1932, and *Wild Boys of the Road*, 1933), innovative gangster films (*Public Enemy*, 1931, and *The Secret Six*, 1931), and backstage musicals (*The Gold Diggers of 1933* and *Footlight Parade*, 1933). But from a box-office point of view, those films only helped the company lose more than thirty million dollars during the Great Depression.

Once the U.S. economy recovered, steady profits came from such Warners films as the Bette Davis and James Cagney comedy *The Bride Came C.O.D.* (1941); the romantic *Christmas in Connecticut* (1945) starring Barbara Stanwyck and Dennis Morgan; the film biography of Cole Porter, *Night and Day* (1946), starring Cary Grant and Alexis Smith; the Broadway hit *Life with Father* (1947), starring Irene Dunne and William Powell; and Jane Wyman's Oscar-winning performance in *Johnny Belinda* (1948). Mainstream feature films like these propelled Warner Bros. to such profits and power that when the Studio Era drew to a close in 1949 Warners ranked behind only Paramount and Twentieth Century–Fox.

Yet, in good times or bad, the fundamental principle of Warners' California studio remained the same: cut-rate moviemaking. Notoriously tightfisted elder brother Harry operated on a volume basis, seeking a small profit on all films, not a big score on several blockbusters each year. But Warners was not simply a conservative clone of Paramount or Loew's. For example, Harry Warner was among a handful of business executives to call for intervention by the United States into what would become the Second World War. He also enthusiastically supported Franklin D. Roosevelt. Harry Warner and his family were no wild-eyed radicals but, rather, strongly patriotic and pragmatic businessmen who did not have to answer to stockholders.

Harry Warner embraced the profits which came from genre films. Backstage musicals included *42nd Street* (1933) starring Dick Powell and Ruby Keeler, and *Wonder Bar* (1934) starring Al Jolson and Kay Francis. Top-selling novels inspired *Oil for the Lamps of China* (1935) and *Anthony Adverse* (1936); Errol Flynn played a swashbuckling romantic hero in *The Adventures of Robin Hood* (1938) and *The Charge of the Light Bragade* (1936). The studio earned a measure of prestige (and a rare Oscar) for its bio-pix: *The Story of Louis Pasteur* (1936) and *Juarez* (1939), both starring Paul Muni. The Second World War inspired the combat films *Air Force* (1943) and *Destination Tokyo* (1944), both tops at the boxoffice. Postwar America seemed to enjoy Warner's fatalistic *film noir* creations as typified by *Mildred Pierce* (1945) and *White Heat* (1949).

More than Paramount, MGM, or Fox, Warners milked profits from its "B" unit under Bryan Foy. Warner stars such as Humphrey Bogart learned their craft under Foy whose biggest money-makers were the *Nancy Drew* detective films. Warner Bros. did not have to take a back seat to any Hollywood company when it came to short subjects. Having innovated sound through vaudeville shorts, it continued recording top talent through the 1930s and 1940s. Most of the big bands of the swing era performed for Warner's Vitaphone cameras.

But animated cartoons proved the company's greatest success in short subjects. Warner's cartoons of the 1940s (starring Bugs Bunny, Elmer Fudd, and Daffy Duck) stood for the best.

Jane Wyman in her Oscar-winning performance in *Johnny Belinda* (1948).

● ●

Warners had begun animation in the 1930s but spent that decade trying to "out-Disney" Disney—Disney's *Silly Symphonies* inspired Warner's *Merrie Melodies* and *Looney Tunes*. Gradually Tex Avery, Chuck Jones, Bob Clampett, and Frank Tashlin perfected an irreverent visual style, more cutting than Disney's, more topical than MGM's *Tom and Jerry* or Paramount's *Popeye the Sailor*. Warner Bros.' animated short subjects embraced the patriotic fever of the Second World War more than did any other part of Hollywood, and as such probably offered more direct social commentary than did any single feature of the era.

• radio-keith-orpheum •

Radio-Keith-Orpheum (RKO) had the shortest, least profitable life of any major studio. RKO was formed so that RCA could market its sound equipment, Joseph P. Kennedy could sell his FBO studio for a big profit, and the Keith-Albee-Orpheum vaudeville theatres could be converted into movie houses. In the first two years (1929 and 1930) of its existence, it reached an artificial peak. Thereafter RKO struggled along; it ranked as a major studio only because of its nationwide theatre chain.

RKO produced the best and worst feature films because its owners and managers were always under the gun to find a way to make money. Rarely was a management team in place for more than a few years when it was let go and replaced by studio bosses with different ideas. Production executives came and went with regularity. David O. Selznick's tenure at the helm lasted from 1932 to 1933 and saw the creation of *King Kong* (1933), *What Price Hollywood?* (1932), and *Bill of Divorcement* (1932). He brought Katharine Hepburn to RKO for her Oscar-winning performance in *Morning Glory* (1933). But Selznick was soon fired, replaced by the creator of *King Kong*, Meriam C. Cooper, who lasted sixteen months. Cooper lasted long enough to initiate the Fred Astaire–Ginger Rogers musicals, among RKO's greatest contributions to film history.

When George Schafer came on as head of production in 1938, he brought to RKO noted figures from Broadway to produce prestige films and make RKO the next MGM. For example, Max Gordon and Harry Goetz re-created their stage hit *Abe Lincoln in Illinois* (1940) for RKO, and Orson Welles and his Mercury Company journeyed west to fashion *Citizen Kane* (1941). Unfortunately *Citizen Kane* was a public relations nightmare, and Welles' contract was terminated following his next film, *The Magnificent Ambersons* (1942). Schafer's top maneuver was to sign independent producer Sam Goldwyn to distribute through RKO. That is how the studio managed to latch on to the box-office powerhouse (and now critically revered film) *The Best Years of Our Lives* (1946).

But Schafer was gone by 1942, and Charles Koerner, his successor, immediately abandoned prestige fare for the cheaply done, predictably profitable "B" films. His first big hit was *Hitler's Children* (1943), an anti-Nazi melodrama which cost two hundred thousand dollars to make but grossed more than three million dollars. Not all the "B" features were created by second-rate talents. The many films produced by the Val Lewton horror unit, Jean Renoir's *This Land Is Mine* (1943), and Robert Siodmak's *The Spiral Staircase* (1946) all were made during Koerner's tenure. Koerner died in 1946 and Howard Hughes moved in to create his special brand of corporate chaos.

RKO offered exhibitors the usual assortment of short subjects. Its Pathé newsreels never matched Fox's Movietone News, but they were consistent, solid attractions. The crown jewel of RKO's shorts was the animation it distributed for Walt Disney from 1937 to 1954. (Before that Disney used United Artists.) The feature-length *Snow White and the Seven Dwarfs* proved an unexpected hit in 1938. Then Disney poured too much money into *Pinnochio* (1940) and *Fantasia* (1940), and although they did well at the boxoffice, little actual profit was made. Unlike the competition, Disney did not prosper during World War II, relying on government contracts to keep the studio afloat. In the 1950s when Disney hit it big in television and theme parks, RKO was well on its way out of the movie business.

• • • • • • • • • • • • • • • •

hollywood's minor studios

• • • • • • • • • • • • • • •

Universal Pictures, Columbia Pictures, and United Artists constituted the Studio Era's Little Three. These corporations could never match the economic muscle of the Big Five because they did not own theatres. Even less powerful and more specialized were Monogram and Republic Pictures, only creating low-budget fare for marginal theatres. The Big Five and the Little Three willingly gave over the least profitable theatres in the United States to Republic and Monogram.

• universal •

Universal Pictures could trace its roots to founder Carl Laemmle's successful fight against the Motion Picture Patents Company. But this company would play only a marginal role during the lucrative Studio Era. Indeed, in the 1930s and 1940s Universal prospered only with low-budget comedies from Abbott and Costello, weekly serials including *Flash Gordon* and *Jungle Jim*, a discount newsreel service, and cheaply made Woody the Woodpecker cartoons. Occasionally during those years Universal's management did become ambitious, and sought prestigious works such as *All Quiet on the Western Front* (1930) to temporarily challenge the Big Five. But the company never succeeded and fell back again.

German immigrant Carl Laemmle formed Universal in 1912 and opened Universal City Studios in 1915, creating the largest, most modern moviemaking operation in the world. But while Famous Players–Lasky moved up to number one in the industry by signing top stars and expanding its feature-film budgets, Laemmle maintained a conservative business posture. He continued doing what had worked so well in the past: low-budget formula films. Indeed the studio became famous as a place for developing professionals such as director John Ford and studio executive Irving Thalberg, and then losing them to the more prosperous Paramount Pictures or MGM.

The Great Depression further battered the already ailing Universal. In 1929 the elder Laemmle appointed his son, Carl Laemmle, Jr., as head of production at the studio. The inexperienced twenty-one–year–old "Junior" Laemmle turned the company from a marginally profitable operation into a gigantic corporate loser. His father stepped in to help, but by 1936 Junior had done his damage as an inept studio manager. That year his father had to sell the studio to J. Cheever Cowdin's Standard Capital Corporation. Cowdin's management team had better luck, especially during the prosperous period of the Second World War. But after the war the studio went on the skids again and merged with independent producer International Pictures in 1946. This merger was not

Universal's *Buck Privates* (1941), starring Bud Abbott and
Lou Costello. This was the studio's biggest money maker of the
1930s and 1940s.

successful, and in 1952 Cowdin sold Universal to Decca Records.

Universal's managers under the Laemmles and the Cowdin regime prospered by specializing in low-budget features. Indeed, if one thinks of a successful Universal picture, the image which ought to come to mind is the comedy *Buck Privates* (1941), starring Bud Abbott and Lou Costello. Abbott and Costello were the lone Universal stars to ever make it into the annual top ten polls during the 1930s and 1940s.

But Universal produced many other types of low-budget films, including horror classics like *Dracula* (1930), *The Mummy* (1932), *The Invisible Man* (1933), and *The Bride of Frankenstein* (1935); Deanna Durbin musicals such as *One Hundred Men and a Girl* (1937) and

Mad About Music (1938); and inspired comedies such as *Never Give a Sucker an Even Break* (1941) and *You Can't Cheat an Honest Man* (1939), both starring W. C. Fields. None of these films ever made a great deal of money. The company did benefit from the general industry prosperity associated with the Second World War and indeed the mid-1940s would prove Universal's apex.

• columbia •

In the 1920s, before the coming of sound, dozens of fly-by-night Hollywood producers attempted to break into the elite circle of the Big

Five. Distributing through a loosely knit confederation of independent agents around the United States (collectively known as states rights), independent producers proffered their films to small, independently run neighborhood theatres. Only one of these small Hollywood operators ever made it to the big time. While the rise of Warner Bros. is the greatest success story, almost as important and equally as inspiring as a rags-to-riches tale is that of Columbia Pictures.

The image of Columbia during the Studio Era focuses squarely on Harry Cohn, the archetypal, cigar-chomping movie mogul. Cohn is reputed to have claimed that if a certain part of his anatomy twitched with excitement when he previewed a picture, then the American public would love it. If he was not moved, the film invariably would turn out to be a dud. In truth, Harry Cohn was a tough negotiator, a ruthlessly successful businessman. He (along with his brother Jack, who handled distribution from New York City) scratched and clawed his way along the hard road through the coming of sound and past the Great Depression into Hollywood prosperity during the 1940s.

Columbia's origins lay in a partnership formed in 1924. Slowly the brothers Cohn marshalled their forces to create first a national system for distribution and by 1931, an international one. Columbia had a small studio plant, beginning with two stages on Gower Street in what was then known as Hollywood's "Poverty Row." The Cohns never had the resources to consider buying theatres. But during the Great Depression the lack of a theatre circuit turned out to be a blessing, since as its larger competitors struggled to pay the mortgages on theatres, Columbia single-mindedly concentrated on making profits from movie production.

Columbia's founders, Jack (left) and Harry (center) Cohn.

● ●

Columbia came of age in 1934 with the release of Frank Capra's *It Happened One Night*, starring Clark Gable and Claudette Colbert. Harry Cohn was able to sign these two stars only because MGM and Paramount wanted to "punish" the pair for refusing certain parts and loaned them to this backwater studio. *It Happened One Night* swept the 1934 Academy Awards. But such a coup was not business as usual for Columbia. Typically, during the 1930s, Columbia relied on its low-budget "B" westerns and its even lower-cost shorts, serials, and cartoons for the bulk of its profits. Columbia is too often remembered only for its few high-cost productions, principally the work of Frank Capra, including *Mr. Deeds Goes to Town* (1936),

Lost Horizon (1937), *You Can't Take It with You* (1938), George Stevens' *Penny Serenade* (1941) and *Talk of the Town* (1942), *The Jolson Story* (1946), and *Jolson Sings Again* (1949).

The efforts of Columbia's "B" Western stars—Buck Jones in the 1930s and Gene Autry during the late 1940s—consistently added to the studio's coffers. But Columbia's low-budget fare included more than men on horses. Popular characters such as Blondie (based on the perennially favorite comic strip character), Boston Blackie (from a popular radio show), and the Lone Wolf detective (from a successful novel) drew in millions of fans. Serials with continuing stories and characters became a Columbia staple after 1937. *Batman* and *Terry and the Pirates*, both inspired by popular comic characters, were particular favorites.

Columbia's comic short subjects were a mainstay for small, neighborhood theatres. In 1934 the Three Stooges launched their first experiment in madness. With scripts that were constantly done and done again; filming that rarely lasted more than a week; and brisk editing and post-production work, films could move from studio to theatre in less than a month. As a consequence, Columbia's comedy shorts always made money, even though less than half the theatres in the United States even booked them. Small-town America never seemed to get enough of Curly, Larry, and Moe.

• united artists •

The founders of United Artists—stars Mary Pickford, Douglas Fairbanks, and Charlie Chaplin, and director D. W. Griffith—sought a corporate apparatus for film distribution for their independent productions. United Artists never had a studio per se; rather it distributed features made by filmmakers at their own studios or on rented facilities. United Artists' heyday came during the 1920s when founders Fairbanks, Pickford, and Chaplin actively created films.

Its greatest success during the Studio Era came during an unlikely period—the Great Depression. In the early 1930s Joseph M. Schenck headed company operations; he was a skilled independent producer and had important connections to Loew's theatres through his younger brother Nicholas. In fact, Loew's theatres served as a patron to United Artists during the early 1930s. But in 1933 Joe Schenck grew tired of constantly haggling with UA's founders about how to split up the profits he was generating. He found a new partner (Darryl F. Zanuck), formed an independent production unit (Twentieth Century Pictures), did very well, and then left United Artists for Fox in 1935 to create Twentieth Century–Fox. United Artists was left high and dry.

Throughout the remainder of the Studio Era, Schenck's successors at United Artists struggled to obtain enough films to fill a meaningful distribution schedule. Many notable producers came and went, including Walter Wanger, Alexander Korda, and David O. Selznick. But only Sam Goldwyn created his best work for United Artists, including *Dead End* (1937) and *Wuthering Heights* (1939). But Goldwyn did not want to remain the lone contributor to corporate profits and in 1941 moved his independent production unit to RKO. Thereafter United Artists plunged into the red ink and played a minor role in the film industry throughout the 1940s. The company even managed to lose money during the Second World War, when profits in the American film industry reached record levels.

• monogram and republic •

The Great Depression caused many practices to change in the American film industry. During the lean times of that economic calamity independent theatres needed a way to attract away customers from theatres owned by the Big Five. Borrowing techniques from the dime store, neighborhood houses began to regularly offer two films for the price of one—the double feature. But these houses needed more films. In stepped Monogram and Republic.

Monogram had barely survived the coming of the Great Depression, and new demand for low-cost fare to fill the bottom half of double features came just in time. Keeping costs at twenty thousand dollars per feature (one-tenth that of an average Paramount film), Monogram ground out profits. Monogram produced cheap versions of standard genre fare including Westerns (starring Bob Steele and Tex Ritter, among others), the Bowery Boys series, and during the Second World War, tales of espionage and intrigue.

Monogram's principle rival was Republic Pictures, whose founder, Herbert J. Yates, began his career in film processing in 1915. Indeed, his Consolidated Film Laboratories reigned as a major in its field. But the Great Depression saw many small producers go under, owing Consolidated thousands of dollars in film processing bills. Yates took what remained of these small producers and in 1935 created Republic Pictures.

Republic's output included Westerns, serials, and assorted low-budget genre pictures. Singing cowboys (Roy Rogers and Gene Autry) were the studio's dominant stars. In fact, during the Studio Era, the singing cowboy symbolized Republic to moviegoers. Serious filmmakers looked down on this lowbrow fare, but in rural America few stars had more drawing power than Autry did during the 1930s or Rogers during the 1940s. Indeed, during the Second World War, Republic did so well that profits soared beyond one million dollars per annum, a figure unheard of outside the Big Five. Yates then set out to become "respectable," and produced several prestigious pictures including John Ford's *Rio Grande* (1950), Orson Welles' *Macbeth* (1948), and Frank Borzage's *Moonrise* (1948). Only a handful, in particular John Ford's *The Quiet Man* (1952), ever made money.

socio-economic shocks

The corporate hegemony of the Big Five and the Little Three, plus Monogram and Republic, proved a resilient industrial structure. This studio system survived the social upheavals caused by the greatest economic calamity of the twentieth century, the Depression of the 1930s.

John Ford's *My Darling Clementine* (1946) opening at San Antonio's Majestic Theatre.

Indeed, during the 1930s the film industry was one of the nation's most visible economic and social institutions, dominating the field of popular entertainment. The coming of the Second World War also caused a number of significant changes in the socio-economic fabric of the United States, including the country's return to prosperity. Moviegoing increased, reaching its highest rate in the history of the United States.

• the great depression •

Although the Great Depression caused social and cultural transformations in all phases of American life, the Hollywood studios endured. As Americans had less money to spend, they went to the movies less frequently. Reliable box-office figures from that era do not exist, but best estimates indicate that total take at the box-

office fell by approximately 25 percent from 1930 to 1934. To attract patrons and generate more revenues, exhibitors offered more and more double feature shows, gave away dishes and other prizes, and began to sell popcorn and candy.

Movie producers reacted as well. The studios laid off workers and pushed those still under employment to work longer hours for less pay. Memoirs of stars, directors, and other craftspersons who labored for the studios during that era recount anecdote after anecdote of dawn-to-dusk working days, with few breaks off for creative reflection. For example, the Busby Berkeley musicals, projecting innocent and naive fun on the screen to help a nation forget its woes, only emerged from the sweat of regular fourteen-hour days, six days a week.

In response, workers began to organize, and the unions and guilds so famous today (like the Screen Actors Guild and the Writers Guild)

The Das Kino Theater, Milwaukee, Wisconsin.

originated and expanded. There were some strikes and work stoppages, but the studios held so much power that workers made only marginal gains. The International Alliance of Theatrical Stage Employees and Moving Picture Operators (IATSE) easily made the most advancement because of its ability to pull out projectionists and thus close down America's theatres. Hollywood craftspeople posed far less of a threat.

The Big Five worked well together to squeeze the maximum in profits from the studio system. During the early 1930s, through their representative in Washington, D.C., the Motion Picture Producers and Distributors Association, they successfully sought and obtained relief through special bankruptcy laws and lenient provisions in the National Recovery Act. As a consequence, the fly-by-night producers, so common in Hollywood during the 1920s, as well as nearly five thousand independent movie theatres around the United States, went under.

With less competition the Big Five simply made even more money as the nation dug its way out from the Great Depression.

The growing lure of the movies to America's youth during the 1930s signaled to educators, religious leaders, and social workers the rise of a new social problem. Frustrations due to a lack of economic opportunity were blamed on the evil influences of the movies. Gangster films, they declared, not only entertained, they also inspired and even trained a generation of crooks. Mae West's indulgent attitudes toward fun and frolic, claimed leaders of the Catholic church, diverted a nation from hard work and Christian attitudes. Conservative religious groups pointed to a generation of youth wasting their lives in movie theatres. Women's clubs devoted to improving society asserted that the movies taught the youth of America bad manners, even antisocial behavior.

To counter these criticisms, Hollywood hired apologists to publicize the positive virtues of going-to-the-movies. The few objective social scientists studying the situation found that movie attendance seemed not to fundamentally influence the youth (or adults) of America very much, if at all. Most moral and religious leaders ignored these studies; they *knew*, first-hand, of the harmful effects movies had on America's young. The more important matter was what to do about this menace.

As economic conditions worsened during the Great Depression, the conservative moral and religious community in the United States took the offensive against Hollywood. Censorship of the movies by various state boards and community panels had existed around the United States since the nickelodeon era. In 1922 Hollywood organized the Motion Picture Producers and Distributors Association to prevent the creation of a national censorship law. This association was popularly known as the Hays Office after its longtime president, former postmaster general Will H. Hays. During the 1920s Hays was able to head off all efforts to legally constrain the film industry on the federal level.

But in 1930 religious and moral leaders mounted a serious new offensive to significantly restrict Hollywood's subject matter. That year a Catholic Jesuit priest, Daniel Lord, S.J., and a prominent Catholic layman, Martin J. Quigley (who also published the influential trade paper *Motion Picture Herald*), revised and strengthened the Motion Picture Code by which Hollywood was supposed to police itself. Trying to head off trouble, the Hays Office embraced this new set of guidelines, but in practice it did little to enforce them.

In 1933 the Catholic church, reflecting the growing despair associated with the Great Depression, pushed for mandatory enforcement. Hollywood agreed to submit scripts to the Hays Office and get approval prior to filming. The Legion of Decency was formed through which the Catholic church began to advise its members on what films to avoid; at times it even called for boycotts of theatres to make sure Catholics did not attend certain films. The B'nai B'rith, the Elks, the Masons, the Odd Fellows, and the National Education Association joined in to pressure the film industry "to clean up its house."

In July 1934 the Hays Office formally established the Production Code Administration. Joseph Breen, a prominent Catholic layman, was placed in charge, and the Motion Picture Producers and Distributors Association agreed that none of its members (specifically the Big Five and the Little Three) would distribute a film unless it had first been approved by the Production Code Administration.

The Production Code forbade scenes which projected a positive image of "crime, wrongdoing, evil, or sin." Criminals had to be portrayed in an unsympathetic fashion; murders had to be presented so as to discourage imitation, and the same held true for sexual activity. But when the Production Code became specific, many found it somewhat laughable:

> No approval shall be given to the use of words and phrases in motion pictures including, but not limited to the following: Alley cat (applied to a woman); bat (applied to a woman); broad (applied to a woman); Bronx cheer (the sound); chippie; cocotte. . . .

and so on, to the end of the alphabet. Indeed, David O. Selznick needed a special exception to have Clark Gable say (as Rhett Butler) in *Gone with the Wind*: "Frankly, my dear, I don't give a damn."

The Production Code had the force of law because the Big Five and Little Three held so much economic power. It was a system of self-regulation policed by its own members. Its goal was not so much to foster good deeds but to create a public relations mechanism to ward off a national censorship law. No federal law was ever passed, and the Production Code ruled as long as the Studio Era lasted, that is until the early 1950s.

• world war two •

The Second World War compelled most nations of the world to devote most of their resources to survival. In this atmosphere of restriction, the movies in America prospered as they never had before. The Hollywood corporate hegemony collected back in spades all the losses it had accumulated during the Great Depression. The movie business in the United States made money almost as fast as it could be collected. It would take an inflation-bloated era of block-busters—the 1970s and 1980s—to match these boxoffice records. In terms of theatrical attendance, per capita records were set in 1945 and 1946 which may never be broken.

But at first the war in Europe hurt the film industry because foreign business declined. As hostilities spread around the world during the late 1930s and into the early 1940s, Hollywood saw overseas box-office revenues plummet. To offset these losses the movie industry focused on South and Central America. The U.S. Department of State's "Good Neighbor Policy" attempted to promote features with positive Latin American figures. Films with Latin stars and Latin locales flooded American screens. Such eminent leaders as Benito Juarez and Simon Bolivar; such stars as Carmen Miranda, Desi Arnaz, and Cesar Romero; such films as *Weekend in Havana* (1941) and *Down Argentine Way* (1940) became commonplace. The Office of Inter-American Affairs, under Nelson Rockefel-

ler, took the task of spreading movie goodwill seriously, supplying technical assistance to the Hollywood studios and paying for promotional trips to film on location, such as Orson Welles's visit to Brazil.

In the United States, where no actual combat took place, film fans flocked to the movies in record numbers. As the expanding war economy nearly wiped out unemployment, people had more money to spend. The severe restrictions of a war economy limited production of some goods (like automobiles) and limited the purchase of others (like gasoline for existing cars). New housing and household appliances were simply not available. But no real limitations on moviemaking or moviegoing were ever established. The administration of President Franklin D. Roosevelt encouraged overworked war employees to see as many movies as possible in their free hours. New movies poured out of Hollywood and attendance records were shattered from coast to coast. In cities like Detroit, where auto factories were churning out airplanes and tanks twenty-four hours a day, movie shows were held around the clock to accommodate workers who worked on evening or morning shifts.

Hollywood made money as never before. The Big Five saw their profits soar into the multi-million-dollar range, totals unmatched since the prosperity of the late 1920s. Male movie stars who were not eligible for the draft worked around the clock. Female stars had greater opportunities than ever before. Independent producers, who had struggled in the 1930s, prospered. No one wanted to admit it, but the war—with all its horror—was a good thing for Hollywood. Everyone involved hoped that its prosperity would never end.

Indeed, Hollywood had anticipated the coming of war in the late 1930s. Newsreels were the first form to confront the impending global conflict, although generally they glossed over the complex negotiations to present exciting battle scenes. When a fictional film praising the loyalists in the Spanish civil war, Walter Wanger's *Blockade*, came out in 1938, there was a storm of protest by anti-Hollywood elements who did not want the film industry to take sides. Isolationists accused the film industry for being propagandists for war. But *Blockade* was the exception. Day-to-day features were hardly inflammatory; they concentrated on non-war, non-controversial genre films.

All this changed on 7 December 1941. The question then became, what can Hollywood do to help win the war? An Office of War Information was established by the federal government to serve as a liaison with the film industry. The desirability of making movies was not an issue; everybody wanted them. The main problem was a lack of film stock, since silver, a significant ingredient in film stock, was also basic to so many war materials. On 8 February 1942 the selective service director, General Louis Hershey, declared the motion picture industry an "essential industry," which meant that its male employees could apply for deferments as "irreplaceable" workers. Still, most men volunteered; Hollywood was oftentimes left de-

pendent on dogs (Lassie), horses (Flicka), and aging heroes (sixty-six–year–old Charles Coburn won the Academy Award for Best Supporting Actor in 1943).

Movies were shipped abroad and shown there even before they were shown in theatres at home. For example, within days of the capture of Bougainville, a tent theatre was set up and Hollywood's latest fare was on the screen. Shells were still bursting within earshot. Pinups decorated the walls of tents and sides of bombers. The famous pose of Betty Grable, her back to the viewer, looking over her shoulder, was known throughout the world.

The studio system was a great economic force, and it spawned a grand era for Hollywood moviemaking. The American film industry was also a powerful cultural force, attracting millions of fans throughout the world to the twentieth century's newest art form. Indeed the studio system represented a particular style of moviemaking. It made the Classic Hollywood Narrative style the standard by which audiences around the world judged the success or failure of a motion picture. The following chapter treats the development of the Classic Narrative style through its Golden Age of the 1930s and 1940s.

· ·

7

the golden age of hollywood moviemaking

During the 1930s and 1940s Hollywood studio moviemakers, from producers and directors to prop movers and costume creators, helped create hundreds of popular feature films annually plus even more short subjects. The American film industry reached this Golden Age by adapting to sound the Classic Hollywood Narrative style developed during the silent era. Throughout the 1930s and 1940s the Hollywood studios churned out films which followed certain repetitive patterns of storytelling and film style. These familiar Westerns, musicals, gangster films, comedies, horror movies, and war films employed the Humphrey Bogarts, the Katharine Hepburns, the Cary Grants, the Bette Davises to add that distinctive touch and in addition help sell the film to millions and millions of patrons.

This rigid Classic Hollywood Narrative system of production defined the parameters within which a filmmaker could work. He or she had to accept these constraints and then could attempt to fashion complex, interesting motion pictures. Certain American studio filmmakers (such as directors Frank Capra and Alfred Hitchcock) presented the public with distinctive movies so popular that in time their names went above the title. To film historians thcsc spccial film authors (or *auteurs*) of Hollywood's Golden Age represented rare talents who were able to work within the system but still wield enough power to regularly leave a distinctive stamp on the films they made. Through a recognizable, patterned use of editing, camerawork, sound, and mise-en-scène, they defined what critics have praised as a "personal vision" within the highly regulated studio atmosphere of Classic Hollywood Narrative movie production.

adapting the classic hollywood narrative style for sound

Hollywood filmmakers established the Classic Hollywood Narrative film style during the silent era. With the introduction of sound they reworked the formula to establish a Classic Hollywood style for the talkies. First the studios had to reorganize to integrate sound into their operations. The new sound-recording technology complicated standard silent techniques. Editing in the silent era simply required a shears, glue, and rewinds; for sound films, an elaborate and expensive apparatus known as a Moviola was required to match and meld sound and image.

The studios for the first time had to hire university-trained engineers to help deal with problems of sound. Some day-to-day difficulties could be resolved at the studio level. So, for example, MGM technicians developed a flexible microphone boom to record moving camera shots. A prototype boom was built in a studio shop, and once it was perfected, the actual manufacture was farmed out, in this case to Mole-Richardson.

But simple tinkering hardly resolved all problems. Adjustments were required in film stocks, and sound equipment was continually improved to enhance fidelity of recording. This could only be done through the resources and staff of multimillion dollar corporations such as Eastman Kodak, RCA, and Western Electric. RCA and Western Electric, then a subsidiary of AT&T, throughout the 1930s worked to perfect directional microphones, increase the frequency range of sound recording, and reduce interference from ambient noise. The Second World War brought technological change to a halt, but after the war came sound recording on magnetic tape, while sound-on-film technology continued to be used for release prints in theatres.

Hollywood never considered abandoning the Classical Narrative style which had worked so well during the glory days of the silent cin-

Studio editor Owen Marks using a moviola at the Warner Brothers Studio, 1937.

● ●

ema. Instead methods were sought to insert sound into the existing moviemaking process. Metaphorically Hollywood filmmakers equated the camera with the eye, the microphone with the ear. Thus, if the camera (eye) could see into the depth of the space, so the microphone (ear) ought to be able to hear in both the foreground and the background. Boom microphones were innovated early on to allow the microphone as well as the camera to follow action continuously while maintaining the proper distance.

In using sound to help tell stories, filmmakers identified the human voice as the center of action. Sound could add character traits whereas in the silent cinema the director could rely only on body and facial characteristics and movements to establish the psychological states of characters and the changes they underwent. In talkies, modulations of the human voice (as well as noises and music) led to more fully developed characters. For example, directional microphones drew out dialogue in heretofore hard-to-reach locales, and improved sound equipment enabled voices to be clearly distinguished from noises in the scene.

Music helped with character development as well. By the 1940s passages of music were used most effectively to identify certain characters, connect scenes, and/or to underscore tense action sequences. Leitmotifs (a repeating configuration of notes) connecting music with character had been part of orchestral scores sent out with silent films; sound filmmaking formalized this technique. In terms of production, music was added last, in the post-production phase. Properly crafted music polished the narrative highlights and cemented the story together so that audience members (humming as they left the theatre) remembered the highlights of the picture, and recommended it to their friends.

With the coming of sound, then, the Classic Hollywood Narrative cinema took on aural equivalents of the visual elements which had long been in use. Some devices were eliminated, intertitles for example, and so this necessitated slightly longer takes to spin out the story. Spoken dialogue also made talkies longer than their silent film predecessors and increased the need for cutting from character to character. The Hollywood cinema of talkies continued to be a cinema of editing: a scene was established and then analyzed through editing to produce the appropriate story values.

During the end of the silent era, multiple-camera filming enabled several shots to be made simultaneously and cut together at a later time. For talkies this technique proved too cumbersome, and so Hollywood looked for ways to adapt single camera filming. The camera was blimped (wrapped to eliminate the recording of internal noise); more flexible cranes and dollies further enhanced the possibilities of camera movement. The coming of sound led to more movement of the camera, not less.

Once the Classic Narrative style was adopted for talkies, Hollywood did not sit still, but innovated technologies it thought would add to profits. New technologies were continually introduced, even though they did not have the "overnight" impact of the coming of sound. For example, deep focus photography came into common use during the 1940s. Film historians have long celebrated the use of deep focus in Orson Welles' *Citizen Kane* (1941). In that film Welles composed with a flare for depth of composition not typically found in films of the 1930s.

Camera operators can adjust for greater depth by manipulating settings and props, camera position and light sources, film stock and film lenses. In deep focus photography, depth is created through combination of a lens that is smaller than 50mm, fast film stocks, complex optical processes, and particular shutter speeds and openings. In the classical Hollywood silent film, rules for composition in space seemed straightforward enough. Actors and actresses performed in one plane of action, two planes at most. The mise-en-scène provided general background reference points, helping to situate the characters in the space of the scene.

Of course, multiple plane spaces were used, but almost exclusively in long shots. Buster Keaton, emphasizing the comic reactions of his deadpan character to his surroundings, often composed his long take (in time) shots in extensive and expressive depth. But his style remained the exception, not the rule. On the whole, the single plane techniques of the 1920s continued to be the norm throughout the 1930s

as filmmakers struggled with finding ways to better use sound.

But by the late 1930s sound had been fully incorporated into the Hollywood cinema, and filmmakers were beginning to seek a new visual look by which to differentiate their films. Thus, in 1940 and 1941 a number of movies (*Citizen Kane* was only one among many) were released in which deep space was used to emphasize tension, as in *The Maltese Falcon* (1941) with its ominous ceilings. But the employment of deep space did not radically disrupt the Classic Hollywood Narrative style because depth was often focused in the center of the frame, or it was used as a dramatic highlight in an establishing shot, or as part of a mystery or horror film.

Citizen Kane (1941) was not the first film to use deep space in a complex manner. But it certainly did incorporate this stylistic possibility to highlight the story of Charles Foster Kane. Cinematographer Gregg Toland utilized wide angle lenses, fast film stocks, arc lighting, and an improved Mitchell camera to create a brand new Hollywood look. Toland had experimented with the elements of deep focus during the 1930s but stuck with the principle of using it only for establishing shots. Toland is justifiably lauded for *Citizen Kane* because he brought fame to the technique (including an article in *Life* magazine) and used deep focus to dramatize shots which lasted far longer than was then the Hollywood norm. These static, beautifully composed shots (such as Susan Alexander's music lesson or Kane signing away his newspapers) were considered stunning sensations in their day.

Consider but one famous example: the shot in which Kane's mother signs over her young son to the banker Thatcher. As the scene begins, Kane as a boy is playing with his sled in the

Orson Welles' *Citizen Kane* **(1941).**

snow. Then the camera pulls back to reveal first a window, then Kane's mother inside the house, on the left of the frame; finally Thatcher joins her at a table to sign the papers. Kane's father stands powerless in mid-distance while the boy, now at the center of the frame, continues to play blissfully in the snow outside. In the distance, throughout the long shot, we see how unaware the young Kane was of the plans being made for his future. In what would have been done in several shots in the traditional Classic Hollywood system, Welles and Toland crafted in one complex unit.

Toland had sought out Orson Welles to get the assignment to shoot *Citizen Kane*. He claimed credit for the film's radical look and was labeled a heretic by his fellow cinematog-

raphers for it. Yet he deserves less credit than he has normally been given since some of the most famous credited deep focus shots (for example, Susan Alexander's attempted suicide) were not done by a cinematographer adjusting the camera, lighting, and lenses, but rather in a special effects laboratory by manipulating the optical printing processes. But Toland and other RKO technicians did highlight through *Citizen Kane* the possibilities of a new style of deep space which, through the rest of the 1940s, came to be accepted as yet another option in the package of possibilities of the Classic Hollywood Narrative cinema.

Being a conservative economic institution, Hollywood rarely permitted such radical experiments to continue very long. After *Citizen*

William Wyler's *The Best Years of Our Lives* (1946).

• •

Kane, deep space was principally used to add a flare to horror films or provide necessary establishing shots, but never as a flourish to stand alone. In Toland's own camerawork for *The Best Years of Our Lives* (1946), a milder, more restrained deep space cinematography amplified the story of three returning servicemen, never exaggerating or calling attention to itself. The most famous use of deep space in *The Best Years of Our Lives*, a scene in Butch's tavern when Al (Fredric March) looks from Homer at the piano in the foreground to Fred (Dana Andrews) in the phone booth in the distance, served only to establish the scene of the action, not to depict at any length changes in character relationships. Director William Wyler

followed this stunning establishing shot by then analyzing the scene with Classical continuity editing.

After the Second World War, a new sense of realism was also absorbed into the Classic Hollywood cinema. The moviegoing public seemed to want locations to look as though they had been recorded on the spot. One way Hollywood accommodated this urge was with deep space photography. Locations seemed more open and spacious when highlighted by deep space photography, for the viewer could take in all the action important to the story, not just focus on one plane. Faster stocks also made images look sharper, and portable equipment permitted the filmmaker to go to a suitable location, not simply rely on studio sets in sound stages. Yet this thrust toward realism did not change Hollywood storytelling on film. The Classical Hollywood Narrative cinema, with modifications, continued to set the standard.

film genres
and movie stars

During the 1930s and 1940s the Classic Hollywood cinema remained dominant, absorbing sound and deep space photography, and the new look of realism. However, the types of stories told did change in order to fashion new appeals to film fans throughout the world. Studios employed ever-changing types of stories to differentiate one film from another. Gangster movies with Jimmy Cagney were quite popular in the early 1930s while detective yarns starring Dick Powell drew in millions of patrons in the 1940s. The Hollywood studios continually worked and reworked familiar stories (such as the Western) in order to gain the greatest share of the boxoffice. Not only did these film *genres* (French for "kinds") tell and retell well-known stories, but audiences came to look out for familiar situations and endings. Moviegoers who went to see a Western *expected* that the hero would vanquish the villains at the end. If the hero did not, the film might be labeled an anti-Western.

Film genres required that audiences and filmmakers agree on certain expectations. Some were distinguished by common theme and narrative. For example, the Western told of the heroic actions of pioneers and cowboys who settled the frontier of the United States between 1845 and 1900. Genres dictated specific settings and objects (their look or iconography). For example, a gangster film of the 1930s required a Chicago-like urban milieu, machine guns, and fast automobiles. Still other genres centered around unusual forms of behavior. In musicals seemingly ordinary folks went about their business, then spontaneously broke into song and dance.

Stars provided the most common way to differentiate genres. Certain figures became the very icons of that particular formula. James Cagney will always be identified as the gangster, despite numerous other, often distinguished movie roles. Frequently a star's persona would change as the public's fascination moved in one direction or another. Joan Crawford played smitten, humble women in the 1930s, and then worked hard to change her image and became the hardened, bitter woman in mystery films of

Ernst Lubitsch's *The Love Parade* **(1929).**

the 1940s. It was the job of the studio boss to figure out which stars belonged to which genres.

• the musical •

The coming of sound made possible the film musical. Numbers could feature dancing, singing, or both, and could be inserted into any number of stories. Thus, the musical can be defined by its use of flourishes of sound and patterns of human behavior and movement we call dance. Once the genre began, with Al Jolson in *The Jazz Singer* (1927) and *The Singing Fool*

(1928), it gave rise to dozens of subgenres as studios looked for ways to differentiate their musicals from those of their competitors.

Early talkies borrowed liberally from stage sources for such revues as *King of Jazz* (starring Paul Whiteman) and *Paramount on Parade* (directed by, among others, Dorothy Arzner and starring everyone on the lot at the time), both released in 1930. The nineteenth-century operetta inspired Ernst Lubitsch's *The Love Parade* (1929), his *The Merry Widow* (1934), and Rouben Mamoulian's *Love Me Tonight* (1932).

In the early 1930s Warner Bros.' Busby Berkeley, a Broadway veteran, created a musical of spectacle centered around backstage stories. Berkeley mounted vast musical numbers for

Fred Astaire and Ginger Rogers in *Top Hat* (1935).

● ●

Footlight Parade (1933), *42nd Street* (1933), *Dames* (1934), and the "Gold Digger" series (of 1933, 1935, and 1937). Backstage musicals differed from revues and operettas in that they told of struggling performers, often set in Depression America. Characters had to be tough and brash, not sentimental and romantic. Their musical performances featured new popular songs within extravagant, spectacular dance numbers, often staged in geometric patterns. Berkeley added this latter touch by choreographing dances with a military, mechanical precision and shooting them from above.

In the mid-1930s a new musical form emerged from RKO, a studio which could not afford to match even Warner Bros.' cut-rate spectacles. Fred Astaire and Ginger Rogers, from 1934 to 1939, created one delight after another: *The Gay Divorcée* (1934), *Top Hat* (1935), *Follow the Fleet* (1936), *Swing Time* (1936), and *The Story of Vernon and Irene Castle* (1939), among others. RKO did not completely abandon the backstage story. Invariably Fred Astaire played a sometimes successful, sometimes out-of-luck performer who somehow always wound up wooing the Ginger Rogers character. The beauty of the Astaire-Rogers form of the musical came from the complex, fanciful integration of song and dance Astaire used to romance Rogers. The plot saw the Astaire character almost lose the Rogers character, but then they would be reunited at the end, often after a modest (compared to Berkeley's finales) but yet spectacular production number. Fred Astaire and Hermes Pan designed the dances in these films, and in their day they were considered great popular talents. A half century later Astaire is ranked among the greatest dancers the United States has ever produced.

The Astaire and Rogers' musicals took the first crucial step toward a musical form in which the song, dance, and story were fully integrated. This type of musical, often filmed in Technicolor, reached its peak in the years just after the Second World War at MGM. However, other studios' musicals were often more successful at the boxoffice. Indeed, the most popular musical stars of the day were Betty Grable at Twentieth Century–Fox, and Bing Crosby at Paramount. But with Vincente Minnelli's *Meet Me in St. Louis*, released in 1944, starring Judy Garland and produced by Arthur Freed, the integrated film musical found a formula which made for great delight.

Producer Arthur Freed brought together talents such as Minnelli and Garland and Gene Kelly and Stanley Donen to help create MGM's most noted musicals. From the first, Freed permitted Kelly to do his own choreography and then later to codirect (with Donen) *Singin' in the Rain* (1952). Garland created one hit song after another. But most importantly Freed was committed to original, integrated film musicals, developed in Hollywood by his in-house talent, matched with the regular output of remaking Broadway hits. During the final years of the studio era great musicals emerged from the Freed unit: *The Pirate* (directed by Vincente Minnelli, starring Gene Kelly and Judy Garland, 1948), *On the Town* (directed by Stanley Donen, starring Kelly and Vera Ellen, 1949), *Singin' in the Rain* (1952), *The Band Wagon* (directed by Minnelli, starring Fred Astaire and Cyd Char-

isse, 1953), and *It's Always Fair Weather* (directed by Donen and Kelly and starring Dan Dailey, Michael Kidd, and Cyd Charisse, 1955).

• the gangster film •

During the early 1930s Hollywood turned out a new form of crime melodrama, the gangster film. The films in this genre depicted the rise and fall of a gangland figure associated in the public's mind with, and indeed inspired by, the notorious career of the 1920s Prohibition era Chicago boss, Al Capone. Warner Bros., taking its stories from yesterday's newspaper headlines, opened this cycle with *Little Caesar* (starring Edward G. Robinson, 1930). The basic narrative was then retold to the delight of movie audiences in *The Public Enemy* (starring James Cagney, 1931) and Howard Hawks' *Scarface* (starring Paul Muni, 1932).

From these three boxoffice hits the fundamental elements of the genre were established. The large American city (by implication Chicago) provided the milieu for the rise of the gangster-hero. In an inversion of the traditional rags-to-riches Horatio Alger fable, he begins life as a poor boy from the slums but rejects the straight and narrow for a career of crime. As he makes his fortune, conflicts arise when rival gangs try to protect their territories. (The intergang warfare featured the marvels of modern technology, from machine guns to high-speed automobiles, to sophisticated communication devices.) But when the gangster reaches the crest of his new power, he becomes lackadaisical and slothful, and a new poor boy arrives to kill him and begin a new ascent.

Not all sectors of American society applauded these exciting tales of lawlessness and

Howard Hawks' *Scarface* (1932), starring Paul Muni (with the gun).

• •

violence. Moral and religious leaders condemned what they saw as the glorification of a hoodlum hero. They insisted that, whatever else transpired during the film, the gangster-hero die at the end. The Production Code of 1934 wrote in such a required ending. In 1935 Hollywood turned to a narrative approved by the "forces of good" in which the FBI was the protagonist. *G-Men* (1935) was iconographically indistinguishable from the classic gangster efforts except that the FBI now brought law and order to the city.

The cycle was reworked in yet another permutation during the late 1930s. In the original efforts the gangster was born a lawbreaker. Few thought about the implications of his environment and social milieu. Society's only choice

was to eradicate this menace. Reform was not an option. But during the late 1930s Hollywood introduced the gangster-hero as the victim of a poor, underprivileged social environment. The gangster in *Crime School* (1938) and *Angels with Dirty Faces* (1938) was represented as a product of the slums of America's cities. He was not simply born a criminal; he was the outgrowth of the failure of society to deal with the lack of low-income housing, poverty, and ineffective schools.

John Huston's *The Maltese Falcon* (1941) continued the iconography of the city milieu and re-used the gangster-villain, but it replaced the gangster-hero with the private eye. This hard-boiled detective, working alone, operated between the world of the police on one side and the world of warring gangs on the other. Isolated, he had to navigate a hellish city, often overwhelmed by the multitude of evils of urban America. But he always triumphed, to move on to another case.

After the Second World War, hard-boiled detective films continued to be popular. Directors, seeking a new look, began to film on location. For example, the new interest in out-of-door, location shooting was applied to a genre staple in *The House on 92nd Street* (1945) which told of an FBI investigation of a German spy-ring in the United States. Moreover, the genre began to investigate itself; that is, it became self-reflexive. In *White Heat* (1949), for example, Cody Jarrett (played by James Cagney) the gangster-hero is an Oedipal figure, not victimized by a slum environment, but rather crippled by a mental condition.

• horror films •

On Valentine's Day 1931 a struggling Universal Pictures released *Dracula*. An American stage production of the Bram Stoker novel of a blood-sucking count had been mounted on Broadway in 1927, starring Bela Lugosi, and despite unfavorable reviews ran for a year in New York and two years on tour. Universal used the same star and veteran director Tod Browning to create the top grossing film of 1931 of that ailing studio. As a result, the invasion of the normal world by the supernatural was off and running as a popular genre of the 1930s.

Universal followed with a version of the Mary Shelley tale, *Frankenstein* (1931), starring Boris Karloff as the monster. This film established the icons of the mad scientist, the out-of-control monster, and the dangerous, murky

foreign setting, usually lacking daylight. After the twin success of *Frankenstein* and *Dracula*, the floodgates opened for more horror films. In 1932 Paramount released *Island of Lost Souls* (with Charles Laughton and Lugosi) and *Dr. Jekyll and Mr. Hyde* (starring Fredric March); Warner Bros. issued *Dr. X* (with Lionel Atwill), and Universal followed with *The Mummy* (starring Karloff) and *The Old Dark House* (also with Karloff and directed by James Whale, director of *Frankenstein*).

During the rest of the 1930s major and minor Hollywood studios regularly issued horror films. *The Bride of Frankenstein*, directed by James Whale and starring Boris Karloff, came out in 1935. New antagonists were developed—*Frankenstein Meets the Wolf Man* in 1943 starred Lon Chaney, Jr., and Lugosi—and studios began to mix genres—*Abbott and Costello Meet Frankenstein* (1948) and *Abbott and Costello Meet the Killer, Boris Karloff* (1949). The attraction of the horror film seemed widespread; audiences wanted to be frightened in socially acceptable ways.

The costs of production were low. Screenplays were easy to develop since the literary sources were no longer copyrighted. Horror film stars may have been well known, but never commanded the salaries of stars of other genre fare. For example, Boris Karloff was paid only one-tenth as much as musical star Betty Grable. In addition, the genre could make efficient use (with judicious placement of light and shadow) of existing studio sets, and thus save thousands of dollars.

The horror film did take on a complex new form in the 1940s. The tales produced by Val Lewton at RKO, beginning with *Cat People* in 1942, stood out as cinematic gems among an increasingly predictable formula. In 1942, returning to a policy of producing more and more

Val Lewton's *Cat People* (1942).

● ●

low-budget B films, RKO created the Lewton unit to specialize in horror films. The studio moguls placed Val Lewton, a former script editor for David O. Selznick, in charge. For these B films Lewton was expected to use already existing sets, employ contract actresses and actors, and find and develop inexpensive scripts. Lewton created several classic horror films with this unit before he left for Paramount: *I Walked with a Zombie* (1943), *The Leopard Man* (1943), *The Seventh Victim* (1943), *The Ghost Ship* (1943), *The Curse of the Cat People* (1944), *The Body Snatcher* (1945), and *Isle of the Dead* (1945).

To take advantage of a multitude of standing sets at RKO, Lewton situated his horror films within the modern world. Fear of the unknown and terror generated by surviving ancient superstitions replaced threatening vampires and werewolfs. In *Cat People* a woman cannot deal with her obsession with cats; in *The Seventh Victim* the heroes are menaced by diabolic cults. Lewton did not have the resources to overwhelm the audience with the shocks of spectacular sequences of terror, so he encouraged his screenwriters to create and maintain tension throughout the film. But after World War II RKO again changed its feature film production policy to emphasize larger budget fare; Lewton's interlude of B horror films came to an end as did an era of innovation in the horror film genre.

• the western •

The Western certainly represents one of the richest of genre traditions in the history of the American film. Thousands of stories of settling the Old West regularly came forth from Hollywood, beginning with the film factory of Thomas Ince and the star power of William S. Hart. The Western as popular culture actually began in the late nineteenth century in dime novels, newspaper serials, the Buffalo Bill Western show and even in Broadway plays. Westerns were regularly produced in the Hollywood of the silent era, but with the coming of sound the film industry turned to other genres, most notably the musical, the gangster film, and the horror film. Indeed the 1930s and 1940s, Hollywood's Golden Age, saw a decline in the Western.

As talkies took over, the Big Five made few big budget Westerns. MGM scrapped its Tim McCoy series; RKO retired Tom Mix. It was the smaller studios, Republic and Monogram, which took on the Western series firmly during the 1930s, establishing the B movie staple. Tom Mix, Buck Jones, Tim McCoy, and Ken Maynard had all been important stars in the 1920s; in the 1930s they became actors who could gain work only in low budget B fare.

Republic Pictures relied on the singing cowboy to generate the largest box office for that minor studio. The popularity of its Gene Autry films commenced in 1935. Autry was far more than a routine cowboy star who could carry a tune. He was a major musical star. Autry regularly issued million-selling records and is properly recognized as a pioneer in country and western. Autry had his own network radio show on CBS; his traveling rodeo played to packed audiences throughout the country; and

he even ranked in the top ten of most popular movie stars before he temporarily retired to serve in World War II.

To generate new products in the late 1930s the Big Five studios considered higher budget Westerns. No one film signaled this renaissance, but John Ford's *Stagecoach*, released in 1939, symbolized the renewed interest in the Western film. Cecil B. deMille contributed *Union Pacific* in 1939, and Warner Bros. issued Errol Flynn's *Virginia City* in 1940. But director Ford, working for Twentieth Century–Fox and later his own independent production company, directed many of the best Westerns of this period. His *My Darling Clementine* (1946), *Fort Apache* (1948), and *She Wore a Yellow Ribbon* (1949) helped make Henry Fonda and John Wayne into major movie stars and set the stage for the renaissance of the Western which would take place in the 1950s.

• the war film •

The coming of the Second World War renewed interest in the war film and brought on a new film genre, the World War II combat film. Variations of film narratives about war had existed since the beginning of the American film industry. But in the midst of World War II Hollywood set out on a war film binge, making dozens of tales of Americans fighting in the air, on land, and in the sea. While the method of fighting may have differed, the basic narrative pattern was similar: a group of men from different backgrounds are brought together and in the heat of battle these men grow close, united against the onslaught of the enemy. In the end, a decisive battle is fought, and the

Howard Hawks' *Air Force* **(1943).**

• •

Allied forces triumph once again. As would be the case with any new genre, this one added a complete new set of icons: the jeep, the combat helmet, the P-41 fighter plane.

The date of the emergence of the combat war film can be firmly established. The attack on Pearl Harbor on 7 December 1941 led to the official entry of the United States into the war, and signaled to the film industry to commence producing war-related films. (Before that the film industry had been falsely accused by isolationists of advocating America's entry.) It took Hollywood about one year to begin to reach its stride. In 1943 came *Air Force* (starring John Garfield and Gig Young, directed by Howard Hawks), *Stand By for Action* (starring Rob-

ert Taylor), *Crash Dive* (starring Tyrone Power and Dana Andrews), *Action in the North Atlantic* (with Humphrey Bogart and Raymond Massey), and *Bataan* (with Robert Taylor and Lloyd Nolan).

Bataan can now be recognized as the seminal work. It is the story of a hastily assembled group of volunteers who bravely attempt to hold off an overwhelming Japanese force. These fighting men, representing the American melting pot, soon grow into a cohesive fighting group and use common strengths to win for the common good. The audience knew the story (the holding of the Bataan peninsula so that Allied forces could regroup and return to recapture the Philippines), and flocked to the

A classic film noir, *Out of the Past* (1947), starring Robert Mitchum and Kirk Douglas.

● ●

film. The formula for the combat film was thus established, and the genre thrived and continued well after the end of the war.

• film noir •

Not all genres are as easy to define as the musical, the gangster film, the horror film, the Western, or the war film. Consider the case of the *film noir* (French for "black film") of the 1940s. Unlike the classic film genres, film noir was not recognized as a genre in the 1940s. Later critics located and labeled this body of Hollywood films which have a common film style, tone, and mood. And forty years later, film

historians do not seem to agree on even which films constitute proper examples. Possible film noir candidates include *Double Indemnity* (1944), *The Postman Always Rings Twice* (1946), *Out of the Past* (1947), and *They Live By Night* (1948).

Certainly film noir is not a genre in the classical sense of the term. Hollywood in the 1940s did not set out to make film noir; nor did moviegoers choose to see one in the way they might have chosen to attend a Western or musical. Film noir can best be characterized as a deviation from the norm of the Classic Hollywood Narrative style of filmmaking. The label *film noir*, coined by the French after World War II, has always been used to designate Hollywood films that were somber in tone, absent of daylight, and unhappy in the end, that is, different from the more optimistic fare of the period. Stylistically, film noir is characterized by dappled lighting, frequent flashbacks, omniscient voice-over narrators, and threatening off-beat settings (often shot on location). Typical film noir stories feature psychologically unstable heros, the lack of traditional romantic relationships among the characters, and resolutions which do not fit the required tradition of the "happy ending."

An examination of film noir takes us away from a consideration of film genres back to the consideration of the Classic Narrative film style. If film noir differed from the norms of the Classic Hollywood Narrative film, so too did the work of a handful of filmmakers. The so-called *auteurs* provide examples of the most fascinating work of Hollywood in its Golden Age.

auteurs

During the Studio Era individual filmmakers struggled to add distinctive touches to Classic Hollywood Narrative films. In the feature films released in Hollywood during the 1930s, the contributions of producers, writers, directors, and others behind the camera (including cinematographers, set designers, composers, and editors) can be analyzed by seeking out common stylistic traits, formal permutations, and thematic constructs within that individual's opus of films. During the Golden Age of Hollywood, we can consider three types of auteurs:

1. Certain auteurs are associated with the recurring use of complex patterns of film style, while remaining generally faithful to the rules of the Classic Hollywood Narrative cinema. For example, an Alfred Hitchcock film is usually filled with sophisticated editing touches while a Welles' effort typically contains complicated camera flourishes.

2. On the level of storytelling, the auteur could develop unique characters in innovative narrative situations. The common traits of the bashful hero (played by Jimmy Stewart) highlight the films of Frank Capra.

3. Finally there is the level of thematic complexity. John Ford's films moved from a flattering, glowing vision of the settling of the American West in *She Wore a Yellow Ribbon* (1949) to a somber, dark portrait in *The Man Who Shot Liberty Valance* (1962).

No Hollywood auteur could break with the rules of the Classic Hollywood Narrative without the risk of being forced out of the system altogether, as some were. But certain individuals were able to survive and even thrive within the rigid constraints of the Hollywood studio system, regularly turning out intense, moving films. Producers, since they worked directly for the studio chiefs, had the most opportunities for innovation, but proved the least venturesome. The multitude of workers behind the camera, at the opposite end of the scale, had precious little power and formed unions and guilds with strict rules for conduct to maximize what leverage they possessed. However, directors, who regularly turned out popular fare, were most able to manipulate the Classic Hollywood Narrative system to create stunning, fascinating films that were fully appreciated only decades later.

Sam Goldwyn (left) meets his fellow moguls, William Paley of CBS (center) and Alexander Korda from Great Britain.

• •

• producers •

The producer within the Hollywood studio system supervised the creation of a slate of films each year. Depending on the particularities of the studio, he or she may have been in charge of turning out a group of unrelated films or of overseeing a handful of films in one particular genre or with one star. By and large, producers who prospered in Hollywood played it very conservatively.

Consider the case of Henry Blanke of Warner Bros. During his tenure he produced such varied works as *The Story of Louis Pasteur* (1936), *The Adventures of Robin Hood* (1938), *Jezebel* (1938), *The Maltese Falcon* (1941), and *The Fountainhead* (1949). In all of his work no clear pattern of story, theme, or style emerged. Blanke fully embraced the Classic Hollywood Narrative system and worked to create movies that would guarantee the greatest profits for his bosses, the brothers Warner.

The exceptions within the community of producers of the Studio Era seem to rest with independent operators such as Sam Goldwyn and David O. Selznick. Each learned his trade at a major company and then split off, distributing films through an RKO or United Artists. Both sought to make the most money for themselves by trying unique combinations of story material and talent.

Samuel Goldwyn in the 1930s took his inspiration from popular Broadway plays and acclaimed novels. From Broadway came the controversial bleak study of the negative side of the American city, *Dead End* (1937), and later the musical *Guys and Dolls* (1955). But Sam Goldwyn will probably be best remembered for *The Best Years of Our Lives* (1946), based on a MacKinley Kantor novel, adapted to the screen by Robert Sherwood. This timely film took advantage of the interest in the returning World War II veterans to create a work of unique charm, richness, and beauty. Through this tale of three servicemen returning home after World War II, Goldwyn harnessed the best from his long-term alliance with director William Wyler and cinematographer Gregg Toland.

David O. Selznick also came to the film business early on and chaffed working under a number of strong studio bosses, including his own father-in-law, Louis B. Mayer. In the 1930s Selznick went off on his own and produced a collection of top pictures for his own company, Selznick International. He is most remembered for the highest-grossing film of the studio era, *Gone with the Wind* (1939). Without a doubt, David O. Selznick controlled all phases of that film's production. In the process he hired and fired three directors and any number of screenwriters. But while no one can deny the economic and social importance of *Gone with the Wind*, that civil war epic did not break with Classic Hollywood Narrative filmmaking. After *Gone with the Wind*, Selznick then squandered his career by spending the rest of his life unsuccessfully trying to make a film to best it.

In the end, the most successful producers of the Studio Era were those who were able to work within the constraints presented them. Indeed, it seems the more difficult the restrictions, the greater chance for success. This certainly was the case with Val Lewton and Arthur Freed (discusssed earlier), who supervised a number of the finest genre films Hollywood has ever released. **Val Lewton** experimented with the conventions of the horror film genre and under severe budget restrictions produced some of the most complex, most interesting films of the studio era. **Arthur Freed** was able to fashion a unit for musicals at MGM which produced a number of gems. Lewton and Freed proved that by carefully working within Hollywood's prescribed rules, they could produce films with a distinctive style and flare, recog-

nized then by audiences and critics, and later by film historians.

• the hollywood crafts •

The producers may have had the power, but they were greatly outnumbered by the studio craftspeople, from hairdressers to grips, camera operators to editors. Unfortunately most labored under strict orders from above, and only through unionization were they able to gain even a measure of control over their careers. But there were exceptions.

Cinematographers made fundamental contributions to any film by planning the lighting, supervising camera placement and movement, and instructing those who operated the cameras which recorded the images. We have seen how **Gregg Toland**, discussed earlier, played a significant role in introducing deep space cinematography. For a time during the early 1940s, Toland even became as well-known as most directors and producers, recognized and praised as a cinematographer-artist by both movie fans and critics alike.

But more typically the cinematographer of the Studio Era skillfully served the director, producer, and studio. His or her job required the creation of images which fit within the accepted boundaries of the Classic Hollywood Narrative system. James Wong Howe noted that the only function of cinematography is to express the story in its own dramatic terms. Thus, the cinematographer, even when doing a first-rate job, simply served as a member of a team whose goal was to create a Classic Hollywood Narrative text.

Ernest Haller, for example, helped photograph *Gone with the Wind* and earned an Oscar for his lush Technicolor images. Over a forty-five-year career (which spanned the complete Studio Era), Haller worked on more than one hundred films, principally for Warner Bros., from *The Dawn Patrol* (1930) to *Jezebel* (1938) to *Mildred Pierce* (1945). But these films stand as star vehicles (for Errol Flynn, Bette Davis, and Joan Crawford, respectively). Few would have anticipated that the Haller of *The Dawn Patrol* would become the Haller of *Mildred Pierce*. As a cinematographer, he adapted to the dominant trends of the day.

Cinematographers were not the only craftspeople who helped create a distinctive look in the Hollywood films of the 1930s and 1940s. Costume designers certainly assisted in creating the look of a star. **Edith Head**, possibly the most famous costume designer of her era, worked at Paramount, fashioning costumes for Marlene Dietrich, Carole Lombard, Gloria Swanson, Mae West, Bob Hope, and Bing Crosby. Her career included her "Latin look" for Barbara Stanwyck in *The Lady Eve* (1941), and her "sarong look" for Dorothy Lamour in the top grossing *Road* pictures of the 1940s. Edith Head won eight Oscars and helped set fashion trends for two decades.

During the post-production process of filmmaking, editors assembled the final film. They had to insure the narrative continuity, and they often helped to add flair in dramas and comedies. The studio's chief editor served as an extension of the production boss. **Margaret Booth**, for example, trained in the era of D. W. Griffith, and rose to head the MGM editing department where she remained throughout the Studio Era. She actually cut few films but assigned, supervised, and checked on all product that left the studio. As Louis B. Mayer's assistant,

Hollywood's most honored costume designer, Edith Head.

● ●

she was the final arbiter in preserving the rules of the Classic Hollywood Narrative cinema.

Screenwriters have long been the most vocal in claiming their rightful due within the Hollywood system of the 1930s and 1940s. Frequently Hollywood's finest work of the Studio Era came from directors who also wrote their own scripts (Orson Welles, Billy Wilder, and Preston Sturges, for example), or writer-director combinations (for example, John Ford with Dudley Nichols and, later, Frank Nugent). All too often, however, a screenwriter worked

Music Director Bernard Herrmann working with Orson Welles.

• •

at the whim of an uncaring producer, serving as yet another employee in the mass production scheme of the studio system.

One overlooked Hollywood craft, however, created a component of the feature film which could stand on its own: film music. The finest composer of the Studio Era may have been **Bernard Herrmann**. This extraordinary talent added music to many a fine film from *Citizen Kane* (1941) and *The Magnificent Ambersons* (1942) to *Vertigo* (1958) and *Psycho* (1960). Herrmann's rich leitmotifs and dark sounds

added an additional dimension to films directed by Orson Welles, Robert Wise, Joseph L. Mankiewicz, and Alfred Hitchcock. Herrmann worked best when assigned to a collaborator who appreciated his extraordinary gifts. Herrmann never controlled the complete thematic or stylistic destiny of a film, but few on which he worked were not made more memorable because of his unique talents.

• directors •

A number of influential and important directors of the Studio Era trained in the silent era, although they would claim their fame and fortune within the Hollywood system of the 1930s and 1940s. Howard Hawks, John Ford, and Frank Capra were directors who prospered in the Golden Age of the Classic Hollywood Narrative cinema.

Howard Hawks represented Hollywood filmmaking at its best. He could make films in every genre and make them well. Gangster films (*Scarface*, 1932), detective films (*The Big Sleep*, 1946), and Westerns (*Red River*, 1948) regularly were turned out by this ace director. The independent-minded Hawks (he rarely worked for any one studio very long) was able to infuse his particular vision of the world into all of these seemingly disparate formulae. Hawks always stuck to the rules, but through subtle permutations in editing, dialogue, character, and space, he created many of the most complex and interesting films of the Golden Age of Hollywood.

Hawks always started with an elegant, tightly woven script in whose creation he had invariably played a dominant role. He never hesitated to hire top writers, including William Faulkner,

Ben Hecht, and Jules Furthman. His narratives often centered on a group of men, usually professionals, who were fervently committed to their careers and skilled at what they did. Less dedicated characters were not admitted to an inner circle which was headed by a tough old pro and his much younger protégé. The tension between characters led to terse conversations; there were few long speeches or rigid pronouncements. Actions, not words, define Hawks' body of films.

Within this Hawksian world, the director masterfully manipulated the personae of many a noted star. Seemingly disparate personalities such as John Wayne and Humphrey Bogart did their best work under Hawks' tutelage. But many directors were able to work with top stars. Hawks was also able to take seemingly bad actors and fashion characters often more appreciated abroad than in their home country. Even as late as 1959, he could sign an unappreciated Angie Dickinson and teen heartthrob Ricky Nelson and have them create the memorable characters Feathers and Colorado in *Rio Bravo*.

John Ford made a specialty of the Western, but also directed other types of films. Early in the 1930s Ford directed a number of popular films starring his employer's (Twentieth Century–Fox) top star Will Rogers: *Dr. Bull* (1933), *Judge Priest* (1934), and *Steamboat 'Round the Bend* (1935), Rogers' final film before his tragic death. John Ford also directed a number of features set in his parents' native Ireland. *The Informer* (1935), a serious tale of the Irish rebellion, received many an award in its day. In retrospect, it seems stodgy when compared to the vitality of *The Quiet Man* (1952), a less pretentious film about an Irishman returning to settle in his native land after a stay in the United States. Ford also undertook basic American his-

tory with *The Prisoner of Shark Island* (1936), *Young Mr. Lincoln* (1939), *Drums Along the Mohawk* (1939), and the celebrated *The Grapes of Wrath* (1940).

But arguably Ford created his best work in the Western; some even maintain he fashioned the greatest Westerns in American cinema history, from *My Darling Clementine* (1946) and *She Wore a Yellow Ribbon* (1949) to *The Searchers* (1956) and *The Man Who Shot Liberty Valance* (1962). In creating the archetype for the genre in *My Darling Clementine*, he specified the classic cinematic shoot-out, the famous final gunfight at the OK Corral where Wyatt Earp and his brothers avenge the murder of their youngest brother. Against the harsh background of the buttes and desert of Monument Valley, Ford plays out the drama of the settling of the West. The Earps ally with Clementine Carter and Doc Holiday to rid the town of the evil Clantons and in the end leave Clementine as the new schoolteacher, the very heart of the civilizing of the Old West.

Ford examined all facets of the settling of the West: from the perspective of the military itself in *Fort Apache* (1948), through the eyes of a crazed madman in *The Searchers*, from the perspective of Native Americans in *Cheyenne Autumn* (1964). By the time of *The Man Who Shot Liberty Valance* (1962) he was viewing the dark side of the coming of civilization, fully abandoning his optimism of *My Darling Clementine*. *The Man Who Shot Liberty Valance* emphasizes the hypocrisy and sham of the myth of the Western.

John Ford managed to make many of the best films ever to come out of Hollywood, and he managed to make some of the worst. Only by focusing on certain works, like those noted above, can we truly underline his greatness. But

Frank Capra's *It's a Wonderful Life* **(1946), starring James Stewart and Donna Reed.**

● ●

there remain questions. Why did he not have a more consistent output? Why did he make the turgid *Mogambo* (1953) or the indulgent *Wings of Eagles* (1957) before and after *The Searchers*? Certainly John Ford stands as an auteur of the highest order, but it remains for historical analysis to ferret out all the ambiguities and inconsistencies in his long career.

Frank Capra celebrated the common man caught up in a world he did not understand. Indeed Capra so honored the small-town American that his narrative form and themes have been labeled Capra-corn. Upon close examination, the Capra canon reveals a director who skillfully used actors (Jimmy Stewart and Gary Cooper) and formulated narratives with an ideological understanding of America that even, the most cynical could not resist. During the 1930s and 1940s Capra constantly pulled and tugged the heartstrings of American moviegoers.

His initial hit, *It Happened One Night* (1934), is the story of a runaway heiress befriended by a self-confident, even cocky, journalist who at first only wants her story but by the film's close ends up marrying her. The celebration of middle class values and the blending of the rich and poor set up fundamental narrative parameters which would endure in Capra's films for twenty years. Whether it was *Mr. Smith Goes to Washington* (1939), *Meet John Doe* (1941), or *It's a Wonderful Life* (1946),

Orson Welles' *The Magnificent Ambersons* **(1942), featuring Tim Holt.**

the Capra hero was able to convince the cynics of the world that simple values and true friendship are what count, not wealth and fame.

This theme receives its darkest treatment in *It's a Wonderful Life*. The film's title is misleading, with the happy ending more ironic than optimistic. The hero's (Jimmy Stewart) joyous reunion with his family and friends in the end caps a film of pain and despair; his fulfillment of the American dream hangs by a bare thread. He has missed out on going to war, making a fortune, and traveling around the world. But somehow he is told that, without him, all the small town glories of trust and friendship would have never come about. The ambiguity of the American dream received one of its most bril-

liant renderings in a film first seen by men and women who had just spent four long years fighting World War II.

Not all the successful and talented Hollywood directors of the Studio Era learned their craft on the job as did Hawks, Ford, and Capra. A good number came from outside the system, generally from the New York stage.

Orson Welles came from a world of radio and the stage. Although he was able to make precious few films during the Studio Era, his first, *Citizen Kane* (1941), has come to rank among the most lauded of Hollywood's Golden Age. Yet through the remainder of the 1940s, largely because of his fabled battles with studio chiefs, Welles directed only *The Magnificent*

Ambersons (1942, released in a truncated form) and *The Lady from Shanghai* (1948). In these films Welles seems obsessed with understanding the relationships between power and the powerful. (Possibly the subject fascinated him so much because he so misunderstood Hollywood's use of power.) In his handful of great films, certainly in *Citizen Kane* and *The Magnificent Ambersons*, Welles explored how an egotistical man tried to live outside the law, above society, or both. These figures were not innocent, but seemed to be haunted by an innocence lost in a bygone era.

To explore the ambiguity of the world faced by these characters, Welles pushed and tugged at the bounds of the Classic Hollywood Narrative, never quite breaking the norms, but certainly never fully accepting them. In the end, his complex use of deep space, matte work, and camera movement in *Citizen Kane* and *The Magnificent Ambersons* provided Hollywood with a "new look," but not one so radical that Hollywood could not release these films and make money from them. Welles ought also to be given credit for exploring all possibilities of film sound, especially the complex relationship of his own voice as the omniscient narrator and the moody, dark tones of the music of Bernard Herrmann.

The European film industry provided yet another type of directoral training ground. Alfred Hitchcock, from England, and Fritz Lang, from Germany, provide two examples of talented filmmakers who learned and perfected their directorial skills abroad but then came to Hollywood to do their best work.

Alfred Hitchcock directed a body of Hollywood films which deal in some way with the act of looking at and re-seeing the world. His characters, in film after film, seem to be caught up in situations they do not understand and

spend a good deal of the story trying to make sense of a complex, mixed-up world. In the process of working out a "happy ending," Hitchcock carefully led viewers into his web through intricate narrative plotting and skillful use of temporal, spacial, rhythmic, and graphic editing. His editing flourishes (such as the shower scene in *Psycho*, or the plane threatening Roger Thornhill in *North by Northwest*) represent the best of Hollywood's use of Classic Narrative techniques of continuity editing. But Hitchcock also paid careful attention to sound and hired Bernard Herrmann to compose and orchestrate *The Birds* (1963), including all its special noises and the shrieks of the birds themselves.

Hitchcock constructed unified (even overdetermined) narratives, constantly reworking plot twists and character identification. In *Shadow of a Doubt* (1943), one of Hitchcock's favorite themes, that of the double, is expressed through a plot in which one character "transfers" guilt to another. Similarly in *Strangers on a Train* (1951) one character takes on traits of another so that the question of the identity of a murderer falls into doubt. In both films Hitchcock employed film noir mood lighting to underscore the ambiguity between the guilty and the innocent. In the end, the ultimate voyeur, the movie audience itself, has trouble distinguishing the seemingly clear-cut oppositions of good and evil.

On a more general level, Hitchcock's dramas of visual exchange spill over into a theme of obsession with guilt and paranoia. By including the audience in this interchange, Hitchcock forces moviegoers to acknowledge heretofore unrecognized moral ambiguities. Contemporary critics take this analysis one step further, using psychoanalytical concepts to argue that Hitchcock's work is exemplary of a cinema of voyeurism and scopophilia (the

Alfred Hitchcock's *Shadow of a Doubt* **(1943),**
starring Joseph Cotton.

Freudian drive to look). The male gaze (by characters, Hitchcock, and spectators) predominates, thus raising questions of the place of women in Hitchcock's cinema. Hitchcock's narratives always seem to be resolved in favor of the male, confirming the patriarchal ideology of the Hollywood film.

Fritz Lang worked as a screenwriter and director at the height of the German Expressionist film movement of the 1920s. Fleeing the Nazis in 1933, he made his way to Hollywood and steadily found work in the studios through the 1940s and beyond. It has often been asserted that we should embrace Lang's German work and dismiss the bulk of his Hollywood hack efforts. But upon re-examination it can be seen that Lang continued to use the Expres-

sionist style (with its emphasis on a complex manipulation of mise-en-scène) to create many a first-rate psychological thriller within the confines of Hollywood moviemaking.

In the Western *Rancho Notorious* (1952, starring Marlene Dietrich), Lang reworked the conventions of that genre, creating what some labeled the first fully realized adult Western. A self-reflexive film, its songs and fragmented episodic formula help draw the attention of the audience to the Western form as a particular, stylized type of filmic creation. Moreover, by borrowing elements from the thriller, Lang created a Western hero who, upon closer examination, functioned more as a hard-boiled detective following a trail of clues. His complex use of camerawork and mise-en-scène further

A publicity still from Fritz Lang's *The Big Heat* (1953), starring Lee Marvin and Glenn Ford.

• •

complicates this seemingly ordinary Western by constantly reminding those who know of Lang's origins in German Expressionist cinema.

The Big Heat (1953) offers viewers a familiar tale of a revengeful cop bringing the syndicate down. Because they murdered his wife and child, the film's central figure becomes obsessed, almost psychotic. Indeed, he becomes as evil in his methods as the men he is pursuing. A stylized mise-en-scène overwhelms the seemingly innocent world of the hero's suburban home and links him with the heavily shadowed, dappled world of the city. This blending of light and shadow clues us to Lang's dominant theme of a merger of good and evil. Morality, clear-cut as the film opens, seems ever so murky as the film comes to an end.

Other talented Europeans besides Hitchcock and Lang journeyed to Hollywood to make a significant impact as directors. For example, Billy Wilder and Ernst Lubitsch permanently took their place within the Hollywood system and made comedies from a slightly oblique perspective. Lubitsch's *Trouble in Paradise* (1932), *Design for Living* (1933), and *Ninotchka* (1939) defined a new style of sophisticated comedy. Wilder fled Nazi Germany, arriving in the movie colony in the mid-1930s. There he served an apprenticeship as a screenwriter (including on Lubitsch's *Ninotchka*), and in 1942 began a directorial career which included the film noir classic *Double Indemnity* (1944) and the cynical examination of Hollywood itself in *Sunset Boulevard* (1950).

Historians will long argue over which directors ought to be elevated to the status of auteur. Cases have been made for Frank Borzage, George Cukor, Otto Preminger, Preston Sturges, King Vidor, and Raoul Walsh. Certainly they and other candidates ought to be seriously considered as we begin to make sense of the filmmaker within the Hollywood studio system of the 1930s and 1940s. But there were also films being made outside of Hollywood during this time, and we ought to survey this important work.

outside the hollywood system

To most Americans of the 1930s and 1940s, Hollywood films defined the entire world of the cinema. Yet we ought not ignore filmmakers who struggled to establish a different framework for making movies. All had to operate outside the Hollywood system, seeking funds from nontraditional sources, releasing films to be shown in only a handful of theatres, or more likely in a union hall, or a school basement. Little fame or acclaim came their way, but documentary and experimental filmmakers of the 1930s and 1940s did offer a distinct alternative to the Classic Hollywood cinema.

Filmmakers operating outside the mainstream can be clustered into two categories. On the one hand, there were the documentary filmmakers, who recognized the power of the cinema to record reality and sought to take full advantage of this unique trait. Further outside the Hollywood mainstream were a group of renegade artists, who argued that the potential of motion pictures went far beyond an ability to record reality. Avant-garde or experimental filmmakers saw in the cinema the power to create a vision of the world unlike that available through the traditional means of artistic expression.

• documentary films •

Hollywood did produce films of reality in its weekly, highly entertaining newsreels and in the interpretative "March of Time" series of exposés. Begun in 1935, "March of Time" presented the news behind the headlines. Producer Louis de Rochemont, a veteran of *Time* magazine, sought to combine the strengths of Hollywood's visuals with journalism's interest in headlines. Each monthly entry of the series took a point of view, usually in line with its parent, *Time* magazine. Moving past traditional standards of documentary filmmaking, events were re-created so that players on the world stage could be seen acting out events crucial to contemporary history.

The voice-of-God narrator, Westbrook van Voorhis, underlined and added cohesiveness to what were dramas of history. While *Time* founder and Republican stalwart Henry Luce insisted upon repeated examinations of the presidency of Franklin D. Roosevelt (for example, *Story of the White House*, 1936), there also were in-depth examinations of American demigods (*Huey Long*, 1935, and *Father Coughlin*, 1935), and the evils of Fascist Germany (*Inside Nazi Germany*, 1938).

To counteract this Hollywood view of the proper role of the documentary film, during the late 1930s a group of liberal and progressive filmmakers formed Nykino, and undertook a series known as "The World Today." Far less well-known than "March of Time," "The World Today" did lead to an important development in the history of American documentary filmmaking. From Nykino came the Frontier Film Group, which sought more than an alteration of public opinion. The Frontier Group wanted to change the world. However, their films espousing radical action never had more than limited distribution and exhibition.

But during the late 1930s and early 1940s, prior to America's entry in World War II, Frontier Films did demonstrate that it was possible to craft powerful statements on film about the economic ills brought on by the Great Depression. Their films were even bold enough to suggest solutions to fundamental economic problems. The Frontier Film Group also proffered two analyses on film of the Spanish civil war (*Heart of Spain* and *Return to Life*, both

1937), a look at organizing efforts in the Tennessee mountains (*People of the Cumberland*, 1938), and a sympathetic treatment of a major auto strike (*United Action*, 1939).

Most observers reserve their greatest praise for the final work of Frontier Film, Paul Strand and Leo Hurwitz's *Native Land*, released in 1942. Contrasting the freedom promised by the United States' Constitution with the struggles of American labor during the 1930s, Strand and Hurwitz concentrated on four segments of American society: the midwestern farm, the urban metropolis, the southern small town, and the industrial city. With Strand's somber lighting, constantly moving camera, and ironic juxtapositions created through the editing added to the booming tones of Paul Robeson's spoken narration, *Native Land* was able to indict U.S. society as a whole but no one person in particular. *Native Land* celebrates the downtrodden at the expense of the rich and powerful.

The late 1930s was a heyday for radical activity in the United States, but the national unity demanded by the outbreak of the Second World War put an end to criticism. In addition, sources of funding completely dried up. Thus in 1942 the Frontier Film Group disbanded. The experience proved that documentary filmmaking in the United States needed a steady source of funds, which would be available on a regular basis only from the United States government, an institution hardly interested in the radical analysis of the country's problems.

The federal government had come to documentary filmmaking through the back door. Agencies like the Post Office, the Department of Agriculture, the Office of Education, and the U.S. Army had long used films to recruit and train workers and to spread the message of their accomplishments. These films were seen as simple extensions of what had previously been accomplished through speeches, the written word, and photography. But the emergency of the Great Depression led the administration of President Franklin D. Roosevelt to begin to consider the use of documentary films to inform the populace of the fundamental problems of the day, tender analysis, and then offer Roosevelt administration programs as the solution.

In 1935 President Roosevelt created the Resettlement Administration to help America's farmers. Roosevelt adviser Rexford Tugwell became its initial administrator. Tugwell set up an elaborate information bureau to convince the public of the need for such programs. Roy Stryker, Dorthea Lange, and Walker Evans provided photographic evidence of the plight of the farmer. Pare Lorentz sought to accomplish even more with motion pictures. Tugwell hired Lorentz, a former movie critic, precisely because of his background as a journalist. Lorentz had no experience making movies, so he hired Ralph Steiner, Paul Strand, and Leo Hurwitz, all of Frontier Films, as cameramen. Lorentz scripted the initial effort, *The Plow That Broke the Plains* (1936), and thus began the creation of what most consider the first true documentary backed by the U.S. government.

In the fall of 1935 Lorentz, Steiner, Strand, and Hurwitz toured the American Midwest capturing the thousands of feet of footage necessary to flesh out Lorentz's script. Virgil Thompson penned the music for the film. *The Plow That Broke the Plains* premiered in Washington, D.C. in May 1936. Lorentz wanted to convince the powerful men and women of the nation's capital to push the distribution of this film beyond the usual circuit of army posts, naval vessels, Civilian Conservation Corps

***Native Land* (1942), a documentary about the struggles of American Labor.**

• •

camps, Sunday schools, universities and colleges, and women's clubs.

The stumbling block was Hollywood ownership of America's movie theatres. The moguls of the film industry saw no need to play "Washington propaganda" in their movie theatres, and so the most publicly visible presentation of *The Plow That Broke the Plains* came in a handful of specialized theatres in America's largest cities (for example, the Fine Arts in Boston and the Little Theatre in Washington) and in several circuits in the Midwest, which presented the film as a show of local pride. Still *The Plow That Broke the Plains* did prove that the government could create a documentary film on a social problem such as the plight of farmers.

A second Lorentz effort, *The River* (1937), followed. This poetic story of how run-off eventually made its way to the Mississippi River hailed the Tennessee Valley Authority (TVA) as the solution to constant flooding and the lack of electricity, two problems which plagued rural

America of the 1930s. In eleven segments, by careful repetition, Lorentz built a case for the necessity of the TVA. The river builds from drops of rain into a mighty force of economic and social power. By the fourth section of the film, the problems that too much water has caused in the past are depicted, showing good comes from the river but so do flooding and erosion. The TVA can prevent this, the audience is told at the film's end, as well as provide cheap electrical power. By the end of *The River*, dams successfully harness the water, and to the swelling strains of Virgil Thompson's music, the narrator celebrates the effectiveness of government action.

The success of *The Plow That Broke the Plains* and *The River* backfired. Republicans throughout the country opposed to President Roosevelt questioned the government's entry into the movie business. "Doesn't the federal government have anything better to do than make movies?" many sarcastically asked. The Roosevelt administration toned down its efforts and had the United States Film Service return to limited scale, neutral training and educational films that were not intended for widespread use or impact.

It would take another crisis—the Second World War—to again spark the interest of the United States government in documentary filmmaking. After Pearl Harbor, impressed with the achievements of Nazi and British film programs, American military and civilian authorities reasoned that perhaps motion pictures might be used to inform the people and assist in the conversion to a war society and economy. The films were made primarily for presentation to government workers and employees, but some were made to be distributed to the general public.

The United States military, not surprisingly, proved to be the largest user of movies during the Second World War. Training films accompanied recruits through every step of their careers in the military: induction, training, combat, overseas living, demobilization, and preparation for re-entry into a postwar world. These films, as had been true of past government films, proved to be no more than routine information texts that showed how to best dress or how to use a training manual.

But there were exceptions. Carlton Moss and Stuart Heisler's *The Negro Soldier* (1944) tried to tell of the importance of blacks in American culture, of course overlooking the racial segregation which then existed in the United States. This U.S. Army–sponsored documentary directly advocated racial harmony. Late in 1942 the Army had determined to make a film to deal with deteriorating race relations in and around southern posts where whites viewed black soldiers with a great deal of suspicion. In addition, white officers needed to reinforce the common goal to fight an enemy abroad.

Unhappy with the initial script by Marc Connelly, the author of Hollywood's *The Green Pastures*, Army authorities turned to Moss, a young black working in the Federal Theatre project. Veteran Hollywood screenwriters Ben Hecht and Jo Swerling softened the original script, and yet another Hollywood veteran, Stuart Heisler, under Frank Capra's supervision, directed. The film celebrated black pride, presenting boxer Joe Louis besting German Max Schmeling, black heroes helping win the Revolutionary War, and Booker T. Washington, George Washington Carver, and Jesse Owens moving to the top of their respective professions. The overall message was so mild that even southern whites could approve. *The Negro Soldier* proved that, when motivated, the white-dominated institutions of the United States could deal, if blandly, with African-American history.

One series of compilation films (films assembled from available footage in the same fashion as an edited book of essays) stood out for the power of its argument and its impact on its soldier audiences: Frank Capra's seven installments of "Why We Fight." Compiled by talent on leave from Hollywood, these seven one-hour films explained why and how the United States became involved in a global war. From 1942 through 1944 (in order) came *Prelude to War*, *The Nazis Strike*, *Divide and Conquer*, *The Battle of Britain*, *The Battle of China*, *The Battle of Russia*, and *War Comes to America*. "Why We Fight" stressed the rise of the threats from abroad (principally the Germans), the major battles of the war, and, in the final edition, the impact of the war on the citizens of the United States.

Prelude to War (1942) opened the series by directly answering the question of why America was in the war. Contrasting a free world (the Allies) with the slave world (the Axis), the film integrated captured footage of the atrocities with newsreel footage positively portraying life in the United States. In sequence after sequence, Capra (assisted by editor William Hornbeck), using techniques of the Classic Hollywood cinema, contrasted the destruction of churches with the free worship of Americans, the terror abroad with the peace at home. *Prelude to War*, and those installments which followed, produced a simple but effective message: it's either us or them. Hitler was represented as the villain the United States Armed Forces must conquer. Indeed, the soldiers who saw these films were made to feel part of the narrative, inspired to go out and function as a member of the heroic army.

But the United States government sponsored more than films to inspire and train the troops. Hollywood veterans ventured into the field and helped record footage of Allied victories. Director John Ford's *The Battle of Midway* (1942) celebrated that Pacific triumph, underscored by the narration of Hollywood stars Donald Crisp, Jane Darwell, and Henry Fonda. Ford's boss in civilian life, Twentieth Century–Fox production chief Darryl F. Zanuck, supervised *At the Front in North Africa* (1943). Director John Huston, in a rare color effort, filed his *Report from the Aleutians* (1943) about the missions of an isolated bomber squadron, and then moved on to tell the story of *The Battle of San Pietro* (1945).

• experimental cinema •

Experimental or avant-garde cinema stood in stark contrast to the Classic Hollywood cinema. The artists who created these films strove to work "underground" and purposely sought to shock and disturb their audiences, to defy conventional values, and to cause viewers to examine their lives and ideologies in a way that modernists in the other arts had been doing since the turn of the century. They saw the single artist, rather than the studio, as the proper creator of cinema.

Amateur 16mm equipment, introduced during the 1920s, had gradually become cheaper, lighter, and more portable. The need of the military during World War II to film battles fostered the introduction of universally available, inexpensive 16mm cameras and projectors. The experimental filmmaker, then, could plan a short film, shoot it with a handful of friends, edit it into its final version, and through a net-

Robert Florey and Gregg Toland's *The Life and Death of 9413—A Hollywood Extra* (1928), an early experimental film.

● ●

work of fellow film enthusiastists offer it for rent to museums and schools throughout the United States. More often than not, the filmmaker would accompany the film to viewings held at specialized film societies or in college auditoriums.

There was precious little funding for an American avant-garde film in the 1920s. Still filmmakers did produce the beginnings of a movement. In 1928 Robert Florey directed and Gregg Toland photographed *The Life and Death of 9413—A Hollywood Extra* in which, in nonnarrative fashion, they satirized America's obsession with Hollywood. Ralph Steiner made H_2O in 1929 to rhythmically examine the shapes and textures of ordinary water. Florey and Toland then went west to Hollywood, and Steiner started Frontier Films.

The equipment requirements of sound movies and the drying up of funds because of the Great Depression eliminated budding interest in the avant-garde cinema. Serious filmmakers, inspired by the plight of the poor, concentrated on documentary efforts. Not until 1943, with prosperity and cheap cameras, did a new era of avant-garde filmmaking in the United States commence. Maya Deren and Alexander Hammid's *Meshes of the Afternoon* (1943) is usually credited with beginning this revival. A nightmare of terror, this film does have a loose narrative structure but certainly does not follow the rules of Classic Hollywood Narrative filmmaking. After the war, in Los Angeles, three more filmmakers—Kenneth Anger, Curtis Harrington, and Gregory Markopoulos—began to turn out experimental films: Anger's *Fireworks* (1947), Markopoulos' *Psyche* (1947–48), and Harrington's *Fragment of Seeking* (1946).

Documentary filmmakers and avant-garde cineastes hardly presented the sole alternatives to Classic Hollywood filmmaking. Filmmakers in France, Britain, and Germany would fashion the first art films of the sound era, motion pictures far different from those coming out of Hollywood. The pre-World War II cinema of France, Great Britain, and Nazi Germany are the subjects of the following chapter.

8

• •

pre–world war II alternatives to hollywood: france, britain, and germany

Filmmakers in other countries were able to create and offer complex, exciting, distinctive cinema; the two most successful European cinemas emerged from France and the United Kingdom. French directors Jean Renoir and René Clair led their native film industry to a filmic glory recognized around the world before the coming of World War II. Producer Alexander Korda and director Alfred Hitchcock did the same for the British cinema. The Nazis in Germany revitalized propaganda filmmaking. Although other nations were able to nurture miniscule film industries, and lived under the thumb of Hollywood, in the 1930s and 1940s the French, British, and German film industries made the most noticeable contributions.

The coming of sound initiated a new cinematic era in Europe as elsewhere. All other film industries in the world trailed the American introduction of talkies by two to five years. The potential for a flood of new American talkies increased pressure on the European film industries to convert to sound as quickly as possible or lose their markets totally to Hollywood. To maintain its competitive edge, for a time in 1929 and 1930 Hollywood even produced German and French versions of features. By 1931 the American producers realized that films dubbed in foreign dialogue made just as much money, and cost far less than creating special versions. A year later American distributors standardized dubbing.

But before European film industries could convert to talkies, they argued about a standard technology. They could have adopted the American systems, either from Western Electric or the Radio Corporation of America (RCA), but they did not want to help these American allies of Hollywood. An alternative lay with a German system, Tri-Ergon. Executives from Tri-Ergon, which was owned by a German cartel, argued for continental unity. During late 1929 and early 1930 Tri-Ergon secured injunctions against Western Electric and RCA for patent infringement in the most important countries in Europe, effectively arresting the diffusion of sound.

After more legal threats and counterthreats, the American sound manufacturers and their Hollywood allies agreed to meet with Tri-Ergon and the top European film companies and negotiate. During July 1930 the parties huddled in Paris and decided to create a cartel. The Paris Agreement divided the world market into four parts. In Europe the Germans would have dominion. In the Americas Western Electric and RCA could compete without interference. In Britain the Americans and the Germans split the market—two-thirds for American firms and one-third for Tri-Ergon. The rest of the world was declared open territory. This agreement held until 1939, when the outbreak of the Second World War effectively erased all such international covenants.

Once the Paris Agreement had been signed, theatre owners in Europe raced to wire for sound to present Hollywood talkies as well as the handful which had been created in France, Britain, and Germany. Native industries throughout Europe scrambled to recapture their markets by appealing to national pride and by mocking Hollywood's inability to re-create dialogue in the correct accent. But quickly leaders of the major European film industries learned that Hollywood would not give up easily. During the 1930s no country was able to totally regain the screens of their native cinemas. Hollywood remained the dominant player.

As a consequence, as they had during the 1920s, the leaders of European film industries again turned for help from their governments. During the 1930s Great Britain, France, and Germany reaffirmed legal restrictions on the number of Hollywood films that could be shown in theatres within their respective countries. In France the Quota Commission required that one French film be produced before seven Hollywood films could be admitted into the country. The British law specified that exhibitors and distributors reserve a certain portion of screen time for native productions. The Germans required import permits.

The force of the restrictions never proved as crippling as European filmmakers would have liked. Throughout the 1930s Hollywood successfully exploited loopholes in the rules by enlisting the help of local theatre owners who stood to make huge profits showing Hollywood, not native, features. Filmmakers hoped talkies would "liberate" the film industries of Europe. As the Great Depression battered Europe, in the years before the Second World War, the French economy, to a major extent, and the British, to a lesser degree, stagnated.

Only the rearmament of Europe for World War II brought the economies (and movie business) back to life. But the boost in business was short-lived, for soon war was everywhere.

Throughout the continent cinemas shuttered as Germany conquered. As soon as the Nazis captured a nation, they re-opened cinemas only for "approved" (principally German) films. The British had to shut cinemas during the battle of Britain, but re-opened them once the tide turned, for Hollywood features. The British made precious few films themselves, using resources for war production. War-weary Britons appreciated the release moviegoing afforded and jammed the country's theatres.

In short, the Second World War had a significant impact on film production. By and large, European film industries closed down, but they did not completely give up. Censorship existed, but surprisingly a handful of significant films were made under the most trying of circumstances, including in France the celebrated *Children of Paradise* (1945). For their part, the Germans moved full speed ahead, producing both fiction and documentary fare in the service of the Nazi state. The British also kept some film production going and, during the war, created *Henry V* (1944) and *In Which We Serve* (1942).

france

France initiated a new era of filmmaking in 1928 when it instituted a quota law to help native producers survive the Hollywood juggernaut. In response, Hollywood (led by Will Hays) evoked a temporary boycott of French films. The Hollywood studios hoped to pressure French theatre owners who made so much money showing Hollywood films to, in turn, pressure to have the law watered down. The strategy worked. The French government passed an altogether weakened law. In October 1931 Hollywood talkies flowed into France in record numbers, generating howls of protest. Public debate ensued once again, and after nearly two years, in August 1933, the French instituted a ceiling on the number of Hollywood films which could be imported. Had the full effect of the law ever been felt it would have lowered the flow of American films into France by twenty-five percent. However, French lawmakers, again under pressure from theatre owners, had written in dozens of loopholes.

During the late 1920s, France ranked third in European filmmaking, behind Great Britain and Germany. The coming of sound, which many thought would benefit France because of its obsession with language purity, proved disastrous. To continue to cater to the French market, Hollywood began to produce "foreign versions" of its features at the rate of one per month. Rather than create these French versions in Hollywood, the major studios set up shop in a suburb of Paris.

In March, 1930 Paramount opened up its Joinville studio and installed Robert Kane, long a Paramount distribution representative in France, as head of operations. For the next twelve months Paramount shared the facility with other American companies and Joinville cranked out one hundred features and fifty shorts. The noted French director Julien Duvivier worked there, as did Hungarian expatriate Alexander Korda, who directed Marcel Pagnol's *Marius* (1931). But early in 1932, as Paramount teetered on the verge of bankruptcy in the United States, executives decided to close down Joinville's filmmaking activities and turn it into a dubbing facility to cheaply convert already-made Hollywood productions into fare acceptable for French audiences.

In 1929 Tobis-Klangfilm purchased a studio outside Paris, equipped it with Tri-Ergon sound equipment, and began to lease space and equipment to all comers. For its own productions Tobis-Klangfilm simultaneously created German and French versions of the same film, matching Hollywood's foreign versions. At the Tobis-Klangfilm complex French director René Clair directed his first talkies, including the widely admired *Sous les Toits de Paris* (1930) and *A Nous la Liberté* (1931). Clair's case offers a typical example of how the Europeans differentiated themselves from American efforts at Joinville. The Europeans concentrated on films aimed at the continental market, while Hollywood aimed for the world.

The French on their own could not really compete with Hollywood, but did manage to continue a marginal native industry. Pathé turned out less than a dozen films in 1930 and 1931, but in 1932, the year Joinville became a dubbing center, Pathé was able to increase to nearly twenty. Independent producers struggled as best they could. For example, Pierre Braunberger sponsored a number of films including Jean Renoir's *La Chienne* (1931).

France did not begin to suffer the ravages of the Great Depression until 1932. But once the Depression struck in France, it did not soon leave. The French economy would only, temporarily, come back to life in 1938 as the country began to re-arm for World War II; France did not achieve a complete recovery from the Great Depression until well after the end of the Second World War. Numbing economic stagnation was the order of the day, from 1932 onward.

The Popular Front government, elected in May of 1936, promised the best hope for recovery. Indeed, for its first few months in office (during the summer of 1936), the administration of Léon Blum seemed to be breaking the back of the economic downturn. The Blum government did bring a new sense of spirit to the French people and offered modest government assistance to the poor and unemployed. Hope for a better future sprang up in all parts of the economy; boxoffice receipts showed an upsurge. But by the spring of 1937 it had become clear to all observers that the Popular Front experiment had failed. The French economy returned to stagnation. French attendance at the cinema again fell.

On the production side the French seemed to be thriving. Since Paramount and Tobis-Klangfilm had in 1933 decreased their activities, French producers once again had a free run at expansion in their native land. In 1934 the French produced more than one hundred

A theatre on the Champs-Elysées in Paris, 1935. Note the narrow entry.

• •

films, a figure well above the 1929 total. They continued to produce between 110 and 130 features per annum until the war broke out.

Still, in 1936, the very year of the coming of the Blum government, financial adversity finally caught up to the pillars of film production. Pathé toppled, and rival Gaumont almost collapsed. Pathé, the largest company, fell because of a financial scandal. Bernard Natan had tried

to save his company through dubious financial maneuvers, but failed. Production came to a standstill. Gaumont survived, but only because of intervention by the government.

With the absence of these two former giant companies, the state of French film production could be best characterized as openly chaotic. Hundreds of companies were formed to make a single film; more often than not, they lost money and went out of business. Top talents such as Jean Renoir and Marcel Pagnol operated in this fashion. Fragmentation also existed in film distribution. Individual companies took on a handful of films, went into the red, and then went bankrupt. The lack of a centralized power crippled France's ability to sell its films abroad, especially in the United States, and made it easy for Hollywood distributors to appeal to profit-conscious French theatre owners.

The French film industry stagnated until 1938 when France began to prepare for war. The German invasion of Poland in 1938 signaled the beginning of hostilities. Between September 1938 and March 1939, the French mobilized twice. They would go to war in response to the signing of the German-Soviet non-aggression pact in August 1939. This wreaked havoc with all aspects of French society, including the film industry. Film production, by and large, shut down; Parisian theatres enacted an eight in the evening curfew. For eight months, during a "phony war," enemy armies camped on opposite sides of the border but did not engage in battle.

Film producers gradually went back to work. The civilian population (and the standing armies) wanted to be entertained. During this interlude the French government took direct command of filmmaking. The Service du Cinéma commissioned both feature-length fiction films and documentaries. The government banned all films (old or new) concerning pacifism (for example, Hollywood's *All Quiet on the Western Front*, 1930), films depressing or distressing to children, and all films which in any way could be seen as demoralizing to the military. "Pseudo-documentaries" (which intercut newsreel footage with staged sequences) underscored the evils of France's duel enemies: Hitler and Stalin.

In May 1940, bypassing the "invincible" Maginot line, the Germans poured across the borders into the Netherlands and Belgium. A little more than one month later the Germans marched into Paris. French filmmaking once again came to a halt; the filmmaking community, by and large, did not wait for what they felt would be a foregone decision. Instead they fled, usually to the United States. Director Max Ophuls, and actors Marcel Dalio and Jean-Pierre Aumont, all Jews, navigated the dual hazards of gaining a visa and passage to Hollywood. Directors René Clair and Julien Duvivier, and Michele Morgan, France's leading star, joined them. Noted American documentary filmmaker Robert Flaherty assisted Jean Renoir's escape.

The Germans quickly took over the French film industry. Less than three weeks after they had marched into Paris, the German military authority in France established a propaganda section to oversee the opening of theatres and ensure the presentation of German features and newsreels and the deletion of any faintly anti-German or pro-Allied material (including all Hollywood and British films). By the end of the summer of 1940 nearly all Paris theatres had re-opened under German control. The Germans lorded over the French cinema until the Allies retook Paris in August 1944.

Thus, the French film industry of the 1930s and early 1940s managed to survive a great deal, including (1) the coming of sound, (2) the Great Depression, (3) regularly changing governments, (4) the collapse of its major company, Pathé, and (5) the Second World War. Amidst all that flux the French managed to create many of the most important films of film history. Talented directors René Clair, Jean Vigo, Jean Renoir, and Marcel Carné thrust France into the forefront of world filmmaking.

René Clair had a distinguished career in the silent film, but it was his production of innovative features during the early sound period that placed him in the forefront of European film production. These films reveal Clair's particularly exciting way of manipulating the virgin medium of talkies. Hollywood had only begun to codify what would become the classic way to use sound; Clair took advantage of a changing Classic Hollywood Narrative style to explore an alternative practice for combining sound and image. Clair recognized that language, noises, and music had a power nearly equal to that of the image, and his early efforts are marked by his attempts to employ sounds and image together rather than have sounds simply support the story line. Clair sought counterpoint.

Sous les Toits de Paris (*Under the Roofs of Paris*, 1930) is a textbook of examples of how *not* to synchronize sound and image. Filmed entirely within a studio, Clair tells the story of two men in love with the same girl, Pola. He introduces his characters through song. The film's most famous sequence opens the film proper (after a prologue not shown in most current prints). Following a series of static views of the roofs of Paris, the camera pans across chimney tops then moves down a street, pulling up to Pola. We follow her as she leaves her house to hear a street singer (Albert) and his customers singing the title song of the movie. As the song continues, a pickpocket

René Clair's *Le Million* **(1931).**

● ●

works the crowd, and Albert (who turns out to be the other central character in the film) gestures to Pola (whom he will pursue through the film) that she is about to become a victim.

In the film, Clair consistently presents an object, but has the "wrong" sound connected with it. For example, the morning after Albert and Pola have shared his apartment, his alarm goes off. He reaches out to shut it off and instead touches his shoe. The alarm stops. We learn why when Clair cuts to Pola as she actually turns off the alarm.

Despite these innovations, the French critical community and filmgoing public did not embrace *Sous les Toits de Paris* upon release. Since Clair worked for a German company, the film also had a Berlin premiere. There the film was hailed as a masterwork. He moved to his next film, *Le Million* (1931), made largely with the same crew as *Sous les Toits de Paris*. *Le Million*, a musical, conveyed all its dialogue through song, introduced by a chorus of tradespeople who comment on the action even though they seem to have little to do with the actual narrative. (At times the chorus even expresses what is in a character's mind.)

Sometimes he would have the characters mime a situation to rhythmical accompaniment on the soundtrack. At times Clair went so far as to have figures move their lips in speech while viewers heard only music. The confrontation between Michel (the seeker of the lottery ticket) and local merchants (to whom he owes money) is rendered in choral music rather than spoken language.

Le Million proved a critical as well as a box-office success. Still working for Tobis-Klangfilm and with the same crew, Clair then directed *A Nous la Liberté* (*Liberty for Us*, 1931). In a more serious tone, he set out to explore the idea of industrial progress through a scenario, like *Le Million*, which blended music, satire, and farce. The studio found it too much a critique and almost did not let him make it. But at this point Clair ranked as the top director in France and had his way.

A Nous la Liberté is hardly a serious social manifesto. The film explores the lack of personal liberty in a modern industrial world. Clair depicts a mythical twentieth-century Europe in which freedom has become a meaningless word. The film centers on two characters who make a lot of money but eventually give it all up and go off to become hobos. In *A Nous la Liberté* Clair continued his complex use of sound and image but without any of the innovations of the earlier two films.

Jean Vigo made only four films before his tragic death at age 29 in 1934. He had been one of the pioneers of the ciné-club movement in France, and his first two films connect directly with the experimental movements of the 1920s. *A Propos de Nice* (1930), made with cinematographer Boris Kaufman, documented the resort city of Nice in some forty minutes. Funded

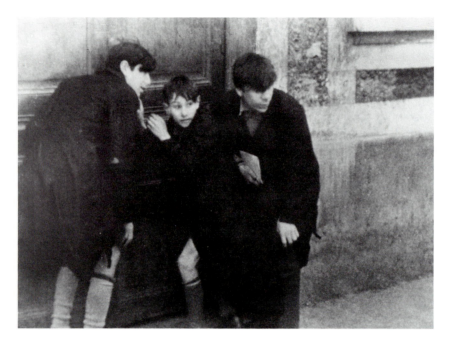

Jean Vigo's *Zero for Conduct* (1933).

• •

by Vigo's father-in-law, this film shocked those who expected a typical promotional travelog. Instead Vigo, the son of a murdered anarchist, depicted a city filled with death, overrun by gamblers, and filled with lifeless monuments and hideous cemeteries, a vision which reminded many of the Surrealists of the 1920s.

After *A Propos de Nice*, Vigo began combining his unique brand of Surrealism with what would come to be called poetic realism. With *Taris* (1931), a short documentary about a champion swimmer, Vigo took his camera underwater as the swimmer Taris clowned at the bottom of the pool and blew water at the lens. But this work, only eleven minutes in length, simply provided a preview of the two remark-

able films which would complete, sadly, this director's oeuvre.

Zéro de Conduite (*Zero for Conduct*, 1933) made Vigo's reputation. This independently produced, forty-four–minute film tendered an exposé of the horrors of the French school system. Hardly a polished narrative, *Zero for Conduct* consists of a series of fragmented fictional impressions of life at a French boarding school. Gradually the boys revolt and take over. The adults who run this school are all caricatures, including the undersized headmaster. The only sympathetic teacher, Huguet, does Chaplin imitations. A delightful, delicate, charming film, French authorities banned its showings until after the end of the Second World War. During the 1950s *Zero for Conduct* was carefully studied by the French New Wave.

Vigo shot his final work, *L'Atalante* (1934), while dying of tuberculosis. Remarkably, this film celebrates the human condition. Depicting the journey of a husband and wife on a barge, the film combines images of the harmony of marriage with the grimness of the Great Depression's unemployed and starving; it creates a poetry of realism. Michel Simon performs in its most vivid passages as an eccentric sailor. The most straightforward of Vigo's films, *L'Atalante* evokes a powerful response in viewers. The fact that it is Vigo's lone feature film does not lessen its status. Vigo pioneered poetic realism; Jean Renoir would make this style world famous.

Jean Renoir, the second son of the great French Impressionist painter, led France to cinematic glory. His style has been characterized as simultaneously lyric and realist. His films reveal a web of interrelationships between figure and space, material life and inner feeling. And these relationships seem to spill out of the frame, asking the viewer to question what is transpiring outside the range of the camera. Renoir seemed to want to explore the metaphysical side of our world through its details.

An obsession with lower-class life provided the thematic core of poetic realism. We see a dark world in which objects seem to overwhelm the characters. In film after film the decor creates the psychology of the hero. Indeed, poetic realism, as exemplified by the work of Renoir, suggested a new way to look at decor in the cinema. With the help of music and lyrical dialogue, poetic realism fashioned an ambience of metaphysical doom.

Jean Renoir discovered the cinema while convalescing from a battle wound during World War I. By 1924 he had directed his first film, *La Fille de L'Eau*, starring his wife Catherine Hessling. Acknowledging his influences (D. W. Griffith, Eric von Stroheim, and Charlie Chaplin), Renoir considered his retelling of the Emile Zola novel *Nana* (1926) his most important contribution to the silent cinema. However, during the 1930s Renoir created one masterwork after another.

Boudu Saved from Drowning (1932) presents the story of a tramp invading the home of a middle-class couple. Stylistically, through long takes, elongated camera movements, and careful use of deep space, Renoir was able to contrast character with action, action with character. Renoir constructed *Boudu Saved from Drowning* as a dialectic of life and nature. The film contrasts the natural freedom of the tramp Boudu with the bourgeois artifice of his host. Visually Renoir contrasts shots of sunlight on water with the artifice of the host's house filled with stuffed birds. To link nature and artifice, Renoir repeatedly framed shots through windows of the bourgeois house as they are constantly being opened to the natural world.

But in *Boudu Saved from Drowning* Renoir did not want to confront the implications of the dichotomy of nature and artifice. On the one hand, his comic mode enabled him to avoid the misery associated with the bourgeois lifestyle. On the other, Boudu never really represents a serious threat to the capitalist middle-class lifestyle. Renoir criticized through comedy but did not go so far as to offer a radical solution.

Le Crime de Monsieur Lange (*The Crime of M. Lange*, 1935) did offer a solution, and, in doing so, solidified Renoir's reputation as a director of the Left. In sympathy with the Popular Front government which was about to rise to

Jean Renoir's *The Crime of M. Lange* (1935).

power, Renoir tried to depict the lives and problems of the ordinary working man and woman. The narrative demonstrates how a cooperative enterprise (a publishing co-op) can, through united action, overcome the tyranny associated with capitalism.

To emphasize a sense of community, Renoir centers all the action of the film in a courtyard which is surrounded by the publishing company and the homes of the workers. The courtyard becomes a sort of stage. By the end of the film, characters who had formerly disagreed come together, a unity reflected in the style of editing and cinematography as well. In the beginning of the film, characters are shown in isolation, joined only through juxtaposed shots; by the film's close, they are grouped together in long takes in deep space. A celebration of

the human spirit with a touch of black humor, *The Crime of M. Lange* also directly attacks class superiority and prejudice. It honors the group effort, showing how united action can lead to a better world for all.

Renoir would then move to make directly political films. *La Vie Est à Nous* (*People of France*, 1936) came about because of the rise of the Popular Front government. In preparing for the May 1936 elections, the leaders of the French Communist party decided to commission a film. Having just finished *The Crime of M. Lange*, Renoir seemed the logical choice to direct. But the creation of *La Vie Est à Nous* was a cooperative effort. Jacques Brunius directed the newsreel sequences, Jean-Paul Le Chanois a factory sequence, and Jacques Becker an episode on the farm. Many who worked on the

Jean Renoir's *La Vie Est à Nous* **(1936).**

• •

film belonged to the French Communist party; most did not.

In the spirit of cooperation of the Popular Front, the crew and cast worked for free, supporting themselves with other jobs, and so with contributions, the film cost only one-tenth of the usual French feature. (The French Communist Party took up collections at its meetings.) Completed several weeks before the election of the Blum government, *La Vie Est à Nous* was more often than not shown (without credits) at political meetings and rallies held before the election. It premiered at the Bellevilloise Theatre, a movie house owned by the French Communist party, in a working-class district of Paris.

Conceived as a propaganda piece for an election, *La Vie Est à Nous* does not tell a story

per se but rather makes an argument. To present their case, the filmmakers combined documentary footage with staged scenes. The beginning presents images of the richness of France contrasted with the poverty of its population. A character tells us: "France does not belong to the French; France belongs to the two [richest] families." The images may be beautiful, with a texture of poetic realism, but no audience member would miss the film's message: The French people ought to do something about their suffering—elect a Popular Front government!

Renoir would make one more overtly political film before the coming of World War II: *La Marseillaise* (1938). While the camaraderie of the Popular Front still remained fresh, Renoir's friends on the Left dreamed of a spectacle

Jean Renoir's *La Grande Illusion* (1937).

• •

celebrating the people of France. Plans, supported by labor unions, called for finance by subscription. Millions were asked to contribute two francs to a project celebrating France. Even after the Blum government was toppled during the spring of the 1937, Renoir and his allies, with no direct government sponsorship, pressed on.

As with *La Vie Est à Nous*, actors and crew offered their time for free, but in the end the creators of this historical epic of the French Revolution were forced to appeal to bankers for loans and had to distribute it through traditional theatrical channels. Since the story of the French Revolution was so well known, Renoir structured *La Marseillaise* as a series of tableaux centered around a battalion from Marseilles and its famous song. *La Marseillaise*,

while celebrating the efforts of common men and women to change society, reworked the brilliant camera movements and realistic use of mise-en-scène so much a part of Renoir's work of the 1930s.

As the Second World War inexorably approached, Renoir felt compelled to fashion a rational appeal against war. For three years, while at work on other projects, he tried to interest producers in *La Grande Illusion*. Only when the major star of the French cinema, Jean Gabin, agreed to appear did backing come through. But probably the character in the film who is best known is the doomed German commander, Rauffenstein, played by Erich von Stroheim. Initially this was to be a small role, but when Renoir learned his idol von Stroheim was in France seeking to revitalize his career as an actor, Renoir eagerly hired him and expanded the part. By suggesting the iron corset and chin strap (to indicate the severity of the character) and by contributing bits of dialogue, von Stroheim gave the most famous performance of his life.

La Grande Illusion (1937) tells the story of French prisoners living in and then escaping from a German prisoner-of-war camp during the First World War. Renoir used this story to compare and contrast men who sought to uphold honor in the face of the horror and insanity of war. No one person could win in this situation; only the human spirit could triumph. Renoir's appeal for humanitarianism went unheeded. Joseph Goebbels, the Nazi minister of propaganda, referred to *La Grande Illusion* as "Cinematographic Enemy Number 1," and had the film banned.

Examining *La Grande Illusion* today we see a film that is more than a tract against war, but like Renoir's following film, *Rules of the Game* (1939), it is an examination of the fundamental structures of French society. On the formal level both have a similiar four-part structure, ending with a final segment which moves outdoors to a much quieter, more intimate scene. *La Grande Illusion*'s four parts develop a network of shifting relationships which at first emphasize difference but in the end present characters who overcome their seeming incompatibility of class and nationality. The French aristocratic officer, de Boeildieu, and the common worker, Maréchal, both prisoners of war, are linked by their nationality; the German commandant, Rauffenstein, and the French aristocrat by their class. When the French are captured and taken to the POW camp, a fourth major character, the Jew Rosenthal, is introduced. Stylistically the initial section of the film in the prisoner of war camp, through frequent use of windows,

stresses separation of men by class and nationality.

Rosenthal and Maréchal (Jean Gabin) escape because de Boeildieu sacrifices his life. The German commander Rauffenstein shoots his comrade because he, as the enemy, defies him. The proletarian and the nouveau riche Jew escape to a world in which the upper class is doomed, a favorite Renoir theme more complexly explored in *Rules of the Game*. *La Grande Illusion* tells of an escape to a new and different world, a society which may or may not be "better" than in the past.

Rules of the Game (1939) would prove to be the final film Renoir made before he left for the United States. He had formed his own independent production company, La Nouvelle Edition Française, for a project he planned to film in Technicolor. Shooting commenced in February 1939 in black and white; filming ended in May, 1939, less than a year before the Germans overran Renoir's native land.

The richness of *Rules of the Game* is, in part, due to abundant references to painting and theatre. The mood of the film, especially the celebrated hunt sequence, transports the viewer back to the scenery of Renoir's father's paintings; its acting style calls up French boulevard comedy. Renoir reasoned that the elegant form of eighteenth-century French comedy might serve as a suitable vehicle in which to comment on the expected collapse of Europe. The music also takes the viewer back to an earlier time. Indeed, Mozart's elegant, graceful music opens and closes the film.

Thematically *Rules of the Game* presents life as an ever-changing game, played by rules which never stand still. No one has the time to stand back and figure out what the world is really about. The story of the weekend in the country almost seems incidental. The film plays

Jean Renoir's *Rules of the Game* (1939).

on tensions and paradoxes and in the end celebrates humanity as the French nation braces at a crucial historical juncture, the end of one era and beginning of another.

Renoir's masterly organization of camera movements and his striking use of deep space orchestrate a swirling set of contrasts between an ensemble of characters. His mobile camera constantly seems to capture several characters in simultaneous foreground and background action. Figures enter and exit, seemingly transgressing the borders of the frame. Close-up and point-of-view shots rarely attract attention away from this multiplicity of action and movement. The beautifully edited hunt sequence, humans taking up violence for pleasure, stands apart

because of its rapid rhythmic editing and brutal reality of defenseless rabbits dying.

When *Rules of the Game* opened in two Parisian theatres in July 1939 audiences booed and critics groaned. Renoir cut the film from 113 minutes to 85 minutes, but it was eventually banned by the French censors as too demoralizing and withdrawn from circulation. Renoir's company went bankrupt, and he fled, to work for the American film industry during World War II.

Marcel Carné remained in France and led a limited "French" film industry during the Second World War. The coming of the war ended whatever glories the French cinema could hope to obtain. The depressed economy of the 1930s

Marcel Carné's *Quai des Brumes* (1938), starring Jean Gabin.

• •

was one thing, occupation by the Germans another. French filmmakers struggled as best they could. Two hundred films were produced under the most trying of circumstances. One quite remarkable film, Carné's *Children of Paradise* (1945), would be made.

Marcel Carné received training in film direction as an assistant to René Clair on *Sous les Toits de Paris*. During the years immediately before the outbreak of the Second World War, he established a collaboration with leftist poet-screenwriter Jacques Prevert. The pair hit their stride with *Quai des Brumes* (*Port of Shadows*, 1938), *Hôtel du Nord* (1938), and *Le Jour se Lève* (*Daybreak*, 1939). These three films represent the best in French studio filmmaking,

with a deeply felt sense of realism, scripts filled with witty dialogue, and noted players Jean Gabin, Michele Morgan, Michel Simon, and Arletty. Here were popular films à la Hollywood—with a French twist.

Carné and Prevert stressed themes of fatalism and melancholy, stylistically fashioned in ever-present shadows. *Quai des Brumes* takes place in a modern (non-specific) port city which seems ever shrouded in shadow and fog. We follow Gabin from his arrival to his death. *Le Jour Se Lève* continued the theme of bitter-sweet fatalism, dark tone, and drab settings. (The parallel to the mood of pre–World War II France, awaiting an almost certain defeat, has often been drawn, and seems, indeed, hard to avoid.) In the opening seconds of *Le Jour Se Lève* a man is shot, and the killer (Jean Gabin again) barricades himself in his attic room. Through a long night he recalls (in flashback) the events which led up to the crime. As dawn breaks, the police assault, and a final shot is heard. A cloud of tear gas creeps over the lifeless body bathed in the rays of a rising sun.

Le Jour Se Lève was banned under the Vichy regime as too fatalistic. As a consequence Prevert and Carné took on a new style to work within the Nazi system. They continued within the studio, but left behind the urban gloom to fashion elaborate theatrical spectacle. The medieval fable of *Les Visiteurs du Soir* (*The Devil's Envoy*, 1942) proved a big hit with Frenchmen worried at a dark moment in history. But the duo's masterwork, *Les Enfants du Paradis* (*Children of Paradise*), proved to be one of the more ambitious undertakings in the history of the French cinema. Running three hours, *Children of Paradise* is set in nineteenth-century worlds of Parisian boulevard theatre and petty crime. The film was shot entirely at the Studios de la Victorine in Nice with whatever plaster, nails, and wood could be scrounged to create a set five hundred feet in height. Shooting was interrupted in 1944 by the Allied recapture of France and was completed at Joinville outside of Paris.

Children of Paradise is a tribute to the theatre. Two of the main characters, based on historical figures, are men of the stage: pantomimist Debureau and the ambitious romantic actor Frédéric Lemaître. Their meeting ground, near the Parisian theatre Funambules (also known as the Boulevard of Crime because of its numerous unsolved thefts and murders), brings them together with the ruthless criminal Lacenaire and the beautiful actress Garance.

Children of Paradise moves effortlessly from tragedy to humor to passion, and has, since World War II, represented the best of French cinema struggling against the Nazi occupation.

There were other directors working in France in the 1930s, two of whom stand out.

Julien Duvivier created *Poil de Carotte* in 1932. He had worked in the silent cinema and, indeed, directed a silent version of *Poil de Carotte* in 1925. But this story of an unloved red-haired boy was far more successful as a talkie. Realistic and scathingly honest, it depicts the animal instincts of children with a cutting edge that was in sharp contrast to the popular Hollywood image of the child-as-angel. Between 1932 and 1937 Duvivier directed ten films; he was one of the stalwarts of the French cinema. He reworked *Le Golem* in 1936; he directed *La Belle Equipe* (1936) in the spirit of the Popular Front government; he made *Pépé-Le-Moko* (1937) in the same style and theme of the best work of Carné and Prevert. In *Pépé-Le-Moko* Jean Gabin's performance established him as a star, the desolate individualist living outside the law.

Jacques Feyder reached the pinnacle of his fame in 1935 with the release of *La Kermesse Héroïque* (*Carnival in Flanders*). For this farce set in 1616, Feyder studied the paintings of the Flemish and Dutch masters of the period. Then he and set designer Lazarre Meerson spent six months supervising the re-creation of Boom, a village in Antwerp. In the comic narrative, loosely based on *Lysistrata*, the women save the town from possible Spanish plunder after their weak husbands offer no resistance. The film proved a great hit throughout Europe and won prizes at the Venice Film Festival and from the New York Film Critics.

• • • • • • • • • • • • • •

great britain

• • • • • • • • • • • • • •

The cinema industry of the British Isles provides a second example of the glories of European film of the 1930s and 1940s. Given the common language and heritage, the American film during the silent era had made significant inroads into the British market. British producers suffered, but theatre owners did not, making millions of pounds by regularly projecting Hollywood films. A crisis finally arose in 1926. Nationalists demanded that the government do something to protect the country from the Hollywood invasion, to save filmmaking in Great Britain. In 1927 Parliament passed the Cinematograph Films Act, which required that a quota of British films be screened.

In 1928 Hollywood brought the first talkies to Britain. Warner Bros. exported *The Jazz Singer* (1927) and *The Singing Fool* (1928) to London. Like audiences in the United States, British film patrons loved them, and British theatre owners scrambled to wire their cinemas. Then the Great Depression struck, lowering attendance at British movie houses. In addition, because of religious pressure throughout 1931, cinemas were forced to close on Sundays, thwarting attendance on a crucial day of the week. In 1932 a new law was passed allowing local choice regarding Sunday closure. In London, movie theatres opened immediately; in Scotland and Wales only a handful of theatre

owners were willing to open and buck protests by religious zealots. After the initial decline, cinema-going shot back up and remained steady as the British economy gradually recovered during the 1930s. Oscar Deutsch commenced building his Odeon chain of art deco super cinemas ("movie palaces"). Thus, the finest, most ornate theatres were constructed in Great Britian during the 1930s, not the 1920s as was the case in the United States.

With protection and new theatres, the British experienced a Golden Age of filmmaking. Production increased to fill the new super cinemas, and profits grew. But British film producers were unable to find a way to expand abroad, particularly into the United States. Hollywood, through its theatre ownership, never permitted the widespread presentation of British films in the United States. The British film industry had expanded as far as it could on its own isles, a very limited home market. This became evident in 1937 when, buoyed with success, British producers had taken on too much debt. As a result, Twickenham studios went bankrupt, and the most successful producer, Alexander Korda, had to order salary cuts at his London Films.

The short-lived Golden Age of British filmmaking ended in 1938, but once again the government came to the film industry's rescue. A

Goodbye Mr. Chips **(1939), starring Robert Donat.**

1938 renewal of the Cinematograph Films Act strengthened the effectiveness of import restrictions, and Hollywood moved in to make "British" films to meet new quota standards. MGM's British subsidiary, in particular, sought to create features bookable even in U.S. theatres. Two efforts, *A Yank at Oxford* (1938), starring Robert Taylor, Maureen O'Sullivan, and Lionel Barrymore, and *Goodbye, Mr. Chips* (1939), starring Robert Donat and Greer Garson, accomplished the assigned goal, but in 1939 the coming of the Second World War soon ended MGM's experiment.

With the outbreak of war in 1940, the British government closed all cinemas to avoid the possibility of a bomb falling on a crowded theatre. But the citizenry protested, and in short time theatres reopened. (No new theatres were built during the war, and by the close of the war 5 percent of the cinemas had been destroyed by German bombs.) Everywhere exterior lights were shut off to avoid detection by German bombers. Despite these restrictions, the movies took on a central place in British life during the Second World War, and as a consequence attendance increased dramatically, reaching a peak of thirty million patrons per week by 1945.

During the war, British film production was cut back. The war effort siphoned needed supplies, so the number of active studios fell from twenty-two to nine. Some shut down altogether and were turned into warehouses; others switched to the production of training or propaganda films. Feature production, nearly two hundred films per year during the mid-1930s, fell to less than fifty by 1942, but these were prestige pictures such as Noel Coward's *In Which We Serve* (1942), Laurence Olivier's *Henry V* (1944), and David Lean's *Blithe Spirit* (1945).

• the golden age of the 1930s •

The 1930s would prove to be a vital and vibrant period for British filmmaking. In November 1931 a young Hungarian producer, Alexander Korda, arrived in London with a contract to direct two films for Paramount; a year later he formed his own company, London Films. With his younger brothers, Vincent, who became a noted director in his own right, and Zoltan, an art director, Alexander Korda began producing "quota quickies," films made on a shoestring by Britains to meet legal screening requirements in British theatres, which really wanted to show only Hollywood fare. Korda discovered while creating these cheap films two stars, Merle Oberon and Robert Donat, who went on to become two of the biggest names in the British studio system of the 1930s.

By 1933 Korda began an effort to go big time. His initial production, *The Private Life of Henry VIII*, starred Charles Laughton along with Donat and Oberon. Costing only sixty thousand pounds, *The Private Life of Henry VIII* quickly grossed more than eight times that amount. Korda was proclaimed the new genius of British film, and the Prudential Assurance Company (an insurance company in the United States) stepped forward to bankroll him. Korda built a studio at Denham and produced more costume epics including *The Scarlet Pimpernel*

(1935) starring Leslie Howard and Raymond Massey, and *Rembrandt* (1936) starring Charles Laughton.

Alexander Korda alone did not engineer the renaissance of the British cinema during the early 1930s. Michael Balcon, head of production at Gaumont-British, achieved his greatest successes during the same period with a string of musicals starring Jessie Matthews: *Evergreen* (1934), *First a Girl* (1935), and *Head Over Heels* (1937). More significantly, in 1934 Balcon lured Alfred Hitchcock away from British International Pictures to direct two British films which would make Hitchcock (and the British cinema) world famous: *The Man Who Knew Too Much* (1934) and *The Thirty-Nine Steps* (1935). More than any filmmaker in Britain of the 1930s, Hitchcock created motion pictures which appealed to audiences both in Britain and throughout the rest of the world.

Alfred Hitchcock had begun working in the British film industry in the early 1920s. His first job had been to write intertitles for silent films. Hitchcock directed his first feature, *The Pleasure Garden*, in 1925. Indeed, through the late 1920s, into the coming of sound, and up to the beginning of the Golden Age of the British film of the 1930s, Hitchcock completed an on-the-job apprenticeship, mastering the Classic Hollywood Narrative style by working in a number of different genres, and learning to work within strict budgets.

In 1934, as the British film industry began to enter its Golden Age, Hitchcock moved to the forefront of his craft with *The Man Who Knew Too Much*. Knowing Hitchcock's proven track record producer Michael Balcon offered him a virtual carte blanche. *The Man Who Knew Too Much* established the Hitchcock style the world would come to love and admire. A relatively short (eighty-four minutes), tightly woven narrative, this first version (a Hollywood remake came in 1956) included a generous portion of Hitchcockian black humor and the requisite amount of suspense. In the gripping climax, a diplomat is almost shot during a concert in the Albert Hall. It is a sequence of great tension, as an ordinary family is drawn into global conflict only by being in the wrong place at the wrong time.

The Thirty-Nine Steps (1935) made Hitchcock an international celebrity. Its pacing set it apart from other thrillers of the era, holding the attention of its audiences throughout the entire eighty-one minutes while the hero (Robert Donat) works himself out of a web of events he does not fully understand. (On the strength of this role Robert Donat became the biggest star of British film.) In fact, *The Thirty-Nine Steps* proved too popular; it led to Hollywood successfully wooing Hitchcock to California. He completed the requirements of his British contract with the films *The Secret Agent* (1936), *Sabotage* (1936), *Young and Innocent* (1937), *The Lady Vanishes* (1938), and *Jamaica Inn* (1939). In 1939 he signed a contract with David O. Selznick.

Cary Grant, Alfred Hitchcock, and Ingrid Bergman.

• •

• the coming of war •

The economic depression which hit the British film industry in 1937 ended the Golden Age, but not filmmaking. Relying on European talent which had fled Hitler, Alexander Korda somehow continued to turn out big budget films, but without the measure of success he had in previous years. Jacques Feyder directed *Knight Without Armour* (1937), for example. Producer Gabriel Pascal was able to persuade George Bernard Shaw to permit his play *Pygmalion* to be filmed. Anthony Asquith and Leslie Howard directed; Howard also played Professor Higgins, and Wendy Hiller played Eliza Doolittle. For Shaw's *Major Barbara* (1941) Pascal produced and directed. Michael Balcon took over the Ealing studio; directors Michael Powell and Carol Reed began careers which after the war would bring glory to the British screen.

With the inevitability of the second major European war of the twentieth century, at first the British film industry wished to remain neutral and not deal with the Nazi menace. Remarkably, the British Board of Censors even banned one of the few exposés from the United States, the March of Time's *Inside Nazi Germany* (1938). But once hostilities commenced, a number of important figures left for America.

Alfred Hitchcock's *The Thirty-Nine Steps* (1935), starring Robert Donat.

Alexander Korda, for example, formed a partnership with United Artists and made his way to Hollywood with British stars Vivien Leigh and Laurence Olivier.

Once it became clear that Germany would not march directly onto the British Isles, a renewed spirit overtook the British filmmakers who remained. In 1942 Noel Coward created *In Which We Serve*, a story that follows a naval destroyer from the day it is commissioned until the day it is sunk. *In Which We Serve* was based on the experiences of Coward's friend Lord Louis Mountbatten, who had commanded H.M.S. *Kelly*, sunk during the battle of Crete. Coward produced, directed, wrote the script, and played the lead in the film. *In Which We Serve* presented carefully drawn characters in a semi-documentary style. Coward was ably assisted by associate director David Lean and cameraman Ronald Neame, both of whom later had careers as directors.

Although a handful of run-of-the-mill comedies and melodramas were turned out during the war, so were some of the most complex and fascinating films ever created by the British cinema. In 1945 the team of director David Lean and playwright Noel Coward created *Blithe Spirit* from Coward's long-running comedy. It was filmed in Technicolor and starred Margaret Rutherford and Rex Harrison. Lean followed up with *Brief Encounter*, the story of a frustrated love affair which captured the tension of trying to maintain a meaningful relationship during the chaos of war.

On a grander scale was the filming of George Bernard Shaw's *Caesar and Cleopatra*, which became the most extravagant film ever made in Britain to that date. Despite the fact the filming took place coincident with the D-Day landings and the German V-2 attacks, producer-director Gabriel Pascal went to incredible (often absurd) lengths to create what the British would call a super-production. He cast thousands, headed by Vivien Leigh and Claude Rains, to create his own *Gone with the Wind*, British style. After six months of filming in England, Pascal even took a crew to Egypt. Critics of the day hailed *Caesar and Cleopatra* as a Technicolor masterpiece; the public disagreed.

Far more successful on all counts was Laurence Olivier's film of Shakespeare's *Henry V*. J. Arthur Rank, an executive of a British flour company who had turned to financing movies, backed this production. *Henry V* proved to be a box-office success in Britain as well as in many overseas markets, including, best of all, the United States. The plot of *Henry V*, a British army invading France, certainly had a topical ring to audiences at the end of the Second World War. Olivier directed himself ably and commissioned a brilliant score by William Walton. Critics complained of an odd mixture of Hollywood and non-Hollywood film styles, but the British hailed it for the glory and profits it brought an industry looking past the end of a global conflict.

• british documentaries •

The British feature film industry certainly had its high points during the 1930s and 1940s. But, surprisingly, so did British documentary filmmakers. Indeed, in the 1930s Britain set the standard for realizing film's power to record reality. The British documentary enjoyed the backing of the government and big business, both of which wished to use the low-budget, shorter documentary form to change attitudes. Remarkably, a Scottish academic, John Grierson, set in motion the documentary movement in Great Britain in the 1930s. (Indeed, he had coined the term documentary in 1926 in a review of Robert Flaherty's *Moana*.)

For the Empire Marketing Board, a governmental organization which promoted British agriculture business, Grierson produced and directed his first film, *Drifters* (1929). The film, which examined North Sea herring fishermen, identified the work and play of ordinary people as the proper subject of the documentary. *Drifters* was the only film Grierson ever directed. He quickly learned that greater power, even in the documentary field, lay in producing. With total supervisory power he could (and did) select projects, monitor their creation, and judge the final cut. Through experiments in camerawork and editing, many inspired by Soviet filmmakers of the 1920s, British documentary filmmakers of the 1930s and 1940s made the commonplace come alive for audiences.

Grierson possessed considerable supervisory skills. He was able to attract a number of talented individuals to his production unit, including Basil Wright, Paul Rotha, and Harry Watt. His staff, which in three years grew from two to thirty, created hundreds of short documentaries covering all facets of British life. The filmmakers of the Empire Marketing Board structured their films not to tell stories but to teach viewers about the lives and problems of the British working class. Grierson argued that cinema was neither entertainment nor art, that it best served the public as a form of pedagogy. He believed that the filmmaker ought to strive to assist the common good, to show how traditional English values could be modified and made useful in the real world of the 1930s economic calamity.

But the realities of the Great Depression affected documentary filmmaking as well as other facets of British life. In 1933 the government closed down the Empire Marketing Board and transferred Grierson's film unit to the Government Post Office (GPO). His mission was transformed from teaching about British trade and commerce to examining the complexities and impact of modern communications. The new base at the GPO provided stable funding and made monies avaliable for the transition to sound.

Still Grierson stressed pedagogy. For example, Alexander Shaw's *Under the City* (1934) told of the workers who maintained the telephone wires which ran beneath London's streets. The voices of the workers were juxtaposed with the explanations of an omniscient narrator. Basil Wright and Harry Watt's *Night Mail* (1936) provided another memorable GPO production. Benjamin Britten composed the music, poet W. H. Auden the verse narration. *Night Mail* examined a typical express train which transported the mail from London to Glasgow. The filmmakers did not stress narrative drama here, but an analysis of modern technology serving the nation. The key to the appeal of *Night Mail* lay in its complex rhythms. Underscored by Britten's music and Auden's staccato-like verse, *Night Mail* stressed the race to deliver the mail with all the speed possible. The pace of the film matches the velocity needed to move mail across the British Isles. *Night Mail* fulfilled all of the attributes Grierson sought to achieve in a documentary by combining an explanation of the modern world with cinematic experimentation.

The British documentary movement drew added support from British promotional boards. These boards hawked all sorts of products, from air and cruise boat lines to gas and oil products, and with their investment in documentaries they increased funds far beyond what Grierson could ever have hoped to extract from governmental ministries. The documentary of institutional advertising can be understood by examining Basil Wright's *Song of Ceylon* (1934). Produced for the Ceylon Tea Board, the film sought to present a favorable view of Ceylon (now Sri Lanka) and its major export. Wright accomplished his goal by drawing the viewer into an examination of the island's culture by skillfully juxtaposing sound and image. Structurally he moved from a general presentation of the dominant Ceylonese culture to an examination of the harvesting of tea. *Song of Ceylon* taught viewers a great deal about a foreign culture even though it presented a particular point of view favorable to its sponsor.

The success of these various documentary forms led the more adventuresome to tackle more controversial social problems, such as inadequate shelter and poor schools, from uncompromising and often critical points of view. For example, *Housing Problems* (1935), directed by Arthur Elton and Edgar Anstey, and produced for the British Gas Association, examined operations to clear a London slum. In apparently unrehearsed interviews, residents vividly told of overcrowded housing, streets filled with vermin and rats, and the lack of adequate sanitation. Tenants of the newly built housing laid out different stories of cleanliness and safety in their new quarters.

The skills developed by the British documentary movement during the 1930s proved of great value to the nation when it entered the

Basil Wright's *Song of Ceylon* (1934).

● ●

Second World War and the government called for the production of training and morale boosting films. The wartime Ministry of Information enlisted the nation's five thousand movie houses to regularly allot two minutes for films which would help the war effort. Early efforts, for example, stressed conserving public transportation and collecting scrap metal.

The logical choice to organize a wartime documentary unit, John Grierson, had emigrated to Canada to build that country's National Film Board. In 1940 Grierson's old GPO Film Unit was taken over by the Ministry of Information and renamed the Crown Film Unit. Former advertising executive Jack Beddington was placed in charge. Immediately he began to produce a series of fifteen-minute documentaries that would be shown monthly in every British theatre. Crown Film Unit took on a variety of subjects including battle reports, industrial training, maternity instruction, and morale boosting. Humphrey Jennings and Harry Watt's *London Can Take It* (1940) was recorded one night during the first German blitz bombing of London. Harry Watt's *Target for Tonight* (1941) followed a routine bomber raid over Germany. *They Also Serve* (1940) examined the role of the housewife in the war effort. *Airscrew* (1940) related the experiences of workers manufacturing airplane propellers.

Humphrey Jennings, a former painter, became the leading wartime documentary filmmaker. He worked with record speed to create *Spring Offensive* (1940), a skillful effort that shows how British agriculture worked overtime to supply needed food for civilians and troops alike. In *Listen to Britain* (1942), Jennings captured through a complex soundtrack the feel of a nation standing resolute against the Nazis. In twenty minutes, natural speech, poetic commentary, dance hall songs, and noises created a symphonic look at Britain preparing for war yet still going about its everyday activities. Jennings' eighty-minute *Fires Were Started* (1943) examined a day in the life of the National Fire Service as it attempted to put out the fires of the blitz. After establishing the individuality of the firemen, Jennings followed them as they prepared the fire equipment and then put out a warehouse blaze.

Jennings' strength as a documentary filmmaker lay in his ability to assemble the images and sounds of everyday life, to construct vivid sketches of the ordinary world. His soundtracks integrated snatches of popular music, radio programs, and seemingly overheard conversations, pioneering what later would be called cinéma verité. Jennings reduced spoken narration to a minimum and let the images and sounds create their own explanations.

· · · · · · · · · · · · · · ·

nazi germany

· · · · · · · · · · · · · · ·

During the 1930s the Fascist government which arose in Germany enveloped filmmaking, and treated it as simply another part of its totalitarian regime. Adolph Hitler took over an industry which had been the most powerful and among the most innovative on the European continent since the close of the First World War. But the Great Depression did batter the German film. Cinema attendance began to drop in 1930 and numerous cinemas were shuttered. The Nazis decreed that no new theatres be built, thus preserving the business of those already in existence. Attendance slowly increased and at mid-decade rose dramatically as the Nazi war economy began to return the country to prosperity.

During the 1920s the Germans had instituted a quota against Hollywood films. In 1933 Hitler commenced to strengthen the law, resulting in the strongest anti-Hollywood stance of any government in Europe. For instance, all dubbing had to be done in Germany, by Germans. Minister of Propaganda Joseph Goebbels held the power to refuse showing of any foreign film with what he considered an anti-Nazi theme.

In 1930 Germany seriously initiated the production of talkies, despite the constraints of devastating problems caused by the Great Depression. For example, producer Erich Pommer, at actor Emil Jannings' suggestion, invited American director Josef von Sternberg to direct

Marlene Dietrich and Jannings in *The Blue An-gel* (1930). Fritz Lang's *M* (1931), the noted si-lent film director's first sound film, and G. W. Pabst's *The Threepenny Opera* (1931), derived from Bertolt Brecht's play with Kurt Weill's songs, added to the prestige of the early Ger-man sound cinema. But the film industry re-mained in the doldrums.

Hitler was pleased to aid the German film industry. In return he demanded filmmakers conform to his overall propaganda. Control-ling the film industry meant he could dictate films with a unified, single line of thought. In May 1933 Hitler installed Goebbels as Minister of Propaganda and Public Enlightenment in charge of all public expression including film. The Nazis had made wide use of newsreels be-fore they officially took power; once in office Goebbels directly supervised newsreel pro-duction. Goebbels did not disband the already existing institutions of the film industry, but instead absorbed them under a central bureau.

But the Nazis were not able to prevent the talent which had made the German film indus-try so important in the 1920s from fleeing the country. Directors (for example, Fritz Lang and William Dieterle) and stars (Marlene Dietrich, Conrad Veidt, and Luise Rainer) emigrated to Hollywood. But some stayed, especially those who had a direct stake in industrial renewal promised (and ultimately delivered) by the Na-zis. Beleaguered theatre owners, devastated by the coming of sound and the economic depres-sion, generally embraced Hitler. Only in 1942 did the Nazis formally absorb the film industry into the central government.

In the 1930s, German film companies pro-duced one hundred features per year. This dropped to sixty once hostilities commenced, even though German citizens, like their coun-terparts in the United States, increased their rate

Leni Riefenstahl's *Triumph of the Will* (1934).

● ●

of movie-going. The average movie bill during the war included a heavy dose of pro-Nazi newsreels as well as musicals, comedies, and historical epics the Nazi authorities considered harmless. Many pro-Nazi party newsreels were also shown on mobile equipment in schools and at mass outdoor rallies.

Of all the efforts at Nazi-sponsored film-making, Leni Riefenstahl's *Triumph of the Will* (1934) stands as the most famous filmic cele-bration of Adolph Hitler. The Führer had per-sonally requested that a positive "documentary" record be made of him; he even chose the title. Riefenstahl's response to this request is a glor-ification of Hitler never again matched in Nazi cinema. Sixteen cameramen and 120 assistants recorded the desired images; whole sequences were staged to create the correct "documen-tary" look. The result was a "record" of the Nuremberg rallies with thousands of the Ger-man people cheering their new leader.

The opening sequence of *Triumph of the Will* is an apotheosis of the cult of Hitlerism.

Through a break in the clouds, an airplane suddenly appears, intercut with the spires and towers of ancient Nuremberg below. The old Germany gives way to the new, a message is reinforced and underscored through musical flourishes. Then thousands of people fill the streets of the old city, celebrating the coming of the new leader. Throughout the film, Hitler is shot from below, emphasizing his great stature. Careful editing separates him from the crowds to underline his special place in the proceedings.

The film records a speech of the Fuhrer who tells those amassed that he will take the German people away from the evils of the past and lead them to renewed triumphs. Resonant symbols (uniforms, bands, and flags) blend with powerful musical marches and are juxtaposed by skillful editors to establish the relentless pace which makes *Triumph of the Will* one of the most chilling films ever made. Some have likened it to a ballet in praise of Fascism.

After *Triumph of the Will* no other documentary celebrating Hitler was needed or commissioned. Hitler had been lionized in a style and mode which would last longer than the Third Reich itself. But Goebbels wanted to keep the theme of leader before the public. He did this covertly through fiction films rather than overtly through more staged documentaries. (It must be remembered that Goebbels did not originally support the making of *Triumph of the Will*; he always called for more subtle ways of

glorifying his Führer.) Generally these pro-Nazi fiction films featured characters from German history modeled on the Führer's image to invite an obvious comparison. They entertained the masses in a traditional manner, and there is some evidence that this genre actually enthralled German moviegoing audiences, especially younger people.

One of these films is *Bismarck* (1940), a tale of the well-known German leader who defeated Austria and France and then united a rejuvenated German nation in the 1870s. The historical parallel to Hitler, the genius as leader, seems obvious. For example, Bismarck, like Hitler, immediately strengthened the army upon assuming power, modernizing it so as to protect the new Germany. Similarly, Bismarck, like Hitler, signed a pact with Russia to safeguard Germany's eastern front while the nation grappled with nations to the south and west. Whatever Bismarck and Hitler did, all was justified in the name of nationalism.

The world survived the onslaught of the Nazis, after a five-year struggle. In 1945 Europe lay in ruins (as did Japan). The Allies moved in to help re-structure the economies and societies of the defeated nations. The post–World War II world market for movies seemed Hollywood's for the taking. No one expected Italy and Japan to soon rise and take a distinguished place in international cinema. But they did, and the reasons for their re-birth are taken up in the following chapter.

· ·

9

....

post–world war II alternatives to hollywood: japan and italy

The end of the Second World War in 1945 signaled a new era for international cinema. Germany, Italy, and Japan were in a state of disarray. The Soviet Union and much of Eastern Europe had also been reduced to rubble—despite being on the "winning" side—since so many battles had been fought within their borders. The Eastern bloc countries were annexed by the USSR, and struggled with new socialist governments. China was in the throes of a civil war. In those countries in which it was allowed free trade (particularly non-communist Europe, Africa and the Far East), Hollywood re-established its power, in some cases with direct assistance of the United States government.

For example, in Germany, long the most powerful film industry in Europe, Hollywood worked hand-in-glove with the U.S. Department of State to try to prevent a re-emergence of the German film industry. The Nazi government had prohibited the exhibition of Hollywood films; in August 1945, for the first time in nearly a decade, Hollywood films were again shown in theatres in Berlin. Hollywood demanded it be able to buy German studios and theatres. This would require special permission since at the time U.S. companies were not permitted to purchase German real estate, nor to secure items in short supply such as the chemicals

251

necessary to develop and print films. The Allied military authorities, trying to help Germany rebuild, turned Hollywood down.

In 1947 a compromise was finally negotiated. The American movie companies would be allowed to distribute films in West Germany, but could not own theatres nor acquire film stock. The effect was that Hollywood set up a powerful, but not complete, monopoly. In February 1948 the Motion Picture Export Association (MPEA), an organization owned and operated for the benefit of the major Hollywood companies, began distributing films in West Germany, taking over duties formally handled by the military government. The MPEA booked in theatres in the British, French, and American zones, but the USSR zone was off limits.

Hollywood was able not only to make money from current films, but also to exploit fully the backlog which had built up during the war. The German film industry could do little except stand back and helplessly watch. The U.S. government, in cooperation with the MPEA, made sure no quotas were raised and that the giant UFA cartel, which had dominated the German film industry since the 1920s, was broken up.

Not surprisingly, film production in Germany simply stagnated. It was not from a lack of trying; there were plenty of companies which sought to make movies, but financing and equipment were nearly impossible to obtain. Of the fifty-seven companies listed in the filmmaking business in West Berlin, only fourteen had made a single film by 1950. Film studios lay idle for months at a time. Audiences seemed happy to catch up with the best of Hollywood.

The German experience illustrates one extreme of Hollywood's takeover of a foreign nation's film business. The British, on the other hand, fought back but in the end also failed to keep Hollywood at bay. During the war Hollywood had never abandoned British screens. After the war Hollywood saw an opportunity to gain even more profits; the American movie companies stepped in, filled screens from one end of the nation to the other, and began to draw out some sixty million dollars per annum from the British market. But an ever worsening balance of payments required the British to cut imports somewhere, and in August 1947 the British Treasury announced a customs duty of 75 percent on earnings of Hollywood films shown in Britain.

In response, Hollywood announced an indefinite suspension of shipments of movies into Britain. This boycott lasted seven months and cut two ways through the British film industry. On one hand it was devastating for British theatre owners who had long relied on Hollywood product to fill their seats. At the same time the boycott did provide an opportunity for British producers, who for the first time in more than thirty years had free access to their own theatres.

Negotiations were held, and early in May of 1948 an agreement was reached. The customs duty was removed, but for two years hence Hollywood could withdraw only a limited amount of revenue from the United Kingdom. All other earnings were "frozen," and Hollywood was forced to produce films in Britain in order to spend these accumulated monies. The agreement also re-instituted the quota (which had been in existence from 1927 to 1942) and guaranteed that for theatres in Great Britain the ratio of films screened would be one-third British, two-thirds American.

The new law also established the National Film Finance Corporation (NFFC) to help subsidize (up to a quarter of the budget) mainstream British filmmaking. From 1950 to 1967 the NFFC advanced some seventy million dollars for nearly seven hundred features and more than 150 shorts. In 1952, at its high point, the NFFC supported seven out of every ten British films. Quickly, however, Hollywood had learned how to play the NFFC game and began to finance "British" films which would be "good enough" to play in the American market. In this first wave of what came to be known as "runaway" productions, Hollywood learned that foreign studios, technicians, and even actors and actresses were in certain cases as good as what was available at home. Thus the British government helped fund such films as *The Guns of Navarone* (1961), *Born Free* (1966), *Lawrence of Arabia* (1962), and *Dr. Strangelove* (1964). By one estimate Hollywood was receiving some three-quarters of the British subsidies during the 1960s.

During the 1960s one British producer summed it up this way: "We have a thriving film production industry in [Britain] which is owned lock, stock, and barrel by Hollywood." Since British unionized film workers demanded less than their Hollywood counterparts, the same film could be produced in London at considerable savings. This proved beneficial to workers in the industry, but surely did not provide the climate for a creative re-naissance in *British* filmmaking. The situations in Germany and Great Britain would prove altogether too common. If the Germans and British could not effectively stand up to Hollywood, one could hardly expect stiff resistance from a Belgium or Spain.

There were two important exceptions, surprisingly from two of the defeated Axis powers. Certainly Hollywood moved in and attempted to exploit these markets, as it had in Germany and Great Britain, but both Japan and Italy, with long traditions of native industries, were able to keep the Americans at bay. After the Second World War, the Italians and the Japanese revived interest in film as art, raising enthusiasm not seen since the 1920s with the films of the Germans, French, and Soviets. Their post-war efforts in turn inspired the French New Wave and other exciting national film movements of the 1960s and 1970s. Indeed, the godfather of the French New Wave, André Bazin, passionately championed Roberto Rossellini's *Open City* (1945), while for movie buffs in the United States there probably was no more celebrated a film, in the decade after World War II, than Akira Kurosawa's *Rashomon* (1950).

• • • • • • • • • • • • • •

japan

• • • • • • • • • • • • • •

After the Second World War, Japan lay in ruins. Yet there was a strong economic and social base from which to begin to rebuild.

Japan also had a long and rich history of filmmaking and of interest in the cinema. Before the turn of the century both Thomas Edison and the Lumière brothers had sent films into Japan. By 1920 there were hundreds of movie theatres and a studio system dominated by Nippon Katsudo Shashin (Japan Cinematography Company, usually known as Nikkatsu) and the Shochiku Cinema Company, which was turning out more than seven hundred films per year.

Shochiku led the way by ordering American equipment and sending executives to Hollywood to study production methods. The company was formed from a monopoly which dominated the stage in Japan. Two brothers, Matsujiro Shirai and Takejiro Otami, developed a chain of theatres, and (like the Shuberts in the United States) controlled important troupes of actors for Kabuki and other forms of popular theatre. From its base of theatres Shochiku expanded into movie production.

By 1930 the Japanese had mastered the Classic Hollywood filmmaking methods. But instead of imitating Hollywood genres such as the Western and gangster film, the Japanese studios created their own versions of repetitive stories. They divided films into historical (*jidai-geki*) and contemporary (*gendai-geki*). Within the historical category the most popular genre was the sword fight film (*chambara*), or what has come to be known as the samurai film. The Japanese studio system turned out hundreds during the 1930s and 1940s as Hollywood was cranking out Westerns and musicals. Within the contemporary category there were comedies, films about modern day office workers, and family dramas. Most major studios maintained two headquarters, one near Tokyo for the production of contemporary films and one near Kyoto for the production of historical motion pictures.

During the years preceding the Second World War the Japanese film industry was one of the largest in the world, often outproducing

Hollywood. And this was done without a major export market. To make profits the Japanese made studio features for far less—on average—than Hollywood did, some ten times less. The Japanese shot their films faster than Hollywood did by creating production units that consisted of a director, writers, and cameramen who, through constant practice together, learned to shoot smoothly and efficiently. Actors, actresses, technicians, writers, and other film workers would stay with a single company for years, even decades.

The coming of sound changed the way Japanese films were shown and made. In the presentation of silent films, men stood beside the screen and commented on what was going on, even vocalizing a number of characters. These *benshi* were extremely popular; some even had fan clubs. With the coming of sound, theatre owners gradually laid off the benshi. The structure of the industry was also transformed. A new company, Toho, formed through a series of mergers, rose to challenge Shochiku as the dominant studio. Affiliation with Kobayashi's theatres guaranteed Toho a powerful base.

Toho's vertical integration was typical during the 1930s. All the major Japanese studios, like their American counterparts, owned theatres. These theatres frequently changed programs, sometimes daily. Double and even triple bills took several hours to view but were relatively inexpensive to attend compared to live theatrical attractions. By the outbreak of World War II nearly all movie houses had abandoned benshi and in most aspects matched their American counterparts, with comfortable seats, vast balconies, and even counters in the lobbies selling snack foods.

During the 1930s the cinema industry in Japan was able to expand, despite the effects of the world-wide Great Depression which ravaged Hollywood. From 1933 to 1937 the number of theatres in Japan doubled to more than two thousand, with more than half playing only Japanese films. Still, at this point in history Japan was a relatively poor country. Even as late as 1937 more than ten percent of the cinemas played silent films. Only recently had some gotten air conditioning and other creature comforts which would make them compare favorably to the luxury and splendor of the typical American movie palace.

Hollywood had had a strong presence in Japan before 1937. Through the early 1930s Shochiku had an exclusive arrangement with Paramount, booking the popular American films in its extensive network of theatres. By 1937 Toho and Shochiku monopolized Japanese exhibition and split the importation of Hollywood features. Shochiku handled Warner Bros., Columbia, Universal, and RKO in its theatres while Toho booked films from MGM, Twentieth Century–Fox, and United Artists for its growing theatre empire. Similar agreements were made with German, French, and British film companies.

In September 1937 the Japanese government instituted a ban on all foreign films. By keeping out Hollywood films, the major Japanese studios prospered as never before. Shochiku, Nikkatsu, Shinko, and Daito made nearly two features each week, fifty-two weeks a year. But this prosperity was short-lived; this Golden Age of the Japanese studio system ended with the coming of the Second World War. As the Japanese military machine moved from an invasion of China in 1937, to signing agreements for mutual protection with Italy and Germany, to the December 1941 attack on Pearl Harbor, the Japanese government began to lay down stricter and stricter rules for filmmaking. Direct governmental control became the order of the day; all films were expected to support the military.

Ultra-militarism ruled until the Japanese surrender in 1945. Once the Japanese lost the war, the Americans occupied the country and instituted their own version of strict governmental control until 1950. Under General Douglas MacArthur, the American occupation forces professed a strategy of reform, and would try to bring to Japan a parliamentary model of government with an infrastructure patterned on the cultural and social institutions of the United States. Gradually the Japanese began to rebuild their nation, including its film industry. Theatres re-opened, but to strict censorship by the Occupation Force.

Although Allied bombing destroyed more than half the country's movie theatres, remarkably the film studios survived virtually intact, and so production could begin again immediately. The problem was that necessary equipment (lights, film stock, and camera parts) were in short supply. Slowly, during the 1950s, a dominant set of companies took charge, led by Shochiku, Toho, and Daiei. By 1955 the Japanese film industry had fully recovered. The number of theatres in operation was up to nearly four thousand. Shochiku was making more than fifty films a year, as were Daiei and Toho. Indeed, by the mid-1950s the companies dominating Japanese cinema seemed remarkably similar to those which controlled the film business before the war.

The Golden Age of studio filmmaking might have returned save for the innovation of television. Regular television broadcasts were first made in 1953 by the publicly owned Japanese Broadcasting Corporation (NHK) and the privately owned Nippon Television Network (NTV). Both grew quickly, and soon the Japanese market had millions of television sets.

Theatrical film attendance peaked in the late 1950s and then declined, falling to a sixth of that acme a decade later. As in the United States, in recent years cinema in Japan has fallen from its status as a mass medium but remains a vital component of the nation's culture.

• japanese directors •

The Japanese studio system was grounded on themes, stories, and visual style of a non-western, Oriental world. This was reflected in the cinema. For example, smooth Hollywood-like camera movements were not always necessary. A samurai film might find its climax recorded with an unsteady, hand-held camera. In addition, the Japanese discovered the virtues of deep space long before it became popular in 1940s Hollywood. Alternative cultural traditions made these stylistic manifestations possible.

But it should be remembered that in the post-war era, Japanese filmmakers worked within a studio system. This was not some Asian artistic colony, but an industry trying to make money. And indeed, at times, Japanese filmmakers have crafted films of which Hollywood certainly would have approved. We ought not forget that Japanese directors grew up watching American films and Akira Kurosawa, for one, certainly acknowledges his debt to such directors as John Ford.

But the historical analysis also seeks to understand alternative ways Japanese directors crafted their stories within their studio system. Kenji Mizoguchi, Yasujiro Ozu, and their fellow filmmakers provided some of the most complex, striking films in the history of cinema. In their own nation they worked in an industry, but with stuctural and stylistic possibilities not found in Hollywood films, the world's dominant filmmaking mode. Not surprisingly, Japanese films were seen as art films in the west. That is, these directors, like the Expressionists, the Soviet Montage school, and others discussed earlier, provided an alternative to the Classic Hollywood Narrative cinema.

Akira Kurosawa is the most famous Japanese director outside his own country. In 1951, when he won the Grand Prize at the Venice Film Festival for *Rashomon*, Kurosawa's fame quickly spread throughout the United States and Europe. However, by the time the West learned of *Rashomon*, Kurosawa was already a well-established director in his own country. Kurosawa started to dabble in the movies, first as a benshi. In 1936 he joined the Photo Chemical Laboratory Studio (later a part of Toho) as an assistant director. He became a Toho director in 1942, under the supervision of Kajiro Yamamoto, noted director of comedies and war films.

Kurosawa initiated his best work in 1948 with *Drunken Angel*, in which he teamed Takashi Shimura (as a blustery alcoholic doctor) and a young Toshiro Mifune (as a hotheaded gangster). These two actors would create testy relationships in numerous Kurosawa films during the late 1940s and early 1950s, including *Stray Dog* (1949), *The Quiet Duel* (1949), and the classic *Seven Samurai* (1954). Indeed, Kurosawa followed the typical Japanese studio practice of employing the same cast and crew production after production, including cinematographer Asakazu Nakai and composer Fumio Hayasaka.

His own consistent drawing power at the Japanese (and, later, international) boxoffice and his long-term studio contract provided Kurosawa with power matched by few directors in Japan. Audiences loved the famous final bat-

Akira Kurosawa (right) helping direct a scene.

tle scenes in *Seven Samurai*. Cineastes praised his use of long lenses and multiple camera set-ups. Kurosawa added wide-screen imagery to his lexicon in 1958 with another samurai film, *The Hidden Fortress*. A firm believer in trying new technologies, during the 1960s and 1970s he would experiment with color, Panavision cameras from the United States, and multi-track Dolby sound.

Since Kurosawa incorporated elements from European culture in his films, they were easier than those of many Japanese directors for Western audiences to appreciate. Frequently he used symphonic excerpts from Beethoven rather than traditional Japanese music. He drew his stories from the classics of Western literature, including Dostoyevski's *The Idiot* (1951), Gorky's *The Lower Depths* (1957), Shake-speare's *Macbeth* (*Throne of Blood* in 1957), and *King Lear* (*Ran* in 1985). Indeed, he has stated his admiration for the films of Frank Capra, D. W. Griffith, Jean Renoir, and John Ford.

Drunken Angel was both a popular and a critical success, placing first in the *Kinema Jumbo* poll in Japan. But it was *Rashomon* which made Kurosawa a praised director around the world. The film combines an exotic Japanese story with the appearance of profundity that Western intellectuals have tended to latch onto to demonstrate the cinema is an art form equal to the novel or theatre. In the West, *Rashomon* is praised for asking "What is truth?" and showing that the answer has many sides.

Superficially a courtroom drama, *Rasho-mon* presents in a most direct manner a ban-dit's violent attack on a traveling warrior and

Akira Kurosawa's *Seven Samurai* (1954).

• •

the warrior's lady. A foraging woodgatherer discovers the warrior's corpse, the authorities capture the bandit, and charge him as the killer. They bring the lady to police headquarters to provide testimony. The dead warrior (through a medium), the bandit, the lady, and the woodgatherer present their versions of what happened. Each story differs from the others.

But *Rashomon* is far more than an exploration of a philosophical doubt. Through alternating long shots and close-ups, the film explores how people try to deal with the harsh truth of the world. Using a style that was different from that of Hollywood, yet not too different, Kurosawa fashioned a tale about human egoism (with its pettiness and duplicity) jux-

taposed against the positive side of the human spirit. The first three versions of the story (the bandit's, the lady's, and the warrior's) are preliminary to the final version told by the woodgatherer. Indeed, the woodgatherer seems to be the film's hero because he alone is able to rise above the self-serving egoism at the core of the narrative.

If *Rashomon* established Kurosawa as a master director, *Seven Samurai* proclaimed to the world his skills as a director of complex action films. From its opening shot of silhouetted horsemen galloping across a horizontal plane, *Seven Samurai* tells us that the director of this film has seen many a John Ford Western. Kurosawa organized *Seven Samurai* like a Western, with the savage brigands (corresponding to the Native Americans), the civilized town folk, and the samurai who live in between (the "cowboy" heroes). This is myth, for these are not traditional samurai allied with a royal house, but warriors with no masters.

Kurosawa emphasized the unbridgeable differences between the villagers and their hired defenders. Although allied momentarily, the samurai and the townspeople actually seek far different goals. Villagers fight for home and family; samurai for honor. Thus, the samurai form their own separate professional group. Once the suitable leader is found in Kambei, the other members fill appropriate roles. To distinguish one warrior from another, Kurosawa used characteristic gestures. Kambei rubs his scalp, Kituchiyo leaps and whoops, and so on. Kurosawa even went against the conventions of the Japanese samurai film in which the samurai themselves represent civilization. Here they stand between chaos and enlightenment, as so often seen with the Western heroes from Hollywood. Stylistically Kurosawa carefully positioned his samurai figures away from the community, but also away from the forces of evil. A primary visual motif is one of boundaries, both natural (mountains, woods, flooded rice paddies), and man-made (fences, doorways).

The final battle sequence in the rain climaxes this powerful film. The confusion in the fierce storm and ever present mud fills in the spaces that Kurosawa had previously carved up, creating continuity from foreground to background. The rain had begun the night before the battle, during the peak of the division between townspeople and the samurai, when one of their number wanted to court a village girl. The camera begins to pan wildly, following the details of this struggle to the death. But then suddenly the combat is over; the samurai stand

before the graves of those who fell, and the villagers have returned to planting rice. The world again is "normally" divided.

Kurosawa continued with period films long after most Japanese filmmakers had abandoned films about Japan's past. *The Shadow Warrior* (1980) is set against a background of sixteenth-century feudal Japan and relates the story of Shingen, warlord of one of three clans struggling for control of Japan, who installs his younger brother as his double to ensure that his control over the clan will continue. A nameless thief, who is the exact double of the elder leader, appears and, when the real Shingen is killed, takes his place. Through this epic story Kurosawa explores classic themes of the nature of friendship, the continuity of culture, and the necessity for self-sacrifice. But this is no simple, straightforward Hollywood film; for one thing it begins with a static six-minute shot in which Shingen sits facing the camera.

But Kurosawa has made more than brilliant period pieces. *Ikiru* (1952), a drama of contemporary Japanese life, is the story of the end of the life of an older man who gradually learns to live only as he is dying. The film opens as he is told he has an incurable disease. Indeed, the first shot of *Ikiru* is an x-ray of his stomach. We then learn that he has been enduring a living hell because of his bureaucratic job, carefully sketched by Kurosawa in almost documentary style.

The bulk of the film is a series of flashbacks revealing the man's family history, with scenes of his children and his wife's death. These memories inspire him to try a new life; he goes to a baseball game, meets a young girl, and begins to enjoy life. This is probably Kurosawa's most famous *gendai-geki* (contemporary drama), popular in the West because of its serious treatment of a universal subject. *Ikiru* also ought to be praised because of its play with narrative, which includes ten flashbacks.

Kenji Mizoguchi is best known for *The Life of Oharu* (1952), *Ugetsu* (1953), *Sansho the Bailiff* (1954), *Crucified Lovers* (1954), and *Street of Shame* (1956), his last film. But Mizoguchi did not begin his career after the Second World War. He directed films continuously from 1923 through 1956, the year of his death, completing eighty-five in all. He was an honored, respected director, regularly receiving industry awards. In short, Mizoguchi is the Japanese equivalent of the Hollywood professional.

In 1920, at age 22, Mizoguchi signed with the Nikkatsu studio to be an actor. He moved quickly to screenwriting, then to assistant director, and in 1923 director. Between 1923 and 1935 Mizoguchi labored vigorously, directing an average of four films per annum. This twelve-year span served as Mizoguchi's apprenticeship. But he would experiment as well. For example, with *Mistress of a Foreigner* (1930) he began to employ the long take which would be so identified with him.

Mizoguchi's career reached a plateau in 1936 when he teamed with screenwriter Yoshikata Yoda for *Osaka Elegy*, and *Sisters of the Gion*, stories of exploited women in contemporary Japan. They were made during a period of intense debate about the role of prostitution in Japanese society in particular and outrage against corrupting Western influences in general. Mizoguchi funded these two films through Dai-Ichi Eiga, an independent operation he set up. The two films received uneven distribution and bankrupted his new company, but they did impress the critics and cement his relationship with Yoda which would last well into the 1950s.

Stylistically Mizoguchi adopted an alternative, non-Hollywood style which utilized very long takes (in terms of time), and complicated camera movements, often involving cranes and dollies. In 1942, for example, with his two-part *The Loyal Forty-Seven Ronin* Mizoguchi held his shots for several minutes or more at a time, when Hollywood rarely had a take over thirty seconds.

After working for the government during the Second World War, Mizoguchi returned to his interest in the emancipation of women. With Yoda and star Kinuyo Tanaka, he set to work creating dramas about women in both historical and modern settings including *The Victory of Women* (1946), *Utamaro and His Five Women* (1946), *The Love of Sumako the Actress* (1947), and *Women of the Night* (1948). After the war such films were seen as old fashioned. With *The Life of Oharu* (1952), however, Mizoguchi won a prize at the Venice Film Festival, and with it critics in Europe "discovered" a Japanese master. "Overnight" he became a hero to the influential French journal *Cahiers du Cinéma*.

Mizoguchi had struggled long and hard to adapt *The Life of Oharu*, taking nearly a year for filming and spending far more than for the normal feature. *The Life of Oharu* is stunning, even though Japanese audiences and critics could not seem to pigeonhole it. What made it so exceptional was its camerawork. This is a film of the long take and moving camera which follows Oharu as she falls from a privileged life at court to that of a nameless nun, achieving nobility and wisdom in the process. While Europeans praised *Ugetsu* and the Japanese lauded *Crucified Lovers*, in retrospect *The Life of Oharu* certainly represents a third high point in this great director's long career.

But with *Ugetsu* and *Sansho the Bailiff* we have a filmmaker near the end of his career turning away from socio-political critique to contemplations of an old master. The crux of this change can be seen in Mizoguchi's treat-

Kenji Mizoguchi's *Sansho the Bailiff* **(1954).**

● ●

ment of women. In his earlier films he protests the plight of women, while in these later films he depicts the woman as a self-sacrificer and mother. In general *Ugetsu* seems to advocate the acceptance of one's given lot in the world. An earlier Mizoguchi film might have argued for struggle; *Ugetsu* favors a spiritual transcendence. Mizoguchi's conversion to Buddhism in the early 1950s seems to explain part of this thematic shift in his films.

Sansho the Bailiff is yet another in the string of Mizoguchi's celebrated artistic triumphs of the early 1950s, earning the Silver Lion at the Venice Film Festival in 1954. The film features the long take which Mizoguchi had been using so effectively for more than two decades. Moreover, in *Sansho the Bailiff* the camera moves in

a majority of shots, sometimes linking the audience to the characters, sometimes withdrawing the audience from them. (Some in Japan criticized Mizoguchi for not cutting enough, not being enough like Hollywood.)

Sansho the Bailiff's famous closing sequence contains particularly beautiful examples of complex camerawork. In the final shot of the film, for example, the camera moves upward away from the reunited couple to reveal a vast seascape and the solitary figure of the old seaweed gatherer, his task now completed. With the long take and fluid camera movement comes a complex use of deep space, with action taking place both in the foreground and background simultaneously. Again and again, the mother and her children are visually separated, even before the full impact of the actual kidnapping which takes place at the center of the story.

Yasujiro Ozu is yet another Japanese filmmaker, who although he became famous in the West after World War II, had begun his career as a director in 1927. Often the most praised Japanese director outside Japan, Ozu is another longtime professional who made films for more than forty years in the mainstream Japanese film industry. He considered himself, like John Ford in the United States, just a filmmaker, regularly producing saleable films for Japanese audiences. Early Western critics fastened on his complex portrayals of the details of everyday Japanese life; today no director is ranked higher for artistic moviemaking.

Like Mizoguchi, Ozu spent the early part of his career learning his craft in the Japanese studio system. In 1923 at age 20 he signed on to work for Shochiku as an assistant cameraman. Four years later came his first directing credit, *The Sword of Penitence*. Between 1927 and 1935 Ozu directed some thirty-two films, principally college comedies and gangster films but modern dramas as well. By 1936 he had earned a place of respect and began to specialize in the *shomin-geki*, the "home drama," focusing on the blues and bliss of middle-class Japanese life. Typical films dealt with raising children, finding employment, settling marital conflict, marrying off sons and daughters, and becoming grandparents. It was in this genre that Ozu made his greatest films.

During his long career Ozu often seemed to be making the same "home drama" over and over again. Indeed, he made *Floating Weeds* twice, in 1934 as a black and white, silent film, then again in 1959 in color with sound. In both versions his "family" consists of an itinerant actor, a woman whom he is visiting for the first

time in twelve years, and their teenage son, who does not know who his father is. The latter version reflects Ozu at the height of his powers. His style of long takes, of neverending space, of carefully structured mise-en-scène adds tension and complications to the story of a man trying to find his family.

Ozu manipulated the home drama in fascinating ways. He suggested that many family problems extended far beyond generational squabbles, that rather, Japanese society imposed constraints which the individual had to live by. In his pre-war films of the late 1930s, Ozu even went so far as to criticize Japanese industry and government bureaucracy. After the war he shifted to a more mystical level. A cycle of nature (uncontrollable by materialist forces), for example, establishes the melancholy found in *An Autumn Afternoon* (1962) and *Tokyo Story* (1953).

Ozu meticulously manipulated his narrative structure to create an endless stream of permutations and combinations of the same story. It is his complex style of camerawork, editing, and mise-en-scène that infatuates today's critics. Some argue he transcended the ordinary, that his formalized compositions, rigorous cutting, and static camerawork function to reveal the beauty in everyday life. Through this unique style, Ozu subtly evoked the mental states of his characters.

But the source of Ozu's style can be found in Hollywood. Ozu was fascinated with the Classic Hollywood cinema and built his unique style from a deliberate imitation of and reaction to Hollywood, in particular the films of Charlie Chaplin and Ernst Lubitsch. But rather than let the story be told invisibly, he maintained a fairly consistent ratio of camera height to the subject, thus permitting a narrow range of camera changes. Ozu loved depth of field and shot

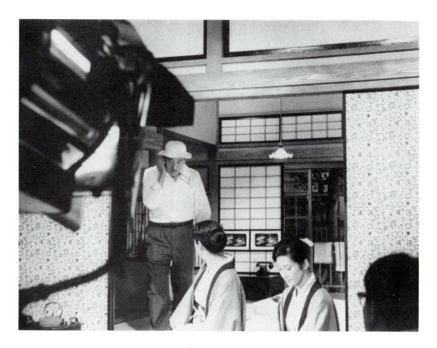

Yasujiro Ozu (left) directing a scene.

down the complete length of a corridor or street. He abandoned the Hollywood 180-degree rule in favor of a 360-degree space. To the trained Hollywood eye, this technique resulted in "incorrect" matches, but it allowed Ozu to explore the complete locus of action. He also frequently employed shots of empty spaces, not as establishing shots, but to punctuate the action. He rejected fades and dissolves. With these traits Ozu was able to fashion a unique, masterful style within the confines of a popular mass production entertainment industry.

Tokyo Story (1953) is a complex work which illustrates how Ozu's films differ from the Classic Hollywood films or European artistic alternatives. For example, sometimes the important story events are disclosed only indirectly as in

the case when the grandmother, a central character throughout, falls ill. The viewer learns of the illness only when her son and daughter receive the news in a telegram. Likewise her death occurs off-screen. In once scene she is alive; in the next her children are mourning her death. If *Tokyo Story* skips details Hollywood would center on, it lingers over other moments which Hollywood would consider less dramatic. For example, characters at various moments stroll and talk yet add no new information to the story.

In an Ozu film, scenes do not begin and end with establishing shots. Instead of classic wipes or dissolves, Ozu often employed shots of spaces not important to the story, only close-by to the action. In the opening of *Tokyo Story*, for example, there are five shots of the port

Yasujiro Ozu's *Tokyo Story* (1953).

● ●

town of Onomichi (the bay, school children, a passing train) before the central characters of the film, the grandparents, are introduced as they pack for a visit to Tokyo. Ozu also cuts in a non-Hollywood manner. For example, he violates the typical Hollywood sense of staging action by constantly crossing over into unknown screen space. He matches on movement, but often across the plane of action. To an audience trained on Hollywood's rules, it takes some time to locate where you are.

Ozu remained faithful to his unique style and popular genre to the end. *An Autumn Afternoon* (1962), his final film, opens with a series

of shots of chimneys from different angles, and only then proceeds to the corridor of an office building in preparation for our introduction to Shuhei Hirayama, a company executive. This editing pattern of the slow rhythmic pace is characteristic of Ozu at his best. *An Autumn Afternoon* continues a style of low angled, static shots cut to emphasize the complete 360-degree space, punctuated by shots of rooms, streets, or landscapes in which no human is present. To the end Ozu was a filmmaker who was able to work and even thrive within a studio system, yet create a cinema which today seems almost radical in its style.

• • • • • • • • • • • • • • • •

italy

• • • • • • • • • • • • • • • •

The Italian film industry had a rich tradition long before its Neo-realism movement. In the 1910s the Italians actively competed in the international film trade with the French, Germans, and Americans. When prosperity came to a grinding halt due to the First World War, Hollywood moved in and took a dominant place. Indeed a year after coming to power in 1923, the Fascists passed a decree which gave the government power to limit Hollywood's ability to bring in films.

Gradually, Fascist dictator Benito Mussolini took more and more interest in Italian film. Italian Fascism proved more tolerant towards all types of filmmakers than was Hitler's Nazism, and so few filmmaking talents emigrated. Still Fascism supported a dictatorship in which final control rested with the state. By the late 1920s the Italian Fascists realized the propaganda power of film and instituted greater controls through a series of state subsidies and censorship. They centralized all educational filmmaking activities in one authority, L'Unione Cinematographica Educativa (LUCE). Not surprisingly one early effort of LUCE was the three-part documentary *Il Duce*, chronicling Mussolini's rise to power. The Fascists took control of the production and distribution of newsreels, and in 1930 LUCE sent Europe's first mobile sound recording truck to follow and record the speeches of Il Duce.

Serious state control began in 1933 when a board of censors began to review all film scripts and projects and regulate the international trade of Italian films. The board banned foreign films (for example, Howard Hawks' *Scarface*) to appease the Catholic church. Filmmakers soon learned to work with this board to produce and distribute approved motion pictures. The Fascist-run Banco del Lavoro could advance 60 percent of the money needed to make a state-approved script. It even loaned the full amount for a handful of pro-Fascist films.

The Fascists poured money into filmmaking. In 1937 Mussolini and his son-in-law, Galeazzo Ciano, dedicated a complex of sixteen new studios, called Cinecitta, outside Rome. It became the Italian Hollywood. In the mid-1930s the government opened a film school, Centro Sperimentale, to train filmmakers. With permanent facilities also outside of Rome, students included Roberto Rossellini, Michelangelo Antonioni, and producer Dino De Laurentis. With the formation of a national agency monitoring the film industry (ENIC), the Fascist takeover of filmmaking, distribution, and exhibition (with a state-owned chain of movie theatres) was complete. To help pay for these ventures, the government instituted a tax on imported films (when they were dubbed) and used this money to underwrite native production. It became illegal to show a foreign film without dubbing approved by the Italian government, which disinfected and sanitized offensive dialogue.

With this new money and governmental support, film production boomed. The Great Depression had cut the annual number of Italian feature films to twelve in 1931. The coming of sound had not helped the Italians keep Hollywood at bay, since the small country did not have a common language or the economic power of Great Britain, France, or Germany. The Italians completed their first sound film, *The Song of Love*, in 1930, but were slow to adopt the new technology. Mussolini's sponsorship of filmmaking did the trick. Production increased steadily, from more than thirty in 1933 to more than sixty in 1938 to nearly ninety in 1941. During the Second World War, with no competition from Hollywood, Cinecitta grew to nearly three hundred fiction films plus eighty-five shorts each year.

Since the Fascists guaranteed virtually any venture into film production would make money, hundreds of "good Fascists" suddenly developed an interest in becoming movie producers. Mussolini's son Vittorio even formed his own company, Europa. The new producers concentrated on turning out standard genre fare, principally comedies and historical epics. But this Golden Age began to come apart in July, 1943. That month the Allies invaded Sicily and Mussolini fled to the northern resort town of Salo to run his government. He shifted the center of filmmaking from Rome to Venice. Thus, when the Allies entered Rome in June of 1944, they found Cinecitta deserted, but intact. They turned it into a refugee camp.

By April 1945 Italy was completely under the administration of the Allies, pending transition to civilian rule. The conquering forces, dominated by representatives from the United States, quickly opened Italy to Hollywood films. Italian exhibitors, long restricted to only Fascist-approved fare, welcomed this deluge. Native production withered and for a time it seemed that Italy would become another outpost of Hollywood. In 1946 alone, Italy imported some six hundred Hollywood films.

But as Italians re-took control of their government, they passed the Andreotti Act in 1949. This measure set a tax on Hollywood imports and used this pool of monies to support native filmmaking. In addition, a quota effectively reserved 25 percent of screen time in Italian theatres for native films. Hollywood imports fell by 50 percent, and Italy began to reclaim its native screens. Specifically, under the Andreotti Act, to dub a Hollywood film, the distributor had to deposit a sum of lire into the Banca Nazionale del Lavoro and to keep it there for ten years. Italian producers could draw on this fund which the government regularly augmented. Italy, more than Germany or Great Britain, effectively subsidized its native film industry which guaranteed Hollywood would be kept in check.

But Hollywood attempted to circumvent these restrictions through co-productions. By carefully structuring the financing and the hiring of talent in front and behind the camera, a producer could draw on Italian subsidies as well as those from other nations. Co-productions began in the 1950s and gradually grew to include one-half of all Italian productions in the 1960s. Italian producers had strong relations with filmmakers in Spain and France. Italian-Franco co-productions had begun as early as 1949, and in twenty years some several hundred films were financed this way.

Typically co-productions gave rise to low-budget genre films, aimed at the drive-in market in the United States. There were gladiator films such as Sergio Leone's *Last Days of Pompeii* (1959) starring muscleman Steve Reeves, and *The Colossus of Rhodes* (1961), starring Rory Calhoun. Italian Westerns nearly always were co-productions, including Leone's *A Fistful of Dollars* (1964) and *For a Few Dollars More* (1965). But the co-production method of film finance also gave rise to Federico Fellini's *I Vitelloni* (1953), *Il Bidone* (1955), *Nights of Cabiria* (1956), and *La Dolce Vita* (1960), Roberto Rossellini's *General della Rovere* (1959), and Michelangelo Antonioni's *La Notte* (1961) and *L'Avventura* (1960).

But in 1945 the Italian film industry lay in rubble. Out of this chaos emerged the influential film movement, Neo-realism. A style of filmmaking which stressed the re-examination of reality was only possible because traditional production was in shambles. But this was also a period of political and social ferment. The radical thrust of Neo-realism was embraced by those who had fought in the Italian underground and after the war were looking for the re-birth of the Italian nation-state. Neo-realist films would always only represent a small share of the Italian box office. Critics bitterly rejected the Neo-realist's claim that they spoke for the nation. But to the world of film, Neo-realism symbolized an exciting, new way of making movies and the re-birth of the Italian cinema.

After the war, Neo-realism would last a decade. By the mid-1950s, the forces of conservativism in Italy united the country and muted social criticism. The social critique of Neo-realism was out; the traditional genres of comedy and melodrama were encouraged and funded. The conservative Italian government looked to divert all funds to mainstream film-making and so began to subsidize the type of moneymaking co-productions noted earlier.

During their heyday, the Neo-realists argued for a break from the past, a departure from traditional subject matter and the cinematic style of Hollywood. This new interest in a cinema of reality actually originated during the Second World War as anti-Fascists sought ways to break with all conventions of Fascist culture, including filmmaking. Mussolini praised innocuous comedies, historical epics, and sentimental melodramas. Neo-realists looked to the poetic realism of Jean Renoir. According to Neo-realism, films should deal with the common man and woman; they should be shot out-of-doors in real-life settings; they ought to be in the same manner as a documentary. Out was the studio production of glossy, well-lighted images.

Indeed, the goal of Neo-realist filmmakers was an anti-studio look. Rejecting Hollywood-style lighting, the Neo-realists made do with the natural light at the location site. They abandoned costume epics and stage-inspired melodramas and moved to the streets of their war-ravaged country. With non-actors who provided the look and behavior filmmakers desired, Neo-realists stressed the ordinary gesture, the expression which fit the mise-en-scène, rejecting images solely contrived to fit a pre-conceived story, as was done in Hollywood. Actors and actresses were asked to improvise as the camera operators looked for the proper angle to best capture the reality of the moment at hand. Framing and camera movement took on a flexibility unknown in the Italian cinema of the 1930s. The Neo-realists abandoned the use of even a unified film stock. Rossellini told interviewers how he bought different film stocks from whatever sources he could find to piece together enough footage for his seminal *Open City*.

But the Neo-realists never broke completely with the past. It was nearly impossible at this time to record natural sounds on location. Ambient noises often masked dialogue, for example. Therefore, even in Neo-realist classics dialogue, music, and noises were added later, in post-production. Deep focus photography was also not discovered by the Italian Neo-realists. The creation of action in the layers of deep space in shots of longer than Classic Hollywood average duration also could be found in contemporary Hollywood, in films of Orson Welles and William Wyler. Moreover, classic analytical editing, a trait at the heart of the Classic Hollywood Narrative style, is common even in the fabled work of Roberto Rossellini.

As for film form, the Neo-realists did abandon the intricately formulated stories so common to the Italian cinema of the 1930s. The narratives were looser; they did not directly tie up all narrative threads. Prerequisite happy endings were abandoned; closure more common to the harsh experience of life became the rule. The most radical of the Neo-realist works, such as De Sica's *The Bicycle Thief* or Rossellini's *Paisan*, include accidental details that are never fully resolved within the story. *Paisan*, for example, presents six episodes of life in Italy during the Allied invasion. There is no single story; some events are never "wrapped up."

For the Neo-realists reality had two distinct attributes. First, the poverty, unemployment, and economic chaos of post-war Italy defined the actions of all characters. Their life was taken up by trying to gain a place to live, something to eat, basic transportation. *The Bicycle Thief*, for example, ends with the two central characters, a worker and his son, wandering down the street still looking for their sole means of transportation, a bicycle stolen long ago. The future is uncertain, determined by economic and social forces over which they certainly have no control. This ending reflects the Neo-realist's second attribute of nature—its ambiguity. Italian cinema of the 1930s presented a fixed, stable world; in Neo-realist films no one seems to know or understand how the world works, where things will lead. This open-ended narrative quality contrasted dramatically with the closure required in the Hollywood films flooding Italy after World War II.

As soon as it was clear that the Allies would liberate Italy, these new ideas about the cinema began to circulate. Umberto Barbaro issued a manifesto of four points which challenged post-war filmmakers to rid themselves of clichés, abandon fantastic and grotesque fabrications, dispense with historical set pieces and fictional adaptations, and exclude stereotypes. This manifesto, a reaction against the Mussolini government, was also a moral stand that valued integrity and the accurate reporting of the lives of ordinary people. Through their writings Neo-realists sought to fashion a new and better Italy. Cesare Zavattini argued that, ideally, Neo-realism ought to operate without narrative, acting, or convention; that cinema should view real people in actual settings performing ordinary actions. He was arguing for a documentary style, one with minimal manipulation of mise-en-scène.

The champions of this new realism were all veterans of the Italian studio system of the 1930s. Roberto Rossellini, Vittorio De Sica, and Luchino Visconti all had been trained by Mussolini's film school. As friends they shared ideas and helped formulate the principles which would make the Italian cinema so famous. They wrote for the film journals *Cinema* and *Bianco e Nero*. They formed independent production companies and after the war Luchino Visconti created *La Terra Trema* (1948), Roberto Rossellini *Open City* (1945) and *Paisan* (1946), and Vittorio De Sica *Shoeshine* (1946) and *The Bicycle Thief*—the major works of Neo-realism.

Luchino Visconti (right) directing.

• italian directors •

Luchino Visconti inspired the Neo-realist movement with his *Ossessione* (1942), made while the Fascists still controlled Italy. *Ossessione* applied a realist mise-en-scène to the formulaic constraints so familiar to Italians through their frequent viewing of Hollywood films. Visconti's film was directly inspired by an American hard-boiled detective novel, James M. Cain's *The Postman Always Rings Twice*. The setting was simply changed to the Romagna region of Italy. The monochrome, dismal, provincial countryside is seen through the long-take style, inspired by Visconti's mentor, Jean Renoir. In the flat marshy country where the Po River begins to widen out into its delta, the film's

central characters are transformed from unhappy folks grubbing out a menial existence to murderers who destroy human life. The husband is a middle-aged, fat, kindly man; the wife is an Italian Madame Bovary, moved by something more than lust and less than love. The lover is caught up in forces he only barely understands.

It was the depressing setting, lives, and story which attracted young Italian filmmakers to this film. Visconti made a movie about people in a mundane world. One can almost taste the red wine and feel the burning sun. At its first showing *Ossessione* outraged the Catholic Church and Fascist censors with its psychological realism and sexual explicitness. Visconti appealed directly to Mussolini, and Il Duce passed it with only a few minor cuts. But with the imminent Allied invasion, the film was not shown and had to await the liberation of the country to make its appearance on Italian screens. In 1944 it was hailed as a masterwork, and the initial spark of Neo-realism had been struck.

Visconti was no son of the working class, having been born into a family of wealth. He did not come to an interest in the cinema until 1936 (at age thirty) when he left to work with Jean Renoir in France. At first in charge of costumes, Visconti then served as Renoir's third assistant director on *Une Partie de Campagne* (1936) and *Les Bas-Fonds* (1936). After a visit to Hollywood, he returned to Italy and worked on the magazine *Cinema*, where he railed against the insipidity and conformity of the contemporary Italian cinema and argued for a cinema of realism.

At the end of the war, Visconti journeyed to Sicily with funds from the Communist Party to record a short documentary of a fishing collective. He stayed seven months and the short subject grew to feature length. He found in the village of Aci Trezza (on the eastern coast) a proletariat not ready for revolution. He fashioned a story of struggle in which a family trying to better itself is continually exploited by fish wholesalers and boat owners. In the end the bank appropriates the family home, the grandfather dies, one brother flees, a sister is disgraced, and the central figure, 'Ntoni, and his brothers return to the sea as hired hands. The film's principle theme is that fundamental change can come only with collective action.

The characters of *La Terra Trema* were played by the locals of Aci Trezza. The language they speak is the Sicilian dialect of their village, hardly more comprehensible to the speaker of standard Italian on the mainland than to a non-Italian. True to a spirit of realism, Visconti used a voice-over narrator to translate the film's story from the dialect of Aci Trezza into the Italian which Sicilians of that region call the "tongue of the continent."

For the film's two-plus hours, the camera remains confined to the village itself, its church square, and the two large rocks which form a gate to the harbor. The film is filled with magnificent panning and tracking shots which integrate figures, decor, and landscape. Depth of field allows action to occur in several planes through real time. With this sort of camera work Visconti was able to record the integrity of the villagers and their dependency on the sea.

Visconti and his screenwriter Giuseppe De Santis, both Marxists, believed that the simple portrayal of ordinary life was only the first step in analyzing what was wrong with Italian society; they needed to analyze the ruling class, and so the two crafted *Senso* (1954), a costume drama which examines class conflict in the nineteenth century. A radical change from the earthy contemporary realism of *La Terra Trema*, *Senso* was influenced by serious Italian Marxist thought of the day as found in the *Prison Notebooks* by Antonio Gramsci. But *Senso* also fit into the genre expectations of the new Italian film industry. Industry officials, as well as most audiences, simply saw *Senso* as another high-class entertainment with big stars (Farley Granger and Alida Valli) and a story of a love affair between an Italian countess and a young Austrian officer, complicated by the countess's betrayal of her husband, her brother, and her political allegiance for her new lover. A complex use of camerawork characterizes *Senso*. The opening shot, for example, moves from the stage of an opera house across the audience to examine all tiers of the seats from which protest against the Austrians will soon erupt.

After *Senso*, Visconti then became more and more interested in operatic theatricalism and lavish romanticism. It was with these new elements that he felt he could best examine class conflict in Italy. But *Senso* was a failure at the boxoffice, and to appease producers Visconti began to make films which were far different from what had been called for by the Neo-realists. He began to film in a studio, with constructed sets and with soft focus to provide a "beautiful Hollywood" look. Indeed, his *White Nights* (1957) was denounced by the adherents of Neo-realism as was *The Leopard* (1963) which he filmed on a multi-million dollar budget provided by Twentieth Century–Fox, the epitome of Hollywood itself.

Roberto Rossellini probably achieved the greatest expression of the ideals of Neo-realism with his *Open City* (1945) and *Paisan* (1946). During the early part of World War II Rossellini made feature films about war and service life which were backed by the government but were not excessively Fascistic in their point of view. After the fall of Mussolini in 1943, he joined the Resistance underground and fought the occupying Germans. It was in this context that he made the first feature about the Resistance, *Open City*. This remarkable film tells of the struggles of a priest and a Communist partisan and ends with the death of both. While the film celebrates the alliance of the Catholic church and the Communists against the Germans, the focus is on the spiritual—since the priest, not the Communist, emerges as the hero of the film. Nearly all of *Open City* was shot on location.

Open City emerged from the ashes of the Second World War to become the first recog-

nized masterwork of the Neo-realist movement. Remarkably, Rossellini produced this important film from scraps which survived an economy and society decimated by war. *Open City* was begun within two months of the Allied liberation of Rome. Nonprofessional actors, save former music hall performer Anna Magnani, acted out re-creations of incidents which had actually transpired. This insistence dictated a flexible use of the camera.

Where *Open City* seems to diverge from the basic tenets of Neo-realism is in its narrative structure; it is highly melodramatic, in the worst sense of the word. Characters are drawn in black and white. One is either for the Resistance or a hated Fascist sympathizer. Faith in a better Italy is rewarded; cynicism becomes a corrupt philosophy. Rossellini's use of his brother Renzo's music adds to this emotional manipulation as do the frequent shots of children used to represent the hope for the future. Indeed the film ends with children neatly juxtaposed against a shot of the dome of St. Peter's, as they file away after the execution of the priest Don Pietro.

Open City had only a mixed reception in Italy but was hailed as a masterwork throughout the world. Rossellini next explored recent Italian history in *Paisan* in 1946. (The title of the film comes from the term that American soldiers used to affectionately greet all Italians.) This film of six episodes traced the American invasion of Italy from the Allied landing in Sicily in 1943 to the surrender of Italy a year later. Through what seem to be unrelated incidents, Rossellini presents the conquest not in terms of armies heroically marching toward victory, but rather as a tragedy causing the suffering and death of millions of his fellow countrymen and countrywomen caught up in forces far greater

Roberto Rossellini's *Paisan* **(1946).**

• •

than they would ever again know. *Paisan* is no doctrinaire, simple-minded manifesto; it is a film that takes a fresh look at a tragic situation.

Improvisation in shooting *Paisan* was carried even further than in *Open City*. The script was written on a day-to-day basis. With huge gaps in the narrative, the film was lavishly praised as an alternative to Hollywood's treatment of the war experience. Rossellini worked with long takes and hand-held cameras always seeming to be in motion. *Open City* and *Paisan* represent two of the foundation works of Neo-realism.

Rossellini, like most Neo-realists, was originally allied with the Italian Left. But the left-of-center coalition government broke up in 1947, and the Christian Democrats, allied with the

Catholic church, took charge in a right-of-center government. Of all the Neo-realists, Rossellini was the only individual to align squarely with the Christian Democrats. And in his films of the 1950s Rossellini broke from Neo-realism and produced dramas about guilt and redemption, investigating the impact of Christianity on the long path of history. Only the grimy setting and the nobility of the poor remained from his Neo-realist days. He undertook a series of films starring his new wife, former Hollywood star Ingrid Bergman. Beginning with *Stromboli* (1949), and even more so with *Francesco* (1950), Rossellini distanced himself further and further from the concerns of Neo-realism.

Vittorio De Sica created three films central to the Neo-realist movement: *Shoeshine* (1946),

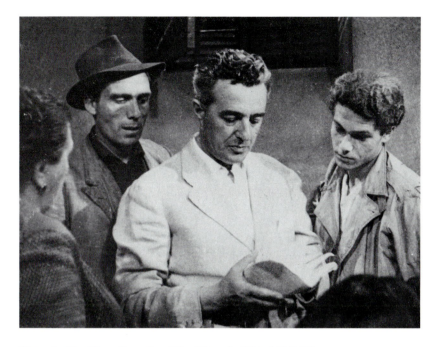

Vittorio De Sica directing *The Bicycle Thief* (1948).

● ●

The Bicycle Thief (1948), and *Umberto D* (1952). These three films were strongly humanist and reformist in impulse, not radical analyses or revolutionary works. According to De Sica, the honest portrayal of ordinary life ought to prove strong enough to inspire audiences to alter their view of the world and to understand on their own how to change it for the better. His narratives, co-scripted with Cesare Zavattini, dramatically contrasted life in bleak, post-war Italy with the potential for a better life.

Like Visconti and Rossellini, De Sica did not simply burst on the scene after the Second World War. He had had a long film-acting career, beginning in the 1920s. Indeed, during the 1930s he was considered quite the matinee idol. He has been labeled the Italian Cary Grant.

In his lifetime De Sica acted in more than one hundred films, using the monies from this lucrative side of the profession to finance the films he wanted to direct.

His first directorial efforts came in the early 1940s, in transforming stage plays to feature films. With his fourth directing project, *The Children Are Watching Us* (1943), he teamed with Zavattini, who would become his principal collaborator for the next three decades. But it would take the conditions present at the end of the Second World War to enable De Sica and Zavattini to fashion their most influential Neorealist films.

Shoeshine (1946) certainly represents a landmark collaboration of director De Sica and screenwriter Zavattini as well as a core work in

Vittorio De Sica's *Shoeshine* (1946).

• •

the Neo-realist opus. It is an uncompromisingly tragic indictment of the social conditions in post-war Italy. The film was inspired by De Sica's observation of the shoeshine boys of Rome plying their trade to American GIs, the only men who had the money for such luxuries. He used two non-professional actors and shot his film on the streets of Rome. The grainy newsreel quality of Anchise Brizzi's cinematography and the seemingly unrehearsed, natural acting provided the feel and mood of a war-torn city trying to recover.

Shoeshine was hailed by the critics of the day, but it lost nearly a million lire. In fact, few people in Italy actually saw the film because theatres had overbooked with Hollywood movies. But as it was shown in art theatres around the world, its reputation grew. Orson Welles,

who praised its realistic view of the world, remarked: "I ran *Shoeshine* recently and the camera disappeared, the screen disappeared; it was just life."

But to make their next work, *The Bicycle Thief* (*Ladri di Biciclette*), De Sica and Zavattini had to beg, borrow, and use the monies gained from De Sica's acting. *The Bicycle Thief* is certainly the most accessible of the core works of Neo-realism. It is the story of Ricci, who finds work after a long period of unemployment and then has his only means of transportation stolen. As he struggles to find his bicycle, the film follows him through his encounters with the denizens of the black market, men preparing for a strike, poor people praying at church, a crowd lamenting a drowned child, and roars of street gangs and mad soccer fans.

Nowhere is a solution presented. Beyond the fleeting glimpses of preparations for a strike, *The Bicycle Thief* does not suggest political struggle to improve the world. De Sica uses the hunt for the bicycle as a means to organize the flow of the narrative, an odyssey by which the director could examine and record the everyday world of post-war Rome, the "star" of the film.

Likewise *Umberto D* (1952) is the story of an ordinary man, one Umberto D (no last name), a retired civil servant who cannot stand to live any longer and makes several attempts at suicide. He fails, and thus has no recourse but to continue on in his hopeless situation. The film's story sounds mundane and banal, but De Sica took measures to distance the viewer from the events at hand by focusing on realist mise-en-scène with a flowing, open camera style.

Umberto D drew harsh reaction from Italian authorities who accused De Sica and Zavattini of presenting too negative a view of Italian society. In fact, following *Umberto D*, the government began to hold up exportation of films which presented Italy as a depressed country lacking justice for its citizens. In other words, the government sought to stymie the flow of Neo-realist films. Critics in Italy went along; Italians seemed to want to have a positive view of the future for their country. It was acceptable to criticize the Fascists when they were in power, but now, in the early 1950s, it was asserted that the best foot ought to be put forward.

Neo-realism ended as a concerted movement, thereafter serving as inspiration and influence for some of Italy's major filmmaking talents for years to come, including Federico Fellini and Michelangelo Antonioni. Fellini played an instrumental part in the development of Neo-realism as a screenwriter. From 1945 to 1949 he worked as a writer and assistant director for Rossellini as well as De Sica, Lattuada, and Germi. He helped Rossellini write the scripts for *Open City* and *Paisan*. For Rossellini's *The Miracle* (1948) Fellini not only wrote the script, he also played the tramp hero who is mistaken by a peasant girl (Anna Magnani) for St. Joseph.

The films which Fellini directed reveal traits of the Neo-realist approach. He opted for location shooting, used non-professionals in his casts, and paid close attention to details of costume and gesture. But from the beginning he modified the tenets of Neo-realism to fashion his own unique style. In *I Vitelloni* (1953), Fellini's third film, a story of middle-class punks who banded together to amuse themselves at the expense of their neighbors in lieu of settling down into responsible but demeaning lives of work, he certainly utilized non-professional actors and location shooting. But Fellini did stray from the thematic concerns of Neo-realism by focusing on the individual as a member of society.

The career of Michelangelo Antonioni represents another off-shoot of Neo-realism. He began his career with the Neo-realist film publication *Cinema*, source of many of the basic writings about the tenets of the movement. Although he had written screenplays as early as 1939 Antonioni began his career as a maker of documentary shorts. His first, *Gente del Po* (*People of the Po*) was begun in 1943 at a site near where Visconti was shooting *Ossessione*. Antonioni acknowledges the influence. In 1948 Antonioni made *N. U.* (short for *Netteza Urbana*) about a day in the life of the street cleaners of Rome. We see ordinary workers doing ordinary jobs, as the swirl of the city surrounds them. There is none of the overt social criticism common to Neo-realism, only an interest in the texture of the real world.

At the beginning of his feature film career Antonioni continued to be influenced by the tenets of Neo-realism. A good example can be seen in his *Cronaca di un Amore* (*Story of a Love Affair*, 1950). In this genre piece he directed against convention as did Visconti seven years earlier in *Ossessione*. He used the genre form to inquire into the morals and psychology of the class enriched by Italy's post-war economic miracle. The film relies on the long take to record its action. This surely was inspired by the tenets of Neo-realism, but Antonioni went far beyond what even Neo-realists would have been comfortable with. He was exploring in different ways the use of the medium and, like Fellini, moved on to construct films far different from those which served as the core of the great wave of Neo-realist filmmaking.

But a greater force for change in the world of cinema soon arose in the post-war world. A new technological reality, television, was innovated. The coming of this new medium would effect the way Hollywood did business. It was the era of the innovation of Cinema-Scope, VistaVision, Panavision, and 3-D. Filmmaking in Hollywood would never be the same again, and major changes in Hollywood would eventually provide a new world for filmmaking throughout the planet. Like the coming of sound, the introduction of television defines a new epoch of film history, and properly we must again turn to see how Hollywood and then foreign filmmakers handled this alternative medium. That is the subject of the following section.

III

•••••••••••••••••••

the television era
1951 to 1975

•••••••••••••••••••

1951
1952
1953
1954
1955
1956
1957
1958
1959
1960
1961
1962
1963
1964
1965
1966
1967
1968
1969
1970
1971
1972
1973
1974
1975

· ·

10

· ·

television, wide-screen, and color

After the Second World War, the American film industry began to change. Loyal film fans began to look for other things to do: starting families, finding nicer homes in the suburbs, buying cars, refrigerators, or the elusive pair of nylons not available during the war. Weekly movie attendance in movie theatres in the United States crested in 1946 and then began to steadily fall, so by the early 1960s it was one-half what it had been in the glory days of World War II. Boxoffice revenues never fell as dramatically because ticket prices surged ever upward. By 1960 thousands of formerly flourishing neighborhood theatres had closed up shop forever.

The causes of this decline in moviegoing have been much debated. Commentators generally blame television, with a clear, simple straightforward argument. Once television programming commenced in the United States after World War II, the standard argument goes, movie fans stayed home, attracted by the free entertainment. Going out to the movies suddenly became a relatively expensive (admission fees plus parking and baby-sitter costs versus nothing for over-the-air television) night out, requiring a long journey downtown. Television entertainment was so much cheaper that millions of Americans simply stayed home.

This analysis is flawed, for it ignores the fact that in most parts of the United States television signals did not become available until long after the decline in moviegoing was well under way. In most parts of the United States, broadcast television only became a viable entertainment alternative after the Federal Communication Commission allocated the majority of television licenses in 1952. In the late 1940s and early 1950s, only one-third of the nation had sets. But this was precisely when millions upon millions stopped going to the movies. Television has long provided a convenient, visible villain, but it was simply not available in most parts of the United States where abandonment of going out to the movies reached a mass scale. Thus, film historians have begun to look for other reasons to explain the vanishing movie audience.

One simple explanation is that many Americans had less money to spend after the war. The prosperity of the war years turned into a stagnant post-war world, with millions of returning veterans looking for that ideal job. Moreover, these same veterans took what money they had saved during the war and spent it on new cars and other big ticket items which had been unavailable since Pearl Harbor day.

But what those who had sacrificed during the war wanted most of all was a new home. The ideal was to move to the suburbs, free from city congestion and noises, close to good schools for the children. Americans moved in record waves to new suburban subdivisions that were underwritten by government-backed GI loans. Home ownership in the first five years after the Second World War increased by 50 percent and then by another 50 percent again during the following five years. By 1960, just as moviegoing was hitting a nadir not experienced since the days of the nickelodeon, more Americans owned homes than rented for the first time in the nation's history.

There were other economic distractions as well. Americans filled these new homes with children in record numbers. Women married at younger ages, and the birth rate increased as never before or since. Better-educated couples had larger families. Indeed, the typical moviegoer of the past (better-educated, richer, middle class) was precisely the individual who most embraced the suburban ideal with its sizable mortgage and the family of four or five children.

These two factors—suburbanization and the baby boom—directly affected moviegoing and would have done so even without the coming of television. The waves of suburbanization moved moviegoers far away from the downtown movie palace, and poor public transportation from the suburbs made it difficult to routinely journey downtown. In any case, the family had fled the city and its attractions for the new world of Little League and backyard barbecues. The automobile replaced the streetcar as the principal means of transportation, and everyone knew it was *impossible* to park downtown.

The American film industry was not oblivious to these trends. It saw that it needed to provide new auto-oriented theatres, and once the necessary building materials became available, they did. Although drive-ins had been around since the 1930s, thousands of new drive-in theatres opened in the suburbs of the United States between 1945 and 1950. The drive-in theatre offered a pleasant, open space where parked cars filled with movie fans could watch double and triple features on a massive screen. By the early 1960s, the very height of suburbanization and the baby boom, the number of drive-ins in the United States had increased from approximately one hundred at the end of World War II to more than four thousand. During one week in June of 1956, for the first time, more people went to the drive-ins than to the

An early post—World War II drive-in. Note the 35-cent admission price.

traditional "hard-top" theatres, initiating a pattern in which summer is the peak moviegoing season of the year.

A longer-term and more permanent reaction to the suburbanization of America came with the shopping center theatre, but this phenomenon did not occur until shopping centers were opened in record numbers in the 1960s. By the late 1960s, with thousands of new shopping centers in place, the locus of movie attendance shifted to what we know today as the mall. With acres of free parking and ideal access by highway, the shopping center—America's new downtown—accommodated thousands of indoor screens and became the center of America's moviegoing habit.

At first one or two theatres were housed together near or as part of a planned shopping center. Gradually, the multiplex of six to twenty screens became the focus of Hollywood's movie producers. Traditional, one-screen cinemas downtown became harder and harder to find; many cities were left with only a handful of theatres within their proper borders. The movies had moved to the suburbs.

Raising baby boom families also took away from moviegoing a core group of young adults who before had formed a disproportionate share of the moviegoing population. Well-educated, middle-class Americans looked to entertainment at home (in the suburbs) for the whole family. In the late 1940s and even into the first few years of the 1950s, they found cheap fun listening to the radio, whose Golden Age in terms of profitability and listenership came during the years immediately following the war. In fact, listening to the radio was the first replacement for going to the movies.

During the 1950s along came something far superior to radio for home entertainment— television. Middle-class suburbanites, who had already abandoned the movies, substituted television watching for radio listening. After buying a TV set, they put the kids, the baby boomers born between 1945 and 1964, in front of it to be entertained.

Suburbanization and the baby boom had dramatic, dampening effects on movie attendance in the United States. But Hollywood had other problems which exacerbated the situation. During Hollywood's Golden Age of the 1930s and 1940s, the major studios directly controlled their own destinies by owning the most important theatres in the nation. But just as suburbanization and the baby boom were fundamentally altering the way Americans lived, the United States Supreme Court, pressured by the Department of Justice, forced Hollywood to sell off its theatres; as a result, it lost direct control of and access to what remained of the movie market.

The antitrust case against the Big Five and the Little Three had its origins in the administration of President Franklin D. Roosevelt. In Roosevelt's second term, he turned to renewed enforcement of existing antitrust laws to help bring the nation out of the Great Depression. Independent exhibitors, allied with women's groups and religious leaders who blamed the movies for all evils in society, had long complained of Hollywood's excesses of power, its domination of film exhibition. Get Hollywood out of the theatre business, they argued, return control of theatres to hometown merchants, and the evil producers would begin making good, clean family movies.

An antitrust suit charging Paramount Pictures, Twentieth Century–Fox, RKO, Loew's/

MGM, Warner Bros., Universal, Columbia, and United Artists with multiple violations of the antitrust laws was filed by the United States' Department of Justice on 20 July 1938. Hollywood lined up the best lawyers money could buy for what turned out to be a ten-year struggle.

Before Pearl Harbor brought the United States formally into the Second World War, each side maneuvered for advantage. In 1940 the government and the major companies seemed to have come to an accommodation. Both signed a consent decree which lasted three years. The government backed off from prosecution; the majors promised to eliminate certain abuses of power and arbitrate more fairly disputes between themselves and independent exhibitors. But with the prosperity of the war years, Hollywood grew too rich, too brazen. Independent exhibitors saw millions of dollars flow directly to Hollywood-owned theatres, away from their own box offices. The independents complained loudly and bitterly and the government re-opened the case. Hollywood felt confident it could win a court battle, but Hollywood was wrong.

In August 1944 the government reactivated the *Paramount* case, pressing for complete divorcement and divestiture of theatre chains. Simply put, the government wanted to split the major companies in two. One division would handle production and distribution; a separate company would handle theatre operations. That was the divorcement part. Divestiture meant that the two new companies had to have separate owners. No common parties could control them. They had to become two distinct operations. Also part of the government demands was the abolishment of trade practices that favored the big Hollywood companies and the major theatre chains, regardless of who owned them.

After numerous decisions and appeals, the United States Supreme Court finally ruled in May of 1948. The major film companies lost. Out went all the trade practices favorable to them. But more importantly the majors were ordered to divorce and divest themselves of their theatres. Howard Hughes, who had just purchased RKO, embraced such a forced sale. He wanted the cash. Barney Balaban, the chief executive officer of Paramount, went along. He wanted the proceeds for investment in television. Both these powerful businessmen reasoned that the fight was over, that selling the theatres might not be so bad.

Consequently, in 1949, after all possible appeals had been exhausted and all extensions granted, RKO and Paramount agreed to sell their theatres. Warner Bros. and Twentieth Century–Fox stalled a bit longer but eventually spun off their theatre chains in the early 1950s. Loew's, parent corporation of MGM, struggled and resisted at every turn. Final divorcement

was not reached until March of 1959, two months shy of two decades after the filing of the complaint by the United States Department of Justice. Loew's took over the theatres, MGM the moviemaking.

The breakup did open up the market to independent exhibitors. Many new circuits were started, especially those centered around the only new type of profitable theatre, the drive-in. However, Hollywood film companies retained direct control of their markets through distribution. They still had the best films and dictated to whom they sold them. Thus Hollywood was not broken by the *Paramount* decision, just wounded. Although the major companies probably would have done far better in adjusting to the new world of suburban entertainment had they still owned theatres, they still held sway because they had the films exhibitors wanted. Now the issue became how to make popular films which could draw suburbanites out of the house.

· · · · · · · · · · · · · · ·

technological innovation

· · · · · · · · · · · · · · ·

Hollywood sought change through new technology, and its first choice was television. The movie moguls did not ignore television; in fact, they all sought to enter the television industry which started up at the close of World War II. Indeed, Hollywood had been

interested in television even *before* the outbreak of the war.

In 1938 the Academy of Motion Picture Arts and Sciences (better known for its annual Oscar fetes) and the Motion Picture Producers and Distributors Association (or the Hays office) jointly initiated a comprehensive study of the state of television technology and possible movie industry actions. Reports were commissioned, strategies formulated and debated. Hollywood needed to be ready. To protect their interests, consultants for both the Academy and the Hays Office advised the movie studios to gear up to produce the bulk of the television programs and to own and operate local stations, in the same manner that they had previously run theatre circuits. The motion picture industry, rather than competing radio interests headed by NBC and CBS, should take control.

Paramount Pictures stepped forward first. In 1938 it invested nearly five hundred thousand dollars in the DuMont Corporation, a small manufacturer of television sets and then an applicant for an experimental over-the-air license. Paramount's President Barney Balaban, a veteran exhibitor, foresaw the day that television technology would take its place in Paramount theatres. With a formal connection to one of Hollywood's most powerful companies, DuMont gained a leg up on the competition. It now had exclusive access to Paramount movies and the vast Paramount production facilities in southern California. With DuMont's stations in New York and Washington, D.C., Paramount controlled four of the nation's first nine television stations.

Paramount also began to formulate plans for a nationwide Paramount television network. The strategy called for Paramount's theatre chains to apply for and then establish stations throughout the United States. Television Productions, Inc., a new Paramount subsidiary, would supply the programs. New England Theatres, Inc., a Paramount-owned chain, applied for a station in Boston; the Blanke circuit in Iowa applied for a license in Des Moines. Soon the company had applications in for television stations throughout the Northeast, the Midwest and the South.

Paramount, however, was not the only interested movie company. Its Big Five rivals all sought a niche in the ownership of new stations. For example, Twentieth Century–Fox applied for licenses for stations in cities from New York to Los Angeles. And Loew's (parent company of MGM) and Warner Bros. both sought television stations in Chicago and Los Angeles.

The dominant radio networks of the day, CBS, NBC, and ABC, were also applying for licenses. The Federal Communications Commission (FCC) was in line to decide among these applicants, but in stepped another Washington agency, the Department of Justice. As the Paramount case was winding its way through the courts at the same time the applications for television stations were pending, the Department of Justice forced the FCC to postpone any decisions on the applications of the movie studios until that case was settled. The communications law prohibited granting broadcast licenses of any type to corporations convicted of monopolistic practices.

Once the Supreme Court ruled against the Big Five in May of 1948, the FCC declared the major Hollywood companies ineligible for the prized television licenses because they were part of a convicted industrial trust. Hollywood's dream of ownership and direct control of television never materialized. The motion picture industry had to seek other ways to deal with a world of suburbanites staying home to have families and watch television.

One strategy was the presentation of large-screen television images in movie theatres—theatre television. The film industry would entice the public away from their small TV screens at home by offering live television on the massive screens of the neighborhood movie house.

Spyros Skouras (right), CEO of Twentieth Century–Fox helping install theatre television, 1952.

The development of large-screen television had commenced in 1930 when the Radio Corporation of America (RCA) held a demonstration at Proctor's Theatre in Schenectady, New York. Throughout the 1930s RCA worked with Warner Bros. and Twentieth Century–Fox toward the day when the technology could be used in movie palaces.

In 1943 Paramount invested an alternative technology known as the intermediate film method. This technique allowed television signals to be sent to a theatre and then be converted—in 66 seconds—into a standard film image that could be shown in the traditional manner on a 35mm projector.

In 1948, once Hollywood learned that it could not directly own and operate over-the-air stations, it pushed to make theatre television

the preferred option for the use of the new technology. The programming attractions would be up-to-the-minute newsreels and exclusive televising of sporting events. Home television could offer neither. Twentieth Century–Fox and Warner Bros. ordered theatre television for their chains. Even the normally conservative Loew's chain signed up.

Paramount led the way. Since it owned and operated a television station in Chicago, that is where it chose to initiate experiments. It would work out the problems in Chicago, and then proffer the system throughout the United States. Launching day was 16 June 1949 at the mammoth (4500 seat) Chicago Theatre in the heart of the Loop. Television equipment recorded live stage acts in a studio and broadcast signals to the theatre where the images were turned into 35mm film. A capacity audience showed up and saw themselves, in the opening short subject, for the premiere.

But subsequent presentations in picture palaces in Chicago's neighborhoods failed to draw large enough crowds to cover expenses. Sporting programs did well enough, especially baseball's 1949 World Series. Championship boxing matches proved the only consistent money-making draw. Big Ten football, even when it featured local favorites from Northwestern University and the University of Illinois, was a dismal failure. After two years Paramount gave up on its experiment in theatre television and turned to other possible new technologies. The other Hollywood studios followed Paramount's lead. Hollywood would have to seek other methods to make its mark in the television business.

· · · · · · · · · · · · · · · ·

wide-screen images in color

· · · · · · · · · · · · · · · ·

In a classic case of product differentiation, Hollywood looked to new *film* technologies to tempt patrons back to the theatres. That is, the American film industry would seek to make films which looked very different from the black and white video images television sets were broadcasting into homes throughout the United States. The first of the so-called new film technologies were inventions which had been long available to the movie industry but had not been required for profit making during Hollywood's heyday of the 1930s and 1940s.

· technicolor ·

One innovation—color—had long been available to the American movie industry. By 1950 the best-known name in that field was Technicolor. Developed in 1917 by Herbert Kalmus, a scientist trained at the Massachusetts Institute of Technology (MIT), Technicolor had been constantly improved. At first it could produce only crude two-color images recorded with bulky special equipment. By the 1930s Technicolor had become one of the stars in such spectacles as *Gone with the Wind* (1939) and such treats as Mickey Mouse and Donald Duck cartoons from Walt Disney. Indeed, the full-color (or three-color) Technicolor process was first introduced in 1932 for Walt Disney's animated short subject *Flowers and Trees*.

Through the 1940s Technicolor was used in a select group of feature films, principally historical epics and lavish musicals. But Technicolor was expensive, kept that way so Herbert Kalmus and his investors could reap extraordinary returns from their years of experiments. The Technicolor company not only rented the

Three frames from *2001: A Space Odyssey* **(1968). These are actual frames from the film and give a sense of the full impact of the use of widescreen.**

All That Heaven Allows **(1955)**

Rear Window **(1954)**

The Birds **(1963)**

Filmmakers who moved to Hollywood from other countries often had unique perspectives on color. *All That Heaven Allows* was directed by Douglas Sirk, who came to Hollywood from Germany. Alfred Hitchcock came to the United States from Great Britain in 1939. *The Birds* and *Rear Window* represent two of his finest color productions.

Singin' in the Rain **(1952)**

The Bandwagon **(1953)**

West Side Story **(1961)**

● ●

Musicals provided Hollywood with a genre that lent itself to the manipulation of color. Consider the examples pictured here.

Once Upon a Time in the West (1969)

She Wore a Yellow Ribbon (1949)

The Searchers (1956)

Costumes, decor, and locations provided the opportunity for filmmakers to create with color. Three of the finest color films ever made are pictured here.

The Sherman Theatre of Milwaukee, Wisconsin advertising an early technicolor movie.

● ●

filmmaker the camera, but also the cameraman and a consultant, usually Natalie Kalmus, the wife of the company's founder, to make sure the film was made their way. One paid dearly for the privilege of using the equipment and experts.

In 1947 the United States government filed an antitrust suit against Technicolor to open up the market for owners of other color systems. A consent decree was signed three years later; Technicolor lost its monopoly. In the early 1950s giant Eastman Kodak surged into the market, introducing Eastman Color, which required only one, not three separate negatives. The studios began to widely adopt this cheaper alternative. The studios brought out Eastman Color under a variety of names. Soon Technicolor, which was forced to bring out its own single-strip process, had been reduced to simply one supplier among many.

In the late 1930s, fewer than 5 percent of all Hollywood films had been made in color; thirty years later, virtually all movies were made in color. In 1971 when *The Last Picture Show*

was released in black and white, director Peter Bogdanovich was hailed for creating a throwback to the old days, to the Hollywood masters of the past. Black and white images were forever clearly identified with Hollywood's Golden Age.

Color features certainly differentiated Hollywood's offerings of the 1950s from the grainy black and white images then available on television. But Hollywood went one step further and made its movies bigger and thus even better. Wide-screen images would certainly catch the public's attention and draw the lost audience back to the theatres.

● cinerama ●

In 1952 Cinerama offered spectacular wide-screen effects by melding images from three synchronized projectors on a vast (specially designed) curved screen. To add to the sense of overwhelming reality, Cinerama also included multi-track stereo sound. Theatres which contracted for the new process were required to employ three full-time projectionists and invest thousands of dollars in new projectors, special sound equipment, and the new screen.

Cinerama was not new. First displayed at the 1939 New York World's Fair, it was then known as Vitarama. The process was reintroduced as Cinerama on 30 September 1952 at the Broadway Theatre in New York. *This Is Cinerama*, a two-hour travelogue, featured scenes ranging from a gripping roller coaster ride at New York's Rockaway Amusement Park to a plane flying through the Grand Canyon. Its backers, including radio and newsreel star Lowell Thomas and former MGM president Louis B. Mayer, touted Cinerama as far superior to television.

At first business was brisk in the few Cine-rama installations around the United States. Backers followed the model of the theatrical road show, long used by touring Broadway shows. Only one large house was converted; tickets were sold on a reserved-seat basis at top dollar. The backers sought long, profitable runs, hopefully lasting a year or more.

At first they seemed right on target. *This Is Cinerama* grossed more than $20 million. In New York City it played for more than two years, the longest movie run in Broadway history. *Cinerama Holiday*, the company's second pro-duction, premiered in October 1953 and was nearly as popular. But the third effort, *Seven Wonders of the World*, issued in 1955, experi-enced poor box-office returns. By then Holly-wood had begun to release its own wide-screen films in CinemaScope and VistaVision. Cine-rama did well only when it had the market to itself.

• 3-dimensional films •

Close on the heels of Cinerama came another innovation—3-dimensional movies or, simply, 3-D. The process for creating 3-D effects had been around since the 1920s; it premiered as Plasticon on 27 September 1922 with *The Power of Love*. Two years later came a series of shorts advertised as Plastigrams. But the films crafted with the new process did not prove enough of a draw to lure the public away from black and white silent features. During those salad days there was little reason for the major studios to stray from the regular profits associated with standardized 35mm films.

In November 1952 Milton Gunzburg, a Hollywood-based entrepreneur, and Arch Oboler, a veteran radio producer, launched *Bwana Devil*, a crude African adventure story

A model setup for Cinerama, approximately 1952. Note installations for three projectors.

• •

starring Robert Stack. The narrative and stars may not have been top drawer, but the 3-D process caused quite a stir. Box-office take at premieres around the United States was good, and United Artists agreed to distribute the film during 1953.

During 1953 and into 1954, 3-D was hailed as the savior of the American film industry. The majors jumped in head first. In April 1953 War-ner Bros. issued what was to remain the most successful of these efforts, *The House of Wax*, starring Vincent Price, which grossed $1 million during its first week of release. Classic genre fare followed: MGM's musical *Kiss Me Kate* (1953), Columbia's crime tale *Man in the Dark* (1953), and Universal science fiction efforts *It Came from Outer Space* (1953) and *The Crea-ture from the Black Lagoon* (1954).

But by mid-1954 it had become clear that the added expense of special 3-D attachments to projectors and glasses which had to be issued to patrons was never matched by the extra take at the box office. The public's interest in 3-D waned and by 1955 the technology was back on the shelf. It remained dormant, only sporadically revived through the 1960s and 1970s. No innovation of 3-D has ever been successful and the heyday remains the brief interlude of late 1953 and early 1954.

• cinemascope •

The failures of Cinerama and 3-D did not discourage Hollywood. Since color clearly helped draw back audiences, maybe some cost-effective wide-screen process could also help. What was needed was a wide-screen process without the added complications and prohibitive investment of Cinerama and 3-D. The search for such a cost-effective system initiated a second phase in Hollywood's attempt to innovate "new" technology for the movies that was superior to home television.

The premiere of the most famous wide-screen process came on 16 September 1953 with CinemaScope. This wide-screen process used an anamorphic lens attached both to the camera and the projector to expand the size of a normal image. Thus the extra investment required was small. The first CinemaScope film, *The Robe*, was a biblical tale starring Richard Burton and Jean Simmons. Audiences of the day were dazzled. CinemaScope seemed to be the answer, a new technology to accomplish what theatre television, Cinerama, and 3-D had failed to do—win back the audience.

Like its predecessors, CinemaScope was not new. French inventor Henri Chretien had begun working on an anamorphic process in the 1920s but had failed to interest any major movie company. Spyros Skouras, president of Twentieth Century–Fox, learned of the Chretien system in December 1952. He hired the inventor to develop a lens which could be fitted to existing equipment. The resultant CinemaScope

did not require more than the normal crew of projectionists and the cost for a theatre's conversion could be kept under twenty thousand dollars.

The Robe so impressed MGM that it took out a sub-license from Twentieth Century–Fox. Warner Bros., after trying and failing with a similar anamorphic lens dubbed SuperScope, also signed as a sub-licensee of Twentieth Century–Fox. By the end of 1953 every major studio—save Paramount with its VistaVision process—had jumped on the CinemaScope bandwagon. The process also included, at least for the first year, stereophonic sound. By November 1954 it was reported that nearly half the existing theatres in the United States had facilities to show CinemaScope.

But equipping theatres proved more expensive than anticipated. To cut costs many theatre owners abandoned the stereophonic sound component; in 1954 Twentieth Century–Fox also commenced using monaural sound. From 1953 through mid-1956 all of Twentieth Century–Fox's CinemaScope movies were in color. But even that feature was abandoned with the black and white *Teenage Rebel* (1956). This made the product even cheaper.

• vistavision •

VistaVision was Paramount's answer to CinemaScope. VistaVision utilized a camera through which a traditional 35mm film traveled horizontally rather than vertically. This technique resulted in an image three times the size of the normal four by three negative. VistaVision premiered on 27 April 1954 at New York's Radio City Music Hall with a major Paramount film, *White Christmas*, starring Bing Crosby. All major Paramount films of the next few years were shot in VistaVision, and the process was even used by other studios, including MGM for *High Society* (1956). With Paramount's backing, Vista-Vision remained in use until 1961, when the last VistaVision film, *One-Eyed Jacks* starring Marlon Brando, was released.

In the mid-1950s other even more dramatic solutions were proposed. In 1955 Mike Todd brought out his Todd-AO which used 65mm film in the camera and a 70mm image for theatre projection. Todd-AO was exploited for *Oklahoma!* (1955) and *Around the World in 80 Days* (1956), each of which cost $5 million to make. But Todd died, and without a promoter Todd-AO fell into disuse. Technicolor offered Technirama, with an anamorphic lens and 35mm film traveling horizontally through the camera. *The Monte Carlo Story* using this process premiered in 1956. Cinemiracle, requiring three projectors and three cameras, joined in a complicated arrangement, was experimented with at both New York's Roxy and Grauman's Chinese Theatres for *Windjammer* during April of 1958 with limited success.

• panavision and eastman color •

The solution to wide-screen images in color would finally come with the merging of two products: Panavision lenses and Eastman Color film stock. Panavision was a small Hollywood company whose owner, Robert Gottshalk, had developed the MGM Camera 65, an anamorphic system, for *Raintree County* (1957). MGM used the Panavision innovations to even greater advantage with the 70mm *Ben-Hur* (1959). Panavision anamorphic projection attachments differed from the ones Baush and Lomb made for Twentieth Century–Fox for CinemaScope in that the optics allowed a change in the ana-

morphic power of the lens with a simple turn of a knob.

Panavision attachments soon became the most popular in the world, the industry standard. Licensees of Twentieth Century–Fox's CinemaScope welcomed an innovation; it freed them from the contractual servitude to a moviemaking rival. By the late 1960s Panavision became the standard for lenses and camera equipment to make Hollywood films. It provided a superior but standardized product for wide-screen images, one which continues to be used into the 1990s.

Eastman Color negative and color print film stock was introduced by the Rochester giant in 1950 to rival Technicolor. Its monopack form signaled the end of the three-pack (three different strips of film) Technicolor system because it was easier to handle and was far cheaper. Eastman Color was happy to service any new customers and so by the mid-1950s had become the industry standard. In fact, since the mid-1950s all (color) films have used Eastman Color. The name may read Metrocolor (owned by MGM), Warner Color, or Color by Deluxe (owned by Twentieth Century–Fox), but the basic stock is from Eastman Kodak. Only the processing differs. Indeed, Color by Technicolor came to mean only that Technicolor developed the negative using Eastman Color stock.

One problem eventually surfaced with Eastman Color: unstable dyes caused negatives to permanently fade. A new, low-fade process was introduced in the 1980s, but not before the colors in many films were lost forever. But in the 1950s this problem was not anticipated. The film industry was happy that Panavision plus Eastman Color enabled it at relatively low cost to provide a product far superior to the black and white images offered by America's television networks.

hollywood on television

Hollywood eventually made peace with the television industry. But the transition proved to be a slow and often painful one. The American film industry had been riding high in 1946; many movie executives who had helped shape the very origins of the film business found it hard to deal with the upstart competitor. But slowly, systematically, the Hollywood movie industry found a niche by making and selling films and series to television. In time it helped establish a new television genre—the movie made for television.

In the early 1950s the major Hollywood studios stonewalled the television industry as they attempted to establish their own stations and networks and then to innovate theatre television. Before it became clear that none of these business strategies would work, the studios logically refused to sell or rent their films to television. They held out for the greater profits which could be realized in a Hollywood-controlled television network. In 1954 it became clear that Hollywood would have to be satisfied as a program supplier for American television.

The corporate stonewalling by the major Hollywood giants did not prevent minor Hollywood companies, which were always looking for ways to make a quick buck, from offering their wares to television. In 1951, for example, Columbia Pictures established Screen Gems as a wholly owned subsidiary to proffer filmed material (existing and original) to television.

Such was the success with such early series as "Father Knows Best," that Columbia, long a supplier of B films to rural theatres, ceased producing Western and crime serials altogether.

The small Hollywood studios willingly also rented their backlots to fledgling television program producers and unemployed actors and craftspeople took up television work. But as the theatrical boxoffice continued to decline, the major studios also had vacant space. Thus, in 1955 the majors plunged ahead into television production. Warner Bros. led the way with "Cheyenne," "77 Sunset Strip," and "Maverick," all series episodes based on scripts and films the studio already owned. Overnight, Hollywood replaced New York as the center of program production for television. By 1960 film companies supplied the majority of prime-time fare.

As this jockeying for power in television production was taking place, feature films were being shown on American television. Initially they came from abroad, the bulk from struggling British film studios, especially Ealing, Rank, and Korda. Never able to break into theatres in the United States, the British capitalized on American television's willingness to show any available entertainment.

Monogram and Republic jumped on board the television bandwagon with a vengeance. These two (plus a multitude of even smaller producers) took their libraries of four thousand titles and made them available for television presentation before the end of 1950. Typical fare included Westerns (Gene Autry and Roy Rogers from Republic, for example), and thrill-a-minute serials ("Flash Gordon," also from Republic). Younger viewers loved these action adventures, but their crude production values (such as the repeated use of stock footage) only served to remind longtime movie fans of the extraordinary number of treasures still resting comfortably in the vaults of MGM, Paramount, Twentieth Century–Fox, and Warner Bros.

• the late show •

To understand how and why the long-dominant Hollywood studios finally agreed to rent (or sell) their vast libraries of film titles to television, one must go back to May 1948 when eccentric billionaire Howard Hughes purchased control of the ailing RKO. In five years Hughes ran RKO into the ground. Debts soared past $20 million; few new productions were approved to generate needed new revenues. By late 1953 it was clear that even Hughes, by then full owner of RKO, could not afford the financial bloodletting taking place at RKO.

Thus few were surprised in 1954 when Hughes agreed to sell RKO's film library to the General Tire & Rubber Company for $25 million. General Tire wanted the RKO back titles to present on its independent New York television station, WOR. WOR then set up its "Million Dollar Movie" series. To milk more cash from its deal, General Tire then peddled rights to RKO's seven hundred features and one thousand short subjects to C&C Television, which in turn rented them to stations throughout the United States in markets in which General Tire did not own stations. Overnight, General Tire made an additional $15 million. In one year

General Tire realized a profit of nearly $10 million from Hughes' fire sale.

These profit figures impressed even the most recalcitrant movie mogul. Thus, in the next twenty-four months, all the remaining major companies released their pre-1948 titles to television. (Pre-1948 titles did not require the payment of residuals to performer and craft unions; post-1948 titles did.) For the first time in the sixty-year history of American film, a national audience was able to view, at its leisure, a broad cross section of the best and worst of Hollywood talkies. Silent films were only occasionally presented, usually in the form of compilations of the comedies of Charlie Chaplin and Buster Keaton.

From the sale or lease to television of these libraries of films, Hollywood was able to tap a significant source of pure profit. This infusion of cash came precisely at a time when Hollywood needed money to support its innovation of wide-screen film spectacles. Television deals followed one after the other. Columbia Pictures, which had early on entered television production, quickly aped RKO's financial bonanza. In January 1956 Columbia announced that Screen Gems would rent packages of feature films to television stations; the initial package comprised 104 films. Columbia realized an instant profit of $5 million.

In March Warner Bros. followed suit. Two months later Twentieth Century–Fox engineered a similar deal. MGM followed in August with a $34 million contract with CBS which tendered the rights to the most famous feature regularly shown on television, *The Wizard of Oz*.

Paramount held out the longest because its management still thought the company had a chance to establish an independent presence in television, at this point in pay-television.

(HBO would prove Paramount right, but not for twenty years.) Finally, disappointed from its numerous failed forays and experiments, in February 1958 Paramount *sold* rather than rented its pre-1948 library. The initial returns were substantial—$50 million. But in the long run the buyer, MCA, then a talent agency, collected far more, enough, in fact, to purchase the ailing Universal Pictures and join the ranks of the major Hollywood studios.

From this point on, the pre-1948 largely black-and-white films functioned as the mainstay of innumerable "Early Shows," "Late Shows," and "Late, Late Shows." A decade later more than one hundred different films aired each week on New York television stations, smaller numbers in less populous cities. The three television networks booked feature films, such as CBS with *The Wizard of Oz*, only as occasional specials, not as regular programming.

The networks did want to show post-1948 Hollywood features in prime time, but this required agreements from the Hollywood craft unions. In a precedent setting action the Screen Actors Guild, led by its president, Ronald Reagan, went on strike and won guaranteed residuals for televised airings of post-1948 films. This guarantee set the stage for movie showings to become staples of prime-time television.

• saturday night at the movies •

NBC premiered "Saturday Night at the Movies" on 23 September 1961 with *How to Marry a Millionaire*, starring Marilyn Monroe, Betty Grable, and Lauren Bacall. Ratings were high. Of the thirty-one titles shown during this initial season, fifteen were in color, and all were post-1948 Twentieth Century–Fox big-budget releases. All had their television premiere on "Saturday Night at the Movies." NBC especially liked the color titles. RCA, pioneer in television color, owned NBC and used the network to spur sales of color television sets.

After CBS and ABC saw how their shows (CBS's "Have Gun, Will Travel" and "Gunsmoke" and ABC's "Lawrence Welk") fared against "Saturday Night at the Movies," they quickly moved to negotiate their own "nights at the movies." ABC, generally a distant third in the ratings during the 1960s, moved first. A midseason replacement, "Sunday Night at the Movies," commenced in April 1962. CBS, the longtime ratings leader in network television, remained aloof and did not set in place its own "Night at the Movies" until September 1965.

But with CBS joining the fray at the beginning of the 1965–1966 television season, the race was on. Television screenings of recent Hollywood movies became standard practice. High ratings were achieved with Alfred Hitchcock's *The Birds* (1963) in 1968 as nearly 40 percent of all television sets in use at the time tuned in. *The Bridge on the River Kwai* (1957), shown in 1966, and *Cat on a Hot Tin Roof* (1958), shown in 1967, achieved ratings almost as high. Clearly, recent feature films shown on television were as popular as anything the medium had to offer. Indeed, when *Gone with the Wind* (1939) was shown in two parts in early November of 1976, half the nation's television sets were tuned in.

By the fall of 1968, movies were shown every night of the week on either ABC, NBC, or CBS. This success of the movie showings on the networks caused the number of "Late" and "Early" shows to fall by 25 percent. Stations not affiliated with one of the three television networks built their schedules around pre-1948 features. Films like *Casablanca* (1943) and *King Kong* (1933), spaced judiciously throughout the viewing year, would year-after-year draw large audiences, but routine B thrillers and wacky low-budget war musicals spent their drawing power after one or two screenings. This unprecedented wave of movie programming quickly depleted the stock of attractive features which had not played on television. On the network level, the rule was to run a post-1948 feature twice ("premiere" and "re-run") and then release it into syndication so that local stations could air it on their "Late" or "Early" shows.

Soon there were too many scheduled movie showings on television and too few new films to fill the schedules. Hollywood knew this, and the studios began to charge higher and higher prices for television screenings. Million-dollar price tags became commonplace. For the widely heralded September 1966 telecast of *The Bridge on the River Kwai* (1957), the Ford Motor Company put up nearly $2 million as the sponsor. The film attracted some sixty million viewers against formidable competition. Hollywood wags predicted that $10 million price tags would appear shortly.

• television movies •

Network executives sought a way to create their own movies. They could closely track costs, and even use these TV movies to test new shows which might then be downsized to appear as regular series. Early in 1966 NBC contracted with Universal to develop a series of "World Premiere" TV movies. NBC stipulated that all films be in color, again to reinforce its leadership in manufacturing television sets. Once

the TV movie was shown twice on the network, rights reverted back to Universal, which could release the TV movies in theatres in the United States (a rare occurrence), then to foreign theatres (more common), and finally to U.S. television stations for their "Early" and "Late" shows (a common occurrence). The initial entry, "Fame Is the Name of the Game," starring minor luminaries Jill St. John and Tony Franciosa, was presented on a Saturday night in November 1966.

Thus, NBC led the way with the innovation of TV movies. Once ABC saw a successful trend, it followed close behind. Eventually CBS, smug with years of constant ratings leadership with traditional series, jumped on board. TV movies took only five years to become a mainstay genre of American network television programming. By early in the 1970s, movies made for television outnumbered theatrical fare shown on the three networks.

A typical movie made for television cost three quarters of a million dollars, far less than what Hollywood was demanding for rental of its recent blockbusters. And the ratings were phenomenal. Few expected that millions upon millions would have tuned in for "The Walton's Thanksgiving Story" (1973), "Night Stalker" (1972), "A Case of Rape" (1974), and "Women in Chains" (1972). Such fare regularly outdrew what were considered the biggest films of the era like *The Graduate* (1973 television premiere), *West Side Story* (1972 premiere on television), and *Goldfinger* (1972 premiere on television).

One TV movie in particular heralded the coming of age of movies made for television. During the 1971–1972 television season the ABC "Movie of the Week" (all TV movies) was the fifth most-watched series of the year. On 30 November 1971 ABC presented a little publicized TV film, "Brian's Song." One third of the households in the county watched, and half the people watching television that Tuesday night selected that movie about a football player who dies of cancer over the television fare on CBS and NBC.

This relatively inexpensive movie vaulted into tenth place on the list of *all-time* movie screenings on television. With *The Wizard of Oz* accounting for five of the top ten ratings up to that November night, "Brian's Song" joined *The Birds* (1963), *The Bridge on the River Kwai*, *Ben-Hur* (1959), and *Born Free* (1966), demonstrating that TV movies could win Emmys (five), prestigious George Foster Peabody awards, and citations from the NAACP and the American Cancer Society. When then President Richard M. Nixon declared "Brian's Song" one of his all-time favorite films, ABC reaped an unexpected publicity bonanza.

"Brian's Song" offered nothing special to distinguish it from the typical early ABC movies made for television. It cost less than a half million dollars to make: stock footage from Na-

tional Football League games and unknown actors and actresses kept expenses at a minimum. Shooting lasted only two weeks. "Brian's Song" was shot as written, just as Hollywood had produced low budget fare during the 1930s and 1940s.

The impact of the first-run of "Brian's Song" nearly equaled the publicity bonanza associated with a successful feature film. Books about the film's hero became best-sellers. The film's music moved onto *Billboard*'s charts. ABC showed it a second time to equally high ratings. The success of "Brian's Song" sent a strong message to the three television networks. From then on, they prepared for unexpected hits, instituting publicity campaigns to take advantage of twists and turns in public opinion, even to shape it, as only theatrical films had done in the past. Longer mini-series and novels for television were innovated. The success of the TV movie proved that Americans had an almost insatiable desire to watch feature-length films, whatever their origin, on their home television sets.

the new studio system

The transformation of America into a land of suburbs and drive-ins, the innovation of wide-screen movies in color, and the integration of the film and television industries led to a reformation of the Hollywood studio system. No studio was unaffected, but only one,

RKO, actually went out of business, and that was because of a very odd situation. Eccentric billionaire Howard Hughes bought an ailing RKO in 1948 as a plaything. He fired production chief Dore Schary and seven hundred more employees. He sold off the theatres. He stringently insisted on non-communist purity for studio personnel and product. Hughes managed to accumulate more than twenty million dollars in losses, and in 1953 the studio all but ceased production.

All the other studios survived. Indeed, given the ups and downs of the business, they did fine. What changed were the rankings. The Big Five and the Little Three were no more. After RKO's fall, the remaining seven were equal. They all distributed films and found independent producers to make the films. They all expanded into television. There was one new kid on the block, the Walt Disney operation. But despite all the changes, the new eight controlled the box office just as tightly as had the pre-war majors.

• mgm •

MGM almost went out of business. Nicholas Schenck took over Loew's in 1927 (upon the death of the company's founder) and thereafter ruled the Loew's/MGM empire with an iron hand. He clung to "his" theatres long after the other majors gave in to the decision of the U.S. Supreme Court, delaying their sale for almost a decade. It was 1959 before the company agreed to a plan to split off its theatres from the MGM production and distribution unit in California.

Schenck had long relied on Louis B. Mayer to run the studio on the West Coast. During the 1930s Mayer did a fine job. The 1940s proved more problematical for a man who seemed more interested in developing champion thoroughbreds than movie stars. In July of 1948 Schenck threw out Mayer and installed Dore Schary, a former writer, as head of production in July of 1948. Schary introduced more serious

subjects to MGM's production schedule. For example, MGM released *Intruder in the Dust* (1949), *Quo Vadis?* (1951), and *Ivanhoe* (1952), all based on famous novels. Schary struggled to find hits. By 1954 the studio of Leo the Lion had only one entry in the year's top-ten grossers, *Seven Brides for Seven Brothers*. Too often Schary efforts lost millions. *Jupiter's Darling* (1955), starring Esther Williams, went more than $2 million in the hole; *Plymouth Adventure* (1952), starring Spencer Tracy and Gene Tierney, lost $1.5 million.

Late in 1955, Schenck retired and his protégé Schary lasted only a few months more. This exodus set off a violent corporate struggle for power. After months of proxy fights and rumors, Arthur Loew, the son of Loew's founder, stepped forward from his long-held position as chief of international distribution to become president. However, Loew proved unsuited for the job and within a year gave way to veteran theatre executive, Joseph Vogel.

Vogel took charge, but had to grapple with an outside takeover attempt, rather than concentrate on making hit films. Joseph Tomlinson, a Canadian road builder, Stanley Meyer, a television producer, and Louis B. Mayer himself tried to wrest the company away. But they did not succeed. The result of the year-long struggle for power was that the once-mighty MGM was but a shell of its former self.

During the late 1950s, hits emerged infrequently from unexpected sources. Elvis Presley starred in *Jailhouse Rock* (1957); longtime MGM favorite Elizabeth Taylor projected a new image in *Raintree County* (1957) and *Cat on a Hot Tin Roof* (1958). Vogel gambled $15 million to re-make *Ben-Hur*, and it turned out to be the top-grossing film of 1960. Unfortunately Vogel also approved the $30 million spent to re-make *Mutiny on the Bounty* (1962), and this bust at the box office precipitated his ouster.

Vogel's successor was Wall Street executive Robert O'Brien. O'Brien approved the popular *Doctor Zhivago* (1965), directed by David Lean and starring Omar Sharif and Julie Christie. Indeed, during his first three years at the helm, from 1963 through 1965, O'Brien did quite well. Earnings actually began to climb, but soon calamity struck once again because of yet another outside takeover attempt lasting three years. O'Brien was able to rebuff this attempt only to lose the company in the end to Kirk Kerkorian, who simply wanted the shell of a studio as a symbol for his new Las Vegas hotel.

In 1969 Kerkorian appointed James T. Aubrey, Jr., formerly with CBS, as MGM's chief of production. Aubrey immediately cancelled fifteen films about to begin production, including the Carlo Ponti–Fred Zinnemann production of André Malraux's *Man's Fate*, which was scheduled to go before the cameras within days. In May of 1970, in a widely publicized action that many then interpreted (incorrectly it turned out) as a signal of Hollywood's imminent demise, Aubrey supervised the sale of much of the famed MGM back lot and the thousands of props from by-gone MGM classics. He also disposed of MGM's studio in Great Britain, of its theatres in Australia, South Africa, and England and of the MGM phonograph record subsidiary.

In the early 1970s under Aubrey, MGM turned to low-budget films. Some, like the black exploitation film *Shaft* (1971), starring Richard Roundtree, made money. But this strategy (as well as other corporate maneuvers) did not help in the long run. Once the sales were over, profits began to fall. In October 1973, just before he resigned, Aubrey took MGM out of movie distribution—the once-mighty Leo the Lion was out of the movie business and would remain so for almost a decade.

• warner communications •

In July 1956 founding brothers Harry and Abe Warner sold their share in Warner Bros. to a syndicate headed by Boston banker Serge Semenenko and New York investment banker Charles Allen, Jr. The sale caused a major rift between the two brothers who had sold out and Jack, who stayed on to help with the transition and then to become an independent producer. (Five years earlier, as required by the United States Supreme Court, the Warner theatres had been spun off into a separate company known as the Stanley Warner Corporation.) The new owners of Warner Bros. had no ties to the past and quickly moved into the television business. The new Warner Bros. tendered its pre-1948 feature films for an instant profit. With the production of the pioneering television series "77 Sunset Strip" and "Maverick," the languishing studio lot hummed once again.

But during the remainder of the 1950s and into the 1960s, Warner the movie company struggled, able to attract only a handful of hits from independent producers. In particular *Camelot* (1967) and *The Great Race* (1965) became big boxoffice successes. Risky ventures such as *Bonnie and Clyde* (1967) and *Who's Afraid of Virginia Woolf?* (1966) also made money. Even Jack Warner contributed a hit, the film version of *My Fair Lady* (1964). But together these efforts were not enough, and Warners' balance sheet moved into the red, making it at risk of a takeover. Seven Arts Productions, Ltd. of Canada distributed Warner films to television stations, and gradually Seven Arts came to represent the only healthy part of the company. In 1966 Jack Warner retired and sold the bulk of control to Seven Arts.

But this would not prove to be a long-term solution. In July of 1969 Kinney National Services, Inc., a New York conglomerate engaged in parking lots, car rental, construction and funeral homes, purchased Warner Bros.–Seven Arts. Steven Ross, son-in-law of Kinney's founder, put together the deal in part to attract the services of super-agent Ted Ashley. In his rush for new acquisitions, Ross not only picked up Warners and the Ashley agency, he also acquired National Periodical Publications (comic book publishers of *Superman* and *Batman*), and Panavision, the manufacturer of lens and camera equipment which were (and are) the standard in Hollywood. Ross wanted to create the ultimate media conglomerate.

Ted Ashley took charge of all operations. Warners' Burbank studio let go hundreds of employees and consolidated operations with Columbia Pictures. John Wayne's independent company, Batjac, settled at Warners. Ashley produced a string of successful films; *Deliverance* (1972), *What's Up Doc?* (1972), and *The Summer of '42* (1971) swelled corporate earnings. The last cost only $1 million but grossed more than twenty times that amount. The studio's biggest hit of the Ashley years proved to be the chilling *The Exorcist* (1973), based on William Peter Blatty's best-selling novel. As a division of Warner Communications, Warner Bros. the film operation settled into a period of consistent earnings.

• paramount •

Paramount had owned and operated the largest theatre chain during the Golden Age of Hollywood. That power came to an end late in 1949. Barney Balaban, the longtime successful president, saw no reason to fight with the Supreme Court's divorcement and divestiture order, and so split his empire in half. Paramount Pic-

tures retained ownership of the production and distribution arms; a new theatre company emerged as United Paramount Theatres under former Balaban aide, Leonard Goldenson.

United Paramount Theatres slowly transformed itself from a movie exhibitor to a television enterprise. The new company sold theatres and used the cash to purchase the ailing ABC television network in 1952. Money from the sales of even more theatres was directly injected into the ABC network and television stations through the 1950s and 1960s. United Paramount Theatres became American Broadcasting/Paramount Theatres, which in the 1960s became simply American Broadcasting Companies.

Paramount Pictures centered its operations at the studio in Los Angeles. Throughout the 1950s Paramount Pictures followed a fiscally conservative strategy. Barney Balaban, longtime corporate chieftain, kept a tight rein on budgets, always looking for ways to trim expenses and add to profits. For example, when Twentieth Century–Fox successfully innovated CinemaScope, Balaban countered with Paramount's less expensive VistaVision, a process which could be used on traditional projectors and thus required a smaller investment on the part of the exhibitor. Moreover, VistaVision enabled Paramount to keep pace with rivals using CinemaScope while never having to take out a license with and pay royalties to Twentieth Century–Fox.

But such skillful maneuvering did not work for long. Surely Paramount still produced the occasional hit. Producer Hal Wallis contributed steady profits from such efforts as *Gunfight at the O.K. Corral* (1957), starring Burt Lancaster and Kirk Douglas, and *Becket* (1964), starring Richard Burton and Peter O'Toole. Wallis' series of films starring Elvis Presley were the most profitable in the history of the movie musical, but still, in 1963, red ink appeared on the Paramount balance sheet for the first time.

Outsiders, seeing an undervalued enterprise, attempted to take over the company in a proxy fight. They pointed to such Balaban mistakes as selling rather than renting the pre-1948 films to television, underinvesting in television production, and failing to attract a consistent flow of films from independent producers. Rather than struggle on, Balaban retired in 1964, and immediately takeover attempts commenced. In the fall of 1966 a giant conglomerate, Charles Bluhdorn's Gulf + Western Industries, purchased Paramount. Bluhdorn installed himself as Paramount's president and hired former press agent Martin S. Davis to run things in New York and former actor Robert Evans to revitalize the studio in California.

Evans increased film production and had the studio buy the adjacent lot (formerly owned by RKO) from Desilu. But disasters came early on, with such mega-budget failures as *Darling Lili* (1970), starring Rock Hudson and Julie Andrews, and *Paint Your Wagon* (1969), starring Clint Eastwood and Lee Marvin. These two spectacles drove Paramount further into the red. But slowly the company reorganized and reemerged as an industry leader, its comeback secured by the 1972 release of Francis Ford Coppola's *The Godfather*. For the first twenty-six days of release, *The Godfather* brought in an unheard of one million dollars per day. Paramount was back.

• twentieth century—fox •

Twentieth Century–Fox began its transition to a new era in 1951. That year the company signed its court-ordered consent decree and began to spin off its theatres. For a time this new chain, National Theatres, still worked closely with Fox the moviemaker because Spyros Skouras, the chief executive officer of Twentieth Century–Fox, worked closely with his brother Charles, who ran the new National Theatres chain. Generally during the 1950s Twentieth Century–Fox had done well under Skouras' guidance. CinemaScope and Marilyn Monroe films led the way, as did newly established television operations.

When longtime studio boss, Darryl F. Zanuck, resigned in 1956 to enter independent production, the company seemed strong. Spyros Skouras tried out a number of replacements (most notably Buddy Adler) but none could match Zanuck's record. Soon Fox began to lose money. To help prop up the balance sheet, Skouras sold part of the famed back lot to Alcoa to be developed into Century City, presently home to any number of Hollywood agents. The deal which climaxed as "Saturday Night at the Movies" also helped add needed cash.

The red ink swelled in 1963 with the bloated production and subsequent boxoffice debacle of *Cleopatra*, starring Elizabeth Taylor and Richard Burton. Originally budgeted at $2 million (not extravagant for that period), the cost escalated to a record $30 million. To break even, at this cost, the film would have had to draw in more than $75 million at the box office. That meant *Cleopatra*'s popularity would have to rival that of *Gone with the Wind*. It never came close.

Anticipating the *Cleopatra* disaster, Spyros Skouras gracefully retired in July 1962. His replacement was none other than the longtime production boss of the company, Darryl F. Zanuck, who brought along his twenty-seven-year-old son, Richard, as his assistant. This choice surprised many since Zanuck had had little luck as an independent producer; his *The Sun Also Rises* (1957) and *The Roots of Heaven* (1958) fared poorly at the boxoffice. Moreover, Zanuck had little experience in the crucial financial side of running a studio. But he was a major stockholder in the company and, many believed, the only realistic choice.

The Zanucks swept in, temporarily closing down the studio and laying off hundreds of workers, and thus instantly saving millions of dollars. Zanuck senior plunged in and re-edited *Cleopatra*, and thus cut losses by millions. But in the longer run the management techniques Zanuck senior had used so successfully during the 1930s and 1940s did not work in the 1960s. *The Sound of Music* (1965) was only a temporary savior, and the multi-million dollar investments *Doctor Dolittle* (1967), *Star!* (1968), *Hello, Dolly!* (1969), and *Tora! Tora! Tora!* (1970) all failed at the boxoffice.

In 1970 Twentieth Century–Fox lost a record $77 million. A corporate struggle ensued and the Zanucks (father and son) were ousted, just as the company seemed on the verge of having to declare bankruptcy. Luckily, there were several hits already in the pipeline, including *Patton* (1970) and *M*A*S*H* (1970). When Dennis Stanfill, a corporate banker, came on as chief operating officer, he hired Gordon Stulberg as production chief. This duo supervised such blockbusters as *The French Connection* (1971), *The Poseidon Adventure* (1972), and *The Towering Inferno* (1973). Thus Fox was ready, in 1977, to fully exploit *Star Wars* and move to the top of the Hollywood studio hierarchy.

• columbia pictures •

MGM, Warners, Paramount, and Twentieth Century–Fox had to deal with jettisoning massive theatre chains as they adjusted to the new Hollywood economics of the 1950s. However, members of the former Little Three never owned theatres and could plunge into the television age "full steam ahead." Columbia Pictures reacted well and thus prospered during the 1950s. With the establishment in 1951 of its Screen Gems subsidiary to produce television series, Columbia began to back independent moviemakers who sought a place to distribute their work. Producer-directors Sam Spiegel, David Lean, Elia Kazan, Otto Preminger, and Fred Zinnemann all found a home at Columbia and created such hits as *From Here to Eternity* (1953), *The Caine Mutiny* (1954), *On the Waterfront* (1955), and *The Bridge on the River Kwai* (1957).

The Cohn brothers ruled Columbia until their deaths in 1956 (Jack) and 1958 (Harry). Abe Schneider and Leo Jaffe succeeded the Cohns, and under their leadership the company continued to prosper with such successes as *Lawrence of Arabia* (1962), *A Man for All Seasons* (1966), *Guess Who's Coming to Dinner?* (1967), *To Sir, With Love* (1967), *In Cold Blood* (1967), *Oliver!* (1968), and *Funny Girl* (1968). Ray Stark, producer of *Funny Girl*, moved to Columbia as its main hit maker. The studio differentiated its products with low-budget British films such as *Georgy Girl* (1966) and Joseph Losey's *The Go-Between* (1971).

A flexible Columbia found hits in unexpected places. In 1969 Columbia released *Easy Rider*. This story of hip young Americans searching for meaning in a crazy world cost less than one-half million dollars and grossed more than $25 million. Bert Schneider, son of the head of the company at the time, had backed the film and was able to convince his father to pick up this independently made film starring Jack Nicholson, Dennis Hopper, and Peter Fonda. But much of the credit for Columbia's successes during the 1960s has to be credited to executive

Robert Benjamin (left) and Arthur Krim (center), creators of the new United Artists, with Max Youngstein, approximately 1955.

Mike Frankovich, who served as head of production from 1964 through 1968.

The 1970s were not kind to Columbia. The studio lost $30 million in 1971, $4 million the next year, and $50 million in 1973. Cost cutting became the order of the day. In 1972 Columbia sold its studio lot and moved in to share operations at Warner's Burbank studio. Columbia remained a viable entity but only became a Hollywood powerhouse again in 1980 when Coca-Cola took it over and injected needed financial support.

• united artists •

United Artists entered the 1950s in the worst shape of any major movie company. Awash in red ink, founders Charlie Chaplin and Mary Pickford (still owners of controlling interest in stock) agreed to sell. In February, 1951 a syndicate took charge, headed by two New York entertainment lawyers, Arthur Krim and Robert Benjamin. The two lawyers struck a unique bargain with Chaplin and Pickford. If new management could turn a profit in any one of its first three years of operation, Krim and Benjamin could then acquire controlling interest. Timing could not have been better for the New York *wunderkinds*. The new United Artists hung out its shingle just as a number of independent producers began to seek out distributors to handle their creations. Within the first year of operation Krim and Benjamin picked up Stanley Kramer's *High Noon* and John Huston's *The African Queen*.

Krim and Benjamin took United Artists, which had not earned a profit in nearly a decade, to the top of the movie business. Krim and Benjamin attracted the work of such stars as Burt Lancaster and Robert Mitchum. Later they worked out deals with the Mirish brothers to distribute the films of directors Billy Wilder, John Sturges, Robert Wise, and Otto Preminger. All liked the freedom and services the new United Artists offered. Benjamin and Krim handled the financing, distribution, and publicity, freeing the creative talents to make movies.

Profits soared under the new management. Black ink averaged $12 million per annum in the 1960s. The "James Bond" series, produced by Albert Broccoli, commenced in 1962 with *Dr. No*. This series added millions to the United Artists' profit sheets. Unlike all its major competitors United Artists entered television in a limited way, principally by acquiring in 1957 Warner Bros.' library of pre-1948 shorts and features for release to television.

Krim and Benjamin cashed in on the conglomerate boom of the 1960s, selling for a handsome profit to Transamerica Company in 1967. This giant San Francisco–based insurance and financial services company had plenty of cash on hand and sought diversification. Krim and Benjamin stayed on to run the United Artists division, an arrangement which proved good for both sides until 1978 when Krim and Benjamin resigned.

• universal •

Universal was only a marginally profitable movie company during the Golden Age of the 1930s and 1940s. When the company was sold in 1952 to Decca records, Edward Muhl became head of production and looked for independent deals in much the same way United Artists and Columbia did. James Stewart came on

board to create a number of fine Westerns, all directed by Anthony Mann including *Winchester '73* (1950) and *Bend of the River* (1952).

Other stars lured to independent deals with Universal included Tyrone Power, Gregory Peck, and Alan Ladd. Universal still ground out low-budget series starring Percy Kilbride and Marjorie Main as "Ma and Pa Kettle" and Donald O'Connor playing opposite Francis the Talking Mule. But in the 1950s the shining light of the studio proved to be the efforts of producer Ross Hunter. His melodramatic fare made consistent money: *Written on the Wind* (1956), *Imitation of Life* (1959), and *Tarnished Angels* (1958), all directed by Douglas Sirk and starring Rock Hudson, Lauren Bacall, Dorothy Malone, Lana Turner, and Robert Stack. Hunter was also responsible for the successful Doris Day–Rock Hudson comedies of this era.

But in 1958 Universal's fortunes took a turn into the red. A year later the MCA talent agency acquired the Universal back lot, and three years later, the whole company. Under government pressure of an anti-monopoly suit, MCA spun off its talent agency and moved into the movie business full time. Under Lew Wasserman, Universal became a powerhouse of television production. Wasserman attracted such talents as Alfred Hitchcock to the massive back lot. Universal initiated the first TV movie series for NBC and crafted its famous and highly profitable tour of the back lot. The attractions seen on the studio tour had little to do with the actual production of films or television programs, but they drew millions of fans and skillfully promoted upcoming Universal films and television programs.

In the 1960s Alfred Hitchcock was Universal's most famous director, but a number of top filmmakers joined him at the studio. Clint Eastwood contributed *High Plains Drifter* (1973),

A young Walt Disney getting ready to merchandise *The Three Little Pigs* (1933).

● ●

and a young George Lucas made *American Graffiti* in 1973. The Mirish Company, Robert Wise, Richard Zanuck, and David Brown all left other studios to join Universal. By the time Universal released the blockbuster *Jaws* in 1975, MCA ranked at the top of the Hollywood film business.

• disney •

The one new player on the block was the Walt Disney Corporation. This studio had existed on the fringes of the American film industry since the 1920s, specializing in animation. But with the transition to the era of television, theatres cut off shorts and forced Disney to move into new arenas. In 1953 Disney formed its own distribution arm, Buena Vista. To fill this new channel, Disney began to commission and release non-animated films. Indeed, the first effort for the new Buena Vista was a documentary, *The Living Desert* (1953). Made for three hundred thousand dollars, it quickly grossed more than $1 million. Thereafter came live-action adventure films aimed at a family audience, including *20,000 Leagues Under the Sea* (1954) and the wildly successful *Mary Poppins* (1964). The final part of the Disney movie strategy included the regular releases of animated classics such as *Snow White and the Seven Dwarfs* (1938) and *Pinocchio* (1940).

But Walt Disney and his brother-partner Roy reasoned that the company would never make it solely as a film producer and distributor. They were probably right. So they branched out. In the 1950s Disney entered television and the theme park business. A struggling ABC television, under Leonard Goldenson, convinced Disney to create a weekly show. The program, under a number of names, including "The Wonderful World of Disney," offered the company a way to advertise upcoming movies as well as its theme park. Davy Crockett and later Zorro were film characters heavily promoted on television. The Disneyland theme park was

opened in 1955 and was an instant hit, providing the bulk of corporate profits.

Disney continued to make movies after the founder's death in 1966, but more and more the company relied on the profits of its theme parks. During the 1970s the company made millions, but less and less from its movie operations. During the 1960s, after the release of *Mary Poppins*, the company was less and less influential in the movie business, although certainly a power in the world of popular culture. But the company never fully left the film business, and so when new management took over in the 1980s, Disney was able to leap back into the serious filmmaking fray, and even to the top of the industry.

hollywood as a changing social force

The social impact of the movies in America changed significantly during the television age. Young Americans between the ages of 12 and 30, the baby boomers, came to dominate the theatrical audience; and consequently, their expectations and desires increasingly influenced the types of films released. To broaden the audience base, Hollywood loosened censorship standards as well. College students began to embrace films as an art form. In the two decades after World War II, movies in America

came to be seen not just as a mass entertainment form, but also as an art to be studied and analyzed in the same way that music, literature, and dance had been for centuries.

The nature of the new audience for the movies in the 1950s was different because people over thirty stayed at home; they deserted the movies for television. Teens and young adults had always gone out to the movies in disproportionate numbers. What was different in the 1950s, 1960s, and beyond was that the young people remained the only reliable, loyal audience for movies in theatres, and now the sheer number of these young people was greater than ever.

This new demographic was recognized by Columbia University social scientist Paul Lazerfeld as early as 1947. He argued that age had long been the most important variable for understanding the composition of the movie audience. And movie opinion leaders, those fans who "picked" the new blockbusters and spread the news by "word-of-mouth," had always been well-educated young people. In most art forms the old dictated tastes to the young; for the movies, the youth set trends for their elders.

But moviemakers in Hollywood, dominated by aging former exhibitors such as Nicholas Schenck of Loew's and Barney Balaban of Paramount, insisted otherwise. They had grown up in the era when movies had to struggle to establish themselves as the dominant form of *mass* culture. They struggled to take the family audience away from vaudeville shows and succeeded. That was how they learned the business, not through some sort of statistical analysis. No upstart social scientist, even at Columbia University, was going to tell them who did or did not go to the movies. Thus, after the Second World War, Hollywood continued to seek out a family audience, believing that parents still selected the movies to see.

The new youthful movie audience was first spotted by exhibitors who stood at the box office and noticed who was and was not anteing up their dollar for a movie show. In 1956 a survey noted that the greatest need voiced by exhibitors was for pictures appealing to the 15-to-25 age group. The same poll showed that Hollywood still doubted that this new audience constituted a significant portion of the theatrical audience. The good news was that this young,

well-educated audience was willing to pay more and more to go out to the movies. This quarter of the population paid for seven-eighths of the tickets, even with prices at the boxoffice steadily climbing past two dollars. Young people alone remained loyal to "going-out-to-the-movies."

The recognition of the so-called youth audience shifted the debate over the social impact of the movies. In the late 1940s the movies were still considered a mass medium, one which was significantly affecting values and beliefs of the American society as a whole. Indeed, this assumption lay at the heart of the investigation of the movie industry's ties to Communists, the witchhunt of the late 1940s and early 1950s. Anti-communists found Communists at work in Hollywood, and since it was *known* that the movies influenced society in important ways, it was permissible to identify and blacklist these radical moviemakers.

The witchhunt against Hollywood came from right wing factions in the United States Congress, particularly those on the House Un-American Activities Committee. There were two sets of so-called hearings, one in 1947, the other in 1951. The latter was more a part of the McCarthy red-baiting era and caused the film industry reams of bad publicity. However, the 1947 hearings were far more serious, since screenwriters who refused to answer questions were sent to jail.

Representative J. Parnell Thomas, head of the House Un-American Activities Committee in 1947, wished to prove that Communists dominated the Screenwriters Guild and, from their positions as writers of scripts, forced left-wing propaganda into Hollywood movies. Witnesses friendly to the committee, such as Jack L. Warner and Louis B. Mayer, told of the evil residing in "sin city," reinforcing the prejudices. By the end of the hearings the committee had cited ten men (nine writers and one director) for contempt because they were unwilling to declare under the glare of television lights and for the next day's headlines whether they had been (or still were) Communists.

But at no time did the House Un-American Activities Committee ever prove Hollywood issued left-wing films. Quite to the contrary. The investigation was really a public show, meant to generate publicity. The committee wanted to use Hollywood to show it was working to ferret out the Communist evil in the United States. Hollywood was considered so important a social force that this display, in the tradition of witchhunts after wars in the United States, was deemed successful. The committee only underscored what Americans already "knew": in the late 1940s Hollywood was a major social force in transmitting ideas and beliefs through the American culture.

But the 1950s signaled the end of one era and the beginning of another for Hollywood's role as a social influence and indicator. In 1955 the movie industry began to realize and exploit the realiable teenage market. The success of *Rock Around the Clock* in 1956 proved there was real money to be made from a teen film. Indeed, a new genre commenced—the teenpic. By 1960 the majors had absorbed the teenpic and made it their own. Successive generations of teenagers have demanded and received such films as an updated "Romeo and Juliet" in *West Side Story* (1961), regular Elvis Presley fare such as *Blue Hawaii* (1961), the Beatles in *Help!* (1965), and explorations of the meaning of life in *The Graduate* (1967), *Easy Rider* (1969), and *Woodstock* (1970).

It took an outsider to show the major studios that there was money in the "new" teenage market. Sam Katzman had earned his spurs with the "Jungle Jim" series of low budget films, starring the former swimming champion and ex-Tarzan Johnny Weissmuller. MGM jumped on the bandwagon and made a killing with *The Blackboard Jungle* (1955), starring Glenn Ford. The same year Warners issued Nicholas Ray's *Rebel Without a Cause* (1955), starring James Dean and Natalie Wood. Purportedly adult films examining juvenile delinquency problems, *The Blackboard Jungle* and *Rebel Without a Cause*, quickly found teen audiences as well. But over the titles of *The Blackboard Jungle* director Richard Brooks played "Rock Around the Clock," and this rock and roll tune soon became a million-seller. Surveys of the day reported high school students' favorite new star was James Dean. These two films gave rise to the youth movies of the late 1950s and 1960s which dealt with juvenile delinquency, drag racing, high school vice, and dating rituals.

To recapture more serious college-age filmgoers, Hollywood loosened censorship standards. The strict code of censorship so powerfully self-enforced during the 1930s and 1940s broke down. Movies became more and more an open medium. Television took the place as the more restricted "family" entertainment. On 26 May 1952 the U.S. Supreme Court announced its decision in the case officially known as *Burstyn v. Wilson*. This case, dealing with the presentation of Roberto Rossellini's *The Miracle*, established for the first time a constitutional basis for challenging the rulings of state and local censorship boards. It declared that motion pictures should be treated as "a significant medium for the communication of ideas." With this ruling the U.S. Supreme Court granted movies the same status as magazines, newspapers, and other means of speech pro-

Glenn Ford in *The Blackboard Jungle* (1955).

tected by the First Amendment of the United States Constitution. In the decade after *Burstyn*, the U.S. Supreme Court heard six movie censorship cases and, with each ruling, the powers of the censors were further reduced. Social reformers turned to television to locate the source of all evils in the American culture.

But to moviemakers the real censorship force had long been the Hays code maintained by the major companies themselves. With the rise of the new era of movie economics and the power allowed filmmakers by the Supreme Court rulings, the threat of self-regulation lessened. Exhibitors, looking for profits, could no longer be coerced into showing only films which followed the strict guidelines set up in

the 1930s. Under its new owners, United Artists defied the code by releasing two of Otto Preminger's films, *The Moon Is Blue* in 1953, and *The Man With the Golden Arm* in 1955, without the prior approval of the Production Code Administration. One mentioned virginity; the other openly showed drug abuse. Later producers also sought to provoke controversy with films dealing with formerly banned subjects. In 1965 there was *The Pawnbroker*, containing female nudity. In 1966 came *Who's Afraid of Virginia Woolf?*, with its excessive profanity. In that same year *Alfie* even took on the long prohibited subject of abortion.

In November 1968 the United States became the last major western nation to have some kind of systematic age classification of motion pic-tures: "G" denotes suitability for general audi-ences; "PG" suggests parental guidance; "R" is restricted to persons under 17 unless accom-panied by an adult; and "X" says no one under 17 will be admitted. Jack Valenti, successor to Eric Johnston as the head of the Motion Picture Producers Association of America, who had suc-ceeded Hays, developed and heralded the rat-ing system. In 1984 "PG-13" was added to indicate excessively violent films which might normally be rated "PG." Most films tend to get a "PG" or "R" since they are expected to mean adult fare, not to be found on television. There are regular disputes, but they usually only serve to heighten boxoffice interest.

By the late 1960s the movies in America had come to an altogether new plateau, one which elevated some films into the category of art. Film began to be analyzed by serious critics and taught in universities where students stud-ied the classics as they would the great works of literature. Indeed, movies replaced the novel as the dominant arbiter of social mores and cultural trends among the best-educated mem-bers of society. As the television set took up the place as the mass popular form, filmmaking began to acquire a special niche in American culture, and film-as-art became the password of the contemporary, post-1975 age.

A new economics and sociology of Holly-wood was in play by 1975, the beginning of our contemporary age. This transformation did not mean great changes in the films Hollywood made. Indeed, the form and style of the classic Hollywood film remained firmly intact, even with the rise of wide-screen films in color and the advent of television. But genres changed, new filmmakers entered the system, and Hol-lywood moved from studio production to a mode of independent production. But the tele-vision era did permit an opening, and so for the first time a serious documentary and un-derground film movement emerged in the United States.

What Everyone Should Know About The Movie Rating System.

GENERAL AUDIENCES

Nothing that would offend parents for viewing by children.

PARENTAL GUIDANCE SUGGESTED

Parents urged to give "parental guidance." May contain some material parents might not like for their young children.

PARENTS STRONGLY CAUTIONED

Parents are urged to be cautious. Some material may be inappropriate for pre-teenagers.

RESTRICTED

Contains some adult material. Parents are urged to learn more about the film before taking their young children with them.

NO ONE UNDER 17 ADMITTED

Patently adult. Children are not admitted.

11

· ·

a transformation in hollywood moviemaking

The Hollywood cinema of the television age—the 1950s, 1960s, and early 1970s—continued to employ the style and form of the Classic Hollywood cinema with the new technologies and new audiences. That basic style was re-adapted to wide-screen techniques and color by the mid-1960s. But the central fact of life was that the entertainment business had changed. More people would watch films on television than in theatres by the early 1970s. To lure patrons back to theatres filmmakers could not stand still. They had to offer something new.

The "New" Hollywood took on more daring themes, but crafted them in the classical style. To fashion these films, the director was touted as an artist, recognized and praised as the center of the creative process. He or she came to be considered an author of a film, like the author of a novel or the composer of a piece of music. His or her name regularly appeared before the title. By the beginning of the contemporary era (which I date from *Jaws* in 1975 and *Star Wars* in 1977) Hollywood filmmakers such as Francis Ford Coppola, George Lucas, and Steven Spielberg became the cultural idols of a generation in the same way novelists had only two decades earlier. College students began dreaming about creating the great American movie, becoming an *auteur*.

But the basis of the "New" film industry remained the regular production of genre films. These could most easily be sold on a mass scale and, remarkably with the new technologies and new audiences, the various fundamental types of genres hardly changed. Only their relative popularity fell or rose. For example, the West-

ern reached its acme at the box office in the 1950s, only to fall out of favor by the time the contemporary era commenced in 1975. And the contemporary era is best understood as beginning with the "re-birth" of the science fiction film with *Star Wars*. To understand filmmaking of the television era is to probe the changes in the Classic Hollywood film genres.

the classic narrative film in the television era

Movies made in America during the 1950s and 1960s continued to be created in the Classic Hollywood Narrative mode, albeit in color and in a Panavision wide-screen format. For all the tales of experimentation (and there were some), Hollywood continued to construct its films around principles which had been in place for more than thirty years. For example, Hollywood's use of color by Technicolor was almost entirely motivated by genre conventions. Through the 1940s and into the age of television, Technicolor was almost entirely identified with the musical, tales of adventure and romance, and films of fantasy. These three represented genres of spectacle. Try to imagine *Around the World in 80 Days* (1956) or *Singin' in the Rain* (1952) without color. From the late 1930s when *The Wizard of Oz* (1939) contrasted the fantasy world of Oz in color with

the stark black and white world of Kansas, Technicolor was restricted to specific generic uses.

Since it was realized early on that Technicolor must add to, not distract from, the sweep of the story, the "proper" rendering of the human complexion became central to the development of Technicolor cinematographic technique. Max Factor became a household name because he and his assistants were able to design the required make-up. To highlight actors and actresses, backgrounds were kept soft, in low contrast, and diffuse in texture.

Gradually color was adapted to all genres and all films. But as soon as color became widespread, crafty veteran directors, like John Ford and Alfred Hitchcock, began to experiment with other uses, and in a short time produced many of the greatest color films. They wedded color to the Classic Hollywood model. With the widespread adoption of Eastman Color during the 1950s, this process of change was further simplified.

Hollywood's use of wide-screen images offers yet another example of how the Classic Hollywood style was marginally adjusted to meet the needs of new technology and still produce seamless, continuous narratives. At first wide-screen processes were closely associated with a particular set of genres, those associated with sweep and grandeur: travelogues (*This Is Cinerama*, 1952, and *Cinerama Holiday*, 1954), biblical pageants (*The Robe*, 1953), and musicals (*Seven Brides for Seven Brothers*, 1954, and *Oklahoma!*, 1955). Hollywood wanted to overwhelm and impress the viewer, to emphasize the grand difference between the tiny, monochrome television image, in a width by height ratio of four by three, and the wider, vast color image.

But the early wide-screen efforts (before Panavision solved this crucial problem) lacked depth of field. It seemed that after the significant experiments with deep space in the 1940s, movies had a flat feel again. To compensate, early CinemaScope productions emphasized the long take, underscoring the vast, elaborate mise-en-scène of the spectacle. But once it became clear that there was no turning back and that wide-screen films would become the norm, traditional cutting styles re-emerged once again. By the late 1950s it was possible to see remarkably rapid editing, indeed as fast paced as any Warners' film of the 1930s, in Henry Levin's popular *Journey to the Center of the Earth* (1959) or Elia Kazan's more celebrated *Wild River* (1960).

Television also altered the way Hollywood made movies; if anything, it forced feature filmmaking to become simpler. The center of the frame (for both the wide-screen and television)

became the focus of all but the least important narrative actions. All significant information had to be centered so it could be seen on a television re-broadcast. Narrative continuity had to be so tight that viewers could go out of the room and still follow the story when they returned moments later. Television produces a viewing experience filled with interruptions for advertisements. The Classic Hollywood cinema, which had been created to offer a narrative flow without interruption, had to learn to accomodate them.

As the rigid era of studio control came to an end, most directors were able to form their own companies, distributing through a major company. With loosening censorship restrictions, it was possible to employ the modified Classic Hollywood style to fashion features dealing with more complex themes. With all the changes, many argue that the 1950s may have been Hollywood's greatest era: it produced the Westerns of John Ford, the melodramas of Douglas Sirk, and the thrillers of Alfred Hitchcock.

New models of moviemaking from Europe added a new dimension to Hollywood filmmaking, at least on the margin. To those who remembered the silent film days of the 1920s, this European influence seemed not very different from the invasion of the German Expressionists. Hollywood learned, absorbed, and adapted and came away with a new look for the narrative cinema.

In European films there was a looser, more tenuous linkage of narrative events, for which absolute closure was not necessary. Stories were located in real settings and dealt with the contemporary (often psychological) problems of confused, ambivalent, and alienated characters. Whereas characters in the Classic Hollywood cinema had to be well rounded, operating with clear-cut traits and characteristics, the European influence allowed for the possibility of confused characters, without clear-cut goals. At the same time, jump cuts gave a new look to comedies and sequences of violence. The possibility of playing with narrative conventions formed the core of Robert Altman's *Nashville* (1975) and Francis Ford Coppola's *The Godfather, Part II* (1974). Some American filmmakers went so far as to copy European masters, and thus from Woody Allen we received an homage to Ingmar Bergman in *Interiors* (1978).

But the Hollywood institutional structure would not permit filmmakers to fashion an idio-syncratic style totally apart from the tenets of the Classic Hollywood text. The mass audience could still understand these different-looking films. The classical premise of continuity of time and space remained in force: any radical departures were encompassed within inventions within the genre. Indeed, the European cinema may have provided alternatives (outlined in detail in the following chapter) which gave Hollywood a new facade, but it never for a moment shook the foundations of the Classic Hollywood rules.

new and old directors in hollywood

For longtime Hollywood filmmakers the television age proved to be an era of transition, a time when the last of the veterans from the silent era were replaced by new directors. By the mid-1970s, the beginning of the contemporary era, "movie brats" such as George Lucas and Steven Spielberg signaled to the world that Hollywood filmmaking had finally reached a new epoch. The old studio system had been supplanted by a more flexible means of independent production. But this transition did not occur before a number of great talents—often with long experience in the industry—led Hollywood through the television era. Indeed the John Fords, Howard Hawks, and Alfred Hitchcocks offered up their best work during the early years of the television era.

But the 1950s did see the sad ending to the careers of many talented directors, including such influential old-timers as Cecil B. deMille, Frank Capra, and King Vidor. DeMille, who had directed his first film in 1914, continued to mint money with his *The Greatest Show on Earth* (1952) and *The Ten Commandments* (1956). But critics noticed a considerable decline in the complexity and polish of his films. The same was true for Capra and Vidor. Frank Capra, who had directed his first film in 1926, continued on with marginal boxoffice efforts, including the delightful *It's a Wonderful Life* (1946) and *A Pocketful of Miracles* (1961). King Vidor had begun in 1919. His post-war efforts, including *The Fountainhead* (1949) and *War and Peace* (1956), only reminded many that his best work had been done two decades earlier.

At the boxoffice and in the Hollywood community probably the most successful of these old timers was William Wyler, who during the 1930s was noted for his adaptations of popular novels and plays, principally for producer Sam Goldwyn: *Dodsworth* (1936), *These Three* (1936), *Dead End* (1937), *Wuthering Heights* (1939), and *The Little Foxes* (1941). But greater success came after the war. Few films have been more honored by Hollywood than his *The Best Years of Our Lives* (1946). This achievement enabled Wyler to break his longtime association with Goldwyn and strike out on his own.

Wyler's *The Heiress* (1949), *Roman Holiday* (1953), *Friendly Persuasion* (1956), and *Ben Hur* (1959) earned a number of Oscars and millions of dollars. The critics praised his offbeat work in *The Collector* (1965) and *The Children's Hour* (1962). Wyler's work in the television era certainly does not rank with the best of Hitchcock or Ford, but to the moviegoing public of the time William Wyler represented the quintessential director, the crafty filmmaker who continued to find ways to make money despite the seeming decline of the American film industry.

Wyler certainly was not the lone talented craftsman still at work. Some, like Clarence Brown, Victor Fleming, Frank Borzage, and Charlie Chaplin, made only a handful of films after the Second World War. Chaplin's *Limelight* (1952), a nostalgic look at pantomime comedy of yesteryear, and Fleming's *Joan of Arc* (1948) were probably the most famous works of this collection of Hollywood filmmakers whose careers went back to the early 1910s.

Some directors continued working nearly until the day they died. Consider the case of Michael Curtiz. With *Casablanca* (1943), *The Adventures of Robin Hood* (1938), and so many other Warner Bros. classics, Curtiz was the ultimate Hollywood insider, largely unknown to the public. After the war Curtiz continued turning them out at Warner Bros.: *Mildred Pierce* (1945), the award-winning film noir tale of death and greed, starring Joan Crawford; *The Breaking Point* (1950), a remake of the more famous *To Have and Have Not*; *White Christmas* (1954) for Paramount, starring Bing Crosby and Danny Kaye; *King Creole* (1958) for his old mentor, producer Hal Wallis, starring Elvis Presley. Curtiz died of cancer only a few months after completing *The Comancheros* (1961), starring John Wayne.

Michael Curtiz was not the only director who worked into his seventh decade. Henry King retired in 1962 at age 74. In the 1950s he directed *The Snows of Kilimanjaro* (1952), *Love Is a Many-Splendored Thing* (1955), and his final film, *Tender Is the Night* (1961). George Stevens, Raoul Walsh, William Wellman, and Billy Wilder all continued to make films for a fourth or fifth decade. But two veterans of the film business, Alfred Hitchcock and Howard Hawks, top this list because they crafted their best work during the 1950s.

Alfred Hitchcock directed an impressive list of films after the Second World War including *Notorious* (1946), *Rope* (1948), *Strangers on a Train* (1951), *Rear Window* (1954), *The Man Who Knew Too Much* (1956), *Vertigo* (1958), *Psycho* (1960), *The Birds* (1963), and *Marnie* (1964), among others. Hitchcock also moved directly into television and crafted a popular weekly series. He arguably became the

The set of Alfred Hitchcock's *Rope* (1948).

most famous director in the United States, if not the world. Surprisingly, despite his fame and fortune, few deny that Hitchcock produced his best work through the 1950s into the 1960s. Hitchcock was that rare filmmaker who was able to craft masterworks of the cinema while retaining popularity with movie fans at large. Few directors have ever directed such a string of popular works that have also been celebrated by the critics as well. For example, celebrated French filmmaker François Truffaut called *Notorious*, Hitchcock's first film after World War II, "the very quintessence of Hitchcock," combining "a maximum of stylization and a maximum of simplicity."

Hitchcock's *Rope* has long been celebrated as one of the most involved, most complex tech-

nical exercises in Hollywood history. Not content with shooting in color for the first time, Hitchcock also decided to film the eighty-minute picture in seemingly one continuous take— with no cuts. No camera could hold the required eighty minutes of film, so at the end of each standard reel, Hitchcock tracked to a dark surface, changed the reel, and then moved out to begin the action once again. The intricate logistics of each ten-minute take were carefully planned and exhaustively rehearsed, with furniture and walls moved to accommodate actresses, actors, and action. With *Rope*, Hitchcock pushed up against the rules of the Classic Hollywood cinema. Although the film is brilliant as a technical exercise, the storytelling suffered. Hitchcock acknowledged placing technique over telling the story, saying "I undertook *Rope* as a stunt."

He limited his experimentation thereafter. The eleven films he made between 1951 and 1960 certainly rank among his (and the cinema's) finest. The 1950s also saw Hitchcock consolidate his public image as the Master of Suspense. Year after year he was able to draw in millions of fans through his skillful re-working of the theme of the individual entangled in events beyond his or her control or comprehension. Hitchcock seemed to be in touch with times during which many suffered from teeming insecurities below a surface of complacency.

For example, Hitchcock's *Strangers on a Train* (1951) played with an intricate pattern of doubling and parallels between an obsessive man who sought to murder his father and a tennis player who desired to divorce his wife to marry another woman. The "normal" tennis player and the psychopathic murderer frequently seem to have a great deal in common and, indeed, are linked from the beginning of the film by shots of their shoes arriving at Washington's Union Station. The success of *Strangers on a Train* restored Hitchcock's reputation as a master of the cinema and a popular Hollywood storyteller. It enabled him to become his own producer and thus, for the rest of his career, to closely supervise his filmmaking.

In *Rear Window* (1954) Hitchcock again took up a technical challenge, but this one was carefully embedded within a story of voyeurism and paranoia. Confining his camera to the point of view of Scotty (James Stewart), who is confined to his apartment with a broken leg, Hitchcock crafted a suspenseful tale of murder interspersed with black humor. The story focuses on Scotty, who is bored and frustrated during his recuperation and begins to spy on

his neighbors. In the process of recording Scotty's rear-window drama, Hitchcock made a film not only about "looking" but about filmmaking as well.

Hitchcock was hardly an elite artist and in the mid-1950s continued active filmmaking while throwing himself wholeheartedly into television production as well. In October 1955 the first "Alfred Hitchcock Presents" appeared on CBS, and the series ran for a decade. Of the approximately 350 episodes, Hitchcock directed only twenty, but he introduced them all, and his wry prologues and epilogues, delivered in a deadpan style to identifiable theme music (Gounod's "Funeral March of a Marionette"), made this moviemaker a national celebrity, with his own widely selling magazine and fan club.

All this activity did not seem to hamper Hitchcock's skills as a filmmaker. Masterworks of cinema regularly appeared from this artist who was at the top of his form. In 1956 Hitchcock remade *The Man Who Knew Too Much* with two of the biggest names in the business at the time, Doris Day and James Stewart. In 1960 he released *Psycho*, which, although on the surface appeared to be a cheaply made, black and white effort, was in fact one of the greatest examples of Classic Hollywood filmmaking. Staying strictly within the bounds of genre filmmaking he made the ordinary, bland world of Fairvale, California into the center of horror. *Psycho*, as a consequence, is now considered a classic of its genre, and in its day made millions of dollars.

Vertigo (1958), with James Stewart and Kim Novak, has become even more famous and revered. Some argue that it belongs in any list of the most important films ever made. With its stark, haunting images suggesting moods of drifting obsessions and hallucinatory dreams,

Vertigo has been interpreted and praised by critics of all stripes. *The Birds* (1963) and *Marnie* (1964) proved Hitchcock had not lost his touch as he moved into the 1960s. In these two popular efforts, Hitchcock played out his by-now familiar themes of guilt and paranoia with his trademark stylistic flourishes of rapid editing, subtle camera movements, and carefully chosen mise-en-scène.

Howard Hawks also made great films in a number of different film genres after the Second World War. He directed complex, elegant Westerns in *Red River* (1948), *Rio Bravo* (1959), *El Dorado* (1967), and *Rio Lobo* (1970), his final film. He also made hilarious comedies such as *Monkey Business* (1952), gripping adventure tales in Africa with *Hatari!* (1962), and even lavish musicals such as *Gentlemen Prefer Blondes* (1953). Through the 1950s and 1960s Hawks worked with some of the film industry's best known stars including John Wayne, Montgomery Clift, and Marilyn Monroe. Fans of the day flocked to his work, little realizing that these were the works of a cinematic master, a filmmaker more admired outside his own country than within. Like Hitchcock, although less famous to the general public at large, Howard Hawks did his best work in the television era.

If the decade of the 1940s (actually 1938 to 1952) marked Hawks' "Cary Grant" period, the 1950s and 1960s marked his "John Wayne" period. Wayne was, in fact, the centerpiece of Hawks' trilogy of *Rio Bravo*, *El Dorado*, and *Rio Lobo*. In *Red River*, audiences had one of the first looks at Wayne in a complex role. In this tale of one of the first successful cross-country cattle drives, Hawks helped (with John Ford) shape the essential John Wayne persona—a man of honor and courage, faithful to his ideals. *Rio Bravo*, one of the most celebrated Westerns

ever made, is actually a Western about Westerns, what critics call a meta-Western. The genre is really the vehicle for a story of the testing of friendship, honor, and courage under duress. Three different generations of men, the aging Walter Brennan, the mature Wayne, and the teenaged Ricky Nelson, struggle to free a community under the grip of an evil regime.

Popular and lucrative at the boxoffice, *Rio Bravo* is filled with the conventional Western archetypes, including the infallible sheriff, the lady with a shady past, the handsome sidekick, and the comic sidekick. And Hawks carefully used the Classic Hollywood style to extract great performances from John Wayne and Ricky Nelson. But in the end *Rio Bravo* is simply a retelling of the Hawks' film, the film he had been making and re-making since *Only Angels Have Wings* in 1939: A band of independent men form a bond and help a community recover from some crisis and return to civilization. For Hawks the filmmaker, the story of the bonds of friendship between the men are stronger than the bonds that civilization can offer in marriage, home, and family. *Rio Bravo* is a supreme achievement in its manipulation of the complex determinates of the Classic Hollywood system: story, stars, and studio style.

Howard Hawks of the 1950s represented the most "Hollywood" of Hollywood directors. He understood the rules so well that he could mold films which flowed so smoothly, so naturally that the viewers could forget that they were actually watching carefully constructed movies. He manifested the full potential of Hollywood genre filmmaking. It was Hawks of the 1950s in general, and *Rio Bravo* in particular, which inspired the Americanization of the *auteur* theory. Hawks was a director who was well within the Hollywood mainstream but who still could create brilliant personal visions, working and re-working the same themes and forms over and over again. Indeed, the early advocates of auteurism in the United States maintained that *Rio Bravo*, more than any other work, represented the best of filmmaking.

But as time passed in the era of television, new directors were needed to staff Hollywood's feature film production. There simply were not enough veterans hanging on. One clear-cut avenue into the ranks of directing started in New York, in the world of live television. Sometimes new talents moved overnight to Hollywood; more often they labored to establish themselves in television and hoped to be among the select handful who were called to California.

Sidney Lumet offers a vivid example of a television director becoming a feature filmmaker. A product of the Yiddish theatre of New York City, Lumet began his show-business career as an actor and then gravitated to directing. In 1950 he was offered a position as an assistant director at CBS television, and along with John Frankenheimer, Robert Mulligan, Martin Ritt, Delbert Mann, and George Roy Hill, directed a number of the live broadcasts of the Golden Age of Television. In fact, Lumet adapted a television script for his first feature film, *Twelve Angry Men* (1957), which was such a commercial and critical success that it earned Lumet an Academy Award nomination. His career in Hollywood was off and running.

Lumet became famous for his adaptions of plays into films, including Arthur Miller's *A View from the Bridge* (1962) and Eugene O'Neill's *Long Day's Journey into Night* (1962). Although Lumet preferred to operate from a base in New York City, ever disdainful of the Hollywood scene, he became a mainstream director in the American film industry of the 1960s. His most successful boxoffice attractions included *Fail Safe* (1964), *The Pawnbroker* (1965), and *Serpico* (1973). Indeed, his career seems to have been characterized by the seeming contradiction of creating an alternative to the optimistic themes of many a Hollywood genre film while never veering away from the confines of the Classic Hollywood style.

Stanley Kubrick is the exception to the typical image of the New York–trained director. From New York City and by *2001: A Space Odyssey* (1968) wildly successful, he remained ever the outsider. His background was not typical for he first worked as a photographer, not in television. He typified the company rebel who was able to work within the system but still retain a measure of independence. Blending influences from Europe and his own vision of the Hollywood spectacle, Kubrick was able to gain control over his own films. One significant hit was *2001: A Space Odyssey*.

Kubrick moved from the still image to the movies by making two documentary shorts for RKO and two low budget features, all in the early 1950s. Through these projects he learned his craft. In 1955 he met James Harris, an aspiring producer, and together they created *The Killing* (1956), a classy crime film about a group of small-time crooks who rob a racetrack only to see their money literally blown away at the end by airplane propellers. *Paths of Glory* (1957) was an uncompromising anti-war film, made at the height of the 1950s anti-Communist paranoia. This film led the way to Kubrick's darkly humorous films of the 1960s: *Lolita* (1962) and *Dr. Strangelove or How I Learned to Stop Worrying and Love the Bomb* (1964). These two films attacked the sexual mores and war interests of American society of the 1950s just as the liberal era of the 1960s was beginning.

2001: A Space Odyssey overwhelmed the new film generation. Here was a complex work, but one which was enjoyable and beautiful to behold. More than any other work of its day, *2001: A Space Odyssey* signaled that Hollywood could learn to appeal to a younger, television-reared audience. After *2001: A Space Odyssey* Kubrick returned to his darker-edged, biting examinations of the human condition. *A Clockwork Orange* (1971), *Barry Lyndon* (1975), and *The Shining* (1980) are remembered more for their use of music and striking visual moments than any unified view of the world or alternative film style. Like many (including most of the New York-based directors) Kubrick sought to combine the style of the European art cinema with the Hollywood style, and he was never able to circumvent the contradictions in that task. Kubrick is best thought of as an updated Orson Welles, able to achieve a touch of great cinema but unable to consistently deliver it.

There were other ways to become a director in the 1950s and 1960s. It was possible, for example, to enter Hollywood from the inside, a path that required some sort of edge. Each case was different, exposing the cracks that began to develop at the edges of Hollywood during the television era.

Samuel Fuller, a newspaper reporter who went to Hollywood as a screenwriter before World War II, represents the renegade who was willing to work cheap and take on any project, however small the budget. At first he toiled on low budget films, at the margin of the industry and did not get his chance to direct a feature until *I Shot Jesse James* (1949). But rather than take advantage of early successes and go to work for a studio, Fuller stubbornly clung to the edges of an industry looking for ways to make films in the television era. His independence first brought him to the notice of French auteurists François Truffaut and Jean-Luc Godard. Through the 1950s into the 1960s,

Fuller toiled in a number of genres including Westerns (*Run of the Arrow*, 1957 and *Forty Guns*, 1957), war films (*The Steel Helmet*, 1950 and *China Gate*, 1957), and crime films (*Pickup on South Street*, 1953 and *The Naked Kiss*, 1964). In all these films, Fuller was ever the gripping storyteller, drawing from his experiences as a crime reporter and an infantryman during World War II.

Stylistically Fuller certainly stayed with the rules of the Classic Hollywood cinema, but he became deft at provoking the emotions of the audience through what at first glance seemed to be shocking transgressions. For example, *I Shot Jesse James* is constructed almost entirely in close-ups, with few establishing shots. His films also are extremely violent, but always stay within the bounds of convention of that particular genre. In short, Fuller thrust and parried with the rules and standards of the Hollywood cinema, always remaining at the edge of accepted dictums.

Otto Preminger trained as a studio contract director during the 1940s, but by the 1950s he was far more famous to the public at large for his social provocation with such works as *The Moon Is Blue* (1953) and *The Man with the Golden Arm* (1955). To those who cared to notice, he also took on an idiosyncratic style, emphasizing the long take. But Preminger never openly defied the system which made him a rich and famous man. He simply took advantage of the possibility of a more adult cinema and made an all-black *Carmen Jones* (1954), an anti-military *The Court Martial of Billy Mitchell* (1955), and a jaundiced look at Washington power and politics in *Advise and Consent* (1962).

John Huston became another example of the studio-trained director who, in the 1950s, turned out a Hollywood-version of the "art-

Publicity material from Sam Fuller's *Shock Corridor* (1963).

● ●

film." After finishing obligations for Warner Bros. and MGM, Huston, with producer Sam Spiegel, founded Horizon Films and released *The African Queen* (1952), starring Humphrey Bogart and Katharine Hepburn. Taken from C. S. Forester's novel, adapted by writer James Agee, *The African Queen* told a bittersweet tale of love and war in Africa at the outbreak of the First World War. Suddenly Huston was a "new, hot" talent. He then moved to other important projects with *Moby Dick* (1956), based on the great novel, *The Misfits* (1961), Marilyn Monroe's last film, and *Freud* (1962), the popular biography of the famous psychoanalyst. Although all these films strained to make serious statements, they rigorously followed the rules of the Classic Hollywood cinema. Huston's im-

age always had him at odds with the Hollywood establishment, but in truth he never broke with it.

Stanley Kramer broke the ground for the serious Hollywood film with his simple tales with clear-cut humanist messages. With his overt liberal themes, Kramer symbolized the adult film to a new, serious film audience. He began his career as a writer but soon realized that the true power lay in producing. He produced *The Men* (1950), *High Noon* (1952), and *The Member of the Wedding* (1952) for director Fred Zinnemann and *The Sniper* (1952) and *The Caine Mutiny* (1954) for director Edward Dmytryk. Kramer then went on to produce and direct *Not as a Stranger* (1955), *The Defiant Ones* (1958), *On the Beach* (1959), *Inherit the Wind*

(1960), and *Judgment at Nuremberg* (1961). Through these works he tackled such formerly forbidden subjects as mental illness, racism, juvenile delinquency, and nuclear war. More than any Hollywood talent, Stanley Kramer set out to create the serious adult issue-oriented film, in which the spirit of the characters triumphed over the injustice in the world. The economic, social, and political system worked fine, if only permitted to work. Kramer should be remembered, along with Otto Preminger and John Huston, for proving that there was money to be made in an adult market.

recycling hollywood's genres

Before the movie brats could re-invent and re-charge the movie genres, Hollywood went through an era when genre films offered the best the industry could and did produce. In the Western, the melodrama, the musical, a number of talented directors fashioned their best work, Hollywood's contribution to the art of the cinema of the 1950s and 1960s. Such important talents as John Ford, Fritz Lang, and Douglas Sirk all did their finest work within the strict confines of film genres.

The 1950s represented a decade when Hollywood expended a great deal of time and energy trying to figure out which genres would work on the big screen and which would have to be ceded to television. As tastes changed, so did the movie audience's interests in certain genres. For example, the musical gradually fell from favor, and the Western reached a crest of popularity. Even as most filmmakers went off on their own as independents, they continued to produce forms of genre cinema, for that is what the studio distributors sought; a talented group of filmmakers through the 1950s and 1960s were able to fashion among the most complex films in the history of the Classic Hollywood Narrative system.

• the western •

The Western continued to be strong in the 1950s, even with the genre's constant exposure on television. Indeed, the 1950s and early 1960s can be labeled the Golden Age of the American Western film. For the movie-going public, stars defined the Western. John Wayne ranked as the biggest boxoffice star in Hollywood and with rugged macho portrayals starred in such hits as *How the West Was Won* (1962), *The Sons of Katie Elder* (1965), and *True Grit* (1969). For a time during the early 1950s Gary Cooper ranked up there with Wayne. Then came the "new," serious Jimmy Stewart. The laconic star, usually best remembered for his comedies of the 1930s and 1940s, surely drew in more fans to theatres during the 1950s with *The Man From Laramie* (1955), *Bend of the River* (1951), and *The Naked Spur* (1953).

After the Second World War the Western needed a new twist to compete with television. Looking toward an adult audience, Hollywood struggled with and began to release more and more adult Westerns. The simple, clear-cut mythology of good versus evil gave way to themes of racism, moral ambiguity, and the proper understanding of manifest destiny. Delmer Daves' *Broken Arrow* (1950), starring James Stewart and Jeff Chandler (who won an Oscar nomination), was a sympathetic tale set in the 1870s when Apache chief Cochise sought peace with the white man. *Broken Arrow* proved so successful for Twentieth Century–Fox it later was turned into a television series.

But the quintessential adult Western remains the Fred Zinnemann-directed and Stanley Kramer-produced *High Noon* (1952). Gary Cooper, as a lawman who struggles to save a town, won an Academy Award as did Dmitri Tiomkin for his haunting, pulsating popular theme music which soared to the top of the charts. The theme of the individual against the mob was sharpened by screenwriter Carl Foreman as a direct attack on the witchhunts of the McCarthy era, which were just reaching their infamous apex (nadir?) at this point.

Other experiments went beyond the innovation of the adult Western. A number of filmmakers sought to infuse the Western with elements from other genre forms. The Arthur Freed unit at MGM brilliantly crafted a musical Western in *Seven Brides for Seven Brothers*

(1954), directed by Stanley Donen. Arthur Penn, a television-trained director, combined the psychological thriller with the Western for his *The Left-Handed Gun* (1958), a psychological study of Billy the Kid, starring Paul Newman.

But the traditional Western hero never went away. *Shane*, for example, was one of the most popular Westerns of the 1950s, number three at the boxoffice in 1953. Alan Ladd played Shane in the traditional manner of the gunfighter with the questionable past, trying to go straight, but being forced to use his guns again to help clean up a helpless town. The location shooting (at Jackson Hole, Wyoming) and the beautiful use of Technicolor enabled this traditional Western to successfully compete with the wide-screen spectacles flooding American movie screens that year.

Some argue that television may even have helped the popularity of the Western feature film. Gene Autry, Roy Rogers, and Hopalong Cassidy renewed their careers as Western stars in reruns (as well as some newly made episodes) which flooded the television air waves. Once the Hollywood apparatus began to crank out prime time series, Westerns proved the popular subjects during the 1950s and into the early 1960s. Series such as "Wagon Train," "Wyatt Earp," "Bonanza," "Cheyenne," and the long-running "Gunsmoke" seemed to be on every night of the week. This was the era when Clint Eastwood first came to the public's attention in television's "Rawhide," James Garner in "Maverick," and Steve McQueen in "Wanted: Dead or Alive." All then successfully made the transition to stardom in feature films.

The film industry was able to support two of its greatest directors of Westerns at the same time: John Ford and Anthony Mann. Both carefully crafted Westerns which appealed to both mass audiences and discriminating movie fans.

John Ford's *My Darling Clementine* **(1946).**

• •

They stuck with top stars (John Wayne and Jimmy Stewart), but both tested and examined the very basic tenets of the Western mythos, and indeed, at times, the very rules of the Classic Hollywood cinema.

John Ford after World War II made *My Darling Clementine* (1946), *Fort Apache* (1948), *She Wore a Yellow Ribbon* (1949), *Wagonmaster* (1950), *The Searchers* (1956), *Two Rode Together* (1961), *The Man Who Shot Liberty Valance* (1962), and *Cheyenne Autumn* (1964). *My Darling Clementine* is the Western many single out as *the* classic exposition of the genre. Wyatt Earp (Henry Fonda) and his brothers help clean up wild Tombstone and in the process enable civilization to take hold. They leave at the film's ending, with Clementine (Cathy Downs) set-

tling in as the school marm. Civilization has come to the wilderness, ever holding an optimism found in the mythos of progress.

In retelling the familiar story of the Earp brothers standing up to the evil Clanton family, Ford demonstrated that Hollywood genre films could be fashioned into complex, popular artifacts. The structure of the film is straightforward and symmetrical, from the ominous opening confrontation between the Earps and the Clantons to the climactic gunfight at the OK Corral. The historical facts were bent to present a classic tale of action and adventure. Doc Holliday became the man caught in the middle. Like the central figures in *The Searchers* and *The Man Who Shot Liberty Valance*, he stood tragically between the forces of ever-advancing civilization and the retreating primitive West. Unlike the Earps, Doc Holliday never is able to locate his proper role in this changing world and thus dies at the end of the film.

To create this proper Western tale in *My Darling Clementine*, Ford, at times, bent the Classic Hollywood Narrative rules. For example, closely viewed, *My Darling Clementine* frequently lacks proper spacial continuity. For example, in sequence after sequence, Ford implies buildings off-screen that in later sequences we learn are not there. No matter, breaking the rules only served to make a better and more exciting story. *My Darling Clementine* represents a complex visual artifact, establishing a style that would appear in more complex form in *She Wore a Yellow Ribbon*, *The Searchers*, and *The Man Who Shot Liberty Valance*.

She Wore a Yellow Ribbon is the second of the three films that have come to be known as Ford's cavalry trilogy: *Fort Apache*, *She Wore a Yellow Ribbon*, and *Rio Grande* (1950). The films all deal with the United States cavalry and star John Wayne, but are only loosely related in terms of other story-elements. In *She Wore a Yellow Ribbon* John Wayne, in one of his first complex, subtle roles in a Ford Western, is the aging hero of a melancholy tale of the hardships of cavalry life. He plays Captain Nathan Brittles, who is to retire from the only life he knows. The complexity of detail pays homage to the life of the average soldier, whether on the winning or the losing side. In a haunting night scene Trooper Smith is buried by his fellow soldiers as General Clay, late of the War Between the States. Indeed, the sadness of the Civil War overlays the complete film in a way that recent veterans of the Second World War must have keenly felt three years after VJ-Day. *She Wore a Yellow Ribbon* is also often singled

out for its brilliant use of Technicolor. The hues are rich and muted, the tones mellow, and the richness often somber, intensifying the nostalgia and elegy for a cavalry caught on the edge of the civilized world.

The Searchers (1956) has been hailed as one of the greatest films ever made, despite the fact it was a boxoffice hit in American drive-ins and starred John Wayne. *Auteur* critics have canonized it as the *great* American film; contemporary directors as different as Paul Schrader, Steven Spielberg, Martin Scorsese, and George Lucas cite it as an inspiration. *The Searchers* certainly is a Western, a rousing adventure tale. But it is also a sad, almost melancholy examination of the contradictions of settling the Old West, filmed in haunting, shadow-filled hues.

At the center of the film stands Ethan Edwards (John Wayne), a bitter, ruthless, and frustrated veteran of the Civil War who engages in a five-year quest to retrieve an orphaned niece, Debbie, who was taken by a Comanche raiding party. The neurotic Edwards belongs neither with the civilized settlers hanging on at the edge of Monument Valley nor with the proud and heroic but doomed Native Americans he pursues. Edwards is torn between his respect for and his hatred of the Comanches he follows. He speaks their language and is at home with their customs, yet he ever seeks revenge for his murdered family.

Never in a Ford film has the wilderness seemed so brutal, civilization so tenuous and threatened. There are no towns, only outposts and isolated homesteads, tiny specks of existence amidst the towering buttes of Monument Valley. The imagery in vivid Technicolor is stunning. The massacre of Ethan's family is foreshadowed by a startled covey of quail, a cloud of dust, and a breathtaking red sunset. And few have not been moved by the image of the grown-up Debbie (Natalie Wood) running down a distant dune, unseen by her searchers.

The film dramatically ends with a battle framed from inside a cave; after turning away the Indian charge, Ethan emerges into the light, lifts Debbie in his arms, and only then (we think) decides not to kill her. Instead he takes her home—to a family long dead, a homestead long deserted. The closing of the film recalls the opening: Ethan stands just outside the doorway, able neither to enter nor to leave. The outsider is to wander the desert forever.

If *The Searchers* is one of the most beautiful films ever made, *The Man Who Shot Liberty Valance*, in black and white, is surely one of the most barren, the most bleak. This was a blockbuster project, bringing John Wayne and Jimmy Stewart together for the first time in what turned out to be a dark vision of the West as a place of deceit and lying. The stunning Technicolor vistas of Monument Valley are replaced by barren, rickety buildings and false hopes of glory.

In *The Man Who Shot Liberty Valance* the Old West has lost its epic proportions and moved into a ramshackle town, and the heroic deed (the shooting of evil Liberty Valance, revealed in flashback) is shown to be a lie. Ransom Stoddard (Jimmy Stewart) is hailed as the hero and elevated to a position of political power, while the true hero dies a pauper. Indeed, we learn that Tom Doniphon (John Wayne), former Western hero, has been unable to navigate the modern order of civilization. The motto "when the legend becomes fact, print the legend" becomes a cynical motto here in the swan song of the greatest maker of the Westerns. It seems appropriate that *The Man Who Shot Liberty Valance* challenges Westerns which have come before it and that the style of the film is so sterile, so artificial looking. The stark stylization of the mise-en-scène, and the nightmarish lighting render this Western a critique of Westerns which have come before it.

Anthony Mann was another Hollywood veteran, having first worked as an assistant on Preston Sturges' *Sullivan's Travels* (1941). *Devil's Doorway* (1950) was his first Western, and between then and 1960 out of a total of eighteen films he made, eleven were Westerns, five of which starred James Stewart: *Winchester '73* (1950), *Bend of the River* (1951), *The Naked Spur* (1953), *The Far Country* (1955), and *The Man from Laramie* (1955). At the time, Stewart was independently producing films and distributing them through Universal. These five Westerns underscore, as with John Ford and John Wayne, how the marriage of star and director can forge a great series of genre films.

Mann's Westerns center around an ambivalent, morally flawed hero (Stewart) who is driven in an almost hysterical psychopathic manner to destroy a villain who mirrors his own worst impulses, his spiritual (and sometimes physical) double. The danger to the hero comes not from the usual threats of Indians or forces of nature, but from emotions locked in his own personality. The disturbed psychological state is reflected in Mann's distinctive use of landscape. The story takes its figures from lush territories to parched deserts where the climactic struggle can take place in the most desolate of craggy rock formations. No civilization here, only the primitive struggle to find oneself.

Winchester '73 depicts a battle between brothers who are linked together in their race to find a prized gun. After finishing necessary obligations, Mann made his next seven films (from 1952 through 1955) in partnership with Stewart. Here audiences experienced a new Jimmy Stewart persona. Before he had been a faltering, perpetual adolescent. Now from that endearing small-town fella came a colder, edgier individual, an obsessed neurotic distrustful of the conventions of society. The public embraced this new screen image and the Mann-directed films proved successes at the box office. Later in the same decade Alfred Hitchcock would take advantage of the "new" Stewart in *Rear Window* and *Vertigo* as did John Ford a few years after that in *The Man Who Shot Liberty Valance*.

Budd Boetticher was not as famous as John Ford, or even as consistently successful at the box office as Anthony Mann. But during the 1950s Boetticher crafted a number of fine Westerns starring Randolph Scott, including *The Tall T* (1957) and *Ride Lonesome* (1959). Boetticher worked in other genres but is most noted for the seven Westerns known as the Ranown cycle. Ranown was the independent production company formed by actor Randolph Scott and producer Harry Joe Brown, who hired Boetticher. Each was made in twelve to eighteen days and followed a classic formula. Boetticher and screenwriter Burt Kennedy elaborated and played with the genre conventions like variations of a musical theme in which we find an isolated, self-reliant individual struggling to survive in a hostile world. Often, as in *The Tall T*, the story moves from seemingly harmless comedy to convincing savagery. The evil is no cartoon effect, but primitive men who kill to live. Hero Randolph Scott stands as the perfect representative of the calm, aging cowboy trying to bring a sense of order to a world which is inherently chaotic.

The 1960s saw the end of the Western as a popular genre form. There were significant films made in this era, but in general public taste turned to other genres. Indeed, the Western had begun to play upon itself, to become self-reflexive. For example, Sam Peckinpah's *Ride the High Country* (1962) and *The Ballad of Cable Hogue* (1970) examined the myth of the Western itself. John Ford's *Cheyenne Autumn* (1964) and Arthur Penn's *Little Big Man* (1970) went further to take the side of Native American values over those brought in from Europe. The Western even began to make fun of itself. *Cat Ballou* (1965, starring Jane Fonda), *Support Your Local Sheriff* (1968, starring James Garner), and Mel Brooks' *Blazing Saddles* (1974, starring Cleavon Little) all were comic spoofs. In George Roy Hill's *Butch Cassidy and the Sundance Kid* (1969) the likable heroes, played by Robert Redford and Paul Newman, die at the end in ignominious circumstances. After they flee to, of all places, Bolivia following a botched train robbery, they are unceremoniously gunned down by the Bolivian Army.

The end of the genre actually came when foreigners began to do Westerns better than filmmakers in the United States. Italian (or spaghetti) Westerns developed into a thriving industry after the Second World War as the Spanish and West Germans as well as Italians attempted to outdo Hollywood. The best of their work ranks with the best of Hollywood's, both in artistic complexity and boxoffice attraction.

Sergio Leone proved Westerns made by an Italian could surpass nearly all of those coming from Hollywood. Leone had entered the Italian film industry in 1939 and even, for a time, worked for Vittorio De Sica, in whose *The Bicycle Thief* (1949) he had a small role. He also learned Hollywood methods by working on spectacles shot in Italy such as *Quo Vadis?* (1951), *Helen of Troy* (1955), and *Ben-Hur* (1959). With *A Fistful of Dollars* (1964), *For a Few Dollars More* (1965), and *The Good, the Bad, and the Ugly* (1966), shot in Italian and English, Leone became internationally famous for his self-reflexive, complex Westerns.

Leone reached his acme in his unique style with *Once Upon a Time in the West* (1968), starring Charles Bronson, Henry Fonda, Jason Robards, Jr., and Claudia Cardinale. This film, co-produced by Hollywood's Paramount Pictures, signaled, for many, the end of the Western as a viable form. The film set a standard for the use of wide-screen cinematography and a complex narrative which encompasses nearly all the fundamental elements of the Western myth. In fact Leone journeyed to Monument Valley so his ultimate Western could have location shooting in the land John Ford made so famous. With its swooping camera movements, extreme close-ups, and haunting music, there are those who argue that no Western since *Once Upon a Time in the West* has been made which even approached its complexity, texture, and careful understanding of the Western movie form.

• film noir •

The film noir, so vital during the 1940s, extended into the 1950s but ended with the coming of television. The film noir of the 1950s found its place in darker science fiction films and anti-communist diatribes. The wide screen format did not seem to lend itself to film noir. Still, the close of the cycle did see the creation of a number of important films in this tradition, in particular Orson Welles' *Touch of Evil* (1958), Robert Aldrich's *Kiss Me Deadly* (1955), and some of the best work of Fritz Lang and Don Siegel.

Fritz Lang labored skillfully not only in the German Expressionist cinema of the 1920s but also in Hollywood during its Golden Age. With *The Big Heat*, released in 1953, he created one of the most important examples of film noir. With Glenn Ford, Lee Marvin, and Gloria Grahame, *The Big Heat* told of a dehumanized

quest for vengeance by a renegade policeman against a remote master criminal whose power extended throughout a whole city. Here was the lone individual struggling in a chaotic urban environment against hopeless odds. Morality is shattered; no one knows who is good and who is bad. Lang's dappled lighting and skilled use of seemingly every possible icon of urban America reinforce the split.

The Big Heat played off a conventional story of a crusading police officer seeking revenge for the murder of his wife. The characterization and heroic ending are conventional enough, but the portraits of crime figures, from the gun moll Debby (Gloria Grahame) to the hood Vince Stone (Lee Marvin), were outlined in uncharacteristic detail, almost as if the criminals were more important than the dull, bumbling police chasing them. Violence is as integral to this world as brushing one's teeth or eating lunch. Bannion (Glenn Ford), the renegade cop, stands alone outside both the law and the crime world, willing to do anything to achieve his vengeance. But like Dirty Harry twenty years later, he is a master of violence, a haunting figure with absolutely no moral restraints.

Don Siegel, the creator of Dirty Harry, almost single-handedly kept alive the film noir during the 1960s. In the 1950s he was better known for his quintessential science fiction film, often read as an allegory of the paranoia of the McCarthy years, *Invasion of the Body Snatchers* (1956). *Invasion of the Body Snatchers* presents a world taken over by mindless pods who on the surface appear to be normal. In the 1960s Siegel turned almost exclusively to the crime thriller, the successor to the film noir, and created *The Killers* (1964), *Madigan* (1968), and *Dirty Harry* (1971). All these films are bleak examinations of policemen who work

Gloria Grahame and Glenn Ford in a production still from Fritz Lang's
***The Big Heat* (1953).**

• •

effectively only on their own, despite, not because of, the effectiveness of the political system.

• the musical •

The musical did not survive the television era. Only a Broadway hit such as *Oklahoma!* (1955), *South Pacific* (1958), *Pajama Game* (1957), or *Damn Yankees* (1958) seemed to guarantee popularity. In fact, in the 1960s only Broadway hits seemed to be produced, including *West Side Story* (1961), *My Fair Lady* (1964), and *The Sound of Music* (1965). The extraordinary success of *The Sound of Music* led to a number of

expensive imitations including *Finian's Rainbow* (1968), *Paint Your Wagon* (1969), and *Darling Lili* (1970). All failed at the boxoffice, officially ending the thirty-year run of the studio musical. But during the 1950s one director did craft significant contributions to this genre with his musicals from MGM.

Vincente Minnelli provided popular, complex, fascinating musicals, including *An American in Paris* (1951), an Academy Award winner, *The Band Wagon* (1953) with Fred Astaire, and *Gigi* (1958), the final major musical from the MGM factory of producer Arthur Freed. *An American in Paris* was a Technicolor spectacle starring Gene Kelly and Leslie Caron and is best known for a seventeen-minute ballet choreographed by Kelly and marking Caron's film debut. *The Band Wagon* emerged from a witty, engaging script by Betty Comden and Adolph Green, starred Fred Astaire and Cyd Charisse, and was given extraordinary life by Michael Kidd's inspired, innovative choreography. Classic tunes of the past were revived in numbers centered around "Dancing in the Dark" and "That's Entertainment." *The Band Wagon* used a true, backstage set piece, at the same time spoofing the conventions of the genre itself.

• comedy •

The comedy genre never vanished. Indeed, in the late 1950s the light comedies of Doris Day and Rock Hudson reached the top of Hollywood money lists, grossing millions against television's situation comedies. *That Touch of Mink* (1962), *Irma La Douce* (1963), *The Apartment* (1960), *Operation Petticoat* (1960), *Some Like It Hot* (1959) all finished as top ten box-office attractions for their respective seasons. Likewise, the films of Dean Martin and Jerry Lewis were consistent top ten boxoffice attractions. Comedies of the 1950s and 1960s came in all forms. Audiences could choose between the dark cynicism of Billy Wilder in his *The Apartment* (1960, starring Jack Lemmon and Shirley MacLaine), and the lightweight teenage tales best characterized by the vehicles of Sandra Dee. Director Frank Tashlin was able to fashion many of the era's most interesting comedies by spoofing the excesses of Hollywood, the nation's newfound obsession with television, and the continuing pervasiveness of the mass culture society.

Frank Tashlin may have made his best film with *Will Success Spoil Rock Hunter?* (1957), starring Jayne Mansfield and Tony Randall. In a style of the theatre of the absurd, he produced a brilliant critique of the ideal male and female image during the conservative 1950s. The movie is filled with quotations, filmic and non-filmic references, and in-jokes to such an extent that it verges on modern dadaist art. Tashlin, more than any Hollywood filmmaker, made fun of the new medium of television. His films are also filled with images of comic books and film animation, drawing out the mosaic collective nature of the filmic image itself. Tashlin's admirers argue that at its best his style can be understood as constructing a film from bits and pieces of pop culture in the same way the Surrealists and Dadaists had done it thirty years earlier.

Frenetic comedies of collage became Tashlin's specialty, as can be seen in *Artists and Models* (1955), *The Girl Can't Help It* (1956), *Rock-a-Bye Baby* (1958), *Cinderfella* (1960), and *The Disorderly Orderly* (1964). Tashlin's animation background allowed him to see everyday life as a visually surreal experience, as a kind of cartoon itself. In fact, Tashlin's features often resemble live versions of the Warners' cartoons he supervised. Jerry Lewis, the star of a number of Tashlin's best remembered feature films, can best be understood as a cartoon character, trapped in an irrational, deformed world not of his own making. Tashlin's stylistic trademarks included complex wide-screen images in radiant color, a frenzied pacing made possible through intricate editing, and, above all, the exploration of all the possibilities of mise-en-scène, not simply actors in front of a set.

Thematically Tashlin's films deal with the decay of the modern world. The traditional is overwhelmed by the icons of the new pop culture of the 1950s—rock 'n' roll, comic books, Jayne Mansfield. For example, in *Will Success Spoil Rock Hunter?* the popularity of Tina Marlowe (Jayne Mansfield) causes all other women to engage in dangerous bust-expanding exercises to the point of nervous exhaustion. The cartoon-like Marlowe is best understood as an animated parody of Marilyn Monroe. The ultimate contradiction of Tashlin's work lies in the fact that while pursuing these themes he worked in the very factory of their creation, Hollywood.

• melodrama •

Hollywood-style melodrama, long an industry staple, thrived in the 1950s as well. Its formula relied on tales of wrenching social problems, repressive small-town milieus, and a preoccupation with sexual fantasies. The narratives may have extended beyond simple excess, but in the end, as called for by convention, the family, the centerpiece of civilization in the melodrama, had to be temporarily stitched together, only to be torn apart in a succeeding film.

Douglas Sirk took the melodrama back to the basics, making films which looked old-fashioned even during the repressive 1950s. On the one hand, Sirk would create films of complete illusion, fully absorbing the viewer. But Sirk was a European left-wing intellectual with a background in Expressionism; thus he was familiar with the power found in the manipulation of mise-en-scène, how through gesture, light, and color he could undercut the very illusion he was denoting in his stories. Sirk was able to impose his own style and interests onto

scripts handed to him by producers Ross Hunter and Albert Zugsmith.

Sirk's remarkable skills enabled him to work within this most oppressive of genres and yet to critique it at the same time. *All That Heaven Allows* (1955) is a tale of a woman (Jane Wyman) who, after the death of her husband, chooses her gardener over a more appropriate suitor, thereby threatening the fundamental values of her middle-class existence. The film plays out this family crisis from the woman's point of view, focusing on her conflicting desires. Ron Kirby (Rock Hudson), the gardener, is a fantasy hero to women—tall, dark, self-contained, at work in the background, but attentive, gentle, even authoritative. He is a romantic figure precisely because he presents an alternative image to "proper" masculinity, challenging middle-class notions of social class and symbolizing an acceptance of the codes of romantic fiction. Skillfully Sirk uses mise-en-scène to indicate the mental states of its characters and to comment on the conservative values supposedly adhered to as part of the "correct" functioning of society.

Written on the Wind (1956) was the film which, two decades after its release, led to the critical rediscovery of the melodramas of Douglas Sirk. Film scholars in the 1970s began to notice Sirk's ironic use of figures, decor, costume, and lighting. We see a massive family mansion and oil pumps working incessantly against the skyline, vividly contrasting with the striking reds associated with Marylee (Dorothy Malone) in her sports car, flowers, and negligee and the cool greens associated with Lucy (Lauren Bacall). Sirk broke with all accepted Hollywood uses of color and instead went back to the basics of German Expressionism.

Sirk found inspiration for his use of space in Expressionism. Hallways and landings offer continual sites to play out the expected conflict. Characters constantly cross each other's paths and in the process exchange confidences, malicious innuendo, and accusations. The mise-en-scène is organized around strong primary colors, contrasts of dark and light, and exaggerated movement and gestures to produce a world dominated by physical and psychological violence, and marked by material and emotional excess which threatens to overturn the fragile stability of the established order. Sirk also played with cliché. For example, he cuts to a nodding mechanical horse and grinning child after Kyle's recognition of his impotence.

Sirk may have been the master of the melodrama, but others played the form in more standard fashion. Indeed, even with all the changes in Hollywood during the late 1960s and early 1970s, this traditional genre never fully went away. For example, the hit *Airport* (1970) offered the viewer little new in melodramatic twists or turns; it was simply a throwback to adventure films of the past. This and other "disaster" films—*The Towering Inferno* (1973) or *The Poseidon Adventure* (1972)—focused on a group of people in danger because of the failure of modern technology and then traced their survival. The dreaded disease of cancer became the outside menace in *Love Story* (1970), the first film to break the $50 million mark since *Gone with the Wind* (1939).

top grosser of 1964 was *From Russia with Love*; third in 1965 was *Goldfinger*; first in 1966, *Thunderball*. Bond, the fictional British Secret Service agent, hero of a succession of Ian Fleming novels, is the center of these fast-paced, extravagant entertainments, throwbacks to the Hollywood of the 1930s and 1940s plus superior special effects, location shooting around the world, and an overt sexuality not permitted under the Hays code.

Having captured the public's fancy with the initial entry—*Dr. No* (1962, directed by Terrance Young)—the Bond films have bridged into the era of contemporary cinema. Through the 1980s, all have been the creations of producers Harry Saltzman and Albert R. Broccoli. But the era of Bond's greatest popularity certainly came in the 1960s with Sean Connery as Bond in *From Russia with Love* (1963, directed by Terrance Young), *Goldfinger* (1964, directed by Guy Hamilton), and *Thunderball* (1965, directed by Terrance Young). Indeed an indicator of the extraordinary popularity of the Bond series during the mid-1960s is *Casino Royale* (1967), a spoof created by five directors (Ken Hughes, John Huston, Robert Parrish, Joe McGarth, and Val Guest), with no less than six Bonds, including Peter Sellers and Woody Allen. Since many saw the Bond films themselves gradually becoming self-parodies, *Casino Royale* provided those who cared with a double barrel of absurdity.

• james bond •

The James Bond spy thrillers, a genre unto themselves, have been the longest-running series of profitable cinema, going strong into the late 1980s. In the early 1960s the Bond films began to earn serious money: the seventeenth

• 'new' genres of the 1960s •

The 1960s, after the death of John F. Kennedy, was an era of questioning, of re-examining past values, including the tenets of film genres. A great many of the most faithful of film fans were seeking alternative lifestyles, new ways to look at and understand their turbulent world. To offer films attractive to this new audience, Hollywood began to release meta-generic cinema, that is, films which comment on past genres, trying to make sense of cinema's history. The most talked about example of this phenomenon was a gangster film about gangster films, *Bonnie and Clyde* (1967, directed by Arthur Penn), which turned expectations on their head.

In 1967 *The Graduate* (starring Dustin Hoffman and directed by Mike Nichols) set off a wave of new youth-oriented films. With the music of Art Garfunkel and Paul Simon, *The Graduate* proved a film aimed at college students could make millions of dollars. In 1969 came *Easy Rider*, a film which cost less than a half-million dollars but finished eleventh in the box-office standings. This motorcycle odyssey across the southern United States focused on two drop-outs from society searching for meaning in life. Backed by another haunting musical score, *Easy Rider* was conceived by Peter Fonda and directed (his debut) by Dennis Hopper. Then came Paul Mazursky's hip look at modern sexuality *Bob & Carol & Ted & Alice* (1969), Robert Altman's anti-war black comedy *M*A*S*H* (1970), the documentary of the world's biggest musical festival *Woodstock* (1970), and Mike Nichols' ultimate black comedy, from the Joseph Heller novel of the same title, *Catch-22* (1970).

Arthur Penn exemplified the trend of reaching out to a college age audience, often with films about the very basic genres of Hollywood. A product of the New York world of live television and Broadway, Penn had begun ten years earlier by examining the Western in *The Left-Handed Gun* (1958), the film noir thriller in *Mickey One* (1965, starring Warren Beatty), the police drama with *The Chase* (1966,

starring Marlon Brando), and the most praised of his films, the meta-gangster film *Bonnie and Clyde*. Penn's *Alice's Restaurant* (1969, based on Arlo Guthrie's whimsical song) saw him tilting against the establishment, making a name for himself as a Hollywood auteur. Penn proved one could make serious films that would also draw millions of college students to the boxoffice.

A new era—the current one—in contemporary cinema dates from the 1975 release of Steven Spielberg's *Jaws*. This film marked the entry of a new, younger generation of Hollywood directors. These "movie brats" and their followers have defined the new movie generation and contemporary cinema. Although they have not taken over, they have created a new era in filmmaking. But *Jaws* and Spielberg hardly appeared out of the blue one day. At the end of the television era, in the late 1960s and early 1970s, filmmakers working in the 'new' genres, with no ties to the Hollywood studio system, began to signal a new era in filmmaking.

Francis Ford Coppola, who provided the transition to the contemporary era, was the first movie brat to succeed as a Hollywood director. He made his entry, possible only because the American film industry had reached its lowest point since its creation, through a door which seemed open to young talent for an ever-so-brief period. His *You're a Big Boy Now* (1967) and *The Rain People* (1969) proved he could make interesting films; *The Godfather*, both parts (1972, 1974), proved he could make money by re-examining the genres from Hollywood's past. Coppola discovered that with careful re-working of the elements of the classic Hollywood genres, he could make blockbusters. George Lucas and Steven Spielberg would follow in Coppola's footsteps.

• • • • • • • • • • • • • • • •

renewing the
documentary form

• • • • • • • • • • • • • • • •

Maybe those outside Hollywood understood that mainstream filmmaking was changing even before insiders did. They found that a Hollywood in flux left openings for the work of alternative filmmakers and the release of documentary and experimental films in the United States. For the first time a serious, independent documentary film movement emerged, as did a thriving avant-garde film movement. Neither would grow too large, but they opened up significant, influential possibilities for new forms of moviemaking.

The origins of the interest in documentary filmmaking in the 1950s came about, in part, because of changing technology and movie economics. With the coming of wide-screen filmmaking, Hollywood turned to expensive cameras (plus new stereo sound equipment) to fashion required gloss. Such equipment was bulky, weighing in excess of one-hundred pounds. No wonder few in Hollywood even dared to think beyond an aesthetic of carefully staging scenes. Producers, to keep expenses at a minimum, insisted on strict observance of the rules of classic Hollywood filmmaking.

But outside Hollywood, filmmakers were beginning to experiment with newly available lighter, portable, inexpensive movie-making apparatus with which two people (one working the camera, one the sound equipment) could make movies. This technology had come into being because of the Second World War. In that conflict both armies demanded and got portable, durable filmmaking equipment to record battles, photograph equipment tests, and exhibit training films. It was the United States Armed Forces that began to "professionalize" 16mm equipment, formerly associated only with "amateur" filmmaking.

Soldiers who had worked with and seen 16mm images returned after the end of hostilities. A combat style became associated with war footage of real events over which the camera operator had no control. The Second World War sped up the innovation and diffusion of magnetic tape for sound recording. The Germans had pioneered this technology; the Americans brought it home as part of the spoils of war. Not only did the United States Army find that magnetic sound was better in tone and quality, but the equipment was portable and could be used with fewer snarls and problems. An even more far-reaching change came during the 1950s when the innovation of the transistor made tape recording equipment even lighter.

By the 1960s a filmmaker could go out with a lightweight, shoulder-mounted 16mm camera with a zoom lens. The reflex system enabled the camera operator to "observe" the action while shooting. A second person carried a compact tape recorder that used one-quarter-inch magnetic tape. A tiny radio transmitter kept the two pieces of equipment in synchronization. Like a journalist looking for the "facts" carrying only a note pad, the filmmaking team could go out and seek "the truth" unencumbered by the drag of heavy, expensive equipment.

But it took more than inexpensive, portable equipment to give rise to what would be labeled the "cinéma verité" (literally, film truth) movement. It also took significant changes in movie economics, in particular new places for film presentation. Television stations brought the nonfiction form to millions, with ever-increasing allocations of time to daily news reports and documentary series such as "See It Now" and "CBS Reports." A handful of theatre owners were willing to try something new, including documentaries. By the mid-1960s, campus film societies regularly presented 16mm documentaries to college audiences. Although these two venues never attracted the numbers still going to Hollywood films, for the first time the audience for documentaries constituted a base numbering in the millions.

Cinéma verité emerged during the late 1950s and early 1960s to dominate the attention of audiences and critics alike. The adherents of this style stressed capturing ongoing events, with minimum interference by the filmmaker. The new documentary filmmakers wanted to take advantage of the power of lightweight equipment to create a record of reality. Live sound tracks replaced the then dominant voice-over commentaries. The filmmaker was encouraged to make every effort to stay out of the way and not to influence ongoing events. To practitioners of cinéma verité, the filmmaker ought not to consciously present a point of view, but rather let the events recorded on film "speak for themselves."

Aesthetically, cinéma verité contrasted dramatically with the Classic Hollywood cinema. Hollywood unabashedly proclaimed itself a wellspring of popular entertainment; cinéma verité stressed the power of cinema to teach. These documentary filmmakers believed they could use their medium to explore details which could be captured only on film and could then understand and, they hoped, improve the world in which they lived. Education had traditionally been done with the written and spoken word. Cinema would not replace either of these traditional forms of communication, but it could help us analyze and comprehend in new ways.

In terms of film style and production, cinéma verité differed significantly from Hollywood techniques. Cinéma verité documentaries were always shot on location. They told stories, but they were based in reality and often lacked the happy ending required by Hollywood producers. In the best examples of cinéma verité, the events recorded by the filmmaker dictated the flow of the action. There could be central characters and logical transitions because cinéma verité did not abandon all Hollywood Narrative cinematic conventions. The theory of cinéma verité simply stressed that to learn the most from a documentary the facts should be able to speak for themselves.

The cinéma verité style was described as "rough." That is, the smoothly flowing camera movements, glossy textured images, balanced lighting, and Hollywood gloss and glamour were missing. Indeed, it became a virtue within the cinéma verité school of documentary filmmaking to embrace what Hollywood called mistakes. If the camera jiggled while someone was talking, that was good, for it proved that the action had not been staged.

Robert Drew headed a team which completed some of the first cinéma verité films made in the United States. In the late 1950s, working for Time, Inc., Drew and Associates created documentary films for television. These wcrc mcant to bc TV analogics to *Life* magazinc, pictorial reviews of major social events. Drew attracted to his project a number of talents, including at least four who would become famous exponents of the cinéma verité movement: D. A. Pennebaker, Albert Maysles, his brother David Maysles, and Richard Leacock.

For a while Drew and his associates crafted films which were presented on CBS, NBC, and ABC. But in the 1960s the three television networks began to establish their own documentary divisions (influenced by the success and style of cinéma verité). After its moment in the mainstream spotlight, documentary filmmakers moved to alternative distribution through college and university film societies, specialized theatres, and, later, public television.

Robert Drew came to filmmaking from the world of journalism. He was working for *Life* magazine when, in 1954, he became interested in documentary filmmaking. His idea was to bring the excitement of a photo-essay to television. Time, Inc. owned several television stations and through them Drew had a market for an exciting new form of photo-journalism. One of his first projects was a documentary of the 1960 Wisconsin Democratic presidential primary contest between Hubert H. Humphrey and John F. Kennedy. They were in a close race and the Wisconsin contest might be crucial.

The film, *Primary*, proved to be unlike anything most Americans had seen before. The filmmakers followed the candidates and their entourages appearing at rallies, greeting folks on street corners, preparing for radio interviews, even catching naps in cars and in hotel rooms. They also filmed the usual plethora of speeches and prearranged hullabaloo. But the filmmakers, perhaps because the candidates were less media conscious than they would be ever again, were also able to document Humphrey directing a rehearsal of his own television program, Jacqueline Kennedy nervously fidgeting while she tried to impress a Polish-American audience in Milwaukee, and John Kennedy anxiously awaiting the results of a contest he would win by a two-to-one margin. *Primary* seemed to offer a balanced report; it favored neither candidate but supported the two-party system. The distinction between this and previous election reports was in the newness of the film style, not in the subject matter or basic themes.

With *Eddie* (1960), Leacock, Pennebaker, and Albert Maysles turned their cameras on auto racing in general and championship driver Eddie Sachs in particular. This was a personal portrait. Eddie Sachs had lost two Indianapolis 500 Memorial Day races, even though he won the time trials and started first in line. The filmmakers photographed the races from fixed positions but achieved a new point of view by intercutting racing footage with extended interviews with the driver himself.

Drew and his associates then moved to ABC-TV to do the "Close-Up" series. This venture established what we know today as "the up close and personal" style, although Drew and his compatriots covered more than simple biographies. Indeed, first was "Yanki, No!" which dealt with anti-Americanism in Latin America. Their second effort, "X-Pilot," looked at the trials and tribulations of jet test pilot Scott Crossfield. "The Children Are Watching" examined the school desegregation controversy in Louisiana. The final effort in this particular series, "Adventures on the New Frontier," offered a "day in the life" of President John F. Kennedy. By this second look at the President, the cinéma verité style had become one of the mainstream tools of the television documentarian.

Richard (Ricky) Leacock began his career as documentary filmmaker long before he worked with Drew and Associates. Indeed, he worked with Robert Flaherty as a cameraman on *Louisiana Story* (1948). Leacock then perfected his craft through assignments for the United States government and on the "Omnibus" television series. Then in the early 1960s he became a vital part of the Drew team.

After *Drew and Associates*, Leacock went on to make the acclaimed *A Stravinsky Portrait* (1964). The challenge was to make a film about one of the great composers of this century without resorting to the usual one-on-one interview interspersed with concert footage. Leacock simply followed Stravinsky around. Throughout the film Stravinsky seems totally oblivious to the camera. We see the musical master at lunch, in discussions with musicians Robert Craft and Pierre Boulez, planning a ballet. Today such an approach would not seem that unusual, but in the mid-1960s it was considered a radical approach to honoring a great man.

D. A. Pennebaker turned away from the political matters of *Drew and Associates* and made films about the cult of rock music of the 1960s. *Monterey Pop* (1968) was a record of a concert, with performances by The Who, Otis Redding, Ravi Shankar, Janis Joplin, and the Mamas and the Papas. This one film helped bring the cultural revolution of the 1960s to the forefront; it stands as a reminder of the joy, freedom, and discovery we now associate with the Age of Aquarius. In vivid colors, *Monterey Pop* created a filmic sensation, regularly appearing at college film societies each spring.

But it was with *Don't Look Back* (1966) that Pennebaker found the perfect subject for his interest in a cinéma verité portrait of an influential musical artist. *Don't Look Back* is a record of Dylan's 1965 tour of England. It paints a vivid portrait of the young star through candid interviews with newsmen, informal chats with teenage fans, concert after numbing concert, arguments with hotel managers, and the end-

less hassle of budding international stardom. The grainy, poor quality of many of the film's images plus the frequently inaudible soundtrack combine to create the strong impression that this is truly a candid look inside the murky world of a rock star's tour. One is never sure when Dylan is "on," for he seems throughout the film to be constantly performing.

Albert and **David Maysles** were also Drew alumni. Like Pennebaker, they focused on portraits of talented individuals and became famous for their character studies including *Showman* (1962, about movie mogul Joseph E. Levine), *What's Happening: The Beatles in the USA* (1964), *Meet Marlon Brando* (1965), *Salesman* (1969, about Bible salesmen), and *Gimme Shelter* (1970), a look at the Rolling Stones concert in which a spectator was killed by the Hell's Angels hired to maintain order. The Maysles' films helped define a set of 1960s heroes, media images for a media age.

Fred Wiseman was not a Drew product, but he may have become, in the end, the most famous exponent of cinéma verité. (Indeed, he was still working in the late 1980s.) He moved directly to political events, making his reputation through a series of exposés of what mainstream America considered its most sacred of institutions. He took apart a mental institution in *Titicut Follies* (1967), a city police department in *Law and Order* (1969), a suburban, upper-middle-class secondary school in *High School* (1968), New York City health care in *Hospital* (1970), and military values in *Basic Training* (1971).

Wiseman brought his skeptical point of view to all subjects. He never offered a radical solution for bringing down the institution; he offered only the comments of a cynic. In each of his films we see the many faces of the institution. A handful rules, everyone else takes orders, few rebel. The average citizen simply goes

A publicity still from Frederick Wiseman's *Basic Training* (1971).

along, adapting as best he or she can. He ignored the stars (be they the liberal politicians of the Drew films or the musicians of Pennebaker) in order to reflect on nitty-gritty problems of the average American's life.

To do this Wiseman broke with the notion that cinéma verité could simply show the facts and then help us discover truth. When he took his audiences inside a selected institution, he carefully chose what he would show. The result was Wiseman's view of truth; he did not claim general legitimacy. To accomplish his goal, he extensively relied on the tools of cinéma verité: hand-held cameras and portable sound recording. But by imposing his structure through editing and avoiding an omniscient narrator, he made it seem as if he were bringing his viewers

inside the institution to make the analysis on their own. In reality, this former lawyer had chosen carefully, leading the viewer to carefully conceived conclusions.

In every institution Wiseman found the same abuse: the misuse of power. *Hospital* lays out the powerlessness of the poor who cannot afford adequate health insurance; *Basic Training* examines the indoctrination of new recruits. And so on. Instead of showing how an institution should work, as would have been the case in a typical instructional film, Wiseman shows us how it doesn't work.

The problem with cinéma verité, in general or in Wiseman's version, was that it offered up no solutions for the multitude of problems it so vividly documented. These documentary filmmakers wanted to somehow remain objective; they did not want to tender a position or a set of solutions. They assumed, instead, that whatever problems were shown could be solved through adjusting the social, political, and economic system, presumably through better governmental programs. Critics of cinéma verité accused the filmmakers of naive optimism. Radicals accused them of selling out.

the new american cinema

A more radical option to Hollywood filmmaking opened up during the television era when the United States saw its greatest activity in the creation and presentation of experimental cinema, principally from artists in New York City and San Francisco. Underground filmmakers had always operated on the fringes of the American culture, but in the 1950s and 1960s they worked with more intensity than ever before. As artists, they defied the norms of American society and culture, those of Hollywood in particular.

A truly experimental cinema became more and more possible during the 1950s and 1960s as camera equipment became more portable and less expensive. An underground film was nearly always 16mm wide; the theatrical standard of 35mm had always been far too expensive. The smaller 8mm "home movie" proved too fragile and could not capture all the information which these film artists sought to present. But this did not stop Stan Brakhage and Ken Jacobs, among others, from trying the cheaper 8mm medium to make films, which they would frequently blow up to 16mm for screenings.

Unlike Hollywood, the American underground has never been driven by profit. Underground filmmakers have, instead, attempted to fashion personal statements about the world for presentation to sympathetic members of a bohemian culture. While Hollywood standardized the length of its features at two hours, underground films have no standard length. They were finished when the filmmaker "ran out of money." Some run less than one minute (for example, Robert Breer's *A Miracle* is fourteen *seconds* long). Others run to lengths Hollywood-trained audiences consider excessive, like Andy Warhol's eight-hour study of the Empire State Building, *Empire* (1964).

In the 1950s as more and more intellectuals began to consider film an art form, foundations and grant providers began to offer funds to makers of art cinema. Even the United States government became involved in the late 1960s with the founding of the National Endowment for the Arts. An institutional network followed. In 1950 Amos Vogel had founded Cinema 16, an influential New York film society which promoted the viewing of experimental cinema. Then, with this model, as more and more colleges and art schools began to teach and study film, experimental filmmakers finally had a circuit of places to regularly show their works outside New York City.

The New American Cinema did concentrate on certain subject matter, usually filling gaps left by Hollywood. One popular genre came from a romantic tendency to take quite seriously one's personal life. Thus, portraits of family and friends were popular. In Andy Warhol's *Henry Geldzaher* (1964), this member of the Warhol group lay motionless on a couch for forty minutes. Stan Brakhage, in one of his 8mm *Songs* (1969), presented his daughter Crystal in her many moods. Indeed Brakhage, probably the most famous filmmaker in the New American Cinema of the 1960s, has recorded his diaries on film. He extended the home movie into what might be called a poetic study, making sketches of his children from the day of their birth.

The New American Cinema protested against social norms. A favorite topic was the insane activity of 1950s America preparing for nuclear war, as is seen in Stan VanDerBeek's *Breathdeath* (1964). But above all, the New American Cinema was vitally interested in cinema itself. These filmmakers prided themselves on seeking to understand what was essentially cinematic and on forcing the medium beyond what Hollywood held were its proper limits. Thus, Andy Warhol made films in which there was no movement, like the aforementioned *Empire*. Robert Breer took on frame-by-frame cutting in *Images by Images I* (1954). Tony Con-

rad made flicker films by simply alternating black and white frames. Stan Brakhage painted on film, deliberately scratching individual frames. To these artists, a film was like a musical composition, filmmaking a process by which to explore the basic parameters of the medium rather than to tell a Hollywood-like story.

In general, Hollywood-trained audiences reacted negatively to their first viewings of these films. There was no narrative to follow, no opening and closing to define the work. Underground filmmakers demanded that their audiences watch their films several times in order to make sense of them. The style tended to be as anti-Hollywood as possible. If Hollywood prided itself on narrative continuity through editing, the adherents of the New American Cinema sought discontinuous editing. If anything, the more disruptive, the quicker the pace, the better. The same was true for camerawork, sound, and mise-en-scène—break the rules and discover a new language of film. Activity centered in New York and San Francisco.

• new york •

The largest contingent of the New American Cinema worked in and around New York City where the mentor to many was Jonas Mekas. In 1962 he helped found the Film-maker's Cooperative to distribute the films of the New York underground. Two years earlier he helped create "The New American Cinema Group." Mekas was a filmmaker himself as well as publisher of the highly influential magazine *Film Culture*. Under his leadership, the Film-maker's Cooperative distributed all films submitted, making no judgments about quality, length, or subject matter.

At the same time, Mekas skillfully promoted series of exhibitions of underground cinema, commencing with the famous Monday night screenings at the Charles Theatre on New York's Lower East Side. Later, this became the Filmmakers' Cinematheque, open every night of the week. In addition, Mekas unabashedly proclaimed the virtues of the American avant-garde through his column "Movie Journal" in the influential weekly, *The Village Voice*.

Mekas' first film, *Guns of the Trees* (1960–1961), a 35mm feature-length project, presented aspects of the 1950s Beat culture in New York through the lives of four fictional characters. At the time he felt it might be able to construct a new wave on the model of the French. But this soon proved too ambitious. Mekas' next film was a documentary of Ken Brown's stage play, *The Brig* (1964). By this time he had shifted to a more personal mode, the diary on film. Staccato, single-frame flashes composed entirely in the camera were counterpointed with longer sketches of weddings, trips to the circus, and meetings. Inter-titles were inserted. Musical accompaniment was interrupted by speeches of the filmmaker. Mekas was thus working in the same mode as his influential colleague, Stan Brakhage.

Kenneth Anger did not always live in New York City, but for extensive periods of time made his base there. Anger grew up in Hollywood and developed a lifelong interest in the camp side of the movie business. His two books, *Hollywood Babylon*, I and II, expose an underground history of Hollywood that the studio executives sought to cover over. Anger's films explored the same issues of sexual and cultural deviance, of cultural convention and social myth.

Indeed, Anger was a holdover from the wave of experimental film which took place in the 1940s. He continued his filmmaking in the 1950s with *Eaux d'Artifice* (1953), and *Inauguration of the Pleasure Dome* (1954), but in 1955 he left the United States and did not return until 1962. At that point he commenced work on what many consider his most influential film, *Scorpio Rising* (1962–1964). This complex work, dominated by images of fetishism and sado-masochism, may be the most seen and most appreciated underground film of the era. Rock songs of the 1950s provide the sound track and comment on the actions of a motorcycle gang. The film lovingly focuses on the chains, belts, and leather of bikers as well as popular culture icons (James Dean, Marlon Brando), and right-wing political enthusiasms (through film clips of Hitler). *Scorpio Rising* offers a riveting portrait of violence, an exercise in mocking humor, and a spectacular celebration of alternative lifestyles.

Far more ambitious, however, was Anger's master opus *Lucifer Rising* (a first version released in 1974 and a second in 1980). This project was cut short when, at a 1967 San Francisco screening of the work-in-progress, the single print was stolen by one of the actors, Manson cultist Bobby Beausoleil, and was supposedly buried somewhere in Death Valley, California, never to be recovered. Anger then "retired." But by 1974 he had completed another version, a dense meditative work shot mostly in Egypt and filled with mystical images such as pinkish flying saucers hovering over the ancient pyramids. A far more complete, even bolder, version was released in 1980 and presently stands as a major work of this pioneering experimental filmmaker.

Robert Breer produced animated films, defining cinema's basic unit as the frame and a complete motion picture as thousands of frames arranged in sequence. In his collage films, thousands of disparate images rush by, in rapid fire, causing visual overload, even in the most experienced viewer. Breer began experimenting with collage style in 1953; a year later came *Images by Images I* (1954), 240 completely unrelated single frames squeezed into a ten-second film. His *Jamestown Baloos* (1957) extended the collage technique, as did *Horse over Tea Kettle* (1962), a wacky cartoon, and *Fist Fight* (1964), a cultural document of the 1960s.

From the beginning Breer worked in opposition to mainstream animation. The Hollywood cartoon made use of the continuous movement of characters in the same way that the Classic Narrative feature film did. Breer's films, on the other hand, are full of disjunctive breaks, multiple and discontinuous spaces and rhythms, and acknowledgements, often made in jest, of the animator's presence. He sought to expand the possibilities of rhythm and editing, of the soundtrack, and of meaningful noises and speech. The effect is a cinema of surprise.

Jack Smith may have been the most famous of the 1960s experimental filmmakers, if only because of the controversy surrounding his *Flaming Creatures* (1963), eventually banned by the state of New York's official censorship board. Smith found his creatures in people from the darkest corners of the nation's largest city. So androgynous were his characters that their sex could be determined only in shots of their genitals, the very shots of penises and vaginae that prompted the state's ban.

Hollis Frampton began as a photographer and turned to filmmaking in New York in the mid-1960s; in 1973 he moved to Buffalo to teach and continue his filmmaking career. Frampton crafted his films in an almost mathematical structure. *Zorn's Lemma* (1970), his best-known work, has a long central section in which alphabetized signs are gradually replaced with wordless images. Through this technique Frampton sought to carefully investigate the epistemology of cinema (the philosophy of how we know cinema) and pursued his study with mathematical rigor.

Before *Zorn's Lemma*, Frampton explored any number of cinematic possibilities, from the simplest use of black and white film stock (*Manual of Arms*, 1966) to the effects of abstract shapes (*Palindrome*, 1969) to the explorations of the re-structuring of photographic imagery (*Artificial Light*, 1969). Even those who praise the American underground cinema find Frampton tough going because he espouses so different a goal from that of the personal cinema artists like Stan Brakhage. Instead, Frampton approached his task almost as a mathematician might, theorizing about the fundamental nature of his medium.

Ernie Gehr, a minimalist, is often lumped into the same category as Frampton. He too has tried to radically re-examine the horizons of the cinema. To Gehr, film is not a vehicle for ideas, but simply a variable of light used in time and space. His films begin with this premise, and those who seek stories or even personal diaries find them sparse, encompassing a single location, a single scene. Once that world is established, Gehr rigorously re-examines it, one film technique at a time. In this way, his work resembles minimalist art, although Gehr himself disavows that term.

Serene Velocity (1970) is Gehr's most famous work. It was filmed on a single corridor, four frames (about a quarter of a second long) at a time. In structuring his film Gehr rotated between images with different focal length settings so that the corridor appeared to advance or recede, rapidly altering its special locus. By changing the focal length, Gehr was able to fashion a pulsating rhythm for his film. Indeed, the subject of this haunting film is the focal length of the camera. For him, and he hopes for the viewer, the cinema is a beautiful illusion. Unlike Hollywood filmmakers, Gehr foregrounds the techniques and apparatus of the cinema.

Michael Snow is best understood as a minimalist in the same mold as Ernie Gehr. But he presents a far different version of an alternative cinema expression. Based in Canada, but championed in New York and highly influential in that artistic community, Snow set up, examined, and laid bare one basic parameter of the medium after another. His films are organized not around stories but around film techniques themselves.

Consider *Wavelength* (1967). In that film the camerawork overwhelms anything we might label a character or a story, however hard we may search. *Wavelength* is a film about the zoom lens. In the beginning we see a wall and windows in long shot. By the end of the film the camera has zoomed to the wall, and the film ends with a close-up of a photograph. Hollywood has often used the zoom lens to tell a story but has hidden its use behind the conventions of Classic Hollywood storytelling. Snow examined in *Wavelength* the very technological process and possibilities of using variable focal lengths.

But Snow has also considered other fundamental parameters of the cinema. *Back and Forth* (1969) consists of panning shots. *One Second in Montreal* (1969) is composed of a set of still photographs. For *The Central Region* (1971) Snow designed his own specially built, remote controlled camera mount, able to perform intricate camera movements. In *The Central Region* Snow used that special camera to sweep the entire desolate landscape of a section

of northern Canada in alternative variations. This provocative three-hour film again tells no story, but is, rather, about the tensions between camera work, camera movement, and cinematic time.

Andy Warhol was probably the most famous of the New York underground filmmakers. Although more people have seen his paintings than his films and he was even more famous for hobnobbing with rich jet setters, there were roughly three periods in which Warhol made serious underground films. First came his silent, still-life studies in which the camera did not move and neither did the subjects. These included *Sleep* (1963), *Eat* (1963), *Kiss* (1963), *Couch* (1964), and *Shoulder* (1964), all about the subjects indicated by the titles. Studying the world through one particular object or movement fascinated the former fashion illustrator.

His second period focused on satiric looks at changing modern life. Early films in this phase even satirized Hollywood and included *Harlot* (1964), Warhol's version of the life of Jean Harlow, the fabled sex goddess of the 1930s. Warhol cast Mario Montez, a female impersonator, as Harlow. During the mid-1960s he also created dramas inspired by cinéma verité, such as *Beauty Number 2* (1965), and cinema merged with live performance, such as *The Chelsea Girls* (1966).

In the late 1960s and into the 1970s Warhol's interests centered on the sociology of sex. In his camp-parody films of this era he combined his interests in Hollywood and popular culture. In this era he offered up his most famous films, including *Lonesome Cowboys* (1968), about homosexuality and the Western myth, and *Heat* (produced by Warhol, directed by Paul Morrissey, 1972), a sort of *Sunset Boulevard* (1950) for the New York artistic community.

• san francisco •

There were also experimental films being made outside New York City, principally on the West Coast, in the San Francisco Bay area. Indeed, as New York City had its Film-maker's Cooperative for distributing underground films, the West Coast community had its Canyon Cinema, the experimental film community's other principle distribution mechanism. The godfather of Canyon Cinema was filmmaker Bruce Baillie. Canyon also published a newsletter, the *Canyon Cinema News*, and held screenings in various locations around the Bay Area.

Bruce Baillie concerned himself with the economics of independent filmmaking, and, in his own work, often seemed to be an outsider trying to understand —with compassion and concern—how people could and did survive in modern America. These films were not balanced, objective documentaries, but rather personal statements about the struggle of life. Baillie's *Mass for the Dakota Sioux* (1963–1964), a film dedicated to the Dakota Sioux Indians of his native South Dakota, deals with all aspects of an alien, contemporary America. Baillie shot footage off television and movie screens, overexposed it for effect, and did all he could to make the world of his film diffuse. He continued his personal exploration with *Quixote* (1964–1965), which tells of a trip across the United States on a motorcycle. Bruce Baillie represented a synthesis of many of the currents of expression of West Coast underground filmmaking.

Bruce Conner took the stuff of reality and image to create what may be among the most accessible and funny of the experimental films of the 1960s. He rummaged through films thrown out by laboratories and theatres and re-edited this "found footage" into a filmic collage.

The popularity of his films stems from the stream of humorous juxtapositions, overkill of the spectacle of destruction, and a scatological attitude toward uptight sexual attitudes, all compiled with ironic effect.

Conner located in San Francisco from his native Kansas and completed his first film, *A Movie*, in 1958. This film consisted of pirated stock footage of disasters and assorted bizarre documentary material. Planes drop bombs and torch the planet; tanks and soldiers kill; automobiles race around tracks toward ultimate death; the Bomb is detonated. Through his rhythmic, spatial, temporal, and graphic juxtapositions, *A Movie* becomes a comic collage about death.

But his most famous work is *Report* (1964–1965). Made with monies from a Ford Foundation grant, Conner took stock footage of the assassination of President John F. Kennedy and repeated key scenes to a rhythmic effect. Indeed, Conner re-edited the film at different times, so there are at least eight (maybe more) versions of *Report*.

• an american original •

Stan Brakhage, not based on either coast, probably represents the most famous and celebrated experimental filmmaker of his era. Brakhage's films combine the raw power of photography with a record of his life and family. These interests are repeatedly transformed and reworked in a turbulent swirl of color, light, and movement. Brakhage's purpose is to expand the world of vision to include not only re-viewings of what we normally see but also flashing abstract patterns, imaginations, hallucinations, daydreams, and night dreams. He represents, more than any filmmaker of his generation, the full-time commitment of the artist who works solely for the personal and the visual, who needs no meaning from literature or history to justify his creative project.

Brakhage spent his early career in San Francisco and New York. He learned his craft at the San Francisco Institute of Fine Arts; in 1955 he journeyed to New York City to collaborate with Willard Maas, Marie Menken, and Joseph Cornell. But it was when he returned to his home in Denver and married (in 1958) that Brakhage began to craft his own unique brand of film art.

He began filming his own family with *Wedlock House: An Intercourse* (1959). In *Window Water Baby Moving* (1959), he documented the birth of his first child. The films continued in an almost endless stream. Many consider *Dog Star Man* (1962–1964) Brakhage's most important work. This seventy-eight minutes of cinema basically follows one action: a woodsman (Brakhage) climbing a hill and chopping down a tree. But the film spreads out and explores this simple action. We see and re-see the landscape, the sun, the moon, the family, the beating heart, the lungs, even microscopic cells. This is a long work of four parts plus a prelude, with themes and variations worked and re-worked as they might be in music. Superimpositions, collages, "cutting within the frame," and triple impositions add to the film's complexity.

But whether from New York City, San Francisco, or Stan Brakhage's home in Colorado, documentary and experimental films, in all their various shapes, designs, and manifestations, did not provide the only alternative to the Classic Hollywood cinema during the 1950s and 1960s. Indeed, throughout the world, after the end of the Second World War, filmmakers began to experiment more and more with the various possibilities of filmmaking. The most serious challenge to Hollywood came from Europe where decades-old film cultures were based in a solid economics of production, distribution, and presentation. This challenge took the form of the "art cinema" movement, whose most influential and complex component could be found in the French New Wave, the initial subject of the following chapter.

12

· ·

the art-cinema alternative

European filmmakers were forced to adapt in the television age. Not only did they still have to battle Hollywood, they also had to test the new world of filmmaking in an era when television was taking over as the favored mass medium. During the 1950s and into the early 1960s, in Europe as in the United States, over-the-air television broadcasting grew to encompass the landscape. Film production and presentation in theatres declined. More and more filmmakers began to seek alternatives, in particular formulating a vision of film as art. More and more filmmakers self-consciously began to make art films, aiming to make observations and statements about the human condition. Filmgoers, often intellectuals looking for new ways to express themselves, abandoned traditional modes of "high art" (literature, music, and drama) and embraced the new film art.

Gradually through the 1950s and 1960s film took on the characteristics of an accepted art form. That is not to say the predominance of the classical Hollywood film in Europe lessened. Hollywood still pulled in millions of dollars from distribution in Europe with films in new wide-screen and color formats. But increasingly Europeans gave up trying to best Hollywood on its own terms and sought an alternative. Indeed, during the 1950s and early 1960s a resurgence in world cinema seemed to be taking place in Europe with films like Ingmar Bergman's *The Seventh Seal* (1957), Federico Fellini's *La Dolce Vita* (1960), and Michelangelo Antonioni's *L'Eclisse* (1962). These were labeled art films and shown in specialized theatres in the United States and elsewhere. They provided a distinct alternative to the look and narrative formula continuously coming from Hollywood.

European directors became international stars. Alain Resnais, François Truffaut, and Jean-Luc Godard, the key members of the French New Wave, emerged as "names-above-the-title" on the art-house circuit. In the 1960s, in Europe and increasingly in the United States, it was *de riguer* in university circles to have seen the latest Fellini or Bergman film and to be able to discuss it intelligently. Directors became so famous they even became known by a single name: "I'm going to see Tati's latest film," or "I hear the new Buñuel is in town."

At the same time there developed the appropriate cultural apparatus. At first in specialized magazines and then regularly in the arts and leisure sections of the major metropolitan newspapers, the work of European auteurs was discussed in the same way one might consider a serious new novel or the work of an important playwright. Film had come of age, although there was always the feeling that it was still a stepchild to more serious artistic endeavors.

Whatever one might think of these art films, few fans could fail to tell the difference between a classical Hollywood text and an art film. The European art films have a unique sense of style; they still tell a story, although with gaps Hollywood would have never condoned. The difference is that they do it with a style which dares to be different. The European art cinema is not as easy to follow as the continuity-minded Hollywood cinema, but that is part of its pleasure. In contrast to the Hollywood version of a consistent, linear reality, the European art film worked from an assumption that the laws of nature are not so easily knowable, and that the psychology of characters rarely operates in a straightforward cause-and-effect pattern.

European art filmmakers sought to "de-dramatize" story-telling by presenting both climactic *and* trivial moments, to emphasize the inherent possibilities of all film techniques, not simply those valorized by Hollywood. In particular, art-cinema filmmakers loosened (but usually never abandoned) cause-and-effect story-telling, created episodic narratives, and enhanced the possibility of making symbols by emphasizing abstractions in character behavior—all prohibited techniques within the Hollywood cinema of the 1950s.

The tight Hollywood story logic was replaced by a looser, more tenuous linkage of events and character actions. The art-cinema presented stories centering around the contemporary psychological problems of alienation and the difficulty of communication. Characters are lost and never found, for example Anna in Antonioni's *L'Avventura* (1960). Endings are not necessarily closed, as in Jean-Luc Godard's *Masculine-Feminine* (1966). Indeed art films seemed to flow along as a series of chance encounters, such as along the journey in Federico Fellini's *La Strada* (1954), stressing the episodic, open nature of the world.

These art films do not lack characters. But they behave very differently from the regulars of a Hollywood film. What defines these art-cinema characters is a lack of consistent motivation. Missing are clear-cut character traits. Narrative patterns also play down clearly motivated cause-and-effect actions and results. Indeed, at times, protagonists even question their purpose in life as does Professor Isak Borg in Ingmar Bergman's *Wild Strawberries* (1957). The central characters in an art film appear in a series of loosely connected episodes; they slide from one crisis to another. Connections are made, but often in the form of a biography (for example, François Truffaut's Antoine Doinel series), or a slices-of-life chronicle, as in almost any of Godard's early films.

The art-cinema is more concerned with the psychological effects of events than with their physical causes. Filmmakers encouraged viewers to become interested in a character's changing mental state through dream sequences, flashbacks of memories, scenes of hallucinations, and frequent fantasies. Flashbacks and flash forwards tell the audience what a character is thinking. Furthermore, these and other filmic devices provoke audience interpretation and analysis.

The international art-cinema deliberately set itself apart from the Classic Hollywood style. This had become possible because there were now openings for marketing non-Hollywood cinema. Hollywood's domination of distribution and exhibition, both at home and abroad, began to lessen, if ever so slightly. The door to new possibilities, which had been firmly shut during the 1930s and 1940s, came ajar. Film companies and filmmakers throughout Europe espoused film as art.

In the United States through the 1950s many a theatre owner began to seek alternatives to closing for good. These entrepreneurs rarely espoused film as art, but they did provide sites for showing European art-cinema in every major American city and at universities and colleges across the nation. Only a handful of theatres presented European films in the United States in the years before World War II. By 1956 the number had reached two hundred;

ten years later it was five hundred; by the late 1960s (including film societies presenting the best of the European art-cinema) the total exceeded one thousand.

Institutions to house film collections (in particular the Museum of Modern Art) and to formalize the study of cinema prospered. Film libraries and departments of film studies mushroomed during the 1960s and early 1970s. Students began to write seriously about film for such publications as *The Velvet Light Trap* (the University of Wisconsin) and *The Film Reader* (Northwestern University). By the end of the television era in 1975, there were thousands of film majors in institutions from the smallest junior college to the hallowed halls of the Ivy League.

The coming of the European art-cinema also provoked the issue of film censorship. The Hays Production Code of Hollywood never knew what to do about serious art films and often handled them as pornographic materials. With the transformation of Hollywood in the 1950s, the Hays Code began to lose its effective control. Independent filmmakers in Hollywood began to ignore it. Desperate theatre owners, seeing possible controversy and additional profits, cooperated.

But local censorship boards throughout the United States did not give up their power without a struggle. In the era of the Red Scare, they got a great deal of mileage from attacking foreign films. So Alain Resnais' *Hiroshima mon Amour* (1959) was banned for its controversial look at the effects of the atomic bomb; Jack Clayton's *Room at the Top* (1958) was suppressed in several communities for its frank sexuality. It was Roberto Rossellini's *The Miracle* (1948) which precipitated the Supreme Court case that led to the loosening of the legal sanctions against free expression in movies.

In Europe the end of the Second World War reestablished international commerce in films. Knowing that their own individual country could not support an industry large enough to compete effectively with Hollywood, filmmakers looked to internationalize their offerings, to sell these new films in as many countries as possible. In France, for example, with the rise of the New Wave in the late 1950s, film exports to the U.S. art theatres had become a flourishing part of the industry. France's efforts to crack the American market had actually begun in 1951 when the government agency in charge of film set up a French film office in New York.

But it was not film as art which first created public interest in French films in the United States. It was a new star—Brigitte Bardot—in Roger Vadim's *And God Created Woman* (1956). This film earned four million dollars in the United States in 1957, a year in which all other French films shown in the United States altogether took in another four million. Theatre owners scrambled to book "off-beat" French films to lure back the lost movie audience. Brigitte Bardot made possible the mass importation of films into the United States, which made feasible the international economic basis of the French New Wave.

American audiences were changing. Film was finally considered an art form. College-educated Americans transferred their loathing for television into a respectable love affair with the movies, especially the European art film. During the 1950s middle-class cinephiles stepped forward to regularly patronize films from Europe with qualities and themes Hollywood seemed to ignore.

During the late 1950s and early 1960s the international art cinema reached an apogee.

In just five years celebrated efforts included Federico Fellini's *Nights of Cabiria* (1956), Ingmar Bergman's *Wild Strawberries* (1957), Michelangelo Antonioni's *L'Avventura* (1960), Alain Resnais' *Hiroshima mon Amour* (1959), François Truffaut's *The 400 Blows* (1959), Jean-Luc Godard's *Breathless* (1960), and Luis Buñuel's *Viridiana* (1961). The European film director rose to the status of international celebrity, talked about in the same breath with noted novelists or composers. Fellini, Antonioni, Bergman, Truffaut, and Godard, to name but five, became stars within this new form of cinema.

So did the film critic. Since the art-cinema stressed ambiguity, the meaning of a film is not as explicit as it is in a straightforward Classic Hollywood tale. Some apparatus had to be set up to interpret art films through such publications as the *New York Times* and the *Saturday Review*. The task of the Hollywood reviewer had been to serve as an extension of the industry to promote films and stars. During the 1960s film critics were expected to explain the meaning of films. Gaps were to be filled in, symbols explained, meaning extrapolated. Ingmar Bergman, for a time the most discussed filmmaker in the Western world, understood this, and in his *Now About These Women* (1964) he inserted a title after a shot of a man running down a corridor waving fireworks warning critics not to interpret this shot symbolically.

So strong was the influence of the art film as a statement about the world that many began to reconsider what criteria constituted a good film. At first it was realism that became the valued trait. In contrast to the regular Hollywood genre products, the imports of Italian Neorealism, beginning with Roberto Rossellini's *Open City* (1945) and *Paisan* (1946), were

Alain Resnais' *Last Year at Marienbad* **(1961).**

● ●

praised for their realistic examination of the world. Their style was designated the apotheosis of serious filmmaking.

Indeed, since the international art cinema so insisted on personal statements, it emphasized the role of the director in making important comments about the status of a postwar world seemingly always in crisis. The filmmaker was praised for profoundly commenting on significant issues and ideas. In retrospect, Alain Resnais' *Last Year at Marienbad* (1961) must be seen as a key work because it pushed the art film toward an extreme exposition of subjectivity. Constructed around the principle of commenting on its own form and origins, *Last Year at Marienbad* went beyond the conventions of a simple realistic art film. Narrative

cues were either eliminated or were often contradictory. Cause-and-effect exposition was abandoned. Character and story were open to almost any interpretation. Art-cinema seemed to have reached a stage of modernism equal to the new novel where the story did not matter.

But *Last Year at Marienbad* pushed the art-cinema to an abyss which later films rarely ventured beyond. In general, filmmakers seemed satisfied to play cognitive games with the spectators, modifying and formalizing a regular set of alternative, non-Hollywood cinematic traits of style and form. Bergman and Fellini became almost brand names. In some cases the alternative was codified through the collective efforts of a nation's filmmakers, and appropriately a label was attached to movements such as the

French New Wave, the New German cinema, and the New Australian cinema.

Eventually the influence and power of the European art-cinema made its way to Hollywood, and we had the "New Hollywood" of the late 1960s and early 1970s. Everything from freeze frames and slow motion to intentional gaps in the narrative were appropriated by filmmakers like Dennis Hopper, in the youth cult film *Easy Rider* (1969); Francis Ford Coppola in *The Rain People* (1969); Mike Nichols in *Catch-22* (1970); and Robert Altman in *Images* (1972). The New Hollywood then went on to parody classic genres. The Westerns of Arthur Penn's *Little Big Man* (1970) and Robert Altman's *McCabe and Mrs. Miller* (1971) offer telling examples. By the 1970s, François Truffaut and Michelangelo Antonioni, valued members of the European art-cinema filmmaking community, had journeyed to work in Hollywood.

the archetypal modern film movement: the french new wave

The classic expression of the European art-cinema came in France with its *nouvelle vague* or "New Wave." Directors Jean-Luc Godard, François Truffaut, and Alain Resnais began as critics, centered around the Paris film journal *Cahiers du Cinéma*, who attacked the French film establishment of the early 1950s. Truffaut, for example, who went on to make such important films as *The 400 Blows* (1959), *Shoot the Piano Player* (1960), and *Jules et Jim* (1961) declared in his early writings that: "I consider a [film] of value only when written by a *man of the cinema*. Aurenche and Bost [two leading French screenwriters of the day] are essentially literary men and I reproach them here for being contemptuous of the cinema by underestimating it."

As can be seen from this typical statement, the French New Wave had its start as a reaction against the French filmmaking establishment which existed after World War II. Truffaut disdained the "tradition of quality" (subsidized by the government) of well-known members of the filmmaking establishment who crafted stories of psychological realism, frequently within the adaptation of noted literary works.

Through their writings, Truffaut, along with fellow cineastes Jean-Luc Godard, Claude Chabrol, and Eric Rohmer, championed directors considered out-of-date (Max Ophuls and Jean Renoir, for example) or "strange" (Jacques Tati and Robert Bresson, to name but two). Even more scandalous was their unabashed love for selected mainstream Hollywood films. These angry young men of Paris of the mid-1950s boldly proclaimed their admiration and respect for certain Hollywood auteurs, ranking them far above the filmmakers in their own country.

The *Cahiers* writers discovered the Hollywood auteurs because the American cinema, absent from France during Nazi occupation, flooded the market in the late 1940s and early 1950s. Unlike Americans who saw films in the order in which Hollywood released them, France took on a filmic tidal wave as Hollywood tried to exploit this rich overseas market. Indeed the 1950s seemed to be a decade of near obsession with things American in France, possibly the result of the heartfelt gratitude the French felt toward the liberators of their country.

An auteur in Hollywood would work within the system to make films which reflected a particular world view. In this way the artist in Hollywood could transcend the constraints of the studio system. The *Cahiers* group championed the films of Sam Fuller, Otto Preminger, and Nicholas Ray as well as some of Hollywood's most famous and honored filmmakers, including Howard Hawks, Alfred Hitchcock, and John Ford. Each was praised for creating a unique vision of the world on film. According to Truffaut: "There are no works, there are only auteurs."

Such ideas became the very foundations of the New Wave. First, they believed individuals could and should author movies in the same way a novelist writes a book or a composer crafts a piece of music. Second, they proposed that a new language of cinema be sought, different than Classic Hollywood filmmaking. These ideas seem tame today, but in the mid-1950s, after Hollywood had dominated for so long (really only four decades), these propositions were considered a bit radical.

But these young men of Paris of the mid-1950s wanted to do more than critique the work of fellow French filmmakers or Hollywood auteurs. Despite their lack of any real experience in film production, they set out to show the world the proper way to make movies. They solicited funds wherever they could find them and shot on improvised locations in and about Paris. Their first works were typically short subjects, but by 1959 Truffaut, Godard, and Resnais all had begun to create feature-length films. By 1960 Godard had crafted *Breathless*, Truffaut *The 400 Blows*, and Resnais *Hiroshima mon Amour*. In April of 1959 Truffaut won the Grand Prize at the Cannes Film Festival with his *The 400 Blows* and the French New Wave was off and running.

The French press of the day seized upon this group of youthful rebels and named it the *la nouvelle vague* (the New Wave). This would be the first of the many recognized "new waves" in the art-cinema world which would come to notice in subsequent years. But few ever matched the initial output of the *Cahiers* group. Between 1959 and 1966 François Truffaut, Jean-Luc Godard, Claude Chabrol, and Eric Rohmer made more than twenty films. Add this to the on-going work of Jacques Tati and Alain Resnais, and the French industry ranked among the most creative and prolific in the world.

• the french film industry •

The French film establishment eventually embraced this New Wave, but it took time. The post-World War II years had been good ones for the mainstream French film industry. In shambles after the war, through government support (quotas against Hollywood and loans to filmmakers), the French film industry began to prosper. The Centre National de la Cinématographie (hereafter the CNC) had been established in October of 1946 and was charged with reviving and regulating the film industry. The CNC not only organized and financed film production, distribution, and exhibition, it was also responsible for non-commercial cinema, represented France at film festivals, and oversaw the training of film technicians. The CNC encouraged co-productions with companies from other European nations, in part to spread the risk, offer the film technicians from participating nations a chance for steady work, and match Hollywood's multi-million dollar budgets. For example, Alain Resnais' *La Guerre est Finie* (1966) was a French-Swedish production while Jean-Luc Godard's *Pierrot le fou* (1965) was a French-Italian co-production.

In 1956 Roger Vadim's *And God Created Woman* was an unexpected commercial success but did not translate into long-term fortunes for the French. In the years immediately preceding 1959, cinema attendance fell off as television slowly infiltrated French homes. The theatrical business tried to maintain a holding action as patronage declined. Movie industry bankers were willing to back Truffaut and Godard because they kept costs down by using unknown actors and limited production schedules. The films of the New Wave cost so little, why not take a chance? In turn the CNC changed its formula for aiding filmmakers; it became more flexible. A prize for first films was set in motion to encourage new talent. These changes in film finance initiated, in the minds of many at the time, the very possibility of the New Wave. In 1959 the bulk of the 130 features turned out in France that year were by first-time directors. These first features achieved extraordinary success, not only in film festivals around the world,

but also in general international distribution. For example, Truffaut's *The 400 Blows* brought in one-half million dollars for distribution rights in the United States alone.

By the early 1960s the New Wave had become the heart and soul of the French film industry. Soon thereafter New Wave filmmakers began to enter the mainstream of international commercial filmmaking. In 1965 Truffaut journeyed to England to make *Fahrenheit 451* for Hollywood's Universal Pictures. Godard made *Contempt* (1963) for an avowed commercial producer, Italian Carlo Ponti. This signaled to many that the New Wave had joined the filmmaking establishment. Indeed, mainstream directors around Europe had begun to imitate characteristics of the New Wave form and style with a surprising amount of commercial success.

But after the events of 1968, in which left wing political forces disrupted French life, the members of the New Wave went their separate ways. Truffaut would make his way to Hollywood while Godard moved on to set up an experimental film and video studio in Switzerland, where he sought to make works which would upset the status quo and critique the capitalist system. This split after 1968 signaled that the movement was over and another phase of French cinema history had begun. But in its day, the New Wave had made a substantial contribution to the history of film during the television era.

• the new wave aesthetic •

New Wave directors crafted many films, often highly disparate in form and style. But there were enough similarities in how they told their stories, edited their work, used mise-en-scène, and manipulated sound and camerawork to identify a common thread, a shared set of characteristics, the tenets of a film movement.

They drew their inspiration from cinema's history, which they found in an extraordinary Parisian institution, the Cinémathèque Française. This film museum not only saved as many films as it could, it also screened them nearly around the clock. Founder Henri Langlois represented the highest order of cinephile, asserting that film history ought to be studied as closely as traditional literary or art history. New Wave filmmakers, therefore, were not taught filmmaking in school, rather they learned by watching as many films as possible, by studying the great directors of the past.

A theory by which to pull this acquired knowledge of the cinema together was provided by their mentor, writer André Bazin. Bazin had been a co-founder of *Cahiers du Cinéma* and through its pages argued that the cinema was an important art form, an art of realism. He maintained that one had to use the strength of the cinema, its affinity with reality, as the basis for a new style of filmmaking. The New Wave surely did not follow all the tenets preached by Bazin, but it drew needed inspiration from his passion and intellect.

From Bazin New Wave filmmakers recognized that cinema was not a neutral object but an artifact created by humans. The Classic Hollywood cinema stressed a seamless, polished look so that the viewer would forget that he or she was watching a movie. French New Wave films avoided this sheen, stressing instead an almost casual, sloppy look. The New Wave directors wanted to avoid what they considered Hollywood's artificiality.

Aping Bazin's hero, Roberto Rossellini, they took to the streets, in this case, Paris. Indeed

Paris became a "star" of the New Wave cinema, a recognizable icon in almost every film. In Truffaut's *The 400 Blows* and *The Soft Skin* (1964) and in Godard's *Breathless* and *Masculine-Feminine* (1966), one saw Parisian cafes and streets. One might argue that Paris itself (or at least sights familiar to American tourists) became a draw equal to actors and actresses such as Jean-Paul Belmondo, Jeanne Moreau, and Jean-Pierre Leaud.

In addition, by shooting in Parisian locations and using friends as performers, New Wave filmmakers required flexible, portable, cheap equipment. Eclair's inexpensive camera freed them to take to the streets, providing a freedom being exploited in the United States only by documentary filmmakers at the time. In Truffaut's *Jules et Jim* we find a 360 degree pan; in his *The 400 Blows* the camera goes into the family apartment and reveals its cramped quarters. In *Breathless* Godard had his camera operator hold an Eclair while seated in a wheelchair to follow Jean-Paul Belmondo and Jean Seberg as they strolled down a Parisian boulevard.

Shooting in natural light on the streets avoided the crafted look of glossy Hollywood studio lighting. Indeed in 1973 Truffaut made a film that examined how Hollywood had long fooled audiences by shooting day for night, that is, shooting night scenes during the day with heavy filters to create darkness. In *Day for Night* (1973) this practice is the central metaphor for Hollywood illusionism, for the Classic Hollywood system of narrative production.

New Wave directors loved to play with the seemingly infinite possibilities of editing, camerawork, sound, and mise-en-scène. Often cited is the scene in Truffaut's *Shoot the Piano Player* in which a character swears that he is telling the truth. He says "May my mother drop dead if I'm not telling the truth." Truffaut then cuts to a shot of an older woman (the mother?) keeling over.

They also loved to "quote" from their favorite films. Both Godard and Truffaut, for example, had characters in films refer to a particular favorite, Nicholas Ray's *Johnny Guitar* (1954), a Republic Western which starred Joan Crawford and Mercedes McCambridge. Such references stressed the links to film history, ignoring allusions to other arts. At times the citations became obscure, at best. For example, Godard had one of his characters take the name of Arizona Jules. Ardent movie fans knew the reference was to Arizona Jim in Jean Renoir's *The Crime of Monsieur Lange* (1935) and one of the central characters in Truffaut's *Jules et Jim.*

New Wave films tell stories, but in a manner which is quite different from the Classic Hollywood Narrative. For example, New Wave characters behave with very little consistency. Why does Michel (Jean-Paul Belmondo) in Godard's *Breathless* act the way he does? A Hollywood version of this film, made in 1983 and starring Richard Gere, carefully motivated Michael's actions; in Godard's film he just seems to wander, drift, and engage the world only at the spur of the moment. Narrative sequences do not flow seamlessly into one another—the viewer never knows what to expect next. A comic scene may be followed by a murder, for example. Editing is crucial. Godard made famous his jump cuts in which characters remained the same as backgrounds constantly changed. The Hollywood-trained viewer would become confused.

New Wave films rarely come to neat closure; they just end. In the Classic Hollywood cinema, all elements of the story ought to be resolved at the end. Perhaps the most famous example

of New Wave ambiguity comes in *The 400 Blows.* Our young hero, Antoine Doinel, has run and run, at last reaching the sea. He stops, and Truffaut freezes the frame of the boy's confused face. The film then ends; the viewer never learns what happens to him. There are no clues of where he will go from there.

Within the typical New Wave narrative there is little contact between the individual and society, nor are the characters placed in any broader context within which they could be understood. Subjective and objective worlds are fused, as are fantasy and reality. The egoism of the central figures reaches a point of solipsism and so the interiority of the subject seems lost, depersonalized. Here are marginal men and women, disaffected intellectuals and students focusing on their own relationships, with no family ties or political affiliations. They move about Paris for their own pleasure; they have no long-term goal, no motivation.

In France these open narratives and themes of nihilism were operating in other art forms as well. Thus the New Novel in literature, which debunked the past, developed at the same time as the New Wave in cinema. The downbeat themes were also related to the conservative rule of Charles DeGaulle, the colonialist war in Algeria, and the crisis of the French intellectual.

A number of filmmakers worked within the New Wave, but three offered the most complex films: Alain Resnais, François Truffaut, and Jean-Luc Godard. But to concentrate on these three is not to negate the contributions of others, Claude Chabrol and Eric Rohmer, for example.

Claude Chabrol was a member of the original *Cahiers du Cinéma* group, and, in 1957, with Rohmer authored the book, *Hitchcock.* From that point on, most critics have compared Chabrol and Hitchcock and have sought to identify the influences of Hitchcock on Chabrol's films. Like Hitchcock, Chabrol's best work seems to be a cross between the unassuming, popular genre of the thriller and the complexities of the New Wave. In short, Chabrol is best known for his self-conscious tales of murder that are developed through a sensuous use of decor and complex camera movements.

Le Beau Serge (1958) is generally acknowledged as Chabrol's first film, and some label it as the precise start of the New Wave movement itself. But it was his second feature, Les Cousins (1959), a melodramatic tale of murder, that made him famous. During the following decade, as the critical praise grew for Truffaut and Godard, Chabrol's work was seen too often as uneven; he was considered simply a director of art-house thrillers who pointed out the falsity of bourgeois relationships. Most singled out his skill in directing his wife, actress Stéphane Audran, in Les Biches (1968), La Femme Infidèle (1968), Le Boucher (1970), and Ten Days Wonder (1972). In these films Chabrol studied the difficulty of establishing personal relationships within the enclosures of family and community, using violent death as the central focus.

For example, Le Boucher was a French and Italian co-production with Stéphane Audran starring as Helene, a beautiful schoolteacher who rejects the advances of the town butcher. He then goes on a rampage of killing. Both the schoolteacher's withdrawal and the butcher's savage reactions are seen as the products of the same frustrated love affair. Here is a small town out of control in the same manner as the American small town in Alfred Hitchcock's Shadow of a Doubt (1943).

Eric Rohmer, after the death of André Bazin, took over as chief editor of Cahiers du Cinéma, a position he held until 1963. Rohmer made his first feature in the influential year of 1959, The Sign of the Lion, and then during the 1960s embarked on what he called his six moral tales: Suzanne's Profession (1963), La Boulangère de Monçeau (1963), La Collectionneuse (1966), My Night at Maud's (1968), Claire's Knee (1970), and Chloë in the Afternoon (1972). The overriding fascination of the films, and of Rohmer as a filmmaker, lies in the affection and humor of seemingly trival situations and choices (often non-dramatic), the fascination with pure conversation, and the actions of two or three central figures. Rohmer worked on location and through the careful camerawork of Nestor Almendros was able to draw the audience into an intimate relationship with the characters. He took advantage of snowstorms (in My Night at Maud's) and rain showers (in Claire's Knee) to fashion his tales of temptations.

His moral tales all have the same plot: a young man on the verge of committing himself to one woman meets by chance another whose charms cause him to question his initial choice. His entire way of thinking, his very moral center, seems to unravel. The vacillations of the young man, who often functions as the narrator of the film, are the whole of the action. Rohmer thus uses a cinema of objectivity to portray a film interested in interior change. By effecting minute changes in landscape and gesture he is able to convey strong emotional change. Each of the six moral tales was shot on the location and "at the time" of the story. Indeed, Rohmer postponed the filming of My Night at Maud's for nearly a year so that Jean-Louis Trintignant would be available during the Christmas season, the moment the scripted story commenced. Although he is classified with the New Wave because of his writings and editorship at

Alain Resnais' *Night and Fog* **(1956).**

● ●

Cahiers du Cinéma, his films are more of a throwback to French film of the 1930s, the poetic realism of Jean Renoir.

• three new wave directors •

Alain Resnais, a decade older than either François Truffaut or Jean-Luc Godard, came to cinema not through writing for *Cahiers du Cinéma* but through an interest in documentary filmmaking. In the years immediately after the end of the Second World War, he made a number of films (both in 16mm and 35mm) about artists. His *Van Gogh* (1948) earned international awards. Through 1958, he crafted docu-

mentaries regarded as among the best ever made, including *Guernica* (1950), about the painting and the air raid during the Second World War, and *All the Memories of the World* (1956), about the French National Library.

But it is his work about the concentration camps of the Second World War, *Night and Fog* (1956), which is probably his best known. This powerful film deals with a horror that was then less than a decade old by skillfully juxtaposing contemporary views of the camps in color with past newsreel footage in black and white. Through a complex series of images Resnais takes the viewer far beyond just another gruesome depiction of the Nazi atrocities (although the film certainly does that as well). He is concerned with the recollection of the Holocaust and its image in our collective history. How should we deal with such horror which on the surface seems so innocent?

Many of this remarkable film's formal strategies and thematic concerns would become characteristic of Resnais' New Wave features. For example, the relationship between the past and present and the ability of memory to traverse time as well as space, are persistent preoccupations in *Hiroshima mon Amour* and *Last Year at Marienbad*. Many might argue that in his documentary phase Resnais actually dealt with these themes in images and sounds in a more haunting, more complex manner than he would deal with them in his more famous, avowedly fictional works.

The power of *Night and Fog* moves it past a simple retelling of the facts. The final moments are extremely moving. As we follow the post-war trials, we are led through the hierarchy of authority of the death camps. At every level, responsibility is denied. We are then left with the question: who is responsible? We can only answer that it is ourselves. As long as certain social, political, and economic conditions are allowed to exist, then such atrocities could happen again. *Night and Fog* is both a moving and disturbing motion picture.

Night and Fog was certainly not some exception among Resnais' documentary work. In *All the Memories of the World*, Resnais takes what seems to be a mundane subject—an exploration of the stacks of the largest library in Paris—and with skillful camerawork raises the fundamental question of how as a society we remember. The short film explores the library building and its processes for cataloguing and preserving the documents, books, and artifacts of France. For Resnais this library is both a living monument to cultural memory and a horrible bureaucratic monster. By the film's end the

building and its workers seem to be from another planet, suggesting Resnais' interest in science fiction. In 1968 he would make a "science fiction" film, *Je T'Aime, Je T'Aime*, in which a human serves as a guinea pig for scientists experimenting with space travel.

Resnais directed his first feature in that pivotal year of 1959. *Hiroshima mon Amour* tells of a love affair juxtaposed with the memories of the dropping of the atomic bomb at Hiroshima which helped end the Second World War. A casual romantic encounter between a Japanese architect ("He") and a French actress ("She") working in Hiroshima on a film about peace provides their loose narrative basis for an exploration of the nature of memory, reality, and experience. The love affair is important because it triggers the memories, as the woman gradually discloses the story of an earlier love affair, a tale she has told no one of before. During World War II, in France She fell in love with a German soldier who was later killed. Because of her "collaboration" She was humiliated and imprisoned.

Through editing and an emphasis on formal repetition, Resnais constructed complex conjunctions of past and present, fantasy and reality, trying to unite what are usually considered distinct parts of the human experience. For example, the quivering hand of the woman's sleeping Japanese lover in the story's present is directly followed by an almost identical image of her former German lover. Tracking shots of the streets of Hiroshima merge with similar shots of her home village in France. The past seems to become the present; reality merges with memory; but what have we learned?

This is not straightforward Hollywood narrative. Rather Resnais reveals his story in stages as he establishes an intricate web of metaphoric relations between past and present. As the film

Alain Resnais' *Hiroshima mon Amour* **(1959).**

● ●

progresses, the terms of association become more abstract as France and Japan converge through intercutting. *Hiroshima mon Amour* was heralded in its day because it exemplified a modernist aesthetic by rejecting a linear, causal narrative. Its "characters" are only human representations, and viewers are continually asked to question what they know, what they understand, indeed, what they are seeing on the screen.

Resnais extended these themes and filmic experimentation to an even greater degree in *Last Year at Marienbad*. Based on a screenplay by the major French writer, Alain Robbe-Grillet, *Last Year at Marienbad* tells of a man and woman only named "X" and "A," who seem to be lost in a baroque palace. The film is a pro-

foundly ambiguous mixture of an individual's real and imagined past and present; we are never sure which is which.

A radical trait of the film is its frequent inclusion of flashbacks and flash-forwards, which may just be subjective visions of either A or X, we can never be sure. At times descriptions by the characters do not correspond with what is seen on the screen. In short, no one has ever confused *Last Year at Marienbad* with a traditional Hollywood narrative. Rather, this beautiful film of haunting black and white cinematography and dizzying camera movements must be purely appreciated for the use of filmic parameters.

Last Year at Marienbad is about the process of understanding reality. Its major theme seems to be an exploration of how people "construct" reality. But it also asks us to ponder the nature of art and artifice. In other words, how do we seek to understand the art of the cinema, including the very film we are watching? *Last Year at Marienbad* was a watershed film because it stood as a serious, complex art work, one which critics of the more traditional arts could not simply dismiss as "just another movie."

Thanks largely to *Last Year at Marienbad* filmmakers seemed to be free to follow the basic tenet of modernism in the arts and explore the nature of their medium as other modern artists had long before done. The film was judged an artistic product of a serious filmmaker and a serious novelist; it was seen by millions around the globe, although, candidly, understood by few. What was clear, however, was that film had arrived as an art form to be discussed and taken as seriously as any other art in the modern cultural spectrum.

François Truffaut stood at the heart of the French New Wave movement. He was the brashest of the young film critics for *Cahiers du Cinéma* and loudly proclaimed his opposition to then current French studio filmmaking conditions. He heralded the idea of the *politique des auteurs* (the auteur theory) and honored his favorites in cinema, which included French directors Jean Renoir, Jean Vigo, and Jacques Tati, as well as Americans Howard Hawks, Orson Welles, and John Ford. Andrew Sarris may have made the auteur theory famous in the United States, but it was François Truffaut who first brought the term into cinema's theoretical currency.

Truffaut learned his craft in the viewing room at the Cinématheque. He is a traditionalist, in the end making no radical formal break like Resnais or radical political break like Godard. It is not surprising that Truffaut ended his career in Hollywood as part of the studio system. Indeed he is probably best known to contemporary movie fans for his portrayal of the French scientist in Steven Spielberg's *Close Encounters of the Third Kind* (1977).

In the late 1950s Truffaut made several short films, served as an apprentice to Roberto Rossellini, the master Italian filmmaker so admired by the New Wave, and worked on the script of Godard's pioneering first work *Breathless*. But his status certainly changed with his creation of *The 400 Blows*. As the "enfant terrible" of French film criticism, in 1958 he had been barred from the Cannes Film Festival; in 1959 he won the best director award at Cannes for *The 400 Blows*.

The 400 Blows is a tale of an adolescent, Antoine Doinel, who struggles with the constrictions of 1950s French society and flees to face an uncertain future. Truffaut went on to make four more films featuring this same character, who was always played by Jean-Pierre Léaud: an episode of *Love at Twenty* (1962), *Stolen Kisses* (1968), *Bed and Board* (1970), and *Love on the Run* (1979). Over nearly two decades, Truffaut, the character Doinel, and the actor Léaud "grew up together."

The 400 Blows is a film of paradoxes. Paris has both affluence (the many shop windows into which Doinel peers) and squalor (his own home environment). Film history is a constant referent. For example, there is a bit of playfulness inspired by Jean Vigo's *Zero for Conduct* (1933), which also dealt with adolescents and their rebellion from society. The Vigo film certainly took a different tack, by focusing almost exclusively on the school, while Truffaut showed Antoine facing authorities at school and a juvenile detention center. Truffaut's debts to Roberto Rossellini and Jean Renoir are evident in the film's style. Truffaut took his characters

François Truffaut's *The 400 Blows* (1959).

● ●

outside the studio setting and permitted them to express themselves in longer than normal Hollywood takes. The result added up to a look of realism far different than the studio epics of French cinema of the 1950s and the Hollywood films which poured into the country.

But there are homages to Hollywood in *The 400 Blows*. For example, the booking of young Antoine recalls in sequence and detail the arrest of Henry Fonda in Alfred Hitchcock's *The Wrong Man* (1957). In stark, documentary fashion questions are asked, fingerprints and mug shots made, and the innocent victim taken off to his cell. Like his fellow *Cahiers* critics Chabrol and Rohmer, Truffaut long admired Hitchcock and interviewed him at length, publishing the interview as a book in 1967.

The rebellious teen of *The 400 Blows* grows up to become a shy, clumsy, awkward suitor in the "Antoine et Colette" episode of *Love at Twenty*. Here Truffaut picks up the story of Antoine as an adult, living on his own, working in a record factory, and unsuccessfully pursuing love. In the next episode, the feature *Stolen Kisses*, Antoine is six years older, but not much wiser. He has just been kicked out of the army, Christine has replaced Colette in his affections, and he marries. Two years later with *Bed and Board* Antoine and Christine struggle with their marriage. Antoine still seems on the run. And in the final entry, *Love on the Run*, Antoine is still running, although he has completed his own autobiographical novel. Thus the fictional Antoine Doinel and the filmmaker François

Truffaut both have closure on their autobiographical quests for understanding their place in the cosmos.

Truffaut made other films which explore the boundaries of art and life, fact and fiction. In two of his early films, his second and third features, *Shoot the Piano Player* and *Jules et Jim*, the main characters try to turn themselves into fictional figures. Both confront life by escaping into a world of fiction.

In *Shoot the Piano Player*, drawn from a detective novel *Down There* by David Goodis, Truffaut sought to emulate the American cinema and make a film noir. But throughout, he gleefully upset the film noir conventions. For example, he cast an introspective, timid singer, Charles Aznavour, in the role of the "tough hero." In the beginning of the film a gangster named Chico (after Chico of the Marx Brothers) is chased down a dark street and runs into the only available light source, a lamppost. This seeming incongruity is followed by a lengthy conversation with a stranger (whom we never see again) about tenderness and love. But the whole film continues this way with serious speeches intercut with ridiculous comic actions. Indeed, alternation is key to its stylistic whole. Truffaut seems intent on contrasting blacks and whites in the manner of the hero's piano keys. Life is shown to be one impossible set of contrasts, one large space of time in which savagery and horror (such as a suicide, shown in flashback) are alternated with comedy and joy.

Jules et Jim made Truffaut an international celebrity; it is the film many still consider his best. The narrative of *Jules et Jim* spans thirty years, opening in La Belle Epoque and closing during the grimness of the Great Depression. This would hardly seem to be the stuff of a New Wave auteur, but the film did tap a different

aesthetic, a new way of looking at the world. For example, during the first third of the film Truffaut interjects a plethora of cinematographic and editing effects, from stop frames to swish pans to jump cuts.

Jules et Jim begins as Catherine (Jeanne Moreau) accepts a proposal of marriage from Jules (Oscar Werner). The film then follows its three main characters up to the beginning of World War I. The brutality of that "war to end all wars" puts a sudden end to any joy in the relationships among the three friends. Catherine and Jules' marriage does not go well because his ideal of her clashes with the reality of her fickleness and cruelty. By the final third of the film, as the three seem to be gaining wisdom, Catherine drowns herself. Jim continues as the romantic, ever searching for a new and better world after the horrors of World War I while Jules is the patient scientist who loves life in its details.

If this narrative structure seems to suggest pathos and decline, its joy of images and sounds undercuts that melancholy. The music, the constant play of shape and design, the expanded use of CinemaScope make *Jules et Jim* a delight. In its day it was hailed as a radical experiment. In retrospect *Jules et Jim* offered no radical break, but reexamined Hollywood and traditional French filmic conventions. It tears them apart and remakes them, but with a new, truthful look at the world and at the joyful potentials of cinema.

Through the 1960s and 1970s Truffaut went on to explore the differences between fact and fiction, reality and Hollywood, in a number of different ways. His *The Bride Wore Black* (1967) offered a deliberate eulogy to Hitchcock. *Fahrenheit 451* (1966) explored the implications of a society in which written fiction, in the form of books, was purposely destroyed. But the best of the films of this period remains *Day for Night*

(1973), a complex self-reflexive film about the travail and anguish of making a movie. *Day for Night* lays out the various ways in which Hollywood employs artifice to convey illusion in the Classic Hollywood style. Truffaut himself plays a film director, frustrated with the pleasure and pain of moviemaking, contemplating his craft as did Federico Fellini in *8½* (1963) and Ingmar Bergman in *Persona* (1966).

Truffaut was also much concerned with the process of education and learning. This is evident early on in the carefully crafted schoolroom sequences in *The 400 Blows*, but it is explicitly addressed in *The Wild Child* (1969) and *Small Change* (1976). The former explores the tale of a child who was abandoned in the forest and apparently raised by wild animals. Recreating a true nineteenth-century historical episode, Truffaut plays the teacher-scientist who carefully instructs the boy, skillfully trying to teach him the ways of civilization. *Small Change* examines a child's life at school and his relationships with others, both adults and other children. This portrait, from a man who savaged the French school system in *The 400 Blows*, offers a more reflective portrait, one in which parents are seen as doing the best they can.

Through his career, unlike his contemporary Jean-Luc Godard, Truffaut stuck to the interests first explored in *The 400 Blows*. As the techniques and concerns of the New Wave were absorbed into mainstream international filmmaking, Truffaut became one of the most important and famous filmmakers in the world. He continued to grapple with the proper role of the arts, the nature of filmic fiction, and the place of education in a civilization, all concerns of traditional liberal humanism. Truffaut seemed to lay out his philosophical position most clearly in *The Last Metro* (1980) in which he examines a theatre troupe in occupied Paris. He seems to confess, like those performers in

that time of great emergency, that he must make art in the way he knows how, committed to a certain formal excellence. If he tried to make political art, he would make bad art and bad politics.

Jean-Luc Godard had no such trepidations and took a very different career path than did Truffaut. By 1970 he abandoned the concerns which gave rise to the New Wave movement and reasoned that cinema should be a tool to assist a radical transformation of the world. Godard challenged the world directly, looking to strip away its basic assumptions, demanding a new and different form of politics, economics, communication, and filmmaking. Godard believed that film could provide the impetus for this revolution.

Godard made many influential films during the 1960s. His first feature film, *Breathless* (1960), has long been considered the film which set the New Wave in motion. His more radical works, such as *A Married Woman* (1964), *Masculine-Feminine* (1966), and *Weekend* (1968), challenged not only Hollywood but also the tenets of the New Wave which had been considered so radical just a few years earlier. His New Wave films, from *Breathless* to *Weekend*, can best be seen as the first of three phases of a most productive career. Godard gradually abandoned the tenets of the New Wave movement, which Truffaut stuck to, and sought "truly radical cinema." The final caption in *Weekend* announces "Fin de Cinéma" (the end of the cinema) and proclaims the second phase of Godard's filmmaking career as a political radical.

His first feature, *Breathless*, proved not only an artistic success but also a financial one. It cost so little because Godard wrote the screenplay, directed it, and edited, with the help of friends Chabrol, Truffaut, and the extraordinary camera operator Raoul Coutard. On the surface, *Breathless* offers an homage to Hollywood through a plot based on a conventional gangster film. The film's hero, Michel (Jean-Paul Belmondo), models himself on Humphrey Bogart through gesture and costume. He even identifies with the posters of Bogart he sees all over Paris. For instance, early in the film Michel is seen standing by a movie poster admiring his hero's image, while doubting his own masculinity. To many of the fans of early Godard, such moments were taken as in-jokes, understood only by the truly dedicated cinephile.

The very style of *Breathless*, its subjective point of view underscored by hand-held camera shots, reflects the degree of individual freedom praised by the New Wave. Godard achieves a new look in *Breathless* by rejecting continuity editing in favor of long-take sequences and jump cutting. The film's free-wheeling camera style celebrates the possibilities of new lightweight cameras, the constraints of low budgets, the richness of location shooting throughout Paris, and the use of actors and actresses who were not movie stars. But in the end Godard stuck to convention and had Michel die, betrayed by his American girlfriend Patricia (Jean Seberg).

Godard made nearly twenty films before the events of May 1968 led him to a commitment to become a radical filmmaker. The seeds of change, however, can be seen in nearly all films after *Breathless*. Gradually he began fashioning a more radical style, while still clinging to traits of the New Wave. In *Band of Outsiders* (1964), for example, Godard crafted a film about a renegade group of thieves who prey on respectable members of society. Although these renegades, like Michel in *Breathless*, are doomed to failure as required by convention, Godard stripped his plot down to its bare essentials and offered a critique of the thriller. He wished to distance the audience, to remind them they are watching a film, not real life.

In the same year, with *A Married Woman*, Godard again employed a well-known, banal plot, but dismantled all the shifts and turns so well known in Hollywood melodrama. This film follows an affair between a middle-class housewife and an actor. Godard again uses the structure of film genre and its conventions to explore the theory of cinema he used to write about when at *Cahiers du Cinéma*. *A Married Woman* plays with disjunctions of sound and image, visual and verbal signs, subjective monologues and documentary realism, as well as positive and negative images, to explore how meaning is generated in cinema. His goal was simple. Godard sought a completely new form of cinema.

Alphaville (1965) performs a similar critique of the cinema, this time of the science fiction genre. This story unfolds in a utopian world of the future where a totalitarian system of government rules and the individual counts for almost nothing. This alienated society has no room for art, love, poetry, or thought; people have been reduced to robots, without their own will, ideas, or feelings, identified only by numbers. Godard stresses that this world of the future is not so far away. He even forgoes futuristic mise-en-scène, portraying a future that looks very much like the present. Godrad's distant world is Paris of 1965 in which (with Raoul Coutard's camera) the contemporary buildings of glass and concrete are made to look like edifices of future terror. Reinforcing this are complex, monotonous sounds of the music of the future.

Alphaville continued Godard's interest in references to the over-reaching influences of films in particular and cultural artifacts in general. The lead, Eddie Constantine, was a popular actor in the French cinema, especially in roles as a gangster. One can also find references to the films of Jean Cocteau, passages which seem

Jean-Luc Goddard's *Alphaville* (1965).

straight out of Franz Kafka, and even Nazi icons from the days when the Germans controlled Paris.

By 1965 Godard had come a long way from his playful New Wave origins. In *Pierrot le fou* his gangster plot has become so thin as to be almost nonexistent. The protagonists are predictably doomed, but who cares? The film seems to be more about the cinema, in particular the effects of CinemaScope and color, than about character development or narrative resolution. The look of *Pierrot le fou* is one of an idyllic paradise interrupted constantly by a harsh and evil reality. The characters try to escape this evil but are eventually driven back to the real world and killed. *Pierrot le fou*, one of Godard's most popular of his 1960s films,

pushed the manipulation of cinematic codes to an extreme while still not advocating a radical break.

But Godard would go one step further, inspired by the aesthetic theories of playwright Bertolt Brecht, and argue that a radical social message ought to lay at the heart of any desire for true freedom. In *Masculine-Feminine*, released in 1966, Godard seems to be looking forward to films of direct political concerns. The film centers around the relationship between the political and the personal. The hesitant, tentative relationship between two young people (a young man involved in Communist party politics and a woman involved with pop music) is used to explore not so much the narrow concern of film theory, but general cultural ideas about sexual relations and their representations in modern culture.

Masculine-Feminine is divided into sections (or "acts"), which denotes Godard's increasing interest in Brecht's theories of epic theatre and the distancing of the spectator from the artwork. Interviews are spaced through the film to remind the viewer that this is a human-made construction, not some natural symbol of the truth. This technique, coupled with long takes and sweeping camera movements, gives the viewer the sense that this is not the New Wave any more, but something very different. Godard has abandoned traditional pleasure construction for political education.

The general thrust of this phase of Godard's career found him foregrounding the very process of story-telling on film. He dissolved the usual relationships (always at least loosely maintained by the rest of the New Wave filmmakers) and traditional distinctions between fiction and documentary, actor and character, and narrative and experimental films. Persons appeared as themselves in works of fiction, actors addressed the camera in monologues, and the viewers were constantly reminded that what they were watching was a movie made from celluloid by people. To emphasize this point in *A Married Woman* he turned the image from negative to positive; in *Two or Three Things I Know About Her* (1967) he turned off the sound track; in *La Chinoise* (1967) he showed the clapper-board on screen. All these actions would be considered mistakes in Hollywood. Godard sought to remind the viewer that he had made the film; he could make the rules.

Godard's *Weekend* (1968) shatters the notion of cinema as truth, pleasure, and individual expression. The viewer is overwhelmed by references to filmmaking, including specific references to Luis Buñuel's *The Exterminating*

Angel (1962), Nicholas Ray's *Johnny Guitar* (1954), John Ford's *The Searchers* (1956), and Sergei Eisenstein's *Battleship Potemkin* (1925). *Weekend* is filled with printed captions, digressions, direct address, and camera techniques which remind the viewer that they are movements of a camera, not the invisible following of characters in a story. *Weekend* is an openly modernist text.

From 1968 into the mid-1970s (the beginning of contemporary filmmaking), Godard collaborated almost exclusively with Jean-Pierre Gorin and the radical Dziga Vertov group (named after the Soviet filmmaker discussed in Chapter 5) which sought to overthrow the capitalist world and create a new Marxist society. What marked this second phase was a complete indifference to the typical audience. In the New Wave, Godard was trying to reach a general public, although hardly the mass audience that we associate with Hollywood. In his Dziga Vertov period, Godard's films were meant to stimulate the revolution.

The watershed political events of 1968 had profoundly affected Godard. Before that spring he had made films with leftist themes, such as *La Chinoise* and *Weekend*, but was willing to use capitalist modes of distribution to specialized art theatres. The events of 1968 changed all that. With his colleague Jean-Pierre Gorin, Godard formed a cooperative for filmmaking. Between 1968 and 1971 Godard, Gorin, and their colleagues of the Dziga Vertov collective made a number of short films on 16mm, highly critical of the status quo. They were distributed through a leftist underground network.

The films of the Dziga Vertov group signal the end of the New Wave as a cohesive film movement. Godard's films of this era deal only with basic social concerns, the means of production. The events treated in the films—from the political scene in Czechoslovakia in the 1969 film *Pravda* to the trial of the Chicago Eight in the 1971 film *Vladimir and Rosa*— become secondary to the question: how does one properly make a revolutionary film? Godard distinguished between political films [those about political events, such as *Z* (1969) by Costa-Gavras or *The Battle of Algiers* (1966) by Gillo Pontecorvo] and films that are part of the process of political and social change. Godard declared that one cannot put a radical message into a traditional form.

With *Tout va Bien* (1972) Godard and Gorin decided to "go aboveground," grappling with the proper way to make movies. Although distributed to traditional art theatres, *Tout va Bien* is no *Day for Night*. *Tout va Bien* is about the process of making that film itself, right down to even showing the checks to cover the expenses of production. Through the film the narrative never flows smoothly but is always interrupted to remind the viewer about the film's production or to make a point about the real politics of the film business as Godard and Gorin saw it from the Left.

If continuity is the bedrock of the Hollywood film, then discontinuity (with a political aim) is the salient feature of *Tout va Bien*, indeed of all Godard's work of the early 1970s. The film is filled with mistakes by Hollywood standards: figures sit down "twice," and sounds from off-screen interrupt the "dialogue." Godard wants the spectator to shed his or her usual way of sitting back to enjoy a seamless, Classical Hollywood film, and to actively engage and participate with the film as a mode of production as it "unreels."

In this latter phase, Jean-Luc Godard, more than any of his New Wave contemporaries, strove to construct an authentic modernist cinema. This attempt went far beyond the artistic explorations of Alain Resnais, or François Truffaut. It is this thrust that has made him the one filmmaker who is usually considered a true modern artist of the cinema, comparable to John Cage in music, James Joyce in literature, or Bertolt Brecht in drama.

the individual as international film artist

Although no single country seemed to be able to match the breadth of the output and innovation of the French, other important filmmakers, dedicated to their art, also found a place in the art-cinema of the 1950s and 1960s. Ingmar Bergman from Sweden, Spanish-born Luis Buñuel, and Federico Fellini, trained in Italian Neo-realism, became famous worldwide. The auteur theory, which celebrated the filmmaker as artist, offered a new way to sell cinema. These and other film directors were promoted as "stars," as had long been done in the world of literature, music, and painting. Models of analysis and study were also appropriated from the other arts; directors grew rich and famous, and toured the world, moving from film festival to interview to conference.

Ingmar Bergman certainly represents the most famous, the most visible of the art-cinema directors. Thousands of cinephiles through the 1950s and 1960s, disgruntled with Hollywood formulae, embraced Bergman's *The Seventh Seal* (1957). Here was a film and a director who took film seriously. And there was more where that came from, for this Swedish director was incredibly productive. From the close of the Second World War until his announced retirement in 1982 (after completing *Fanny and Alexander*), Bergman made some forty features, a number of television programs, and helped fashion the careers of Max von Sydow, Bibi Andersson, and Liv Ullmann. In 1960 he stood as the most famous film artist in the world.

But fame did not come overnight for Bergman; it took more than a decade. Indeed, even during the 1950s, he worked seven months per year as a theatre director to ensure a stable financial base. Most critics seem to locate his important early work in *Summer Interlude* (1951), *Summer with Monica* (1953), and *Smiles of a Summer Night* (1955). These are films of memory that reveal moments of happiness, tranquility, and sensual pleasure. For about one hundred thousand dollars (a fraction of what a Hollywood film cost) Bergman crafted *Smiles of a Summer Night*, which won a Special Prize at the Cannes Film Festival (for Poetic Humor), and thus lifted himself into the pantheon of the international art-cinema.

Smiles of a Summer Night is a formalized, theatrical comedy in the vein of Mozart's opera *The Magic Flute* (which Bergman later filmed in 1974) or *The Marriage of Figaro*. Four men and four women circle around each other, constantly changing partners in an elaborate dance of love played out in a turn-of-the-century country mansion. The plot wittily and skillfully interweaves such archetypal Bergmanesque themes as the difficulty of finding love, the question of one's true identity, and the frustration of being unable to find lasting emotional commitment. As often would be the case in Bergman's films, the female characters fare far better in the end than do their male counterparts.

Smiles of a Summer Night is a unified work, complete with the studied elegance of a smoothly flowing camera. The cast complement each other, and nearly all would later become world famous as Bergman's repertory company: Bibi Andersson, Harriet Andersson, Ingrid Thulin, and Gunnar Bjornstrand. Many critics see this comedy as the high point of Bergman's early work, a marked contrast to the image of a purveyor of Nordic gloom, the inwardly introspective serious artist. Bergman, indeed, injected comedic moments into *Wild Strawberries* (1957) and *The Devil's Eye* (1960). But as he became more and more famous, feature length comedies became rarer and rarer.

Indeed, films filled with gloom and symbols of frustration first drew Bergman lavish praise in the world of the art-cinema. In 1958 he won the Golden Bear at Berlin for his portrait of the frustrated life of a professor in *Wild Strawberries*; three years later he earned an Academy Award for Best Foreign Language Film for the medieval tale of a brutal crime and sadistic retribution in *The Virgin Spring* (1960); a year later he was given another Academy Award for Best Foreign Language Film for a story of loneliness and vulnerability in family relation-

Ingmar Bergman's *The Seventh Seal* **(1957).**

ships in *Through a Glass Darkly* (1961). By the early 1960s, these three films and *The Seventh Seal*, the archetypal art house film of angst, had made Bergman the most noted serious filmmaker of his generation.

In these works he began to tap his experience in the theatre. For example, *The Seventh Seal* was based on a short play, *Painting on Wood*, which Bergman had written for his acting students at Malmo. The theatre seemed to inspire him to turn inward. So, for example, disillusionment about religion became a theme he attacked with vigor in the 1950s. *Wild Strawberries*, *The Seventh Seal*, *The Virgin Spring*, *Through a Glass Darkly*, *Winter Light* (1963), and *The Silence* (1963) lead progressively through the rejection of religious beliefs, leav-

ing only a conviction that life is haunted by a virulent, active evil. Thus, the crusading knight of *The Seventh Seal*, who cannot face death once his faith is lost, survives only to witness the cruelty of religious persecution.

Most proponents of the art-cinema still look back to *The Seventh Seal* as one of the films which most signifies the Bergman style. Having been reared in a strict Lutheran family headed by a father who was a pastor, Bergman was constantly struggling with religious doubts and problems. *The Seventh Seal* is the first of three (with *The Magician*, 1958, and *The Virgin Spring*) which helped him personally purge what he considered the ugly side of religion. As the film makes clear from the beginning, the title refers to God's book of secrets fastened by seven seals; only after the seventh seal is broken will the secret of life be revealed.

The plot concerns a fourteenth-century knight returning home after a decade of Crusades in the Holy Land. He finds his native country striken by plague and haunted by guilt, witch hunts, and self-persecution. In constant low-key light, in stark surroundings, the knight begins to have his own doubts, and eventually confronts "Death," a cloaked figure who tells him his time has come. But the knight wins a reprieve by playing a game of chess for his soul.

The imagery set symbol-hunting film viewers to their history books. Stark Christian imagery, based on mural paintings which were common in Swedish churches, comes to life in *The Seventh Seal*. To contrast the knight's frightful dilemma, Bergman inserted a sub-plot of a poor couple making their way through the world as best they can. (Symbol hunters see them as the Virgin Mary and Joseph.) Bergman himself, in program notes for the film, emphasized that the conflict and dread of the fourteenth century allegorically foreshadowed the fear and trepidation of the atomic bomb and the cold war of the 1950s. He believed we all know that we will die, but not before we struggle within ourselves about the meaning of life.

As was evident from his work with comedies, there seems to be no single, unified Bergman. Consider *Wild Strawberries*, which signaled yet another turn in Bergman's career. In this film, he concentrated on psychological dilemmas and ethical issues in human and social relations. In the tale, an aging Professor Isak Borg (played by noted Swedish director Victor Sjöström in his late seventies) learns of his past through a succession of dreams he has while driving to Lund to receive an honor. His daughter-in-law rides with him and, as a new member of the family, is unafraid to pose the unasked

questions. Much of the film is narrated by Professor Borg and thus comes off as an "analysis of dreams," highly influenced no doubt by Strindberg's *Dream Play*, which Bergman had directed in the theatre. The title, "Wild Strawberries," refers to the fruit which for Swedes symbolizes rebirth in spring. In the film the wild strawberries remind Borg of his youth, of a past love.

Bergman's psychological puzzle takes a different tact in *Persona* (1966), fashioned at the height of his fame as a director. Perhaps his most influential film, many consider this Bergman's most psychologically complex, controversial, and significant work. *Persona* offers a version of Brechtian analysis, a surreal treatment of dual personalities which grapples with themes of failed love and the horrors of a world seemingly self-destructing around us. It was not until he made *Persona* that Bergman felt he could come to grips with the dark forces of human nature which sexual urges can inspire. Indeed, Bergman claims that his films after *Persona* concern his ceaseless fascination with women.

Persona presents a dramatic conflict between two women—Alma (Bibi Andersson), a young nurse, and Elizabeth Vogler (Liv Ullmann), her patient, an actress who has withdrawn into silence. The tension between the two women and the power of the silence remind many of yet another Strindberg source, *The Stronger Persona* is the most successful of Bergman's self-reflexive work. That is, it is as much about the nature of the cinema as about the fundamental problems of the two women. *Persona* announces its interest in film theory at the very beginning with an image of the ignition of an arc projector and the threading of a film. The film ends with the projector being turned off. Certainly one of the most shocking

Ingmar Bergman's *Persona* **(1966).**

moments in Bergman's entire oeuvre comes in the middle of *Persona* when we see a film rip (or appear to rip) and then burn.

Bergman would again deal with psycho-sexual relationships, successively and uncompromisingly, in *The Touch* (1971), showing a married woman driven out of her mind by an extra-marital affair; *Face to Face* (1976), concerning the nervous breakdown of a cold-natured woman analyst and the hallucinations she suffers; and in a film made for television but later shortened and released as a feature film, *Scenes from a Marriage* (1973), dealing with the troubled long-term relationship of a professional couple who are divorced but unable to actually separate. The female stars of these films became international celebrities, in particular Bibi Andersson in *Persona* and *The Touch* and

Liv Ullmann in *Scenes from a Marriage* and *Face to Face*.

Luis Buñuel became an international celebrity with the rise of the art-cinema, but he had been making films since 1928 when he and Salvador Dali unleashed *Un Chien Andalou*. Spain has produced few truly international film-makers and most summaries of Spanish cinema begin and end with Buñuel. Yet any close examination of his oeuvre reveals that Buñuel worked far more in Mexico and France than in his native Spain. Wherever he could find receptive conditions, he worked—in any number of genres, from realist documentaries to serious art films to bitter, dark satires.

Perhaps the easiest way to analyze this unique talent is to divide his career into the four periods which cover his fifty-year career.

In the first, as discussed in chapter 4, Buñuel is the Surrealist who slit the eyeball in *Un Chien Andalou* and attacked French society in *L'Age D'or* (1930). Equally as interesting, but far less noted, are two remarkable political documentaries: *Land Without Bread* (1932) is about the sufferings of Las Hurdes, an impoverished region of Spain; *Madrid '36* (1937) is about the Spanish Civil War. Critics have long praised *Land Without Bread* as a powerful investigation of the squalor and poverty of people living in an isolated region of Spain. But this film offers more than a straightforward analysis of injustice and wretched living conditions. It is also about the nature of the documentary itself. In this twenty-seven-minute black and white film, Buñuel adopts the tone of a traditional travelogue, with a dispassionate voice-over and the incongruous music of Brahms, while stunning the viewer with horror in every image.

Cues abound in *Land Without Bread* to alert the viewer that this is hardly an innocent documentary recording reality. For example, from two different points of view we see a goat fall off a mountain. To achieve a view from above and a view from the side of the "same" event would require two cameras being in the right position for this "accident." To make sure we "get it" Buñuel adds a puff of gunsmoke to remain in the frame to explain how this mishap took place. Unabashedly manipulating images for shock, Buñuel placed diseased men and women before his camera. The views are terrifying: the chronically ill, the dead. The sympathetic audience member is expected to feel sorry for these poor people. But Buñuel, in a cruel joke, seems to mock himself because while he is there, he does nothing to help. He sees his fellow Spaniards simply as subjects for his camera, not victims. He used and manipulated them, as he did the actors and objects in his earlier Surrealist films, to shock but not to

offer suggestions for political or social change.

In the third phase of his career Buñuel was an anonymous journeyman filmmaker. At the end of the Second World War he wound up working in the relatively small but consistently productive Mexican film industry. Indeed the short-lived Golden Age of the Mexican studio system is closely identified with Buñuel. In 1942 the Mexican national government had created a centralized credit agency to encourage film production. The Second World War had so boosted economic activity in Mexico that in 1945 when Buñuel arrived the nation was in the process of becoming the leading filmmaking country in the Americas outside Hollywood.

Buñuel directed twenty films in Mexico from 1946 to 1964. Because of the existing studio system Buñuel most often had to work with players and scripts that he did not choose. In time he became a fast-working and efficient director, able to finish low-budget films on time. *The Young and the Damned*, for example, was one such low-budget effort, finished in three weeks. But this film of serious social criticism won the 1951 Cannes Film Festival Prize for Best Direction, thereby placing this "new" talent (Buñuel was fifty-one years old) on the international art-cinema map.

In a realist style, *The Young and the Damned* depicts the brutal world of Mexico City slum children. Their lives are impoverished, violent, and devoid of a stable home. Buñuel, also the co-screenwriter of the film, personally researched the lives of these children before the filming took place. *The Young and the Damned*, influenced by Italian Neorealism, has a documentary look, the result in part of its mode of production. It was low-budget, filmed on location in three weeks in actual slum districts of Mexico's capital city. Moreover, its episodic narrative structure portrays the mundane activities of a workaday existence on the edge of starvation. A multitude of problems are sympathetically underscored, but no solutions offered.

But it should be stressed *The Young and the Damned* was hardly a typical Buñuelian effort during this period. As a hired studio director, he did what he was told, including musicals such as *Great Casino* (1947), melodramas like *Daughter of Deceit* (1951), *Death in the Garden* (1956), and *Republic of Sin* (1959), and fanciful comedies such as *Mexican Bus Ride* (1951) and *The Illusion Travels By Streetcar* (1953). Buñuel helped bring color films to Mexico in the form of a co-production with Hollywood, *Robinson Crusoe* (1952). Although there are touches of cynicism reminiscent of Surrealism, in the end Buñuel was able to manipulate elements of form and style only as budget and producers allowed.

Buñuel began his fourth phase, as an internationally known filmmaker, in Mexico. *The Exterminating Angel* (1962) is a social satire in which a group of elegant upper-class guests are, for no clear reason, trapped at a formal dinner party in an elegant mansion. But as fear and hunger take over, the marooned guests see their hypocritical facades crumble and polite behavior give way to acts of cowardice, lust, sadism, and degradation. To attack the bourgeoisie's moral and religious hypocrisy Buñuel employed the Surrealist weapons of surprise (through careful use of editing and mise-en-scène), dream imagery, bizarre gags, images of comic horror, and unexpected assaults on narrative logic and order.

The successes of such films as *The Exterminating Angel* enabled Buñuel to make his way back to Europe during the 1960s. He began by making films in France, even as he continued to work in Mexico, and critics took notice. With *Viridiana* (1961) Buñuel became a director of

note, an aged venerable link to the Surrealist period. *Viridiana*, made in Spain, won Best Film at the Cannes Film Festival in 1961. The conservative Franco government, seeking to liberalize its image, invited its native son to return to make whatever film he wanted. Buñuel shot *Viridiana* in a matter of weeks, and knowing he had settled a long-held score with the Catholic Church, he then fled the country, anticipating the uproar. The dictator Franco raged and dismissed his minister of culture, cursing the day he ever permitted the faithless ex-patriot Buñuel to return with official approval.

The film's heroine, Viridiana, has completed her novitiate, and is about to commit her life to the Catholic Church. But before she can do this her mother superior asks to visit her uncle Don Jaime, who had paid for her education. During the stopover, the Don rapes Viridiana and then kills himself. Viridiana leaves the Church and takes in beggars and castaways to the uncle's home, which she has inherited. But they only take advantage of her to hold orgies. The final climatic scene is a visual parody of Da Vinci's painting of the Last Supper, accompanied by the singing of the "Hallelujah Chorus." This Surrealist juxtaposition of icons of the Church in what was considered a sacrilegious narrative impressed the art-cinema world of the early 1960s.

Buñuel continued his irreverent examinations of a world gone crazy with *Simon of the Desert* (1965), *Belle de Jour* (1966), *The Milky Way* (1969), and *The Discreet Charm of the Bourgeoisie* (1972). The latter, which won the Academy Award for Best Foreign Language Film in 1972, was a French, Spanish, and Italian co-production, shot in France. *The Discreet Charm of the Bourgeoisie* follows a carload of people trying to go to dinner. This seemingly simple

Luis Buñuel's *Viridiana* (1961).

journey narrative is constantly interrupted; scattered about the film are four dreams, but since the "real" action is so implausible, we are almost not sure when dreams begin and end. This is more a film about telling stories on film than it is a coherent movie tale.

Buñuel was able to rise to fame and influence only with the ascent of the art-cinema. That is, it took the re-structuring of world cinema in the television era to enable Buñuel, near the end of his career, to gain an international following. In the 1960s as audiences of young people began to flock to his work for its Surrealist perspective that ceaselessly attacked the dominant social order, Buñuel suddenly was discovered and celebrated as an aging master of cinema. But with a close look one recognizes

in *Tristana* (1970) the same merciless attack on accepted mores as found in *L'Age D'or* or *Land Without Bread*. To the end of his career, with *That Obscure Object of Desire* (1977), Buñuel maintained his jaundiced, Surrealist view of the world.

Federico Fellini had begun his career as Neo-realism, as a movement, in fits and spurts came to an end during the 1950s. As the reaction to the events of World War II had fully played out and the Italian economy returned to normal, perhaps it was inevitable that the Italian cinema would return to its commercial roots. Hollywood controlled the world market for filmmaking and the powers of the cinema industry in Italy began to actively solicit American co-productions. Shooting in Italy saved

Hollywood money, for the Italians it meant jobs. The results usually meant costume epics: *Ulysses* (1954), *Ben-Hur* (1959), and *Cleopatra* (1963).

This Hollywood invasion has been labeled the death knell of Neo-realism by some, but in fact it was just a transition to further international fame in the art-cinema. Crucial to this transformation were the early films of Federico Fellini. His *I Vitelloni* (1953) continued the Neo-realist interest in social problems through its portrait of six provincial characters. For a true Neo-realist these six figures would have been the jumping-off point for a condemnation of society's ills. Fellini instead concerned himself with the clash of illusion and reality in the dreary life of these characters.

This implicit interest in psychology looms even larger in two films which established Fellini's reputation as a master of the art-cinema: *La Strada* (1954) and *Nights of Cabiria* (1956). In both works Fellini moved beyond simply recording the particulars of the somber reality of life to a more personal vision, one motivated by an interest in a particular mythology concerned with spiritual poverty and the necessity for grace and salvation. Thus *La Strada*'s central figure, Gelsomina, and the plucky prostitute Cabiria in *Nights of Cabiria* are more concerned with the failure of human communication and a lack of love than with political and social ills. Each was portrayed by Giulietta Masina, the director's wife, and each functions within Fellini's poetic universe as a unique individual with the potential to receive spiritual grace. In each film Fellini used a loose picaresque plot in which the "road" (in Italian, "la strada") leads to personal fulfillment.

With *La Strada* Fellini began a strong interest in autobiographical filmmaking by casting his wife in the film. This highly symbolic work has been read as everything from a manifesto on civil rights to a treatise on woman's liberation. Certainly it is a step away from Neo-realism, as a highly personal parable about the relationship between a man and woman. Whatever it meant to audiences at the time, *La Strada* proved to be a huge critical success, encouraging Fellini to take more of an interest in autobiographical films.

In *La Strada* Fellini extensively used circus imagery, which would appear in any number of later films. Three central characters inhabit this world of a small traveling circus. Gelsomina is a self-sacrificing, doe-eyed simpleton who becomes the chattel of Zampano, the animalistic strongman (played by Hollywood actor Anthony Quinn). There is also the Fool, who eventually helps Gelsomina see her value as a human being. We follow the episodic journey of these three until Gelsomina's death. A moving camera constantly follows the three through their struggles with their own troop and then with a larger circus. *La Strada* won more than fifty international awards, including praise from the Venice Film Festival, a prize from the New York Film Critics, and an Academy Award as Best Foreign Language Film.

Fellini focused international interest on this new Italian cinema, and during the decade of the 1960s the Italians, led by Fellini, achieved a reputation that nearly equaled the French of the New Wave. But this was no Italian new wave, but rather a collection of filmmakers working independently in Italy, making films for an international market. Fellini's best work comes at this time with *La Dolce Vita* (1960), *8½* (1963) and *Juliet of the Spirits* (1965).

In *La Dolce Vita* Fellini transforms the tinsel world of Rome's Via Veneto and the paparazzi searching for photos of stars and starlets into a metaphor for an entire civilization. Set against the magnificent ruins of earlier times (classical Rome, Christian Rome, baroque Rome), Fellini

Federico Fellini's *La Strada* (1954).

● ●

shows us a culture based on meaningless intellectual debates, sterile love affairs, and publicity stunts. Sylvia (Anita Ekberg), the sensual Hollywood actress in Rome to make a film, seems to embody American go-getting-ness while Marcello (Marcello Mastroianni) just flows along with life.

Through the 1960s Fellini became increasingly preoccupied with his role as a filmmaker and, as a result, the autobiographical manifestations in his films became more and more introspective. His *8½* is a dazzling example of cinema as individual expression. Fantasy rather than reality is the director's proper domain. Thus, after establishing Marcello Mastroianni as his alter ego in *La Dolce Vita*, Fellini cast him again as the central character, the moviemaker in *8½*.

Indeed, *8½* achieved a certain importance because Fellini made a film about filmmaking.

Self-reflexivity had long been a hallmark of the modern novelist, but filmmaking had to achieve a certain stature before films about the creative process of making cinema could be taken seriously. Many saw *8½* simply as a self-indulgent but thoroughly creative attempt to fill a void in the director's filmmaking career, which had reached a certain end with *La Dolce Vita*. But today it is seen as a classic example of the filmmaker seriously taking on the tenets of his own creative process.

Structurally *8½* moves backward (dealing with preparation of the film) in order to go forward, so that the end of *8½* comes when the director begins to make a new film. Guido, a motion picture director not unlike Fellini himself, has lost the inspiration for his art and life. Through the film he turns inward to examine the major influences on his life—his boyhood, his church, his relationship with his

Federico Fellini's *La Dolce Vita* **(1960).**

● ●

parents, his relationships with certain women, all revealed in elaborate flashbacks. These dream sequences are seen as both the best of times and the worst of times. It is only when he contemplates suicide at the end of the film that he can be reborn. Like an artistic phoenix, Guido arises from the ashes of his frustration, inspired to fashion a new type of film from the experiences of his past. But then we realize that the very film he is inspired to make is the film we have been watching, his eighth-and-a-half work (counting a short as half).

Juliet of the Spirits (1965), Fellini's next film, was almost a sequel to *8½*, since it examined the psychological struggles of his wife. Both films, therefore, explored the same problems from different sexual perspectives, while on a deeper autobiographical plane, the two character studies express and explore two different sides of Fellini's mythic ego. But Fellini's subsequent films, while complex and often popular with critics and fans of the art-cinema, never matched these earlier efforts. The flamboyant imagery continued, but to what purpose? Fellini continues to work, principally for television, but without the influence he had during the 1960s as a central figure in the rising world of the international art-cinema.

Jacques Tati worked in film in France before, during, and after the New Wave, but always seemed to exist outside any movement. Because he began in the music hall (French vaudeville) in the 1930s doing mimes of tennis players and soccer stars and then made films which loosely are called comedies, Tati has never been given the serious credit of a Bergman or Fellini. But in terms of complex, creative manipulation of the basic parameters of the cinema—editing, camerawork, sound, and mise-en-scène—there may have been no greater master of the medium.

Tati moved to film from the stage, filming shorts of his music hall routines such as *Oscar the Tennis Champion* (1932). His first feature would not come until after the Second World War with *Jour de fête* (1949). This film, just over an hour long, tells of the life in a small French village disrupted by a travelling fair and transformed by the introduction of a modern, technologically sophisticated high-speed mail delivery service imported from the United States. The local postman, played by Tati, with his ancient bicycle becomes involved in mishap after mishap. The creative inanity of *Jour de fête* has been compared appropriately to the classic silent comedies of Charlie Chaplin and Buster Keaton.

Honors on the art-cinema circuit began to flow Tati's way with the premiere of *Monsieur Hulot's Holiday* (1953) and *Mon Oncle* (1958). Tati played the central figure in both, Mr. Hulot. On the surface, both appealed to audiences around the world as gentle, satirical observations of the incongruities and impersonality of modern life, whether the rituals of France's annual summer vacations or the "work-saving" gadgets imported from the United States after the Second World War.

In particular *Monsieur Hulot's Holiday* presents a portrait of a holiday week at an unnamed middle-class seaside resort, climaxing with a massive fireworks display (accidentally set off by Mr. Hulot). The film's structure is remarkably symmetrical. For example, in the opening the vacationers make their way to the site of fun;

in the final scenes they are returning home. The story has come full circle. The film contains very little actual dialogue but is rather an orchestration of sounds of doors squeaking, tennis balls meeting racquets, and automobiles puttering along (identifying Hulot's car in particular).

Monsieur Hulot's Holiday is a tour de force of camerawork, with seemingly all possible angles and placements tried at least once. The remarkable feature of this film is that Tati was able to craft a story which appealed to nearly all moviegoers, while offering the serious cinephile a rigorous exploration of the possibilities of camerawork and sound. And *Monsieur Hulot's Holiday* is funny, appealing to a middle-class world which tries to "get away" but can never leave the cultural apparatus at home.

Mon Oncle was Tati's first film released in color. Hulot, the angular everyman in the tan raincoat, pipe, argyle socks, and hushpuppy shoes, is now an uncle to the archetypal middle-class family, the Arpels, who live in the most up-to-date, gadget-filled home. Hulot forms a bond with his young nephew, who prefers the ways and the picturesque flat of his simpler, "pre-technological" uncle. Both feel caught in a world that they do not really understand. When the well-meaning Arpels try to find a job and wife for Hulot, their plans backfire. But there is a bonus—through the experience they do grow closer to their son.

Mon Oncle offers less sight gags then either *Jour de fête* or *Monsieur Hulot's Holiday*. Instead it is formed of quiet satire, of the "modern" world gone a little bit mad. The contrast between the soulless up-to-date environment of the Arpels and the haphazard warmth of Hulot's surroundings is emphasized and underscored through all the parameters of the filmmaker's art. Tati fashioned vivid images of

Jacques Tati starred in and directed *Monsieur Hulot's Holiday* (1953).

clashing colors, added a vast array of sounds of gadgets, and filmed them from a nearly infinite variety of camera angles. The film has an almost mathematic structure as the Arpels speed about their days, getting as much as possible done while Hulot spends time contemplating, observing the ways of this strange world.

Tati's master work, ten years in the making, surely has to be *Play Time* (1967), a loosely constructed tale of a group of American tourists rushing to visit a traditional Paris they never seem to find. The wry comedy grows out of Hulot's trying to help, as they all wander around a version of "Paris" created with a number of vast sets built outside the real Paris in what came to be known as "Tativille." This film too

is remarkably structured. Consider, for example, the pattern of changing color schemes. In the first section of the film the settings and costumes are principally grays, blacks, and browns, giving Paris a cold, drab look. By the end of *Play Time* the "same" locales have turned bright red, pink, and green, making this Paris look like a circus ride or garden. The subtle change in color represents a most overt example of Tati's careful use of film structure and style to craft insights about the effects of an inhuman, uninhabitable, sterile cityscape and how only we can transform it into a bright receptive city of pleasure.

In *Play Time* Tati stands at the height of his powers as a filmmaker. The film is not simply a creative use of mise-en-scène but upon close analysis almost a dissertation about the possibilities of camerawork in the modern cinema. In one particularly funny shot a group of American female tourists is enjoying themselves at the opening of a new restaurant. At one point in this longest sequence in the film Tati places the camera behind a counter and at a low angle, so that it seems that the waiter is pouring champagne into the flowers on the women's hats rather than into the glasses they hold, just out of sight. To audience members looking for an amusing film, the humor is everywhere. To anyone interested in the possibilities of the cinema, the skill at camerawork and mise-en-scène (as well as sounds and noises plus unobtrusive editing) is almost overwhelming.

Jacques Tati can best be understood by comparing his use of the long shot with that found in the typical Hollywood film. Hollywood uses the long shot to establish a scene, always returning to the figures and decor found in these establishing shots. Tati, in obsessive and elusive fashion, layers and layers deep space, offering so much information that no one viewer in a single sitting could catch it all. But the overall comic effect is never lost. Tati choreographed his long shots as one might plan an intricate dance. Dialogue is minimal, but the sound track is filled with rich noises: splats of mud, creaking briefcases, doors opening with more than a simple swish. Tati's passion for his version of filmic perfection was not matched in *Traffic*, his final film. But his *Play Time* stands as one of the most important films in the television era, indeed in the history of cinema.

Robert Bresson is another French director, another perfectionist, another filmmaker to come to fame during the 1950s. He represents the independent film artist, one who began after the Second World War, and offered inspiration to, but never worked as part of, the French New Wave. With *Diary of a Country Priest* (1950), Bresson achieved fame in art-house circles. But his career began in the 1930s when he started to dabble in short films. During World War II he spent eighteen months as a prisoner, escaped, and made his first feature *Angels of the Streets* (*Les Anges du Péché*, 1943), a spiritual drama concerned with a convent. Despite its moral seriousness, *Angels of the Streets* made back its costs, as did *Les Dames du Bois de Boulogne* (1945).

But Bresson, ever the perfectionist, would spend six years finding his next project. *Diary of a Country Priest*, the spare tale of a young, dying priest in a small village, is certainly not Hollywood's idea of an exciting subject for a film. The solitude of the priest and his struggles with sin and life are seen in frequent close-ups and are articulated in a constant monologue juxtaposed by poignant, pointed sounds. Bresson's renunciation of professional actors and actresses dates from this film, which marked the beginning of his now famous austere style, free of dynamic music or wild gestures or Hollywood excitement. Many found this style almost spiritual, religious in feeling.

It would be five more years before he completed his next film, *A Man Escaped* (1956), the title of which describes its story. But *A Man Escaped* contains precious little action, simply a man alone with his feelings and desire to flee prison.

The film displays a meticulous attention to detail, having actually been shot in a prison. The style emphasized the close-up, with the central figure, on screen throughout most of the ninety-minute film, played by a twenty-seven-year-old philosophy student. Pacing is

Robert Bresson's *A Man Escaped* **(1956).**

crucial. François Truffaut has likened its style and structure to pure music, with the film's essential richness embodied in its rhythm.

While waiting for his death sentence to be carried out, Fontaine concocts an escape plan. He spends days carefully loosening the boards of his cell door and making crude ropes to climb down the high prison walls. Just as he is ready to put his plan into action, a boy, Jost, is put into the cell with Fontaine. Deciding that Jost is not a spy and can be trusted, Fontaine reveals his plan and both, in the film's most elaborate sequence, escape.

As he did in *Diary of a Country Priest*, Bresson relies heavily on close-ups. The close examination of Fontaine and his continuous voice-over commentary reveal a mind ever alert, working with a contemplation equal to the aspiring novitiate. Throughout this seemingly simple story, Bresson brilliantly fuses sound and image. It is most often Bresson's complex and dazzling use of the soundtrack which keeps the viewer informed of activities, inside and outside the prison, at the same time that Fontaine experiences them. At certain points in the film Bresson even permits his sound track to dominate since there is little light in the shot to permit the viewer to take in important details.

A Hollywood film would have used a group of men to play off each other. *A Man Escaped*, until near the end, concentrates on only a single man. Indeed the commentary, camerawork and mise-en-scène draw us to his tiny gestures and interaction with ordinary objects that become crucial to his escape. In the middle of the film, when Fontaine breaks his door and uses the wood to make implements for escape, we see close-ups of his hands sharpening a spoon handle into a chisel and hear loud scraping sounds suggesting the rubbing of the spoon against the boards of the door. We see and hear the ripping of cloth with a razor to make ropes and even the swish of straw as Fontaine cleans up slivers of wood to hide his work from the guards. To Hollywood, such "action" would be considered boring and would be cut out before release. To Bresson, it was crucial, central to the type of film he wished to make.

At times in the film Bresson's use of sound pushes it beyond the power of the image. Some of the sequences in *A Man Escaped* are so dark that sound carries the narrative. For example, after Fontaine falls asleep for the first time in prison there is a fade to black and, with the screen still dark, we hear his now familiar voice saying: "I slept so soundly, my guards had to awaken me," followed by a loud sound of a bolt and hinge. The light let in by the opening of the door allows the viewer to finally see a faint image of a guard's hand shaking Fontaine.

Ever complicating the film is the use of music, especially passages from Mozart's Mass in C Minor, which seems unmotivated and out of place. Indeed, after it is heard over the credits, we do not hear it again until well into the film at the point when Fontaine walks with his fellow prisoners to empty their slop buckets. As the music plays, Fontaine explains: "Empty your buckets and wash, back to your cell for the day." This juxtaposition of ceremonial religious music with the degrading routines of prison life

provides a crucial and dramatic reminder of the harsh life in prison and the desire for freedom.

The spare Bressonian style continued with *Pickpocket* (1959) and *The Trial of Joan of Arc* (1962). Through the 1960s and 1970s Bresson made relatively few films, always on his own terms, and always with a style admired by film purists. His spare style favored black and white, and so Bresson did not make his first color film until 1969 with *Une Femme Douce*. But the thematic impetus remained. Bresson's belief in the Catholic Church has long provided a stable base to his work. The characters in his films can achieve a state of grace only through suffering. His figures are defined, however, by a minute interest in detail, whether trying to escape or picking pockets. Complicated dialogue is avoided in favor of voice-over narration. The narratives are unexciting, pared down to the essentials, often constrained by one setting (a prison) or a set amount of time (that needed to escape). And the films are his. Bresson makes films on his own terms and so he is famous for not letting his actors and actresses contribute. They do what they are told.

Michelangelo Antonioni had begun his film career in the Neo-realist era, but like his countryman Federico Fellini he achieved his greatest fame after that movement had ended. Antonioni became a star of the international art cinema with *L'Avventura* (1960), assisted by the outcry of protest which came at the Cannes Film Festival of 1960. Festival attendees did not know what to make of a film so elliptical in style, so mysterious in theme. *L'Avventura*, an Italian-French co-production, presented an unprepared viewer with an ever so loosely told story of a couple who are traveling among the islands of Sicily when the woman disappears. Her husband and friends search for her but in the end never find her. Antonioni's refusal to close the film drew the wrath of critics; it was acceptable to make an art film, but it should tell a coherent story, with a beginning, middle, and end.

L'Avventura is paced very slowly when compared to Hollywood films, with much of its action occurring in real time; that is, the time passing in the film equals the time elapsed by all the events which transpired. Antonioni did not take advantage of ellipses to "speed up" to include only the most exciting bits of action. The characters communicate, but with very little dialogue. More often than not they are seen looking away into the bleak Sicilian landscape. If Hollywood tried to involve the viewer in the story, Antonioni sought distance from the audience. Yet the basic theme of *L'Avventura* is straightforward enough: modern society lacks the moral codes to support even the most basic of human relationships.

Because of the success of *L'Avventura*, for his next two films, which followed similar themes and utilized parallel stylistic traits, Antonioni was able to employ several of the major stars of the international art cinema: Jeanne Moreau, Marcello Mastroianni, Monica Vitti, and Alain Delon. *La Notte* (1961) featured Moreau and Mastroianni as a couple confronting the stresses of their marriage and not finding any real solution. Hollywood would have provided an appropriate happy ending; Antonioni again provided no closure. The film covers twenty-four hours in the lives of Giovanni and Lidia Pontano in which the events—visiting a dying friend, going to a night club, attending a party— seems to lead nowhere, just as their relationship is at a standstill.

The final film of his so-called trilogy, *L'Eclisse* (1962), starring Vitti and Delon, features the modern couple again drifting into nothingness

in their relationship. Yet this Italian-French co-production offered more action, often through editing, including a remarkable fifty-eight shot sequence at the end. Still overall like the other two films of this trilogy, *L'Eclisse* is characterized by a number of deliberate cinematic features. Pictorially all three of the films are formally beautiful, and all employ natural time, offering a pacing unfamiliar to traditional Hollywood-trained viewers.

In *Red Desert* (1964) Antonioni worked in color for the first time. (Like Tati and Bresson, he came late to this innovation which was commonplace in Hollywood films by then.) *Red Desert* presents yet another portrait of neurotic crisis, in a pictorial frame of stunning beauty, with elegant subdued colors, especially reds and greens. To be sure, although critics do not rate this film as highly as the previous trilogy, it must be judged a remarkable step in the use of color cinematography.

After *Red Desert* Antonioni's career took a significant turn. He moved to England to make *Blow-Up* (1966) for MGM. Against the backdrop of the swinging pop scene of 1960s London, Antonioni fashioned an avowedly popular work in which he asked viewers to contemplate a complex question: what is the nature of the cinema? *Blow-Up* tells a slightly elliptical tale of a photographer who thinks he has inadvertently photographed a murder. But he is not sure since the photographic evidence never tells him the complete answers to the questions he poses. *Blow-Up* was a major international hit that was booked into mainstream theatres.

Antonioni took the next logical step and journeyed to Hollywood to make *Zabriskie Point* (1970). For members of the art-cinema set, this marked the end of significant interest in Antonioni's work. Here was another European who was lured to Hollywood by the promise of fame and fortune; but in the end he achieved neither and fled back to his native land to continue to work, but never with the success abroad that he had achieved during the 1960s.

Pier Paolo Pasolini was another Italian who created films of stark beauty within the context of the art-cinema. An avowed intellectual, working in both film and literature, he studied under the masters, including Fellini for whom he authored parts of the script for *Nights of Cabiria*. Pasolini's first feature was *Accattone!* (1961), a grim depiction of the life of a pimp who falls in love, tries to go straight, but in the end is killed in an accident. Pasolini's film closely examines the sub-proletarian culture of Rome using no professional actors or actresses. Throughout *Accattone!* the suffocating urban milieu is sharply counterpointed by the elegant classical music of J. S. Bach.

Pasolini reached greater fame during the mid-1960s with *The Gospel According to St. Matthew* (1964), a Marxist version of the story of Christ. This French-Italian co-production is based on direct quotations from the gospel text. The familiar drama is etched against an arid landscape and accompanied by sacred music. A similar directness was brought to a pagan myth in Pasolini's version of the Greek drama *Oedipus Rex* (1967). This color version is faithful to Sophocles in text, but does not utilize the traditional emphasis and pacing. Pasolini added a prologue and epilogue, and set the story in modern times. Filmed in Morocco, against vast stretches of bleak desert, the use of primitive music emphasizes the primeval reverberations of the subject.

But Pasolini would gain a different form of notoriety through his clashes with Italian authorities and the Catholic Church because of generous doses of explicit sex and violence in *The Decameron* (1971), *The Canterbury Tales*

(1972), *A Thousand and One Nights* (1974), and *The 120 Days of Sodom* (1975). *The Decameron* became an international boxoffice hit because of its explicit content. Indeed the images of degradation in all four films are so explicit, so vivid, so wrenching, audiences found themselves fascinated, repulsed, and horrified at the same time.

Bernardo Bertolucci is the youngest of this group of talented Italians, and probably came to the attention of more contemporary movie fans with his Academy Award winning, Hollywood-financed *The Last Emperor* (1988) than with his early efforts in Italy. To the art-cinema world he was the boy wonder when at age 24 he crafted *Before the Revolution* (1964), a unique mix of radical politics and pure emotion. He kept up his political critique with *The Spider's Stratagem* (1970) and *The Conformist* (1970), both filled with camera movements which are among the most elaborate, most beautiful in the history of cinema of the television age.

Bertolucci surfaced in the mainstream film business with his *Last Tango in Paris* (1972), which became a cause célèbre of the pornography crisis in the United States during the early 1970s. Starring Marlon Brando, Jean-Pierre Leaud (of Antoine Doinel fame), and Maria Schneider, *Last Tango in Paris* depicts a brutal, explicit sexual intimacy and art in an era when the makers of *Deep Throat* (1972) were arguing that explicit sexual films could also be judged works of high art.

The Angry Young Men were filmmakers in Great Britain who during the 1950s sought a gritty realism in the cinema through films which closely examined British working-class life. This was a new class consciousness, inspired by the dramas of John Osborne, the films of the Italian Neo-realism, and the successes of the French New Wave. The films of the Angry Young Men emphasized an explicit sympathy with the working class. Suddenly instead of adaptations of great British literary classics, or the light-hearted Ealing comedies made famous in the years immediately following World War II, a handful of British filmmakers filled the screen with smokestacks, uneducated heroes, and lost souls who had no real control over their own lives. The heroes of these films struggled as best they could, but in the end returned to the poverty from which they came.

The cycle of Angry Young Men films had its direct origins outside the cinema industry. Indeed the filmic movement took its name from the theatrical movement of Osborne, Wolf Mankowitz, and Shelagh Delaney; from the novels of John Braine and David Storey; and from a new generation of actors including Albert Finney, Rita Tushingham, and Richard Harris. Since this aesthetic, in part, stressed an interest in reality, the cinema seemed to have some potential that the artifice of the stage or the written word inherently lacked.

Jack Clayton directed *Room at the Top* (1958) which, with its seemingly uncompromising view of the underside of British society, caused a sensation in its day. With major stars in Laurence Harvey and Simone Signoret, *Room at the Top* followed the hero of John Braine's best-selling novel as he fought to move in an upper-class environment through his skillful pursuit of women. The film's realistic treatment of cluttered dreariness and frank sensuality (for the time) made it a major hit in the art houses around the world.

Tony Richardson had staged *Look Back in Anger*, the John Osborne play, at the Royal Court Theatre. *Look Back in Anger* was filmed in 1959. Richardson then moved on to produce Karel Reisz's *The Loneliness of the Long Dis-*

tance Runner (1962) and craft his own works in *A Taste of Honey* (1961) and *Saturday Night and Sunday Morning* (1960). *Look Back in Anger* (1959) starred Richard Burton and Claire Bloom and did feature the class conflict and the tragic events of the play. Another adaptation of a play, *A Taste of Honey* by Joan Littlewood, seemed more successful. Then Richardson was off to Hollywood, following the success of *Tom Jones* (1963).

● ● ● ● ●

The events of 1968 signaled the end of the French New Wave and with it the close of the art-cinema as a distinct epoch. To be sure, the name directors continued to create, but, more often than not, with less a burst of creativity. They often worked in Hollywood or certainly as part of the mainstream cinema. Soon Hollywood itself embraced many of the traits which made the art-cinema of the late 1950s and early 1960s so distinctive: location shooting, non-continuous stories, naturalistic acting styles, and experimental cinematography and editing in such films as *Bonnie and Clyde* (1967) and *M*A*S*H* (1970). Hollywood diffused the uniqueness of the art-cinema for the mass audience, as it had with German Expressionism forty years earlier, by absorbing a number of its valued techniques and employing a number of its name filmmaking talents.

But the European based art-cinema did not provide the only alternatives to Hollywood during the television era of 1950 through 1975. Through the 1960s filmmakers throughout the world aspired to the fame and prestige of the New Wave, to become the next Fellini, Bresson, or Bergman. But though always hampered by less secure industrial bases from which to begin, filmmakers from Germany and Eastern Europe did on more than one occasion demonstrate that all the interesting and significant cinema was not being made in Hollywood, France, Italy, and Great Britain. Even filmmakers in Third World countries—although more sporatically—were able to create fascinating cinematic alternatives. These new stylists of the television era are the subject of the following chapter.

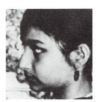

13

searching for alternative styles

From 1950 to 1975 through the television age every couple of years critics in Europe and the United States seemed to uncover some "New Wave," or major as-yet-undiscovered talent. The 1960s saw the rise of true internationalism in the cinema. But the realities of politics and economics meant that not all nations were equal. Filmmakers from countries under strict Soviet domination, from poorer developing nations, and from countries which had no recent history of cinematic production did not begin from the same base as their European counterparts dealt with in the preceding chapter. Yet they all had one thing in common. Their economies, movies as well as other goods and services, were dominated by one of the world's two superpowers: the United States and the USSR.

defining influences: hollywood and the ussr

To best understand world cinema of the television era (1950–1975) one has to first examine the dynamics of world film power.

389

In the West the defining force continued to be Hollywood. After the Second World War, country after country sought to impede Hollywood and develop their own filmmaking tradition; none succeeded completely. The Second World War temporarily crippled Hollywood's ability to export films as markets in Europe and Asia, the best the American film industry had, were cut off for the duration. As the Second World War drew to a close, the major Hollywood companies formed the Motion Picture Export Association (hereafter MPEA) to present a united front to foreign markets. The MPEA, which operated as the sole bargaining agent for members by setting prices and terms of trade, became the center of Hollywood's renewed thrust in a post-war world. Since the United States government used Hollywood films to help project America's best face around the world, the U.S. State Department and the succeeding presidents supported Hollywood's continuation as the world's dominant film seller.

But after the Second World War foreign governments had to face problems which required immediate solutions which would impinge on Hollywood's ability to trade. For example, if a nation let Hollywood take out precious currency, it severely upset that country's balance of payments. They literally could not afford the luxury that Hollywood wished to provide. As a result, treaties were made with a number of countries (Britain and France, to name but two) that allowed Hollywood to draw out some currency and take the rest through the production of films. That is, a film with an American cast, director, and producer was shot overseas with monies made at foreign theatres showing American films. Films featuring exotic locations as well as certain types of genre films (in particular Westerns) were often shot in Europe through the 1950s and 1960s. Hollywood soon learned the value of "run-away" productions, the shooting of films outside the confines of their studio backlots.

The development of faster film stocks, better and more portable sound recording, and techniques which facilitated location shooting made it cheaper to shoot a film in England, Spain, or Italy than to recreate sets in the studio. Audiences, probably reacting against television's crude studio production qualities, came to prefer features shot on locations. There were also significant cost savings since the expenses of making a feature in Hollywood rose dramatically after World War II as craft unions asserted their demands, and actors and directors used their leverage to extract greater payment. It simply became easier and cheaper to shoot a film anywhere but Hollywood. Foreign governments cooperated, supplying armies (sometimes literally) of extras to people spectacles. It was rumored in the 1960s that the Spanish army was a profit-making enterprise because of its frequent use in Hollywood movies.

Moreover, once the Second World War ended and economic emergencies of currency stabilization could be set aside, Hollywood began to consider how much it was actually extracting from foreign markets. Fully half of the dollars for a typical feature release during the 1960s came from abroad, principally from the United Kingdom, Italy, Canada, West Germany, France, Japan, Spain, Australia, Brazil, and South Africa, in that order. No longer was it enough to please audiences in Peoria, Illinois, and Allentown, Pennsylvania; a filmmaker also had to consider patrons in Munich, Belgrade, and Tokyo.

By the mid-1960s co-productions had become a fact of movie-making life. Since all Western countries had some form of governmental assistance scheme in place to encourage "native" production, a co-production deal enabled a Hollywood company to gain a governmental partner to share the financing risk. A good example is Bernardo Bertolucci's *Last Tango in Paris* (1972), starring Marlon Brando and Maria Schneider. This film was an Italian-French co-production, on paper 60 percent Italian and 40 percent French. In reality it was an Italian-Hollywood co-production. The "French" partner was in fact Productions Artistes Associes, a subsidiary of United Artists, one of the major Hollywood movie companies.

Through the MPEA, Hollywood went to any lengths necessary to open up new markets. During the 1960s many African countries achieved their independence from European domination. Hollywood adjusted as best it could, usually by simply trying to maintain the same terms of trade it had under the former colonial power. The American film industry's first organized effort came in April of 1961 when the MPEA set up an African office, and began distributing films to the English-speaking countries of Ghana, Gambia, Sierra Leone, Nigeria, and Liberia. (All but Liberia were newly independent.) This five-nation market then contained about sixty million people, a population equal that of the United Kingdom. The new office enabled Hollywood to successfully head off possible governmental restrictions and keep its films flowing into these potentially lucrative markets.

Later in the 1960s the MPEA moved to the French-speaking republics south of the Sahara Desert. In 1969 the MPEA created the West African Film Export Company (later Afram Films, Inc.) to distribute films to fifteen French-speaking African countries with nearly sixty million inhabitants. Thus through the late 1960s we had the spectacle of not only Hollywood but also the French film industry fighting to plunder the developing nations of Africa. As expected Hollywood eventually took the dominant role.

The impact of this monopolistic behavior stifled the growth of African cinema. It was hard enough for such poor countries to make films at all, but Hollywood's sales monopoly made it just that much harder. Many African filmmakers had to go to non-African festivals to see the work of their colleagues. Indeed, even powerful European countries could not keep Hollywood at bay. Some had hoped that the European Economic Community (the Common Market) might have the collective strength to deal with Hollywood. It did not.

In all countries native filmmakers battled stiff opposition from theatre owners who embraced Hollywood films because they made more money from them than booking native productions. Governmental officials often allied with theatre owners because they liked the tax revenues they collect from successful theatres. In addition, as nations set up television operations, they saw less of a need to subsidize a native film industry. But there they again encountered Hollywood. Of the television programs exported around the world, the bulk come from the United States and were made by the major Hollywood film companies.

As the television era came to an end in 1975 (and the age of video and satellite transmission began) several thousand feature-length movies were produced annually worldwide, less than 10 percent of which came from Hollywood. Yet American films occupied about half the screen time around the world in a declining theatrical market. For example, when color television was introduced in Australia in the early 1970s, the urban-based and suburban cinemas continued to draw customers, but smalltown and rural theatres went out of business. In many countries in the developing world, however, only the rich could afford a television set and so in India, for example, a thriving theatrical film industry continued on, with a studio system and theatres prospering throughout that vast sub-continent.

In sum, although many factors influence movie attendance, it is clear that once television became established in nation after nation around the world, theatre audiences significantly declined. Film industries adapted, often showing much of their output on television. Yet Hollywood reacted skillfully to preserve its share of the theatrical business as well as take a dominant role in the new television technologies.

But the United States was not the lone super-power. The USSR held influence over the socialist countries of the world. Invariably an agency of the government controlled film production, distribution, and exhibition, usually through some part of an education or interior ministry. In its way, the USSR held sway over the film policies of Eastern bloc socialist countries as strongly as Hollywood influenced filmmaking and theatrical screenings. For example, filmmakers in Eastern Europe often had no choice but to toe the line. There were periodic thaws, but to understand the workings of Eastern European cinema after the Second World War, it is necessary to first learn about the workings (and foreign policy) of the Soviet film industry.

In the 1950s Josef Stalin supported the goals of socialist realism, which reflected a unique national spirit and tenets proclaimed by the Communist Party. Stalin had permitted some freedom of expression outside this rigid formula of socialist realism during the Second World War, but as soon as that conflict was over he consolidated his power once again, taking rigid control over the film industry. Director Leonid Lukov's *A Great Life* (1946) was attacked for creating a "false" picture of the Soviet people by presenting images of lazy, immoral, and corrupt citizens. (In reality it was a mild portrait of harsh conditions in the society.) Under Stalin's policy of socialist realism, a film's style could not call attention away from the party-approved themes.

The Communist party severely limited subjects filmmakers could treat in the years immediately after the war. Safe subjects included World War II films in which the united Soviet people defeated the Germans, with no mention made of help from the Allies. This re-enactment of the war on film, complete with proper heroes and villains, became standard fare in all of Eastern Europe after the war. Another safe formula included anti-American plots in which the villains were U.S. troops or spies from the CIA. Biographies of important Russians of the past, including *Lenin* (1948), *Academician Ivan Pavlov* (1949), and *Mussorgskii* (1950), were approved as well.

Stalin silenced the greats of the Soviet cinema, from Sergei Eisenstein to Alexander Dovzhenko to V. I. Pudovkin. Eisenstein, who died in 1948, made no more films after *Ivan the Terrible*. Dovzhenko's lone post-war effort, *Life in Bloom* (1948), one of the first Soviet color films, was decimated by the censors. Pudovkin was accused of lack of commitment to the Russian heritage for his *Admiral Nakhimov* (1946) and was forced to revise the film. His final work, *The Return of Vasili Bortnikov* (1953) was heavily supervised by party functionaries.

The early 1950s saw the steady decline of the number of films released. For example, in 1952, the year before Stalin died, only five feature films were produced. Part of the reason for that extremely low number was that a year earlier the state authorities had issued an edict that the production of black and white films would be curtailed in favor of color (Agfacolor,

The Cranes Are Flying (1959) from the USSR.

● ●

called Sovcolor in the USSR). Gradually the necessary film stock was produced, and in 1953 production rose to thirty films, many simple recordings of Moscow stage performances.

A gradual thaw and industry expansion came after Stalin's death in 1953. But at first the upheavals in Communist party leadership and accompanying purges gave filmmakers only a feeling of insecurity. Occasionally, seemingly controversial works were released, even heralded, while at other junctures less confrontational films were still suppressed. In the West this was the era of the emergence of the art-cinema and two Soviet exports won considerable fame. *The Cranes Are Flying* (1957), directed by Mikhail Kalatozov, won the Golden Psalm Award at the Cannes Film Festival in 1958. A tale of suffering during the Second World War (an acceptable subject in Soviet cinema), the heroine's tragedy symbolized the collective tragedy of the Soviet nation. More famous was *Ballad of a Soldier* (1958), a tale of a six-day leave. The rewarded soldier falls in love, re-

turns to the front line to fight again, and is killed. Grigori Chukhrai's poignant film won the Best Film Prize at the 1959 San Francisco Film Festival. Both *The Cranes Are Flying* and *Ballad of a Soldier* showed one and all the vast potential of the Soviet cinema.

The Soviet cinema did open up further during the 1960s, but hardly to the degree as was seen in more independently minded nations of Eastern Europe. Soviet authorities continued to stress safe, predictable fare. They encouraged safe genres, not as formulaic as socialist realism, through direct allocation of necessary finance. Satires were even permitted, but they were always carefully orchestrated by the party. It was acceptable to make fun of officials from the Stalin era, but not all of them. For example, the frustrations of bureaucratic red tape provided an easy, acceptable target in *True Friends* (1954), *The Girl Without an Address* (1957), and *The Businessmen From the Other World* (1963).

More typical were epics based on Soviet literature including works of Tolstoy, Gorki, Gogol, and Chekhov. The most lavish of this type of production came with *War and Peace* (1964, released in two parts in the United States in 1968), based on the Tolstoy novel. Directed by Sergei Bondarchuk, it was made in four parts, ran eight hours, and took five years and an estimated equivalent of forty million dollars to be filmed in 70mm. Shakespearean plays, including *Othello* (1955) and *Hamlet* (1964), also made their way to the Soviet screens, as well as numerous operas and ballets, including *Boris Godunov* (1954), *Romeo and Juliet* (1955), *Swan Lake* (1957), and *Sleeping Beauty* (1964). These latter epics usually were financed in wide-screen formats in color to feature the Bolshoi and Kirov theatre troupes.

After the departure of Nikita Khrushchev in 1964, Leonid Brezhnev ushered in a period of stability. This détente enabled increased cultural communication, but still the state authorities held a firm grip over filmmaking. As the USSR moved into the 1970s the Soviet cinema industry was fully nationalized, with control resting, from 1963 on, in the hands of the Cinematography Committee of the USSR Council of Ministers. That particular committee controlled all of the country's thirty-nine film studios, the largest four being Mosfilm, the Gorkeii (also in Moscow), Lenfilm (in Leningrad), and the Dovzhenko studio (in Kiev). In a typical year in the early 1970s, more than one hundred feature films were produced plus hundreds of documentaries, news films, and films for television. Of the features, a small number (less than five in each case) were co-productions with Czechoslovakia, Yugoslavia, East Germany, and Bulgaria.

The Soviet film industry officially imported no Hollywood films; instead it brought in features from North Korea, East Germany, Czech-oslovakia, Poland, Yugoslavia, and other smaller members of the Eastern bloc as well as France, Egypt, and Italy. By controlling theatres and television networks, Soviet authorities were able to keep Hollywood out. The Soviet Union held dominion in export to its socialist allies as well. Hollywood films did appear in these countries, but hardly in the same numbers as in Western nations.

The USSR was also one of the few countries in which, because of state control, the role of the film industry was not reduced because of television. As the number of cinemas declined in the West (with the introduction of television), in the USSR the number of theatres remained constant. The state managed theatrical film-making and presentation as well as the production, distribution, and presentation of television programs. Under this system, film-making held its own long after television had seized the day in the West.

• • • • • • • • • • • • • • •

eastern europe

• • • • • • • • • • • • • • •

Filmmakers in Poland, Czechoslovakia, Hungary, and Yugoslavia were somehow remarkably able to work in a world dominated by Hollywood to the west and the USSR to the east. Struggling with state-run bureaucracies, creative moviemakers managed to seize particular moments of history and fashion complex, fascinating feature-length films. But it must be emphasized that these were brief breaks in history and in the end the power of the USSR and USA reasserted the status quo. Thus, predictably, after bursts of creativity, the film industries in Poland, Czechoslavakia, Hungary, and Yugoslavia returned to routine efforts of state-sponsored, conservative films fitting the socialist realistic formula.

• poland •

The Polish film industry had to make a completely new start at the end of the Second World War. In the previous five years the nation's limited production facilities had been almost totally destroyed, as had many of the nation's movie houses. Production slowed to a crawl; only seven features were made in 1950. But once rebuilt, by the mid-1950s, a modestly liberal system of decentralized production facilities with some degree of local autonomy was set up. The state, of course, remained the exclusive producer-distributor-exhibitor, but a consequence of the same social and political forces which led to the October 1956 uprising against the USSR also marked an end to strict Stalinist-type controls.

By the late 1950s Polish filmmakers had more creative freedom than existed elsewhere in Eastern Europe. In fact, the films made during this period of time in Poland were rarely shown in other Soviet satellites because authorities considered them in violation of the conservative, state-serving, optimistic tenets of accepted socialist realism. Its reputation rests on the work of a handful of directors working during this historical break.

Andrzej Wajda emerged in the mid-1950s with a trilogy of films exploring the shape of postwar Poland. Indeed, the Polish film usually cited as the first breakthrough work is Wajda's *A Generation* (1955). This powerful portrait of resistance fighters stressed sacrifice for one's

country, not correctness of political views. Wajda's *Kanal* (1957) followed, a story of the 1944 Warsaw uprising against the Germans.

But *Ashes and Diamonds* (1958) is most often considered his masterwork because it is filled with both realistic touches and Bergman-esque symbols. Not unexpectedly *Ashes and Diamonds* became a particular favorite on the art-cinema circuit, for it tells a relatively straightforward story but does not look like a typical Hollywood film. With *Ashes and Diamonds*, Wajda took a strong stance against what was then the accepted Communist party line. He took his story from a novel in which the politics were exemplary of orthodox Polish Communism of the period and stood it on its head. The film's theme stressed that simple allegiance to the state only served to divide the Polish people.

With these three films Wajda announced the beginning of a new Polish cinema, one which broke decisively with the traditions of prewar and Stalinist filmmaking. Wajda set the tone of the 1950s with films which, instead of chronicling the struggle to build socialism in conservative Soviet fashion, analyzed struggles for national independence or honor. Nationalism was stressed; the issue of communism was simply avoided. In retrospect, it seems that Polish film artists rejected the claims of a communist state more thoroughly and completely than others in the Eastern bloc. Polish film became an expression of Poland rather than Polish socialism, which explained the almost continuous tension between the filmmaking community and the state authorities. For example, the apparent relaxation of governmental controls through the early 1960s was followed by the tightening of controls in 1968.

Andrzej Munk rivaled Wajda during the late 1950s. His second feature, *Man on the*

Andrzej Wajda's *Ashes and Diamonds* (1958).

Track (1957), deals with the consequences of a world in which issues of political shifts are constantly intruding into everyday life. When an elderly railroad engineer is killed in an accident, his heroism is ignored during the investigation because authorities are more concerned with his political allegiance. Munk's masterwork, *The Passenger*, was unfinished when the director died in 1961, but the film was "completed" in 1963 with still photographs. *The Passenger* is about a Polish woman in a German concentration camp, told from the point of view of one of the camp's guards. In this film too, the heroes survive a rigid, uncaring system, not committed to the official goals of the Communist party.

Jerzy Skolimowski dealt with the frustrations of coming of age in a rigid socialist environment in *Identification Marks: None* (1964), for which he earned his degree from the official film school. He had started as a scriptwriter for Wajda on *Innocent Sorcerers* in 1959. His student films, *Identification Marks: None* (1964) and *Walkover* (1965), used a limited number of shots, hundreds less than Hollywood would have used. But his potential would be developed elsewhere. Skolimowski left for the West in the late 1960s. Unfortunately for the serious film community in Poland, Skolimowski was neither the first nor the most famous director to flee.

Roman Polanski is probably the most famous exile from the Polish cinema of the television era. He made his first film in Poland in 1957, his last there five years later. *Knife in the Water* (1962) was denounced by the Polish

Roman Polanski's *Knife in the Water* **(1962).**

• •

Communist party, and Polanski's funding was cut off. As a student and filmmaker contributing to the Polish Golden Age of filmmaking, he learned to make films with limited resources—with few actors and only a hand-held camera. This was a minimalist type of Hollywood cinema. He would later become far more famous for the films made in France, Italy, Britain, and finally, those made in Hollywood including *Repulsion* (1965), *The Fearless Vampire Killers* (1967), *Rosemary's Baby* (1968), and *Chinatown* (1974).

Poland's moment in history was finished by the mid-1960s. Consider that Wajda did not even work then in his native land, making his lone film, *The Siberian Lady Macbeth* (1962), during the 1960s in Yugoslavia. (He would go on to make *The Wedding* in 1972 and *Danton* in 1982.) As Poland entered the 1970s, the age of the coming of increased importance of television, the control of the production, distribution, and exhibition of all films rested firmly in the hands of the state authority, Film Polski, under the Central Film Office of the Ministry

of Culture and the Arts. In 1972 feature filmmaking accounted for twenty-five titles while films for television numbered more than one hundred. With only fifteen hundred operating theatres (for a nation of some thirty million people), more and more Polish theatres turned to the films from the USSR and even Hollywood to fill remaining screen time.

• czechoslovakia •

The modern era of filmmaking in Czechoslovakia began on 11 August 1945 when the Communists in the government forced the nationalization of the cinema, a mere three months after the formal close of World War II. It was the first Eastern European industry taken under direct governmental control. The film industry languished until the coup of 1948 established the Communist party's solidification of power. The state bureaucrats at the Barrandov studios received carte blanche; they had at their disposal the resources of the state and the finances to use cinema to educate Czechs in the service of the Communist party. The method they planned to employ was socialist realism, which would remain the dictating force until 1957.

The Golden Age of the Czech cinema had its roots in the 1950s when several leading filmmakers tried to make films like those being made in Poland, more closely in tune with real day-to-day life. The death of Josef Stalin in 1953 made possible a more liberal attitude toward filmmaking, but this came to an end in 1959 when three of the twenty-nine films produced the preceding year were banned and their directors blacklisted. But the seeds of a new cinema were taking root in the National Film

Academy. Unlike the rest of the population (except the party elite who had private cinemas where they watched Hollywood Westerns and musicals), Academy students spent their time watching contemporary European and American films: the work of Orson Welles, the Neorealists, and later the French New Wave. In these films they found the models for the New Czech cinema.

From 1957 to 1963 a gradual change took place: filmmakers were seeking new cinematic styles, new ways of telling stories. But the change did not take place overnight. Although the Czech New Wave is usually dated from the release of Vojtěch Jasný's *September Nights* in 1957, the great divide came in 1963 with the release of Jaromil Jires' *The First Cry*, Věra Chytilová's *Something Else*, and Miloš Forman's *Black Peter*. These films offered exciting alternatives to socialist realism; contemporary Czech life was given a chance to become subject matter for the first time since before the Second World War. Except for Jires, none of these directors were party members. In the years immediately following 1963, directors Jan Nemec, Evald Schorm, Ivan Passer, Jiří Menzel, Pavel Juracek, and Ester Krumbachova helped define an alternative cinema. These figures and their work during the 1960s became known as the Czech New Wave even though their differences as filmmakers made this wave less a stylistic and formalistic whole when compared to the homogeneous traits of, say, the early French New Wave.

Miloš Forman is the most famous of the Czech New Wave directors. With his focus on contemporary working-class Czechs, he seemed to be less interested in Communist party affairs than in the unchanging problems of the human race. The heroes of *Competition* dream of pop stardom; the plain factory girl in *Loves of a Blonde* (1965) struggles with her love affairs; the uncouth working-class characters of *The Firemen's Ball* (1967) try to have fun in a dull, lifeless world. These films reflected the contemporary Czech working class from a position of realistic empathy. They were attacked by the state, but not suppressed.

Forman shot on the streets using nonprofessional actors. Indeed, his style is characterized by his sensitive use of non-actors and professionals speaking natural sounding dialogue. *Loves of a Blonde* and *The Firemen's Ball* work as humorous stories of mild social criticism. After the Soviet invasion in 1968, *The Firemen's Ball* was banned, and Forman decided to move permanently to the West. By 1975 Forman had made *One Flew Over the Cuckoo's Nest* (1975), the most honored Hollywood film in its year of release.

Věra Chytilová, more eclectic and formalist than Forman, became noted as something of a stylistic virtuoso. She gained prominence with her second feature, *Daisies* (1966). Stylistically, *Daisies* emerged from a collage of influences, from the Lumière brothers to Abel Gance to Charlie Chaplin. *Daisies* offers a dazzling display of montage, tinting, and color manipulation; it is a multi-faceted tour de force. Chytilová used this film as a veritable tableau of experimentation. Against the complex form and style, it evokes the youthful ennui of two girls who revolt against their drab world and find no simple solutions to their dilemmas. The themes were so powerfully felt that complaints reached the Czech parliament; the film's ban dutifully followed. But unlike her compatriots in Poland and Forman in her own country, Chytilová stayed in Czechoslovakia and struggled to remain in favor and make films.

Jiří Menzel made the most famous film of this era, at least in Western Europe and the

Miloš Forman's *Loves of a Blond* (1965).

United States. His *Closely Watched Trains* (1966), a tale of a young railway apprentice's sexual struggles, won the Academy Award for Best Foreign Film in 1968 but was banned in Czechoslovakia after the Soviet invasion in that year. Menzel eventually saved his career by recanting and publically disassociating himself from his pre-invasion films. Menzel's pervasive theme, the vicissitudes of sex, can be seen in his *Capricious Summer* (1968) and his *Crime at the Nightclub* (1968). But his *Larks on a String* (1969), about the sexual yearnings of a working-class boy, was banned before its release and prevented the director from actively working in the cinema until the mid-1970s.

The seeming contradiction of the Czech New Wave came through the experience of the film academy, where colleagues could study film together and not worry much about making only acceptable socialist realist films. They sought to appeal to a wider audience, not simply to function as tools of the state. The state at this time, the mid-1960s, tolerated these experiments, but the end came in 1968 with the Soviet military intervention. When, a year later, the regime of Gustov Husak established power, it proclaimed a summary ban on almost an entire year's output of the Czech cinema. Husak returned the cinema to one function: to educate through socialist realism, the state-approved style.

The impact on the film industry was devastating. Miloš Forman, Ivan Passer, Ján Kadár, and Jan Nemec, among others, left the country

Jiří Menzel's *Closely Watched Trains* (1966).

never to return. Forman, Passer, and Kadár moved to the West and made films in Europe and the United States. Indeed, Forman became one of the leading directors in Hollywood in the 1970s. So did Passer, who made *Born to Win* (1971), with George Segal and Karen Black, and *Law and Disorder* (1974), with Carroll O'Connor and Ernest Borgnine. Ján Kadár, who died in 1979, achieved less success in Hollywood but did direct *Lies My Father Told Me* (1975) and *Freedom Road* (1978).

Of those who remained in Czechoslovakia, only Menzel and Chytilová struggled against the state. Menzel, after a pause of six years and a public recantation of his "sins," including the winning of an Oscar, made *Short Cut* in 1980 and *Snowdrop Festival* in 1985. Véra Chytilová

made *The Apple Game* (1977), *An Apartment House Story* (1982), and *Calamity* (1982), which combine comedy and formal experimentation. By 1968 the Czech New Wave was clearly over, a brief glowing moment in the history of the Czech cinema.

• hungary •

Hungary, one of the world's smaller nations, has had a far greater influence in filmmaking than its size would indicate. This fact is all the more remarkable considering that Hungary's language and geographical location have isolated it from the Western European capitals of

Paris and London. For that reason, the national cinema has been particularly unified, dominated by one or two artists. Like the cinema in other countries in Eastern Europe, Hungary's film industry had to begin virtually from scratch after World War II. The industry produced less than one hundred films during the 1950s, but some proved remarkable.

Somewhere in Europe (1947) is one film that stands out in the years immediately after World War II. This film about the lives of a marauding group of children displaced by the war first attracted international attention to the Hungarian cinema. In addition, it gave several of Hungary's future directors, Felix Mariassy and Karoly Makk in particular, a chance to work. But *Somewhere in Europe* is most famous for its screenwriter, noted film theoretician Bela Balazs, who collaborated with Mariassy on the screenplay. Balazs had written one of the first influential books on film theory, *Theory of the Film*, and had been a pioneering proponent of film as an art form.

Somewhere in Europe thematically anticipated most of the tensions which would come to dominate the Hungarian cinema through the 1950s. The narrative concerned displaced children who were forced to live like animals to survive. Only after some help from adults are they able to integrate themselves into society. The film was influenced by Italian Neo-realist concerns with realism and Soviet ideas of what was a proper subject for Marxist filmmakers. But although these influences came to a fine confluence in this film, they too often led to muddled work in future Hungarian efforts.

The script became the intellectual peg on which authoritarian bureaucracies were able to structure their control of a film early on, before actual production commenced. Thus, in the 1950s Hungarian filmmakers were assigned scripts, their task simply to film them. This system was indeed much like Hollywood's, but it was used to advance the interests of the state. Hungarian studios became film factories. Filmmakers thus began to stress cinematography and, indeed, Hungarian cinema of the 1950s and later is noted for the complexity and verve of its cinematography.

In the 1950s, as Hungary recovered from the effects of World War II, three major directors emerged to rank with the world's best: Zoltán Fábri, Andras Kovács, and Miklós Jancsó. There were others, but these three put the Hungarian cinema on the world map of the art-cinema during the late 1950s and into the 1960s.

Zoltán Fábri chronologically came first. His first important film, *Fourteen Lives Saved*, was released in 1954. Virtually all his films concerned a group of individuals subjected to extreme stress such as the struggle with a natural disaster in *Fourteen Lives Saved*. Fábri demonstrated that a Hungarian filmmaker could treat important themes even though state authorities had to approve each script.

The Hungarian cinema of the 1950s, as reflected in the work of Fábri, remained conservative at best. During the 1960s the situation changed dramatically. Hungarian cinema became more aesthetically innovative, more intellectually demanding, more socially revolutionary. The social criticism of earlier periods became more analytical of Hungarian society and culture in particular.

Andras Kovács emerged as a filmmaker at this time. Like his fellow filmmaker Miklós Jancsó, Kovács had a long career in filmmaking before he started directing features in 1960. Kovács' work is firmly grounded in the documentary, and his general theme is how history shapes the individual. His first significant film was *Difficult People* (1964), which marked a decisive turn in the Hungarian cinema, since it was hardly a prescriptive state tale of the joys of communism. Instead, *Difficult People* tells the story of inventors thwarted by the red tape of bureaucracy, brilliant persons throttled by the state which funded the film. The film saw the shift from the confining constraints of the immediate post-war era. By relying on documentary principles Kovács avoided the twin tyrannies of prescribed scripts and formulaic cinematographic style.

Kovács continued his concern with historical analysis in his later work. His *Cold Days* (1966) memorializes the massacre of the villagers of Ujvidek (now Novi Sad in Yugoslavia) during the Second World War. Films about war atrocities were hardly unique, but this particular effort focused on the collaboration of Hungarian Fascists. Kovács not only reminded Hungarians that the Second World War was a civil war in their country but underscored the responsibilities of the common man in that struggle. The film does support the need for a socialist state in the face of fascism, but the film is really about the ease with which authoritarian regimes take power.

Miklós Jancsó is certainly the most famous of the Hungarian filmmakers. Anyone who has seen his impressive work can recognize his distinctive style. The films have little in the way of conventional acting. Music is always diegetic; that is, the source of the music must be specified in the film itself on camera. But the stylistic trait that most people notice right away is the lack of editing. These are films of very long takes; often ten minutes elapse without a cut. In *Red Psalm* (1972), for instance, there are some twenty shots in all. And during these long takes, the camera is constantly moving.

In films like *The Red and the White* (1967), *Agnus Dei* (1970), and *Red Psalm* (1972), Jancsó employed his very lengthy camera movements that roam across and among groups of people—tracking, craning, zooming, and changing focus. Jancsó's movies are as much about camerawork as they are about the past. Along with Orson Welles, Carl Dreyer, Andy Warhol, Jean Renoir, and Kenji Mizoguchi, Jancsó is one of the cinema's great masters of the long, moving take. Jancsó even built whole sequences of stories around a single moving camera shot.

But Jancsó is no minimalist filmmaker simply interested in formalist technique. His films, like those of Kovács, reveal a deep-seated interest in the problems of Marxism on the intellectual and theoretical level. Jancsó's chief interest is the history of Hungary seen through the eyes of a Marxist analyst. This is not to say that his films are historical works in the conventional sense of socialist realism, in which the workers optimistically triumph over their capitalist exploiters.

In contrast, Jancsó employs Marxist analysis in two very different ways. First his actual historical situations are stripped of all the particulars which might individualize them. Although it may be simple enough to recognize that such films as *The Round-Up* (1965) and *Agnus Dei* refer to actual historical moments in Hungary's past (the aftermath of the failure of the Kossuth rebellion or the failure of the Republic of the Councils), one has to know Hungarian history reasonably well to identify the actual situations. Nor are the events and individuals portrayed realistically. Jancsó never reveals particulars in the way Kovács does, but rather seeks the "why" behind the events.

By stripping away traditional realism, Jancsó sought to identify the basic principles of a society. He wanted to know why people do what they do. People are not villains but can do villainous acts. This view accounts for the fact that, in a Jancsó film, characters who seem attractive at first later act in puzzling and terrible ways.

Another question Jancsó's films seek to answer is why so many idealistic revolutions have spawned totalitarian states. In *Red Psalm*, he looks at the nature of the revolutionary process. *Agnus Dei* tries to make sense of the Stalinist regime of terror in the USSR in the 1930s. *The Confrontation* (1969) deals with the role of intellectuals and students in shaping a socialist society, while *The Red and the White* (1967) examines the realities of Hungarians caught up in an armed struggle for socialism.

The metaphysical situations Jancsó's films portray end in betrayal, slaughter, and despair. Far from giving the viewer a neat sense of closure, they portray closed circles of violence in which redemption comes, if it ever does, through self-sacrifice. This is a director who combines an unusual style of filmmaking with an unusual view of Marxist analysis. Many admire him, but frankly few, if they are honest, can pretend to say they fully understand this very nontraditional director. Jancsó stands outside both the Hollywood system and the system of socialist realism. This explains why, although he is widely admired, he has not been terribly influential.

• yugoslavia •

Although there existed a Yugoslav cinema long before 1945 (the Lumière brothers had projected their shorts in Belgrade before they were in New York), the Yugoslav cinema begins anew at the close of World War II. At that time filmmakers shared the struggle against Fascism with Marshall Tito and helped form a united country composed of six republics and two autono-

mous Serbian provinces with five major languages, three religions, and two alphabets. Yugoslavia's films reflect the diversity of this complex social matrix.

At the close of the Second World War, there was no film industry in Yugoslavia. From this beginning, twenty-two filmmaking companies were formed and more than one thousand movie houses built. At first the film industry was to be centralized at Koshutnyak, a huge studio complex outside Belgrade. But this Yugoslav Cinecitta never prospered and was transformed into a television production facility. Instead, the Yugoslav film industry decentralized, as did the government of the nation in the 1950s. According to the 1956 Film Law, each of the five republics was to have its own film center and absorb the numerous existing companies.

This plan seems apropos for this country that is neither a planned socialist state like the USSR nor a market capitalist nation like the United States. Yugoslavia's mixed economy is reflected in its film industry. Films are financed through a complicated mosaic of grants from the cultural committees of each republic and from funds generated at the box office. In recent years additional monies have come from television. Since the film industry is nationalized, all film production, distribution (import and export), and exhibition is handled by Jugoslaijafilm. In the 1960s, the government increased subsidies, thus spurring on the production of feature films.

In the years since 1960 this mixture of capitalism and socialism has resulted in two types of films: routine efforts for the small home market, typically social comedies or celebrations of the victories of the partisans in World War II; and for export, a handful of films aimed at the art-cinema market. The latter tend to be more individualistic, less about Yugoslavia in particular and more about the joys and frustrations of social and personal relations.

Marshall Tito broke with Moscow and the Soviet bloc in 1948 and thus the Soviet-dictated style of socialist realism played an increasingly less important role in Yugoslavia in the 1950s than in Poland, Czechoslovakia, and Hungary. By the mid-1950s a more pluralist, open-minded policy toward the film industry had been established in Yugoslavia. Of the film-making nations of the Eastern bloc, Yugoslavia was the most open. But this openness has cost the Yugoslavs in the international art-cinema export market. They have won numerous awards but have not achieved a national identity in the way the Poles did with Wajda and the Czechs did with Forman and other members of their New Wave of the 1960s.

Five years after the close of the Second World War young Yugoslav filmmakers had produced more than 250 documentaries covering all phases of the country's reconstruction after the war. Indeed each of the six republics had an established documentary unit. Somewhat surprisingly the impetus of the documentary movement survived post-war reconstruction and served as an important training ground for later feature filmmakers including Dušan Makavejev, Karpo Godina, Krsto Papic, and Zellimir Zilnik.

Yugoslavia became best known for its work in animation. Influenced by Walt Disney Studios from Hollywood and the more experimental efforts of Czech and Pole cartoonists, the Yugoslavs sought to create their own creations on film. But they lacked finance and supplies. Thus Zagreb filmmakers abandoned classical animation techniques, best known through the work of Disney, and developed a method of reduced animation, which required fewer drawings but resulted in a less full, less realistic look. Reduced animation is however faster, cheaper, and more flexible.

Dušan Vukotić had much to do with establishing the Czech reduced animation style through his experiments with simple line drawings and semi-abstract comic characters. Thematically he dealt with the influence of Western goods and modern civilization coming to Yugoslavia. In *Ersatz* (1961), for example, a line figure of a man can create any object he desires—air mattresses, fish, even humans. When the woman he has created runs off, to vent his wrath the hero begins to "unplug" the world, including the film we are watching. This is a satiric film with a lovely jazz accompaniment which delighted many critics with its self-reflexive jokes on the process of animation itself.

The feature films that have been produced in Yugoslavia follow three phases of development. From the close of the war through the 1950s the industry had to establish itself. The first feature made after the war, Vjekoslav Afric's *Slavica* (1947), took its story from the partisan defense of the country against the Nazis and the Italians. Although this film employs an interesting mix of documentary and classic narrative techniques and of Hollywood and Soviet influences, after that effort the partisan film settled down into a native, formulaic genre in which the evil German and the Italian Fascists were overwhelmed by the good Yugoslav nationalists. Throughout this early period the partisan film dominated the feature film in Yugoslavia.

But there were some more complex treatments of the war. France Stiglic moved from the documentary to the feature film with *The Valley of Peace* (1956), lyrically playing off the war experience as seen through the eyes of two children who rescue a downed American pilot. His *The Ninth Circle*, coming four years later, told of a Zagreb Jewish woman who falls in love and then is taken away to a concentration camp. This was the first Yugoslav film to directly treat the concentration camp issue and the atrocities committed by the Ustashis, the Croatian collaborators who murdered more than one hundred thousand Jews and one-half million Serbs during the war.

During the New Wave of Yugoslav cinema in the 1960s, a number of directors emerged to create individualistic works which made their mark around the world in art cinemas. It was no accident that this New Wave coincided with a liberalism in the Yugoslav society in general and was coupled, as was the case in many countries around the world, with a degree of social unrest and the rise of a youth culture. Although the New Wave of Yugoslavia was heralded in 1957 with the release of *Saturday Night*, directed by Vladimir Pogacic, it was 1961 which inaugurated a new era in both the quantity (thirty-two features in one year) and quality (numerous awards won). Once the new decentralized constitution was put into place in 1963 a new spirit of Yugoslav feature filmmaking commenced, centered on the works of Alexander Petrović, Zivojin Pavlović, and Dušan Makavejev.

Alexander Petrović, like many of his fellow Czech New Wave directors, had come through the ranks of the documentary movement. But it was his third feature, *Three* (1965), which earned him international recognition. This triptych of the partisan film genre so common at the time presented three encounters with death during the Second World War, each starring Bata Zivojinovic, the leading actor in Yugoslavia at the time. In the first he observes the execution of an innocent man; in the second he himself is the victim of a tense chase by the Nazis, who kill another partisan instead; finally,

he plays a partisan officer who must sentence to death a young woman to whom he is quite attracted. This is a tightly drawn set of narratives which won First Prize at the Karlovy Vary Festival and was nominated for an Academy Award for Best Foreign Film of the year.

Even more well known outside Yugoslavia is his next film, *I Even Met Happy Gypsies* (1967), which was also nominated for a Foreign Film Oscar and won the International Critics Award at the Cannes Film Festival. Shot in rich colors by Tomislav Pinter, a leading Yugoslav cinematographer, this is a realistic story of the lives of gypsies in modern-day Serbia. It was voted by Yugoslav critics in 1983 as the best Yugoslav film ever made.

Zivojin Pavlović has made more than a dozen films, none better than a partisan drama *The Ambush* (1969), which follows the growing disillusionment of a young partisan with the new socialist state immediately after the war. Stalin is the villain here. Pavlovic opens and closes the film with stark images of Stalin coupled with Russian marches on the sound track. He unmercifully exposes the shortcomings of overzealous Communist authorities who committed crimes in the name of state solidarity. The film proved to be too powerful for the Yugoslav authorities even in the liberal days of the late 1960s, and they banned the film before widespread release. They did let Pavlovic continue to make films which were less offensive.

Dušan Makavejev challenged the world of film style and form. Using forms of collage and compilation techniques, Makavejev juxtaposed images out of order and constantly played with disjunctions in time. Influenced by the writings of Wilhelm Reich, Makavejev interrelated personal and sexual relationships with continuing economic and political struggles. His most acclaimed work was *W. R.: Mysteries of the*

Organism, released in 1971 as the era of liberalism in filmmaking was coming to a close in Yugoslavia. This work synthesized the various experimental techniques he had dabbled with during the 1960s in such films as *Man Is Not a Bird* (1965) and *Love Affair, or The Case of the Missing Switchboard Operator* (1967). The film's almost surreal flow of images juxtaposes everything from sex and politics to Freud and Marx to film and "reality." It is humorous, ironic, and liberating.

Makavejev's *Innocence Unprotected* is a fragmented, chaotic, interrupted film. The Classic Hollywood cinema requires tying up all the loose ends; this film celebrates its lack of closure. *Innocence Unprotected* is collage rather than a classic narrative, an experiment in an alternative way to make films. He uses a wide range of the possible filmic materials, including the 1942 film *Innocence Unprotected* made by

Aleksic, a Yugoslav acrobat. A second source of filmic material comes from a mass of newsreels from the 1940s, and also posters and newspaper clippings from the period. This film challenges us to examine our notions of what is a proper film. Makavejev also asks us to consider what and how we know the past.

W. R.: Mysteries of the Organism (1971) deals with sexuality of politics and the politics of sex. As with *Innocence Unprotected* it challenges the viewer to think, to ponder. Consider that it criticizes both Stalin and Western capitalism. Makavejev looked to philosopher Wilhelm Reich (the "W. R.") to examine the individual's place in the correct road to socialism. This film too assaults the established codes of Hollywood to look at fundamental relationships of filmmaking. *W. R.: Mysteries of the Organism* may be the most celebrated of the films of Yugoslavia from the 1960s and early 1970s.

the developing world

During the television era, from 1950 through 1975, European nations were not the only countries making movies. Nearly all nations of the world had some sort of film production going at some point in time. But the larger nations, such as India, Brazil, and Argentina, certainly had the most active film industries following a capitalistic, profit-making form of production, distribution, and exhibition. In the socialist world, a much smaller nation, Cuba, dedicated a large amount of its resources to filmmaking and through the 1960s took center stage in the cinema of Latin America.

• india •

The cinema in India has long been a main-stream part of popular culture, but in the West, apart from the art-cinema of Satyajit Ray, little is known of the films of this subcontinent which regularly produced more films than any other nation in the world during the past forty years. The Lumière brothers reached Bombay only months after dazzling Paris with their cinematographe projector. The first completely Indian feature came in 1913; sound in 1931. Talkies were even able to survive, despite the numerous sub-cultures and multitude of languages of India.

India's cinema industry centers in Bombay and Madras. Bombay, the original locus, concentrates on film in Hindi, the most widely spoken Indian tongue (of some twenty-six) and the official language since independence. In the south, the state of Madras developed its own massive industry with the production of films in Tamil, the chief southern tongue. These two categories, the Hindi film in the north and the Tamil film in the south, constitute the mainstream of Indian cinema. With little penetration of television, the film industry of the 1950s and 1960s resembled Hollywood of the pre-television era. The power of the star system was coupled with the repetition of popular formulae or genres. Particularly popular were films which we might call musicals, with popular songs, a variety of dance numbers, and noted musical stars.

While other capitalist nations produced fewer and fewer films during the 1960s, the Indians produced more, showing a one-third increase during the decade. By 1971, Indian films approved by the censor amounted to more than four hundred. These productions included 118 films in Hindu, 83 in Telegu, 73 in Tamil, 52 in Malayalam, 33 in Kannada, 30 in Bengali, 23 in Marathi, and the remainder in 11 other languages, including English. A remarkable 250 filmmaking companies, using more than sixty studios, produced the films. The central government encouraged the making of Indian films by requiring all commercial cinemas to show at least one Indian film per show. The government also offered grants, loans (through the Film Finance Corporation), and a system of prizes to reward the "best" films.

Exhibition was concentrated in a fixed number of theatres augmented by more than two thousand mobile operations which served a series of rural circuits throughout the country-side. In addition, hundreds of 16mm theatres were operated by central and state governments, principally showing thousands of shorts, newsreels, and documentaries. In these cinemas, the ratio of Indian to Hollywood films was four to one. India also imported a small number of films from Italy, the USSR, Japan, and other western countries. Through the 1950s and 1960s India's was a theatrically dominated, homegrown film industry.

At the close of World War II the Indian film industry, like the country as a whole, was in a state of transition. The war had a devastating effect on the society in general and on the film industry in particular. The major studios of the 1930s had collapsed; independent producers, working irregularly, became the norm. After India achieved independence in 1947, filmmakers began to celebrate the new nationalism. There was an increase in patriotic historical films and films which honored India's mythological past.

One reason for the popularity of these films was the success of S. S. Vasan's Madras-made costume drama *Chandralekha* (1948). The story of two princes fighting over a throne and a princess, its lavish spectacle, skillfully choreographed dances, and dazzling sword fights made it a national hit. Similar historical costume films would get a great boost from the introduction of color in 1952. *Aladdin and the Wonderful Lamp* (1952) and *Alibaba* (1954), among others, helped historical fantasies make up 30 percent of the native box office. Melodramas, love stories, and light romances were saved for cheaper black and white.

There were any number of filmmakers working at this time. Raj Kapoor, as star, director, and producer, combined lavish spectacle, magnificent sets, dazzling locations, and frequent fantasy sequences to make his name popular throughout the nation. Bimal Roy turned to melodrama and song. Mehboob Khan made *Mother India* (1957), a classic of popular entertainment which enjoyed continuous revivals. This tale of traditional rural life presented the struggle for survival of a poor village woman who, left alone with her children, defended her self-respect and womanhood against famine, floods, corrupt money lenders, and finally her rebellious outlaw son. Combining realism, Hollywood melodrama, and Hindu religious and folk imagery, it appealed to Indian nationalism and traditional sentiment in the context of an ever-changing post-colonial world.

But all filmmakers had to work within a rigid set of defined genres similar to those in Hollywood of the 1930s and 1940s. The largest category, the social film, dealt with contemporary times, and its structure was defined by melodrama or comedy. Historical films were predominantly epic displays of ornate grandeur, often set in Mughal court life, with lavish settings and big stars—leading to large takes at the boxoffice. Mythological films employed

trick photography to bring to life stories from folk tales. Stunt films were about rural outlaws of the past and were played as broadly as possible. There were also frequent costume, magic, and fantasy films. Although such genre works were highly popular in Indian cinemas, playing to the shouts and cheers of native audiences, they rarely made their way to the West.

Since the inception of a separate Hindi cinema with the coming of sound, there has been a small tradition of socially serious films. The Bombay Talkies Studio, founded in 1934, produced such films as *Untouchable Girl* (1936), which dealt with the bitter realities of the caste system. Bimal Roy's Hindi *Two Acres of Land* (1953) was influenced by Italian Neo-realism and earned the Prix International at the 1954 Cannes Film Festival. Another of Roy's films, *Sujata* (1959), dealt with the caste system in an equally open and honest way. K. A. Abbas, while earning a place in mainstream filmmaking with star Raj Kapoor on such hits as *The Vagabond* (1951) and *Mr. 420* (1955), also crafted experimental films such as *Children of the Earth* (1949) and *Munna* (1954).

Among the minority language cinema traditions, only the Bengali cinema, centered in Calcutta, was able to achieve any recognition. The international fame of one director, Satyajit Ray, proved it was possible to work outside the mainstream, glossy, Hollywood-like cinema. Indeed, in the West, Ray's films were sold as serious art films. He is thus the best-known Indian filmmaker outside his own country.

Satyajit Ray made films more popular in art cinemas in the West than in his native land. There were many reasons for this, including his lack of work in established genres and his work in Bengali, a regional language. In 1947 Ray founded the Calcutta Film Society, where Ben-

Satyajit Ray's *Apu Sansar* (1959).

gali intellectuals and cineastes, dissatisfied with the norms of conventional cinema, looked at films from abroad and discussed alternative filmmaking styles and forms. Thus Ray's influences were not native filmmakers, but Italian Neo-realism, Frenchman Jean Renoir, and even the best directors of the Classic Hollywood cinema.

Ray's reputation rests on the Apu trilogy: *Pather Panchali* (1955), *Aparajito* (1956), and *Apu Sansar* (1959), an epic about a family that moves from a traditional village to a modern city. But Ray has also treated other subjects, including feudal aristocrats in *The Music Room* (1958) and *The Adversary* (1971), and the movies in *The Hero* (1966).

Ray began in the cinema as a hobby in the years immediately after the Second World War. In 1950 Jean Renoir, the great French filmmaker, visited India to make *The River* and encouraged the young Ray to think about filming *Pather Panchali*, a popular book by the Bengali writer Bhibuti Bannerjee. At first Ray found it impossible to raise the monies for a film to be shot with non-professional actors and actresses on location in the manner of Italian Neo-realism. But *Pather Panchali* was completed and released in 1955 to acclaim at the Cannes Film Festival in 1956. The Apu trilogy is characterized by an un-Hollywood like realism, with the mise-en-scène often photographed in deep space and through long takes (in time) and slow, deliberate camera movements. The editing, however, is classic in its continuity of storytelling.

• south america •

The largest nations of South America, Brazil and Argentina, were rich enough to sustain a native industry, but not of the size or impact of India or Japan. They could at times keep Hollywood at bay, but they were hardly typical. Indeed most South American countries, notably Bolivia, Chile, Colombia, Ecuador, Paraguay, Peru, and Uruguay had no regular film production at all. Occasionally, governments would sponsor educational or documentary films, but in the few hundred commercial cinemas in each country, the bulk of the films shown were from Hollywood, Argentina, and Brazil.

The film industry in Brazil, like that in all South American countries, was surrounded by Hollywood as it developed. Before the 1960s there was little happening in the country to give Hollywood exporters any worry. There was one indigenous genre, the *chanchada*, or musical comedy. In the late 1940s Luiz Carlos Barretto and noted documentary filmmaker Alberto Calvalcanti opened the Vera Cruz studio where they produced more than a dozen features before they went out of business. In this and other instances, Brazil proved that no nation could out-Hollywood Hollywood.

That changed in the 1960s with the Cinema Novo. Inspired by the French New Wave and Italian Neo-realism, Cinema Nôvo put Brazil on the international cinema map. Cinema Nôvo came at a time of economic boom and increasing national pride. In Rio de Janeiro and São Paulo filmmakers attempted to plug into the art-cinema interest. Through cineclubs and discussion the Brazilians attempted to construct their own unique contribution to the new wave of cinema.

The Cinema Nôvo movement came in three waves. In the first period (from 1960 to 1964) filmmakers drew on a history of the revolt of the underclasses and folklore of the poor. Glauber Rocha's *Black God, White Devil* (1964) critiqued the banditry and chaos of northeast Brazil; Ruy Guerra's *The Guns* (1964) probed conflicts among peasants, landowners, and the military; Nelson Pereira dos Santos' *Barren Lives* (1963) looked at peasant poverty in the northeastern section of the nation. These and other works sought to be more than film entertainment or an alternative to Hollywood. These socially committed filmmakers wanted to spur downtrodden masses to act and to articulate their outrage. Such revolutionary aspirations were never fulfilled partly because these films never were widely distributed and thus often never reached their intended audiences.

From 1964 to 1968 Cinema Nôvo suffered because the military had seized power from a populist government. Filmmakers re-grouped and tried to figure a next step. Glauber Rocha made *Earth Entranced* (1967), telling of a self-styled revolutionary shot down by the police. Between 1968 and 1972, filmmaking prospects grew bleak. Another right-wing government took power and began to censor movies and arrest filmmakers. Glauber Rocha, Ruy Guerra, and Carlos Diegues took refuge in exile. Those who remained avoided political subjects. Indeed Rocha's *Antonio das Mortes* (1969) signaled the end of the Cinema Nôvo. This lyrical, mythic epic creatively integrated elements of Brazilian popular religious culture, politics, folklore, social history, music, and literature.

Filmmakers in this period pushed for nationalist support of the movies. In 1969 the government created Embrafilm to finance films and even to run theatres. It dictated that any theatre must show Brazilian films 140 days a year and set maximum amounts of currency that Hollywood companies could take out of the country. But it was not until a political thaw during the mid-1970s that this law could be put to any significant use to revitalize filmmaking in Brazil.

The cinema of Argentina, at the end of World War II, was small, aimed only at its own internal market. In truth, Hollywood still dominated, even though the government of General Juan Perón initiated a series of powerful quotas and loans to stimulate native production and exhibition. (These tactics also guaranteed that Perón could keep an eye on what films were made.) Perón fell from power in 1955, but the governments which succeeded his kept tight reins on the film industry.

Argentina, although a large country, had only one-fourth the population of Brazil in the 1970s. Nevertheless, its theatrical film production remained about half again the size of Brazil's. The nation had theatres in all the big cities, including seven American style drive-ins in Buenos Aires. A handful of directors were able to survive in this small market (relative to Hollywood), including one who would make an international reputation during the art-cinema era.

Leopold Torre-Nilsson was one director who was able to survive in the tightly controlled world of Argentine film and achieve a fair degree of fame in the art-cinema world of the early 1960s. Torre-Nilsson came from a movie family; in fact, he co-directed his first feature, *Oribe's Crime* (1950), with his father. He did not make many films (twenty-one in all), but some were quite distinguished. The first Jorge Luis Borges

story was brought to the screen as *Days of Hatred* (1954). For *The House of the Angel* (1957) he first teamed with his novelist wife, Beatriz Guido. She wrote the scripts; he directed. He took *The House of the Angel* to the Cannes Film Festival, and it was hailed by such French luminaries as André Bazin and Eric Rohmer. He won a prize at Cannes in 1961 for his *The Hand in the Trap*, another tale of loneliness and woe.

The House of the Angel proved the turning point in his career. He broke with the routine comedies and melodramas produced to compete with Hollywood imports and made a film which was approved of abroad and easily fit into the art-cinema category. Many compared the intensity of the film to the best of Ingmar Bergman and Luis Buñuel. Torre-Nilsson's themes and his stories of the isolated Europeanized bourgeoisie stifled by a repressive Catholic moral force in Argentina was well accepted by European audiences, and, to a lesser extent, by American filmgoers.

Inspired by the success of Torre-Nilsson and the French New Wave, a generation of 1960s directors appeared in Argentina, often referred to as the New Argentine cinema. Noted directors included David Kohon, Rodolfo Kuhn, Jose Martinez Suarez, Lautaro Murua, Simon Feldman, and Manuel Antin. The Argentine New Wave lasted only two years (1960 to 1962), until the government changed hands and began to clamp down on its critics. Suarez's *The Ace* (1960) exposed corruption in the world of soccer; Kuhn's *Little Bird Gomez* (1964) exposed the seedy side of the entertainment industry. These New Wave directors were linked by a sense of disenchantment with the status quo in Argentine society.

The most famous of the Argentine New Wave films inspired worldwide attention. *The*

Hour of the Furnaces (1968), more than four hours long, was banned for years, yet this three-part documentary skillfully combined newsreel footage, dramatic sequences, and printed slogans in a cinematic collage to win awards in Italy, West Germany, and Great Britain. The film was not meant to entertain but to incite revolution. Building on the nationalism of the Peronists, it sought a left-wing revolution to put an end to underdevelopment and exploitation. It failed in that task, and thereafter the Argentine cinema returned to sporadic production, too often aimed at besting Hollywood, an impossible task.

• cuba •

Since its revolution, the Cuban film industry has ranked as the most powerful in Latin America because of the state support from the Castro government. Before Fidel Castro, who came to power on 1 January 1959, Cuba offered little more than a site for location shooting by Hollywood. The best that Cubans could hope for was the occasional Cuban-Mexican co-production. In their theatres, before the revolution, Cubans saw films from Hollywood, Brazil, and Argentina.

After the revolution the Castro government set up the Cuban Film Institute or ICAIC. Although it created no Hollywood in the Caribbean, Cuba's eight million inhabitants did generate a lively, influential film industry. During the 1960s, after a start-up period, it produced nearly fifty feature films and hundreds of documentaries, educational films, animated cartoons, and newsreels. The ICAIC operated the country's nearly five hundred cinemas plus seventy-five mobile units which went out into the countryside. Imported films were strictly

regulated but drawn from the USSR and Hungary as well as Hollywood and Western Europe.

ICAIC served (and still serves) as a film production facility, as a training ground for filmmakers, as the distributor of Cuban films around the world, as a cinematheque, and as the publisher of *Cine Cubano*, one of Latin America's leading film journals. ICAIC was founded because Castro realized the importance of film in his plans to transform Cuba from a capitalist outpost to a modern socialist state. Castro called for filmmakers to inform the revolution and draw on working-class Cuban history. At first ICAIC had little in the way of film equipment, film stock, or laboratory facilities. Slowly, through the 1960s, ICAIC took on the characteristics of a modern film institute, stressing the creation of relatively cheap newsreels and documentaries. Feature films were limited to a handful per year.

Tomás Gutiérrez Alea, one of the founders of ICAIC, is one of Cuba's best-known filmmakers. His *Memories of Underdevelopment* (1968) stands as one of his nation's most noted and praised works. But he did not just begin with this famous, honored work. One of ICAIC's earlier major productions and Alea's first feature was *Stories of the Revolution* (1961). It consists of three autonomous dramatic sketches which portray three different armed insurrections against Batista in a style reminiscent of Italian Neo-realism. *The Death of a Bureaucrat* (1966) presents a very different work. This black comedy features a clever use of off-beat dialogue, animation, and comic parodies of famous moments in Cuban history. This is a rare work because it is a complete satire of the bureaucratic trappings and red tape of this new socialist society.

Memories of Underdevelopment became a symbol of a new cinema in Fidel Castro's Cuba. Sensitively transposing Desnoes' novel to the

Tomás Gutiérrez Alea's *Memories of Under-development* (1968).

● ●

screen, Alea examined the dilemma of the intellectual in post-revolutionary Cuba with a great deal of subtlety and irony through the character of Sergio, a wealthy but alienated middle-class man who stays in Cuba after the revolution. Alea combined documentary footage with traditional fiction techniques and also used selected sequences from the direct point-of-view of the central figure. Through this juxtaposition of visual forms and through the contradictions it raises in the story of one man's reflections, *Memories of Underdevelopment* pushes the viewer to see the function of history in shaping what we are taught and how our history shapes our thoughts.

Alea has continued to make complex films, although less famous ones. His *The Last Supper* (1976) tells of a slave rebellion in a Cuban sugar plantation near the end of the eighteenth century. The references to Christianity underscore the differences between the landowner's life and the existence of the slaves. *The Survivors* (1979) presents another comedy in which, through black humor, Alea shows us a bour-

geois family attempting to live apart from the socialist revolution and ultimately regressing to feudalism and then savagery.

Julio Garcia Espinosa was another founder of ICAIC as well as a major director and writer about the role of the cinema in the Cuban revolution. He has, in addition to his own work, sponsored a number of films, including Chilean exile Patricio Guzman's three-part documentary, *The Battle of Chile* (1973–1977). Espinosa warned his fellow directors to search for a style that would differentiate Cuban cinema from Hollywood. In his own work Espinosa has followed these dictates.

Humberto Solás also tried to create new Cuban forms. His *Lucia* (1968) was made at the age of twenty-six as his first feature film. This historical epic tells three love stories that take place in three different eras of Cuban history, all involving a woman named Lucia. Solás varies the camerawork, music, and narration in the three episodes to contrast the class differences of the main figures and their historical eras. These are not traditional love stories but examinations of the roles of men and women in Cuba before and after the revolution.

Solás has since struggled to match this massive initial effort. His short documentary *Simparele* (1974) deals with the people and customs of Haiti. The feature-length *Cantata of Chile* (1975) traces, through the alternation of styles, the struggles of the working class of Chile. *Cecilia Valdés* (1982) is a feature-length Spanish-Cuban co-production which examines Havana's nineteenth-century slave-holding culture. *Amada* (1983) tells of a bourgeois woman trapped in an unhappy marriage in Havana of 1914. Solás, like many of his compatriots, continues to struggle to find the proper way to make films in a changing socialist society.

Manuel Octavio Gómez has been one of ICAIC's most productive creators of feature films. Like his fellow Cuban filmmakers he has experimented with a variety of narrative and visual styles in order to establish a socialist film-making technique with the appeal of Holly-wood. His *The First Charge with the Machete* (1969) is a historical drama telling of the victory of the machete-wielding Cuban rebels over Spanish forces in the 1868 war of indepen-dence. In his *A Woman, a Man, a City* (1978) Gomez interweaves three narrative threads to explore the lives of three characters. His *Patakin* (1982) is a musical comedy which features social satire and Hollywood-style pro-duction numbers.

Santiago Alvarez is best known as ICAIC's most prolific and influential documentary film-maker. (In addition he has headed ICAIC's Latin American Newsreel division from its inception, producing one news film per week to circulate in the island's approximately five hundred the-atres.) The themes of maintaining international solidarity, combating American imperialism, and supporting the Cuban revolution form the tripartite foundation of Alvarez's documenta-ries. For example, in his *Now* (1965) Alvarez juxtaposes photos and news clips with Lena Horne's singing of "Now" to underscore the racial injustice in the so-called free United States. His 120-minute *April in Vietnam in the Year of the Cat* (1975) also integrates music and montages of photos and news footage, in this case to commemorate the founding of the Dem-ocratic Republic of Vietnam.

Indeed much of Cuban cinema has centered on the use of documentary film. ICAIC annually produces some forty documentaries. These range from the feature-length *I Am a Son of America . . . and Am Indebted to Her* (1972) and *And Heaven Was Taken by Storm* (1973) in which Santiago Alvarez chronicled Fidel Cas-tro's trips to Salvador Allende's Chile, Eastern Europe, and Africa. Pastor Vega made *Long Live the Republic!* in 1972 to re-examine Cuban his-tory prior to the revolution. This is a Marxist interpretation of the United States' imperialism in the Latin American region. In making the film, Vega tapped not only his own country's resources but also the Library of Congress in Washington, D.C. Pedro Chaskel's shorts *A Pho-tograph Goes Around the World* (1981) and *Ché Today and Always* (1983) pay homage to the revolutionary leader Ernesto "Ché" Guevara. But most of Cuba's documentaries are simply shorts about exceptional individuals, like *Cay-ita, Legend and Feats* (1980), about a ninety-six year old woman who lived through and still supports the Castro revolution, and *Pedro Zero Percent* (1980) about a dedicated dairy farmer.

recent new waves

At the end of the television age, as we moved into the era of contemporary cin-ema, the films of Germany and Australia have become critically influential and at times pop-ular around the world. For film historians these two movements represent the latest of film's continuous "new waves." That is, they have been recognized and shown in theatres around the globe. Whether they will have the measure of impact and influence of the French New Wave remains to be seen. But surely here are two movements which define the edge of film history.

• new german cinema •

During the late 1960s and early 1970s three young German filmmakers burst onto the international scene to signal a rebirth of their national cinema. Werner Herzog, in his 1968 *Signs of Life*, Rainer Werner Fassbinder, in his 1969 *Love Is Colder Than Death*, and Wim Wenders, in his 1971 *The Goalie's Anxiety at the Penalty Kick*, signaled to the art-cinema world that a national cinema which had been dormant since the end of the Second World War was positioned to claim a place in the international scene. Gradually through the 1970s the New German cinema did attract a loyal and devoted audience.

But it had been a long struggle since the close of the Second World War. The period from 1945, with the surrender to the Allies, to the early 1960s was one of slow transition. The country was split in two: the Federal Republic of Germany (FRG or West Germany) and the German Democratic Republic (GDR or East Germany). The nation was shattered, its cities leveled, and its populace shamed. The Allies (the United States, England, France, and the USSR) wanted to reeducate the inhabitants, to use film (and other media) to break the Nazi legacy. In the USSR-controlled Eastern zone, the Soviets set about dubbing their own films into German. The Soviets immediately centralized film production, creating the government-

controlled Deutsche Film Aktiengesellschaft (DEFA) in May 1946. Whereas some forty film companies started up after the war in West Germany, filmmaking in East Germany always functioned as a state-controlled industry.

In West Germany the FRG was led by Konrad Adenauer, a fierce anticommunist and an ally of the United States. Adenauer's tenure in office led to economic prosperity and relative political stability. But this success came at a price. The 1950s was a staid era of domestic harmony marked by a fear of nonconformity and opposition ideas. The West German film industry became an adjunct of Hollywood. American interests maintained rigid control over the films that were distributed in the country. Thus, unlike its neighbors, West Germany had no quotas; Hollywood products freely flowed into its theatres.

The FRG government tried to assist the film industry in two ways. First an arrangement of government-secured loans to film producers was established in March of 1950, intended to spur small-scale productions as an alternative to Hollywood. Secondly, attempts began in 1953 to revive the depleted UFA through covert sponsorship of banks. This effort also floundered. Even with government backing, UFA could not compete with Hollywood on its own terms. By 1962 the once-mighty UFA was in liquidation.

All that state-subsidized capitalism did— with its rigid rules and formulations—was to give the power of the purse to a conservative state authority. A state board screened every film and had to approve it before it could be shown. Another state agency provided tax breaks for films which it deemed had "artistic quality." West Germany had no cine-clubs, no film schools, no networks of art theatres. It occupied an arid, state-dominated film landscape.

Consider the most popular film genre of the 1950s—the Heimatfilm, or the Homeland film. Over three hundred such films were made between 1947 and 1960, an estimated one-fifth of the entire West German output. The Homeland films offered comforting images of green fields untouched by the ravages of bombing, mountain villages strongly linked to the past, and picture postcard panoramas of a by-gone era. Untouched nature replaced ruined cities; and church bells broke the quiet serenity, not bulldozers and jackhammers; quaint panel houses offered warmth and comfort in contrast to the lack of adequate safe housing left after World War II. Films such as Hans Deppe's *Black Forest Girl* (1950) and *Green Is the Heather* (1951) soothed audiences whose daily life was actually a constant struggle.

Literary adaptations from safe middle-class literature abounded. These so-called Verfilmungen came from realist novels from by-gone eras which centered on polite civility and domestic tranquility. For example, the novels of Thomas Mann provided the source for costume films featuring popular stars and graced by high production values. Alfred Weidenmann's two-part *Buddenbrooks* (1959) reduced Mann's sweeping epic about the fall of a complete class in society to a stuffy drawing room drama.

Nostalgia can also be seen in the extraordinary number of remakes. A popular comedy such as *The White Horse Inn*, originally done in 1935, was redone in 1952 and 1960. *Vulture Valley*, a Homeland film originally made in 1940, was filmed again in 1956. Revisions of former glories included remakes of the classics of Weimar cinema of the 1920s. But these classics were hardly just done over. Lavish costumes, matinee idols, and vast sets were meant to re-sell *The Last Laugh* (1955) and *Madchen in Uniform* (1958). War films, about ten percent of the total, seemed also to concentrate on the glories of the past. Paul May's popular three-part *08/15* (1954–1955), for example, helped reinstate the military as an admirable modern calling, carefully distinguishing the glories of the average infantry soldier from the evil leadership of the Nazi era.

West Germany encouraged those who fled the Nazis to come back and work. Robert Siodmak's return in the mid-1950s sparked great interest. He had gained renown in Hollywood with such thrillers as *Phantom Lady* (1944) and *The Spiral Staircase* (1945). Of his half dozen efforts in the 1950s and early 1960s, the most successful was *The Devil Strikes at Night* (1957), which received several prizes. He cleverly meshed his heritage of Expressionist style with an oblique commentary on the rampant materialism of the 1950s in West Germany, all in high-contrast lighting with darkened stairwells, frenzied faces, and non-traditional camera angles in a story of Nazi cover-up and greed.

Fritz Lang returned to Germany to make his last film, *The Thousand Eyes of Dr. Mabuse* (1960). In the guise of a pulp B thriller he created a self-reflexive modernist film concerned with the nature of film narrative and the penchant for voyeurism. Many at the time thought it crudely made, but its mis-matches and disjunctive crosscutting project a world in which the authorities keep track of everyone. *The Thousand Eyes of Dr. Mabuse* provides a link back to an earlier Mabuse film (*The Testament of Dr. Mabuse*, 1933), a critique of the Nazis. This was Lang's only film in modern Germany and the final one of his career.

But significant changes commenced in 1963. A public scandal brought down the Adenauer cabinet, and the new government recognized that the film policies of the 1950s had not worked. Against this background the Oberhausen Manifesto appeared. Presented at the Eighth Annual Oberhausen Festival, this angry declaration by twenty-six young filmmakers announced a New German cinema, one which would emphasize freedom of expression and freedom from oppressive state control and interference. "The old film is dead. We believe in a new one." Alexander Kluge, the New German film's most articulate defender, stressed the role of film to explore reality, to document everyday life, to free West Germany from occupation (read "Hollywood") influences. This manifesto was inspired by the successes of the French New Wave, then only a few years old.

But there were major and important differences between the filmmakers of the French New Wave and the New German cinema. The German filmmakers had no central critical or theoretical position on filmmaking; nor did they have a strongly felt opposition to Hollywood-style filmmaking. Instead they united around the desire to develop a new, alternative creative environment so that each filmmaker could fashion films he or she liked. Moreover, they had little sense of the history of the richness of the German cinema. They had no models for inspiration as the French had in Robert Bresson, Jacques Tati, or Jean Renoir.

They sought a source of public funding which would guarantee the autonomy of the director from both a Hollywood-like industry and the political pressure of the FRG state. They may have called for radical action, but they knew (or thought) that they must still obtain state funds or there would be no autonomous West German film industry. In February 1965 the Ministry of Interior, the same state unit which had presided over the failed 1950s subsidy schemes, set up the Kuratorium Junger Deutscher Film (Board of Curators of Young German Film) to supply five million marks for the initial works of the New German cinema. Later in the 1960s came the film academies of Ulm, West Berlin, and Munich.

With Alexander Kluge's first feature, *Yesterday Girl*, Volker Schlöndorff's *Young Torless*,

and Jean-Marie Straub and Daniele Huillet's *Not Reconciled*, all released in 1966, the films of the New German cinema won a number of international prizes. Like 1959 in France, suddenly the New German cinema was everywhere, shown and praised in London, Rome, Paris, and later in the United States. The breakthrough came in 1966 when Volker Schlöndorff's *Young Torless* earned the International Critics Prize at the Cannes Film Festival, Peter Schamoni's *Closed Season on Fox Hunting* gained the Silver Bear at Berlin, and Alexander Kluge's *Yesterday Girl* received the Silver Lion at Venice. These films plus Ulrich Schamoni's *It* (1966) aptly expressed the rage of German youth in general and young German filmmakers in particular. They all concerned private rebellions of angry young people whose elders offer little help or advice.

The problems of funding seemed to end in the mid-1970s with television. The television industry in Germany (as in many European countries) created competition for the services of experienced filmmakers. Since German television was state run and financed, it could fund films regardless of popularity. Indeed, the television executives wanted the films first shown in theatres to gather fame and prestige; and then they would show them on television. Television thus gave the New German cinema a solid basis of support.

Rainer Werner Fassbinder emerged from the underground world of radical stage productions but at the same time looked to Hollywood for inspiration. He shared the dreams and disillusionment of the Hollywood 1940s film noir view of life. Fassbinder had a particular fascination with the crime dramas of Howard Hawks, and this can be seen as an influence in his debut feature *Love Is Colder Than Death* (1969), where characters are caught between tough-guy posturing and the insecurity which motivates such self-stylizing. Staged in a petty criminal milieu reminiscent of Jean-Luc Godard's *Band of Outsiders*, Fassbinder's re-creation of low life in Munich imparted a social dimension to the world of a gangster thriller.

Fassbinder became one of the hardest working, fastest of the New German directors. He turned the constraint of limited budgets into a creative virtue. For example, the lack of contrast in lighting in *Love Is Colder Than Death* creates a world in which there are no shadows, no places to hide. The long static takes and the sparse decor of his *Katzelmacher* (1969) under-lines the world of disenchanted confines of Germany's provinces. *Why Does Herr R. Run Amok?* (1970) forms a radical exercise in which improvisation renders a documentary-like vi-sion of a struggling technical designer faced with changing career demands and domestic troubles. Full of what Hollywood would con-sider mistakes (like overexposed film and out-of-focus shots), the film reveals the harsh reality that moves its protagonist to murder his family and later commit suicide.

Wim Wenders, a graduate of the Munich Academy for Television and Film, also was deeply interested in American film. His career fully expresses the love-hate of Hollywood typ-ical of an occupied nation. His cryptic adapta-tion of Peter Handke's crime novel, *The Goalie's Anxiety at the Penalty Kick* (1971) is full of ref-erences to the American cultural presence in West Germany, including for example, the ever-blaring popular music and "quotations" from Howard Hawks' *Red Line 7000* (1965) and Don Siegel's *Madigan* (1968). *The Goalie's Anxiety at the Penalty Kick* traces a few days in the life of a former soccer player who has blithely mur-dered a cashier at a movie house. But this is a crime tale without Hollywood's penchant for tying together all the loose ends. Wenders' tale is full of red herrings and unfinished bits, el-liptical leaps, missing transitions, and inexact character motivation.

Werner Herzog ranks as the third signifi-cant member of the New German cinema. His feature debut, *Signs of Life* (1968), brought him a State Film prize and considerable attention. In this tale of the gradual undoing of a German soldier stationed in an isolated outpost during the Second World War, the soldier Stroszek goes mad in a valley of inexorably revolving windmills. *Signs of Life* began Herzog's interest in landscape detail, psychological change, and life lived at the edge. His experimental docu-mentary, *Fata Morgana* (1970), set on a des-ert inhabited by bizarre natives, settlers, and explorers, presented an odd mixture of fic-tion and documentary, narrative and non-narrative impulses.

The 1970s would be the decade of the great success of the New German cinema. The works of Wenders, Fassbinder, and Herzog gained an international following, complete with hom-ages in Paris, London, and New York. They be-came among the most celebrated auteurs of the decade. The irony is that as the praise increased abroad, these filmmakers and their compatriots only found more trouble at home.

New German filmmakers had from the be-ginning opposed the dominant cinema of the state and imported Hollywood films. As the days of student rebellion of the late 1960s and early 1970s began to wane, so did the state's toler-ance for underground films. Conservative forces arose, whether in the form of blacklist-ing, state denunciation, or security checks. West German radical filmmakers either left the coun-try (Straub/Huillet to Rome, for example) or stopped making films altogether.

But Fassbinder worked on. He sought a more popular film while maintaining interest in experimenting and formulating art films which would appeal to a market abroad. *The*

Merchant of Four Seasons (1971) was his break-through work. It is a melodrama which owes much to another German expatriate to Hollywood, Douglas Sirk, who in California created some of Hollywood's glossiest work. Fassbinder learned to recast this popular genre (otherwise known, in the 1950s, as the "women's weepies") while still forcing attentive viewers to see the contradictions behind the gloss. The story of a fruit vendor's humble aspirations, disappointments, and suicide are linked via mise-en-scène to the 1950s: stylized clothing, tense family relations, kitsch paintings, and women in the kitchens.

But despite the international triumphs of *Ali: Fear Eats the Soul* (1973) and *Effie Briest* and *Fox and His Friends*, both made in 1974, the director faced constant rejection at home. He was attacked in the conservative press as a leftist anti-Semite for *Garbage, the City, and Death* (1976), saw his agreements with national television cancelled from under him, and even contemplated emigration and suicide. He could not overcome his despair and was found dead in a Munich apartment on 10 June 1982. Some saw it as the end of an era.

The New German cinema was not a stylistic movement in the same sense that the unified French New Wave was. The French New Wave had a set of closely associated filmmakers who worked in similar themes, conventions, and stylistic traits (at least until 1968). The New German cinema, on the other hand, consisted of a talented set of directors, not works in a similar style. The term came about not to denote a unified movement but rather to emphasize the rebirth of the German cinema after lying fallow since the Second World War. The filmmakers of the New German cinema were united in being outside the normal system of finance and distribution; each had specific ideas about how films ought to be made.

• the new australian cinema •

By 1986 even the least observant movie fan had heard of the rebirth of Australian filmmaking through one film, *Crocodile Dundee*. Released in the United States in 1986, this film made Paul Hogan a major star and finished in second place behind *Top Gun* for 1986 grosses. But this burst of creative filmmaking from Australia really began ten years earlier. Since 1970 the Australian cinema has produced a body of varied work. We have seen a major reinterpretation of Australian history in notable films like *Breaker Morant* (1980) and *My Brilliant Career* (1979). *Mouth to Mouth* (1978) and *Stir* (1980) have looked at the morals of contemporary Australian society. These and other films created a stir around the world in the 1970s signaling yet another New Wave.

The beginnings of the Australian cinema date back as far as 1896. But like most countries of small population, Australia of the 1920s and 1930s imported Hollywood productions for their movie screens, occasionally interspersed with films from Great Britain and other members of the Commonwealth. Only a handful of native Australian productions were shown, usually as curiosities or supporting features. During World War II Australian filmmakers did make newsreels and documentaries to support the war effort.

From the close of the Second World War until the mid-1960s the Australian feature film industry almost ceased to exist. Only a handful of feature films were made, often through sponsorship of Hollywood. What work there was came mainly from the documentaries being made at the Commonwealth Film Unit (Film Australia) and the Shell Film Unit, or film companies from abroad who used Australia for location work. In this latter category were Hollywood's *The Kangaroo Kid* (1950) and *The*

Sundowners (1960). In short, Australian movie exhibition was dominated by American and British interests.

Fundamental conditions began to change in the 1960s. Many factors came into play. There was a rise in nationalism in the arts in general and concern that Hollywood domination had gone on too long. A film society movement, particularly strong in Sydney and Melbourne, pushed for indigenous creations. This activity, coupled with a growing experimental film movement and the rise of film publications such as *Film Digest*, *Masque*, *Cinema Papers*, and the *Sydney University Film Group Bulletin*, led to a film culture which did everything but produce films.

The Australian Film Development Office was established by an act of Parliament in 1970 to administer funds to provide loans and assistance to film and television producers. Three films made in 1970 promised an exciting future. British director Tony Richardson's *Ned Kelly* (1970) had rock star Mick Jagger cast as an Australian folk hero. *Walkabout* told of the clash of the white and aborigine cultures. The director, another Brit, Nicholas Roeg, the cinematographer for *The Sundowners*, drew a haunting portrait of the barren, bleak, but beautiful Australian outback. In the third work, Canadian director Ted Kotcheff's *Wake in Fright* (titled *Outback* in the United States) actually used a predominantly Australian cast and crew to tell the story of a schoolteacher in an outback town where violence lay just below the surface of what seems to be a beautiful landscape.

By 1971 the funds from the Australian Development Corporation had begun to have their effect. Oddly the first work funded by the government was no artifact of high culture but the wacky *Adventures of Barry MacKenzie* (1972), followed two years later by *Barry MacKenzie*

Holds His Own (1974). Both offer uproarious parodies of a particular Australian character, the "Ocker," who centers his life on sex and Foster's lager. The humor is sophomoric, but the mise-en-scène colorful and haunting. Both films were big hits in Australia.

Bruce Beresford launched, with these two films, a career and later went on to direct such mainstream Hollywood fare as *Tender Mercies* (1982). A native of Sydney, Beresford learned filmmaking in England but returned to his native land when opportunities opened up in 1971. He followed the two successful MacKenzie films with several fine works, including *The Getting of Wisdom* (1977). His international breakthrough came just before Christmas of 1980 with the release of *Breaker Morant*, a beautifully crafted tale of three Australian soldiers sacrificed by the British government during the Boer War. Like many a successful foreign director before him, Beresford parlayed his success in Australia into a move to Hollywood.

Peter Weir has, perhaps, been the director most responsible for opening the eyes of the world to a new Australian cinema. His first notable effort was a gothic and camp horror film, *The Cars That Ate Paris* (1974). The film was promoted at the Cannes Film Festival, but critics were divided. Roger Corman almost picked it up for distribution which would have guaranteed Weir a degree of fame he had to wait only one more year to achieve. *Picnic at Hanging Rock* (1975) was distributed successfully in the United States, in part because of the valiant efforts of Renée Furst. *Gallipoli* (1981) earned Weir international fame. He went to Hollywood and made the big budget films *The Year of Living Dangerously* (1982), starring Mel Gibson and *Witness* (1985), starring Harrison Ford.

George Miller made his name with the exciting trio of Mad Max movies: *Mad Max*

(1979), starring Mel Gibson, *The Road Warrior* (1981), also with Gibson, and *Mad Max Beyond Thunderdome* (1985), again with Gibson and Tina Turner. He also made what most critics hailed as the best segment of *Twilight Zone, The Movie* (1983)—"Nightmare at 2,000 Feet." His *The Witches of Eastwick* (1987), starring Jack Nicholson and Cher, was a major hit during the summer of 1987. Teamed with producer Byron Kennedy for the "Mad Max" films, Miller created on film a futuristic savage world by using Australia's desolate highways as a setting. Through creative make-up he was able to fashion larger-than-life villains and anti-heros and to help make Mel Gibson an international star.

Miller's mise-en-scène is extraordinary. His highways seem to stretch out for endless miles and lead nowhere. There is no shade, no relief. Dressed in a mixture of football uniforms, leather jackets, and desert wear, the villains are a hard and desperate lot of survivors who know no bounds of violence for survival in the post-cataclysmic world. To counter this evil, Max is the burnt-out anti-hero who is still able to add some civilization to this madness. Miller openly patterned Max after Japanese Samurai and clas-

sic American movie heroes, possibly accounting for some of the popularity of his films in the United States.

One of the other major accomplishments of the Governmental Film Act of 1970 was to open a film school in 1973. Gillian Armstrong was one of the first students of the new school and became the first woman to direct a film in Australia in forty-five years. She has directed *My Brilliant Career* (1979) and *Starstruck* (1983). The latter is a delightful new-wave musical comedy. Phillip Noyce, a classmate of Armstrong's, deftly intercut actual newsreel footage with the fictional story of two newsreel companies in his *Newsfront* (1978).

Many date the end of the New Australian cinema to 1980 when the best talents all seemed to have moved to Hollywood. However, there was no absence of new films, as the government passed yet another law designed to increase production. Here we encounter a problem with historical analysis. The events are too close to us in time, and thus it is impossible to tell if the wave of the New Australian cinema is over or if it continues through the work of others.

14

● ● ● ○ ●

an epilogue: contemporary film history

A new era for watching movies began in the mid-1970s with the popularity of computer-made, sound-enhanced films such as *Star Wars* (1977) by George Lucas. At the same time satellites and video tape recorders initiated a wave of film viewing in homes in the United States and, increasingly, throughout the world. Similarly, recent documentaries and experimental films seem to have become video productions.

With the rise of new technologies—video assisted production, distribution by satellite, exhibition on cable television and directly to the home by satellite—we have entered the world of the contemporary cinema. Cinema since 1975 is so recent that historical analysis is simply not possible. Thus, the epilogue of *Movie History: A Survey* does not present history at all but a survey of contemporary events: first of the still-dominant Hollywood and then of other filmmaking nations. The methods we used in the preceding chapters to analyze the economic, technological, social, and aesthetic aspects of cinema history will still be employed, but without the proper historical distance necessary to clearly identify trends. Thus this survey ends with something more along the lines of "organized journalism," "a review of contemporary events," than history per se.

• • • • • • • • • • • • • • • •

the new hollywood

• • • • • • • • • • • • • • • •

Americans have never been more fascinated with the movies. In 1986, on average, nearly twenty million fans journeyed each week to nearby multiplex cinemas to relish Hollywood studio–sponsored theatrical blockbusters: Paramount's *Top Gun* (1986), *Crocodile Dundee* (1986), and *Star Trek* in its multiple versions (1979, 1982, 1984, 1986, and 1989), as well as smaller films such as director David Lynch's *Blue Velvet* (1986). Today, more than ever, films attract the serious intellectual comment once reserved for plays or novels. In addition, movies like Brian De Palma's *Scarface*, only a modest success during its theatrical release, found new life through home video rentals. And well-publicized, made-for-television motion pictures including "War and Remembrance" (1988) and "Lonesome Dove" (1989) draw millions to their television sets.

As the nature of films and film viewing has changed, so too has the technology of moviemaking changed. Computers, in particular, enable filmmakers to craft special effects to live action and animation, a set of filmmaking parameters simply not possible before. The major hit of 1988, for example, Disney's *Who Framed Roger Rabbit?*, achieves a nearly miraculous interaction of live and cartoon figures. A fountainhead of the possibilities of combining modern technology and traditional narrative filmmaking is George Lucas' Industrial Light and Magic Corporation. Yet, despite these technological innovations, the process of moviemaking remains remarkably the same; the Classic Narrative rules are still firmly in place.

Although important changes occurred in Hollywood moviemaking in the 1970s, even more important were the new ways and places to watch movies. This began with the TV movie expanding into the mini-series and novel-for-television. Some critics dismiss these low-budget productions as the "disease of the week," but in reality today's made-for-TV dramas are successors to Hollywood's B movies of yore. They surely boost ratings, which is why mini-series like *Hollywood Wives* (1987) or *The Thorn Birds* (1983) arrive like clockwork at key ratings-measurement periods. Since the turn-around time from production to presentation is so short, made-for-TV films can deal with topical issues and even like *The Day After* provoke discussion of important ideas.

In the mid-1970s, Time, Inc. changed the world of cable television in the United States forever with its Home Box Office (HBO), which, for a monthly fee of about ten dollars, offered cable television subscribers recent Hollywood motion pictures—uncut, uninterrupted by commercials, and not sanitized to please network censors. For the first time in the television age, a way had been found to make viewers pay for what they watched in their living rooms. As "pay television," HBO drew back the older movie fan who did not want to go out to a theatre but loved watching second-run films on television at home.

But cable television offers the film fan much more than HBO. Ted Turner took a typical independent station, complete with its sports, reruns, and old movies, and beamed it to all America via the satellite to create his famous SuperStation. Turner also purchased MGM, not for its current productions, but for access to its library of old films. Thus, half of WTBS's time is filled with old films. Turner does not operate the only SuperStation. Because of these SuperStations, Americans have a rich, repertory cinema in the home. Old Hollywood films, the best and worst, run all day long.

In 1988 Turner offered the film fan even more with his TNT (Turner Network Television). To the delight of film fans throughout the United States TNT unspools long-unseen films from the vaults of the MGM, Warner Bros., and RKO libraries now under Turner's control. A quick survey of *TV Guide* reveals that about a quarter of the average television broadcast day is devoted to rerunning Hollywood feature films.

The post-1975 video age reached its greatest change in the mid-1980s with the home video revolution. Sony introduced its Betamax half-inch home video cassette recorder (VCR) in 1975. Originally priced at more than one thousand dollars (double that in today's dollars adjusted for inflation), the cost of the Beta machines and their newer rivals from VHS dropped to just over three hundred dollars per machine by the mid-1980s. An enthusiastic American public (plus millions in other nations) snapped up so many machines that by 1989 fully two-thirds of American households were equipped to tape off the air or run pre-recorded tapes.

By the mid-1980s home video had been declared a revolution. Popular news publications hailed the 1980s as the age of home video. The number of cassettes released for home purchase or rental went past one hundred thousand. One and all hailed home video as a mass medium; new releases are regularly reviewed in major newspapers and equal in status to network and cable television. And in the future lies High Definition Television which, although only in the experimental stage in 1990, promises nearly movie quality images in advanced television sets before the turn of the century.

At first, the Hollywood moguls loathed the new machine. Jack Valenti, President of the Motion Picture Association of America, declared that the VCR was a parasitical instrument robbing Hollywood's take at the boxoffice. But quickly enough during the 1980s Hollywood found a way to make the most of this newest of technologies.

The studios vastly underestimated the demand for a movie show at home and tried to sell pre-recorded movies to the public for sixty dollars and up. Few buyers lined up. The significant change came in the early 1980s as local entrepreneurs throughout the United States began to buy multiple copies of pre-recorded movies and to rent them to the public. The terms varied, but usually one anted up to join a "club" and then rented the tape for one or two dollars per day. By the mid-1980s stores renting video tapes seemed to be popping up on every street corner. Even grocery stores jumped into the business.

The Hollywood majors were quick to capitalize on the trend. In 1986, the returns from ancillary video sidelines exceeded the take at the boxoffice in the United States. During the mid-1980s about four hundred new pre-recorded cassettes were being released each month, 70 percent of which are Hollywood feature films. Most observers now argue that the Hollywood movie business has fully absorbed the impact of the VCR and looks forward to the next technological change.

These new ways to watch movies have raised new concerns about pornography going directly into the home. Hollywood's representative in Washington, sensitive to complaints, initiated a new rating category, PG-13, to show that it was concerned about films which should (or should not be seen) by teenagers. Concerns have risen also about the accessibility of video cassettes, since there is a flourishing market for X-rated material on video.

This new and expanded film audience has also drawn in new filmmakers and companies to Hollywood in the 1980s. Fall and spring became the times of the year Hollywood could introduce serious works to the market, saving the blockbusters for the summer, Christmas, and Easter seasons. Thus, a black filmmaker, Spike Lee, was able to distribute *She's Gotta Have It* (1986) through a Hollywood company, and David Lynch's *Blue Velvet*, a violent but brilliant film, could also find a niche. *Platoon* (1986), a serious look at the Vietnam war, could even rise to the status of a hit.

Films dealing with serious themes are also being made for television. Made-for-television movies regularly treat, albeit in a predictable, melodramatic fashion, serious issues from AIDS to the impact of nuclear war. One reason that TV movies can respond to current social issues "overnight" is because the lead time for a TV production is so much shorter than for a feature (six months versus nearly two years). Many speculate as the film generation ages, films with complex themes will more regularly appear in theatres of the future.

Theatre owners will seek ways to differentiate their offerings from videotapes. Paradoxically, more new movie screens have been constructed in the 1980s than at any time since the 1920s. Why? To offer consumers ease of access to the latest first-run Hollywood film. Summer blockbusters like *Batman* (1989) now

open on more than two thousand screens at one time.

All the exposure on videotape and pay television guarantees that the television networks will show less and less theatrical fare and may show only made-for-TV movies or specials by the year 2000. In fact, this trend has already begun. When CBS aired *Star Wars* in February 1984 that all-time blockbuster looked to be a sure-fire ratings hit. Therefore, the network doubled its prime-time ad prices. But *Star Wars* was beaten in the ratings by *Lace*, a steamy, made-for-TV movie which cost only three million dollars to make, less than half of what CBS had paid to rent *Star Wars*.

But whatever the trends of the future, as we move into the twenty-first century, interest in watching movies has never been higher. Only the technology for presentation seems to change, indeed to expand the possibilities for viewing. All of these changes, from cable to pay television, from the multiplex to the VCR, add up to one clear trend. More and more people are going to be watching more and more movies. And to filmdom's majors, that is nothing but good news, for they will still be shaping most of what people watch.

In all the technological transformation for movie viewing, the major movie corporations have lost none of their power. (And nothing seems to loom on the horizon to lessen their hold on the industry.) The majors have a strong track record; these corporations have survived and prospered despite the coming of over-the-air television, cable television, pay television, and the video cassette recorder. All now function as venues through which to sell feature films and make greater profits.

The handful of companies formed more than a half century ago still have hegemony over the creation of the movies and the distribution of them throughout the world. Since the end of the Second World War, they have survived the forced selling of their theatre chains, the rise of network television, the advent of cable and pay television, and, most recently, the video cassette revolution. These companies may have new owners, but they show no signs of weakening. Indeed, if anything, they are getting stronger.

In the 1980s, old-fashioned entrepreneurs own two of the seven major studios—Twentieth Century–Fox and MGM/UA—and their reach vastly exceeds anything ever dreamed of by the moguls of Hollywood's Golden Age of the 1930s and 1940s.

Twentieth Century–Fox had a rough go during the late 1970s despite its *Star Wars* trilogy. Executives came and went. In 1981 Twentieth Century–Fox was purchased by oilman Marvin Davis; four years later he sold the company to the Australian-born press lord Rupert Murdoch, who combined it with the chain of six big-city independent television stations that he had recently acquired from Metromedia Television. This meant that a Fox film such as *Predator* (1987) or *The Jewel of the Nile* (1985) could be shown by the new Fox television stations after it appeared in the nation's theatres, keeping the film's revenues within the corporate family.

Less well-known is the case of MGM/UA, where Kirk Kerkorian, airline magnate and Las Vegas mogul, owns and controls the famous movie empire. In May 1981 MGM Film, Inc. acquired the United Artists Corporation from giant Transamerica. A year earlier MGM had been split apart into MGM Film and MGM Grand Hotels, both controlled by Kerkorian. With this merger, MGM/UA, after languishing in the 1970s and being, for a time, out of movie making altogether, began to reassert itself as a major industry filmmaker. But only a few hits came, including *WarGames* (1983) and the traditional James Bond *Octopussy* (1983).

Kerkorian tried and failed to take the firm private, but in a stunning turn of events four years later, Kerkorian sold the MGM "half" of his movie corporation to Ted Turner of cable television fame. Turner really only wanted the classic MGM movies to show on his cable television SuperStation and had no interest in making more movies. So in 1985 Turner returned MGM (sans the movie library) to Kerkorian. Television power Lorimar-Telepictures took over what remained of MGM's fabled back lot.

Two of Hollywood's major studios are (or through the 1980s had been) linked to large, diversified, multi-national conglomerates. Columbia Pictures Industries, for example, had been a division of soft-drink giant Coca-Cola from 1982 to 1987. In 1987 Coke spun off this ailing subsidiary. Only a tenth of Coca-Cola's profits had come from Columbia, and the giant soft-drink firm had never been able to squeeze sizable profits from the movie (and television) company. The new Columbia Picture Entertainment included Tri-Star Pictures, which it had owned with HBO.

Paramount Pictures, a division of the billion dollar conglomerate Gulf + Western, remained a leader in movie profits through the 1980s. In the mid-1980s the hits flowed from the Melrose Avenue studio in machine-gun fashion: The *Star Trek* films, the Eddie Murphy films, and even television spin-offs such as *The Untouchables* (1987). In 1989 Gulf + Western dropped that awkward corporate title and became simply Paramount Communications, Inc.

Top honors at the box office during the 1980s also went to studios owned by companies that were part of the conglomerates which specialize in entertainment: Warner Bros., owned by Warner Communications, Universal, owned by MCA, and the Disney Corporation. These corporations are media conglomerates. That is, they generate their considerable profits from mass media enterprises such as phonograph records (Warner), theme parks (Disney and Universal), and television production (Universal and Disney), while also holding strong positions in the film industry. And in 1989 when Time and Warner merged, the new Time-Warner, Inc. became the largest media conglomerate in the world.

At MCA longtime company head Lew Wasserman and heir apparent Sidney J. Sheinberg run this television-driven company with a frugality and tight fist that Wall Street has long admired. But in the mid-1980s the company's film division did not do as well as its television shows, recorded music, and theme parks. MCA reached a peak of profitability in 1982 with *E.T.: The Extraterrestrial* and again in 1988 when the video for *E.T.* broke all records for sales of a single tape. But in between Universal has changed managers several times, seeking a formula to regain its former position of power.

Time-Warner is another media conglomerate and, although it has had no hit to rival *E.T.*, during the 1980s its Warner Bros. division rarely offered up boxoffice duds. One star, Clint Eastwood, has added millions to this corporate giant. A major change came in 1989 with the release of *Batman*, which within two months surged to second place on the all-time boxoffice list, right behind *E.T.*

The Disney studio, part of the Walt Disney entertainment empire, became the shining star of the American film industry during the late 1980s. Its new management team of Michael Eisner and Jeffrey Katzenberg took command in 1984. Before that, the motion picture division had been a corporate drain, with such losers as *Tron* and *Nightcross*. The new managers created a new label of adult films, Touchstone, and did well from the beginning with its first effort, *Splash*. With the release of *Down and Out in Beverly Hills* (1986) and *Stakeout* (1987) under its new Touchstone banner, Disney successfully drew adult audiences and posted greater profits than at any time since founder Walt Disney passed away in 1966.

Twentieth Century–Fox, MGM, UA, Paramount, Columbia, Time-Warner, Universal, and Disney remain the "majors." Year in, year out they control almost eighty percent of the movie business in the United States and approximately half the market in Sweden, West Germany, and several other nations in Western Europe, not to mention Asia. Hollywood derives roughly one-third of its theatrical boxoffice revenues from overseas. Every few years a couple of bold pretenders (in the 1980s Orion Pictures and New World) emerge to challenge the majors at home, and as often as not they succeed after possibly creating only a modest hit or two. But no challenger has survived in the long haul. In Hollywood, the dozens of independent producers have no choice but to distribute their films through one of the major studios.

The majors' power derives, as it has since the 1920s, from their ability to distribute films. At considerable expense, they maintain offices in more than a dozen cities in North America (and up to fifty overseas), where their representatives are in constant contact with the heads of the dominant theatre chains. A studio's "hit parade" record at the boxoffice is what impels theatre owners (a conservative lot with most of their assets invested in real estate) to consistently rent its products.

During the 1980s there has been great change in theatrical exhibition, despite the oft-repeated dire predictions of gloom-and-doom because of the coming of cable television and home video. A handful of companies control the film exhibition business, led by General Cinema, American Multi-Cinema, Cineplex-

Odeon, and United Artists Communications (not connected with United Artists film production company in any way), each with more than one thousand screens. (Total screens in the United States soared past twenty-two thousand in 1987.) These new film exhibition giants made their profits and influence when "hard-top" cinemas enjoyed a comeback, usually in the form of mini-cinemas with a couple hundred seats squeezed into a series of plain boxes adjoining a shopping center.

In a way, during the 1980s the exhibition business came full circle; the new multiple theatres are essentially unadorned, chopped-up versions of the glorious Paramounts and Orientals of old. The economics is simple and straightforward enough: a theatre with four screens is four times more likely than a one-screen house to book a hit picture; one with ten is ten times as likely. An unexpected blockbuster can be shifted to the largest auditorium in the complex, a dud to a smaller one.

A few new theatres, principally built by Cineplex-Odeon, are adding frills to again lure customers with architectural splendor. Indeed, the rise of Cineplex-Odeon surely has meant good news to potential movie patrons. Garth Drabinsky, the indefatigable Canadian-born president, believes in bringing back luxury to the movie theatre. Seats in Cineplex theatres are wide and comfortable; the butter on the popcorn is real; the sound and image achieve a standard long forgotten.

The multiplexes are far better suited to today's film release and film viewing patterns. Filmgoing used to be part of the social fabric. People went regularly, except when they were very young or very old. It was a habit, like going to the grocery store. Television took over that habit by the late 1950s, and filmgoing became an impulse purchase. Annual admissions leveled off at about one billion per annum during the 1960s and have remained steady at that number. The future of the movie industry, with steady demand at the theatres and increasing attractions on television, seems very, very bright.

new hollywood filmmakers, styles, and genres

By the late 1970s, filmmaking had finally achieved the status of an art form. The influential *New York Times* reviews movies with a seriousness once reserved for dance and theatre. Once college students who wanted to make an artistic statement sat down to write the great American novel; now they plug in their word processors hoping to fashion the next

Prizzi's Honor (1985, director John Huston) or *Hannah and Her Sisters* (1986, director Woody Allen).

During the 1970s the film generation spawned its own auteurs. The "Movie Brats," led by Steven Spielberg and George Lucas, have studied and consciously aped the masters of foreign cinema. For example, Akira Kurosawa, one of Japan's greatest directors, provided models of complex rhythmic editing and elaborate camera placement in his 1954 masterpiece *Seven Samurai*. Spielberg's *Jaws* (one of the ten highest-grossing films of all time) and Lucas' *Star Wars* (also in the top ten highest-grossing films of all time) seem far removed from Kurosawa's earlier masterpiece of traditional Japanese cinema, but both American directors consciously modeled the pace and look of those popular attractions on Kurosawa's classic.

As expected, the movie generation has created its own set of movie stars. There seem to be two types. The traditional male icons such as Robert Redford and Clint Eastwood, like John Wayne and Henry Fonda from the past, seem only to project "themselves." The movie audience continues to expect an image established decades ago, despite the advancing years of these stars. In contrast, the younger stars seem to adapt to the scripts they are presented. Sissy Spacek, Dustin Hoffman, and Robert DeNiro, to name but three, never seem to play the same part two movies in a row.

Even movie critics have achieved cult status in the present movie age. Gone are the days when a reviewer for a major newspaper labored in anonymity. Indeed, some reviewers who appear on television have become stars in their own right. Roger Ebert and Gene Siskel, hosts of the most popular movie review program, have become more famous than many of the celebrities over whose work they pass judgment and are paid just as well (nearly one million dollars per year). Today's Hollywood recognizes the power of Ebert and Siskel, courting them in a way unmatched since they wooed the 1940s gossip mavens Hedda Hopper and Louella Parsons.

The American film has never been more popular, more studied, more dynamic. Some wax nostalgic about the Golden Age of the 1930s and 1940s. But today's movie-goers have far more choices. We can never be sure where tomorrow's filmmakers will take the American cinema. But it will surely be an exciting and interesting journey as the motion picture industry in the United States moves toward its one-hundredth birthday in 1996.

In the early 1970s it seemed that the film genre was a dead form in Hollywood. (See chapter 11.) But an important change came in 1975 with the release of Steven Spielberg's *Jaws*. Two years later came George Lucas' *Star Wars*. The business of Hollywood production would not be the same. These classically conservative adventure tales sent producers back to make more genre films and revitalized the science fiction genre in one move. From *Jaws* came *Raiders of the Lost Ark* and the other two Indiana Jones films. From *Star Wars* we have gotten two sequels (so far) and *E.T. Grease* proved the musical was a lively and healthy genre; *Beverly Hills Cop*, both parts so far, proved moviegoers still wanted detective dramas. Hollywood aimed these squarely at the teenagers who were their most faithful customers.

We had the cycle of the sequel. There have been (up to the end of the 1980s) four *Rockys* (1976, 1979, 1982, and 1985), four *Supermans*

Play Time (1967), France

Seven Beauties (1976), Italy

Chariots of Fire (1981), Great Britain

Many of the most complex and beautiful uses of color occur in European films.

Bonnie and Clyde (1967)

Rocky (1976)

Annie Hall (1977)

• •

By the time the young directors of the "New Hollywood" began to make their
films, color had become the accepted standard.

Star Wars (1977)

Jaws (1975)

E.T.: The Extraterrestrial (1981)

Three of the highest grossing films of all time are creations of Steven Spielberg and George Lucas.

Bugs Bunny

"War and Remembrance" (1988)

Cineplex Odeon

• •

Color plays an important role in animation, TV movies, and in movie theatre complexes. Bugs Bunny represents Warner Bros.' longest "living" star, having celebrated his fiftieth year in show business in 1990. "War and Remembrance" ended the networks' enthusiasm for television mini-series. The Cineplex Odeon complex, on the edge of the parking lot at Universal Studios, represents today's finest example of theatre building.

(1978, 1980, 1983, and 1987), three *Halloweens* (1978, 1981, and 1983) and eight *Friday the 13ths* (1980, 1981, 1982, 1984, 1985, 1986, 1988, and 1989) with more promised. Indeed, the original *Superman* was conceived with a sequel in mind and partially on film. Other genres made their return in the late 1970s and early 1980s. The horror film was revived early on in the 1970s with *The Exorcist* (1973), which generated a half-dozen spin-offs. Even *Jaws*, with its monster shark, must be seen as part of this wave of horror film. Every kind of monster arose from its Hollywood grave. There were werewolves in Joe Dante's *The Howling* (1981) and John Landis' *An American Werewolf in London* (1981). Also revived were vampires in John Badham's *Dracula* (1979) and Tony Scott's *The Hunger* (1983) and zombies in George Romero's *Dawn of the Dead* (1979) and in *Halloween* and *The Fog* (1980), by John Carpenter, whom many regard as the best director in recent years of the horror film genre.

The monster film has even been crossbred with other genres, particularly the science fiction film as in *Alien* (1979) and *Aliens* (1986). A variation then becomes the alien who is friendly, giving rise to the most popular movie of the 1980s and one of the most popular of all time—Steven Spielberg's *E.T.* (1982). This type of plot can be contrived to appeal to teen audiences because it is a parable about growing up or coming of age. Over and over movies teach younger audiences that it is not enough to gain knowledge (however hard that may be); they must also convince the adult world to take them seriously.

The proliferation of teen fantasies did not happen by accident or because some cynical producer sought a way to exploit the audience. When George Lucas was working on *Star Wars*

he recalled the comic books and Hollywood serials of his youth. Skeptics in the hip mid-1970s scoffed; no one would be interested, the film would be a bust. But Lucas successfully reformulated these myths from the past into what then was the highest grossing film of all time. The commercial success of his comic book fantasies spawned a whole new set of genre films. There were sword-and-sorcery films like John Boorman's *Excalibur* (1981) and John Milius' *Conan the Barbarian* (1982) and its sequel *Conan the Destroyer* (1984). Indeed Lucas and Spielberg teamed together to have the twentieth-century scientist battle forces of evil in *Raiders of the Lost Ark* (1981), *Indiana Jones and the Temple of Doom* (1984), and *Indiana Jones and the Last Crusade* (1989).

Comedy has also changed, redone for the teenage audience. For every comic romance with a light touch, such as John Hughes' *Sixteen Candles* (1984, starring Molly Ringwald) or Paul Brinkman's *Risky Business* (1983, starring Tom Cruise), there have been many more based on the broadest possible humor, such as *Rock 'n' Roll High School* (1979), *Fast Times at Ridgemont High* (1982), and *Revenge of the Nerds* (1984).

Inspired by the antics of Saturday Night Live's "Not Ready for Prime Time Players" (including John Belushi, Dan Aykroyd, and Bill Murray), nothing was too obvious to be done over. The movie that revitalized this genre, John Landis' *National Lampoon's Animal House* (1978), is an irreverent anti-intellectual look at college and fraternity life of the early 1960s. Bluto (Belushi) and his Delta fraternity buddies are kicked out of school and decide to disrupt the homecoming parade in one final "really futile, stupid gesture." In the final credits (which also serve to update the lives of the characters), we learn that Bluto is a United States senator. This certainly sums up the new comedy's attitude toward the official adult world.

But this broad slapstick humor remarkably shares traits with the science fiction films noted above. Both demand that we suspend our belief about the "real" world. Any physical and social act seems possible. The world, past and present, becomes a playground for fun. At times this verges on so broad a sense of humor that it reaches surrealistic heights as in *Cheech & Chong's Next Movie* (1980), *Cheech & Chong's Nice Dreams* (1981), and *The Blues Brothers* (1980, developed by and starring Aykroyd and Belushi). Woody Allen self-reflexively comments on this other world of the movies by having movie characters walk off the screen in *The Purple Rose of Cairo* (1985), introducing Marshall McLuhan in *Annie Hall* (1977), and turning into any character he wants in *Zelig* (1983).

But directors still use comedy in familiar ways. Mel Brooks, probably the most honored comic director after Woody Allen, took on Hollywood of the past with *Blazing Saddles* (1974), *Young Frankenstein* (1974), *Silent Movie* (1976), and *Space Balls* (1987). Hal Ashby seemed to do his best work in comedy, especially *Harold and Maude* (1971) and *Being There* (1979), Peter Sellers' final film. Blake Edwards gave us the dark side of Hollywood in *S.O.B.* (1981) and the 1980s attitudes on sex in *Skin Deep* (1989).

Sports films, long relegated to television, have also made a comeback. Sylvester Stallone turned himself and his character into a one-man industry with *Rocky I, II, III,* and *IV.* This "Philadelphia bum" conquered the world through grit and determination. Suddenly all sports and sports figures were the subject of "beat-the-odds" films. Track and field was fea-

tured in Hugh Hudson's *Chariots of Fire* (1981), bicycle racing in Peter Yates' *Breaking Away* (1979), and the martial arts in *The Karate Kid*, Parts I, II, and III (1984, 1986, and 1989).

But Stallone has also revealed a less positive side of the American drive for success. His two (more in the future) *Rambo* films portray the outsider, the loner, taking on the jobs no one wants. In *Rambo: First Blood Part II* (1985), the rare sequel that out-grossed the original entry, Rambo/Stallone rescues American soldiers missing in action in Vietnam when the official world refuses to acknowledge that such MIAs even exist. Thus we have come full circle. Rambo must convince outsiders as the police chief did in *Jaws.* The real world may have less than a full complement of happy endings, but in Hollywood of the 1980s, heroes in a world of almost absurd narrative logic always triumph.

George Lucas changed Hollywood forever with his *Star Wars.* In 1967 Lucas worked as an assistant to Coppola on *Finian's Rainbow*, and shot a documentary about the making of Coppola's *The Rain People* (1969). It was on the strength of these efforts that Coppola persuaded Warner Bros. to sign Lucas to do *THX-1138* (1971). The result was a science fiction film of great skill (noted for its "white on white" sequence), but unfortunately it proved a dud at the boxoffice. Lucas would have to wait until 1977 with *Star Wars* to kick off the new cycle of science fiction films. He gained a measure of fame and fortune in the meantime with a teenage "coming of age" film, *American Graffiti* (1973). This portrait of the day and night before the hero goes off to college, with its soundtrack of rock and roll songs from a decade earlier, was a winner at the box office. Produced by Coppola, it sparked the careers of Cindy Williams, Harrison Ford, Suzanne Sommers, Ron Howard, and Richard Dreyfuss. It made Universal a great deal of money and made Lucas a force in Hollywood.

Lucas used his newfound power wisely. His next film was *Star Wars* (1977). Based on his enthusiasm for pulp science fiction, comic heroes, and low budget serials of the 1940s, this single film proved that the right vehicle could make millions and millions of dollars. *Star Wars* created a money machine no one foresaw. The spin-offs from the movie generated a new industry, taking away the toy underwriting market from Disney. Using Dolby sound and computer animation and modeling, *Star Wars* and its sequels, *The Empire Strikes Back* (1980) and *Return of the Jedi* (1983), revitalized movies for children and proved one film could make its creators among the richest men and women in the United States.

The record on Lucas sans the *Star Wars* cycle, however, is mixed at best. While his production of *More American Graffiti* (1979) did not live up to expectations, his co-productions with Steven Spielberg of *Raiders of the Lost Ark* and *Indiana Jones and the Temple of Doom* surely did. But then the highly publicized *Howard the Duck* (1986) proved one of the great flops in contemporary Hollywood history. Although after *Star Wars* Lucas was thought to be the Disney of the 1980s, his career as of a decade later seems at a crossroads.

Steven Spielberg had no sponsor per se; rather he broke in by directing television shows and then TV movies (for example, *Duel* in 1971). Coming after one modest film, *The Sugarland Express* (1974), *Jaws* provided one of the most finely crafted Classic Hollywood narratives ever made. This textbook of classic filmmaking proved that genre films, skillfully directed in a traditional style, had returned. Offbeat was out; classic genre films of terror and release were in.

Spielberg has directed several more films in different genres. His *1941* (1979) was a crazy comedy and a true failure, for critics, for movie fans, and for Universal. More successful on all these fronts was the science fiction film, *Close Encounters of the Third Kind* (1977) and the phenomenal fantasy *E.T.: The Extraterrestrial*. The latter film zoomed to the top of the box-office charts and made Spielberg into more of a producer. His mega-hits seemed to follow a consistent pattern. In the typical Spielberg film, the central figure, a male, has his conception of the world undermined and then enlarged as he comes face-to-face with some extraordinary force. In *Duel* it was a monstrous truck driven by an unknown person. In *Jaws* it was Bruce, the shark. In *Close Encounters of the Third Kind* and *E.T.* the extraordinary force was from another world. There is no vision of social concern in these films, only an elementary wonderment reminiscent of Walt Disney's longtime theme song, "When You Wish Upon a Star."

In the 1980s Spielberg became the producer of clout; he sponsored films, filmmakers, and even the television series, "Amazing Stories." His *The Color Purple* (1985), *An American Tail* (1986, an animated feature), and the two *Poltergeist* (1982, 1986) films were good but not great at the box office. Yet the *Indiana Jones* series proves that with the correct formula Spielberg can still make highly profitable films. What is surprising is that this consummate filmmaker—and moneymaker—has been, at least until given an honorary award in 1987, ignored by mainstream Hollywood. The Academy of Motion Picture Arts and Sciences chose as best picture Czech refugee Miloš Forman's *One Flew Over the Cuckoo's Nest* over *Jaws* in 1975; New Yorker Woody Allen's *Annie Hall* over *Close Encounters of the Third Kind* in 1977; the British *Chariots of Fire* over *Raiders of the Lost Ark* in 1981; and another British film, *Gandhi*, over *E.T.* in 1982.

If Lucas and Spielberg are best known for their successes and failures as movie producers, there have been many contemporary directors who have stuck to directing. Indeed probably the most famous American auteur filmmaker in the 1980s, at least to the general public, has been Woody Allen.

Woody Allen achieved filmmaking distinction first as a star, then as filmmaker. Audiences love his humor in *Love and Death* (1975), the much-honored *Annie Hall* (1977), the black and white *Manhattan* (1979), and the-man-of-a-thousand-faces *Zelig* (1983). Allen has also made serious art films in the vein of Ingmar Bergman's *Persona* or Federico Fellini's *8½*, but audiences and critics alike have rejected *Interiors* (1978) and *Stardust Memories* (1980).

In live performance, in records, and on film, for thirty years Woody Allen has fashioned his comic persona as the hip, neurotic New Yorker. Today he is as familiar in his image as Charlie Chaplin was as the Tramp and Jerry Lewis as the American loudmouth fool in earlier eras. Allen began his film career with a parody of a gangster film, *Take the Money and Run* (1969), and continued elements of comic parody in *Bananas* (1971), *Sleeper* (1973), and *Love and Death* (1975).

Most critics have cited *Annie Hall* (1977) as the first major Woody Allen-as-auteur film. Collaborating with screenwriter Marshall Brickman and cinematographer Gordon Willis, Allen created an autobiographical work which, through its meta-narrative filmic devices, stands apart from his earlier comic efforts. For example, subtitles reveal what is really going on; a superimposed Annie watches herself and Alvie (the Woody Allen character) make love; and a split screen shows gentile and Jewish family dinner scenes.

Since then, Allen and his collaborators have tried many ways to express intellectual concerns to a mass audience. *Interiors* is a serious study of human psychology in which Woody Allen does not appear. Modeled on Ingmar Bergman's *Cries and Whispers*, it is a serious psychoanalytical exploration of family life, the influence of one's mother, and the attempt to deal with the real world. *Manhattan*, in black and white, marked Allen's return as the New York Jewish comic. Allen continues to make one film per year, so we can only speculate on how he will be evaluated in the future. He has been recognized in his own time; we cannot be sure what future critics will make of him.

Martin Scorsese, a graduate of New York University's School of Cinema, has had an uneven career. While *Taxi Driver* (1976), starring Robert De Niro, may be his most famous film, it was his fourth, *Mean Streets* (1973), which established his critical reputation. This autobiographical work concerned four Italian-American youths coming of age in modern urban America, struggling with traditional values and modern economics. Critics have found his other work uneven. *Alice Doesn't Live Here Anymore* (1974) is violent; *New York, New York* (1977), a musical, is overblown when compared to the film of the final concert of The Band, *The Last Waltz* (1978); *The King of Comedy* (1983) explores the underside of media hype; and *The Last Temptation of Christ* (1988) generated more controversy than any film of the late 1980s. Perhaps Scorsese's most complex work was the boxing film *Raging Bull* (1979). Starring Robert De Niro, this violent portrait of the boxing world, in black and white, captured the gritty world of basic human struggle.

Certainly other notable directors are at work in contemporary Hollywood. Some critics cite the work of Paul Schrader, whose *Blue*

Collar (1978) is a tight story of corruption in a labor union. Others praise Brian DePalma's *Scarface* (1983). Joan Micklin Silver's low-budget look at the early twentieth century in New York's Lower East Side in *Hester Street* (1974) and her *Crossing Delancy* (1987) mark her as an important talent. But for now we can only speculate as these and other filmmakers continue to create. Only with some historical distance will we be able to sort out their importance and influence.

contemporary world cinema

The contemporary period from the late 1970s through the present has seen some fifty countries regularly produce feature length entertainment of some four to five thousand films per annum. A number of countries in Africa have produced their first features only within the past decade. The bulk of the film productions comes in the form of documentary and educational films, more often than not now made on videotape. In all countries except those in Eastern Europe, the USSR, Cuba, the People's Republic of China, and North Korea, film production, distribution, and exhibition are controlled by private commercial enterprises. But in many other countries, the government provides, directly or indirectly, financial or other subsidies and supervises some form of regulation and restriction of content.

The largest film-producing countries are in Asia. India, for example, continues to turn out nearly five hundred films per year, principally for internal use, with no eye toward the export market. Outside Asia, the United States and the USSR produce the most, dominating their respective spheres of influence. Europe produces less for theatres, but twice as many (one hundred versus two hundred) if one counts films made for television. Most countries today produce less than one hundred films per year, with television production accounting for an ever-increasing share of the market.

The Asian interest in the cinema is also reflected in the large number of cinemas which show films made for that market. Only one outside nation's films ever have the demand necessary to have dubbing done on a regular basis—those from Hollywood. Thus, in many underdeveloped countries, the films shown are from the native country and Hollywood. But other filmmaking nations still struggle to export. The USSR exports to Eastern Europe; Mexico, Spain, and Argentina dominate the trade for the world's twenty or so Spanish-speaking nations; Egypt supplies the Arab-speaking world. Europe continues with co-productions to expand the film market among as many members of the European community as possible, nearly always underwritten by governmental subsidies.

The feature film, dramatic stories in the mold Hollywood has made popular for so long, dominates almost exclusively the creation of films in the 1980s. Other forms common in the past—newsreels, short subjects, and animated films—have almost disappeared from public screens. Instead, these non-feature length works have been taken over by video and are made with television as the principle market. Indeed, increasingly, many features as well are made with television as the first-run showcase.

In Great Britain, for example, film audiences constitute only a tiny fraction (about ten percent) of what they were after the Second World War. Remarkably, a handful of producers have kept the British film industry alive in the face of declining theatre patronage. David Puttnam achieved his first success as a producer with singer David Essex's *That'll Be the Day* (1974) and *Stardust* (1975) and with other musical films, such as *Mahler* (1974). After one success, *Midnight Express* (1978), and one failure, *Agatha* (1979), in Hollywood, Puttnam returned to England and formed Goldcrest. This company put the British film back on the map once again in the early 1980s with *Chariots of Fire* (1981), a tale of two British runners in the 1920 Olympics. It won Hollywood's Oscar for Best Picture that year. But that hit only tempted Puttman away from England and back to Hollywood, this time as head of Columbia Pictures. He lasted little more than a year and was back to England once again in September of 1987.

As the end of the century approaches, the future of the British film industry seems to be in peril. The Conservative government of Margaret Thatcher has cut off the National Film Finance Corporation, which helped to fund fea-

ture films. The hope rests outside the film business, in television's Channel Four, a relatively new, independent station. This institution has sponsored films which premiere on television and *then* make their way, if successful, to specialized art cinemas.

But there have been European filmmakers who have been able to fashion careers as *film-makers* in the age of television and movies made for television. Consider the case of Lina Wertmuller. Her films reflect typical Italian filmic comedic conventions, all the while they are also politically oriented. Few Italian directors in recent years made more of a splash in the international art-cinema world than did Wertmuller in the 1970s with *The Seduction of Mimi* (1972), *Love and Anarchy* (1973), *Swept Away* (1974), and *Seven Beauties* (1976). Wertmuller combined a concern for political issues with finely structured, traditional Italian film comedy. For example, *Seven Beauties* deals with the Holocaust in a politically controversial manner; the hero survives by killing his best friend. Wertmuller's comic treatment of life in a concentration camp upset many who felt this, of all subjects, was just not fitting material for comedy.

But Wertmuller has been the exception. For the key event in recent cinema history in Italy, as in most of Western Europe, has been the coming of television. Through the 1980s Italy has remained more devoted to theatrical exhibition than most countries, but few could deny that television has become a prime showcase for movie viewing. Indeed Italian state television (RAI) has helped sponsor many of the major works of the Italian cinema of contemporary times: *Padre Padrone* (1977), *The Tree of the Wooden Clogs* (1978), Federico Fellini's *The Clowns* (1970), and Bernardo Bertolucci's *The Spider's Stratagem* (1970). And Italian films have been shown as the principle showcase on

U.S. television networks, including Giuliano Montaldo's *Marco Polo* (1982). Certainly, in the 1980s television films have been as important in Italy as TV movies and mini-series have been in the United States.

Smaller European countries struggle to make films as well. They have to deal with Hollywood's distribution power as well as a flood of films from nearby neighbors. Still there has been continued interest in filmmaking in the late 1970s and 1980s, as Swiss Alain Tanner and Belgian Chantal Akerman have proved.

In Switzerland interest in filmmaking came about in the late 1960s as a group of cineastes, based in Geneva, sought to make films and export them around the world. Alain Tanner studied in Britain and began making films in the late 1950s. In the late 1960s, he put the Swiss cinema on the world art film map, achieving international success despite tiny budgets. Tanner, whose hero is Ingmar Bergman, stuck to one principle theme: the individual's role in society. The central character in *Charles—Dead or Alive* (1969) questions her role in bourgeois society; in *The Salamander* (1971) a woman struggles to avoid being pigeonholed by two filmmaker characters casting a movie. He followed with *The Middle of the World* (1974) and a non-narrative comedy *Jonah Who Will Be 25 in the Year 2000* (1976), a bittersweet look at how eight people try to fit into modern society, failing at every turn.

Belgium is a small European country where American and French films dominate theatre screens. Only two or three Belgian features are made each year. Emerging from this environment in the 1970s was Chantal Akerman, an avant-garde filmmaker who writes and directs her films which are made on very low budgets. She took a lead acting role in her first major film, *I, You, He, She* (1974), an explicitly feminist view of a woman's changes in her sexual relations. *Jeanne Dielman, 23 Quai du Commerce, 1080 Bruxelles* (1975) is a 198-minute film which focuses on the exploitation of a housewife who turns to prostitution and is driven to murder one of her clients. This non-traditional film, utterly lacking Classic Hollywood Narrative devices, takes the viewer into the life of this oppressed, exploited female.

Akerman continued to make films through the 1980s. She directed *The Golden Eighties* (1986), a deconstruction of the formula of the traditional Hollywood musical. That is, all aspects of the process of making the spectacle are carefully analyzed by the filmmaker in the film. Akerman ranks as one of the most committed feminist filmmakers, one who uses film to explore the contemporary issues in the feminist struggle to change European culture.

Even in India in the 1980s television has begun to make inroads. With videotape libraries and the government infusion of money into television, film has begun to lose its place in a nation of devoted moviegoers. By 1986 more than three-quarters of the nation had access to television, and the theatrical cinema had begun to adapt to television, as has long been the case in Western Europe. Whether television will take over completely depends on the government media policy, for even to a nation as mad about cinema as India, the 1970s seem to have been a golden age of big budgets, great extravaganzas, and big stars. The star system, like Hollywood's of the 1930s and 1940s, was strong, possibly the last holdout in an age of satellite transmissions.

The 1970s for the Indian cinema had seen a star system the equal of Hollywood's. Rajesh Khanna, otherwise known as "The Phenomenon," was the male idol while Dharmendra and his "dream girl" Hema Malini had an equal following. In 1973 came Hollywood-type gangster films such as Prakash Mehra's *Chains* (1973), about a tormented policeman singlehandedly avenging the murder of his parents, and *The Wall* (1975) which pitted a poor honest policeman against a wealthy corrupt gangster. Crucial to this new genre has been the star power of Amitabh Bachchan, an angry young man and certainly one of the greatest stars in the history of the Indian cinema.

Indian stars worked on several productions at the same time and became enormously wealthy. The multi-star *Flames* (1975) ran for six years in one theatre in Bombay. This "curry Western," inspired by Italian and Hollywood Westerns, which had long been popular in India, features Amitabh and Dharmendra as outlaws hired to capture a sadistic villain. But *Flames* also had its share of comic relief, romance, and song.

Other Asian countries have also been strong producers of film. For example, Hong Kong produces more than one hundred films per year. This tiny country of only four million persons and an area of less than one thousand square miles probably created more films per capita than any nation in the world. In fact, the number of features produced per year has exceeded the number of open movie houses! While Hong Kong's citizens watched Hollywood and native product in about equal numbers, its film producers set out to make films for all of Southeast Asia.

South Korea and the Philippines also produce significant numbers of films, about 200 per year. (Both have nearly ten times the population of Hong Kong, however.) In the 1960s the Philippines may have been the most movie fanatic nation in the world. Its nearly one thousand theatres were jammed, especially in the major cities. Some opened as early as seven in the morning and ran continuously until midnight. Despite the introduction of television,

few homes actually had sets, and so filmgoing continued vigorously in the 1960s.

Such was not the case in Japan. Although this mighty island nation had long been a power in the film industry, television hit the film industry particularly hard. Production had risen from more than five hundred features in 1960 to nearly nine hundred in 1965 but then began to fall dramatically to less than four hundred five years later. Annual cinema attendance, which peaked in the late 1950s, plunged as well; so the count of patronage at Japanese movie houses in 1970 was little more than one-sixth what it had been a decade earlier. The number of cinema houses (7200 in 1960) fell by more than 60 per cent. But the Japanese industry was still in business, and with India and Hong Kong was still functioning through the 1980s.

The principle reason for the decline was television. For example, the bulk of the work of the Japanese Society of Film Directors shifted to television and as in the United States, viewers saw movies primarily on TV, both second-runs of theatrical fare and movies-made-for-television. For theatre owners, who still wanted to make money, Hollywood obliged. By the mid-1970s foreign films (meaning Hollywood productions, by and large) began to attract as many Japanese patrons as native Japanese productions did. Thus, just as the Japanese were exporting their video cassette recorders to change the American movie market, they began watching more and more of what Hollywood produced in their theatres and on their VCRs.

The Japanese studios tried their best to compete. When the first Lucas/Spielberg films hit Japanese theatres, they were very, very popular. Immediately Japanese studios (led by Toho) set out to make their own *Jaws* and *Star Wars*. But because Japanese disaster and science fiction films had much smaller budgets than did their

Hollywood counterparts, they failed to generate the boxoffice take of the Hollywood fare, despite the advantage of being booked by theatres owned by the Japanese studios.

But the Japanese studios hardly gave up. At Toei the formerly popular yakuza (gangster) film series were replaced with docudramas. One of the finest was Kinji Fukasaku's *Fight Without Code* (1973–1976) series to document the struggles of Hiroshima's local yakuza. This realistic portrayal of a gangster's drive for power (with titles to give the look of a documentary) sharply contrasted with the idealized view of the yakuza proffered by the genre films of the 1960s. Kinji Fukasaku and Sadao Nakajima specialized in making popular works out of docudrama exposés of the underworld. Fukasaku's *Prefecture of Police vs. Organized Crime* (1975) gave the audience an action film, but it was also an exploration of the roots of the violence and the nature of the police and gangsters as institutions within Japanese culture.

Toei also made comedies. Its *Truck Drivers* (1975–1979) series of films features the comic tales of a road hauler and his colleague traveling all over Japan in a brightly painted vehicle. The studio also made fairy tale films for children and action adventure tales to compete with American offerings. Rivaling the *Truck Drivers* was the Shochiku studio's *Tora the Tramp*, which made the studio a great deal of money, directed by Yamada. Shochiku also did well with films aimed at high school and college audiences.

But two of the old line studios almost went out of business. In 1971 Daiei went bankrupt and had to be reorganized four years later. Also in 1971 the nearly bust Nikkatsu ceased making conventional films and turned to the production of soft-core pornography or "roman porno" (romantic pornographic films). The directors under contract to Nikkatsu had to create low-budget films filled with scenes of disguised sexual activity since Japanese censorship does not condone direct sexual expression. Thus Nikkatsu roman porno created a unique eroticism of hidden and suggested sexual expression inspired by traditional Japanese erotic art and literature.

Despite the films' restricted subject matter, many critics found the work of the Nikkatsu studio extremely well done. With witty stories, beautiful camerawork, and important social themes, the films have often been voted among the best of the year by Japanese critics. To circumvent censorship, Nikkatsu had its filmmakers feature voyeurism, fetishism, and sadomasochism to avoid explicitly shown sexual organs. Nevertheless, in 1972 the studio became involved in a dramatic censorship case which ended four years later when filmmakers Seiichiro Yamaguchi and Katsuhiko were found innocent.

Several directors worked well within the roman porno system. Tatsumi Kumashiro featured popular music, stories with overt political messages, and comedy to make such hits as *Sayuri Ichijo: The West Desire* (1972), *The Lovers Get Wet* (1973), *The Back Paper of the Sliding Door of a Four-and-Half Tatami Mat Room* (1973), and *The Black Rose Goes to Heaven* (1975). This final work is a self-reflexive comedy about a film company making a cheap erotic film and its struggles with governmental authorities. Noboru Tanaka adapted the same story that Oshima used for his *In the Realm of the Senses* (1976) to make *Document of Sada Abe* (1975). This film, set almost entirely in a small room of an inn, tells the story of a legendary woman in Japan, chronicling through flashbacks her passionate past. His *Stroller in the Attic* (1976) tells of a nihilistic youth who spies on people from his attic.

In the 1980s, its management taken over by its labor union, Nikkatsu has promoted several young assistant directors and has begun to make non-pornographic films. A typical example is *Family Game*, directed by Yoshimitsu Morita, an ingenious comedy about contemporary urban life in Japan that was hailed on the international art-cinema circuit. Shinya Yamamoto has also directed several interesting parodies, including *Close Encounter with Horny Men* (1979), which not only parodied Steven Spielberg's *Close Encounters of the Third Kind* (1977) but combined it with the narrative of Billy Wilder's *The Apartment* (1960) to tell of a Japanese employee dominated by his bosses.

As in the United States, independent filmmakers have tried to crack the studio system. But doing this takes wealth and ingenuity. Consider the case of Akira Kadokawa. In 1976 this young, aggressive publisher began to produce films by adapting narratives from popular books his company had already published. He then promoted these on television to an extent unseen in Japan before, so that the advertising budgets often outweighed the actual costs to make the films. But they have made money and Kadokawa keeps on producing detective films, melodramas, and action-adventure fare.

In the West the reputation of the Japanese cinema rests largely with two filmmakers, Akira Kurosawa and Nagisa Oshima. Although he has made fewer films than in the 1950s, Akira Kurosawa has made several interesting films during the past two decades. *Dersu Uzala* (1975), shot entirely in Soviet Siberia with Russian actors, told the story of a Russian captain and a Mongolian guide. His next film was financed by Twentieth Century–Fox at the insistence of longtime admirers George Lucas and Francis Ford Coppola, who served as the producers of *Kagemusha* (*The Shadow Warrior*, 1980). This

big-budget film reminded fans of the glories of *Seven Samurai* and made a record ten million dollars in Japan alone. Kurosawa received help from France for his next film, *Ran* (1985). Producer Serge Silberman and Kurosawa set Shakespeare's *King Lear* against a background of Japanese civil war to create an epic period piece. With dazzling battle sequences and lavish costumes, *Ran*'s portrait of greed, revenge, and jealousy did far better abroad in the international art-cinemas than in Japan.

Nagisa Oshima, in the early 1970s, crafted a series of experimental narratives about different political and social aspects of postwar Japanese life. *The Ceremony* (1971) treated rituals of funerals and weddings; *Dear Summer Sister* (1972) dealt with the political question of Okinawa; *Three Resurrected Drunkards* (1968) dealt with youths thought to be illegal Korean immigrants; and *The Man Who Left His Will on Film* (1970) examined filmmaking by high school students and what they learned about life and ideology.

But Oshima became world famous (infamous to some) when in 1975 he made the first hard-core film officially produced by a Japanese. Oshima shot *In the Realm of the Senses* in a closed studio and had the film developed and edited in France. The complete film was shown in only the most liberal countries around the world; in Japan it was shown only after certain scenes were treated chemically to obliterate images—a long-standing practice for censoring foreign films. Based on the story of a woman who, after days of intense lovemaking, chops off her lover's penis, *In the Realm of the Senses* caused a scandal in Japan which dragged on for years.

In countries where it was shown, *In the Realm of the Senses* was a hit and made Oshima famous, especially in Europe and the United States. As a result, the film's French producer,

Anatole Dauman, and Oshima teamed up to make another film with a Japanese cast. *Empire of Passion* (1978) is the magnificently shot tale of two lovers haunted by the ghost of a man they murdered. An Englishman, Jeremy Thomas, produced Oshima's *Merry Christmas, Mr. Lawrence* (1983) based on the story of the relationship of Japanese and British officers in a Japanese prisoner-of-war camp during World War II. The casting of two rock stars, Britain's David Bowie and Japan's Ryuichi Sakamoto, contributed to the international appeal of the film, but neither film matched the success of *In the Realm of the Senses*, and thereafter Oshima settled down to being a regular in the international art-cinema circles, more popular outside his own country than in Japan.

Formerly a mighty filmmaking power, Japan today seems to be typical of many nations around the world. Since it is impossible to take Hollywood head-on, nation after nation has turned to television as the major outlet for film-making. That is not to say that there have not been developments in cinema or that new film-makers have not emerged all over the world. For example, one of the most famous of the late 1980s is Ousmane Sembène of Senegal, who began making films in the early 1960s. His *Ceddo* (1978) symbolizes the limited progress of African independent cinema. It was filmed in Wolof, the Senegalese language, and based on the director's personal reconstruction of his country's past. His earlier films had always had one version in French to ensure their export potential.

Set in an unspecified colonial past, *Ceddo* deals with the enslavement of the people. The common people are aroused to resistance when one of them kidnaps the king's daughter. Rivalries are sparked and the people struggle for power as European slave traders and Catholic missionaries move in to take advantage of the situation. The princess is rescued and helps free her people. The pacing is slow, the close-ups infrequent, and the camera often stationary, techniques which distance a viewer used to the Hollywood style. But this is a native cinema of criticism, one which tries to be different from the smooth entertainment of Hollywood.

Many African filmmakers actually work out of Europe to avoid the restrictions of their own countries and the lack of cinema facilities in Africa. Med Hondo, like Sembène, discovered film in Paris and first worked in the theatre, then in film to create dramas of estrangement and alienation. Through Marxist dialectic, Hondo wishes to find an alternative to the Hollywood style to explore his themes. In the documentary, *Dirty Arabs, Dirty Niggers, Your Neighbors* (1973), he criticized the use of North African and Black African workers in France, while *We'll Have All Death to Sleep* (1977) followed the Polisario liberation movement.

The problem lies with the continued domination of Hollywood and its average budgets of 20 million dollars per feature. Like it or not the American film industry continues to dominate the world of cinema, and all others must react. Increasingly, the creation of alternatives outside Hollywood have begun to take place exclusively on video for television. Films will continue to be made, but more and more seen as their first-run on television around the world. In contrast, Hollywood films, as far as we can see into the future, can and will be made with an eye to theatres for the initial screening, then VCRs, cable, satellite-to-home telecast, and television broadcast, to follow. But these are still forecasts, and only when we have the proper perspective will we be able to research and write the history of film in the era since 1975.

appendix one

• •

guide
to further
reading

This appendix is not meant to list every title, but to guide the reader to significant, important works to read with *Movie History: A Survey*.

First, a few caveats:

—The citations are confined to those in English and easily found in most university libraries or large public libraries.

—In most cases the first reference to a concept, idea, or filmmaker will note all the relevant literature. For example, for John Ford, although he is discussed for his contribution in the Studio Era and the Westerns of the 1950s, the first citation, in Chapter 3, contains suggested readings.

—I have not listed screenplays, which can be found by consulting the books suggested.

In the end the reader should consider doing his or her own research. True film history research requires more than simply reading books and articles. The only guide to film research in English is excellent: Robert C. Allen and Douglas Gomery, *Film History* (New York: Knopf, 1985). Research materials for film history are of two kinds: the films themselves (see Appendix 2) and paper documents. Paper documents tend to be associated with economic history, technological history, social history, or aesthetics. The most useful are *primary sources*, that is, documents generated directly at the time and place by the participants.

· · · · · · · · · · · · · · · ·

primary sources

· · · · · · · · · · · · · · · ·

· economic ·

The Department of Special Collections at the University of California at Los Angeles holds the surviving papers of RKO.

The Walt Disney Archive on the studio lot in Burbank, California holds the records of the company.

The University of Iowa Library in Iowa City contains an essential resource of the history of vaudeville in the B. F. Keith Collection.

The Harvard Business School Library contains the business records of the pioneering film organization of Raff & Gammon.

The William Seymour Theatre Collection at Princeton University has the distribution records of Warner Bros.

The corporate records of the United Artists Corporation are held at the State Historical Society in Madison, Wisconsin.

Many local historical societies hold papers about filmmaking in that area. See, for example, the San Diego Historical Society and the State Historical Society of Colorado.

· technological ·

The Academy of Motion Picture Arts and Sciences Library in Beverly Hills, California has papers of the Technicolor Corporation.

The Stanford University Museum of Art in Stanford, California holds papers and materials relating to the work of Eadweard Muybridge.

The Edison National Historic Site in Orange, New Jersey hold the massive collections of inventor Thomas Alva Edison.

The Cayuga Museum of History and Art in Auburn, New York is the resting place for the artifacts of Theodore W. Case, one of the inventors of sound-on-film.

· social ·

The Academy of Motion Picture Arts and Sciences Library in Beverly Hills, California has papers of many involved in the film industry as well as the records of the Production Code Administration, the Hays Office's west coast unit.

The Gone With the Wind Museum in Atlanta, Georgia has the world's largest collection about the most popular film of Hollywood's Golden Age.

The Delyte W. Morris Library at Southern Illinois University in Carbondale, Illinois holds the papers of blacklisted screenwriter John Howard Lawson.

The Indiana State Library in Indianapolis holds the private papers of the founder of the Motion Picture Association of America, Will H. Hays.

The Department of Special Collections at Columbia University Library holds Robert Flaherty's correspondence from the 1920s through the 1940s.

The Jewish Museum of New York City holds a valuable collection of films and materials related to the Jewish experience in the United States.

The New York Public Library's Schomberg's Center for Research in Black Culture is a major collection of materials relating to blacks in film.

• aesthetic •

The Academy of Motion Picture Arts and Sciences Library in Beverly Hills, California has papers of filmmakers Frank Borzage, George Cukor, and John Huston, producer Hal Wallis, and make-up expert Perc Westmore, to name only a few.

The Louis B. Mayer Library of the American Film Institute in Los Angeles holds papers of Robert Aldrich and Martin Scorsese.

The Department of Special Collections at the University of Southern California holds 20,000 scripts in the MGM Screenplay Collection as well as the production records for Warner Bros.

The Manuscript Division of the Library of Congress in Washington, D. C. holds the papers of Miriam Cooper and actress Lillian Gish.

The Newberry Library in Chicago contains the papers of screenwriter Ben Hecht.

The Lilly Library at Indiana University in Bloomington, Indiana holds the papers of directors John Ford and Orson Welles.

• films •

Appendix 2 details holdings of films in the United States.

• guides •

Several books provide the location and status of primary materials, although they seem to go out of date the instant they are published. See Nancy Allen, *Film Study Collections* (New York: Ungar, 1979), Robert A. Armour, *Film* (Westport, CT: Greenwood, 1980), Leonard Maltin, *The Whole Earth Sourcebook* (New York: New American Library, 1983), and Anthony Slide, Patricia King Hanson, and Stephen L. Hanson (comp.), *Sourcebook for the Performing Arts* (Westport, CT: Greenwood, 1988). Two area-specific guides include Linda Harris Mehr (ed.), *Motion Pictures, Television and Radio: A Union Catalogue of Manuscript and Special Collections in the Western United States* (Boston: G. K. Hall, 1977) and Bonnie G. Rowen, *Scholar's Guide to Washington, D.C. Film and Video Collections* (Washington, D.C.: Smithsonian Institution Press, 1980). See also the occasional listings of the opening of new manuscript collections in issues of *Cinema Journal* and *Quarterly Review of Film Studies*.

• • • • • • • • • • • • • • • •

secondary sources

• • • • • • • • • • • • • • • •

Ideally, only when the researcher has exhausted the use of primary sources should
he or she see the secondary sources listed below. However, often we do not have the time
or money to access primary materials. Remember that secondary sources proffer the arguments and analyses of others. When you read
them, be careful to note any bias. The books
and articles below are listed by the subjects
covered in *Movie History: A Survey*.

• preface •

Modestly I state that there is only one book on re-
searching film history and that is Robert C. Allen
and Douglas Gomery, *Film History* (New York:
Knopf, 1985). The other major influence on the
shape and design of *Movie History: A Survey* is
David Bordwell, Janet Staiger, and Kristin Thompson's monumental *The Classical Hollywood Cinema* (New York: Columbia University Press, 1985).

• chapter 1 •
the invention and
innovation of the movies

This and other discussion of the technology of the
movies are based on the invention, innovation,
and diffusion methodology which I developed. For
the best and clearest version of this see Douglas

Gomery, "The Coming of Sound: Technological
Change in the American Film Industry" in Tino
Balio, *The American Film Industry*, Revised Edition
(Madison: University of Wisconsin Press, 1985).
For a comparison of alternative approaches to the
study of the history of technology see Edward
Branigan, "Color and Cinema: Problems in the
Writing of History," originally published in *Film
Reader 4*, 1979, but most conveniently found in
Paul Kerr, *The Hollywood Film Industry* (London:
BFI, 1986).

The invention of the movies is treated in Brian
Coe, *The History of Movie Photography* (New York:
Zoetrope, 1982), Raymond Fielding (ed.), *A Technological History of Motion Pictures and Television* (Berkeley: University of California Press,
1967), and C. W. Ceram, *Archaeology of the Cinema* (New York: Harcourt, Brace, 1965). The basic
bibliography of work on the invention and innovation of the cinema is found in John L. Fell (ed.),
Film Before Griffith (Berkeley: University of California Press, 1983).

For background on the history of photography in
general see Beaumont Newhall, *The History of
Photography* (New York: The Museum of Modern
Art, 1964).

The career of Eadweard Muybridge is closely examined by Gordon Hendricks in *Eadweard Muybridge* (New York: Grossman, 1975) and Kevin
MacDonnell, *Eadweard Muybridge* (Boston: Little
Brown, 1972).

For more on Eastman Kodak see Reese V. Jenkins,
Images and Enterprise (Baltimore: Johns Hopkins
University Press, 1975).

Thomas Alva Edison has certainly been one of the most written-about Americans. For the standard work see Robert Conant, *A Streak of Luck* (New York: Seaview Books, 1979) and Wyn Wackhorst, *Thomas Alva Edison* (Cambridge: MIT Press, 1981). For a less flattering view see Gordon Hendricks' *The Edison Motion Picture Myth* (Berkeley: University of California Press, 1961), *The Beginnings of Biograph* (New York: The Beginnings of the American Film, 1964), and *The Kinetoscope* (New York: The Beginnings of the American Film, 1966). On the Edison films see Jon Gartenberg, "Camera Movement in Edison and Biograph Films, 1900–1906," *Cinema Journal*, Volume 19, Number 2 (Spring, 1980) and Robert C. Allen, "Vitascope/Cinematographe: Initial Patterns of American Film Industrial Practice," in Gorham A. Kindem (ed.), *The American Film Industry* (Carbondale: Southern Illinois University Press, 1982).

The beginnings of the movies in Great Britain is covered in Michael Chanan, *The Dream That Kicks* (London: Routledge & Kegan Paul, 1980).

For what it was like in the early days of movie-making consult Jay Leyda and Charles Musser (eds.), *Before Hollywood* (New York: American Federation of the Arts, 1986) and Fred J. Balshofer and Arthur C. Miller, *One Reel a Week* (Berkeley: University of California Press, 1967).

On the innovation of movies through vaudeville see Robert C. Allen's pioneering work in *Vaudeville and Film, 1895–1915* (New York: Arno Press, 1980) and his "Contra the Chaser Theory," in John L. Fell (ed.), *Film Before Griffith* (Berkeley: University of California Press, 1983). For a dissenting view see Charles Musser, "Another Look at the Chaser Theory," *Studies in Visual Communication*, Volume 10, Number 4 (Fall, 1984).

The career and influence of Edwin S. Porter is treated in Noel Burch, "Porter, or Ambivalence," *Screen*, Winter 1978/79, and Charles Musser, "The Early Cinema of Edwin Porter," *Cinema Journal*, Volume 19, Number 1 (Fall, 1979).

The innovations of the American Vitagraph Company is the subject of Charles Musser, "American Vitagraph: 1897–1901," *Cinema Journal*, Volume 22, Number 3 (Spring, 1983), and Anthony Slide, *The Big V* (Metuchen, NJ: Scarecrow, 1987).

The important contributions of Sigmund Lubin are covered in Joseph P. Eckhardt and Linda Kowall, *Peddler of Dreams* (Philadelphia: National Museum of American Jewish History, 1984).

For more on the brothers Lumière see Alan Williams, "The Lumière Organization and 'Documentary Realism,'" and Marshall Deutelbaum, "Structural Patterning in the Lumière Films," both in John L. Fell (ed.), *Film Before Griffith* (Berkeley: University of California Press, 1983).

The standard works on Georges Méliès are John Frazer, *Artificially Arranged Scenes* (Boston: G. K. Hall, 1979), Paul Hammond, *Marvelous Méliès* (New York: St. Martin's, 1975), and Andre Gaudreault, "Theatricality, Narrativity, and Trickality: Reevaluating the Cinema of Georges Méliès," *Journal of Popular Film and Television*, Volume 15, Number 3 (Fall, 1987). See also Katherine Singer Kovacs, "Georges Méliès and the *Feerie*," in John L. Fell (ed.), *Film Before Griffith* (Berkeley: University of California Press, 1983).

In the earliest years the New York City environs served as a center for film production as described in Paul Spher, *The Movies Begin* (Newark, NJ: Newark Museum, 1977), Anthony Slide (ed.), *The Memoirs of Alice Guy Blache* (Metuchen, NJ: Scarecrow, 1986), and Richard Alleman, *The Movie Lover's Guide to New York* (New York: Harper & Row, 1988).

Filmmaking also took place outside New York as described in Kalton C. Lahue, *Motion Picture Pioneer* (South Brunswick, NJ: Barnes, 1973) for Chicago, and Richard Alan Nelson, "Florida: The Forgotten Film Capital," *Journal of the University Film Association*, Volume 29, Number 3 (Summer, 1977).

A fascinating account of pre-nickelodeon film exhibition is Burnes St. Patrick Hollyman, "The First Picture Shows: Austin, Texas (1894–1913)," *Journal of the University Film Association*, Volume 29, Number 3 (Summer, 1977) and Edward Lowery, "Edwin J. Hadley: Traveling Film Exhibitor," in John L. Fell (ed.), *Film Before Griffith* (Berkeley: University of California Press, 1983).

The best account of the nickelodeon era remains Robert C. Allen's *Vaudeville and Film, 1895–1915* (New York: Arno Press, 1980). For a case study of the impact of the nickelodeon on a single community see Roy Rosenzweig, *Eight Hours For What We Will* (New York: Cambridge University Press, 1983).

• chapter 2 •
the triumph of hollywood

For the possibilities of analyzing the history of a film industry see Douglas Gomery, "Film Culture and Industry: Recent Formulations in Economic History," *Iris*, Volume 2, Number 2, 1984 and "The Economics of Film: What Is the Method?" in Sari Thomas (ed.), *Film/Culture* (Metuchen, NJ: Scarecrow, 1982).

On the Motion Picture Patents Company and the founding of Hollywood see Richard Dale Batman, "The Founding of the Hollywood Motion Picture Industry," *Journal of the West*, Volume 10, Number 4 (October, 1971). For a comprehensive history of the Patents Trust see Robert Anderson, "The Motion Picture Patents Company: A Reevaluation" in Tino Balio, *The American Film Industry*, Revised Edition (Madison: University of Wisconsin Press, 1985).

David Bordwell, Janet Staiger and Kristin Thompson, *The Classical Hollywood Cinema* (New York: Columbia University Press, 1985) extensively treats the rise of the Hollywood system of production including the rise of the feature film.

The star system is treated in Richard de Cordova, "The Emergence of the Star System in America," *Wide Angle*, Volume 6, Number 4 (1985) and Janet Staiger, "Seeing Stars," *The Velvet Light Trap*, Number 20 (1983).

The career of Mary Pickford is treated in Robert Windeler, *Sweetheart* (New York: Praeger, 1974).

The creation of United Artists is covered extensively in the first of Tino Balio's two volume corporate history: *United Artists* (Madison: University of Wisconsin Press, 1976).

For more on the important impact of Thomas Ince see Janet Staiger, "Dividing Labor for Production Control: Thomas Ince and the Rise of the Studio System," *Cinema Journal*, Volume 28, Number 2 (Spring, 1979) and Jean Mitry, "Thomas H. Ince: His Esthetic, His Films, His Legacy," *Cinema Journal*, Volume 22, Number 2 (Winter, 1983).

Adolph Zukor and his Famous Players' Company taught the world how to fashion a movie monopoly. See his *The Public Is Never Wrong* (New York: Putnam's, 1953).

The rise of world distribution is treated in detail in Kristin Thompson's *Exporting Entertainment* (London: BFI, 1985) and Janet Staiger, "Combination and Litigation: Structures of U.S. Film Distribution, 1896–1917," *Cinema Journal*, Volume 23, Number 2 (Winter, 1983).

The career of Roxy is examined in Ben M. Hall's *The Best Remaining Seats* (New York: Bramhall House, 1961).

The career of Sid Grauman is covered in Charles Bearsley, *Hollywood's Master Showman* (New York: Cornwall Books, 1983).

The innovations of Balaban & Katz and the subsequent application in the Publix theatre chain are treated in two articles by Douglas Gomery: "The Growth of Movie Monopolies: The Case of Balaban & Katz," *Wide Angle*, Volume 3, Number 1 (1979) and "U.S. Film Exhibition: The Formulation of a

Big Business," in Tino Balio (ed.), *The American Film Industry*, Revised edition (Madison: University of Wisconsin Press, 1985).

The social reaction to the early movies is treated in Garth Jowett, *Film* (Boston: Little Brown, 1976), and Robert Sklar, *Movie-Made America* (New York: Random House, 1975). Gerald Mast (ed.), *The Movies in Our Midst* (Chicago: University of Chicago Press, 1982) collects contemporary articles about American film history from a social and cultural perspective. All three of these volumes cover all phases of the social history of the American film.

The reaction of the Progressive era to the movies can be seen in Lary May's *Screening Out the Past* (Chicago: University of Chicago Press, 1980), and Kathleen D. McCarthy, "Nickel Vice and Virtue: Movie Censorship in Chicago, 1907–1915," *Journal of Popular Film,* Volume 5, Number 1 (1976). For a perspective of the "new" woman and the movies see Kathy Peiss, *Cheap Amusements* (Philadelphia: Temple University Press, 1986). See also Robert Fisher, "Film Censorship and Progressive Reform: The National Board of Censorship of Motion Pictures, 1909–1922," *Journal of Popular Film*, Volume 4, Number 2 (1975) and Nancy J. Rosenbloom, "Between Reform and Regulation: The Struggle over Film Censorship in Progressive America, 1909–1922," *Film History*, Volume 1 (1987).

The history of censorship is covered in Richard S. Randall, *Censorship of the Movies* (Madison: University of Wisconsin Press, 1968) and Edward de Grazia and Roger K. Newman, *Banned Films* (New York: R. R. Bowker, 1982).

The Hays Office is covered in Leonard J. Leff and Jerold L. Simmons, *The Dame in the Kimono* (New York: Weidenfeld and Nicolson, 1989) and Garth Jowett, *Film* (Boston: Little Brown, 1976).

The social institution of Hollywood is covered in Lary May, *Screening Out the Past* (Chicago: University of Chicago Press, 1982). Hollywood as a place

is chronicled in Bruce T. Torrence, *Hollywood* (New York: Zoetrope, 1982).

• chapter 3 •
hollywood establishes
the classic narrative style

To understand the Classic Hollywood Narrative style, the best book is David Bordwell, Janet Staiger and Kristin Thompson, *The Classical Hollywood Cinema* (New York: Columbia University Press, 1985). For their critique of other work in this area see Kristin Thompson and David Bordwell, "Linearity, Materialism, and the Study of Early Cinema," *Wide Angle*, Volume 5, Number 3 (1983). To gain an understanding of the terms for aesthetic analysis see David Bordwell and Kristin Thompson, *Film Art*, 2nd edition (New York: Knopf, 1986). See also Robert C. Allen and Douglas Gomery, *Film History* (New York: Knopf, 1985) for suggestions. For an overview of interviews of survivors of the period see Kevin Brownlow, *The Parade's Gone By...* (New York: Knopf, 1968). See also George Pratt's *Spellbound in Darkness* (Greenwich, CT: New York Graphic Society, 1973), and Gerald Mast's *The Movies in Our Midst* (Chicago: University of Chicago Press, 1982) for documents from the era.

The career of D. W. Griffith is covered in Joyce E. Jesionowski, *Thinking in Pictures* (Berkeley: University of California Press, 1987), Richard Schickel, *D. W. Griffith* (New York: Simon & Schuster, 1984), Cooper C. Graham, Steve Higgins, Elaine Mancini, and Joao Luiz Vieira, *D. W. Griffith and the Biograph Company* (Metuchen, NJ: Scarecrow Press, 1985). For the experience of working with Griffith see Billy Bitzer's *His Story* (New York: Farrar Straus, 1973). Fred Silva in his *Focus on Birth of a Nation* (Englewood Cliffs, NJ: Prentice-Hall, 1971) offers historical analysis of the director's most influential achievement.

The career of Cecil B. deMille is covered in Richard Kozarski, *The Rivals of D. W. Griffith* (Minneapolis, MN: Walker Art Center, 1976), Charles Higham, *Cecil B. DeMille* (New York: Dell, 1973) and Anne Edwards, *The DeMilles* (New York: Abrams, 1988).

John Ford is covered in Peter Bogdanovich, *John Ford* (Berkeley: University of California Press, 1968), Dan Ford, *Pappy* (Englewood Cliffs, NJ: Prentice-Hall, 1979), Tag Gallagher, *John Ford* (Berkeley: University of California Press, 1985), Joseph McBride and Michael Wilmington, *John Ford* (New York: DaCapo, 1975), Andrew Sarris, *The John Ford Movie Mystery* (Bloomington: Indiana University Press, 1975), Lindsey Anderson, *About John Ford* (New York: McGraw-Hill, 1983) and a special issue of *Wide Angle*, Volume 2, Number 4 (1978).

King Vidor is covered in his own words through his *King Vidor on Filmmaking* (New York: McKay, 1972), and *A Tree Is a Tree* (New York: Monarch, 1976) plus an oral interview in Nancy Dowd and David Shepard, *King Vidor* (Metuchen, NJ: Scarecrow, 1988). Raymond Durgnat and Scott Simmon offer a comprehensive assessment of his work in *King Vidor American* (Berkeley: University of California Press, 1988).

William Wellman offered his views in his autobiography, *A Short Time for Insanity* (New York: Hawthorn, 1974). See also Frank T. Thompson, *William A. Wellman* (Metuchen, NJ: Scarecrow, 1983).

Raoul Walsh is covered in his autobiography, *Each Man in His Time* (New York: Farrar Straus, 1974), and Phil Hardy (ed.), *Raoul Walsh* (Edinburgh: Edinburgh Film Festival, 1974).

Allan Dwan is interviewed at length in Peter Bogdanovich, *Allan Dwan* (New York: Praeger, 1971).

Henry King is covered in Walter Coppedge, *Henry King's America* (Metuchen, NJ: Scarecrow, 1986).

Clarence Brown is covered in Allen Estrin, *Hollywood Professionals, Volume 6* (South Brunswick, NJ: 1980).

Frank Borzage is examined closely by Frederick Lamster in *Souls Made Great Through Love and Adversity* (Metuchen, NJ: Scarecrow, 1981).

More on Tod Browning can be found in Stuart Rosenthal's *Tod Browning* which is Volume 4 of the Hollywood Professionals Series (New York: Barnes, 1975).

Mack Sennett is in Kalton C. Lahue and Terry Brewer, *Kops and Custard* (Norman: University of Oklahoma Press, 1968).

Charlie Chaplin is in David Robinson, *Chaplin* (New York: McGraw-Hill, 1985), Julian Smith, *Chaplin* (Boston: Twayne, 1984), Harry M. Geduld, *Chapliniana* (Bloomington: Indiana University Press, 1987), Wes D. Gehring, *Charlie Chaplin* (Westport, CT: Greenwood, 1983), and Charles J. Maland, *Chaplin and American Culture* (Princeton: Princeton University Press, 1989).

Buster Keaton has been examined by Rudi Blesh, *Keaton* (New York: Macmillan, 1966), Tom Dardis, *Keaton* (New York: Scribners, 1979), Daniel Moews, *Keaton* (Berkeley: University of California Press, 1977), and George Wead and George Ellis, *The Film Career of Buster Keaton* (Boston: Twayne, 1977).

Harold Lloyd has been treated in Adam Reilly, *Harold Lloyd* (New York: Collier, 1977), and Richard Schickel, *Harold Lloyd* (Boston: New York Graphic Society, 1974).

Harry Langdon is covered in William Schelly, *Harry Langdon* (Metuchen, NJ: Scarecrow, 1983).

European directors who made their way to Hollywood in the 1920s is the subject of Graham Petrie's *Hollywood Destinies* (New York: Routledge & Kegan Paul, 1985).

Ernst Lubitsch is covered in Robert Carringer and Barry Sabath, *Ernst Lubitsch* (Boston: G. K. Hall, 1980), William Paul, *Ernst Lubitsch's American Comedy* (New York: Columbia University Press, 1983), Leland Pogue, *The Cinema of Ernst Lubitsch*

(South Brunswick, NJ: Barnes, 1978), and Herman G. Weinberg, *The Lubitsch Touch* (New York: Dutton, 1977).

F. W. Murnau is covered in a special issue of the *Quarterly Review of Film Studies*, Volume 2, Number 3 (1977) plus Lotte Eisner, *F. W. Murnau* (Berkeley: University of California Press, 1973).

Victor Seastrom and Mauritz Stiller are treated together in Hans Pensel, *Seastrom and Stiller in Hollywood* (New York: Vintage, 1969).

Erich von Stroheim is in Thomas Quinn Curtis, *Von Stroheim* (New York: Farrar, Straus, 1971), Joel Findler, *Stroheim* (New York: Praeger, 1968), Richard Kozarski, *The Man You Love to Hate* (New York: Oxford University Press, 1983) and Herman G. Weinberg's reconstructions in *The Complete Greed* (New York: Dutton, 1973) and *The Complete Wedding March* (Boston: Little, Brown, 1974).

Maurice Tourneur is examined by Richard Koszarski in *The Rivals of D. W. Griffith* (Minneapolis, MN: Walker Art Center, 1976) and in "Maurice Tourneur: The First of the Visual Stylists," *Film Comment*, Volume 9, Number 2 (March-April, 1973).

Rex Ingram is covered in Liam O'Leary, *Rex Ingram* (New York: Barnes & Noble, 1980).

The documentary movement before the coming of sound is surveyed in Richard Meran Barsam, *The Non-Fiction Film* (New York: Dutton, 1973), and Jack C. Ellis, *The Documentary Idea* (Englewood Cliffs, NJ: Prentice-Hall, 1989).

Raymond Fielding treats the history of the newsreel in his *The American Newsreel, 1911–1967* (Norman, Oklahoma: University of Oklahoma Press, 1972).

The travel film is covered in Kevin Brownlow, *War, the West, and the Wilderness* (New York: Knopf, 1979). See also Osa Johnson, *I Married Adventure* (Philadelphia: J. B. Lippincott, 1940).

For more on Robert Flaherty see William T. Murphy, *Robert Flaherty* (Boston: G. K. Hall, 1978), Arthur Calder-Marshall, *The Innocent Eye* (London: Penguin, 1963), Paul Rotha, *Robert Flaherty: A Biography* (Philadelphia: University of Pennsylvania Press, 1983), and Richard Meran Barsam, *The Vision of Robert Flaherty* (Bloomington: Indiana University Press, 1988).

• chapter 4 •
influential alternatives to hollywood: european cinema

The idea of a film movement and the concept of a stylistic version of film history are developed in David Bordwell, *French Impressionism* (New York: Arno, 1980) and Robert C. Allen and Douglas Gomery, *Film History* (New York: Knopf, 1985).

For more on Swedish cinema see Peter Cowie, *Swedish Cinema* (Cranbury, NJ: Barnes, 1969).

The Cubist movement in film is treated in Standish B. Lawder, *The Cubist Cinema* (New York: New York University Press, 1974).

Surrealism and film is the subject of J. H. Mathews, *Surrealism and Film* (Ann Arbor: University of Michigan Press, 1971) and Stephen Kovacs, *From Enchantment to Rage* (East Brunswick, NJ: Fairleigh Dickinson University Press, 1980).

Danish director Carl Dreyer is treated in David Bordwell, *The Films of Carl-Theodor Dreyer* (Berkeley: University of California Press, 1981), and Tom Milne, *The Cinema of Carl Dreyer* (Cranbury, NJ: Barnes, 1971).

French Impressionism as a movement is covered in David Bordwell's *French Impressionist Cinema* (New York: Arno, 1980) and Richard Abel's *French Cinema* (Princeton: Princeton University Press,

1984). See also Abel's collection of writings from the period in *French Film Theory and Criticism* (Princeton: Princeton University Press, 1988).

Louis Delluc is covered in Eugene C. McCreary, "Louis Delluc, Film Theorist, Critic and Prophet," *Cinema Journal*, Volume 16, Number 1 (Fall, 1976).

Abel Gance is dealt with by Kevin Brownlow in his *The Parade's Gone By …* (New York: Knopf, 1968) and *Napoleon* (New York: Knopf, 1983). See also James M. Welsh and Steven P. Kramer, *Abel Gance* (Boston: Twayne, 1978).

German Expressionism as a film movement is the subject of several important books including Lotte Eisner, *The Haunted Screen* (Berkeley: University of California Press, 1969), John D. Barlow, *German Expressionist Film* (Boston: Twayne, 1982), Roger Manvell and Heinrich Fraenkel, *The German Cinema* (New York: Praeger, 1973), Stephen Eric Bonner and Douglas Kellner (eds.), *Passion and Rebellion* (South Hadley, MA: J. F. Bergin, 1983), Sigfried Kracauer, *From Caligari to Hitler* (Princeton: Princeton University Press, 1947), Thomas Elsaesser, "Social Mobility and the Fantastic: German Silent Cinema," *Wide Angle*, Volume 5, Number 2 (1982) and Michael Budd, "Retrospective Narration in Film: Re-reading 'The Cabinet of Dr. Caligari,'" *Film Criticism*, Volume 6, Number 1 (Fall, 1979). A good background on Expressionism in general can be found in John Willet's two fine books: *Expressionism* (New York: McGraw-Hill, 1970) and *The New Sobriety* (London: Thames & Hudson, 1978).

Fritz Lang is closely examined by Lotte Eisner, *Fritz Lang* (New York: Oxford University Press, 1977), Robert Armour, *Fritz Lang* (Boston: Twayne, 1978), Peter Bogdanovich, *Fritz Lang in America* (New York: Praeger, 1967), Reynold Humphries, *Fritz Lang* (Baltimore: Johns Hopkins University Press, 1988), Ann Kaplan, *Fritz Lang* (Boston: G. K. Hall, 1981), and Stephen Jenkins (ed.), *Fritz Lang* (London: BFI, 1981).

Georg Wilhelm (G. W.) Pabst is dealt with by Lee Atwill, *G. W. Pabst* (Boston: Twayne, 1977).

• chapter 5 •
the soviet experiment
in filmmaking

Basic information about the Russian Revolution and the implications for the film industry can be read in Jay Leyda, *Kino* (Princeton: Princeton University Press, 1980), Richard Taylor, *The Politics of the Soviet Cinema, 1917–1929* (Cambridge: Cambridge University Press, 1979), Vance Keply, Jr., "The Origins of the Soviet Cinema: A Study in Industry Development," *Quarterly Review of Film Studies*, Volume 10, Number 1 (Winter, 1985). Basic documents from the period can be found in Richard Taylor and Ian Christie (ed.), *The Film Factory* (Cambridge: Harvard University Press, 1988). See also Luda Schnitzer, Jean Schnitzer and Marcel Martin (eds.), *Cinema and Revolution* (New York: Hill and Wang, 1973).

Constructivism and its implications for Soviet cinema are treated in Noel Burch, "Film's Institutional Mode of Representation and the Soviet Response," *October*, Number 11 (1979), a special issue of *Screen* on "Soviet Film of the 1920s," Volume 12, Number 4 (Winter 1971/72), George Rickey, *Constructivism* (New York: Braziller, 1967), Christa Lodder, *Russian Constructivism* (New Haven: Yale University Press, 1983), and Herbert Marshall, *Masters of Soviet Cinema* (London: Routledge & Kegan Paul, 1983).

Lev Kuleshov is covered in Ronald Levaco (ed.), *Kuleshov on Film* (Berkeley: University of California Press, 1974).

Sergei Eisenstein has an extensive literature, part of which includes David Bordwell, "Eisenstein's Epistemological Shift," *Screen*, Volume 15, Number 4 (Winter, 1974). Eisenstein's own writings are collected in Jay Leyda (ed.), *Film Form* (New York: Harcourt Brace, 1949), Jay Leyda (ed.), *The Film Sense* (New York: Harcourt Brace, 1944), *Notes of a Film Director* (New York: Dover, 1970), Jay Leyda and Zina Voynow, *Eisenstein at Work* (New York Pantheon, 1982), and Harry Geduld and Ronald Gottesman, *Sergei Eisenstein and Upton Sinclair* (Bloomington: Indiana University Press, 1970). His basic biography can be found in Yon Barna, *Eisenstein* (Bloomington: Indiana University Press, 1973) and Marie Seton, *Sergei M. Eisenstein* (New York: Grove Press, 1960). For more of his writings see Richard Taylor (ed.), *S. M. Eisenstein*, Volume I (Bloomington: Indiana University Press, 1988). Other biographical details can be found in Leon Moussinac, *Sergei Eisenstein* (New York: Crown, 1970), Ivor Montagu, *With Eisenstein in Hollywood* (New York: International Publishers, 1969), and Vladimir Nizhny, *Lessons with Eisenstein* (New York: Hill & Wang, 1962). See also Kristin Thompson, *Eisenstein's Ivan the Terrible* (Princeton: Princeton University Press, 1981).

Dziga Vertov is dealt with in Annette Michelson (ed.), *Kino-Eye* (Berkeley: University of California Press, 1984), David Bordwell, "An Introduction to Dziga Vertov," *Film Comment*, Volume 8, Number 1 (Spring, 1972), Seth Feldman, *Dziga Vertov* (Boston: G. K. Hall, 1979), Annette Michelson, "The Man with a Movie Camera: From Magician to Epistemologist," *Art Forum*, Volume 10, Number 7 (March, 1972), and Vlada Petric, *Constructivism in Film* (New York: Cambridge University Press, 1987).

Esther Shub can be learned more about in Vlada Petric, "Esther Shub: Cinema Is My Life," *Quarterly Review of Film Studies*, Volume 3, Number 4 (Fall, 1978).

V. I. Pudovkin's writings are gathered as *Film Technique and Film Acting* (New York: Grove, 1960). See also Peter Dart, *Pudovkin's Films and Film Theory* (New York: Arno, 1974).

Alexander Dovzhenko is covered by Vance Kepley, Jr., *In the Service of the State* (Madison: University

of Wisconsin Press, 1986), and Mario Carynnyk (ed.), *Alexander Dovzhenko* (Cambridge: MIT Press, 1973).

• chapter 6 •
the coming of sound and the studio system

For information on the coming of sound see articles by Douglas Gomery in "The Coming of the Talkies: Invention, Innovation, and Diffusion," in Elizabeth Weis and John Belton (eds.), *Film Sound* (New York: Columbia University Press, 1985), and "Warner Bros. Innovates Sound: A Business History," in Gerald Mast (ed.), *The Movies in Our Midst* (Chicago: University of Chicago Press, 1982).

A survey of the studio system is Douglas Gomery, *The Hollywood Studio System* (New York: St. Martin's, 1986). See also Thomas Schatz, *The Genius of the System* (New York: Pantheon, 1989).

Paramount is covered by John Douglas Eames, *The Paramount Story* (New York: Crown, 1985) and Leslie Halliwell, *Mountain of Dreams* (London: Hart-Davis, 1978).

Loews/MGM is treated in John Douglas Eames, *The MGM Story* (New York: Crown, 1976), Bosley Crowther's *The Lion's Share* (New York: Dutton, 1957), Gary Carey, *All the Stars in Heaven* (New York: Dutton, 1981), and Aljean Harmetz, *The Making of The Wizard of Oz* (New York: Knopf, 1981).

Fox has a listing of its films in Tony Thomas and Aubrey Solomon, *The Films of 20th Century–Fox* (Seacaucus, NJ: Citadel, 1988). On Darryl F. Zanuck see Mel Gussow, *Don't Say Yes Until I Finish Talking* (Garden City, NY: Doubleday, 1971).

Warners is covered from the pictorial listing point of view in Clive Hirschhorn, *The Warner Bros. Story* (New York: Crown, 1979). An adequate studio history can be found in Charles Higham, *War-*

ner Brothers (New York: Scribners, 1975). On Warners' films of the 1930s see Nick Roddick, *A New Deal in Entertainment* (London: BFI, 1983).

RKO is treated in a basic pictorial survey in Richard Jewell and Vernon Harbin, *The RKO Story* (New York: Arlington House, 1982). See also Donald L. Bartlett and James B. Wilson, *Empire* (New York: W. W. Norton, 1979) on the career of the studio's final owner, Howard Hughes.

Columbia is treated in Ed Buscombe, "Notes on Columbia Pictures Corporation, 1926–1941," in Paul Kerr, *The Hollywood Film Industry* (London: BFI, 1986) and in Bob Thomas, *King Cohn* (New York: Putnam's, 1967).

Universal has its picture survey in Clive Hirschhorn, *The Universal Story* (New York: Crown, 1983). Its origins are treated in I. G. Edmunds, *Big U* (New York: Barnes, 1977).

United Artists is the lone corporation served by an official biographer in Tino Balio's *United Artists* (Madison: University of Wisconsin Press, 1976). See also Ronald Bergan, *The United Artists Story* (New York: Crown, 1986).

Republic Pictures is treated in Richard Maurice Hurst, *Republic Studios* (Metuchen, N.J.: Scarecrow, 1979). Monogram is treated in Tim Onosko, "Monogram: Its Rise and Fall in the 1940s," *The Velvet Light Trap*, Number 5 (1972) and Ted Okuda, *The Monogram Checklist* (Jefferson, NC: McFarland, 1987). Both studios are covered in Todd McCarthy and Charles Flynn (eds.), *Kings of the Bs* (New York: Dutton, 1975), and Gene Fernett, *American Film Studios* (Jefferson, NC: McFarland, 1988).

The effects of the Great Depression on the American film industry are dealt with in Douglas Gomery, "Hollywood, the National Recovery Administration, and the Question of Monopoly Power," in Gorham Kindem (ed.), *The American Movie Industry* (Carbondale: Southern Illinois University Press, 1982). For more on the effects of both the depression and the war see Douglas

Gomery, *The Hollywood Studio System* (New York: St. Martin's, 1985). The rise of unions in Hollywood came in the 1930s and is treated in Murray Ross, *Stars and Strikes* (New York: Columbia University Press, 1941). See also David F. Prindle, *The Politics of Glamour* (Madison: University of Wisconsin Press, 1988) on a history of the Screen Actors Guild. See also Colin Shinder, *Hollywood Goes to War* (London: Routledge & Kegan Paul, 1982) and Clayton R. Koppes and Gregory D. Black, *Hollywood Goes to War* (New York: Free Press, 1987).

• chapter 7 •
the golden age of hollywood moviemaking

An overall history of the aesthetic effects of the coming of sound on the Classic Hollywood cinema can be found in the latter chapters of David Bordwell, Janet Staiger and Kristin Thompson, *The Classical Hollywood Cinema* (New York: Columbia University Press, 1985). For the approach of the social historian see Andrew Bergman, *We're in the Money* (New York: New York University Press, 1971).

Surveys of film genres can be found in Thomas Schatz, *Hollywood Genres* (Philadelphia: Temple University Press, 1981) and Stuart Kaminsky, *American Film Genres* (New York: Dell, 1977). For background on the concept of a film genre see John G. Cawelti, *Adventure, Mystery and Romance* (Chicago: University of Chicago Press, 1976), Wes D. Gehring, *Handbook of American Film Genres* (Westport, CT: Greenwood, 1988), and Barry Keith Grant (ed.), *Film Genre Reader* (Austin: University of Texas Press, 1986).

On the musical see Rick Altman, *The American Film Musical* (Bloomington: Indiana University Press, 1987), Jane Feuer, *The Hollywood Musical* (Bloomington: Indiana University Press, 1982), and

Rick Altman (ed.), *Genre* (London: Routledge & Kegan Paul, 1981).

The gangster film is treated in Colin MacArthur, *Underworld, USA* (New York: Publisher, 1972), and Eugene Roscow, *Born to Lose* (New York: Oxford University Press, 1978).

Horror films are covered in Barry Keith Grant, *Planks of Reason* (Metuchen, NJ: Scarecrow, 1988), Roy Huss and T. J. Ross, *Focus on the Horror Film* (Englewood Cliffs, NJ: Prentice-Hall, 1972), and Gregory A. Waller, *American Horrors* (Urbana: University of Illinois Press, 1987).

The Western is treated in Ed Buscombe, *The BFI Companion to the Western* (London: Andre Deutsch, 1988), John G. Cawelti, *The Six-Gun Mystique* (Bowling Green, Ohio: Bowling Green University Popular Press, 1971), George Fenin and William K. Everson, *The Western* (New York: Grossman, 1973), Jack Nachbar, *Focus on the Western* (Englewood Cliffs, NJ: Prentice-Hall, 1974), Jon Tuska, *The Filming of the West* (Garden City, NY: Doubleday, 1976), a special issue of *The Velvet Light Trap*, Number 12 from Spring of 1974, and Archie P. Moore, *Shooting Stars* (Bloomington: Indiana University Press, 1987).

The war film is treated in Jeanine Basinger, *The World War II Combat Film* (New York: Columbia University Press, 1986).

Film noir is the subject of Alain Silver and Elizabeth Ward, *Film Noir* (Woodstock, NY: Overlook Press, 1979), Jon Tuska, *Dark Cinema* (Westport, CT: Greenwood, 1984), Foster Hirsch, *Film Noir* (New York: DaCapo, 1981), Lawrence Alloway, *Violent America* (New York: Museum of Modern Art, 1971), Charles Derry, *The Suspense Thriller* (Jefferson, NC: McFarland, 1988), and J. P. Telotte, *Voices in the Dark* (Urbana: University of Illinois Press, 1989).

The application of the auteur theory to the history of the American films is treated in Andrew Sarris' *The American Cinema*, which was first printed in 1968 and is now available from the University of Chicago Press.

Those who supervise the overall finance and creation of a film are called producers. See the accounts in Hal Wallis and Charles Higham, *Starmaker* (New York: Macmillan, 1980) and Joe Pasternak, *Easy the Hard Way* (New York: Putnam's, 1956).

The pre-production process begins with a script. Screenwriters are examined in comprehensive detail in Tom Stempel's *Framework* (New York: Ungar, 1988). Gary Carey's *Anita Loos* (New York: Knopf, 1988) tells of the career of one of Hollywood's most influential early screenwriters. See also Pat McGilligan, *Backstory* (Berkeley: University of California Press, 1986), Frances Marion, *How To Write and Sell Film Stories* (New York: Covici Friede, 1937), and Richard Corliss (ed.), *The Hollywood Screenwriters* (New York: Avon, 1972).

Movie stars are the most visible workers on a film. There have been literally thousands upon thousands of biographies and autobiographies of stars, most of which are easily found in any sizable library. For annual reviews of the newest entries see the December issues of *Communication Booknotes*. On the idea and influence of the movie star please see Richard Dyer, *Stars* (London: BFI, 1979), and Alexander Walker, *Stardom* (New York: Stein and Day, 1970).

Behind the camera are cinematographers, who are treated in Scott Eyman (ed.), *Five American Cinematographers* (Metuchen, NJ: Scarecrow, 1988), Todd Rainsberger, *James Wong Howe* (San Diego: Barnes, 1981), Charles Higham, *Hollywood Cameramen* (Bloomington: Indiana University Press, 1970), Dennis Schaefer and Larry Salvato, *Masters of Light* (Berkeley: University of California Press, 1984), and Leonard Maltin, *Behind the Camera* (New York: Signet, 1971).

Costumers of film stars are detailed in Susan Perez, *Film Costume* (Metuchen, NJ: Scarecrow,

1981) and David Chierichetti, *Hollywood Costume Design* (1976).

Set designers are covered in Leon Barsacq, *Caligari's Cabinet and Other Grand Illusions* (New York: New American Library, 1976).

Make-up experts are examined in Frank Westmore, *The Westmores of Hollywood* (Philadelphia: J. B. Lippincott, 1974).

Composers of film music are covered in Irwin Bazelon, *Knowing the Score* (New York: Arco, 1975), James L. Limbacher, *Keeping Score* (Metuchen, NJ: Scarecrow, 1981), Roy M. Prendergast, *Film Music* (New York: Norton, 1977), Mark Evans, *Soundtrack* (New York: Hopkinson and Blake, 1975), and Tony Thomas, *Music for the Movies* (South Brunswick, NJ: Barnes, 1973).

Sam Goldwyn was certainly one of Hollywood's most important producers. His achievements are reviewed in Carol Easton's *The Search for Sam Goldwyn* (New York: Morrow, 1976), A. Scott Berg, *Goldwyn* (New York: Knopf, 1989), and Lawrence J. Epstein, *Samuel Goldwyn* (Boston: Twayne, 1981).

David O. Selznick tells his own story in *Memo* (New York: Viking, 1972). See also Leonard J. Leff, *Hitchcock and Selznick* (New York: Weidenfeld and Nicolson, 1987), Bob Thomas, *Selznick* (Garden City, NY: Doubleday, 1970), and Ronald Haver, *David O. Selznick's Hollywood* (New York: Knopf, 1980).

Val Lewton is treated in some detail in Joel Siegal, *Val Lewton* (New York: Viking, 1972) and J. P. Telotte, *Dreams of Darkness* (Urbana: University of Illinois Press, 1985).

Arthur Freed is treated in Hugh Fordin, *The Movies' Greatest Musicals* (New York: Ungar, 1975) and Donald Knox, *The Magic Factory* (New York: Praeger, 1971).

Edith Head has penned her autobiography: *Edith Head's Hollywood* (New York: Dutton, 1983).

Bernard Herrmann is dealt with in Tony Thomas, *Film Score* (South Brunswick, NJ: Barnes, 1979).

Howard Hawks is covered in Robin Wood, *Howard Hawks* (New York: Doubleday, 1968), Gerald Mast, *Howard Hawks* (New York: Oxford University Press, 1982), a special issue of *Wide Angle*, Volume 1, Number 2 (Summer, 1976), and Joseph McBride's two books: *Focus on Howard Hawks* (Englewood Cliffs, NJ: Prentice-Hall, 1972) and *Hawks on Hawks* (Berkeley: University of California Press, 1982).

On Frank Capra, first read his autobiography, *The Name Above the Title* (New York: Macmillan, 1971) and then consult Richard Glazer and John Raeburn (eds.), *Frank Capra* (Ann Arbor: University of Michigan Press, 1975), Charles Maland, *Frank Capra* (Boston: Tawyne, 1980), Jeanine Basinger, *The 'It's a Wonderful Life' Book* (New York: Knopf, 1986) and Raymond Carney, *American Vision* (New York: Cambridge University Press, 1986).

Orson Welles is covered in Andre Bazin, *Orson Welles* (New York: Harper & Row, 1978), Robert Carringer, *The Making of Citizen Kane* (Berkeley: University of California Press, 1985), Peter Cowie, *The Cinema of Orson Welles* (New York: Barnes, 1965), Ronald Gottesman, *Focus on 'Citizen Kane'* (Englewood Cliffs, NJ: Prentice-Hall, 1971), Charles Higham, *Orson Welles* (New York: St. Martin's, 1985), Joseph McBride, *Orson Welles* (New York: Viking, 1977), James Naremore, *The Magic World of Orson Welles* (New York: Oxford University Press, 1978), Barbara Leaming, *Orson Welles* (New York: Viking, 1985) and a special issue of *Persistence of Vision*, Number 7 (1989).

Alfred Hitchcock is examined in detail in Albert LaValley, *Focus on Hitchcock* (Englewood Cliffs, NJ: Prentice-Hall, 1972), Eric Rohmer and Claude Chabrol, *Hitchcock: The First 44 Films* (New York: Ungar, 1979), William Rothman, *Hitchcock: The Murderous Gaze* (Cambridge: Harvard University Press, 1982), John Russell Taylor, *Hitch* (New York: Pantheon, 1978), François Truffaut, *Hitchcock* (New

York: Simon & Schuster, 1967), Robin Wood, *Hitchcock's Films* (New York: Barnes, 1975), Marshall Deutelbaum and Leland Pogue (eds.), *A Hitchcock Reader* (Ames: Iowa State University Press, 1986), Tom Ryall, *Alfred Hitchcock and the British Cinema* (Urbana: University of Illinois Press, 1986) and Donald Spoto's two books: *The Art of Alfred Hitchcock* (New York: Hopkinson and Blake, 1976) and *The Dark Side of Genius* (Boston: Little Brown, 1983).

Billy Wilder is treated in Bernard F. Dick, *Billy Wilder* (Boston: Twayne, 1980), Axel Madsen, *Billy Wilder* (Bloomington: Indiana University Press, 1969), Steve Seidman, *The Film Career of Billy Wilder* (Boston: G. K. Hall, 1977), and Maurice Zolotow, *Billy Wilder in Hollywood* (New York: Putnam's, 1977).

George Cukor is examined in Gary Carey, *Cukor and Co.* (New York: Museum of Modern Art, 1970) and James Bernardoni, *George Cukor* (Jefferson, NC: McFarland, 1985).

Preston Sturges is treated in James Curtis, *Between Flops* (New York: Limelight, 1984) and Ray Cywinski, *Preston Sturges* (Boston: G. K. Hall, 1984).

To understand the documentary movement in the United States during the 1930s and 1940s consult Richard Meran Barsam, *Nonfiction Film* (New York: Dutton, 1973), William Alexander, *Film on the Left* (Princeton: Princeton University Press, 1981), and Jack C. Ellis, *The Documentary Idea* (Englewood Cliffs, NJ: Prentice-Hall, 1989).

The highly interpretative "March of Time" series is the subject of Raymond Fielding, *The March of Time* (New York: Oxford University Press, 1978).

For more on Frontier Films see Russell Campbell, *Cinema Strikes Back* (Ann Arbor: UMI Press, 1982).

The federal government had come to documentary filmmaking through the back door and is the subject of Richard Dyer MacCann, *The People's Films* (New York: Hastings House, 1973).

Parc Lorentz has published a book, *Lorentz on Film* (New York: Hopkinson and Blake, 1975). See Robert Snyder, *Pare Lorentz on the Documentary Film* (Norman: University of Oklahoma Press, 1968).

For more on *The Negro Soldier* see Thomas Cripps' *Black Film as Genre* (Bloomington: Indiana University Press, 1979) and *Slow Fade to Black* (New York: Oxford University Press, 1977). For more on the Why We Fight series see Jay Leyda, *Films Beget Films* (New York: Hill and Wang, 1964) and Thomas Bohn, *An Historical and Descriptive Analysis of the 'Why We Fight' Series* (New York: Arno, 1977).

The experimental cinema of the 1930s and 1940s is treated in American Federation of the Arts, *A History of the American Avant-Garde Cinema* (New York: American Federation of the Arts, 1976). P. Adams Sitney has written extensively about this period and his work includes two edited volumes, *The Avant-Garde Film* (New York: New York University Press, 1978), and *Film Culture Reader* (New York: Praeger, 1970), and two thoughtful surveys in *The Essential Cinema* (New York: New York University Press, 1975), and *Visionary Cinema* (New York: Oxford University Press, 1979).

Maya Deren is covered in a special issue of *Film Culture*, Number 39 (1965), and Regina Cornwell, "Maya Deren and Germaine Dulac: Activists of the Avant-Garde," *Film Library Quarterly*, Volume 5, Number 1 (1971).

• chapter 8 •
pre—world war II alternatives to hollywood: france, britain, and germany

For background on the coming of sound to European cinema see Douglas Gomery, "Economic Struggle and Hollywood Imperialism: Europe Converts to Sound," *Yale French Studies*, Number 60, (1980) and Paul Monaco, *Cinema and Society* (New York: Elsevier, 1976). For the experience of the French film industry see Roy Armes, *French Film* (New York: Dutton, 1970).

René Clair is dealt with in Lucy Fischer, "René Clair, *Le Million*, and the Coming of Sound," *Cinema Journal*, Volume 16, Number 2 (Spring, 1977), Cecelia McGerr, *René Clair* (Boston: Twayne, 1980), and R. C. Dale, *The Films of René Clair*, Volumes I and II (Metuchen, NJ: Scarecrow, 1986). See the director's own *Cinema Yesterday and Today* (New York: Dover, 1972).

Jean Vigo is treated in P. E. Salles Gomes, *Jean Vigo* (Berkeley: University of California Press, 1971), John M. Smith, *Jean Vigo* (New York: Praeger, 1972) and William G. Simon, *The Films of Jean Vigo* (Ann Arbor: UMI Press, 1981).

Jean Renoir is dealt with by many writers. See Christopher Faulkner's two books: *The Social Cinema of Jean Renoir* (Princeton: Princeton University Press, 1986), and *Jean Renoir* (Boston: G. K. Hall, 1979). See also Leo Braudy, *Jean Renoir* (Garden City, New York: Doubleday, 1972), Alexander Sesonske, *Jean Renoir* (Cambridge: Harvard University Press, 1980), and Raymond Durgnat, *Renoir* (Berkeley: University of California Press, 1973). The director himself wrote *My Life and My Films* (New York: Atheneum, 1974).

Marcel Carne is dealt with in Evelyn Ehrlich, *Cinema of Paradox* (New York: Columbia University Press, 1985), Edward Baron Turk, *Child of Paradise* (Cambridge: Harvard University Press, 1989), and Andre Bazin, *French Cinema of Occupation and Resistance* (New York: Ungar, 1981).

The history of the British cinema during the 1930s and 1940s can be found in Roy Armes, *A Critical History of British Cinema* (New York: Oxford University Press, 1978), and James Curran and Vincent Porter (eds.), *British Cinema History* (Totowa, NJ: Barnes, 1983).

Alexander Korda is covered in Karol Kulik, *Alexander Korda* (London: Allen, 1975).

The British documentary movement is covered by Alan Lovell and Jim Hiller, *Studies in Documentary* (New York: Viking, 1972), Elizabeth Sussex, *The Rise and Fall of British Documentary* (Berkeley: University of California Press, 1975), Philip M. Taylor, *The Projection of Britain* (Cambridge: Cambridge University Press, 1981), and Paul Sawann, *The British Documentary Film Movement, 1926–1946* (Cambridge: Cambridge University Press, 1989).

John Grierson is treated in Forsyth Hardy, *John Grierson* (London: Faber and Faber, 1979), James Beveridge, *John Grierson* (New York: Macmillan, 1978), and Jack C. Ellis, *John Grierson* (Boston: G. K. Hall, 1986). Grierson's own writings are contained in his *Grierson on Documentary* (Berkeley: University of California Press, 1966).

Paul Rotha wrote *Rotha on Film* (London: Faber and Faber, 1958).

Harry Watt wrote *Don't Look at the Camera* (London: Paul Elek, 1974).

Humphrey Jennings is the subject of Anthony Hodgkinson and Rodney E. Sheratsky's *Humphrey Jennings* (Hanover, NH: University Press of New England, 1982).

The standard accounts of Nazi cinema can be found in M. S. Phillips, "The Nazi Control of the German Film Industry," *Journal of European Studies,* Volume 1 (1971), Renata Pan-Berg, *Leni Reifenstahl* (Boston: Twayne, 1980), David Hinton, *The Films of Leni Reifenstahl* (Metuchen, NJ: Scarecrow Press, 1978), David Stewart Hull, *Film in the Third Reich* (Berkeley: University of California Press, 1969), Erwin Leiser, *Nazi Cinema* (New York: Macmillan, 1974), Julian Pently, *Capital and Culture* (London: BFI, 1979), David Welsh, *Propaganda and the German Cinema, 1933–1945* (New York: Oxford University Press, 1983), and Cooper Graham, *Leni Reifenstahl and Olympia* (Metuchen, NJ: Scarecrow, 1986).

• chapter 9 •
post—world war II alternatives to hollywood: japan and italy

The end of the Second World War in 1945 signaled a new era for international cinema treated in Thomas Guback, *The International Film Industry* (Bloomington: Indiana University Press, 1969).

The history of the Japanese film can be found in Joseph L. Anderson and Donald Richie, *The Japanese Film*, rev. ed. (Princeton: Princeton University Press, 1982) and Richie's *The Japanese Cinema* (Garden City, New York: Doubleday, 1971). See also David Bordwell, "Our Dream Cinema: Western Historiography and the Japanese Film," *Film Reader 4* (1979), and Noel Burch, *To the Distant Observer* (Berkeley: University of California Press, 1979) as well as Alain Silver, *The Samurai Film* (New York: Overlook, 1984) and a special issue of *Journal of Film and Video*, Volume 39, Number 1 (Winter, 1987).

Akira Kurosawa is dealt with in Donald Richie, *The Films of Akira Kurosawa* (Berkeley: University of California Press, 1984), and Richie's *Focus on Roshomon* (Englewood Cliffs, NJ: Prentice-Hall, 1972). See also Patricia Erens, *Akira Kurosawa* (Boston: G. K. Hall, 1979) and the director's autobiography, *Something Like an Autobiography* (New York: Knopf, 1982).

Kenji Mizoguchi is treated in more detail in Dudley Andrew and Paul Andrew, *Kenji Mizoguchi* (Boston: G. K. Hall, 1981), David Bordwell, "Mizoguchi and the Evolution of Film Language," in Stephen Heath and Patricia Mellencamp, *Cinema and Language* (Frederick, MD: University Publications of America, 1983), and Robert Cohen, "Mizoguchi and Modernism: Structure, Culture, Point-of-View," *Sight and Sound*, Volume 47, Number 2 (1978).

Yasujiro Ozu is treated in loving detail by David Bordwell, *Ozu and the Poetics of the Cinema* (Princeton: Princeton University Press, 1988), and Donald Richie, *Ozu* (Berkeley: University of California Press, 1974). See also Paul Schrader, *Transcendental Style in Film* (Berkeley: University of California Press, 1972).

A survey of the history of the Italian cinema, in particular Neo-realism, can be found in Roy Armes, *Patterns of Realism* (New York: Barnes, 1971). See also Mario Cannalla, "Ideology and Aesthetic Hypotheses in the Criticism of Neo-Realism," *Screen* Volume 14, Number 4 (Winter, 1973–1974), Millicent Marcus, *Italian Film in the Light of Neorealism* (Princeton: Princeton University Press, 1987). *Movie History: A Survey* closely examines three key Neo-realist filmmakers, but there were others. See Pierre Leprohon, *The Italian Cinema* (New York: Praeger, 1972) and Mira Liehm, *Passion and Defiance* (Berkeley: University of California Press, 1984) for more. George Huaco, *The Sociology of Film Art* (New York: Basic Books, 1965), and Peter Bondanella, *Italian Cinema* (New York: Ungar, 1983) grapple with what is Neo-realism.

Luchino Visconti is treated in Geoffrey Nowell-Smith, *Luchino Visconti* (Garden City, New York: Doubleday, 1968), Gera Servadio, *Luchino Visconti* (New York: Watts, 1983), Monica Stirling, *A Screen of Time* (New York: Harcourt Brace, 1979), and Claretta Tonetti, *Luchino Visconti* (Boston: Twayne, 1983).

Roberto Rossellini is examined in detail in Peter Brunette, *Rossellini* (New York: Oxford University Press, 1987) and Jose Luis Guarner, *Roberto Rossellini* (New York: Praeger, 1970).

Vittorio De Sica is discussed in Cesare Zavattini's *Zavattini* (Englewood Cliffs, NJ: Prentice-Hall, 1970).

• chapter 10 •
television, wide-screen, and color

The changes in the American film industry after the Second World War are surveyed in Charles Higham, *Hollywood at Sunset* (New York: Saturday

Review Press, 1972) and a special issue of *The Velvet Light Trap*, Number 11, 1974.

Overviews of technological change in the 1950s and 1960s are best found in James Limbacher, *Four Aspects of Film* (New York: Brussel and Brussel, 1969) and Raymond Fielding, *A Technological History of Motion Pictures and Television* (Berkeley: University of California Press, 1967).

For the changes in film exhibition in terms of the effects of suburbanization and the baby boom, see Douglas Gomery, "The Coming of Television and the 'Lost' Motion Picture Audience, *Journal of Film and Video*, Volume 38, Number 3 (Summer, 1985).

Drive-ins are treated in Bruce A. Austin, "The Development and Decline of the Drive-in Movie Theatre," in his *Current Research in Film* (Norwood, NJ: Ablex, 1985).

The Paramount anti-trust case is treated in Michael Conant, *Antitrust in Motion Picture Industry* (Berkeley: University of California Press, 1960).

For more on theatre television, see Douglas Gomery, "Theatre Television: A History," *SMPTE Journal*, Volume 98, Number 2 (February, 1989), and "Theatre Television: The 'Missing Link' of Technical Change in the U.S. Motion Picture Industry," *The Velvet Light Trap*, Number 21 (Summer, 1985).

For more on the history of color see Edward Branigan, "Color and Cinema: Problems in the Writing of History," originally published in *Film Reader 4*, 1979, but most conveniently found in Paul Kerr, *The Hollywood Film Industry* (London: BFI, 1986). In particular Technicolor is treated in Fred E. Basten, *Glorious Technicolor* (San Diego: Barnes, 1980). See also R. T. Ryan, *A History of Motion Picture Color Technology* (New York: Focal Press, 1978) and Gorham A. Kindem, "Hollywood's Conversion to Color: The Technological, Economic, and Aesthetic Factors," in his *The American Film Industry* (Carbondale: Southern Illinois University Press, 1982).

The wide-screen technologies are treated in Robert C. Carr and R. M. Hayes, *Wide Screen Movies* (Jefferson, NC: McFarland, 1988), Brad Chisholm, "Widescreen Technologies," *The Velvet Light Trap*, Number 21 (Summer, 1985), Martin Quigley, Jr., (ed.), *New Screen Techniques* (New York: Quigley Publishing, 1953).

On CinemaScope see essays by James Spellerberg, John Belton and Richard Hincha in *The Velvet Light Trap*, Number 21 (Summer, 1985).

3-D is covered in Dan Symmes, *Amazing 3-D* (Boston: Little Brown, 1982).

For more on Hollywood's selling and leasing of films for the late show and the implications of what followed see Douglas Gomery, "Television, Hollywood, and the Development of Movies-Made-For-Television," in E. Ann Kaplan (ed.), *Perspectives on Television* (Frederick, MD: University Publications of America, 1983) and "Television, Hollywood, and the Evolution of the Made-for-TV Motion Picture," in Horace Newcomb (ed.), *Television: The Critical View* (New York: Oxford University Press, 1987).

The latter years of MGM are described in Lillian Ross, *Picture* (New York: Limelight, 1984) and Dore Schary, *Heyday* (Boston: Little Brown, 1979).

Warner Bros. in the 1950s and beyond is treated in Charles Higham, *Warner Brothers* (New York: Scribners, 1975).

Paramount is examined in John Douglas Eames, *The Paramount Story* (New York: Crown, 1985).

Twentieth Century–Fox is covered in Tony Thomas and Aubrey Solomon, *The Films of 20th Century–Fox* (Secaucus, NJ: Citadel, 1979) and John Gregory Dunne, *The Studio* (New York: Farrar, Straus, 1969).

Columbia Pictures is treated in David McClintick, *Indecent Exposure* (New York: Morrow, 1982).

United Artists is dealt with in Tino Balio's follow-up to his original history, this one taking the company from the early 1950s to the present: *United Artists* (Madison: University of Wisconsin Press, 1987).

Universal is best examined in Clive Hirschhorn, *The Universal Story* (New York: Crown, 1983) and Dan E. Moldea, *Dark Victory* (New York: Viking, 1986).

Disney has generated a great deal of prose, both positive and negative. His supporters would look to Bob Thomas, *Walt Disney* (New York: Simon & Schuster, 1976); his detractors would cite Richard Schickel, *The Disney Version* (New York: Simon & Schuster, 1968). The scholar is best advised to start with the bibliography extensively documented in Elizabeth Leebron and Lynn Gartley, *Walt Disney* (Boston: G. K. Hall, 1979).

Hollywood as a social force changed in the 1950s and this is covered in Larry Ceplair and Steven Englund, *The Inquisition of Hollywood* (Garden City, NY: Doubleday, 1980), Victor Navasky, *Naming Names* (New York: Viking, 1980), Eric Bentley (ed.), *Thirty Years of Treason* (New York: Viking, 1971), Walter Goodman, *The Committee* (New York: Farrar, Straus, 1968) and Robert Vaughn, *Only Victims* (New York: Putnam's, 1972). For more on censorship controversies of the period see Ira H. Carmen, *Movies, Censorship, and the Law* (Ann Arbor: University of Michigan Press, 1966). See, in particular, Leo A. Handel, *Hollywood Looks at Its Audience* (Urbana: University of Illinois Press, 1950), Leonard Quart and Albert Auster, *American Film and Society Since 1945* (New York: Praeger, 1985), and Thomas Doherty, "American Teenagers and Teenpics, 1955–1957: A Study in Exploitative Filmmaking," in Bruce A. Austin (ed.), *Current Research in Film*, Volume 2 (Norwood, NJ: Ablex, 1986).

• chapter 11 •
a transformation in
hollywood moviemaking

The Hollywood cinema of the television age, of the 1950s, 1960s and early 1970s, continued to employ the style and form of the Classic Hollywood

cinema so well treated in David Bordwell, Janet Staiger and Kristin Thompson, *The Classical Hollywood Cinema* (New York: Columbia University Press, 1985).

New ways of independent production are treated in Mark Litwak, *Reel Power* (New York: Morrow, 1986) and David Lees and Stan Berkowitz, *The Movie Business* (New York: Vintage, 1981). For an interesting case study see Andrew Sinclair, *Spiegel* (Boston: Little Brown, 1987) about the independent producer Sam Spiegel.

William Wyler is examined by Axel Madsen, *William Wyler* (New York: Crowell, 1973).

Sidney Lumet is covered in Stephen Bowles, *Sidney Lumet* (Boston: G. K. Hall, 1979).

Stanley Kubrick is dealt with in some detail in Thomas Alan Nelson, *Kubrick* (Bloomington: Indiana University Press, 1982), Alexander Walker, *Stanley Kubrick Directs* (New York: Harcourt, Brace, 1971), Jerome Agel, *The Making of 2001* (New York: Signet, 1970), Carolyn Geduld, *Filmguide to 2001* (Bloomington: Indiana University Press, 1973), Norman Kagan, *The Cinema of Stanley Kubrick* (New York: Grove, 1975), Robert Philip Kolker, *The Cinema of Loneliness* (New York: Oxford University Press, 1980), Michel Climent, *Kubrick* (New York: Holt, Rinehart and Winston, 1983), and Wallace Coyle, *Stanley Kubrick* (Boston: G. K. Hall, 1981).

Sam Fuller is the subject of Nicholas Garnham, *Samuel Fuller* (New York: Viking, 1971), and Phil Hardy, *Samuel Fuller* (New York: Praeger, 1970).

Otto Preminger is examined by Gerald Pratley, *The Cinema of Otto Preminger* (Cranbury, NJ: Barnes, 1977). See also the director's memoirs in *Preminger: An Autobiography* (Garden City, NY: Doubleday, 1977).

John Huston is treated in Gerald Pratley, *The Cinema of John Huston* (Cranbury, NJ: Barnes, 1971), Axel Madsen, *John Huston* (Garden City, NY: Doubleday, 1978), and Stuart Kaminsky, *John Huston* (Boston: Houghton Mifflin, 1978).

Stanley Kramer is dealt with in Donald Spoto, *Stanley Kramer* (New York: Putnam's, 1978).

Francis Coppola is treated in Robert K. Johnson, *Francis Ford Coppola* (Boston: Twayne, 1979), Robert Philip Kolker, *The Cinema of Loneliness* (New York: Oxford University Press, 1980), and Jeffrey Chown, *Hollywood Auteur* (New York: Praeger, 1988).

For more on the Western in the 1950s and 1960s see Jim Kitses, *Horizons West* (Bloomington: Indiana University Press, 1969) and John H. Kreidl, *Showdown* (Urbana: University of Illinois Press, 1979).

Anthony Mann is the subject of Jeanine Basinger, *Anthony Mann* (Boston: Twayne, 1979).

Budd Boetticher is the subject of Jim Kitses, *Budd Boetticher: The Western* (London: BFI, 1969).

Sergio Leone is examined by Robert C. Cumbow, *Once Upon a Time* (Metuchen, NJ: Scarecrow, 1987) and Christopher Frayling, *Spaghetti Westerns* (London: Routledge & Kegan Paul, 1981).

Don Siegel is closely examined in Stuart Kaminsky, *Don Siegel: Director* (New York: Curtis, 1974).

Vincente Minnelli penned an autobiography in *I Remember It Well* (Garden City, NY: Doubleday, 1974).

For more on comedies of the 1950s see Gerald Mast, *The Comic Mind*, 2nd edition (Chicago: University of Chicago Press, 1979).

Frank Tashlin is dealt with in Claire Johnston and Paul Willemen (eds.), *Frank Tashlin* (London: Screen, 1973).

For more on melodrama of the 1950s see Christine Gledhill, *Home Is Where the Heart Is* (Urbana: University of Illinois Press, 1987) and a special issue of *Screen*, Volume 29, Number 3 (Summer, 1988).

Douglas Sirk is the subject of Jon Halliday (ed.), *Sirk on Sirk* (New York: Viking, 1969). and Michael Stern, *Douglas Sirk* (Boston: Twayne, 1979).

For more on the long-running James Bond series see Tony Bennett and Janet Woollacott, *Bond and Beyond* (New York: Methuen, 1987).

Arthur Penn is examined in Robin Wood, *Arthur Penn* (New York: Praeger, 1969), John G. Cawelti, *Focus on Bonnie and Clyde* (Englewood Cliffs, NJ: Prentice-Hall, 1972), Robert Philip Kolker, *The Cinema of Loneliness* (New York: Oxford University Press, 1980), and Joel S. Zuker, *Arthur Penn* (Boston: G. K. Hall, 1984).

The changes in the documentary film in the United States during the 1950s and 1960s are discussed in Alan Rosenthal, *The New Documentary in Action* (Berkeley: University of California Press, 1971), Thomas Waugh, *Show Us Life* (Metuchen, NJ: Scarecrow, 1984), Jack C. Ellis, *The Documentary Idea* (Englewood Cliffs, NJ: Prentice-Hall, 1989), Richard Meran Barsam, *Nonfiction Film* (New York: Dutton, 1973).

Cinema verité is treated in Stephen Mamber, *Cinema Verité in America* (Cambridge: MIT Press, 1974), Louis Marcorelles, *The Living Cinema* (New York: Praeger, 1977), G. Roy Levin, *Documentary Explorations* (Garden City, NY: Doubleday, 1971), and M. Ali Issari and Doris A. Paul, *What Is Cinema Verité?* (Metuchen, NJ: Scarecrow, 1979).

Ricky Leacock is the subject of James Blue, "One Man's Truth—An Interview with Richard Leacock," *Film Comment 3* (Spring, 1965), and his own, "For an Uncontrolled Cinema," *Film Culture*, Numbers 22–23 (1961).

The Maysles brothers are treated in "Cinema Verité: A Survey Including Interviews with Richard Leacock, Jean Rouch, Jacques Rozier, William Klein, the Maysles Brothers," *Movie*, Number 8 (April, 1963).

Fred Wiseman is closely examined in Liz Ellsworth, *Frederick Wiseman* (Boston: G. K. Hall, 1979), and Thomas W. Benson and Carolyn Anderson, *The Films of Fred Wiseman* (Carbondale: Southern Illinois University Press, 1989).

The rise of the experimental film of the 1950s and 1960s is treated in some detail in American Federation of the Arts, A *History of the American Avant-Garde Cinema* (New York: American Federation of the Arts, 1976). P. Adams Sitney has written extensively about this period and his work includes two edited volumes, *The Avant-Garde Film* (New York: New York University Press, 1978), and *Film Culture Reader* (New York: Praeger, 1970), and two thoughtful surveys in *The Essential Cinema* (New York: New York University Press, 1975), and *Visionary Cinema* (New York: Oxford University Press, 1979). See also Gregory Brattuck (ed.), *The New American Cinema* (New York: Dutton, 1967), David Curtis, *Experimental Cinema* (New York: Universe, 1971), Sheldon Renan, *An Introduction to the American Underground Film* (New York: Dutton, 1967), and Malcolm LeGrice, *Abstract Film and Beyond* (Cambridge: MIT Press, 1977).

Jonas Mekas has written *Movie Journal* (New York: Collier Books, 1972) and been interviewed for *October*, Number 29 (Summer, 1984) by Scott McDonald.

Kenneth Anger is treated by Noel Carroll, "Identity and Difference: From Ritual Symbolism to Condensation in *Inauguration of the Pleasure Dome,*" *Millennium Film Journal*, Number 6 (Spring, 1980).

Robert Breer is treated in a special issue of *Film Culture*, Number 27 in 1963.

Hollis Frampton wrote extensively. See, for example, "Mind Over Matter," *October*, Number 6 (Fall 1978). For background see a special issue of *October*, Number 32 (Spring, 1985), and Bruce Jenkins and Susan Krane, *Hollis Frampton* (Cambridge: MIT Press, 1984).

Ernie Gehr is treated by a number of articles in *Film Culture*, Number 70/71, from 1983.

Michael Snow is treated in Peter Lehman, "Michael Snow: The Nature of the Material," *Wide Angle*, Volume 7, Numbers 1/2 (1985), Annette Michelson, "About Snow," *October*, Number 8 (Spring, 1979), and William Wees, "Prophecy, Memory and the Zoom: Michael Snow's 'Wavelength' Reviewed," *Cine-Tracts*, Volume 4, Numbers 2/3 (1981).

Andy Warhol's filmmaking is covered in Stephen Koch, *Stargazer: Andy Warhol's World and His Films* (New York: Praeger, 1973).

Bruce Baillie has a number of his writings and articles about his films collected in *Film Culture*, Numbers 67/68/69 (1979). See also Lucy Fischer, "Castro Street: The Sensibility of Style," *Film Quarterly*, Volume 29, Number 3 (1976).

Stan Brakhage is covered in a special issue of *Artforum*, Volume 11, Number 5 (January, 1973), Robert A. Haller (ed.), *Brakhage Scrapbook* (New Platz, NY: Treacle, 1981) and his own *The Brakhage Lectures* (Chicago: Good Lion Press, 1972). See also Marjorie Keller, *The Untutored Eye* (East Brunswick, NJ: Fairleigh Dickinson University Press, 1986) and William C. Wees, "Words and Images in Stan Brakhage's *23rd Psalm Branch,*" *Cinema Journal*, Volume 27, Number 2 (Winter, 1988).

• chapter 12 •
the art-cinema alternative

For more on the changes in overall filmmaking and exhibition in Europe in the 1950s and 1960s and the rise of the art film movement see Thomas Guback, *The International Film Industry* (Bloomington: Indiana University Press, 1969) for the basic economics. David Bordwell in his *Narration in the Fiction Film* (Madison: University of Wisconsin Press, 1985) lays out the concept of the art film. See also Steve Neale, "Art Cinema as Institution," *Screen*, Volume 22, Number 1 (1981).

For more on the economics, theory and cultural background of the French New Wave see Steve Lipkin, "The New Wave and the Post-War Film Economy," in Bruce A. Austin (ed.), *Current Research in Film*, Volume 2 (Norwood, NJ: Ablex, 1986). On the French New Wave see James Monaco, *The New Wave* (New York: Oxford University Press, 1976), Michel Marie, "The Art of the Film in France Since the 'New Wave'," *Wide Angle*, Volume 4, Number 4 (1981), Roy Armes, *The French Cinema Since 1946*, two volumes (Cranbury, NJ: Barnes, 1970) and Peter Graham (ed.), *The New Wave* (Garden City, New York: Doubleday, 1968). For developments in film theory of the time see J. Dudley Andrew, *Andre Bazin* (New York: Oxford University Press, 1978) and Louis Giannetti, *Godard and Others* (London: Tantivy, 1972). For a study of an influential force in the French New Wave see C. G. Crisp, *Eric Rohmer* (Bloomington: Indiana University Press, 1988). The end of the French New Wave is usually dated with the political events of May 1968 which are covered in Sylvia Harvey, *May '68 and Film Culture* (London: BFI, 1978).

Claude Chabrol is treated in Robin Wood and Michael Walker, *Claude Chabrol* (Praeger, 1970).

Alain Resnais is examined in Roy Armes, *The Cinema of Alain Resnais* (New York: Barnes, 1968), John Francis Kreidl, *Alain Resnais* (Boston: Twayne, 1979), James Monaco, *Alain Resnais* (New York: Oxford University Press, 1978), and John Ward, *Alain Resnais, or The Theme of Time* (Garden City, NY: Doubleday, 1968).

François Truffaut is the subject of Don Allen, *Truffaut* (New York: Viking, 1974), Leo Braudy (ed.), *Focus on Shoot the Piano Player* (Englewood Cliffs, NJ: Prentice-Hall, 1972), C. G. Crisp, *François Truffaut* (New York: Praeger, 1972), Annette Insdorf, *François Truffaut* (New York: Morrow, 1979), and Graham Petrie, *The Cinema of François Truffaut* (New York: Barnes, 1970).

Jean-Luc Godard is probably the most written about of filmmakers of the past thirty years. The basic writings are covered in Julia Lesage, *Jean-Luc Godard* (Boston: G. K. Hall, 1979). Then try Royal S. Brown (ed.), *Focus on Godard* (Englewood Cliffs, NJ: Prentice-Hall, 1972), a special issue of *Camera Obscura*, Numbers 8-9-10 (Fall, 1982), Jean-Luc Godard, *Godard on Godard* (New York:

Viking, 1972), Toby Mussman (ed.), *Jean-Luc Godard* (New York: Dutton, 1968), Ian Cameron, *The Films of Jean-Luc Godard* (New York: Praeger, 1969), Richard Roud, *Jean-Luc Godard* (Garden City, NY: Doubleday, 1968), and Colin MacCabe, *Godard* (Bloomington: Indiana University Press, 1981).

Ingmar Bergman is also written about in much detail. A select bibliography includes Frank Gado, *The Passion of Ingmar Bergman* (Durham: Duke University Press, 1986), Maria Bergom-Larrson, *Swedish Film* (Cranbury, NJ: Barnes, 1979), Stig Bjorkman, Torsten Manns, and Jonas Sima, *Bergman on Bergman* (New York: Simon and Schuster, 1973), Peter Cowie, *Ingmar Bergman* (New York: Scribners, 1982), Robin Wood, *Ingmar Bergman* (New York: Praeger, 1969), Jorn Donner, *The Personal Vision of Ingmar Bergman* (Bloomington: Indiana University Press, 1964), Stuart Kaminsky and Joseph F. Hill (eds.), *Ingmar Bergman* (New York: Oxford University Press, 1975), Vlada Petric (ed.), *Film and Dreams* (Pleasantville, New York: Redgrave, 1981), and John Simon, *Ingmar Bergman Directs* (New York: Harcourt Brace, 1972). Brigitta Steene has written *Focus on The Seventh Seal* (Englewood Cliffs, NJ: Prentice-Hall, 1972), *Ingmar Bergman* (Boston: Twayne, 1978), and *Ingmar Bergman* (Boston: G. K. Hall, 1982). The director's autobiography is *The Magic Lantern* (New York: Viking, 1988).

Luis Buñuel is closely examined in Freddy Buache, *The Cinema of Luis Buñuel* (Cranbury, NJ: Barnes, 1973), Francisco Aranda, *Luis Buñuel* (New York: DaCapo, 1976), Ado Kyrou, *Luis Buñuel* (New York: Simon & Schuster, 1963), and Joan Mellen (ed.), *Luis Buñuel* (New York: Oxford University Press, 1978). The director's autobiography is *My Last Sigh* (New York: Knopf, 1983).

Federico Fellini is dealt with in Hollis Alpert, *Fellini* (New York: Atheneum, 1986), Liliana Betti, *Fellini* (Boston: Little Brown, 1979), Peter Bondanella (ed.), *Federico Fellini* (New York: Oxford University Press, 1978) and Edward Murray, *Fellini the Artist* (New York: Ungar, 1976). For Fellini's own thoughts see *Fellini on Fellini* (New York: Delacourte, 1976).

Jacques Tati is the subject of Brent Maddock, *The Films of Jacques Tati* (Metuchen, NJ: Scarecrow, 1977), Lucy Fischer, *Jacques Tati* (Boston: G. K. Hall, 1983) and Kristin Thompson, *Breaking the Glass Armor* (Princeton: Princeton University Press, 1988).

Robert Bresson is examined in Lindley Hanlon, *Fragments* (Cranbury, NJ: Fairleigh Dickinson University Press, 1986), Paul Schrader, *Transcendental Style in Film* (Berkeley: University of California Press, 1972), Ian Cameron, *The Films of Robert Bresson* (New York: Praeger, 1970) and Jane Sloan, *Robert Bresson* (Boston: G. K. Hall, 1983). See the director's own views in *Notes on Cinematography* (New York: Urizen, 1977).

Michelangelo Antonioni is the subject of Roy Huss, *Focus on Blow-up* (Englewood Cliffs, NJ: Prentice-Hall, 1971), Ian Cameron and Robin Wood, *Antonioni* (New York: Praeger, 1968), and Seymour Chapman, *Antonioni* (Berkeley: University of California Press, 1985). For the director's own words see his *That Bowling Alley on the Tibor* (New York: Oxford University Press, 1986).

Pier Paolo Pasolini is covered in Stephen Snyder, *Pier Paolo Pasolini* (Boston: Twayne, 1980), Oswald Stack (ed.), *Pasolini on Pasolini* (Bloomington: Indiana University Press, 1969), Paul Willemen, *Pier Paolo Pasolini* (London: BFI, 1977), and Louise K. Barnett (ed.), *Heretical Empiricism* (Bloomington: Indiana University Press, 1988).

The Angry Young Men from the United Kingdom are treated in Alexander Walker, *Hollywood U. K.* (New York: Stein & Day, 1974) and Roy Armes, *A Critical History of the British Film* (New York: Oxford University Press, 1978). Cultural background can be found in John Hill, *Sex, Class, and Realism* (London: BFI, 1987).

● **chapter 13** ●
**searching for
alternative styles**

To best understand the dynamics of world film power see Thomas Guback, *The International Film Industry* (Bloomington: Indiana University Press, 1969) and his update "Film as International Business," *Journal of Communication*, Volume 24, Number 1 (Winter, 1974). For Hollywood's viewpoint see Jack Valenti, "The Foreign Service of the Motion Picture Association of America," *The Journal of the Producers Guild of America*, Volume 10, Number 1 (March, 1968). For some background on the USSR see Daniel J. Goulding (ed.), *Post New Wave Cinema in the Soviet Union and Eastern Europe* (Bloomington: Indiana University Press, 1989) and Iu Vronstov, *The Phenomenon of the Soviet Cinema* (Moscow: Progress Publishers, 1980).

On the Eastern European cinema in general see Mira Liehm and Antonin J. Liehm, *The Most Important Art* (Berkeley: University of California Press, 1977), Michael Jon Stoil, *Cinema Beyond the Danube* (Metuchen, NJ: Scarecrow, 1974), and David W. Paul (ed.), *Politics, Art, and Commitment in Eastern European Cinema* (New York: St. Martin's, 1983).

The Polish film industry and culture is treated in Stanislaw Kurzewski, *Contemporary Polish Cinema* (London: Wischhusen, 1980), Boleslaw Michalek and Frank Turaj, *The Modern Cinema of Poland* (Bloomington: Indiana University Press, 1988), and Daniel J. Goulding (ed.), *Post New Wave Cinema in the Soviet Union and Eastern Europe* (Bloomington: Indiana University Press, 1989).

Andrzej Wajda is covered by Boleslaw Michalek, *The Cinema of Andrzej Wajda* (Cranbury, NJ: Barnes, 1973) and the director's own *Double Vision* (London: Faber and Faber, 1989).

The Czechoslovakian film industry and culture is treated in Antonin J. Liehm, *Closely Watched Films* (White Plains, NY: International Arts & Sciences Press, 1974), Peter Hames, *The Czechoslovak New Wave* (Berkeley: University of California Press, 1985), Josef Skvorecky, *All the Bright Young Men and Women* (Toronto: Martin, 1971), and Daniel J. Goulding (ed.), *Post New Wave Cinema in the Soviet Union and Eastern Europe* (Bloomington: Indiana University Press, 1989).

Miloš Forman is dealt with in Thomas J. Slater, *Miloš Forman* (Westport, CT: Greenwood, 1987).

Véra Chytilová is examined in Peter Hames, "The Return of Véra Chytilová," *Sight and Sound*, Volume 48 (Summer, 1979) and Harriet Polt, "A Film Should Be a Little Flashlight: An Interview with Véra Chytilová," *Take One* (November, 1978).

The Hungarian film industry and culture is treated in Istvan Nemeskurty, *Word and Image* (New York: Ungar, 1982), Graham Petrie, *History Must Answer to Man* (London: Tantivy, 1979), and Daniel J. Goulding (ed.), *Post New Wave Cinema in the Soviet Union and Eastern Europe* (Bloomington: Indiana University Press, 1989).

Miklós Jancsó is examined in Roy Armes, *The Ambiguous Image* (Bloomington: Indiana University Press, 1976), Lorant Czigany, "Jancsó Country," *Film Quarterly*, Volume 26, Number 1 (Fall, 1972).

The Yugoslavian film industry and culture are treated in Gertrude Joch Robinson, *Tito's Maverick Media* (Urbana: University of Illinois Press, 1977), Daniel J. Goulding, *Liberated Cinema* (Bloomington: Indiana University Press, 1985), and Michael J. Stoil, *Balkan Cinema* (Ann Arbor: UMI Press, 1982).

The Indian film industry is covered in Erik Barnouw and S. Krishnaswamy, *Indian Film* (New York: Oxford University Press, 1980) and Mira Binford, "The New Cinema of India," *Quarterly Review of Film Studies*, Volume 8, Number 4 (Fall, 1983).

Satyajit Ray is the subject of Marie Seton, *Portrait of a Director* (Bloomington: Indiana University Press, 1971), Robin Wood, *The Apu Trilogy* (New York: Praeger, 1971) and Ben Nyce, *Satyajit Ray* (New York: Praeger, 1988). See the director's own, *The Unicorn Experience* (New York: Dutton, 1987).

Latin America cinema in general is examined in Julianne Burton, *Cinema and Social Change in Latin America* (Austin: University of Texas Press, 1987) and Jorge A. Schnitman, *Film Industries in Latin America* (Norwood, NJ: Ablex, 1984).

The Brazilian film industry and culture are treated in Pat Aufderheide, "Will Success Spoil Brazilian Film?," *American Film*, Volume 8, Number 5 (March, 1983), Randal Johnson, *Cinema Nôvo* (Austin: University of Texas Press, 1984), Randal Johnson and Robert Stam (eds.), *Brazilian Cinema* (East Brunswick, NJ: Fairleigh Dickinson University Press, 1982), and Randal Johnson, *The Film Industry in Brazil* (Pittsburgh, PA: University of Pittsburgh Press, 1987).

Argentina is covered in Tim Barnard, *Argentine Cinema* (Toronto: Nightwood Editions, 1986).

The recent history of the Cuban film industry and culture can be found in Michael Chanan, *The Cuban Image* (Bloomington: Indiana University Press, 1986).

Background on the New German cinema can conveniently be found in Timothy Corrigan, *New German Film* (Austin: University of Texas Press, 1983), John Sanford, *The New German Cinema* (New York: DaCapo, 1982), a special issue of *New German Critique*, Numbers 24–25 (Fall/Winter, 1981–1982), a special issue of *Wide Angle*, Volume 3, Number 4 (1980), a special issue of *Quarterly Review of Film Studies*, Volume 5, Number 2 (Spring, 1980), James C. Franklin, *New German Cinema* (Boston: G. K. Hall, 1983), Klaus Phillips (ed.), *New German Filmmakers* (New York: Ungar, 1984), and Eric Rentschuler (ed.), *German Film and Literature* (New York: Ungar, 1984).

Alexander Kluge is dealt with in a special issue of *October*, Number 46 (Fall, 1988).

Rainer Werner Fassbinder is examined in Ronald Hayman, *Fassbinder* (New York: Simon & Schuster, 1984), Tony Ryans, *Fassbinder* (London: BFI, 1976), Howard Feinstein, "BDR 1-2-3: Fassbinder's Postwar Trilogy and the Spectacle," *Cinema Journal*, Volume 23, Number 1 (Fall, 1983), and Robert Katz, *Love Is Colder than Death* (New York: Random House, 1987).

Werner Herzog wrote *Of Walking* (New York: Tanam, 1981) and is the subject of Timothy Corrigan, *The Films of Werner Herzog* (New York: Methuen, 1987).

Wim Wenders is dealt with by Kathe Geist, *The Cinema of Wim Wenders* (Ann Arbor: UMI Press, 1988).

The history of the Australian cinema, in particular its rebirth in recent years, can be found in Andrew Pike, *Australian Film* (New York: Oxford University Press, 1980), David Stratton, *The New Wave* (New York: Ungar, 1980), Eric Reade, *History and Heartburn* (East Brunswick, NJ: Fairleigh Dickinson University Press, 1981), Glen Lewis, *Australian Movies and the American Dream* (New York: Praeger, 1987), and Brian McFarland, *Australian Cinema* (New York: Columbia University Press, 1988).

• chapter 14 •
an epilogue:
contemporary film history

A new era for watching movies began in the mid-1970s and so what to recommend as reading is not so much history as the first draft of history, to be revised.

There have been many changes in Hollywood, and for more on that see James Monaco, *American Film Now* (New York: Oxford University Press,

1979) and Michael Pye and Lynda Myles, *The Movie Brats* (New York: Holt, Rinehart and Winston, 1979).

For more on the new television technologies as delivery systems for movies see Roy Armes, *On Video* (New York: Routledge & Kegan Paul, 1988), James Lardner, *Fast Forward* (New York: Norton, 1987), George Mair, *Inside HBO* (New York: Dodd Mead, 1988), Douglas Gomery, "The Economics of the New Television Technologies," in Douglas V. Shaw, William S. Hendon and Virginia Lee Owen (eds.), *Cultural Economics 88* (Akron: Association for Cultural Economics, 1989) and Douglas Gomery, "Hollywood's Hold on the New Television Technologies," *Screen*, Volume 29, Number 2 (Spring, 1988).

For more on contemporary Hollywood films see Douglas Gomery, "Hollywood's Movie Business," in Michael C. Emery and Ted C. Smythe (eds.), *Readings in Mass Communication*, Seventh Edition (Dubuque, Iowa: Wm. C. Brown, 1989), Michael Ryan and Douglas Kellner, *Camera Politica* (Bloomington: Indiana University Press, 1988), and Albert Auster and Leonard Quart, *How the War Was Remembered* (New York: Praeger, 1988). Stephen Farber and Marc Green, *Outrageous Conduct* (New York: Morrow, 1988) provide a case study of Hollywood filmmaking practices, both good and bad. For a case study of the Disney company see John Taylor, *Storming the Magic Kingdom* (New York: Knopf, 1987). A case study of Rupert Murdoch's takeover of Twentieth Century–Fox is the subject of Douglas Gomery, "Vertical Integration, Horizontal Regulation—The Growth of Rupert Murdoch's Media Empire," *Screen*, Volume 28, Number 4 (May–August, 1986).

For more on sequels see Noel Carroll, "Back to Basics," in Philip S. Cook, Douglas Gomery, and Lawrence W. Lichty (eds.), *American Media* (Washington, D.C.: The Wilson Center Press, 1989). For more on the rise of contemporary science fiction films see Vivian Sobchack, *Screening Space* (New York: Ungar, 1985). For more on recent horror films see Noel Carroll's *The Philosophy of Horror* (New York: Routledge & Kegan Paul, 1989).

George Lucas is treated in Thomas G. Smith, *Industrial Light and Magic* (New York: Del Rey, 1986) and Dale Pollock, *Skywalking* (New York: Ballantine, 1983).

Steven Spielberg is covered in Robert Philip Kolker, *A Cinema of Loneliness*, rev. ed. (New York: Oxford University Press, 1988) and Donald R. Mott and Cheryl McAllister Saunders, *Steven Spielberg* (Boston: Twayne, 1986).

Woody Allen is treated in Douglas Brode, *Woody Allen* (Secaucus, NJ: Citadel, 1985) and Robert Benayoun, *The Films of Woody Allen* (New York: Harmony House, 1986).

Martin Scorsese is the subject of Mary Kelly (ed.), *Martin Scorsese* (Pleasantville, New York: Redgrave, 1980) and Robert Philip Kolker, *The Cinema of Loneliness* (New York: Oxford University Press, 1980). See the director's own *Scorsese on Scorsese* (London: Faber and Faber, 1989).

Few Hollywood directors have written serious books of film criticism; for a rare example see Paul Schrader, *Transcendental Style in Film* (Berkeley: University of California Press, 1972).

For a useful survey of contemporary world cinema see William Luhr's *World Cinema Since 1945* (New York: Ungar, 1987).

A film industry emerged on mainland China during the 1980s. See Chris Berry (ed.), *Perspectives on Chinese Cinema* (Ithaca: Cornell University Press, 1985), Paul Clark, *Chinese Cinema* (Cambridge: Cambridge University Press, 1987), and George Stephen Semsell (ed.), *Chinese Film* (New York: Praeger, 1987).

For more on filmmaking in the United Kingdom during the late 1970s and 1980s see Martyn Auty and Nick Roddick, *British Film Now* (London: BFI, 1985).

Lina Wertmüller is covered in Gina Blumenfeld, "The Next to Last Word on Lina Wertmüller," *Cineaste*, Volume 7, Number 2 (1976) and Diane Jacobs, "Lina Wertmüller: The Italian Aristophenes," *Film Comment*, Volume 12, Number 2 (March-April, 1976). See an interview in "You Cannot Make the Revolution on Film," *Cineaste*, Volume 7, Number 2 (1976).

Alain Tanner is covered in Jim Leach, *A Possible Cinema* (Metuchen, NJ: Scarecrow, 1984).

On recent Japanese film see David Dresser, *Eros Plus Massacre* (Bloomington: Indiana University Press, 1988).

Nagisa Oshima is treated in Maureen Turim and John Mowitt, "Thirty Seconds Over ... Oshima's The War of Tokyo or the Young Man Who Left His Will on Film," *Wide Angle*, Volume 1, Number 4 (1977) and Stephen Heath, "The Question of Oshima," *Wide Angle*, Volume 2, Number 1 (1977).

For more on African cinema and other parts of the Third World see John D. H. Downing, *Film and Politics in the Third World* (New York: Praeger, 1987), Roy Armes, *Third World Filmmaking and the West* (Berkeley: University of California Press, 1987), Hala Salmane, *Algerian Cinema* (London: BFI, 1977), Françoise Pfaff's *The Cinema of Ousmane Sembere* (Westport, CT: Greenwood, 1984) and her bibliography *Twenty-Five African Filmmakers* (Westport, CT: Greenwood, 1988), and Keyan Tomaselli, *Race and Class in South African Film* (New York: Smyrna, 1988).

For topics not covered above see Hans Jurgen Wulff, *Bibliography of Film Bibliographies* (New York: K. G. Saur, 1987).

To keep up with history in the making, by the categories used in this book, consult the following journals and magazines.

As historians do further research, they publish their findings in books and journals. The leading journals include *Cinema Journal*, the official publication of the Society for Cinema Studies, *Journal of Film and Video*, the official publication of the University Film Association, *Quarterly Review of Film Studies, Screen, Wide Angle, Historical Journal of Film, Radio, and Television, Journal of Popular Film and Television, The Velvet Light Trap, Film and History, Persistence of Vision,* and *Millennium Film Journal*. These and many other articles are indexed on a regular basis in *Film Literature Index*, published from State University of New York at Albany, since 1973. For help see Anna Brady, Richard Wall and Carolyn Newitt Weiner, *Union List of Film Periodicals* (Westport, CT: Greenwood, 1984).

For reviews of film books see *Communication Booknotes* summary every December and the listings every year in Peter Cowie's annual *International Film Guide* series.

To follow the industry around the world read weekly *Variety*.

To follow changes in film technology read *SMPTE Journal* and *American Cinematographer*.

To study the social impact of film from a leftist point of view read *Jump Cut* and *Cineaste*.

To follow changes in film aesthetics read journals of theory and criticism such as *Screen* and *Cinema Journal*. For reviews of current films see *The New York Times, The Los Angeles Times, Sight and Sound* and the *Village Voice*.

No bibliography can be complete; the above listing offers no pretensions in that direction. Thus for further bibliography see Jack C. Ellis, Charles Derry and Sharon Kern, *The Film Book Bibliography, 1940–1975* (Metuchen, NJ: Scarecrow, 1979) and their update, *Film Book Bibliography, 1975–1985* (Metuchen, NJ: Scarecrow, 1988), George Rehrauer, *The Macmillan Film Bibliography* (New York: Macmillan, 1982) for books.

appendix two

• •

filmography

Below, by the divisions used in *Movie History: A Survey*, I list key films and suggest the best sources in English. Titles are in English, except when the foreign title predominates in the U.S.

To locate films not listed here, one can consult the four volumes of *The International Dictionary of Films and Filmmakers*, published by St. James Press of Chicago (dates follow): Volume I—Films (1984), Volume II—Directors/Filmmakers (1984), Volume III—Actors and Actresses (1986), and Volume IV—Writers and Production Artists (1987). Updated revisions are promised for the early 1990s.

The British publication *Film Dope* has compiled filmographies for more than a thousand film artists from Ken Adam and James Agee to Rudolph Mate and Elaine May. Continuing through the alphabet, forthcoming issues promise filmographies of Georges Méliès to Sven Nykvist, with the publisher promising to take the filmographies to *Z*.

The American Film Institute *Catalog* series assembles credits for U.S. productions for the 1910s, 1920s, 1960s, and, next in line, 1930s.

There are any number of fine reference books in the field of film studies, all usually found in any good public or university library. One handy book with which to begin continues to be Ephraim Katz, *The Film Encyclopedia* (New York: Crowell, 1979).

To see films in their original 35mm gauge one must generally go to an archive; those in the United States that hold the bulk of Hollywood's films include the following:

- Department of Film, George Eastman House, Rochester, New York 14607

- The Library of Congress, Motion Picture Division, Washington, DC 20540

- Department of Film, Museum of Modern Art, 11 West 53rd Street, New York, New York 10019

- UCLA Film and Television Archive, University of California at Los Angeles, Los Angeles, California 90024

- The Wisconsin Center for Film and Theatre Research, State Historical Society, Madison, Wisconsin 53706

- U.S. National Archives, 8th and Pennsylvania Avenue, Washington, DC 20408

There are any number of smaller collections. Write Center for Film and Video Preservation, The American Film Institute, 2021 North Western Avenue, Los Angeles, California 90027 for more information or consult Anthony Slide, Patricia King Hanson and Stephen L. Hanson (comp.), *Sourcebook for the Performing Arts* (New York: Greenwood Press, 1988) and Leonard Maltin (ed.), *The Whole Film Sourcebook* (New York: New American Library, 1983).

One can see films on what some have called the inferior gauges, principally 16mm. This is most often the way films are shown to students in large classes. Rental companies include

- Budget Films, 4590 Santa Monica Boulevard, Los Angeles, California 90029

- Canyon Cinema Cooperative, 2325 Third Street, San Francisco, California 94107

- Clem Williams Films, 2240 Nobletown Road, Pittsburgh, Pennsylvania 15205

- Films Incorporated, 440 Park Avenue South, New York, New York 10016

- Images Film Archive, 300 Philips Park Road, Mamaroneck, New York 10543

- The Killiam Collection, 6 East 39th Street, New York, New York 10016

- Kino International, 250 West 57th Street, New York, New York 10019

- Kit Parker Films, 1245 Tenth Street, Monterey, California 93940

- Museum of Modern Art, Department of Film, 11 West 53rd Street, New York, New York 10019

- Swank Motion Pictures, 201 South Jefferson Avenue, St. Louis, Missouri 63166

Movies are now widely available on home video tape. The preferred format has become ½ inch tape in Beta or VHS, with the latter dominating the U.S. field. There are thousands upon thousands of films now out on tape, all easily ordered from one's local video store.

For obscure U.S. titles and foreign films on tape, try:

- Home Video festival, P. O. Box 2032, Scranton, Pennsylvania 18501

- Blackhawk Film and Video, Box 3990, 1235 West 5th Street, Davenport, Iowa 52808

- Video Yesterday, Box C, Sandy Hook, Connecticut 06482

- Facets Multimedia, 1517 West Fullerton Avenue, Chicago, Illinois 60614

- For current releases as they appear check the columns in *Video Review* magazine

To check if a film is on tape, see the latest edition of Leonard Maltin's invaluable *TV Movies* published in updated versions each year by New American Library. It also is the best source for finding the running time, director, and other basic information about nearly every Hollywood title one will come in contact with.

While VHS dominates in the U.S., Beta still delivers a superior picture. Europeans use the PAL standard, which cannot run on VHS just as VHS cannot run on Beta, and so on. The future promises more changes. An 8mm video tape is already on the market, and high definition television promises yet another standard, with a superior picture.

With laser disc, the image is sharper, the sound is better, and one can interact with the images and sounds, going instantly to any spot on the film. They last seemingly forever and are now increasingly used in education. Due to the high cost of the machines, the lack of ability to record and playback, and the limited amount of films available, the laser disc has not had nearly the acceptance of home video tape machines. But with prices coming down, many situations, particularly in university audiovisual centers or libraries, should keep this option in mind. For more information consult Image Entertainment, 6311 Romaine Street, Hollywood, California 90038 or other companies which advertise in such publications as *Video Review*.

In the end even the best television image is a compromise. The present U.S. standard does a fairly good job (but not a perfect one) of enveloping films made on a 4 × 3 aspect ratio, but a television image cannot capture a wide-screen image. So, before it is shown on television, a wide-screen film is panned and scanned so the center of the action, as determined by those who do the panning and scanning, is in the frames you see. A "new" film is created without the consultation of the filmmakers. Beware!

Two other problems should be noted for the home video age. The first and most publicized is colorization. Here a black and white film is recorded onto videotape with all the problems just described. Then using a computer to code certain colors, the film is turned into a color version. Needless to say, in nearly all cases the original filmmakers were never consulted.

The other problem is the movie made for television. For example, *Brian's Song* is often shown in 16mm, but this is as bad a showing a 35mm film on television. One should watch films made for television *on television*.

• chapter 1 •
the invention and innovation of the movies

Edwin S. Porter made *The America's Cup Race* (1899), *Terrible Teddy the Grizzly King* (1901), *The Finish of Bridget McKeen* (1901), *Appointment by Telephone* (1902), *Jack and the Beanstalk* (1902), *How They Do Things in the Bowery* (1902), *The Life of an American Fireman* (1903), *Uncle Tom's Cabin* (1903), *A Romance of the Rails* (1903), *The*

Great Train Robbery (1903), *Rescued from an Eagle's Nest* (1907), and *Tess of the Storm Country* (1914).

J. Stuart Blackton and **Albert E. Smith** made for their Vitagraph Company in the early days such films as *The Battle of Manila Bay* (1898), *Tearing Down the Spanish Flag* (1898), *Jeffries Skipping Rope* (1899), *Boat Race on the Harlem River* (1900), *Panorama of Wreckage on Water Front, Galveston* (1900), *Raffles the Amateur Cracksman* (1905), *Vanderbilt Auto Race* (1905), and *Wrecked Mansions Along Van Ness Avenue* (1906). For an extensive listing see Anthony Slide, *The Big V*, revised edition (Metuchen, NJ: Scarecrow Press, 1987).

Georges Méliès produced *Playing Cards* (1896), *The Czar's Excursion to Versailles* (1896), *Battleship Maine* (1898), *The Man of Heads* (1898), *William Tell* (1898), *Christ Walking on Water* (1899), *The Dreyfus Affair* (1899), *Cinderella* (1899), *The Pillar of Fire* (1899), *Joan of Arc* (1900), *The Man with the Rubber Head* (1901), *Bluebeard* (1901), *Gulliver's Travels* (1902), *The Adventures of Robinson Crusoe* (1902), *A Trip to the Moon* (1902), *The Damnation of Faust* (1904), *The Barber of Seville* (1904), *Paris to Monte Carlo* (1905), *20,000 Leagues Under the Sea* (1907), *The Hallucinations of Baron Münchhausen* (1911), and *The Conquest of the Pole* (1912). For a complete listing see Paul Hammond, *Marvelous Méliès* (New York: St. Martin's, 1975).

• chapter 2 •
the triumph of hollywood

George Kleine produced *Albany, N. Y. Fire Department* (1901), *Mt. Pelee in Eruption and Destruction of St. Pierre* (1902), *Chicago–Michigan Football Game* (1903), *Atlantic City Floral Parade* (1904), *President Roosevelt's Inauguration* (1905), and *Panama Canal* (1907). He released such titles as *Quo Vadis?* (1913), *The Betrothed* (1913), *The Last Days of Pompeii* (1913), and *Anthony and Cleopatra* (1913). For more information see Rita Horwitz and Harriet Harrison, *The George Kleine Collection* (Washington: Library of Congress, 1980).

Mary Pickford starred in *Her First Biscuits* (1909), *In the Bishop's Carriage* (1913), *Tess of the Storm Country* (1914), *A Girl of Yesterday* (1915), *The Pride of the Clan* (1917), *The Poor Little Rich Girl* (1917), *Little American* (1917), *Rebecca of Sunnybrook Farm* (1917), *Stella Maris* (1918), *Daddy Long Legs* (1919), *Pollyanna* (1920), *Little Lord Fauntleroy* (1921), *Rosita* (1923), *Dorothy Vernon of Haddon Hall* (1924), *Sparrows* (1926), *Kiki* (1931), and *Secrets* (1933). For more information see Gary Carey, *Doug & Mary* (New York: Dutton, 1977).

United Artists, the company of the stars, early on released *His Majesty, the American* (1919, with Douglas Fairbanks), *Broken Blossoms* (1919, directed by D. W. Griffith), *When the Clouds Roll By* (1919, starring Douglas Fairbanks), *Pollyanna* (1920, featuring Mary Pickford), *The Mollycoddle* (1920, starring Douglas Fairbanks), *Suds* (1920, starring Mary Pickford), *The Mark of Zorro* (1920, starring Douglas Fairbanks), *Little Lord Fauntleroy* (1921, starring Mary Pickford), *Robin Hood* (1922, starring Douglas Fairbanks), *A Woman of Paris* (1923, directed by Charlie Chaplin), and *The Gold Rush* (1925, directed by and starring Charlie Chaplin). For a complete filmography for United Artists until 1950 see Tino Balio, *United Artists* (Madison: University of Wisconsin Press, 1976).

Thomas Ince as a director made *Little Nell's Tobacco* (1910), *War on the Plains* (1912), *For the Freedom of Cuba* (1912), *Custer's Last Raid* (1912), *The Battle of Gettysburg* (1913), and *Civilization* (1916, with Raymond West and Reginald Baker). He produced *The Coward* (1915), *Hell's Hinges* (1916), *The Aryan* (1916), *Flying Colors* (1917), and *Anna Christie* (1923).

Rudolph Valentino became a star based on *The Four Horsemen of the Apocalypse* (1921), *The Sheik* (1921), *Blood and Sand* (1922), *Cobra* (1925), *The Eagle* (1925), and *The Son of the Sheik* (1926). See Vincenti Tajiri, *Valentino* (New York: Bantam, 1977) for a complete filmography.

• chapter 3 •
hollywood establishes
the classic narrative style

Douglas Fairbanks reached the crest of his popularity with *His Picture in the Papers* (1916), *Flirting with Fate* (1916), *Reaching for the Moon* (1917), *Wild and Woolly* (1917), *When the Clouds Roll By* (1919), *The Mark of Zorro* (1920), *The Mollycoddle* (1920), *The Three Musketeers* (1921), *Robin Hood* (1922), and *The Thief of Bagdad* (1924). For a complete listing see Gary Carey, *Doug & Mary* (New York: Dutton, 1977).

D. W. Griffith directed *The Adventures of Dollie* (1908), *The Call of the Wild* (1908), *The Drive for Life* (1909), *A Corner in Wheat* (1909), *The Usurer* (1910), *Gold Is Not All* (1910), *The Girl and Her Trust* (1912), *One Is Business, the Other Crime* (1912), *The Musketeers of Pig Alley* (1912), *The Battle at Elderbush Gulch* (1914), *Judith of Bethulia* (1914), *Home Sweet Home* (1914), *The Avenging Conscience* (1914), *The Birth of a Nation* (1915), *Intolerance* (1916), *Hearts of the World* (1918), *True Heart Susie* (1919), *Broken Blossoms* (1919), *Way Down East* (1920), *Dream Street* (1921), *Orphans of the Storm* (1921), *America* (1924), *Isn't Life Wonderful?* (1924), *Sally of the Sawdust* (1925), *Abraham Lincoln* (1930), and *The Struggle* (1931). For a complete listing see Richard Schickel, *D. W. Griffith* (New York: Simon and Schuster, 1984).

Cecil B. deMille directed *The Squaw Man* (1914), *The Virginian* (1914), *The Girl of the Golden West*

(1915), *The Cheat* (1915), *Joan the Woman* (1917), *Old Wives for New* (1918), *We Can't Have Everything* (1918), *Male and Female* (1919), *Don't Change Your Husband* (1919), *Why Change Your Wife?* (1920), *Forbidden Fruit* (1921), *The Affairs of Anatol* (1921), *Saturday Night* (1922), *The King of Kings* (1927), *The Sign of the Cross* (1932), *Union Pacific* (1939), *North West Mounted Police* (1940), *The Story of Dr. Wassell* (1944), *Unconquered* (1947), *The Greatest Show on Earth* (1952), and *The Ten Commandments* (1956). For a complete listing see Gene Ringgold and DeWitt Bodeen, *The Films of Cecil B. DeMille* (New York: Citadel, 1969).

John Ford made *Straight Shooting* (1917), *The Iron Horse* (1924), *Three Bad Men* (1926), *Four Sons* (1928), *Dr. Bull* (1933), *The Lost Patrol* (1934), *Judge Priest* (1934), *Steamboat 'Round the Bend* (1935), *The Informer* (1935), *The Prisoner of Shark Island* (1936), *Stagecoach* (1939), *Young Mr. Lincoln* (1939), *Drums Along the Mohawk* (1939), *The Grapes of Wrath* (1940), *How Green Was My Valley* (1941), *My Darling Clementine* (1946), *Fort Apache* (1948), *She Wore a Yellow Ribbon* (1949), *Wagonmaster* (1950), *The Quiet Man* (1952), *Mogambo* (1953), *The Searchers* (1956), *The Wings of Eagles* (1957), *Two Rode Together* (1961), *The Man Who Shot Liberty Valance* (1962), and *Cheyenne Autumn* (1964). For a complete listing see Peter Bogdanovich, *John Ford* (Berkeley: University of California Press, 1978).

James Cruze fashioned *Too Many Millions* (1918), *The Covered Wagon* (1923), *Ruggles of Red Gap* (1923), *Merton of the Movies* (1924), *The Pony Express* (1925), and *Old Ironsides* (1926).

King Vidor made his reputation with *The Big Parade* (1925), and *The Crowd* (1928). Before that he made *The Turn in the Road* (1919), *The Jack Knife Man* (1920), and *Peg O' My Heart* (1922). He later went on to direct *Street Scene* (1931), *Our Daily Bread* (1934), *Stella Dallas* (1937), *Duel in the Sun* (1946), *The Fountainhead* (1949), and

War and Peace (1956). For a complete listing see Raymond Durgnat and Scott Simmon, *King Vidor American* (Berkeley: University of California Press, 1988).

William Wellman directed *The Vagabond Trail* (1924), *The Circus Cowboy* (1924), *The Cat's Pajamas* (1926), *Wings* (1927), *Public Enemy* (1931), *Wild Boys of the Road* (1933), *A Star Is Born* (1937), *The Ox-Bow Incident* (1943), *The Story of GI Joe* (1945), *Battleground* (1949), *The High and the Mighty* (1954), and *Lafayette Escadrille* (1958). For a complete listing see Frank T. Thompson, *William A. Wellman* (Metuchen, NJ: Scarecrow, 1983).

Raoul Walsh directed *The Regeneration* (1915), *The Thief of Bagdad* (1924), *What Price Glory?* (1926), *Sadie Thompson* (1928), *The Cock-Eyed World* (1929), *In Old Arizona* (1929), *The Big Trail* (1930), *The Roaring Twenties* (1939), *They Drive By Night* (1940), *High Sierra* (1941), *Strawberry Blonde* (1941), *Gentleman Jim* (1942), *Cheyenne* (1947), *White Heat* (1949), and *Battle Cry* (1955). For a complete listing see Phil Hardy, *Raoul Walsh* (London: Screen, 1974).

Allan Dwan made *The Spirit of the Flag* (1913), *Robin Hood* (1922), *Manhandled* (1924), *Stage Struck* (1925), *East Side, West Side* (1927), *The Iron Mask* (1929), *Heidi* (1937), *Suez* (1938), *The Three Musketeers* (1939), *Sands of Iwo Jima* (1949), and *Most Dangerous Man Alive* (1961). For a complete filmography see Peter Bogdanovich, *Allan Dwan* (New York: Praeger, 1971).

Henry King directed *Who Pays?* (1915), *Tol'able David* (1921), *The White Sister* (1923), *Stella Dallas* (1925), *The Winning of Barbara Worth* (1926), *State Fair* (1933), *In Old Chicago* (1938), *Jesse James* (1939), *The Song of Bernadette* (1943), *Wilson* (1944), *The Gunfighter* (1950), *The Snows of Kilimanjaro* (1952), *Love Is a Many-Splendored Thing* (1955), and *Tender Is the Night* (1961). For a listing of his work see Clive Denton, Kingsley Canham and Tony Thomas, *The Hollywood Professionals*, Volume 2 (London: Tantivy, 1974).

Clarence Brown made *The Great Redeemer* (1920), *The Last of the Mohicans* (1920), *The Eagle* (1925), *Kiki* (1926), *Flesh and the Devil* (1927), *Anna Christie* (1930), *Inspiration* (1931), *Anna Karenina* (1935), *Idiot's Delight* (1939), *National Velvet* (1944), *The Yearling* (1946), and *Plymouth Adventure* (1952). For more information see Allen Estrin, *The Hollywood Professionals*, Volume 6 (South Brunswick: Barnes, 1980).

Frank Borzage directed *That Gal of Burke's* (1916), *Humoresque* (1920), *Secrets* (1924), *Seventh Heaven* (1927), *Street Angel* (1928), *They Had to See Paris* (1929), *A Farewell to Arms* (1932), *Man's Castle* (1933), *No Greater Glory* (1934), *Three Comrades* (1938), *The Mortal Storm* (1940), *Stage Door Canteen* (1943), *The Spanish Main* (1945), *Moonrise* (1949), and *The Big Fisherman* (1959). For more information see Frederick Lamaster, *Souls Made Great Through Love and Adversity* (Metuchen, NJ: Scarecrow, 1981).

Tod Browning directed *Jim Bludso* (1917), *The Unholy Three* (1925), *The Unknown* (1927), *London After Midnight* (1927), *The Big City* (1928), *The Iron Man* (1931), *Freaks* (1932), and *Miracles for Sale* (1939). For more information see Stuart Rosenthal and Judith M. Kass, *The Hollywood Professionals*, Volume 4 (London: Tantivy, 1975).

Charlie Chaplin made *Kid Auto Races at Venice* (1914), *Tillie's Punctured Romance* (1914), *The Tramp* (1915), *One A.M.* (1916), *Easy Street* (1917), *The Cure* (1917), *A Dog's Life* (1918), *Shoulder Arms* (1918), *Sunnyside* (1919), *The Kid* (1921), *A Woman of Paris* (1923), *The Gold Rush* (1925), *The Circus* (1928), *City Lights* (1931), *Modern Times* (1936), *The Great Dictator* (1940), *Monsieur Verdoux* (1947), *Limelight* (1952), and *A King in New York* (1957). For a complete listing see David Robinson, *Chaplin* (New York: McGraw-Hill, 1985).

Buster Keaton crafted shorts such as *Cops* (1922) and *The Balloonatic* (1923) and then these influ-

ential features: *The Three Ages* (1923), *Our Hospitality* (1923), *The Navigator* (1924), *Sherlock, Jr.* (1924), *Go West* (1925), *Seven Chances* (1925), *The General* (1927), *Steamboat Bill, Jr.* (1928), and *The Cameraman* (1928). For a complete listing see George Wead and George Ellis, *The Film Career of Buster Keaton* (Boston: Twayne, 1977).

Harold Lloyd made *Grandma's Boy* (1922), *Dr. Jack* (1922), *Safety Last* (1923), *The Freshman* (1925), and *The Kid Brother* (1927). This is a partial list; for a complete one see Adam Reilly, *Harold Lloyd* (New York: Collier, 1977).

Harry Langdon appeared in *Tramp, Tramp, Tramp* (1926), *The Strong Man* (1926), and *Long Pants* (1927). For more information see William Schelly, *Harry Langdon* (Metuchen: Scarecrow, 1982).

Ernst Lubitsch directed *Miss Soapsuds* (1914), *Blind Man's Bluff* (1915), *The Merry Jail* (1917), *Gypsy Blood* (1918), *Madame Dubarry* (1919), *The Doll* (1919), *The Flame* (1923), *Rosita* (1923), *The Marriage Circle* (1924), *Lady Windermere's Fan* (1925), *So This Is Paris* (1926), *The Student Prince* (1927), *The Love Parade* (1929), *Trouble in Paradise* (1932), *Design for Living* (1933), *The Merry Widow* (1934), *Angel* (1937), *Ninotchka* (1939), *The Shop Around the Corner* (1940), *To Be or Not to Be* (1942), and *Cluny Brown* (1946). For a complete listing see Robert Carringer and Barry Sabath, *Ernst Lubitsch* (Boston: G. K. Hall, 1978).

F. W. Murnau made *The Boy in Blue* (1919), *The Last Laugh* (1924), *Tartuffe* (1925), *Faust* (1926), *Sunrise* (1927), *Four Devils* (1928), and *Tabu* (1931, co-directed with Robert Flaherty). For a complete listing see Lotte Eisner, *Murnau* (Berkeley: University of California Press, 1973).

Paul Leni directed *Waxworks* (1924), *The Cat and the Canary* (1927), *The Chinese Parrot* (1927), *The Man Who Laughs* (1928), and *The Last Warning* (1929).

Paul Fejos made *Pan* (1920), *The Last Moment* (1928), and *Lonesome* (1928).

Erich von Stroheim directed *Blind Husbands* (1918), *The Devil's Passkey* (1919), *Foolish Wives* (1921), *Merry-Go-Round* (1922), *Greed* (1924), *The Merry Widow* (1925), *The Wedding March* (1927), and *Queen Kelly* (1928). For a complete listing see Richard Koszarski, *The Man You Loved to Hate* (New York: Oxford University Press, 1983).

Maurice Tourneur directed *The Man of the Hour* (1914), *Pride of the Clan* (1917), *The Poor Little Rich Girl* (1917), *The Blue Bird* (1918), *A Doll's House* (1918), *Victory* (1919), *Treasure Island* (1920), *The Last of the Mohicans* (1920), *The Foolish Matrons* (1921), *The Isle of Lost Ships* (1923), and *Aloma of the South Seas* (1926).

Rex Ingram directed *The Great Problem* (1916), *The Four Horsemen of the Apocalypse* (1921), *The Conquering Power* (1921), *Turn to the Right* (1921), *The Prisoner of Zenda* (1922), *Scaramouche* (1923), *The Arab* (1924), *Mare Nostrum* (1925), and *The Three Passions* (1929). For more information see Liam O'Leary, *Rex Ingram* (New York: Barnes & Noble, 1980).

Osa and **Martin Johnson** made *Cannibals of the South Seas* (1923) and *Simba* (1928). See Osa Johnson's *I Married Adventure* (Philadelphia: J. B. Lippincott, 1940) for more information.

Merian C. Cooper, as a documentary filmmaker, made *Grass* (1925) and *Chang* (1927). He is credited as the producer for *King Kong* (1933), *The Lost Patrol* (1934), *Becky Sharp* (1935), *The Long Voyage Home* (1940), *She Wore a Yellow Ribbon* (1949), and *The Quiet Man* (1952).

Robert Flaherty is most famous for *Nanook of the North* (1922), *Moana* (1926), *Tabu* (with F. W. Murnau), *Man of Aran* (1934), *The Land* (1942), and *Louisiana Story* (1948). For a complete listing see Paul Rotha, *Robert J. Flaherty* (Philadelphia: University of Pennsylvania Press, 1983).

• chapter 4 •
influential alternatives to hollywood: european cinema

Victor Sjöström made *Give Us This Day* (1913), *The Kiss of Death* (1917), *The Outlaw and His Wife* (1918), *The Phantom Chariot* (1921), *He Who Gets Slapped* (1924), *The Tower of Lies* (1925), *The Scarlet Letter* (1927), and *The Wind* (1928).

Mauritz Stiller made *Mother and Daughter* (1912), *Thomas Graal's Best Film* (1917), *Bonds That Chafe* (1920), *The Story of Gösta Berling* (1923), and *Hotel Imperial* (1927).

Hans Richter made *Rhythmus 21* (1921–1924), *Rhythmus 23* (1923–1924), *Inflation* (1927–1928), *Dreams That Money Can Buy* (1944–1947), *8 × 8* (1954–1957), and *Alexander Calder* (1963).

Walter Ruttman created *Opus I* (1921), *Opus II* (1920–1923), *Opus III* (1920–1923), *Opus IV* (1920–1923), *Opus V* (1925–1926), *Berlin, Symphony of a Great City* (1926–1927), *Weekend* (1930), and *In the Night* (1931).

Carl Dreyer made *The President* (1919), *The Parson's Widow* (1920), *Leaves from Satan's Book* (1921), *Master of the House* (1925), *The Passion of Joan of Arc* (1928), *Vampyr* (1932), *Day of Wrath* (1943), *Ordet* (1955), and *Gertrud* (1964). A complete listing can be found in David Bordwell, *The Films of Carl-Theodor Dreyer* (Berkeley: University of California Press, 1981).

Louis Delluc scripted *La Fête Espagnole* (1919, directed by Germaine Dulac), and directed *Fumée Noire* (1920), *Le Silence* (1920), *Fièvre* (1921), *La Femme de Nulle Part* (1922), and *L'Inondation* (1923).

Abel Gance created *J'Accuse* (1919), *La Roue* (1923), *Napoleon* (1927), *The Life and Loves of Beethoven* (1936), *The Queen and the Cardinal* (1936), *Louise* (1939), and *Quatorze Juillet* (1954).

For a complete listing see Steven Kramer and James Welsh, *Abel Gance* (Boston: Twayne, 1978).

Jean Epstein fashioned *L'Auberge Rouge* (1923), *Coeur Fidèle* (1923), *Le Lion des Mogols* (1924), *Six et Demi-Onze* (1927), *La Chute de la Maison Usher* (1928), *La Pas de la Mule* (1930), *L'Homme à l'Hispano* (1933), and *Vive la Vie* (1937).

Marcel L'Herbier directed *Rose-France* (1918), *Le Carnival des Vérities* (1920), *L'Homme du Large* (1920), *El Dorado* (1921), *Don Juan and Faust* (1922), *L'Inhumaine* (1924), *L'Argent* (1929), *L'Enfant de L'Amour* (1929), *Bird of Prey* (1933), *L'Aventurier* (1934), *The Great Temptation* (1936), *Rasputin* (1938), *Foolish Husbands* (1941), *The Queen's Necklace* (1946), and *The Last Days of Pompeii* (1948).

Germaine Dulac directed *The Smiling Madame Beudet* (1923), *Le Diable dans la Ville* (1924), *The Seashell and the Clergyman* (1927), *Disque 927* (1928), *Themes and Variations* (1928), and *Etude Cinégraphique sur une Arabesque* (1929).

Fritz Lang made *Halbblut* (1919), *Destiny* (1921), *Dr. Mabuse, the Gambler* (1922), *Die Nibelungen* (1924, in two parts), *Metropolis* (1927), *Spies* (1928), *M* (1931), *The Testament of Dr. Mabuse* (1933), *Fury* (1936), *You Only Live Once* (1937), *The Return of Frank James* (1940), *Western Union* (1941), *Man Hunt* (1941), *Hangman Also Die* (1943), *Ministry of Fear* (1944), *Scarlet Street* (1945), *Rancho Notorious* (1952), *The Big Heat* (1953), *While the City Sleeps* (1956), and *The Thousand Eyes of Dr. Mabuse* (1960). For a complete listing see E. Ann Kaplan, *Fritz Lang* (Boston: G. K. Hall, 1981).

G. W. Pabst filmed *The Treasure* (1923), *The Joyless Street* (1925), *Secrets of a Soul* (1925), *The Love of Jeanne Ney* (1927), *Pandora's Box* (1928), *Westfront 1918* (1930), *The Threepenny Opera* (1931), *The Trial* (1947), and *The Last Ten Days* (1955). For a complete listing see Lee Atwell, *G. W. Pabst* (Boston: Twayne, 1977).

E. A. Dupont directed *The Secret of the American Docks* (1917), *Child of Darkness* (1922), *Variety* (1925), *Love Me and the World Is Mine* (1927), *Atlantic* (1929), *The Circus of Sin* (1931), *The Marathon Runner* (1933), *Ladies Must Love* (1933), *A Son Comes Home* (1936), *The Scarf* (1951), and *Return to Treasure Island* (1954).

• chapter 5 •
the soviet experiment in filmmaking

Lev Kuleshov directed *On the Red Front* (1920), *The Extraordinary Adventures of Mr. West in the Land of the Bolsheviks* (1924), *Death Ray* (1925), *By the Law* (1926), *Horizon* (1932), *Theft of Sight* (1935), *The Siberians* (1940), *The Oath of Timur* (1942), *The Young Partisans* (1943), and *We Are from the Urals* (1944). A complete listing can be found in Ronald Levaco, *Kuleshov on Film* (Berkeley: University of California Press, 1974).

Sergei Eisenstein made *Strike* (1925), *Battleship Potemkin* (1925), *October* (1928), *The General Line* (1929), *Alexander Nevsky* (1938), and the two parts of *Ivan the Terrible* (1944 and 1946). For a complete filmography see Yon Barna, *Eisenstein* (Bloomington: Indiana University Press, 1974).

Dziga Vertov created *Agit-Train* (1921), *Kino-Pravda* (1922–1925), *Cinema-Eye* (1924), *A Sixth of the World* (1926), *Man with a Movie Camera* (1929), *Three Songs of Lenin* (1934), *Famous Soviet Heroes* (1938), *Three Heroines* (1938), and *For You, The Front!* (1943). A complete listing can be found in Annette Michelson (ed.), *Kino-Eye* (Berkeley: University of California Press, 1984).

Esther Shub created *Fall of the Romanov Dynasty* (1927), *The Great Road* (1927), *The Russia of Nicholas II and Leo Tolstoy* (1928), *Today* (1930), *Komsomol—Leader of Electrification* (1932), *Mos-*

cow Builds a Subway (1934), *The Country of the Soviets* (1937), *Spain* (1939), *20 Years of Soviet Cinema* (1940), *Fascism Will Be Destroyed* (1941), and *The Trial in Smolensk* (1946).

V. I. Pudovkin created *Chess Fever* (1925), *Mechanics of the Brain* (1926), *Mother* (1926), *The End of St. Petersburg* (1927), *Storm over Asia* (1928), *A Simple Case* (1932), *Deserter* (1933), *Victory* (1938), *Admiral Nakhimov* (1946), and *The Harvest* (1953).

Alexander Dovzhenko directed *Vasya the Reformer* (1926), *Zvenigora* (1928), *Arsenal* (1929), *Earth* (1930), *Ivan* (1932), *Aerograd* (1935), *Shors* (1939), *Bucovina-Ukrainian Land* (1940), and *Michurin* (1948). A full listing can be found in Vance Keply, Jr., *In the Service of the State* (Madison: University of Wisconsin Press, 1986).

• chapter 6 •
the coming of sound and the studio system

Paramount during the Studio Era was the home to Mae West in *I'm No Angel* (1933) and *Belle of the Nineties* (1934), the Marx Brothers in *The Cocoanuts* (1929) and *Horse Feathers* (1932), Marlene Dietrich in *Blonde Venus* (1932), and *The Scarlet Empress* (1934), Maurice Chevalier in *One Hour with You* (1932), Bing Crosby in *Holiday Inn* (1942), *Going My Way* (1944), *The Emperor Waltz* (1948), and *A Connecticut Yankee in King Arthur's Court* (1949), Bob Hope in *My Favorite Blonde* (1942), *My Favorite Brunette* (1947), and *Monsieur Beaucaire* (1946). Mitchell Leisen contributed *I Wanted Wings* (1941), and Preston Sturges added *The Great McGinty* (1940), *The Lady Eve* (1941), and *The Miracle of Morgan's Creek* (1944). The work of Cecil B. deMille and Ernst Lubitsch is treated in Chapter 3. For a fuller listing see John

Douglas Eames, *The Paramount Story* (New York: Crown, 1985).

MGM during the Studio Era was the home to Marie Dressler in *Min and Bill* (1930) and *Tugboat Annie* (1933), *Tarzan, The Ape Man* (1932), *Tarzan and His Mate* (1934), *Tarzan's New York Adventure* (1942), Stan Laurel and Oliver Hardy in *Sons of the Desert* (1933), the Marx Brothers in *A Night at the Opera* (1935) and *A Day at the Races* (1937), Clark Gable in *Manhattan Melodrama* (1934) and *San Francisco* (1936), and Spencer Tracy in *Test Pilot* (1938) and *Boys' Town* (1938). MGM's Technicolor musicals included *Meet Me In St. Louis* (1944), *Easter Parade* (1948), *Singin' in the Rain* (1952), *The Pirate* (1948), *On the Town* (1949), *The Band Wagon* (1953), and *It's Always Fair Weather* (1955). MGM's British wing produced *A Yank at Oxford* (1938) and *Goodbye, Mr. Chips* (1939). The studio also made the *Dr. Kildare* and *Hardy* family series, and the *Tom and Jerry* cartoon series. See John Douglas Eames, *The MGM Story* (New York: Crown, 1976).

Twentieth Century–Fox during the Studio Era was the home to Shirley Temple in *Little Miss Marker* (1934), *The Little Colonel* (1935), and *Rebecca of Sunnybrook Farm* (1938), Sonja Henie in *One in a Million* (1937), and *Thin Ice* (1937), Alice Faye in *Alexander's Ragtime Band* (1938), Tyrone Power in *In Old Chicago* (1938), and *Suez* (1938), Betty Grable in *Moon Over Miami* (1941), *Song of the Islands* (1942), *Coney Island* (1943), *The Dolly Sisters* (1945), *Mother Wore Tights* (1947), and *When My Baby Smiles at Me* (1948). Critics hailed the social exposés of *Gentlemen's Agreement* (1947) and *Pinky* (1949). For more see Tony Thomas and Aubrey Solomon, *The Films of 20th Century–Fox* (Secaucus, NJ: Citadel, 1979).

Warner Bros. pioneered talkies with *Don Juan* (1926), *The Jazz Singer* (1927), *Lights of New York* (1928), and *The Singing Fool* (1928). During the Studio Era Warners was famous for its social exposé films such as *I Am a Fugitive from a Chain*

Gang (1932) and *Wild Boys of the Road* (1933), innovative gangster films such as *Public Enemy* (1931) and *The Secret Six* (1931), and backstage musicals such as *42nd Street* (1933), *The Gold Diggers of 1933* and *Footlight Parade* (1933). Adventure tales included *Oil for the Lamps of China* (1935), *Anthony Adverse* (1936), Errol Flynn in *The Adventures of Robin Hood* (1938) and *The Charge of the Light Brigade* (1936), and bio-pix *The Story of Louis Pasteur* (1936) and *Juarez* (1939), both starring Paul Muni. Other stars included Bette Davis in *The Bride Came C.O.D.* (1941), Barbara Stanwyck in *Christmas in Connecticut* (1945), Jane Wyman in *Johnny Belinda* (1948), and Joan Crawford in *Mildred Pierce* (1945). Warners also issued *Nancy Drew* detective films, and *Merrie Melodies* and *Looney Tunes* cartoons. For more information see Clive Hirschhorn, *The Warner Bros. Story* (New York: Crown, 1979).

RKO during the Studio Era produced *What Price Hollywood?* (1932), *Bill of Divorcement* (1932), *Morning Glory* (1933), *King Kong* (1933), *Abe Lincoln in Illinois* (1940), *Citizen Kane* (1941), *The Magnificent Ambersons* (1942), *Hitler's Children* (1943), the Val Lewton horror films including *I Walked with a Zombie* (1943), *The Leopard Man* (1943), *The Seventh Victim* (1943), *The Ghost Ship* (1943), *The Curse of the Cat People* (1944), *The Body Snatcher* (1945), and *Isle of the Dead* (1945), and Robert Siodmak's *The Spiral Staircase* (1946). RKO distributed animation of the Walt Disney studio from 1937 to 1954 which included *Snow White and the Seven Dwarfs* (1938), *Pinnochio* (1940), *Fantasia* (1940), *Dumbo* (1941), *Bambi* (1942), and *Cinderella* (1950). See Richard B. Jewell and Vernon Harbin, *The RKO Story* (New York: Arlington House, 1982).

Universal produced during the Studio Era Abbott and Costello in *Buck Privates* (1941), weekly serials including *Flash Gordon* (1930s) and *Jungle Jim* (late 1940s), "Woody Woodpecker" cartoons as well as *All Quiet on the Western Front* (1930), *Dracula* (1930), *Frankenstein* (1931), *The Mummy* (1932), *The Invisible Man* (1933), *The Bride of Frankenstein* (1935), Deanna Durbin in *One Hundred Men and a Girl* (1937) and *Mad About Music* (1938), and *You Can't Cheat an Honest Man* (1939) and *Never Give a Sucker an Even Break* (1941), both starring W. C. Fields. For more information see Clive Hirschhorn, *The Universal Story* (New York: Crown, 1983).

Columbia Pictures produced during the Studio Era Frank Capra's *It Happened One Night* (1934), *Mr. Deeds Goes to Town* (1936), *Lost Horizon* (1937), and *You Can't Take It with You* (1938), George Stevens' *Penny Serenade* (1941) and *Talk of the Town* (1942), and *The Jolson Story* (1946) and *Jolson Sings Again* (1949). Serials included *Batman* (1940s). For more information see Rochelle Larkin, *Hail, Columbia* (New Rochelle, NY: Arlington House, 1975).

Republic Studios will be remembered for John Ford's *Rio Grande* (1950) and *The Quiet Man* (1952), Orson Welles' *Macbeth* (1948), and Frank Borzage's *Moonrise* (1948), as well as the Westerns of Roy Rogers and Gene Autry and serials such as *Zorro Rides Again* (1937), and *Jungle Girl* (1941). For more information see Richard Maurice Hurst, *Republic Studios* (Metuchen, NJ: Scarecrow, 1979).

Monogram produced cheap musicals such as *Lady, Let's Dance*, low-budget Westerns such as *Partners on the Trail* and many a comedy such as *Million Dollar Kid*, all released in 1944, the heyday of the studio. For a complete filmography see Ted Okuda, *The Monogram Checklist* (Jefferson, NC: McFarland, 1987).

• chapter 7 •
the golden age of hollywood moviemaking

Musicals of the early talkie era included *King of Jazz* (1930) and *Paramount on Parade* (1930). The first great wave came with Rouben Mamoulian's *Love Me Tonight* (1932) and Busby Berkeley's *Footlight Parade* (1933), *42nd Street* (1933), *Dames* (1934), and the "Gold Digger" series (of 1933, 1935, and 1937). Fred Astaire and Ginger Rogers appeared in *The Gay Divorcée* (1934), *Top Hat* (1935), *Follow the Fleet* (1936), *Swing Time* (1936), and *The Story of Vernon and Irene Castle* (1939). The musicals of Ernst Lubitsch are treated in chapter 3, while those from MGM and Twentieth Century–Fox are noted above under the appropriate studio. For more information see John Russell Taylor and Arthur Jackson, *The Hollywood Musical* (New York: McGraw-Hill, 1971).

The gangster film cycle opened with *Little Caesar* (1930, starring Edward G. Robinson) and *The Public Enemy* (1931, starring James Cagney). Maybe the best of the lot is Howard Hawks' *Scarface* (1932, starring Paul Muni). The genre was reworked through *Crime School* (1938) and *Angels with Dirty Faces* (1938). John Huston's *The Maltese Falcon* (1941) continued the iconography in the detective film. The gangster film became self-reflexive with Raoul Walsh's *White Heat* (1949, starring James Cagney). For more information see Eugene Rosow, *Born to Lose* (New York: Oxford University Press, 1978).

The horror film cycle of the 1930s opened on Valentine's Day in 1931 when Universal released *Dracula*. Other horror films which followed included *Frankenstein* (1931), *Dr. Jekyll and Mr. Hyde* (1932), *The Mummy* (1932), *The Old Dark House* (1932), *Island of Lost Souls* (1933), *The Bride of Frankenstein* (1935), *Frankenstein Meets the Wolf Man* (1943), *Abbott and Costello Meet Frankenstein* (1948), and *Abbott and Costello Meet the Killer, Boris Karloff* (1949). For more information see Carlos Clarens, *An Illustrated History of the Horror Film* (New York: Capricorn, 1967).

Henry Blanke of Warner Bros. produced such varied works as *The Story of Louis Pasteur* (1936), *The Adventures of Robin Hood* (1938), *Jezebel* (1938), *The Maltese Falcon* (1941), and *The Fountainhead* (1949).

Samuel Goldwyn produced *Kid Millions* (1934), *Dodsworth* (1936), *Dead End* (1937), *Stella Dallas* (1937), *Wuthering Heights* (1939), *The Little Foxes* (1941), *The Best Years of Our Lives* (1946), *Hans Christian Andersen* (1952), and *Porgy and Bess* (1959). For a complete filmography see Alvin H. Marill, *Samuel Goldwyn Presents* (South Brunswick: Barnes, 1976).

David O. Selznick is most remembered for *Gone with the Wind* (1939). He also produced *Spoilers of the West* (1927), *A Bill of Divorcement* (1932), *Dinner at Eight* (1933), *David Copperfield* (1935), *A Star Is Born* (1937), *The Adventures of Tom Sawyer* (1938), *Spellbound* (1945), and *A Farewell to Arms* (1957). For a complete filmography see Ronald Haver, *David O. Selznick's Hollywood* (New York: Bonanza, 1980).

Ernest Haller was the cinematographer for *Love Is Everything* (1920), *French Dressing* (1927), *The Dawn Patrol* (1930), *The Emperor Jones* (1933), *Captain Blood* (1935), *Jezebel* (1938), *Gone with the Wind* (1939), *Mildred Pierce* (1945), *The Flame and the Arrow* (1950), *Rebel Without a Cause* (1955), *Man of the West* (1958), and *The Restless* (1965). For a filmography see *Monthly Film Bulletin*, November, 1969.

Edith Head was the most famous costumer designer of the studio era. Her credits include *Peter Pan* (1924), *Wings* (1927), *The Virginian* (1929), *A Farewell to Arms* (1932), *Love Me Tonight* (1932), *Duck Soup* (1933), *She Done Him Wrong* (1933), *The Glass Key* (1935), *Hopalong Rides Again* (1937), *Union Pacific* (1939), *Northwest Mounted Police* (1940), *Ball of Fire* (1941), *I Married a Witch* (1942), *Double Indemnity* (1944), *Hail the Conquering Hero* (1944), *The Blue Dahlia* (1946), *Road to Rio* (1947), *The Heiress* (1949), *All About Eve* (1950), *The Greatest Show on Earth* (1952), *Shane* (1953), *White Christmas* (1954), *The Man Who Knew Too Much* (1956), *Loving You* (1957), *Teacher's Pet* (1958), *Breakfast at Tiffany's* (1961), *The Birds* (1963), *The Patsy* (1964), *Red Line 7000* (1965), *Hotel* (1967), *Airport* (1970), *Family Plot*

(1976), and *Dead Men Don't Wear Plaid* (1982). For a filmography see her autobiography, *Edith Head's Hollywood* (New York: Dutton, 1983).

Bernard Herrmann wrote music for *Citizen Kane* (1941), *The Magnificent Ambersons* (1942), *The Ghost and Mrs. Muir* (1947), *The Day the Earth Stood Still* (1951), *Vertigo* (1958), and *Psycho* (1960). For a filmography see *Films in Review*, August–September, 1967.

Howard Hawks directed *The Road to Glory* (1926), *A Girl in Every Port* (1928), *Dawn Patrol* (1930), *The Criminal Code* (1931), *Scarface* (1932), *Twentieth Century* (1934), *Ceiling Zero* (1936), *Bringing Up Baby* (1938), *Only Angels Have Wings* (1939), *His Girl Friday* (1940), *Sergeant York* (1941), *Ball of Fire* (1941), *To Have and Have Not* (1944), *The Big Sleep* (1946), *Red River* (1948), *I Was a Male War Bride* (1949), *Gentlemen Prefer Blondes* (1953), *Rio Bravo* (1959), *Hatari!* (1962), *El Dorado* (1967), and *Rio Lobo* (1970). A complete listing can be found in Joseph McBride, *Hawks on Hawks* (Berkeley: University of California Press, 1982).

Frank Capra made *The Strong Man* (1926) and *Long Pants* (1927) with Harry Langdon. At Columbia he directed *American Madness* (1932), *The Bitter Tea of General Yen* (1933), *Lady for a Day* (1933), *It Happened One Night* (1934), *Mr. Deeds Goes to Town* (1936), *Lost Horizon* (1937), *You Can't Take It with You* (1938), *Mr. Smith Goes to Washington* (1939), and *Meet John Doe* (1941). On his own he fashioned *It's a Wonderful Life* (1946), *State of the Union* (1948), *A Hole in the Head* (1959), and *A Pocketful of Miracles* (1961). See for a full listing Charles Maland, *Frank Capra* (Boston: Twayne, 1980).

Orson Welles made *Citizen Kane* (1941), *The Magnificent Ambersons* (1942), *The Stranger* (1946), *The Lady from Shanghai* (1948), *Macbeth* (1948), *Mr. Arkadin* (1955), *Touch of Evil* (1958), and *Falstaff* (1966). For a complete listing of his credits see John Russell Taylor, *Orson Welles* (Boston: Little Brown, 1986).

Alfred Hitchcock directed *The Pleasure Garden* (1925), *The Lodger* (1926), *Blackmail* (1929), *Murder* (1930), *The Man Who Knew Too Much* (1934), *The Thirty-Nine Steps* (1935), *The Secret Agent* (1936), *Sabotage* (1936), *Young and Innocent* (1937), *The Lady Vanishes* (1938), *Jamaica Inn* (1939), *Rebecca* (1940), *Suspicion* (1941), *Shadow of a Doubt* (1943), *Notorious* (1946), *Strangers on a Train* (1951), *Rear Window* (1954), *The Man Who Knew Too Much* (1956), *Vertigo* (1958), *North by Northwest* (1959), *Psycho* (1960), *The Birds* (1963), *Marnie* (1964), *Torn Curtain* (1966), *Frenzy* (1972), and *Family Plot* (1976). For a complete list see Donald Spoto, *The Dark Side of Genius* (Boston: Little Brown, 1983).

Billy Wilder created *The Major and the Minor* (1942), *Double Indemnity* (1944), *The Lost Weekend* (1945), *The Emperor Waltz* (1948), *Sunset Boulevard* (1950), *Stalag 17* (1953), *The Seven Year Itch* (1955), *Witness for the Prosecution* (1958), *Some Like It Hot* (1959), *The Apartment* (1960), *Irma La Douce* (1963), *Kiss Me, Stupid* (1964), and *The Front Page* (1974). For a more complete filmography see Steve Seidman, *The Film Career of Billy Wilder* (Boston: Twayne, 1977).

March of Time in its heyday treated such subjects as *Speakeasy Street* (1935), *Huey Long* (1935), *Father Coughlin* (1935), *Texas Centennial* (1936), *Dust Bowl* (1937), *G-Men of the Sea* (1938), *Inside Nazi Germany* (1938), *Uncle Sam: The Farmer* (1939), *Britain's RAF* (1940), *Peace—by Adolph Hitler* (1941), *The F.B.I. Front* (1942), *Post-war Jobs?* (1944), *Palestine Problem* (1945), *Atomic Power* (1946), and *MacArthur's Japan* (1949). For a complete filmography see Raymond Fielding, *The March of Time* (New York: Oxford University Press, 1978).

Pare Lorentz was the driving force behind only four films: *The Plow That Broke the Plains* (1936), *The River* (1937), *The Fight for Life* (1940), and *Nuremberg Trials* (1946). For more information see Robert L. Snyder, *Pare Lorentz and the Documentary Film* (Norman: University of Oklahoma Press, 1968).

Maya Deren was the creative force behind *Meshes of the Afternoon* (1943), *At Land* (1944), *A Study in Choreography for Camera* (1945), *Ritual in Transfigured Time* (1946), *Meditation on Violence* (1948), and *The Very Eye of Night* (1959).

Kenneth Anger made *Fireworks* (1947), *Eaux d'Artifice* (1953), *Inauguration of the Pleasure Dome* (1954), *Scorpio Rising* (1962–1964), and *Lucifer Rising* (a first version released in 1974 and a second in 1980).

Gregory Markopoulos made *Psyche* (1947–48), *The Dead Ones* (1948), *Flowers of Asphalt* (1949), *Swain* (1950), *Eldora* (1953), *Serenity* (1955–1961), *Twice a Man* (1963), *The Death of Hemingway* (1965), *Ming Green* (1966), and *Mysteries* (1968).

• chapter 8 •
pre—world war II alternatives to hollywood: france, britain, and germany

René Clair directed *The Crazy Ray* (1923), *Entr'Acte* (1924), *The Italian Straw Hat* (1927), *Sous les Toits de Paris* (1930), *Le Million* (1931), *A Nous la Liberté* (1931), *Quatorze Juillet* (1933), *Le Dernier Milliardaire* (1934), and *The Ghost Goes West* (1935). For a complete listing see R. C. Dale, *The Films of René Clair* (Metuchen, NJ: Scarecrow, 1986).

Jean Vigo made *A Propos de Nice* (1930), *Taris* (1931), *Zéro de Conduite* (1933), and *L'Atalante* (1934). P. E. Salles-Gomes, *Jean Vigo* (Berkeley: University of California Press, 1971) provides a useful filmography.

Jean Renoir directed *La Fille de L'Eau* (1924), *Nana* (1926), *The Little Match Girl* (1928), *La Chienne* (1931), *Boudu Saved from Drowning* (1932), *Toni* (1934), *Le Crime de Monsieur Lange* (1935), *La Vie Est à Nous* (1936), *The Lower Depths* (1936), *La Grande Illusion* (1937), *La Marseillaise*

(1938), *Rules of the Game* (1939), *Swamp Water* (1941), *This Land Is Mine* (1943), *The Southerner* (1945), *The Woman on the Beach* (1947), *The River* (1951), *French Cancan* (1955), and *The Elusive Corporal* (1962). For a complete listing see Christopher Faulkner, *Jean Renoir* (Boston: G. K. Hall, 1979).

Marcel Carné made *Jenny* (1936), *Quai des Brumes* (1938), *Hôtel du Nord* (1938), *Le Jour se Lève* (1939), *Les Visiteurs du Soir* (1942), and *Children of Paradise* (1945).

Julien Duvivier created *Poil de Carotte* (1932), *Le Golem* (1936), *La Belle Equipe* (1936), and *Pépé-Le-Moko* (1937).

Jacques Feyder made *Carmen* (1926), *The Kiss* (1929), *Daybreak* (1931), and *Carnival in Flanders* (1935).

Alexander Korda produced *The Private Life of Henry VIII* (1933), *Rembrandt* (1936), *Things to Come* (1936), *Elephant Boy* (1937), *The Four Feathers* (1939), *The Thief of Bagdad* (1940), *That Hamilton Woman* (1941), *Jungle Book* (1942), *The Fallen Idol* (1948), *The Third Man* (1949), and *Storm of the Nile* (1955). For more information see Karol Kulik, *Alexander Korda* (New Rochelle, NY: Arlington House, 1975).

Basil Wright made *The Country Comes to Town* (1931), *O'er Hill and Dale* (1932), *Windmill in Barbados* (1933), *Song of Ceylon* (1934), *Night Mail* (1936), *The Face of Scotland* (1938), and *This Was Japan* (1945). See Elizabeth Sussex, *The Rise and Fall of British Documentary* (Berkeley: University of California Press, 1975) for more information.

Harry Watt made *North Sea* (1938), *Squadron 992* (1940), *London Can Take It* (1940), and *Fiddlers Three* (1944). See Elizabeth Sussex, *The Rise and Fall of British Documentary* (Berkeley: University of California Press, 1975) for more details.

Humphrey Jennings made *Penny Journey* (1938), *Spring Offensive* (1940), *Heart of Britain* (1941), *Listen to Britain* (1942), *A Diary for Timo-*

thy (1945), and *Family Portrait* (1950). See Anthony W. Hodginson and Rodney E. Sheratsky, *Humphrey Jennings* (Hanover, NH: University Press of New England, 1982).

Leni Riefenstahl made *The Blue Light* (1932), *Victory of Faith* (1933), *Triumph of the Will* (1934), *Day of Freedom* (1935), *Olympia* (1938) and *Tiefland* (1954). See Renata Berg-Pan, *Leni Riefenstahl* (Boston: Twayne, 1980) for more information.

• chapter 9 •
post—world war II alternatives
to hollywood: japan and italy

Akira Kurosawa has directed *The Most Beautiful* (1944), *Drunken Angel* (1948), *Stray Dog* (1949), *The Quiet Duel* (1949), *Rashomon* (1950), *The Idiot* (1951), *Ikiru* (1952), *Seven Samurai* (1954), *The Lower Depths* (1957), *Throne of Blood* (1957), *The Hidden Fortress* (1958), *Yojimbo* (1961), *High and Low* (1963), *Dodes'kaden* (1970), *Dersu Uzala* (1975), *The Shadow Warrior* (1980), and *Ran* (1985). For a complete filmography as of the end of the 1970s see Patricia Erens, *Akira Kurosawa* (Boston: G. K. Hall, 1979).

Kenji Mizoguchi is best known for *Mistress of a Foreigner* (1930), *Osaka Elegy* (1936), *Sisters of the Gion* (1936), *The Loyal Forty-Seven Ronin* (1942), *The Victory of Women* (1946), *Utamaro and His Five Women* (1946), *The Love of Sumako the Actress* (1947), *Women of the Night* (1948), *The Life of Oharu* (1952), *Ugetsu* (1953), *Sansho the Bailiff* (1954), *Crucified Lovers* (1954), and *Street of Shame* (1956). For a complete filmography see Dudley Andrew and Paul Andrew, *Kenji Mizoguchi* (Boston: G. K. Hall, 1981).

Yasujiro Ozu directed *The Sword of Penitence* (1927), *I Was Born But ...* (1932), *Passing Fancy* (1933), *A Story of Floating Weeds* (1934), *The Only Son* (1936), *The Brothers and Sisters of the Toda Family* (1941), *There Was a Father* (1942), *Late*

Spring (1949), *Early Summer* (1951), *The Flavor of Green Tea over Rice* (1952), *Tokyo Story* (1953), *Early Spring* (1956), *Tokyo Twilight* (1957), *Equinox Flower* (1958), *Floating Weeds* (1959), *Late Autumn* (1960), *The Last of Summer* (1961), and *An Autumn Afternoon* (1962). For a complete filmography see David Bordwell, *Ozu and the Poetics of the Cinema* (Princeton: Princeton University Press, 1988).

Luchino Visconti directed *Ossessione* (1942), *La Terra Trema* (1948), *Senso* (1954), *White Nights* (1957), *Rocco and His Brothers* (1960), *The Leopard* (1963), *The Damned* (1969), and *Death in Venice* (1971). For a complete listing see Gaia Servadio, *Luchino Visconti* (New York: Franklin Watts, 1983).

Roberto Rossellini created *Open City* (1945), *Paisan* (1946), *Germany Year Zero* (1947), *The Miracle* (1948), *Stromboli* (1949), *Europa '51* (1952), *Voyage to Italy* (1953), *The Rise of Louis XIV* (1965), *Socrates* (1970), and *The Age of the Medici* (1973). For a complete listing see Peter Brunette, *Roberto Rossellini* (New York: Oxford University Press, 1987).

Vittorio De Sica fashioned *The Children Are Watching Us* (1943), *Shoeshine* (1946), *The Bicycle Thief* (1948), *Miracle in Milan* (1950), *Umberto D* (1952), *Gold of Naples* (1954), *The Roof* (1956), *Two Women* (1960), and *The Garden of the Finzi-Contini* (1971).

• chapter 10 •
television, wide-screen,
and color

MGM during the television era produced *Intruder in the Dust* (1949), *The Asphalt Jungle* (1950), *Quo Vadis?* (1951), *Ivanhoe* (1952), *Plymouth Adventure* (1952), *Seven Brides for Seven Brothers* (1954), *Jupiter's Darling* (1955), *Jailhouse Rock*

(1957), *Raintree County* (1957), *Cat on a Hot Tin Roof* (1958), *Ben Hur* (1959), *Mutiny on the Bounty* (1962), *Doctor Zhivago* (1965), and *Shaft* (1971). For more information see John Douglas Eames, *The MGM Story* (New York: Crown, 1976).

Warner Bros. during the television era released *A Streetcar Named Desire* (1951), *The House of Wax* (1953), *A Star Is Born* (1954), *Giant* (1956), *Sayonara* (1957), *The Nun's Story* (1959), *Fanny* (1961), *The Music Man* (1962), *My Fair Lady* (1964), *The Great Race* (1965), *Who's Afraid of Virginia Woolf?* (1966), *Camelot* (1967), *Bonnie and Clyde* (1967), *The Summer of '42* (1971), *Deliverance* (1972), *What's Up Doc?* (1972), and *The Exorcist* (1973). For more information see Clive Hirschhorn, *The Warner Bros. Story* (New York: Crown, 1979).

Paramount during the television era produced *Sunset Boulevard* (1950), *A Place in the Sun* (1951), *The Greatest Show on Earth* (1952), *Shane* (1953), *The Country Girl* (1954), *To Catch a Thief* (1955), *Gunfight at the O.K. Corral* (1957), *Heller in Pink Tights* (1960), *One-Eyed Jacks* (1961), *Hatari!* (1962), *Donovan's Reef* (1963), *Becket* (1964), *The Odd Couple* (1968), *Darling Lili* (1970), and *The Godfather* (1972). For more information see John Douglas Eames, *The Paramount Story* (New York: Crown, 1985).

Twentieth Century–Fox during the television era released *Cheaper by the Dozen* (1950), *Rawhide* (1951), *The Pride of St. Louis* (1952), *The Robe* (1953), *Three Coins in the Fountain* (1954), *The King and I* (1956), *The Sun Also Rises* (1957), *The Roots of Heaven* (1958), *The Diary of Anne Frank* (1959), *Sons and Lovers* (1960), *The Longest Day* (1962), *Cleopatra* (1963), *The Sound of Music* (1965), *Doctor Dolittle* (1967), *Star!* (1968), *Hello, Dolly!* (1969), *Tora! Tora! Tora!* (1970), *Patton* (1970), *M*A*S*H* (1970), *The French Connection* (1971), *The Poseidon Adventure* (1972), and *The Towering Inferno* (1973). For more information see Tony Thomas and Aubrey Solomon, *The Films of 20th Century–Fox* (Seacaucus, NJ: Citadel, 1979).

Columbia Pictures during the television era produced *From Here to Eternity* (1953), *The Caine Mutiny* (1954), *On the Waterfront* (1955), *The Bridge on the River Kwai* (1957), *Lawrence of Arabia* (1962), *A Man for All Seasons* (1966), *Guess Who's Coming to Dinner?* (1967), *To Sir, With Love* (1967), *In Cold Blood* (1967), *Oliver!* (1968), *Funny Girl* (1968), and *Easy Rider* (1969). For more information see Rochelle Larkin, *Hail, Columbia* (New Rochelle, NY: Arlington House, 1975).

United Artists during the television era released *The African Queen* (1951), *High Noon* (1952), *The Moon Is Blue* (1953), *Kiss Me Deadly* (1955), *Around the World in 80 Days* (1956), *Sweet Smell of Success* (1957), *Paths of Glory* (1957), *China Doll* (1958), *Pork Chop Hill* (1959), *The Alamo* (1960), *Dr. No* (1962), *Goldfinger* (1964), *Help!* (1965), *Hawaii* (1966), *Alice's Restaurant* (1969), *Bananas* (1971), and *Sleeper* (1973). For more information see the second volume of Tino Balio's studio history: *United Artists* (Madison: University of Wisconsin Press, 1987).

Universal during the television era produced *Winchester '73* (1950), *Bend of the River* (1952), *The Glenn Miller Story* (1954), *Written on the Wind* (1956), *Imitation of Life* (1959), *Operation Petticoat* (1960), *Lover Come Back* (1962), *Marnie* (1964), *Torn Curtain* (1966), *Madigan* (1968), *Airport* (1970), *High Plains Drifter* (1973), *American Graffiti* (1973), and *Jaws* (1975). For more information see Clive Hirschhorn, *The Universal Story* (New York: Crown, 1983).

• chapter 11 •
a transformation in hollywood moviemaking

William Wyler directed *Anybody Here Seen Kelly?* (1928), *Dodsworth* (1936), *These Three* (1936), *Dead End* (1937), *Wuthering Heights* (1939), *The*

Letter (1940), *The Little Foxes* (1941), *Mrs. Miniver* (1942), *The Best Years of Our Lives* (1946), *The Heiress* (1949), *Roman Holiday* (1953), *Friendly Persuasion* (1956), *Ben Hur* (1959), *The Children's Hour* (1962), and *The Collector* (1965). For a complete listing see Axel Madsen, *William Wyler* (New York: Thomas Y. Crowell, 1973).

Michael Curtiz directed *The Third Degree* (1926), *Noah's Ark* (1929), *20,000 Years in Sing Sing* (1933), *Captain Blood* (1935), *The Adventures of Robin Hood* (1938), *Yankee Doodle Dandy* (1942), *Casablanca* (1943), *Mildred Pierce* (1945), *The Breaking Point* (1950), *White Christmas* (1954), *King Creole* (1958), and *The Comancheros* (1961). For more information see Roy Kinnard and R. J. Vitone, *The American Films of Michael Curtiz* (Metuchen, NJ: Scarecrow, 1986).

Sidney Lumet has directed *Twelve Angry Men* (1957), *Long Day's Journey into Night* (1962), *A View from the Bridge* (1962), *Fail Safe* (1964), *The Pawnbroker* (1965), *The Anderson Tapes* (1971), *Serpico* (1973), *The Wiz* (1978), and *The Verdict* (1982). For more information see Stephen Bowles, *Sidney Lumet* (Boston: G. K. Hall, 1979).

Stanley Kubrick is best known for *The Killing* (1956), *Paths of Glory* (1957), *Lolita* (1962), *Dr. Strangelove or How I Learned to Stop Worrying and Love the Bomb* (1964), *2001: A Space Odyssey* (1968), *A Clockwork Orange* (1971), *Barry Lyndon* (1975), and *The Shining* (1980). For a complete filmography see Thomas Allen Nelson, *Kubrick* (Bloomington: Indiana University Press, 1982).

Samuel Fuller has made *I Shot Jesse James* (1949), *The Steel Helmet* (1950), *Park Row* (1952), *Pickup on South Street* (1953), *Run of the Arrow* (1957), *Forty Guns* (1957), *China Gate* (1957), *Underworld USA* (1961), *Shock Corridor* (1963), *The Naked Kiss* (1964), and *The Big Red One* (1980). For more filmography see Phil Hardy, *Samuel Fuller* (New York: Praeger, 1970).

Otto Preminger directed *Laura* (1944), *Where the Sidewalk Ends* (1950), *Angel Face* (1952), *The Moon Is Blue* (1953), *Carmen Jones* (1954), *The Man with the Golden Arm* (1955), *The Court Martial of Billy Mitchell* (1955), *Porgy and Bess* (1959), *Anatomy of a Murder* (1959), *Exodus* (1960), *Advise and Consent* (1962), and *The Cardinal* (1963). For a complete listing see Otto Preminger, *Preminger* (Garden City, NY: Doubleday, 1977).

John Huston directed *The Maltese Falcon* (1941), *The Treasure of the Sierra Madre* (1948), *Key Largo* (1948), *The African Queen* (1952), *Beat the Devil* (1954), *Moby Dick* (1956), *The Misfits* (1961), and *Freud* (1962). For a list of his films as of the late 1970s see Stuart Kaminsky, *John Huston* (Boston: Houghton Mifflin, 1978).

Stanley Kramer produced *The Men* (1950), *High Noon* (1952), *The Member of the Wedding* (1952), and *The Sniper* (1952), and then produced and directed *Not as a Stranger* (1955), *The Defiant Ones* (1958), *On the Beach* (1959), *Inherit the Wind* (1960), and *Judgment at Nuremberg* (1961). For a listing of his credits see Donald Spoto, *Stanley Kramer* (New York: Putnam, 1978).

Francis Ford Coppola has directed *You're a Big Boy Now* (1967), *The Rain People* (1969), *The Godfather* (1972), *The Conversation* (1974), *The Godfather, Part II* (1974), *Apocalypse Now* (1979), *One from the Heart* (1982), *The Cotton Club* (1984), and *Peggy Sue Got Married* (1986). For a filmography as of the late 1980s see Jeffrey Chown, *Hollywood Auteur* (New York: Praeger, 1988).

Anthony Mann directed *Dr. Broadway* (1942), *T-Men* (1948), *Devil's Doorway* (1950), *Winchester '73* (1950), *Bend of the River* (1951), *The Naked Spur* (1953), *The Far Country* (1955), *The Man from Laramie* (1955), and *The Tin Star* (1957). For a complete filmography see Jeanine Basinger, *Anthony Mann* (Boston: Twayne, 1979).

Budd Boetticher crafted *One Mysterious Night* (1944), *The Bullfighter and the Lady* (1951), *Horizons West* (1952), *The Man from the Alamo* (1953), *Seven Men from Now* (1956), *The Tall T* (1957), *Buchanan Rides Alone* (1958), *Ride Lone-*

some (1959), and *Comanche Station* (1960). For more information see Jim Kitses, *Horizons West* (Bloomington: Indiana University Press, 1969).

Sergio Leone directed *A Fistful of Dollars* (1964), *For a Few Dollars More* (1965), *The Good, the Bad, and the Ugly* (1966), *Once Upon a Time in the West* (1968), and *Once Upon a Time in America* (1984). For a filmography see Christopher Frayling, *Spaghetti Westerns* (London: Routledge & Kegan Paul, 1981).

Vincente Minnelli directed *Cabin in the Sky* (1943), *Meet Me in St. Louis* (1944), *The Pirate* (1948), *An American in Paris* (1951), *The Bad and the Beautiful* (1952), *The Band Wagon* (1953), *Lust for Life* (1956), *Gigi* (1958), and *Bells Are Ringing* (1960).

Comedy as a genre hit a peak at the box office during the television era with *The Apartment* (1960), *That Touch of Mink* (1962), and *Irma La Douce* (1963). See also the films of Jerry Lewis including *The Bellboy* (1960), *The Errand Boy* (1961), *The Nutty Professor* (1963), *The Patsy* (1964), and *The Big Mouth* (1967). For a fuller listing see Gerald Mast, *The Comic Mind*, second edition (Chicago: University of Chicago Press, 1981).

Frank Tashlin directed *Artists and Models* (1955), *The Girl Can't Help It* (1956), *Will Success Spoil Rock Hunter?* (1957), *Rock-a-Bye Baby* (1958), *Cinderfella* (1960), and *The Disorderly Orderly* (1964). For more information see Claire Johnston (ed.), *Frank Tashlin* (London: Screen, 1973).

Douglas Sirk made during his career such films as *Hitler's Madman* (1943), *Sleep My Love* (1948), *Magnificent Obsession* (1954), *All That Heaven Allows* (1955), *Written on the Wind* (1956), *Tarnished Angels* (1958), and *Imitation of Life* (1959). For more information see Jon Halliday, *Sirk on Sirk* (New York: Viking, 1972).

Don Siegel directed *Duel at Silver Creek* (1952), *Riot in Cell Block 11* (1954), *Invasion of the Body Snatchers* (1956), *Baby-Face Nelson* (1957), *The*

Line-Up (1958), *Flaming Star* (1960), *Hell Is for Heroes* (1962), *The Killers* (1964), *Coogan's Bluff* (1968), *Two Mules for Sister Sara* (1970), *Dirty Harry* (1971), and *The Shootist* (1976). For a complete filmography see Stuart M. Kaminsky, *Don Siegel: Director* (New York: Curtis, 1974).

The James Bond series has included *Dr. No* (1962), *From Russia with Love* (1963), *Goldfinger* (1964), *Thunderball* (1965), and *Diamonds Are Forever* (1971). For a filmography see Steven Jay Rubin, *The James Bond Films* (New York: Arlington House, 1983).

Arthur Penn directed *The Left-Handed Gun* (1958), *The Miracle Worker* (1962), *Mickey One* (1965), *The Chase* (1966), *Bonnie and Clyde* (1967), *Alice's Restaurant* (1969), *Little Big Man* (1970), *Night Moves* (1975), *The Missouri Breaks* (1976), and *Four Friends* (1981). For a complete filmography see Robert Philip Kolker, *The Cinema of Loneliness* (New York: Oxford University Press, 1988).

Richard (Ricky) Leacock created *Toby and the Tall Corn* (1954), *How the F-100 Got Its Tail* (1955), *Primary* (1960), *On the Pole* (1960), *The Chair* (1962), *A Stravinsky Portrait* (1964), *Ku Klux Klan—the Invisible Empire* (1965), and *Chiefs* (1969).

Albert and **David Maysles**, brothers, have created *Showman* (1962), *What's Happening: The Beatles in the USA* (1964), *Meet Marlon Brando* (1965), *Salesman* (1969), *Gimme Shelter* (1970), *Cristo's Valley Curtain* (1972), and *Grey Gardens* (1975).

Fred Wiseman may be the most famous exponent of the cinema verité school with his *Titicut Follies* (1967), *High School* (1968), *Law and Order* (1969), *Hospital* (1970), and *Basic Training* (1971). For more information see Liz Ellsworth, *Frederick Wiseman* (Boston: G. K. Hall, 1979).

Jonas Mekas has made *Guns of the Trees* (1960–1961), *The Brig* (1964), *Report from Millbrook* (1966), *Walden* (1968), *Reminiscences of a Jour-*

ney to Lithuania (1972), Lost, Lost, Lost (1976), In Between (1978), and Notes for Jerome (1981).

Robert Breer created Images by Images I (1954), Horse over Tea Kettle (1962), Fist Fight (1964), LMNO (1978), and Trial Balloons (1982). For more information see Lois Mendelson, Robert Breer (Metuchen, NJ: Scarecrow, 1982).

Hollis Frampton is noted for Manual of Arms (1966), Palindrome (1969), Artificial Light (1969), Zorn's Lemma (1970), and Magellan (1972–1984). For more information see Bruce Jenkins and Susan Krane, Hollis Frampton (Cambridge: MIT Press, 1985).

Ernie Gehr has created Morning Wait (1968), Serene Velocity (1970), Shift (1972–1974), Eureka (1974), Table (1976), and Mirage (1981).

Michael Snow has made Wavelength (1967), Back and Forth (1969), One Second in Montreal (1969), The Central Region (1971), and Presents (1982).

Andy Warhol produced Sleep (1963), Eat (1963), Kiss (1963), Couch (1964), Shoulder (1964), Beauty Number 2 (1965), The Chelsea Girls (1966), and Lonesome Cowboys (1968). See Stephen Koch, Stargazer (New York: Praeger, 1973).

Bruce Baillie made On Sundays (1960–1961), David Lynn's Sculpture (1961), The Gymnasts (1961), Here I Am (1962), To Parsifal (1963), Mass for the Dakota Sioux (1963–1964), Quixote (1964–1965), Yellow Horse (1965), Castro Street (1966), Quick Billy (1970), and Roslyn Romance (1971–in progress).

Bruce Conner directed A Movie (1958), Cosmic Ray (1960–1962), Report (1964–1965), Leader (1964), 10 Second Film (1965), The White Rose (1967), Marilyn Times Five (1969–1973), Crossroads (1976), Valse Triste (1977), Mongoloid (1978), and America Is Waiting (1981).

Stan Brakhage has created Interim (1952), Unglassed Windows Cast a Terrible Reflection (1953), The Extraordinary Child (1954), Zone Moment (1956), Daybreak and Whiteye (1957), Wedlock House: An Intercourse (1959), Window Water Baby Moving (1959), Cat's Cradle (1959), The Dead (1960), Blue Moses (1962), Dog Star Man (1962–1964), The Art of Vision (1965), Lovemaking (1968), Songs (1969), Scenes from Under Childhood (1970), and Eye Myth (1972).

• chapter 12 •
the art-cinema alternative

Claude Chabrol has directed Le Beau Serge (1958), Les Cousins (1959), Bluebeard (1963), Les Biches (1968), La Femme Infidèle (1968), Le Boucher (1970), Just Before Nightfall (1971), Ten Days' Wonder (1972), Wedding in Blood (1973), Nada (1974), and Innocents with Dirty Hands (1975).

Alain Resnais began with documentary filmmaking: Van Gogh (1948), Guernica (1950), Night and Fog (1956), and All the Memories of the World (1956). His features include Hiroshima mon Amour (1959), Last Year at Marienbad (1961), La Guerre est Finie (1966), Je T'Aime, Je T'Aime (1968), Stavisky (1974), Providence (1977), and My Uncle from America (1978). For a complete filmography as of the late 1970s see John Frances Kreidel, Alain Resnais (Boston: Twayne, 1977).

François Truffaut directed The 400 Blows (1959), Shoot the Piano Player (1960), Jules et Jim (1961), an episode of Love at Twenty (1962), The Soft Skin (1964), Fahrenheit 451 (1966), The Bride Wore Black (1967), Stolen Kisses (1968), The Wild Child (1969), Bed and Board (1970), Two English Girls (1972), Day for Night (1973), The Story of Adele H. (1975), Small Change (1976), and The Last Metro (1980). For a filmography see Annette Insdorf, François Truffaut (Boston: Twayne, 1978).

Jean-Luc Godard challenged the world with such striking films as *Breathless* (1960), *Une Femme Est une Femme* (1961), *Vivre sa Vie* (1962), *Les Carabiniers* (1963), *Contempt* (1963), *A Married Woman* (1964), *Band of Outsiders* (1964), *Pierrot le fou* (1965), *Alphaville* (1965), *Masculine-Feminine* (1966), *Made in USA* (1966), *Two or Three Things I Know About Her* (1967), *La Chinoise* (1967), *Weekend* (1968), *One Plus One* (1968), *La Gai Savoir* (1968), *Pravda* (1969), *Wind from the East* (1970), *Vladimir and Rosa* (1971), *Tout va Bien* (1972), *Letter to Jane* (1972), *Numero Duex* (1975), and *First Name: Carmen* (1983). For a filmography see Julia LaSage, *Jean-Luc Godard* (Boston: G. K. Hall, 1979).

Ingmar Bergman has directed *Crisis* (1946), *Prison* (1949), *Thirst* (1949), *Summer Interlude* (1951), *Summer with Monica* (1953), *The Naked Night* (1953), *Smiles of a Summer Night* (1955), *Wild Strawberries* (1957), *The Seventh Seal* (1957), *The Magician* (1958), *The Devil's Eye* (1960), *The Virgin Spring* (1960), *Through a Glass Darkly* (1961), *Winter Light* (1963), *The Silence* (1963), *Persona* (1966), *Hour of the Wolf* (1968), *Shame* (1968), *The Passion of Anna* (1969), *The Touch* (1971), *Scenes from a Marriage* (1973), *Face to Face* (1976), *The Magic Flute* (1975), and *Fanny and Alexander* (1982). For a filmography see Frank Gado, *The Passion of Ingmar Bergman* (Durham: Duke University Press, 1986).

Luis Buñuel directed *L'Age D'or* (1930), *Land Without Bread* (1932), *Madrid '36* (1937), *Great Casino* (1947), *The Young and the Damned* (1950), *Mexican Bus Ride* (1951), *Daughter of Deceit* (1951), *Robinson Crusoe* (1952), *The Illusion Travels By Streetcar* (1953), *Death in the Garden* (1956), *Nazarin* (1958), *Republic of Sin* (1959), *Viridiana* (1961), *The Exterminating Angel* (1962), *Simon of the Desert* (1965), *Belle de Jour* (1966), *The Milky Way* (1969), *Tristana* (1970), *The Phantom of Liberty* (1974), and *That Obscure Object of Desire* (1977). For a filmography see Joan Mellen (ed.), *The World of Luis Buñuel* (New York: Oxford University Press, 1978).

Federico Fellini has directed *I Vitelloni* (1953), *La Strada* (1954), *Nights of Cabiria* (1956), *La Dolce Vita* (1960), *8½* (1963), *Juliet of the Spirits* (1965), *Fellini's Satyricon* (1969), *The Clowns* (1970), *Roma* (1972), *Amarcord* (1974), and *Fellini's Casanova* (1976). For a filmography see Edward Murray, *Fellini*, 2nd edition (New York: Ungar, 1985).

Jacques Tati made *Jour de Fête* (1949), *Monsieur Hulot's Holiday* (1953), *Mon Oncle* (1958), *Play Time* (1967), and *Traffic* (1971). For a complete listing see Lucy Fischer, *Jacques Tati* (Boston: G. K. Hall, 1983).

Robert Bresson has made *Les Anges du Péché* (1943), *Les Dames du Bois de Boulogne* (1945), *Diary of a Country Priest* (1950), *A Man Escaped* (1956), *Pickpocket* (1959), *The Trial of Joan of Arc* (1962), *Balthazar* (1966), *Mouchette* (1967), *Une Femme Douce* (1969), *Four Nights of a Dreamer* (1971), *Lancelot of the Lake* (1974), and *L'Argent* (1983). For a listing of his work as of the early 1980s see Jane Sloan, *Robert Bresson* (Boston: G. K. Hall, 1983).

Michelangelo Antonioni has made *L'Avventura* (1960), *La Notte* (1961), *L'Eclisse* (1962), *Red Desert* (1964), *Blow-Up* (1966), *Zabriskie Point* (1970), and *The Passenger* (1975).

Pier Paolo Pasolini directed *Accattone!* (1961), *The Gospel According to St. Matthew* (1964), *Oedipus Rex* (1967), *The Decameron* (1971), *The Canterbury Tales* (1972), *A Thousand and One Nights* (1974), and *The 120 Days of Sodom* (1975). For a filmography see Stephen Snyder, *Pier Paolo Pasolini* (Boston: Twayne, 1980).

Bernardo Bertolucci has directed *The Grim Reaper* (1962), *Before the Revolution* (1964), *The Spider's Stratagem* (1970), *The Conformist* (1970), *Last Tango in Paris* (1972), *1900* (1976), and *The Last Emperor* (1988). For a complete listing as of the mid-1980s see Robert Philip Kolker, *Bernardo Bertolucci* (New York: Oxford University Press, 1985).

The Angry Young Men movement in England included Jack Clayton's *Room at the Top* (1958); Karel Reisz's *Saturday Night and Sunday Morning* (1960); and Tony Richardson's *A Taste of Honey* (1961), *The Loneliness of the Long Distance Runner* (1962), and *Tom Jones* (1963). For more titles see John Hill, *Sex, Class, and Realism* (London: BFI, 1986).

• chapter 13 •
searching for
alternative styles

Soviet films of the post-war period include Dovzhenko's *Life in Bloom* (1948), Pudovkin's *Admiral Nakhimov* (1946), *Lenin* (1948), *The Return of Vasili Bortnikov* (1953), *Academician Ivan Pavlov* (1949), *Mussorgskii* (1950), *True Friends* (1954), *Boris Godunov* (1954), *Romeo and Juliet* (1955), *Othello* (1955), *The Cranes Are Flying* (1957), *Swan Lake* (1957), *The Girl Without an Address* (1957), *Ballad of a Soldier* (1958), *The Businessmen From the Other World* (1963), *Hamlet* (1964), *War and Peace* (1964, released in two parts in the United States in 1968), and *Sleeping Beauty* (1964).

Andrzej Wajda has directed *A Generation* (1955), *Kanal* (1957), *Ashes and Diamonds* (1958), *The Siberian Lady Macbeth* (1962), *Everything for Sale* (1968), *Landscape After the Battle* (1970), *The Wedding* (1972), *Man of Marble* (1978), *Man of Iron* (1981), and *Danton* (1982). For a filmography see his autobiography *Double Vision* (London: Faber and Faber, 1989).

Andrzej Munk directed *Congress of Fighters* (1949), *Art of Youth* (1950), *A Railwayman's Word* (1953), *The Stars Must Shine* (1954), *Sunday Morning* (1955), *Man on the Track* (1957), *Bad Luck* (1960), and *The Passenger* (1963).

Jerzy Skolimowski directed *Identification Marks: None* (1964), *Walkover* (1965), *Le Départ* (1967), *The Shout* (1978), and *Moonlighting* (1982).

Roman Polanski has made *Knife in the Water* (1962), *Repulsion* (1965), *The Fearless Vampire Killers* (1967), *Rosemary's Baby* (1968), *Chinatown* (1974), and *Tess* (1979). For more information see Gretchen Bisplinghoff and Virginia Wexman, *Roman Polanski* (Boston: G. K. Hall, 1979).

Miloš Forman has directed *Black Peter* (1963), *Loves of a Blonde* (1965), *The Firemen's Ball* (1967), *Taking Off* (1970), *One Flew Over the Cuckoo's Nest* (1975), *Hair* (1979), *Ragtime* (1981), and *Amadeus* (1983). For a complete filmography see Thomas Slater, *Milos Forman* (New York: Greenwood Press, 1987).

Véra Chytilová has made *Daisies* (1966), *The Apple Game* (1977), *An Apartment House Story* (1982), and *Calamity* (1982).

Jiří Menzel has directed *Closely Watched Trains* (1966), *Capricious Summer* (1968), *Crime at the Nightclub* (1968), *Larks on a String* (1969), *Short Cut* (1980), and *Snowdrop Festival* (1985).

Miklós Jancsó is well-known for *My Way Home* (1964), *The Round-Up* (1965), *The Red and the White* (1967), *Silence and Cry* (1968), *Agnus Dei* (1970), *The Confrontation* (1969), and *Red Psalm* (1972).

Dušan Makavejev challenged the world with *Man Is Not a Bird* (1965), *Love Affair, or The Case of the Missing Switchboard Operator* (1967), *Innocence Unprotected* (1968), *W. R.: Mysteries of the Organism* (1971), *Sweet Movie* (1974), and *Montenegro* (1981).

Satyajit Ray has created the Apu trilogy: *Pather Panchali* (1955), *Aparajito* (1956), and *Apu Sansar* (1959). His other films include *The Music Room* (1958), *Devi* (1960), *Two Daughters* (1961), *Expedition* (1962), *The Big City* (1963), *The Lonely Wife* (1964), *The Hero* (1966), *The Zoo* (1967), *Days* *and Nights in the Forest* (1970), and *The Adversary* (1971). For a filmography see his book *The Unicorn Experience* (New York: Dutton, 1987).

Brazilian Cinema Nôvo included *Black God, White Devil* (1964), *Barren Lives* (1963), and *Antonio das Mortes* (1969). For a filmography see Randal Johnson, *Cinema Nôvo × 5* (Austin: University of Texas Press, 1984).

Leopold Torre-Nilsson directed *Oribe's Crime* (1950), *Days of Hatred* (1954), *The House of the Angel* (1957), *The Hand in the Trap* (1961), *Homage at Siesta Time* (1962), *Monday's Child* (1966), *The Knight of the Sword* (1969), and *The 7 Madmen* (1973).

Tomás Gutiérrez Alea has made *Memories of Underdevelopment* (1968), *Stories of the Revolution* (1960), *The Death of a Bureaucrat* (1966), *The Last Supper* (1976), and *The Survivors* (1979).

Humberto Solás has directed *Lucia* (1968), *Simparele* (1974), *Cantata of Chile* (1975), *Cecilia Valdés* (1982), and *Amada* (1983).

Manuel Octavio Gómez has created *The First Charge with the Machete* (1969), *A Woman, a Man, a City* (1978), and *Patakin* (1982).

Rainer Werner Fassbinder directed *Love Is Colder Than Death* (1969), *Katzelmacher* (1969), *Why Does Herr R. Run Amok?* (1970), *The Merchant of Four Seasons* (1971), *The Bitter Tears of Petra von Kant* (1972), *Ali: Fear Eats the Soul* (1973), *Effie Briest* (1974), *Fox and His Friends* (1974), *Mother Kusters Goes to Heaven* (1975), *Satan's Brew* (1976), *Chinese Roulette* (1976), *The Marriage of Maria Braun* (1978), *Berlin Alexanderplatz* (1980), *Lola* (1981), and *Querelle* (1982). For a complete filmography see Ronald Hayman, *Fassbinder* (New York: Simon and Schuster, 1984).

Wim Wenders has created *The Goalie's Anxiety at the Penalty Kick* (1971), *Alice in the Cities* (1973), *Kings of the Road* (1976), *The American Friend* (1977), and *Paris, Texas* (1984). For a filmography see Kathe Geist, *The Cinema of Wim Wenders* (Ann Arbor: UMI Research Press, 1988).

Werner Herzog has created *Signs of Life* (1968), *Land of Silence and Darkness* (1971), *Aguirre, the Wrath of God* (1972), *The Mystery of Kaspar Hauser* (1974), *Heart of Glass* (1976), *Nosferatu* (1979), *Woyzeck* (1979), and *Fitzcarraldo* (1982). For a filmography see Timothy Corrigan, *New German Film* (Austin: University of Texas Press, 1983).

Bruce Beresford has made *Adventures of Barry MacKenzie* (1972), *The Getting of Wisdom* (1977), *Don's Party* (1976), *Breaker Morant* (1980), and *Tender Mercies* (1982).

Peter Weir has directed *The Cars That Ate Paris* (1974), *Picnic at Hanging Rock* (1975), *Gallipoli* (1981), *The Year of Living Dangerously* (1982), and *Witness* (1985).

George Miller has made *Mad Max* (1979), *The Road Warrior* (1981), *Mad Max Beyond Thunderdome* (1985), and what most critics hailed as the best segment of *Twilight Zone, The Movie* (1983): "Nightmare at 2000 Feet."

• chapter 14 •
an epilogue:
contemporary film history

Mel Brooks made *The Producers* (1968), *Blazing Saddles* (1974), *Young Frankenstein* (1974), *High Anxiety* (1977), and *Space Balls* (1987).

Hal Ashby made *Harold and Maude* (1971), *The Last Detail* (1973), *Shampoo* (1975), *Bound for Glory* (1976), *Coming Home* (1978), and *Being There* (1979).

Blake Edwards has directed *Breakfast at Tiffany's* (1961), *Experiment in Terror* (1962), *Days of Wine and Roses* (1962), *The Pink Panther* (1964), *The*

Return of the Pink Panther (1974), *Revenge of the Pink Panther* (1978), *S.O.B.* (1981), *Victor/Victoria* (1982), *Micki and Maude* (1984), and *Skin Deep* (1989).

George Lucas forever changed Hollywood with his *Star Wars* (1977) and has also been the creative force behind *THX-1138* (1971), *American Graffiti* (1973), *The Empire Strikes Back* (1980), and *Return of the Jedi* (1983).

Steven Spielberg has directed the TV movie *Duel* (1971) and the features *The Sugarland Express* (1974), *Jaws* (1975), *1941* (1979), *Close Encounters of the Third Kind* (1977), *E.T.: The Extraterrestrial* (1982), *The Color Purple* (1985) and the "Indiana Jones" films: *Raiders of the Lost Ark* (1981), *Indiana Jones and the Temple of Doom* (1984), and *Indiana Jones and the Last Crusade* (1989).

Woody Allen has made *Take the Money and Run* (1969), *Bananas* (1971), *Everything You Always Wanted to Know About Sex but Were Afraid to Ask* (1972), *Sleeper* (1973), *Love and Death* (1975), *Annie Hall* (1977), *Interiors* (1978), *Manhattan* (1979), *Zelig* (1983), *Broadway Danny Rose* (1984), and *The Purple Rose of Cairo* (1985).

Martin Scorsese has made *Mean Streets* (1973), *Alice Doesn't Live Here Anymore* (1974), *Taxi Driver* (1976), *New York, New York* (1977), *The Last Waltz* (1978), *Raging Bull* (1979), *The King of Comedy* (1983), and *The Last Temptation of Christ* (1988).

David Puttnam has produced *That'll Be the Day* (1974), *Mahler* (1974), *Stardust* (1975), *Midnight Express* (1978), *Agatha* (1979), and *Chariots of Fire* (1981).

Lina Wertmüller has created *The Lizards* (1963), *Now Let's Talk about Men* (1965), *The Seduction of Mimi* (1972), *Love and Anarchy* (1973), *Swept Away* (1974), and *Seven Beauties* (1976).

Alain Tanner has created *Charles—Dead or Alive* (1969), *The Salamander* (1971), *The Middle of the World* (1974), *Jonah Who Will Be 25 in the Year 2000* (1976), *Light Years Away* (1980), and *In the White City* (1983).

Chantal Akerman has made *Hotel Monterey* (1972), *I, You, He, She* (1974), *Jeanne Dielman, 23 Quai du Commerce, 1080 Bruxelles* (1975), *News From Home* (1976), and *The Golden Eighties* (1986).

Tatsumi Kumashiro has made *Sayuri Ichijo: The West Desire* (1972), *The Lovers Get Wet* (1973), *The Back Paper of the Sliding Door of a Four-and-Half Tatami Mat Room* (1973), and *The Black Rose Goes to Heaven* (1975).

Nagisa Oshima has crafted *Three Resurrected Drunkards* (1968), *Death By Hanging* (1968), *The Man Who Left His Will on Film* (1970), *The Ceremony* (1971), *Dear Summer Sister* (1972), *In the Realm of the Senses* (1976), *Empire of Passion* (1978), and *Merry Christmas, Mr. Lawrence* (1983).

Ousmane Sembène has made *Borom Sarret* (1963), *Niaye* (1964), *The Money Order* (1968), and *Ceddo* (1977). For more information see Françoise Pfaff, *Twenty-five Black African Filmmakers* (New York: Greenwood Press, 1988).

Med Hondo has created *Dirty Arabs, Dirty Niggers, Your Neighbors* (1973) and *We'll Have All Death to Sleep* (1977). For more information see Françoise Pfaff, *Twenty-five Black African Filmmakers* (New York: Greenwood Press, 1988).

• photo credits •

Pages 5, 8, 9L, 9R, 12, 19, 22, 25, 34: The Museum of Modern Art Film Stills Archive. Page 37: The Kobal Collection. Pages 38, 46: The Museum of Modern Art Film Stills Archive. Pages 51, 62: The Bettman Archive. Pages 64, 76, 79, 81, 82, 83, 84, 85, 86, 87, 89, 91, 92, 94, 100, 106L, 106R, 107, 110, 117, 118, 119, 121, 122, 123, 126, 130, 131, 132, 142, 146, 147, 151, 154, 155, 157, 159, 167, 176, 179, 193, 194, 196, 197, 201: The Museum of Modern Art Film Stills Archive. Page 203: Wisconsin Center for Film and Theater Research. Pages 204, 208, 209, 211, 212, 214, 215, 218, 221, 229, 230, 232, 233, 234, 237, 240, 243, 246, 248, 257, 258, 261, 264, 269, 272, 273, 274: The Museum of Modern Art Film Stills Archive. Page 277: SPG International. Pages 288, 307: The Museum of Modern Art Film Stills Archive. Page 321: Wisconsin Center for Film and Theater Research. Page 329: The Museum of Modern Art Film Stills Archive. Page 338: Photofest. Pages 351, 358, 360, 362, 366, 370, 372, 375, 377, 378, 380, 382, 393, 396, 397, 399, 400, 413: The Museum of Modern Art Film Stills Archive.

Color insert between pages 286 and 287: Page 1 (Top) Photofest, (Middle) The Kobal Collection, (Bottom) The Kobal Collection; Page 2 (Top) The Kobal Collection, (Bottom left) Photofest, (Bottom right) Photofest; Page 3 (Top left) The Kobal Collection, (Top right) Photofest, (Bottom) Photofest; Page 4 (Bottom left) The Kobal Collection, (Bottom right) The Kobal Collection. Color insert between pages 430 and 431: Page 1 (Top right) The Kobal Collection, (Bottom) Photofest; Page 2 (Top left) The Kobal Collection, (Top right) Photofest, (Bottom) The Museum of Modern Art Film Stills Archive; Page 3 (Top) The Kobal Collection, (Bottom left) The Museum of Modern Art Film Stills Archive, (Bottom right) Photofest; Page 4 (Top left) Photofest, (Top right) Photofest, (Bottom) Courtesy of Cineplex Odeon Corporation.

index